THE LETTERS & LIVES OF

THE STRICKLAND FAMILY

CHRISTINE FISHER

Grosvenor House
Publishing Limited

All rights reserved
Copyright © Christine Fisher, 2022
www.thestricklandfamily.org

The right of Christine Fisher to be identified as the author of this
work has been asserted in accordance with Section 78
of the Copyright, Designs and Patents Act 1988

The book cover is copyright to Christine Fisher
Cover Design by Brian Jones

This book is published by
Grosvenor House Publishing Ltd
Link House
140 The Broadway, Tolworth, Surrey, KT6 7HT.
www.grosvenorhousepublishing.co.uk

This book is sold subject to the conditions that it shall not, by way of
trade or otherwise, be lent, resold, hired out or otherwise circulated
without the author's or publisher's prior consent in any form of binding or
cover other than that in which it is published and
without a similar condition including this condition being imposed
on the subsequent purchaser.

A CIP record for this book
is available from the British Library

ISBN 978-1-83975-157-8
eBook ISBN 978-1-80381-155-0

Contents

	Page
Pictures	247–250, 416–419
19th century map of south-eastern Canada	iv
Introduction	v
Part 1: From Lancashire to Suffolk and Ontario	1
Part 2: Life patterns form and fame begins	97
Part 3: Return to Lancashire and difficulties	177
Part 4: Authors galore	251
Part 5: Life changes	331
Part 6: From eight to seven	421
Part 7: From seven to four	513
Part 8: A late flowering	571
Part 9: The sole survivor	615
Part 10: Lasting fame?	651
Acknowledgements	658
Appendix 1: Family members and key dates	659
Appendix 2: Principal works of the Strickland family	660
Appendix 3: References	661
Picture Credits	664

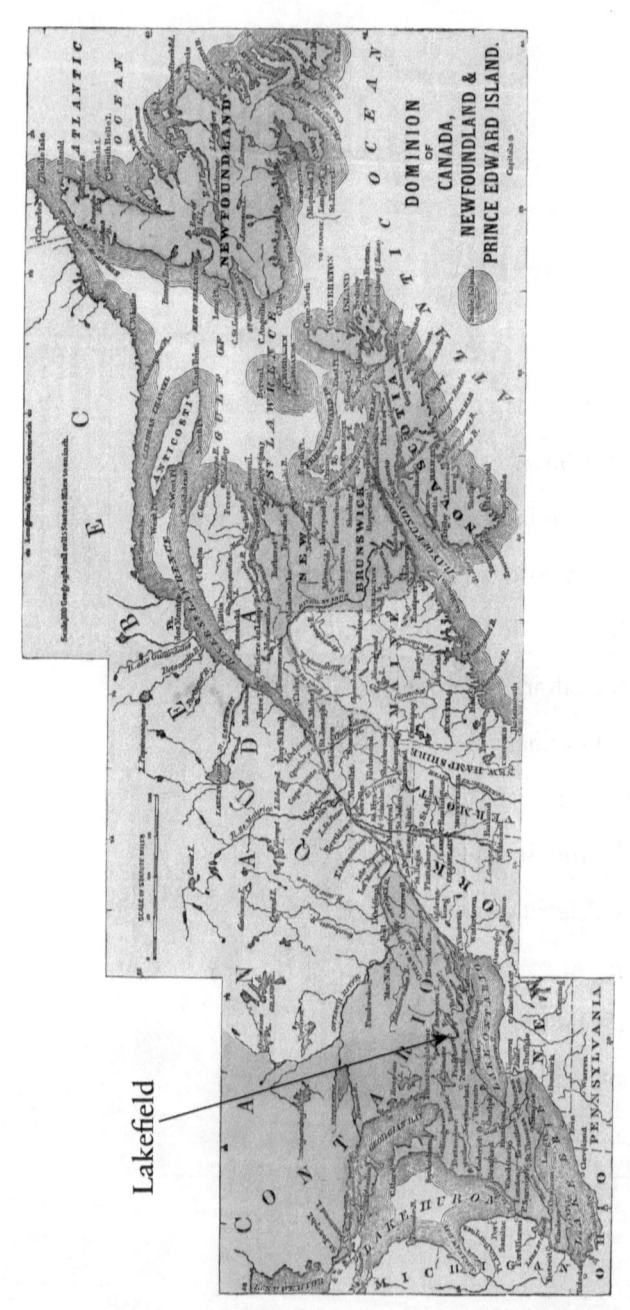

Contents

	Page
Pictures	247–250, 416–419
19th century map of south-eastern Canada	iv
Introduction	v
Part 1: From Lancashire to Suffolk and Ontario	1
Part 2: Life patterns form and fame begins	97
Part 3: Return to Lancashire and difficulties	177
Part 4: Authors galore	251
Part 5: Life changes	331
Part 6: From eight to seven	421
Part 7: From seven to four	513
Part 8: A late flowering	571
Part 9: The sole survivor	615
Part 10: Lasting fame?	651
Acknowledgements	658
Appendix 1: Family members and key dates	659
Appendix 2: Principal works of the Strickland family	660
Appendix 3: References	661
Picture Credits	664

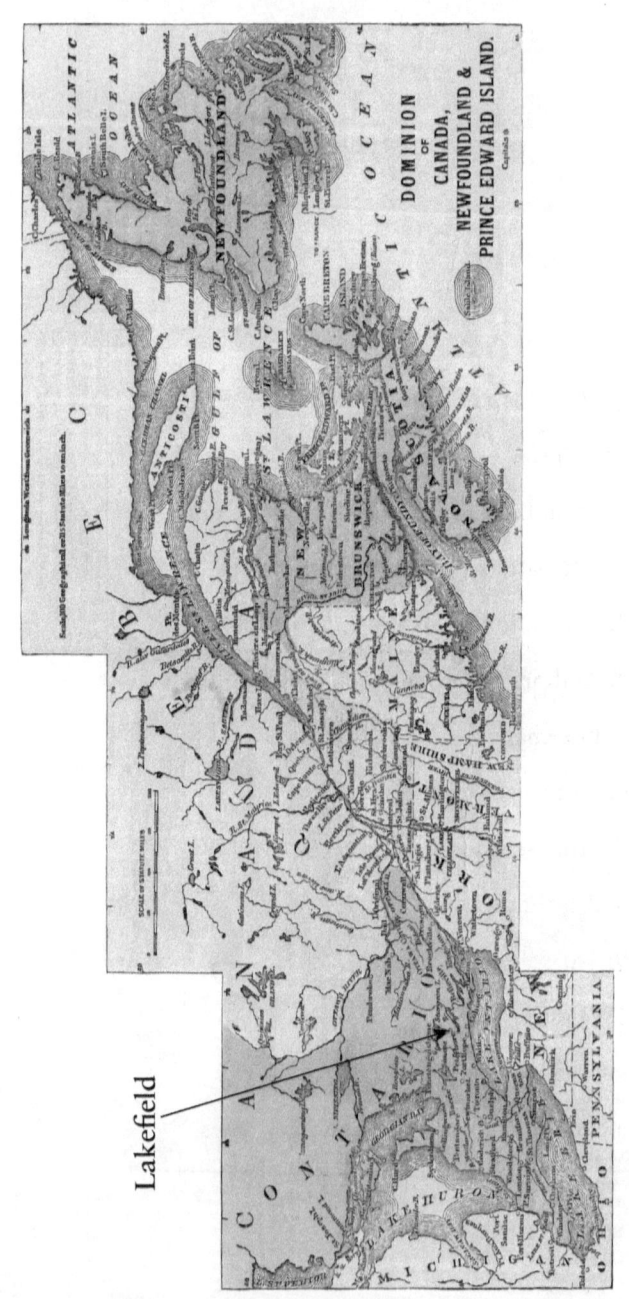

Introduction

This book contains the life stories of six sisters and two brothers, the children of Thomas Strickland (1758-1818) and his second wife, Elizabeth (1773-1864).

The family originated in Lancashire, and believed it had ancestry in common with the Strickland family of Sizergh Castle. Thomas Strickland worked as a dock manager in Rotherhithe, Kent and retired to Suffolk, a wealthy man, in 1803. In 1808 he bought Reydon Hall, a large house with a small estate not far from the Suffolk coast.

Family circumstances changed dramatically in 1815 when Thomas Strickland lost most of his money in a business venture that went wrong. The situation became much worse in 1818 when he died suddenly, leaving a Will which tied his family to Reydon Hall, but without income to maintain it.

This book tells how his widow and children survived and how their lives evolved. It is based on family letters, biographical writings and newspaper articles of the time.

The sisters turned out to be a literary celebrity of the first order in England, and two pioneers of Canadian literature. The brothers became a successful Canadian pioneer and a Master Mariner. One sister married well; one was an author who chose to remain anonymous; and the sixth sister, despite ill health and being the daughter who stayed at home to care for their ageing mother, was also a writer of note.

The Strickland sisters and brothers were intellectually gifted and capable of great feats of endeavour. They had a range of personalities and frailties, and suffered misfortunes as well as successes in the course of their long and varied lives. They experienced romance and heartache, poverty and some wealth, suicide, murder and varying degrees of fame.

This Strickland family was extraordinary, and far more interesting and varied in their achievements than the other literary family of the 19th century – the Bronte family.

Part 1: From Lancashire to Suffolk and Ontario

Family roots in Finsthwaite; ship building in Rotherhithe; gout and family life in Suffolk; financial down-fall; writing careers begin; emigration to Canada; marriages

Strickland family origins

The Strickland family whose lives are chronicled in this book had an ancestral home at Finsthwaite Hall, in the Lake District, to the south-west of Lake Windermere. They believed themselves to be connected in some distant and unknown manner to another and more prestigious Strickland family, one based in Sizergh Castle, which lies about 20 miles east of Finsthwaite village.

It was assumed that the split between these two Strickland families was due to the Reformation in the reign of Henry VIII, the Strickland family of Finsthwaite Hall adopting the new religion, whereas the Strickland family of Sizergh Castle remained Catholic. Although there had been this divergence in terms of religion, both branches of the Strickland family had been Royalist in the Civil War of the 17th century, and to varying degrees continued to support the Jacobite cause after the downfall of James II.

When James II went into exile, the elder son from Finsthwaite Hall joined the exiled king in France. From there he joined the Franco-Spanish army, and fought in the War of the Spanish Succession against allied forces which included England and Portugal. He took part in the Battle of Almanza, in which the Franco-Spanish army defeated the

English and allied army, but then disappeared and it was presumed that he died in battle.

When his father died, the elder brother had long been presumed dead, and the younger brother was assumed to be the rightful heir to the family estates, and behaved accordingly. However, the elder brother reappeared after a silence of 26 years, and successfully claimed his inheritance which dramatically changed the fortunes of his younger brother, who had a family of ten children.

The eldest of these ten children, named Samuel Strickland, was away at school when his uncle returned. Samuel's education, reputedly at Winchester College, was abruptly terminated and he returned to Lancashire, no longer the heir to an estate and income, but merely a son of a younger brother.

Rather than remain in Lancashire and dependent on the charity of his uncle, Samuel Strickland moved to London, and got a job as a Clerk in a London Dock. One of his brothers and three of his sisters subsequently followed his example and moved to London.

Samuel Strickland married and among his children was Thomas Strickland, born in 1758, and father of the eight children whose biographies are the subject of this book.

1758-1791: Thomas Strickland's early life

Thomas Strickland's first wife was a great-niece of Sir Isaac Newton. She died young, and the only child of the marriage, a daughter, died in infancy. However, by means of this marriage, a few of Sir Isaac Newton's belongings passed to Thomas Strickland and remained as treasured possessions in his home.

Thomas married as his second wife Elizabeth Homer, fifteen years younger than himself, having been born in 1773. Together they had nine children, of whom the first eight survived to adulthood but their last child, a daughter named Ellen, died in 1811 at the age of six months.

1792-1803: The Rotherhithe years

The first five of Thomas and Elizabeth Strickland's children were all daughters and were all born at Rotherhithe in Kent. The eldest daughter was named Elizabeth and was born in 1794. She was known as Eliza for much of her life, and, to avoid confusion, will always be referred to in this book as Eliza until after the death of her mother.

Thomas and Elizabeth Strickland's second daughter, Agnes, was born in 1796. At the birth of a third daughter in 1798, Thomas and Elizabeth took steps to preserve the family surname and her full name was Sarah Strickland Strickland. Her family nicknamed her Thay.

The fourth daughter, Jane Margaret Strickland, was born in 1800. The fifth and final child to be born at Rotherhithe was Catharine Parr Strickland, born in 1802. Both Jane and Catharine, although referred to by a single Christian name in this book, generally used both their Christian names when signing letters, including family letters. Catharine's second name of Parr reflected a family belief that the family was, in some unexplained way, descended from or connected with Katharine Parr, the last wife of Henry VIII.

The family home in Rotherhithe was near the south bank of the River Thames to the east of the City of London, at a time when Rotherhithe was a centre for building, re-fitting and repairing ocean-going sailing ships. Thomas Strickland was a manager in the Greenland Dock which had been built to accommodate ships of the East India Company while they were being re-fitted and repaired.

Greenland Dock had been built in such a way that over 100 ships could be accommodated at the same time, every one of which could be moved to be worked on without disturbing any of the other ships. It was, in essence, a long and narrow rectangular basin, with ships moored parallel to each other down the long sides.

When it was built, Greenland Dock was in a rural area and trees were planted along each side to act as wind breaks. The ships were without cargo while they were being worked on, meaning there was little need for warehousing, and Rotherhithe when Thomas and Elizabeth Strickland lived there, was less industrial in appearance than the London Dock area in general. To some extent Greenland Dock still exists today, albeit mainly as a leisure space.

Thomas Strickland's role as dock manager included superintending the mould loft, a large area with a flat floor where detailed ship-building plans, with all their complications, could be brought up to full size prior to construction. A family story, recorded by Catharine, was intended as an anecdote about Agnes, but it actually provides more information about Thomas Strickland and his work at that stage in his life than is available from any other source.

The story goes that in 1802, Earl Stanhope and his nephew Lord Camelford visited Thomas Strickland at his workplace in Rotherhithe. Charles Stanhope, 3rd Earl of Stanhope (1753-1816) was a scientist and a statesman, and was also brother-in-law to William Pitt the Younger, Tory Prime Minister from 1783-1801 and again from 1804 until his death in 1806. Earl Stanhope was a Fellow of the Royal Society, had studied mathematics and spent a considerable part of his income on scientific experiments. Lord Camelford (1775-1804), as well as being Earl Stanhope's nephew, was a cousin of William Pitt the Younger, and had been in command of various ships in the Royal Navy.

Their reason for visiting Thomas Strickland and Rotherhithe was to examine and discuss with Thomas Strickland some particular improvement in one of the models or plans for a ship with which he was involved. Thomas Strickland was therefore a clever, skilled and highly-regarded man in a position of authority, and it was during his years at Rotherhithe that he became wealthy enough to retire in comfort.

The family anecdote was based on Earl Stanhope and Lord Camelford both being tall men, who were accompanied by another man who was unusually short. Agnes (aged 6) intending to be polite, offered chairs to the tall men and her own low stool to the "little gentleman", which everyone, except perhaps the "little gentleman", found amusing. Why Agnes was present at her father's place of work during this important visit was not explained but is, in itself, an interesting point.

Of the five young daughters, Agnes was the most difficult to handle, being a mischievous and adventurous child. At the age of four she had been discovered by Peter (the family gardener) in the branches of an apple tree. The gardener rebuked her saying "Miss Agnes, young ladies should not climb trees" to which she is said to have replied "Peter, if climbing was born in me, then I must climb" and carried on doing so. This quotation and others referring to the early life of the Strickland family, generally derive from Catharine

Parr Strickland's later writings on the Strickland family. Where her writings are verifiable, they almost without exception turn out to have been accurate. It therefore seems reasonable to accept that her unverifiable comments are also true.

Living with the Strickland family at this time, and helping Mrs Strickland look after her young daughters, was a widowed gentlewoman called Mrs Harrison. She had been brought up with Thomas Strickland's first wife but lost all her property in what Jane Margaret Strickland later described as "the great fire that consumed a part of eastern London." By this she would have meant the Ratcliffe Fire of July 1794.

The fire began in the riverside hamlet of Ratcliffe, on the north bank of the Thames, a mile or two nearer the City of London than Rotherhithe. An unattended kettle of pitch boiled over and started the fire, and when the flames reached a barge loaded with salt petre, an ingredient in the manufacture of gunpowder, the barge exploded. Burning fragments shot in all directions and the fire spread through the narrow streets and barge-building yards of the area. With the help of a south-westerly wind, the fire spread rapidly eastwards and northwards.

The Ratcliffe fire was the most destructive event in London between the Great Fire of 1666 and The Blitz of 1940, destroying over 450 houses and making about 1400 people homeless. Those who could not find shelter with friends and relations were given temporary accommodation in tents which were put up in the grounds of the local church and elsewhere.

Mrs Harrison, having been given shelter by Thomas Strickland after the fire, helped look after the children and taught them their first lessons. In Jane's words "she proved a tender but self-constituted nurse."

In 1803 at a time when the Greenland Dock was about to change hands, Thomas Strickland retired at the age of 45. He was a wealthy man through his own endeavours, but he suffered from gout, and hoped that a move to East Anglia would improve his health.

1803-1808: Family life at Stowe House, Bungay

In East Anglia, Thomas Strickland continued to have business interests. These included being an early director of Norwich Union insurance company, which over the course of the next two hundred years evolved into the modern-day company named Aviva.

After their move from Rotherhithe, the Strickland family had a town house in Norwich, and a family home in Bungay, on the northern edge of Suffolk, where the Waveney River forms the boundary between the counties of Norfolk and Suffolk.

Despite the town house in Norwich and Thomas Strickland's business arrangements, nearly all the recorded family memories from this period relate to family life at Stowe House, Bungay, which Thomas Strickland leased from 1803 to 1808.

Stowe House had started life in the 17th century as a plainly-built farmhouse, but had been extended by the addition of a dining room and drawing room with bow windows on the ground floor; a large paved hall with a spiral staircase; and three sets of chambers upstairs. By means of these additions, the nature of the house was changed from a farmhouse into a gentleman's residence. It was linked by an orchard and a meadow to the Waveney River and it was Catharine who left many and detailed memories of family life at Stowe House.

Of the house in general she said there was an upper room, reputed to be haunted by the ghost of an apprentice, whose death had been caused by the cruelty of a former owner of the house. It was used as a store-room, but the servants would only go there in daylight and even then it was a gloomy place, the windows having been covered with whitewash. In addition the outside wall had fruit trees trained against it, so that the limited daylight coming into the room flickered as it filtered through the leaves.

Catharine remembered as a child being taken up to this attic by the young cook who wanted company while she collected some herbs and onions. Catharine wrote: "Alice, or Alls as we called her, had set me down on the floor – when suddenly I called out 'Alls there's a boy over there! There's a boy over there!' and ran to her. No doubt it was my own shadow I saw on the wall but the poor superstitious woman thought it was the ghost of the dead boy. She snatched me up under her arm and rushed down the ladder stairs, and fell in a fit on the kitchen floor – fit after fit followed. At last she got so bad that her mother was sent for, and took the poor girl home."

Catharine described a typical day at Stowe House, which began and ended with prayers: "At 7 o'clock the nurse came and told the children it was time to rise. The first thing before dressing, the little girls knelt down beside the bed, and said their prayers – the Lord's prayer, the Collect for the day, and one or more verses of the beautiful old morning hymn 'Awake my soul and with the sun.' At night they stood up and repeated the Creed, and the Lord's prayer and the evening hymn 'Glory to Thee my God this night' and the collect 'Lighten our darkness' and the Gloria – these were never omitted – even the little ones had to kneel in prayer."

After morning prayers "The nurse took away the youngest ones to wash and dress, but the older ones had to dress themselves, and help one another – and to see that their night clothes were neatly folded, laid by, and the bed opened to air, and the windows opened."

The next marker in the day was breakfast. "At 8 o'clock breakfast was ready in the brick parlour – a room that was a play room and a breakfast room. There was little furniture in it, a queer shaped corner cupboard, some high stools, and a long table – a little iron grate that could hold a few handfuls of coal – and the window was a very small casement of very many small diamond shaped panes.

"The breakfast consisted of oatmeal boiled in milk, not thick like porridge. A slice of dry bread not buttered, was placed beside each basin. That was all these children had for their breakfast. There was no grumbling among these little folk – they were wiser; for they knew what would have been done – the food taken away at once, and no more given to them till dinner – a long while to wait till two o'clock."

Although breakfast was spartan, the mid-day meal was not. "At dinner there was always a plentiful supply of well cooked food – the children were never allowed to ask for anything, they were helped to what was good for them, and if any objection was made – at a word the child was dismissed from the table and dessert.

"The oldest girls only were admitted to the tea table, the other children took their supper of bread and milk at another table. Nor did they ever have tea, except on birthdays, or special holidays – then they had it with cake and other dainties." Catharine said that this way of treating children was the general custom in the early part of the 19th century and in her view it did them no harm: "The children grew up healthy and strong – the treatment suited them."

After breakfast came lessons. Thomas Strickland had a poor view of the way girls were educated in the early years of the nineteenth century, and undertook his daughters' education himself. Catharine wrote: "There was an old fashioned cuckoo clock in the lower hall in Stowe House. When the cuckoo called the hour of ten, the young folks went to the study where their father and mother were ready for them. The three older sisters" (Eliza, Agnes and Sarah) "made their curtseys, as they took their place at the table with slates and copies, ready set, and their reading and spelling books and maps all in due order.

"The younger children" (Jane and Catharine) "went to their mother, where their books, needles, thimbles and work lay ready for them. At three years of age, the education of these little children had already commenced, under the dear mother's care – and she was as strict with her infant class, as the father was with the older ones. There must be no noise, no talking, no crying – and disobedience was punished in the very youngest child."

The punishment could be spending time alone in the brick parlour, having dry bread for dinner or having no dinner at all, or no play hour. Telling a lie, quarrelling with each other, being rebellious to the nurse or any of the other servants, would result in punishment, but again Catharine made no complaint about this treatment, feeling that she and her sisters were as "lively and happy as many other children who have every indulgence and have their own way unchecked."

At twelve o'clock, lessons were finished, everything was neatly tidied away and the children were free to go and play outside. The meadow between the house and the river, as well as being a playground for the children, was where "Colly the cow and Billy the horse fed. Billy was a beauty and so gentle" that he was a great favourite with the children. There was also a tortoise-shell cat, and rabbits in a hutch in the granary for the children to look after.

The children's games were simple – running races, skipping, building with the sand of the river bank and playing with dolls. Even in play the children's education continued for the dolls were "rag dolls or paper dolls – for indeed we had no costly wax dolls – nor even jointed wooden dolls – not any toys but such as we made ourselves – no money was spent on toys."

This was not due to poverty for their father was wealthy and well able to pay for toys: "This was part of the system observed by our parents in the education of their children – to render them independent and to call forth their talents, and to form industrious habits."

Thomas Strickland had a brass-bound wooden tool chest and the little girls were sometimes allowed to watch him making things, and he would suggest things which they could make, providing the necessary tools and materials. Catharine remembered him saying: "There are two ways to make this thing – a right way and a wrong way, now try and find out the right way" with "persevere and you must succeed" and "never give up" being phrases used to encourage them in their attempts.

The children each had a piece of garden to cultivate, as well as pet rabbits and pigeons to care for, all of which helped keep them busy and out of mischief. They were also taught to respect money. Catharine said: "It was one of the peculiarities of our home system – no money was given to us unless it was earned – nor were we allowed to accept money even from our most familiar friends or nearest relations, but every encouragement was given to obtain it by honest labour – The labour was light and such as was easy to be done – the weeding and taking care of vegetables – the gathering of ripe seeds in the garden for which a stated sum was given – liberal pay it was – Such little industries were encouraged."

From Catharine's recollections it seems that Thomas and Elizabeth Strickland, although strict about discipline and education, were kind and loving parents. The family spent their evenings in a half circle in front of the fire, listening to their mother telling stories, hearing accounts of their family history, singing, and reciting the ballads and poems they had learned.

Mrs Strickland, born Elizabeth Homer, had at least three sisters and at least one brother. She had family connections both in London and in Norwich. In the early 1800s Norwich was one of the richest cities in England, its wealth being based on the textile industry, while its geographical location and the condition of the roads meant it had easier links by sea with the Low Countries than by road with the rest of England. Later, during the Industrial Revolution, major manufacturing towns would grow up elsewhere in Britain and the relative wealth of Norwich would decline.

Thomas and Elizabeth Strickland had three more children while the family were living at Stowe House. Their sixth daughter, Susanna was born in 1803, and she was followed by two sons. Both boys carried forward Christian names used by previous generations of the Strickland family. Samuel was born in 1805, and Thomas (known as Tom) in about 1807.

When Susanna arrived there was some doubt about her survival, so she was baptized when only a few days old, at the church of St Mary's in Bungay, in December 1803. Catharine remembered the older girls helping to choose a name for their new sister. Their suggestions were far from straightforward. Eliza, then aged 11: "suggested Cassandra for they were deep in Pope's Homer's Iliad" (which gives a flavour of the education these little girls were receiving). Agnes, aged 9: "insisted on the grand-sounding name of Andromache, her hero Hector's wife" while Sarah, aged 6: "meekly suggested Hecuba." When in later years Susanna objected to the name she had been given, her mother told her the story of what she might have been called, whereupon "Susie was reconciled" to the homeliness of her name "and quite thankful when she heard of her escape."

When Samuel was born in November 1804 Catharine, although only three at the time, remembered the excitement caused by the birth of a son, and the associated puzzlement among his sisters: "The nurse came down and told us that we had a baby brother. She told us nobody would think of _us_ now. We could not understand nurse's meaning – six girls to be made of little account for the sake of one tiny baby boy!! Just eleven months younger than little Susie."

Catharine remembered "being taken upstairs with the rest of my sisters to look at this wonderful little brother, only a few hours old, and hearing him cry when my sister Jane tried to open his tiny hand to present him with a small rag doll as a token of love and good will – but the gift was not appreciated by the ungracious baby, as forcing open the little fingers rather roughly had disturbed the little gentleman's slumbers and caused a noisy demonstration on his part, which alarmed the nurse, who bundled us out of the room in double quick time – and the new baby was voted a cross ugly thing, not half as nice as the old baby."

As a special treat to celebrate the arrival of a son, the cook prepared "sweetened gruel in which a liberal portion of raisins and spice had been boiled". The children each had a small bowlful "As we were not often allowed any indulgence in the way of sweet cakes or luxuries, the plum gruel, or caudle, left an indelible impression on my memory."

Samuel was named after his grandfather and an uncle and "grew to be a lovely healthy little fellow – his cheeks as red as roses, his eyes as blue as heaven and a head covered with golden curls – he was a beauty – and the pride and delight of his sisters' hearts – Wilful and passionate as a child, which was not to be wondered at, all things considered, as he was much indulged by all of us. And no doubt might have been more spoiled, but for the addition to the family of another boy, who was called after my father, Thomas or Tom, as he was always called, who of course diverted some of the attention from his elder brother – which was no doubt a good thing for them both."

Catharine made no other comment on the arrival of Tom and throughout all the family memoirs and letters it is usually the case that Tom is barely mentioned. As a result, written accounts of the Strickland family sometimes say that it was a family of seven children, Tom not having been noticed or counted.

Catharine in her reminiscences described the family's religious observance: "Our Sundays were strictly observed no playing games, no noisy romping – Church service morning and afternoon – the text to be duly remembered and repeated. The Bible was read – even to the genealogies of the Jews – no explanations given – This was customary. Children were to receive all by faith, as truths not to be questioned. This was a firm, but fruitless faith."

The Strickland family attended the church of St Mary's in Bungay: "a fine building – there was a grand organ and choir – and a formidable personage – the Beadle who in a blue serge gown trimmed with yellow stalked up and down the aisles bearing in his hand a long white wand and casting terrible looks as he passed with noiseless steps the matted aisles on all idlers – The Beadle was the terror of us children and I well remember trembling lest he should spy me and take me to the bone-house – that was the fate of delinquents.

"I had an old prayer book which I was accustomed to hold upside down when I was four years old but at five I had made such progress" that Catharine could read the service and take part in the prayers. "One day I let this heavy book fall out of my hands and it fell on the head of a devout maiden Lady in a pew below the gallery. I was in an agony of fright. I saw the white wand moving in our direction and instantly concealed myself under the bench and behind my elder sisters' frocks. The dreaded bone-house loomed in view but the stately official passed us by – but then my beloved book – when should I see it again. Never – for I dared not go to claim it – Great was my joy – next service – to find it in the pew."

The interior of St Mary's Church in Bungay was described by a visitor in 1810 as a wonderful 18th century period piece. The interior was seated with uniform wainscoted box pews and the entire length of the south aisle was filled with a long gallery. On another gallery at the west end of the church was a fine organ, at that time a rarity in parish churches. It had 1,100 pipes and 21 stops and had been given to the church in 1728.

Dominating the interior and filling the east wall was a panelled altarpiece with five compartments. The Ten Commandments were in the centre panel and above that were the royal arms of King William III. This centre panel was flanked by painted figures of Moses and Aaron, which in turn were flanked by the Lord's Prayer and the Apostle's Creed. This description of the royal arms of King William being a dominant feature of the east wall explains Catharine's memory of praying between 1803 and 1808 for King William and the Princess Anne, even though King William III had died in 1702, Princess Anne subsequently became Queen Anne and had died in 1714.

One would have expected the prayers to have been for King George III who had been king since 1760 and was to continue to reign until 1811 when, due to his mental ill health, his son George would be declared Regent. After the death of King George III in 1820, the Regency Period would end and Prince George would become George IV. However, this was in the future when from 1803 to 1808 the Strickland family attended church in Bungay and King George III was on the throne.

Catharine in later life described Susanna as a young child. Catharine wrote: "She early shewed a lively imagination. She lived in a sort of dream world of her own, clothing the fanciful images of her fertile brain in language that often partook of the poetical, rather than plain matter of fact words ... When she was about four years old, she would suddenly look up with her earnest grey eyes and relate some wonderful romance of her own creation ... she used to talk of great rivers, and big trees, and white ants, and snakes and crocodiles – Sometimes it was told in a dream but more often as a fact that she had seen." Susanna's stories would get her into trouble. Catharine wrote: "Susie was one of those children that are little understood, and being a little girl and original in her ways was often in trouble – She was either full of spirits or easily depressed, often seeing things through an excited imagination. As a very young girl she was often unhappy ... seeing things through an unreal medium, either too great or too small."

At about the same time (1808) as 4-year old Susanna was day dreaming her stories, 12-year old Agnes Strickland made her first serious attempt at writing poetry and wrote an historical poem about the powerful Bigod family of Bungay Castle. She worked on the poem in secret for several weeks then proudly read it to her father, expecting to receive praise and encouragement. Instead he told her bluntly that her subject was lacking in originality and her work without merit. He told her not to waste any more time trying to write poetry until she understood what constituted good poetry and what did not. Agnes's enthusiasm for writing poetry was duly crushed, at least for a few years.

However, along with his harsh criticism, Thomas Strickland began to include the reading and study of poetry in his daughters' education, and thus showed the breadth of his own knowledge, and the serious approach he was taking to the education of his daughters. He selected poems for them to read aloud and learn by heart, and he pointed out the features and styles of the various poets so that Agnes soon understood where her own poem had been deficient.

Apart from the morning lessons, Thomas Strickland got his daughters to read aloud to him biographies and works of history, following the readings with discussion of what they had just read. In this way, or so his daughter Jane later claimed, they hardly missed the lighter reading which was not permitted to them.

Agnes had an excellent memory, a characteristic which Jane and Catharine also displayed later in their lives. Agnes would voluntarily learn whole passages of Shakespeare and other works that she enjoyed, simply to have them stored in her memory. Eliza and Agnes had read most of Shakespeare's historical plays before they were 10. As far as the War of the Roses was concerned, Agnes was very strictly a Lancastrian, in keeping with her family history, while Eliza was a staunch Yorkist, and the two sisters sometimes fell out when discussing the associated politics.

Although she had never seen a play in her life, and indeed the books she was allowed to read were very strictly limited, Agnes went through a phase of enthusiasm for acting, and decided to put on plays with the help of her four younger sisters, Eliza refusing to have anything to do with it. All went well and was tolerated by her parents until Agnes decided they would act the murder scene in Richard III, with Agnes playing the part of the doomed prince, while Sarah was "a good listener in Brackenbury" and also "the first nameless villain." At the entrance of the murderers, however, the supposed villains all looked too young and cheerful for their supposed evil intent and they all burst out laughing. The tragic scene degenerated into a comedy, and private theatricals were thereafter discouraged.

Having read Shakespeare's version of history, Agnes wanted to know if his version of events was true and if not, what had really happened, and she studied in great detail the reference books in her father's library. These included Rapin's 'English History' which had originally been written in French. Catharine described this as two great folios which were presented in such a dull form that even many adults would have been discouraged from reading them.

Thomas Strickland's education of his daughters included subjects which were not usually thought necessary or suitable for the female mind, and he wanted at least one of his daughters to be an excellent mathematician but as Catharine observed: "Alas in this he signally failed. He aimed too high and mistook the real talent. Eliza with laudable perseverance became a good mathematician following the rules implicitly and believing with her teacher that numbers represented unchangeable truth. But Agnes who jumped at her conclusion often failed and was often punished, sometimes she proved the sums after a fashion of her own – by a set of rules she worked out in her own brain. She reached the right end but it was not by the regular way and I believe to the very last she pursued this mental code of calculation with success as to results."

The education of the children was very wide ranging. Catharine recalled: "Many of our tastes were formed in our childish days fostered by our parents – The love of flowers, of birds, study of animals and insects with their ways and habits, drawing, architecture (especially that of the ancients) painting and literature were pointed out to our attention by our parents. We each had a garden to cultivate ... Our Father was an earnest disciple of good old Isaac Walton. From his early years he had been a lover of the 'gentle craft' ... When we lived on the banks of the Waveney, he often spent quiet hours with his rod and line and then some of us were in attendance to carry his garden chair, basket and rod, and sit beside him quiet as mice. We each had our own rod and lines and was it not delightful to be taught how to twist the lines with the little brass reel and wheel and to pore over dear old Isaac's 'Complete Angler' ... I have the old book, it is to me a precious one. It was a favourite book of my dear Fathers and I shall leave it to my grandson, also a fisher out in the far Nor-West."

The Strickland family lived at Stowe House until Eliza was 14 years old and Agnes 12, and Catharine felt that the location of Stowe House had a lasting effect on the writing of these two sisters. She wrote: "Stowe House was in the vicinity of the old romantic and historic town of Bungay, with a view of the Castle, Hill and ivied walls, and ruins of that stronghold of the rebellious Bigod, Bungay Castle – from which the defiant Earl Marshall sent forth his refusal to come forth to his irate sovereign's command. No doubt the traditions that still lingered in that neighbourhood and to which they listened with enthusiasm, formed and fostered the tastes of my sisters, and which in after years gave the peculiar tone to their writings."

With the lease of Stowe House coming to an end in 1808, Thomas Strickland bought the Reydon Estate to form the family's permanent home thereafter. The property included a farm together with Reydon House, and was situated in an isolated position, over half a mile inland from the parish church.

In late December 1808 the family moved to their new home, which was 15 miles south and east of their old home, and increased the distance to Norwich from 15 miles to 25 miles. At this time Thomas Strickland was 50 years old and his wife Elizabeth was 35.

Catharine described the family move from Stowe House to Reydon as taking place in two stages. "It had been arranged that the two eldest girls" (Eliza and Agnes) "were to go to the new house some days previous to the rest of the household – It was late in the month of December, and an intensely cold winter had commenced with severe frosts and heavy snow storms when the moving took place. And it was necessary that my eldest sister should be in the house to arrange the furniture as it arrived. There were new servants hired, all the old ones having been discharged. I remember the cheerless look of the dismantled rooms as by degrees all the necessary articles of household use were taken away.

"My father, mother, the baby" (Tom) "and my little brother Sam just three years old, and my sister Jane left in a closed carriage and Sara, Susie and I were to follow later in the day in an open conveyance, under the care of Mr Sallow, the head carpenter and builder who had been engaged for many weeks making the changes and repairs in the new house, and had come the previous day to say all was done and ready for my father's reception – And he undertook to deliver up the keys of the house to the landlord's steward and to drive my sisters and me to Reydon. It was Christmas Eve (1808) we took our last farewell of the dear Stowe House and the old town of Bungay."

1808-1810: Early years at Reydon House

Although they had moved only a few miles, the climate at Reydon was colder and damper than at Bungay. Catharine wrote: "We were not clothed to resist the cold. The bleak sea breezes chilled us, and we soon felt the change in the shape of rheumatic fever which had never visited us in the sheltered vale of the Waveney. Agnes suffered severely from ague which for a long time injured her constitution as it did some other members of the household."

Reydon House, which gradually became referred to as Reydon Hall, had been built of brick in extensive grounds at the end of the 17th century. It had ornate chimneys and Flemish gables and was, and still is, situated in a lonely spot about half a mile inland from Reydon's parish church of St Margaret.

Like Stowe House, Reydon House could boast haunted attics. Catharine wrote: "There was a garret that was said to be haunted by the ghost of an eccentric old bachelor – said to have died in this old chamber which had been his secluded domicile for twenty years. It was a curious place, papered with old almanacs, dated in the last century. There was in this room a tiny iron grate with its rusty bars and the hooks that held up the hangings of the forlorn old recluse's bed. The servants said he never mingled with the family. His brother's wife made him live in the garret, she disliked him and never allowed him to sit at table. All the noises in that old part of the house were attributed to old Martin."

While Martin seems to have been a harmless presence, a second ghost was rather less friendly. Catharine said: "She was a little old woman in grey who occasionally played fantastic tricks. The maidservants who slept on this upper floor, where stood the huge old mangle in its massive oaken frame (it took the gardener or the cook to turn the crank) declared that it used to work by itself and turn the great linen rollers without hands, unless it were those of old Martin's ghost? Or the little old lady in grey? No doubt this restless little woman had been a busy housewife in her day. She must have been a spiteful sort of ghost, by those whose chambers she haunted, that she would come to them and shake her skinny hand in their faces and hiss at them, while a cold blast from her breath chilled, and made their blood freeze."

Reydon House was relatively isolated compared with Stowe House. Catharine wrote: "The chief want that was felt by my mother and elder sisters was congenial company" and their father was adversely affected by the climate. "Our father now suffered from longer fits of gout so from that time he was never able to walk without crutches." On the positive side, the family in the summer could enjoy the pleasures of living near the sea, and from some of the upper windows of Reydon House could see "ships sailing in the offing."

The children's lives were now very different from when they lived at Stowe House. As Thomas Strickland's health deteriorated, Mrs Strickland had to spend increasing amounts of time nursing him, and there was less time and energy to devote to the education of their children. For a while the children were left free to follow their own inclinations, but they began to run wild, and a governess was employed to restore order.

After only six months the governess left to run a school, and was not replaced. Instead, the older sisters were given the task of passing on to their younger sisters the lessons which they had themselves learned. Even so, outside the class-room, according to Catharine: "We younger ones were left a great deal under the control of nursemaids and we were cowed into obedience by terror – Horrible tales of ghosts, murders and highway robberies – gypsies and chimney sweeps carrying off bad children, all of which we listened to and believed."

While the six Strickland girls were proceeding one way or another with their home schooling, their two young brothers were set on a different path of education. They began by attending the small school in the village. Catharine said: "When four years of age and while still wearing frocks and little white trousers, Sam was sent daily to a school in the village kept by an old and very respected couple who for forty years had been the instructors of nearly three generations of children from their earlier years till old enough to take their place in the world." The girls and little boys of the village were taught by Mrs Newsom in one building, while the older boys were taught by Mr Newsom in another building.

Catharine wrote: "My little brother was set on a low bench in front of all the classes of girls, along with three other little boys of about the same age, to be taught his ABC and what else filled up the weary hours from eight in the morning till twelve. A bit of scarlet wool was given to each of these infant scholars, and one of the girls showed them how to wind it from one thumb to another, this was all they had to keep them quiet till the time arrived for their spelling lesson. Then the maid or two of his sisters came to release the poor little prisoner, and take the young animal home – This was our brother Sam's first school" and presumably also the first school for his younger brother Tom.

Catharine continued: "Our eldest sister was his next governess, and after that, he and his brother Tom were placed as day scholars at Dr Valpy's school Norwich." This school was founded in 1547 and was located in the Cathedral Close, Norwich. The school, now called Norwich School, still thrives.

During periods when Thomas Strickland was confined to bed with gout, Eliza and Agnes shared the task of reading their father to sleep. Catharine remembered: "The newspapers were Agnes' expected task. Perched on the foot of the bed, she would read with grave interest the political events of those stirring times, and the long speeches of the Ministers in the House of Commons. Her attention was so deeply engaged that she would arrange our schoolroom into a House of Commons, and give us a grand speech from Mr Canning, whom she was supposed to represent, and we thought it great fun to cheer and cry 'Hear, hear!' " The Napoleonic Wars were in progress, having begun in 1803.

Despite Thomas Strickland's strictness in the classroom, he had no objection to his children having opinions which differed from his own. Catharine noted: "Oddly enough, the Father and his child politician seldom agreed upon historical subjects. He was a Whig and a great admirer of William III, whom she detested being a devout champion of the unfortunate House of Stuart. Yet I never remember any trouble arising out of their opposition. She loved her father and was ever constant in her attachment." Maybe Thomas Strickland was thus teaching Agnes how to marshal and present her facts, and how to be an effective speaker in a debate.

1811: Eliza has a sad romance

In 1811, according to Catharine, Eliza's life entered a very difficult period: "We children were confined for hours to the school room. We did not know that Eliza had had a great trial laid on her which made her grave and impatient of our teasing ways. When yet a gay lively girl of sixteen, she had been asked in marriage – by a gentleman who was greatly attracted by her grace and talents. Captain W- applied to our father for leave to address Eliza. He was on the eve of taking command of a fine new East Indiaman, the Harleston – which was destined for making the long journey to India – a three years absence.

"The leave was granted provisionally and Eliza was thus far engaged to the gallant Captain and he sailed with the proviso that Eliza was to be his wife if nothing prevented. With him also went his younger brother, a bright lad of sixteen. The ship was launched under bright auspices but from that hour she was heard of no more. It was supposed that the vessel was burnt at sea – or perished with her crew in some wild hurricane or cyclone in the Indian Ocean. Our sister Eliza never married – I know not if this first blight that fell on her young heart chilled its affection but though she had many other suitors – she never loved again well enough to give her hand to anyone who sought it."

This is a sad little story and the beginning and the end of it seem to be true, but there is something wrong with the middle of the account. In January 1811, when Eliza was sixteen, two Suffolk newspapers gave an account of the launch of a ship named the 'Harleston'. The Bury and Ipswich Post on Wednesday 30th January 1811 reported: "Friday se'nnight a fine new ship of 580 tons burthen, called the Harleston, intended for the East India trade, was launched from Mr Bailey's yard at Halifax near Ipswich."

The Suffolk Chronicle on Saturday 26th January 1811 gave a more enthusiastic account: "Yesterday the Harleston East Indiaman, of 579 tons burthen, built by Mr Jabez Bayley, of this town, was launched at Halifax Yard, in the presence of a considerable concourse of spectators. She was built for Peter Everett Mestaers Esq and is one of the handsomest and largest vessels ever launched from our yards. The swell of water, occasioned by the launch, rather damped the ardour of many female visitors who stood on the shore ... She went off in a fine style, highly gratifying to the builder, and to all those who witnessed this dashing event."

An article in the Hampshire Chronicle on 20th May 1811 further corroborated Catharine's account, for in this article the captain of the 'Harleston', named by Catharine as Captain W-, was given his full surname: "Wednesday a Court of Directors was held at East India House, when Captain Hine of the Lady Lushington, Captain Templar of the Baring, and Captain Walker of the Harleston took leave previously to departing for Bengal direct." Other accounts gave Captain Walker his Christian name which was Thomas.

The 'Harleston' had been chartered by the East India Company, as was customary, and as in Catharine's account only undertook one such voyage. However at that point Catharine's story and the facts, as established via newspaper archives start to part company. The 'Harleston' under the command of Captain Thomas Walker sailed from Portsmouth on 21st June 1811 and reached Calcutta on 2nd November the same year. Its return journey was reported in stages, being recorded at Saugar on 2nd January 1812, Benkulen on 25th January and St Helena on 12th May 1812.

The 'Harleston' travelled on from St Helena under the protection of a Royal Navy frigate, leaving St Helena on 24th of May 1812, and passing Portsmouth on 20th July 1812 as one in a convoy of nine East India ships returning from Bengal. The 'Harleston' arrived safely at Deal on the Kent coast on 23rd July 1812. Captain Thomas Walker can therefore be presumed to have returned safely from this voyage, whether or not accompanied by a younger brother.

Soon after it had returned to England, the 'Harleston' was sold by Peter Mestaer, its original owner, and it never undertook another voyage for the East India Company. Its new owner Davypersaud Ghose was based in Bengal, and the 'Harleston' was still listed there in 1823. However, in 1813 Peter Mestaer bought another ship, an American vessel which had been launched in 1810, which he also named or re-named the 'Harleston.' This is also the name of two small East Anglian towns, one in Norfolk and the other in Suffolk. This second 'Harleston' was used as a West Indiaman, sailing between England and the West Indies for several years. This 'Harleston' finally became a whaling vessel, but on only its second whaling voyage in 1826 it was condemned at Mauritius as unseaworthy.

Therefore, whatever happened to Captain Thomas Walker, he did not disappear on his return voyage to India in 1811-1812, nor did he disappear on a voyage in either of the ships named 'Harleston'. He returned to England after one year, not three as Catharine had remembered, but can be traced no further, because there were several merchant navy captains surnamed Walker at that time, and it was rare for Christian names to be recorded. What happened to him and to the alleged unofficial engagement is a mystery, but the end of the story was as Catharine recorded. Eliza did not marry a gallant sea captain, and nor did she marry anyone else.

1808-1814: The Norwich and Reydon years

As Thomas Strickland's attacks of gout became longer and more severe, he had to spend the colder months away from the chill of Reydon and in the milder climate of Norwich, where his sons were at school. Catharine recorded: "It was therefore decided that part of the household, with my father and eldest sister" (Eliza) "to superintend it, should remove to Norwich, while our Mother remained at the Hall with the rest of the family to manage the farm and home establishment – Occasional exchanges were made among the young people – This was a pleasant arrangement for us all and it gave us opportunities of seeing a little more of the world than we could do in the lonely country house – my eldest sister came home and my Mother took her place with our father, but as soon as spring advanced the father returned and passed the summer with the Mother at the old house, going back to the city in the autumn."

The daughters who were in Norwich were allowed to borrow books from the circulating libraries, and could read the novels of the day and a wider range of literature than at home. The Waverley novels of Sir Walter Scott were beginning to appear and were very popular.

During these years Agnes went through a period of mental ill health, but which was not recognised as such. Catharine said: "A change came over Agnes that began to affect her health and spirits. Instead of the high-spirited bright creature, she became quietly studious – to shun noise. She was nervously excitable, started at any sudden change. The long rambles she used to enjoy were now weariness, and unfortunately the cause was attributed to want of ability or mental indolence. The poor young thing silently bowed beneath her yoke which for several years pressed heavily upon her, and but for the protecting care of her elder sister, she might have sunk beneath the ill judged severity of those who did not understand, that she was being crushed under the stern rule that was conscientiously thought to be the right one to raise and strengthen the weak. It was in after years acknowledged with deep regret to have been a great mistake." As a result either of this period of mental ill-health or simply as a result of growing up, Agnes changed from being a mischievous and adventurous child, and became a calm-tempered and physically timid adult.

Catharine remembering the year 1814 wrote: "At 18 Agnes's poetical talents began to show themselves. Eliza with many high qualities and acquirements delighted in the development of her sister's talents. So wedded were these remarkable sisters in heart and mind that they often wrote and composed together; one would start an idea and together it would grow into a form and be wrought out – and yet they differed greatly in person and essential points of character and in some especial talents."

1815: Thomas Strickland has a financial blow

The family circumstances changed dramatically in 1815 when Thomas Strickland lost money in a way which Jane Strickland described as resulting from "the misconduct of a near relation of his wife" whose maiden name had been Homer "in whose business he had invested the chief part of his property." Elsewhere the blow is described as Thomas Strickland having acted as a guarantor for a firm which failed, and so his own money was lost.

A notice appeared in the local papers on 2nd June 1815 which gave formal notification that: "the partnership lately subsisting between the undersigned Wm Homer and Thos Strickland, trading in the City of Norwich as Coach Makers under the name of Wm Homer was this day dissolved by mutual consent, their manufactory being at St Giles's Gates, Norwich." Debtors and creditors of the partnership were asked to settle their accounts.

Following the dissolution of the partnership, Thomas Strickland took over the business and continued to run it on his own, presumably in an attempt to repair the financial damage that had been done.

1817: Sarah and Catharine are very brave

With their father's efforts now concentrated in Norwich for financial as well as health reasons, some of the children were at times living at Reydon with both parents absent, and were in a mildly hazardous situation. Catharine wrote: "It chanced that our mother was detained unusually long at the town house during the early part of 1817 – a cold season it was, and an anxious one – the country was full of disbanded soldiers, from the continent." The Napoleonic Wars had ended after the Battle of Waterloo in 1815. "A general feeling of discontent existed, owing to many political causes – and the bad harvest of the previous summer."

Catharine continued: "In our lonely isolated home, we knew little of the outside world, and few strangers came to the house. Still there were tramps and smugglers and loose hands about, which kept us cautious. It was one of the precautions that was enjoined upon my sister, and the servants, to see that all the doors and windows were securely locked and barred, and every room examined each night before going to bed. This was no trifling duty, as the house was large and even the unoccupied garrets were entered every night before dark.

"The wintry winds would shake the windows and doors on a stormy night, and the far off sound of the ocean waves on our coast, added to the loneliness of the situation and made it more gloomy. Nor could we always account for sounds that seemed to have no natural causes and seemed to come from the cellars. These subterranean noises, we found out long afterwards to have been caused by the trusted but treacherous gardener who was in league with a band of smugglers. Their contraband of the lighter, more valuable sort, were often deposited in these underground vaults. The vigilance of the revenue officers of the coast guard had not been sufficiently aroused to keep the coast – a lonely one it was – free from the daring men that carried on their illicit trade.

"The winter of which I speak had been remarkable for reports of daring deeds, not without bloodshed between the smugglers and the coastguard men, and there were many instances in our vicinity of house breaking, but it was chiefly with the view of getting food and clothing. No violence had been shown to the inmates, still it was an alarming situation for unprotected women, but our sister" (Sarah) "was brave, and kept us from being frightened. We made the gardener on whose faith we had the most implicit confidence, instruct us in the art of loading and firing off a pistol that we discovered in a drawer of my father's bureau. Against such an unheard of unfeminine accomplishment our faithless gardener remonstrated. Well we never heeded – but made a good hit one day at a chalked mark on the garden door and felt wonderfully brave afterwards.

"Not many nights after this Sarah and I" (aged 19 and 15 respectively) "were awakened from our sleep by the sound as if someone was trying to pry open the barred shutters in the dining-room and without any thought of fear, Sarah got the pistols, gave me one and armed herself with the other – our design was, to fire off the pistols from a front window, to bring help from the gardener's cottage. We planned as we thought very prudently – the report of the pistols rang through the night air, and echoed back from Reydon Wood – but no aid came – but we detected a figure half bent disappear from the cover of the shrubs, and take a circuitous way across the fields beyond the road. This was no doubt the gardener himself. Then all remaining quiet, we went shivering to bed, and felt we had done great things in defence of the house, and shown ourselves no cowards in the hour of danger.

"Next day we asked Lockwood why he did not come when we fired the danger signal, but he said 'There was no danger, so he did not heed it' but his wife said 'He did not hear it for he was out all night and never came home till near daylight.' After that we had no more nightly noises to alarm us. Lockwood had taken good care that there should be no harm done – for he had only loaded the pistols with powder – so we could not have winged our man in spite of our bravery."

1817: Catharine and Susanna become authors

In the same way that a close friendship had formed between the eldest daughters, Eliza and Agnes despite their different personalities, a similar situation had developed between the two youngest daughters, Catharine and Susanna.

Catharine was placid and steady, and formed a bridge between her older sisters and her younger siblings, Susanna, Sam and Tom. Catharine described Susanna who, Catharine wrote: "was naturally of an impulsive temper, she was often elated and often depressed, easily excited by passing events, unable to control emotions caused by either pain or pleasure, morbidly sensitive to reproof, which if conscious of fault created self-reproach and made her for a time miserable – but if undeserved roused in her a spirit of resistance against what she regarded as tyranny and injustice, and having made her protest against it, she retired into herself and made no concession to the higher powers – I think I must often have acted the part of the brake on a steep hill, for the safety of the inside passengers. A few tender words had the effect that oil poured on water has - it smoothed the waves of irritated feelings, and calmed the rising storm. Susie was controllable by love – it was the magnet that she obeyed – opposition, stern remonstrance produced the opposite effect."

Life for those at Reydon House in the long winter months was dull. Catharine said: "We passed the days in the lonely old house, in sewing, in walking in the lanes, sometimes going to see the sick, and carry food and little comforts to poor cottagers – but reading was our chief resource, we ransacked the library for books. We dipped into the old magazines of the previous century and dull enough much of the contents proved. We tried history and drama – voyages and travels – of which there was a huge folio.

"To break the tedium of the dull winter, Susanna and myself formed the notion that we would try and write something of a novel ourselves – The idea was just to amuse ourselves by reading at night to our elder sister, what we had written during the day – our indulgent sister" (Sarah again) "made no objection to the proposed plan. We next turned our attention to getting the necessary materials for carrying it into execution – The want of the simple articles, pen, ink and paper, being a serious obstacle to our important undertaking. We had no money and even if we had had cash in hand – we should hardly have known what sort of paper to ask for at the shop in Southwold. We were such babes" despite being 14 and 15 years of age.

"Now it so happened that Sarah remembered having seen at the very bottom of the great Indian coffer of papier machee that stood between the windows in our bedroom, and which formed the receptacle of stores of household linen – sheets, blankets and spare quilts – reams of blue paper, blotting paper, and dozens of quill pens, ready cut, which had been sent to our father after the death of our uncle who had been a clerk in the Bank of England – and these had been deposited, by our mother at the bottom of this old Indian chest. The blue paper we pounced upon – for though not exactly the orthodox sort of stationery for such a purpose – it would do for a rough copy – and the ready made pens were just the very thing we wanted, as we knew little of the art of pen-making, we regarded them as real treasures, and as we knew there were cakes of Indian ink in a drawer in the bureau, we managed to make some very respectable ink for our work. Susanna and I stitched up the blank book, folding the paper to a convenient size.

"We had found among the old books a fine atlas, full of maps, and abounding in the most interesting geographical histories of the European countries, legends that we never questioned, and flourishing descriptions that just suited our romantic ideas of countries we had never seen. Susanna chose the period of the 'Thirty Years' War' – the great Gustavus Adolphus was one of her heroes and with her flexible imagination, she laid the foundation of a romantic tale of that period. She finally arrived at a successful and very sensational conclusion to her story while I was wading through a labyrinth of domestic life in Alpine regions, in the days of William Tell. Mine was meant to be an interesting love story, but being a novice in such matters, I found myself somewhat at a loss, and finally, in spite of sundry hints from my elder sister I left my Hero and Heroine in some inextricable muddle, and fell out of love adventures altogether and altered my plan and style, to one that proved far more to my taste and ability, and ended by writing a juvenile tale, which I brought to a successful conclusion.

"Every day we wrote a little of our stories, and every night we read aloud what we had written to our patient indulgent sister and thankfully received any advice and suggestions she offered – And it was thus that we passed the time till our mother's return. We kept our secret closely after she came home, bringing my eldest sister Eliza with her for a visit. Now came the crisis. One morning I was sitting on the step of our dressing-room door, reading to my sister Sarah my last chapter – when the door silently opened – and a very white hand, very gently took my manuscript out of my hand, and disappeared. It was our mother. Not a word she said – With dismay I looked at Sarah's alarmed face – Mamma had suspected that there was some secret hidden from her. She had already taken possession of Susanna's manuscript.

"I was covered with confusion – what would Eliza say? We dreaded her criticism and truly it came in very cutting and sarcastic terms 'I think my dear Katie and Susan you had been better employed in improving your grammar and spelling, than in writing such trash as that.' Up sprang the indignant Susan and snatched the despised manuscript and threw it in the fire – I hung my head and finally made a retreat in tears of shame at the well merited criticism. And then no more was said about our blue paper manuscripts. Now I am sure Sarah and I lamented over the destruction of Susan's story. It had merits far beyond what could have been supposed – a perfect plot, and characters full of fire and interest – so we thought – And it was finished.

"Well a year or two passed by. I had a reluctance entirely to destroy my production so I kept it laid by in secret – a sort of instinctive feeling that there was some merit in it I suppose. Two or three years after, I rewrote the story on good paper and it was sold for ten guineas by my Guardian."

(1817: Literary context - Jane Austen dies)

Jane Austen's first novel 'Sense and Sensibility' had been published in 1811. She died on 18th July 1817, aged 42. The last two of her six novels, 'Persuasion' and 'Northanger Abbey', were published posthumously in 1818.

1817: Agnes returns to writing poetry

Agnes's desire to write poetry re-emerged, stirred into action by the death of Princess Charlotte, who was heir to the throne, being the only legitimate child of the Prince Regent. She was a popular princess who married for love rather than for dynastic reasons, and her first child was due in November 1817. To the shock of the nation, Princess Charlotte died in child-birth and her son was still-born. A period of national mourning followed during which Agnes wrote a poem suitable to the event.

Agnes had been severely ill with some kind of fever in the autumn of 1817, and worked on the poem in secret, for fear of being forbidden on health grounds from carrying on with the task. Her understanding of poetical construction was now on a firm foundation and her poem 'Monody on the Death of Princess Charlotte' was in a different league from the earlier poem which had been so thoroughly rejected by her father.

The family were sufficiently impressed by Agnes's poem that one of her younger sisters persuaded her to show it to someone who Catharine later described as "a literary friend of her father." He in turn showed it to the editor of a local newspaper, the 'Norwich Mercury', who published it anonymously in his paper, making this poem the first published work of the Strickland family.

Agnes now had her father's approval and encouragement in her poetical endeavours, and having written many minor pieces, she set to work on a lengthy poem, a romance set in the time of the War of the Roses which she entitled 'Matilda.' This she read to Thomas Strickland when he had returned to Reydon Hall with Eliza. He was, in Jane's words, delighted and astonished, and Agnes remembered his praise for many years, it being the last poem she read to her father before his death.

May 1818: Thomas Strickland dies

Soon after Agnes had gained her father's approval for her poem, the event was overtaken by one of far greater importance. Thomas Strickland, after his period of becoming increasingly an invalid, died suddenly of a heart attack. Catharine wrote: "In the May of 1818 we lost our dear Father. A sudden attack of the gout seizing his heart was the cause of his death. It was our first great cause of sorrow."

Jane described her parents' marriage and the effect on Elizabeth Strickland of her husband's death. Jane wrote: "The blow was sudden, the bereavement appearing yet more terrible from its being wholly unexpected. The happy union of four-and-twenty years had been in a few moments brought to a close. There had been no discord to mar the wedded life of the couple now separated by the inexorable hand of death." Jane said of her father: "His patience in sickness, and cheerful spirits when convalescent were remarkable. His varied talents and accomplishments, his vast mental stores, fine person, and charming manners, had made her willingly renounce, for his sake, the gaieties of life, though she was nearly twenty years his junior. The loss to her was indeed irreparable, and rendered still heavier by pecuniary losses, which compelled her to practise a rigid and unsocial economy."

Thomas Strickland's death was announced in the local papers with the words: "Died on Monday 18th May 1818, in St Giles, Norwich, Thos Strickland Esq. – respected and esteemed by the world, beloved by those whose nearer approach enabled them to estimate his talents and virtues." In accordance with his wish to be buried in a quiet churchyard if he died in Norwich, he was buried at Lakenham, two miles south of Norwich Cathedral just outside the city walls.

December 1818: Thomas Strickland's Will

When Thomas Strickland died, a Will which had been duly signed and witnessed was officially accepted as his final Will, and work had begun on implementing it, when a hand-written and un-witnessed but later Will was found. The later Will was dated 10th April 1818 and the question of whether or not this should be regarded as his final Will caused legal difficulties and delay.

It was decided that if the hand-writing could be convincingly pronounced as that of Thomas Strickland, the Will written in April 1818 would be accepted in place of the earlier one. The two people who were deemed to be very familiar with Thomas Strickland's handwriting, and who were willing to vouch that they believed Thomas Strickland to be the true author of the document, were both relatives of Thomas Strickland's widow Elizabeth, whose maiden name had been Homer.

The two men were John Homer and William Homer, both of whom lived in Norwich. John Homer described himself as a wine merchant, and William Homer said he was a coach-maker. There can be little doubt that he was the William Homer whose business partnership with Thomas Strickland had been dissolved, and who is implicated as the cause of Thomas Strickland's financial downfall.

It took until 19th December 1818 for the later Will to be legally accepted in Norwich, and a further stage of legal procedure had to be carried out which necessitated Elizabeth Strickland being in London on 7th January 1819, before the three executors could get to work implementing it. The executors to Thomas Strickland's Will were his widow Elizabeth Strickland, Richard Morgan of Norwich, and the Rev John Robinson, Vicar of Southwold.

Thomas Strickland in his last Will did his best to protect and provide for his widow and children, but he must have thought that he had a few more years of life in front of him, with time to repair the financial damage he had suffered, because the wording of his Will was more financially optimistic than was warranted by his circumstances when he died.

His estate was valued at under £4,000 and he left everything to his widow to provide for her during her lifetime, but with some very strict instructions attached. He bequeathed to Elizabeth Strickland all his personal belongings and household contents "either at Reydon

House (or) at my Houses at St Giles's Gates" in Norwich. He also left her his "Freehold and Copyhold estates" at Reydon "to receive the rent profits and income thereof during her life or to cultivate and crop the land herself if she so chooses" for the maintenance of herself and their children.

He then recorded that he held leasehold premises "at or near St Giles Gates ... Norwich and a coach manufactory carried on in the said premises under the firm of Thomas Strickland & Co". His Will was very clear that this firm should be sold at the earliest opportunity and that Elizabeth Strickland should retain absolutely nothing which could in any way associate her with the business. His wording implies a continuing suspicion that his wife/widow, unless clearly prevented, might find herself drawn back into fresh financial problems as a result of the coach-making business and her relative William Homer. His exact words regarding the coach manufactory were that his executors should "as soon as possible dispose of the same to the best advantage turning everything possible into money or good securities for money but on no account to have any concern in the business of coach-making by receiving an annual profit from the business" nor should they "leave any assets on the premises undisposed of" which could be "construed into a partnership at some future time."

Having thus done his best to protect his wife from future difficulties in that direction, he specified that the money so raised was to be used to pay all debts and expenses, and to pay off the mortgage on the Reydon estate. Any remaining money was to be invested "in the Bank of England in the public funds in the names of my executors. The interest of the said stock to be received by my wife" during her life.

Finally, Thomas Strickland left to his wife Elizabeth everything associated with his farm at Reydon – animals, crops, equipment etcetera – if she should wish to cultivate the farm on her own account. If not, money raised from anything sold was also to be invested in government stock and the income from the investment was to be available to Elizabeth during her life.

Thomas Strickland having, as he thought, protected and provided for Elizabeth Strickland during her lifetime, then looked further into the future and specified that on Elizabeth Strickland's death, Reydon

Hall and all its contents should be sold and the proceeds divided equally between his eight children. Unfortunately, this well-intentioned specification had the effect of trapping the family at Reydon Hall, unable to move from or sell it until Elizabeth Strickland herself died. His Will contained very little else apart from the request that Elizabeth Strickland should accept the advice of the two other executors of his Will in case of difficulty.

Once they had permission to act, the executors very soon found a buyer for the coach-making business in Norwich. The business had been sold by February 1819 and notices were placed in newspapers asking people indebted to the estate of Thomas Strickland to settle their accounts. However, selling the business had been a far easier matter than getting customers to pay what they owed, and eighteen months later there were still many bills outstanding, and the executors had to resort to public threats of legal action to try and get the situation resolved.

Unfortunately, the money raised from selling the business was a long way short of clearing Thomas Strickland's debts. There was a mortgage of £1,400 outstanding on the Reydon property, and this mortgage would remain undiminished throughout Elizabeth Strickland's life, all she was able to do was to pay any annual interest on the loan to prevent the debt increasing, but she was never able to reduce the mortgage, not even by a trifling amount.

Elizabeth Strickland, in order to clear remaining debts and pay funeral costs, had to borrow money from Richard Morgan, who was subsequently referred to by the family as their guardian, as well as being an executor of their father's Will. The loan was for £309 16s and was to be repaid, without interest, 30 years later. Thomas Strickland's instruction that excess money should be invested in the Bank of England was therefore an irrelevance. All that Elizabeth Strickland and her eight children had to live on, was any income that could be made from farming at Reydon, plus any rents that could be charged, minus any interest that had to be paid on the mortgage.

Therefore Elizabeth and her eight children had to maintain a large property and exist more or less on thin air, plus what they could earn by other means. The eldest daughters, Eliza and Agnes were 24 and 22 years old when their father died, and the youngest children, Sam and Tom were 13 and 11 years old, and were both still attending a fee-paying school in Norwich.

1819-1820: The family adjusts

Whilst Thomas Strickland's Will was being sorted out, the family continued to have homes in both Norwich and Reydon. Over the summer of 1818 Catharine lived at Reydon under the care of Eliza, while Sam and Tom lived in Norwich to continue their education. The other family members did a certain amount of journeying between the two places. Catharine when referring to this period wrote: "Sometimes Susanna and my mother stayed with us, and sometimes one of our other sisters drove over and remained a few days." However, it must have become clear to Mrs Strickland quite soon after her husband died that this was no longer affordable. The coach-making business having been sold, Sam and Tom's schooling was ended, and the home in Norwich was given up. The Strickland family moved to Reydon as their permanent and only home.

Catharine, who has left such a detailed account of the everyday life of the family up to 1818, quietly drew a veil over the ensuing few years, referring neither to the straightened circumstances in which the family found themselves, nor to any romances involving herself or her sisters. She summed all this up by writing: "Years brought changes in our lives, occupations and friendships. Though still living in the retirement of Reydon House, we were not quite shut out from society – many friendships were formed, and we occasionally left home to visit distant friends."

She added: "It is not my intention to dwell on attachments necessarily arising from a more enlarged sphere of intimacy, with those who were attracted by talent or natural beauty – for among the six sisters there were some who were remarkable for their personal attractions inherited from my father who was remarkably handsome – therefore lovers were not wanting, but we pass those things by, as no matter of interest, to anyone of the present date."

Catharine did, however, leave a description of her two eldest sisters. Of Eliza, Catharine wrote: "In person Eliza was tall, slender and elegantly formed. A brunette with hazel eyes and chestnut hair, her features were small and delicate. Her hands with long slender fingers seemed to excel in all works of skill with pencil or brush – for she became a charming self-taught flower artist, as well as adept at catching likenesses of the human face. She danced gracefully the slow minuet de cour, the cotillon, these were the fashion of the day. She was passionate in temper, quickly roused to anger and had all the pride of the old ancestors and a little added to it." Eliza, self-contained and easily angered, was the most studious of the family, and Catharine later in life regretted not having paid better attention to Eliza's attempts to instruct her in botany and the natural sciences.

Catharine's description of Agnes shows more contrasts with Eliza than similarities: "Agnes on the contrary was a serene and contemplative temper. She had a great share of family pride like her sister and father – the old historical legendary lore that the sisters listened to and the sort of books they read. While Eliza excelled with her pencil in drawing, Agnes could not make the outline of a flower with pencil or even copy a simple engraving, but put a piece of paper and a pair of scissors in her hands, and she could give the exact outline of any face that she studied for a few minutes, her profiles were perfect and she cut the semblance of any animal, bird or object, tree or flower, and produce landscapes that were like shadowy drawings so exquisite was the workmanship."

Another difference between her two eldest sisters that Catharine noted was in dancing. "Agnes did not care for dancing – it did not suit her, she would have excelled in music, but in those days teachers were few and the piano only begun to be introduced – she was disgusted with the inferior instrument in our house and gave up just as she was beginning to master the difficulties of the learner. She abandoned the music to the younger ones. I said her temper was serene. It was so, for I never saw her descend to any violence of speech or gesture. There was a quiet dignity that marked her all through life. She was beloved by the servants who would do anything for dear Miss Agnes – the labouring poor men, women and children held her in deep reverence and affection, she had kind words and looks for them all." Agnes had black or very dark brown hair and eyes rather than the chestnut hair and hazel eyes of Eliza.

At the end of the biography of Agnes which Jane was to write, are Jane's descriptions of her sisters Agnes and of Eliza. That of Agnes reads: "She was attractive, though not to be called beautiful.

She was tall and remarkably upright. Her bust and arms were very fine; her hair black as ebony, glossy and silky in texture, as well as abundant; her complexion somewhat pale, unless brightened by exercise or excitement, when it became roseate."

The written description of Eliza reads: "She was tall, but scarcely appeared so from the symmetry of her form. Her features were small and delicate, her teeth beautiful, her hair dark chestnut, and so profuse that it reached to her knees; her eyes were hazel, the complexion of her face that of a warm brunette. Her bust, hands and feet were remarkable for their beauty; her conversation was lively and intelligent; her disposition generous, her temper warm to faultiness; but she was very unselfish, and willing to help all who needed her assistance."

Of Eliza's abilities, Jane wrote: "She was a fine dancer, an excellent botanist and florist, drew well in many styles, was well versed in heraldry, and found great pleasure in antiquarian research. Unlike Agnes, whose health was often delicate, she possessed a fine constitution, and though so sylph-like in appearance, was personally strong. Well skilled in business. It was to her application was made in case of any difficulty in the family, which, in fact, she ruled, possessing the governing powers in no ordinary degree, and perhaps exercising them not always to the liking of the governed."

With the need to supplement the family income, some of the family turned to writing as a means to earn some money. In 1818 at the age of 16, Catharine had a children's story sold on her behalf by her guardian, Richard Morgan. It was published in London by Harris of St Paul's Churchyard who paid her five guineas, and asked her to write more stories in a similar vein, paying her the same sum each time.

Also thanks to the efforts of their guardian, Agnes had the opportunity to have a long, narrative poem, 'Worcester Field, or The Cavalier' published in monthly parts in 'The London Magazine.' However Agnes did not think the terms were good enough and refused the offer, a decision she later regretted.

1819-1820: Relatives begin to rally round

Although money was always in short supply, the Strickland children had relatives on both their mother and their father's side of the family who were in a position to help, and who soon began to do so. Susanna was an early beneficiary, but with mixed results. In 1819 she caught whooping cough, and she wrote later "for 8 months it hung upon me like a tormenting fiend. I became a perfect skeleton in consequence, and made my first visit to London for change of air which had the desired effect, and gave me my first mortifying knowledge of the world."

Catharine's account of Susanna's early life gave more details. She wrote: "When Susanna was about sixteen, my mother received an invitation from a married sister (whom she had not seen for a number of years) for one of her nieces to visit her. My aunt had not seen any of us since we were babies – It was decided that Susanna should be the one chosen to go to London – This was the first time she had ever been from home.

"The unknown Aunt did not take kindly to her and after a few weeks my sister did not find the sojourn a pleasant one and went to stay with my father's sister who received her kindly and with this Aunt" (Sara Stone) "and Uncle" (Stone) "she remained some months very happily, returning home the following spring."

Catharine, true to her intention of not revealing anything about young romances, said nothing further, but a footnote to Catharine's written account, but not in Catharine's handwriting, added: "The truth is she fell in love with a young man, who was not at all her equal and her Aunt was naturally very much displeased."

1821: Writing begins in earnest

In 1820 King George III died and the Prince Regent became King George IV. In the Strickland household by 1821, Susanna and Catharine were both writing, and were both getting their work published. Catharine said: "It was after Susanna returned home that she began writing some of her earlier productions and we passed very pleasant times, reading, writing and taking big walks and I think it was in that year or the following that she wrote her historic tales of 'Spartacus'. During the following years she published several popular books among them 'Hugh Latimer,' 'Prejudice and Principle' and 'Roland Massingham'." 'Spartacus' is said to be Susanna Strickland's first known work, a romantic historical novel published in 1822 by AK Newman.

In common with her elder sister Agnes, Susanna was writing poetry and getting it published in newspapers, in Christmas Annuals and occasionally in book form. Catharine said: "Susanna also wrote many small poems that appeared in the Annuals of those years which gained friendly notice. On being encouraged by some of her literary friends, she again visited the great city while her volume of poems was passing through the press. This book was published under the title of 'Enthusiasm and other poems' by Susanna Strickland. The first edition was soon exhausted, and it was very favourably reviewed but already the taste for poetry was beginning to decline – Southey, Coleridge, Wordsworth still held the field in poetry but the public began to turn their attention to prose."

Catharine's own work did not include poetry and her written works, whether sketches, short stories or books, were generally intended for children. This was the genre which she had discovered came most easily to her, when she had made her first attempt at writing in 1817. Her early published works were 'Disobedience; or, Mind What Mama Says' published in 1819, 'Nursery Fables' published in 1821 and 'Little Downy; or, The History of a Field Mouse' published in 1822. 'Little Downy' was sometimes wrongly attributed to Susanna.

From 1821 onwards stories written variously by Agnes, Jane, Susanna and Catharine Strickland appeared in the Christmas Annuals which were then very popular, some directed at children and some aimed at adults.

At this time, Agnes and Eliza together wrote 'The Rival Crusoes' and followed this with 'Historical Tales of Royal British Children,' which Jane said succeeded in making them "a little ready money." Jane also had a book published in the early 1820s, entitled 'Harry Percy', while poems by Agnes and by Susanna were appearing in newspapers on a fairly regular basis. By these means five of the Strickland daughters were building a name for themselves in the literary world. Sarah and Tom were the only children of Thomas and Elizabeth Strickland who never made any attempt to earn money by writing.

With income from the farm at Reydon and a little rental income, plus the money the daughters gained from their writing, the Strickland family managed to keep their heads above water.

However, parts of the large house had to be shut up to reduce running costs, while the building as a whole, and even the parts that were still occupied, gradually deteriorated due to the family's lack of money.

1822: Tom is the first to leave home

Sam and Tom having left school, Sam set to work on the family farm at Reydon, and Tom decided that he wanted a life at sea. There were no openings in the Royal Navy in 1822 and so the Merchant Navy was his only option. At the age of fourteen, Tom started his naval life.

How he joined and in what role has not been recorded. But Catharine said that he left home: "in a Merchant ship bound for the South Pacific" and so, from the very start of his career, he was working on the large sailing ships which made long and hazardous voyages, with absences from home which lasted many months or even years.

By the time Tom returned from his first voyage, his brother Sam had left England and as Catharine recorded: "Thus were the brothers separated and they met again only once, many years after."

The early 1820s: Eliza is the next to leave home, followed on a part-time basis by Agnes

The next of the eight children to move out of the family home on a fairly permanent basis was Eliza, who had been born in 1794. In the 1820s she moved to London, lived in furnished rented accommodation and got work as a book reviewer and magazine editor.

Agnes to some extent followed her elder sister's example and lived in London for months at a time but whereas Eliza chose to live independently and more or less permanently in London, Agnes's home continued to be at Reydon. When in London she seems generally to have stayed with relatives. These were mainly her father's cousin, Thomas Cheesman, and her father's married sister, Mrs Leverton.

Thomas Cheesman

Thomas Cheesman had been born in 1760 and was a renowned engraver. His work included making engravings of portraits, including twenty portraits now in the National Portrait Gallery. In her biography of Agnes Strickland, written many years later, Jane described the situation thus: "A new source of intellectual pleasure was opened for (Agnes) by the study of the Italian language – her kind instructor being an elderly cousin of her father, an engraver of some eminence, and a highly accomplished man. He generally passed the summer months at Reydon, where he was a very welcome and beloved guest.

"Being a man of vast acquirements, a fine musician, a great antiquary, and one who had seen much of life, his company enlivened the solitude of Reydon; and he kindly devoted himself to the task of completing the education of his young cousins, who on their parts took some pains to draw him out of his eccentric old bachelor ways, but of course with very little success. Agnes was a great favourite with this amiable old gentleman, with whom she read Petrarca, Ariosto in select portions, and Dante. Of the most obscure passages of the last he could give a learned exposition."

Another description of Thomas Cheesman and his connection with the Strickland family at Reydon House, was left by Catharine when she wrote her memoirs many years later. Elaborating on the family history which has already been referred to, Catharine wrote: "too proud to seek favour of any of his own, our grandfather left the North country and came up to London where he got a situation as confidential clerk in Halletts Dock Yard. After a while his brother William followed his steps and was employed in a large mercantile establishment of which he afterwards became the proprietor. Three sisters subsequently left home and married in London but two were childless – one only left a son" (Thomas Cheesman) "who became a pupil of Frances Bartolozzi – well known as an artist and engraver – now chiefly remembered by his cousins who loved and greatly valued him – he was a solitary eccentric old man, full of knowledge and talent, devoted to music and the fine arts, music, poetry and languages, a man of genius and rare accomplishments but so foreign in his habits and manners that he seemed to stand apart from his fellow men as if he belonged to a different era or another country."

Jane when referring to Thomas Cheesman wrote: "Her cousin painted a fine miniature of Agnes during one of his visits to Reydon, which is now" (1887) "in the possession of her sister." (Sarah) "This was an excellent likeness of her at the time it was taken, as she was then fuller in person than in more mature years."

During the course of the family correspondence, two other miniatures painted by Thomas Cheesman were mentioned, miniatures of Sarah and of Susanna. No mention has been found of miniatures of any of the other three sisters, and only three miniatures have appeared in subsequent publications. These pictures were printed in the first instance in a biography of Agnes Strickland written in 1940 by Una Pope-Hennessy who names them as Agnes, Susanna and Sarah. No firm dates have been attached to the portraits which would appear to have been painted at different times.

Thomas Cheesman's niece lived with him in London, looking after the running of his household. Due to difficulties with handwriting, the niece's name is not known precisely. It will be given as it seems to be on each occasion when it crops up. At this point her name seems to be Miss Standen. Thomas Cheesman's home at the time when Agnes and her sisters were visiting him, was in Newman Street, not far from Oxford Street, where he had previously lived. His last work to appear in an exhibition of the Society of British Artists was in 1834 and he probably died in 1834 or 1835.

Mrs Rebecca Leverton and 'Worcester Field'

The other relative who regularly provided a London home for the Strickland sisters, was Mrs Leverton, a Strickland by birth. In 1803 she had married her second husband, Thomas Leverton, a well-known London architect who died in 1824. Among Thomas Leverton's professional works was the building and internal decoration of his home at 13 Bedford Square in London. He may indeed have been the architect of the whole, or a major part of Bedford Square, which Susanna described in a letter as "a very pretty part of Town, though not quite as fashionable as my ambitious sister poet" (Agnes) "would wish."

Mrs Leverton's contribution to the lives of the Strickland sisters, apart from inviting them to stay in her London home, was to hold

Drawing Rooms at Bedford Square, social events to which she invited the literary people of the day, including editors of the numerous magazines then in operation. In theory this provided the Strickland sisters with contacts for placing their work in fashionable magazines. However Eliza and Agnes soon realised that many magazines were not likely to accept their work because literary ladies, notably Lady Fanny Morgan and Miss Landon (known as LEL), had a substantial influence over the editors or owners of the magazines, and it was necessary to gain the support of these women in order to progress.

As Miss Landon claimed to have an annual income of over £250 from the poems she published, Agnes made another attempt at earning a living through her poetry, believing her own work to be just as good as that of Miss Landen. However Agnes's efforts at publication were markedly less successful than those of LEL, possibly because her private life was less colourful.

Agnes, having turned down the offer to publish 'Worcester Field' which her guardian had obtained, herself managed to find a publisher for the poem. Unfortunately, this publisher went bankrupt while he was working on the poem, and Agnes had to pay to retrieve her own manuscript.

She then found people willing to put their name down for a copy in advance of publication, with the aim of covering costs. Agnes made no profit, and may even have needed the help of Mrs Leverton to draw even, but the publication of 'Worcester Field' enhanced her reputation as a published poet, and from 1827 she was referred to, when subsequent work was published, as "the author of 'Worcester Field' " until a better reference became available.

1820-1830: Agnes and Eliza work with Henry Colburn

One of the men who founded and financed several magazines was Henry Colburn, with whom Fanny Morgan was particularly closely associated. Among his numerous publications were 'The Literary Gazette', 'New Monthly Magazine', 'Court Journal' and 'Athenaeum'. Agnes managed to get work from Henry Colburn as a writer in the 'New Monthly Magazine' with payment at a guinea and a half for a page of poetry, and ten guineas for a prose sketch.

Eliza also worked for Henry Colburn. Lady Morgan may have realised that Eliza Strickland, unlike Agnes, had no literary ambitions, and simply wanted to earn a living. With or without Fanny Morgan's involvement, Eliza started working for the 'Court Journal' and was subsequently appointed as a member of staff. By the time King George IV died in 1830, being succeeded by King William IV, Eliza had become editor of the 'Court Journal' with a regular income and a settled situation in London.

1825: Sam emigrates to Canada

Tom having left home for a life of adventure and hardship at sea, his elder brother Sam also felt he wanted more than the quiet life of a Suffolk farmer, and he decided to emigrate. Catharine recorded the event in her reminiscences, and Sam himself wrote a book 27 years later which described his emigration and life thereafter.

Catharine wrote: "Sam after he returned from school attended to the cultivation of the Reydon farm – But the first wave of emigration had set in, the great depression both in the Mercantile, and Agricultural affairs, had caused people to turn their attention towards making homes for their families in the Colonies – The books and pamphlets that were written set forth the advantages of emigration to Canada in very flattering colours and to this subject my brother turned with all the hopefulness of youth. He was young, just nineteen, full of vigour, strength and as sanguine as could be. Arrangements were made to enable him to reach the land of freedom and the friends to whose care he was consigned by the dear anxious mother." The friend was James Black who had gone out to Canada early in the 19th century and had settled with his family on a half-cleared farm near Lake Ontario.

Sam described his own attitude: "A preference for an active, rather than a professional life, induced me to accept an offer made by an old friend, of joining him in Darlington, in Upper Canada in 1825. I therefore took leave of my family in Suffolk, and engaged a passage in the brig 'William McGilevray' commanded by William Stoddart, an experienced American seaman." The area of Canada that Sam moved to in 1825, known as 'Upper Canada', had changed in name to

'Canada West' by the time he wrote his book in the 1850s. Both names refer to modern-day Ontario.

Sam was to set off at the end of March 1825 and Catharine described his departure: "Mother and some of the sisters bade him farewell over night, but Sarah and I kept vigil, and slept little, that we might prepare a hot breakfast for the dear traveller, who must start on his journey before sunrise to meet the London coach at Yoxford, ten miles from Reydon – we had resolved to accompany him to the coach.

"Well do I remember that day 25th March 1825, the early breakfast that we made as cheerful as we could, not to dampen the spirit of the bright hopeful boy. The glorious sunrise as it broke over the dark Henham woods – it had been by a setting moon that we had left home – the frost glittering on the grass. We reached the picturesque old Town where we parted with this dear one – now for the first time launched on the wide world.

"How well I remember his bright handsome face – smiling as he waved his cap and the light morning breeze lifted his bright sunny curls from his brow as the coach passed us, and we now realised what a parting this was – and it was with saddened hearts we returned home."

Sam gave an account of what happened next: "On the 28th March 1825 we left London Docks, and dropped down the river to Gravesend, and on the following day put our pilot ashore off Deal, and reached down as far as the coast of Sussex where we were becalmed for two days.

"It blew so fresh for two or three days, that we made up for lost time, and were soon out of sight of Scilly. The 18th and 19th of April 1825 were very stormy, the sea ran mountains high; we had a foot of water in the cabin. The gale lasted till the following morning, but though the storm had lulled the wind was against us.

"The weather was foggy near the bank of Newfoundland. We passed over the Great Bank without any danger, though the wind was high and the sea rough. On the 29th April 1825 we fell in with some icebergs" a spectacle which he found "magnificent and imposing" as well as "very fearful and sufficiently appalling. We took care to keep a good look out, but the fog was thick.

"We entered, on the 5th May 1825, the Gulf of St Lawrence. The 6th of May found us in the river St Lawrence" where snow fell all day. "On the 8th of May 1825 we sailed as far as the Seven Islands – we could hear the howling of the wolves at night, to me a new and dismal sound. On the 10th of May we stood for the island of Bic, and took on board a pilot. On our progress through the river – the shores were dotted with farm-houses with fine gardens and orchards, while lovely islands, covered with lofty trees, rose from the river and delighted the eye.

"On the 13th May 1825 we passed the island of Orleans and the Falls of Montmorenci. Quebec soon came into view, with its strong fortress crowning the imposing heights. The next day our brig was taken in tow by the fine steam-boat, the 'Richelieu de Chambley' and we proceeded at a rapid rate. The next day saw us safely moored in the port of Montreal, just forty-five days from our departure from the London Docks.

"The river here is very broad. The Lachine rapids commence immediately above the town. I took my passage in a Durham boat, bound for Kingston, which started off the next day. We had hard work poling up the rapids. The next evening we landed at Les Cedres. I now determined to walk to Prescot to take a steam-boat for Kingston on Lake Ontario. I fell in with an Irishman and we travelled in company for three days. I remained two or three days at Prescot, waiting for the arrival of my baggage from the Durham boat then I left Prescot by boat in the evening for Kingston."

From Kingston, Samuel took the schooner 'Shamrock' which sailed "through the Thousand Islands – the Archipelago of the St Lawrence." Two days journey got him as far as Cobourg, then a small village, from which he walked the last six or seven miles "to my friends in Darlington. I was received with the greatest kindness and, in a few days felt quite at home."

Mr Black's farm consisted of over 200 acres of cleared land, mainly meadows and pasture, and, according to Sam "Mr Black had held a situation under government and had lived in London all his life prior to emigrating to Canada" and had therefore struck a poor deal when buying the land. The township when Sam arrived in 1825 "boasted only a grist-mill, saw-mill, a store and half-a-dozen houses." At this stage Sam was intending to stay with the Black family until the following spring, to learn Canadian ways of clearing land and farming. He then intended to buy land of his own.

Sam soon fell in love with one of Mr Black's daughters. Catharine's version of events, written for family reading, was that Sam "won the affection of one of Mr Black's daughters, a very sweet girl, not quite eighteen, but they said to 'Wait a year or two' but love will venture in where reason says nay and they made a stolen marriage." Sam's version of events, written to be published in a book, was slightly different: "During my domestication under my friend's roof, I became attached to one of his daughters. The affection was mutual, and our happiness was completed by the approbation of our friends. We were married: and it seemed there was a goodly prospect of many years of wedded happiness before us."

Catharine wrote: "In those primitive days in the Colony, young people married at very early ages, and often began life with little more than a shanty roof over their heads. They were contented without luxuries, home made furniture of the roughest description, pork, potatoes, bread with a store of maple syrup and molasses, and tea to furnish the light portion of the menu. It needed much real faithful love to furnish contentment, and cheerfulness – this dear Sam and his pretty young wife thought they possessed in full measure."

1825-1826: Friendship develops with James Bird

It was at about the time Sam emigrated to Canada, that the Strickland family in Reydon began a correspondence with James Bird. He was a sociable man with a wide circle of literary friends and lived in Yoxford, Suffolk with his wife Emma and their children.

James Bird ran a pharmacist shop which also sold stationery and books, and he was also a published poet. Yoxford is a village some ten miles south-west from Reydon, and a stopping point for coaches travelling to or from London.

Some of the letters to James Bird which originated from the Strickland daughters have survived, the letters dating from 1825 until James Bird's death in 1839. The correspondence contained orders for medicines and stationery, requests for news about literary matters, and general family news.

1826-1829: Tom's next voyage

When Sam left Reydon early in March 1825, Tom had not yet returned from his first voyage to the South Pacific, which he began three years previously. There is no record of when he returned but after a period at home he set off again in the autumn of a year which is most likely to have been 1826.

This date is deduced from a letter which Susanna wrote to Emma Bird saying: "I take the opportunity of my dear brother passing through Yoxford on his way to London to beg your acceptance of a basket of apples for the children. Whom I doubt not, like the feathered race whose names they bear, are exceedingly fond of fruit. Mamma would have sent some before but we could not find a conveyance without occasioning a greater expense than such a trifling tribute of our esteem and friendship was worth."

The letter continued: "My brother received a hasty summons last night to rejoin his ship bound for India immediately so that you may imagine the bustle and confusion his sudden departure has occasioned but we are scarcely allowed time to think of the long and painful separation that is about to take place and shall feel his absence more tomorrow than we do tonight. I love him so tenderly that I feel my heart none of the lightest." Silence about Tom and his life in the family chronicles is not, therefore, due to any family antipathy towards him, merely that none of the family have thought fit to record much about his early life. Similarly, and equally to be regretted, there is little about Sarah or Mrs Strickland in family reminiscences, and barely a mention of Jane.

If sailing for India in the autumn of 1826, Tom might not have been expected to arrive back until early in 1829.

1826: Sam becomes a settler

Sam kept to his original intention of helping Mr Black and learning from him for a year, then setting up on his own. In 1826 he began to look for land to buy, but was unable to find anything suitable near to his parents-in-law in Darlington. One of his brothers-in-law had bought land fifty miles away on the banks of the river Otonabee, a mile from the newly laid out town of Peterborough.

Sam and his wife Emma decided to go and settle there, and bought a plot on the river bank adjoining Emma's brother's land.

Sam in his book wrote: "Otonabee contains over 80,000 acres which at that time had just been opened by the Government for location. The only practicable road then to this settlement was from Coburg, distant some 12 miles. The price asked was fifteen shillings per acre, which was high for wild land at that time, but the prospect of a town so near" had put the asking price up, even though the town had only got as far as consisting of a lay-out and a few log houses.

Sam needed £150 to buy the land, plus enough cash to survive on while he did the basic clearing and building work, and turned the land into a farmstead. In his published account written many years later, Sam glossed over how he came by this money, simply stating that money was sent to him by his family in England. When Sam asked for the money in 1826 he would have been well aware how difficult it would be for Mrs Strickland to send him any money at all, but he seems to have asked for, and she seems to have sent, £300.

Mrs Strickland raised the money by putting a value of £300 on the one-eighth share of the Reydon Estate which Sam would inherit on her own death. She then notionally bought it from him, and mortgaged the share in return for the £300 cash which she sent to Sam. Three of her daughters (Eliza, Agnes and Jane) stood as sureties for the repayment of the mortgage. These were Sam's three eldest sisters, two of whom were managing to earn something of a living for themselves. This sounds all very well for Sam, but a bit hard on the female members of the family struggling to make ends meet in Suffolk.

However, with the money promised and subsequently sent to Canada, Sam reported that he: "closed the bargain and became a landed proprietor in Canada West. On the 16th of May 1826, I moved with all my goods and chattels, which were easily packed into a single horse wagon, and consisted of a plough iron, six pails, a sugar kettle, two iron pots, a frying pan with a long handle, a tea kettle, a chest of carpenter's tools, a Canadian axe, and a cross-cut saw. My stock of provisions comprised a parcel of groceries, half a barrel of pork and a barrel of flour. The roads were so bad that it took three days" to go the fifty miles.

Sam's wife Emma was by this time expecting their first child, and remained with her parents while Sam got on with the work of preparing their future home helped by two hired labourers. Their first task was to build a simple shanty hut for immediate shelter whilst they cleared land and built a proper house. The house was to be 36 feet long and 24 feet wide, to be made of elm logs, with three rooms, entrance hall and staircase on the ground floor, leading to three bedrooms upstairs. Sam's aim was to complete the outside walls, roof and chimney before the winter of 1826/1827 set in, so that he would "be able to work at the finishing part inside, and with the benefit of a fire."

One evening in the autumn of 1826 Sam wrote that: "upon returning to my shanty in the evening, I was surprised to find that my brother-in-law had just arrived with the intelligence of the birth of my first-born son, and the dangerous illness of my dear wife. My poor Emma had been safely delivered of a fine boy, and was supposed to be progressing favourably, when some alarming symptoms made it necessary to send for me.

"Long before dawn I was some miles upon my sad journey to Darlington. I had no horse – I had had neither time for rest nor appetite for food. I loved my wife with all the warmth of a youthful husband. I am very fond of small children, and the idea of having one of my own had given a stimulus to all my labours but my first-born seemed dearly purchased now at the cost of his poor mother's peril. Fifty five miles lay between me and my suffering wife. The roads were heavy from the late rains. It was evening by the time I reached Darlington Mills, and I was still some five miles from my father-in-law's.

"It was quite dark, and I was so over-powered by my fifty miles' walk, that I stopped at a tavern and asked for some tea. I had scarcely been seated two minutes before some men entered. They were discussing what was to them merely local news, but the question 'When is the funeral to take place?' riveted my attention at once. Putting down the much-needed but untasted refreshment, I demanded of one of the speakers 'Whose funeral?' My heart at once foretold from its inmost depths what the dreaded answer would be."

So it was that Samuel Strickland became a father and a widower when still only twenty one years of age. A notice was inserted in the

Bury and Norwich Post in England on 6th December 1826 which read: "Died – on the 8th October 1826, at her father's house in Darlington, Upper Canada, 10 months after her marriage, and 9 days after her delivery of a son, in the 22nd year of her age, Emma, fifth daughter of James Black, Esq., and wife of Samuel Strickland, Esq., formerly of Reydon House, in this county."

Summer 1827: Sam returns to his farm and re-marries

After Emma's death, Sam made arrangements for the care of his baby son, and after a few months absence went back to his own farm. He wrote: "I returned in sadness to my lonely and desolate home. I had to begin life again. I had left my land unsown, and therefore the prospect of a crop of wheat for next year's harvest was, I felt assured, entirely gone" but when Sam arrived back at his farm, he found: "My fallow was not only sown but showing green blade, for some kindly hands had been at work that pecuniary losses might not be added to my heavy domestic bereavement."

The kindness had been done by "my excellent neighbour Mr Reid and his sons." Mr Reid on being thanked "said that he had done nothing more than a neighbourly duty, and insisted that I should take up my abode with them. Mrs Reid treated me with maternal kindness, and in their amiable family-circle my bruised heart recovered its peace."

Sam in his later account reflected on Canada in 1827. He wrote: "The country was quite unsettled, excepting here and there the nucleus of a small village appeared, for the clearings were mostly confined to the vicinity of the Great Lake. There were no plank, gravel or macadamized roads then; saw and grist mills were few and far between. It was no uncommon thing for a farmer to go thirty or forty miles to mill, which sometimes detained him a whole week from his family; and even more if any accident had happened to the machinery."

Sam spent the spring and early summer of 1827 in the company of his new friends: "I used to go down to the farm every morning, and return in the evening to a cheerful fire-side and agreeable society. I fenced in my fields, planted my spring crops, Indian corn and potatoes. I had my house nearly finished and considered it time

I should go and reside in it, and not trespass any longer on the hospitality of my friends."

Catharine recorded the life of Sam's son: "On going to visit his baby son, my brother found that the Irish woman in whose care he had left it, had not taken proper care of it, and the child was suffering from neglect and the dear child was kept in a miserable state of dirt. He took the poor child away from its unfeeling, ignorant nurse, and hiring a horse from a farmer, and with a pillow on which the little one was placed as comfortably as could be, he bore his priceless burden, and it arrived none the worse for its long days journey. It was tenderly received by Miss Reid and her sister and devotedly cared for. Very soon little Edward grew healthy, a lovely child, loved by all the young ladies of the family."

Sam, having decided to take up residence in his own house "did not like the idea of living the life of a hermit. I proposed to, and was accepted by my friend's eldest daughter" (Mary Reid) "in whom I found what I sought – a faithful mother for my child, and the most devoted and affectionate wife for myself. A better woman, indeed, never existed."

September 1827: Reydon Farm is rented out and there is an auction

After both her sons left home, Elizabeth Strickland continued working the farm at the Reydon estate for a couple of years. She then rented out the farmland, and sold all the farm equipment and stock.

On 11th October 1827 an agreement was signed in which Elizabeth Strickland leased "several parcels of land containing 72 acres together with a double cottage, barns, stables, neathouse, outhouse and buildings in Reydon" for a period of eight years at an annual rent of £144 to 'William Adams of Brampton, farmer'.

With the land and buildings in the process of disposal, a sale of the livestock and equipment was organised and announced in the local press: "To be sold at auction on Monday 24th September 1827, all the farming live and dead stock, implements in husbandry, dairy utensils &c of Mrs Strickland, who has let her farm."

The main items for sale were "4 capital chestnut mares and geldings, a 2 year-old filly, capital grey pony rising 5 years old fit for saddle or harness, 4 excellent milch cows, sow and 10 pigs, close-bucked wagon 3 ¾ tumbrels, luggage cart, taxed ditto and harness, 2 foot ploughs, 2 wheel ditto, cultivator, 2 rolls, wheel chaff engine, cart and plough harness, numerous hand tools, and agricultural requisites; all the dairy utensils, and 4 iron-bound barrel beer casks, and 5 half barrels."

The auction began at mid-day and after it was over, Agnes wrote an account of it to James Bird. She wrote: "Praised be our stars! That day of fuss, anxiety, bustle, expectation and disappointment is over. And it is our consolation for the low rate at which our prime milch cows, worthy horses, and freshly painted blue and red implements sold, to reflect that they are gone, and cannot return to trouble us with causing another public auction day on their accounts.

"I could not help wishing that Wilkies had been present last Monday to sketch our auction and its attendants, many of whom had about as much business there as your little Catharine, craving the dear child's pardon for coupling her name with that of the company at our auction which consisted mainly of Southwold Pilots, who understanding that our parish Clerk, mine host of the Bear, had set out a board in our meadow, for the purpose of selling cakes, apples and strong beer to the company at 'Madam Strickland's' auction, yielded to the force of the irresistible attraction and followed him hither, which was a complete work of supererogation on their parts as they might have had the facsimiles of the beer, cakes and apples, two miles nearer to their own town had they stopped at the Bear instead of seeking so public a place as our orchard to indulge their sottish propensities.

"However they were of a different opinion, and they sat under the trees on the damp grass, smoking their pipes and drinking till it was dark night and mine host of the Bear carried off his empty kegs and panniers with the full conviction that he, at any rate, had made a good day's work.

"Then every purchaser who had bought anything of the amount of five shillings poured into the house with demands for liquor wine or beer written in legible characters on every feature of their faces, and there were refreshments to be provided (according to their degrees) in parlour and kitchen before they would pay for their respective bargains till we thought there would never be an end of their cravings. It is however all over, and it is well that it is so, and it was a characteristic winding up of poor Mamma's farming campaign."

December 1827: Agnes publishes a book of poems

In 1827 Agnes was still hoping to earn her living as a poet. She put together a volume of fifty poems which was printed for her by Messrs J R & C Childs of Bungay. The Childs family of Bungay, like the Bird family of Yoxford, were sociable people with a wide circle of acquaintances, and became friends with the Strickland family as well as having business dealings with them.

In September 1827 Agnes sent a message asking how the printing was getting on and Robert Childs sent the reply: "Tell Miss Agnes she writes faster than we can print, but she shall have it out before the New Year."

The longest poem in the volume had the title 'The Seven Ages of Woman' and this was used as the title for the book as a whole. The book added to Agnes's reputation as a writer, and for a while thereafter advertisements for anything she wrote carried the reference "author of 'The Seven Ages of Woman'."

Catharine was also busy producing a published volume. In Catharine's case the writing did not necessarily carry her name as her task was to produce the end product, a Christmas annual for children. Agnes sent a copy of the completed annual to James Bird as a present for his 9 year old son, also called James. Agnes wrote: "I have enclosed a copy of 'The Juvenile Forget-Me-Not' for my little friend James if he does not consider it too juvenile for his acceptance. I think I told you when at Yoxford that it was a work of Catharine's with the exception of the poetry, which is by me."

In December 1827 Agnes again wrote to Mr Bird, taking advantage of an opportunity of sending a letter to Yoxford by hand and receiving a reply by the same means, and therefore free of charge. Agnes had been unwell and described her symptoms to Mr Bird in his role as pharmacist: "I have an improving bulletin to announce on my part, since I feel an abatement of the most unpleasant symptoms, and have been able to take the air several times last week, but I am still lamentably feeble, and you may perceive by the character of this exquisite writing, how much my hand trembles.

"I still suffer from bile and flatulence and look very sallow and wan. If you will oblige me by making up the tonic draught as before, or anything else you think would be beneficial in my deranged state of the nervous and digestive system, Mr Adams the bearer of this, will I know take charge of the packet. I think it would be as well to put up a half pint bottle of the mixture which would be giving it a fairer trial. It certainly did me much good while taking it. I suffer much with weakness in the knees, which makes getting up and down stairs a difficult matter. I should much have enjoyed to peep in upon your Xmas party yesterday, and hope you and dear Mrs Bird and the little ones, spent a happy and cheerful day. We were dull enough, the indisposition of Catharine and myself precluding much mirth, and I am generally the merriest of the circle."

Agnes's book of poems was nearing publication and extracts from it had been appearing in newspapers since November. Agnes wanted news of the book's reception and Mr Bird, with his contacts and stationery-cum-book-cum-pharmacy shop, was in a position to help. Agnes wrote: "Mr Seth Stevenson has kindly inserted a second extract from my book in his paper, and the Editor of the Sunday Monitor has inserted 'An Original Greek Song' which I sent him thinking it would come in well after Navarino."

The Battle of Navarino had been fought in October 1827 as part of the Greek War of Independence. It was a decisive victory for allied forces from Britain, France and Russia against the Ottoman and Egyptian forces which were trying to suppress the Greeks. Agnes added, with a mixture of curiosity and despondency: "I am curious to know whether any of the revues and magazines for the ensuing month will notice my volume. I suppose the monthly review will clapper claw it in a remorseless way as they did 'Worcester Field'."

January 1828: A Sunday School is opened at Reydon parish church

The Strickland family attended the local parish church in Reydon, despite the poor spiritual state of the Church of England during the Regency period and thereafter. Catharine many years later described the situation: "The greatest state of deadness and supineness existed, not only in our Parish Church but in all the neighbouring ones – There was a state of spiritual destitution, against which no one lifted up their voice to remonstrate, so indifferent had people become – the parishioners listened patiently to long winded homilies, but this state of things was not always to continue – there are now no fox-hunting horse-riding men in our Suffolk churches. The old race is now dead and gone, and better men fill their pulpits – those were the dark days under the reign of the Georges."

As the Strickland children grew from childhood to adulthood their attitude to the world around them began to change, as also did the nature of the local clergy. Catharine wrote: "As the years went by we began to understand the condition of the people among whom we lived, and that we had duties to perform with them, not only to ease the burden of sickness and poverty, but also to take an interest in their higher welfare. With the aid of our young and enlightened vicar, my sisters and myself succeeded in establishing a Sunday School for the children of the labourers in our parish." The Sunday School at the Reydon parish church of St Margaret came into existence on the first Sunday of 1828.

The Strickland sisters not only helped get the Sunday School at Reydon off the ground, they also taught there. Susanna described the pastime in a letter to James Bird in October 1828, a letter which shows the friendly links between the Bird, Childs and Strickland families. Susanna wrote: "I have increased my cold at the Church this afternoon in teaching eight dunces their ABC. Little Frank Childs is still with us, he helps me not a little with my class in the school and hears the elder children their Catechism while I teach the little ones to read. I am serving my apprenticeship at tuition. Surely all children are not as stupid as my class. I never knew I possessed a grain of patience till today. I do assure you my dear friend it was tried to the utmost."

March 1828: Agnes meets Sir Walter Scott

As the winter moved towards the spring of 1828, Agnes prepared to go to London to visit her aunt, Mrs Leverton. She was to catch the London coach that picked up passengers at Yoxford, which gave her the chance to pay a social visit to the Bird family en route. Her letter to Mr Bird of 28th February 1828 is a combination of sociable and literary chat, including mention of the poem 'Dunwich' by James Bird which was about to be published.

Agnes, who had been ill over the winter, wrote: "My Dear Friend, The period of my visit to London being now determined, and friday week being the day appointed to travel by Yoxford day coach" she asked if it would be convenient for herself and Susanna to visit for a few hours the previous day "we should arrange to sleep at the Inns, which would insure my being up in time for the friday's coach. My health is a little improved within the last week, I am under the care of Mr Tag, our regular man of pills, and am taking bitter draughts, and pills thrice a day.

"On Monday week I was at Bungay, where I mentioned your 'Dunwich' to my friend Mr Childs, who said he would take a copy. I wish he had said 10. Mrs Bardwels 'the stationer at Southwold' asked me to request you to write to her, what would be the price of the book, and when forthcoming, as she thought she could sell some. She has sold up my poems, but I always let her have my book on sale or return, and she has (her own proposal) 20 per cent profit on each volume. This is rather better than the sale of 'Worcester Field' at Longmans, where my 100 copies, have returned considerably less than they cost me for printing and boarding.

"I have been busily employed in writing tales designedly for the annuals and have produced three. I want to write one or two more, but last week I was obliged to visit the mantua maker making and altering my robes for London, and the eternal flounces and furbelows, fitting and re-fitting, frilling and quilling, and all the long etcetera of female costume, chased from the secret chamber of my brain a multitude of excellent ideas – now I am again at leisure, all my imaginative treasures have fled, and I am as dull and incapable of wit or pathos as any Lane and Newman writer". As an afterthought she asked: "Will you have the goodness to enquire for me the inside fare by the Yoxford coach to London. I am told the Saxmundham is cheaper."

However, Agnes had to postpone her visit due to poor health, and a week later she wrote again to James Bird saying: "I am not yet myself, but this weather is as much against me, as it is inimical to the poor snowdrops, who are hanging their heads, in a truly forlorn manner, and shrinking from the bitter blast. All things considered my dear friend I have resolved to postpone my journey till Monday week, longer I cannot on account of Mrs Leverton's impatience to have me in town. I will leave Reydon after dinner on the Monday so I shall not be with you till some time about five o'clock, when I shall with much pleasure, accept an invitation to take tea with Mrs Bird in her chamber, if she be well enough to bear the accession of clack." Emma Bird was expecting a baby in the near future.

Mrs Strickland having sold the family horses at the auction in 1827, the family transport now consisted of a donkey and cart if walking was impractical. Agnes continued: "Susan will probably be my companion. We shall most probably journey to Yoxford with my long eared Pegasus, attended by a mere foot page, most appropriately eclept John Phastar. He seems a very worthy creature, and suits our quiet service much better than that complete prototype of Callum Beg, the late John, whom Mamma has been forced to discharge on account of his incorrigible pranks." It was probably on this visit to London that Agnes met Sir Walter Scott, author of the very popular Waverley novels in which Callum Beg is a character.

There are two versions of how Agnes came to meet the famous man. One version is that Sir Walter Scott was a guest at one of Mrs Leverton's Drawing Rooms and that Agnes met him there. In this version of their meeting, they shook hands and their conversation was about his novels and he said that the idea for them came from his reading an earlier Scottish novel by Jane Porter, a friend of Agnes.

The other version of the meeting was given by Susanna in a letter to Mr Bird. She wrote: "Agnes has introduced herself to Sir Walter Scott at a public exhibition. He shook hands with her and complimented her on her Poems. She is delighted."

April 1828: Sam has a career change

The Canada Company had been set up as a land and colonization company in 1824. In 1826 it bought two and a half million acres of land from the government, about half of which lay in the Huron Tract (western Ontario), the rest being in relatively small scattered areas.

In his auto-biography Sam wrote: "In the spring of 1827 the Canada Company began operations at Guelph, under the superintendence of John Galt, Esq. I had heard a great deal about the fertility of their lands, especially in the Huron tract, containing a million acres in one block. I resolved to go and judge for myself; and as I heard the superintendent was then in Toronto, I determined to call upon him there, and collect all the information in my power.

"My first interview with Mr Galt took place at the Old Steamboat Hotel in February 1828. He received me with great kindness, and asked me many particulars of Bush-life connected with my first settlement. I suppose my answers were satisfactory, for he turned to me abruptly, and asked me if I would like to enter the Canada Company's service. He wanted a practical person to take charge of the outdoor department in the absence of Mr Prior who was to be sent to the Huron tract with a party of men to clear up and lay off the new-town plot of Goderich." Sam was told he would "have charge of the Company's stores, keep the labour rolls, and superintend the road-making and bridge-building, and indeed everything connected with the practical part of the settlement."

Sam accepted the offer at once: "This was just the sort of life I wished. No salary was to be named till I had been three months in the Company's employ" which Sam accepted as he believed he would in due course be paid "according to my deserts."

As agreed at the interview, Sam arranged his affairs then returned to: "meet Mr Galt in Toronto in April 1828 at the commencement of the spring operations." He was sent to Guelph, travelling by wagon and reaching his destination on the afternoon of the second day. At Guelph Sam found "some twenty or thirty log-houses, about as many shanties, a large frame tavern building, a store, two blacksmith's shops and the walls of two stone-buildings. One of these would be the company's offices. Dr Dunlop and Mr Prior each had a good house, and there was the Priory, a large log-building afterwards occupied by the superintendent." Sam wrote that "this was pretty well, considering that only a year had elapsed since the first tree was felled.

"I was fully employed the whole summer in constructing two bridges, one over the Speed, and the other over the Eramosa branch, also in opening a good road to each. These bridges were built of cedar logs, and on a plan of my own, which Mr Galt highly approved." It sounds as though Sam had learnt from his father or through his sisters how to turn his hand to practical work, and how to build things well.

Sam also had other jobs to keep him occupied. He wrote: "We had no medical man in Guelph for some months after my arrival so, for want of a better, I was obliged to turn physician and soon became very skilful in bleeding and tooth-drawing, and as I charged nothing, you may be sure I had plenty of customers." After his three month trial period, Sam was given a salary and a house in which he and his family lived rent-free, and Sam's second wife, Mary was able to join him.

November 1828: Susanna breaks off an engagement

In August 1828 Susanna wrote to Mr Bird to arrange a social visit: "Kitty and I are only waiting for a fine day to pay you a flying visit of a few brief hours but they will be hours of pleasure. Green spots in the desert of life. We propose getting up very early and coming with the donkey to be with you in the forenoon and start for home about seven."

Susanna, aged 25, was engaged to be married, possibly unofficially, but the relationship was ended soon after. At the beginning of September 1828 she told Mr Bird: "Today I had a letter from Asker. He is now in Norwich, but gives me no hope of seeing him again this year. I am vexed with him on many accounts. If he were not Asker I should positively hate him. I query now whether I shall ever be his wife, certainly not if he goes on in his present extravagant career. You will smile and say lovers quarrel. But I abhor selfishness and this trait in a husband of mine would drive me mad."

Two months later she told James Bird: "This day has been a heavy trial, of shuddering agony. I have written him his final dismissal. My eyes were tearless but my brain seemed to burn and my heart to wither but it must be so. I must now strive to forget him. I could not write to him in scorn or anger, and when I signed the warrant that gave the death blow to the hopes of years my heart was overflowing with tenderness to the author of my sufferings. But I will never be his wife – No Never!"

February 1829: Agnes enthuses about phrenology

During much of 1828 Agnes was ill and her letter to James Bird, which she wrote on 19th February 1829 was a mixture of stationery order, exchange of general news and chatter, and a letter to Mr Bird in his role as pharmacist. Agnes wrote: "I am taking a great deal of exercise walking an hour thrice a day but am still so bilious. I look – oh Juno! how I look! – a perfect orange colour and nothing I take does me any good, yet I have no pain in the side, or tension about the liver, I am not subject to affections of that kind, this is a stomach complaint debility indigestion and flatulence. If you think Colosinth pills would be serviceable to me, send a small box. If not I must be guilty of one extravagance of a box of Dixons Antebilious. I would never use any other if they were not so atrociously dear."

The Strickland family was still avoiding postal charges where possible, using whatever means of communication they could find. On this occasion the carriers were members of the local constabulary. Agnes wrote: "I am as normal in a great hurry therefore if you will have the goodness to book the order against the next opportunity of sending I shall be grateful. Perhaps Mr Constable Bringston or the Wangford Constable Bensons may (if there have been any naughty doings in the parish) attend your Yoxford justice sitting, and either would take a parcel for us. Are not the channels of poetical and literary communications between we Suffolk bards remarkably choice and refined!"

This letter also covered the subject of phrenology and the Childs family of Bungay. Members of the Childs family are the only people in Bungay ever mentioned in the Strickland correspondence, so it may be supposed that if any of the family visited Bungay, they would have met at least one member of the Childs family while there.

The printing business of J R & C Childs was long-established and flourishing. It was run by John Childs, and by his younger brother Robert, and by his son Charles. They specialised in printing inexpensive editions of classical works and of the Bible, as a means of increasing public literacy and of raising intellectual standards. The family were prominent non-conformists, and politically they were radicals.

They were also keen phrenologists, believing that the detailed shape of a person's skull gives an indication of character and mental capabilities. The idea had arisen in the 1790s and, after being roundly condemned as nonsense by the Edinburgh Review and defended by its originator, Dr FJ Gall, many people in the 19th century became fascinated by the idea.

The Strickland sisters were among those interested in phrenology, and Agnes encouraged James Bird in the same direction. In her February 1829 letter to James Bird, she wrote: "And my dear friend you have at length visited Bungay and made acquaintance with our worthy Phrenologists. I rejoiced to hear it for I am sure you must be mutually pleased with each other. I can assure you that your excursion has been productive of no small pleasure to me in reading your witty and spirited lines on the occasion of your visit to R Childs's Golgotha as we always call his scull museum, and now confess that you did not leave it untainted with the Phrena-mania.

"It is a very epidemical place for that sort of thing. Few people leave it without experiencing a spice of the infection and however they outwardly protest against giving the slightest faith to the science, may nevertheless be detected from time to time in the act of examining their own bumps and making sly inquisitions upon the craniums of all their acquaintance. Such are the first suggestions of an inclination towards phrenology but they become gradually stronger till the party at length acquires sufficient evidence of the truth of the science (especially if he be blest with a fine head of his own) to acknowledge himself a decided phrenologist."

The phrenology craze could be somewhat unsettling as was later recalled by James Ewing Ritchie who was a son of the Rev Andrew Ritchie of the Suffolk village of Wrentham, and a friend of the Strickland family. When describing John Childs he wrote: "He was a great phrenologist and I well remember how I, a raw lad, rather trembled in his presence as I saw his keen, dark eyes directed towards that part of my person where my brains are supposed to be. I imagine the result was favourable, as at a later time I spent many a pleasant hour in his dining room, gathering wisdom from his after-dinner talk and inspiration from his port."

John Childs was hospitable, and many intellectually adventurous people met around his table. James Ewing Ritchie added a physical description and said that John Childs was: "almost Napoleonic in appearance, with a habit of blurting out sharp cynicisms and original epigrams, rather than conversing."

James Ewing Ritchie also gave a description of Reydon House and the Strickland family as he remembered them in the 1820s, when Thomas Strickland had been dead for a number of years. He wrote: "the widow and daughters kept up what little state they could; and I well remember the feeling of surprise with which I first entered their capacious drawing-room. It must have been, now I come to think of it, a dismal old house, suggestive of rats and dampness and mould – with a general air of decay all over the place, inside and out. It must have been a difficulty with the family to keep up the place, and the style of living was altogether plain; yet there I heard a good deal of literary life in London."

He also mentioned Tom by saying "Then there was a brother Tom, a midshipman – a wonderful being to my inexperienced eyes – who once or twice came to our house seated in the family donkey-chaise, which seemed to me, somehow or other, not to be an ordinary donkey-chaise, but something of a far superior character. I have pleasant recollections of them all."

May 1829: Susanna thinks Agnes is working too hard

As the weather improved, so did Agnes's health and she wrote several poems and short stories during 1829. Some of her poems referred to contemporary events, for example her poem 'On the Conflagration of York Minster.' The Minster had been set alight on 1st February 1829 by an arsonist who had hidden behind a pillar until the building was closed for the night. He then piled cushions and prayers books in the Choir, set fire to them and escaped. By the time the fire was noticed, it had become impossible to extinguish and when it eventually died down, lead on the Minster roof had melted, limestone pillars had cracked, the choir roof had collapsed and the medieval choir stalls, organ and pulpit had been destroyed. The arsonist was soon caught but at his trial he was found not guilty due to insanity. He died in a London hospital a few years later.

Agnes's narrative poem about the fire consisted of ten seven-line verses of which the first is as follows:

> The beautiful, the holy fane
> Wherein our fathers prayed,

Which sap and siege with stern disdain,
And time's dark storms assailed in vain,
Is waste and lowly laid.
And all the pleasant things destroy'd
In which a Christian people joy'd.

It was one of several of Agnes's poems printed in newspapers during 1829 and 1830 with the writer being described as 'Miss Agnes Strickland, Author of The Seven Ages of Woman'.

Agnes's health continued to be precarious as Susanna reported to Mr Bird in a letter dated May 1829: "Dear Agnes left us yesterday on a short visit to Bungay where I hope the change of air will be beneficial. She is indeed in a very poor way, I fear not very long for this world and no inducement will prevail upon her to resign her pen. What use will fame be to her when she is mouldering in the dust. She is killing herself by inches."

With Agnes, Jane, Susanna and Catharine Strickland all having work published, editors and publishers were confused about who-wrote-what and their required rates of pay. Among those who asked for clarification was Frederick Shoberl who produced the English versions of 'Ackermann's Forget-Me-Not.' These were attractively bound Christmas annuals which had previously been launched in Germany and France.

Susanna's reply to his enquiry was dated June 1829, and showed Susanna's feeling that the lives of herself and Agnes had gone their separate ways in both a literary and a social sense. Susanna told Mr Shoberl that she and Agnes "seldom communicate our literary business to each other, as our friends in the world of letters are often of different parties and totally unknown to each other. Her address is 13 Bedford Square." Susanna added "I shall be perfectly satisfied with half a guinea per page for verse and 10 or 12 guineas per sheet for prose, in which both my sisters" (Catharine and Jane) "agree."

June 1829: Sam moves to Lake Huron

Sam's role at Guelph sometimes involved long journeys from home to sell land and to receive payments for the company. By the spring of 1829, he was no longer needed at Guelph and he was transferred to Goderich and was pleased by the move. Goderich, Sam wrote, was: "on the shores of the mighty Huron lake where I had always wished to go – fine lakes, noble forests, and productive soil, have since made it a source of wealth for many a settler."

Sam left his family in Guelph in early June 1829 and made the journey to Goderich with the company's agent, Mr Prior. For most of the journey "the road was a mere sleigh-track through the woods, newly cut out, and rarely exceeding twelve feet in width. At this time we saw only three log-cabins during the whole way, these being about twenty miles apart. These were kept by Dutch or German emigrants, who supplied travellers with whiskey and provisions – when they had any – which was not always the case."

Sam liked what he saw of Goderich: "The upper town is situated on a fine cliff fronting the lake and harbour. The lower town comprised a few acres of alluvial flat, only a few feet elevated above the lake." At the time the newly surveyed town consisted only of "three frame-houses in the process of building, a log-house, beautifully situated on a bold hill overlooking the harbour, and a dozen or so log-cabins."

While Sam was working for the Canada Company in Goderich, he bought a small log-house and town lot there: "The situation was very pretty, commanding a fine view of the lake" but he immediately set to work in his spare time, to build a house which, he said, was "constructed of cherry logs and mortar" suitable to receive his family. "It had no upstairs except for stowage. The ground-storey I divided into a parlour, kitchen, and three bedrooms."

The work progressed well and Sam expected his family to join him as soon as there was sufficient snow for the primitive road to be used as a sleigh-route. However Mary had other ideas. Sam wrote that: "Determined to join me, she hired a settler who was owner of a wagon and a yoke of oxen, which she loaded with the most useful articles, reserving room in the wagon for herself, the child, and nursemaid." The child was their first child, a daughter named Maria.

The road was in such a primitive state that the wagon with the family belongings was upset twice in the first five miles of the journey, and Mary felt safer walking the rest of way carrying the baby, rather than risk being involved in any more wagon upsets.

The journey of 90 miles took her six days which, under the circumstances, seems quite fast

Edward, Sam's son from his first marriage had been left with his parents-in-law at Douro, in the care of Mary's sister Eliza, apparently justified by the explanation "of whom he was so fond that my wife did not like to separate such friends from each other." Baby Edward Strickland and Eliza Reid subsequently, but at an unspecified date, joined Sam's household at Goderich.

November 1829: Susanna fears Agnes's reputation is damaging her own

Thomas Harral was another literary friend of the Strickland family. He had first had dealings with them in the days when he edited the 'Suffolk Chronicle' and the 'Bury Gazette,' and the contact between the families continued after he moved to London in 1823. In London he wrote for, and edited, a court and fashion magazine called 'La Belle Assemblee'. He lived in Clarendon Square in London, where the Strickland sisters, particularly Susanna and Catharine, visited him and his family.

By 11th November 1829, Susanna was trying to separate her writings from those of Agnes and told Mr Bird when she then wrote to him: "Mr Harral is quite in a panic at my dropping my own name but I do not think I was wrong to change my initials. Last year I got into two annuals under the signature of S Strickland. This year I have got into five under the signature of ZZ and was rejected by all under my own name, save by Ackermann, and if I remain SS to Mr Harral I do not think it will at all matter."

Susanna felt that Agnes's reputation was damaging her own, but there is no mention elsewhere that this was the case. Susanna wrote: "I find that there is a prejudice against the name of Strickland, that the prejudice against Agnes extends to me. I shall not stand in her way and a feeling of Xtianity prompts me to relinquish the odious task of competition. My dear friends will recognise their dear Suzy under ZZ and what is all the rest of the world to me."

At about the same time Susanna told James Bird of her feelings towards some of her sisters. She wrote: "my beloved sister Catharine, who is dearer to me than all the world – my monitoress, my dear and faithful friend. I love my Kate – She is absent now for a few days, and I feel lost and lonely without her. We are all authoresses but Sarah, the third; but then she is a beauty, and such a sweet girl withal, that everybody loves her, and I often think she is the best off, for she has elegant tastes and pursuits, and no clashing interests to interfere with the love her sisters bear her." Her feelings towards her sisters Eliza, Agnes and Jane Margaret were not mentioned.

Of her brothers, Susanna wrote: "My eldest brother was a fine, handsome fellow, and promises to do something for himself in Canada. He gives me such superb descriptions of Canadian scenery that I often long to accept his invitation to join him – But I fear my heart would fail me when the moment for separation came." This was the earliest recorded mention of Susanna contemplating emigration. Her brother Tom was not mentioned.

April 1830: Susanna joins the Congregational Church

Susanna in her mid-twenties began to question her religious beliefs. Catharine explained: "Susanna from childhood had an inherent love of freedom of thought and action. She was suddenly awakened from a state of religious indifference, to one of doubtful questioning through the energetic preaching of one clergyman of the English church and a great conflict was going on in her mind at this time. Among her religious friends was one at Southwold. She was a beautiful example of every Christian virtue, making religion captivating to the youthful heart.

"When this clergyman left the neighbourhood, he commended Susanna to the care of a worthy earnest Nonconformist Pastor, in whose Christian teaching he had much confidence. The Pastor" – the Rev Mr Ritchie of Wrentham Chapel – "was a worthy, learned and excellent man and his wife an accomplished woman. My Mother allowed my sister to take lessons in drawing and water colour painting from her – and as Susanna possessed a decided talent in that line, she made good progress in a short time – in after years she became remarkable for her artistic talents."

In June 1829 Susanna in writing to Mr Bird gave vent to her religious anxieties: "Oh! When will these mental struggles be over. When Holy Father will you call your erring child. I sometimes glance on the spot I once chose in our quiet churchyard for my grave. How peacefully the sunbeams sleep upon it."

The following year, Susanna broke from the family tradition of being a member of the Church of England, and on 4th April 1830 she became a member of the Congregational Church. She described the event in a letter to Mr Bird in which she wrote: "And did you really think of me on the 4 of April that memorable never to be forgotten day when I first received the cup of salvation from the hand of my beloved Pastor and felt that I was indeed bound to the Church into which I had been admitted by the indissoluble bond of Christian union.

"I was admitted on the Friday previous – it was a dreadful day – rain, hail, blow and snow. I was obliged to brave all – I was two hours getting to Wrentham and almost drenched to my skin. The kind fatherly welcome I received at the dear Parsonage, the tenderness and care of sweet Amy soon restored my spirits, and I did not feel at all what I had to go through till Mr R gave me his arm to accompany them to Chapel – it was a starless moonless pouring night – and the dreariness of the evening seemed to give an additional gloom to my mind.

"There was no joy in my heart – Like the heavens above me not one gleam of light on my mind. The tenderness of my dear Pastor only made me more sad – The only cheering conviction was, that I was obeying the dictates of conscience and that I was right – The service was beautiful. The sermon most touching, and so deeply was I interested that I never thought of my admission till Mr R came to the pew door, and led me into the vestry.

"He left me alone for about a quarter of an hour whilst he read to the congregation my reason for dissenting from the establishment and proposed me for a member – During this interval my mind underwent all the deep excitement peculiar to my nature. The first five minutes I could not help feeling bitterly that this step would ultimately make me an alien to all my old friends, that I should never kneel down in the same place of worship with any of them again and that I was the first member of my family that had ever become a dissenter – These worldly thoughts were soon banished – Better hopes and feelings succeeded – I prayed long, deeply and fervently, and my whole soul seemed broken and dissolved in tears. But the storm passed away and a sweet calm was beginning to steal over me when Mr R came for me.

"This renewed all my violent agitation. I was placed in a pew opposite the pulpit and stood up. All the rest of the congregation were seated – I trembled from head to foot – Every eye was upon me. I buried my face in my hands and the tears streamed fast through my fingers during Mr R's most pathetic address. He was much agitated and though I did not see him, his faltering voice assured me how deeply he felt for me – But when he gave me the right hand of fellowship in the name of the whole congregation my spirit revived and during the last beautiful prayers I rejoiced that the ordeal was past, that I was the member of a free church and blessed with such a friend and spiritual advisor.

"I am happy now – so happy when I attend our holy little sanctuary. Tis a sweet looking place – One of the first independent chapels ever built. Set some little way from the main street up a beautiful lane – full of fine old trees – The meeting yard is full of old pines and lilac and liburnam trees – covered with velvet sod and spangled over with flowers – I have chosen my grave under two pine trees in which the wind sighs lulaby through the long day – And then there is such a beautiful ash by the gate, that Shakespeare might have eulogized."

There is a description of Wrentham Congregational Church in the 1974 edition of Pevsner's guide to the 'Buildings of England' which recorded that the church was built in 1778 of red brick with a tiled roof. The windows and doorways were arched, and inside the pulpit was opposite the doorway. There were galleries down the sides of the chapel, and the box pews, one of which Susanna occupied in 1830, were still there in 1974.

Spring 1830: Catharine acts as peace-maker

From a letter thought to have been written in the spring of 1830, it seems that Susanna had fallen out with Agnes and maybe others or another in the family, and that Susanna had written a conciliatory letter to Catharine who then acted as a peace-maker. The cause of the row is not explained but the timing suggests that it may have been connected with Susanna's controversial decision to become a member of the Congregational Church. The letter also states the unusual colour of Agnes's eyes.

Catharine wrote to Susanna: "I know my darling I can scarcely give you greater satisfaction than by telling you of the kindness which our dear Agnes expressed to me on reading your letter she was sensibly touched by it and her dear black eyes were full of kindly tears. See dearest Susanna though you have lost one you have yet in the season of adversity gained another and the return of affection (and that a sister) is surely valuable."

June 1830: The reign of King William IV begins

King George IV died and the reign of King William IV began on 26th June 1830. Sam recorded what happened when the news reached Canada. He wrote: "I was busy in the storehouse one afternoon, when Mr Prior entered with a newspaper in his hand which he had just received from the old country. 'I see by this paper, Strickland, that George IV is dead; and that his Majesty King William IV has been proclaimed. Now, I think we must give the workmen a holiday on this memorable occasion – and have a little fete, inviting all the settlers within reach. We will have some refreshments served round.' Upon the appointed day every-one within ten miles assembled, dressed in their best attire; and ready to show their loyalty in any way Mr Prior might think proper to recommend.

"Mr Prior ascended a large stump; and, in a loyal and patriotic speech, informed us 'that he had called this meeting to hear him proclaim his most gracious Majesty King William IV.' He then read the proclamation, which was received with nine rounds of British cheers. Our party then formed a large circle by joining hands; and sang the national anthem, accompanied by the Goderich band, which was composed of two fiddles and a tambourine. 'Rule Britannia' was also played and sung with great loyalty and enthusiasm."

Sam said that His Majesty's health was then drunk by means of a "pail of whiskey, with a tea-cup floating on the surface, being handed round, followed by another pail containing spring water. The eating and drinking part of the festival now commenced in earnest. We had seated ourselves on the ground, under the shade of four or five immense button-wood trees. In the centre of the group, the union-jack waved gracefully over our heads." This was followed by a dance and games.

July 1830: Susanna is engaged to John Moodie

From the summer of 1830, Susanna often stayed with Thomas Pringle and his wife Margaret at their home in Claremont Square, Pentonville, which was then on the northern outskirts of London. The Pringle's had emigrated to South Africa and had lived in Cape Town for a number of years. Thomas Pringle had attempted to establish a magazine there, but the South African government was sensitive to his criticism of their policies regarding slavery, and the Pringle family returned to England in 1826.

Back in England, Thomas Pringle obtained editorial roles, including being editor of the 'Athenaeum,' which published several of Susanna's poems. Susanna became a close friend of the family, sometimes accompanying them when they went to Hampstead for a holiday, and she began to refer to Mr Pringle fondly as 'Papa'.

Catharine recalled of Susanna that she was: "the guest of the poet Thomas Pringle, the Secretary of the Anti Slavery Society, and in his house she met many writers of that day, and she was herself much noticed, her lively manner and bright original turn of thought gained her many friends – nor was she entirely idle. Her pen was employed by Mr Pringle in writing in behalf of the Anti Slavery Cause, in which she felt the greatest interest, entering into the subject with all her heart and soul."

In November 1830 Susanna's poem 'An Appeal to the Free' was printed in the 'Suffolk Chronicle.' It consisted of six verses the third of which is:

> 'Ye children of Britain! Brave sons of the isles,
> Who revel in freedom and bask in her smiles,
> Can ye sanction such deeds as are done in the West,
> And sink on your pillows untroubled to rest;
> Are your slumbers unbroken by visions of dread,
> Does no spectre of misery glare on your bed?
> No cry of despair break the silence of night
> And thrill the cold hearts, that ne'er throbbed for the right!'

It was at Thomas Pringle's home that Susanna met John Wedderburn Dunbar Moodie. Born in 1797 and six years older than Susanna, he had a farm in South Africa and had come to England to negotiate a deal for publishing a book about his colonial adventures.

Catharine has left a cheerful account of Susanna and John's courtship: "Susanna became acquainted with him at Mr Pringle's. He was a constant visitor, almost an inmate in the house from the time of her arrival. They spent their time walking on the heath" (Hampstead Heath) "in sweet converse, listening to music, reading aloud etc. and in short became enamoured of each other. In spite of the warning of her good padre and her Southwold friends to love none but a man of their church, poor Susie became a convert to Lieut Dunbar Moodie."

By the time Susanna returned to Reydon from London at the end of July 1830, she was engaged to be married and keen to have her latest book published. She told James Bird: "I must depend upon my wits to buy my wedding clothes, rather a hard alternative for a smart damsel like me." She hoped that the unsettled situation in France at that time would not end in conflict, as Lieut John Moodie was a half-pay officer in the 21st Royal Scottish Fusiliers, and might have been called back into active service.

Susanna described her future husband to James Bird as: "the gallant fellow whom I love with all my heart and soul. His uncle is now Sir Alex Dunbar and he talks of us living near the good old man in Orkney. In spite of the cold I am sure I should be happy with him anywhere if beneath the burning suns of Africa or building a nest among the eagles of the storm encircled Orkneys. This is my hero's native Isle."

August 1830: Tom marries Margaretta Adela Thompson

Whatever the timing of Tom's voyages may have been, he was definitely in England on 4th August 1830 for this was the day when he married Margaretta Adela Thompson at St Martin in the Fields Church in London. Tom was 22 and Margaretta was 18 years old.

If Tom's mother or any of his sisters attended his wedding, there is no mention of it in any family correspondence which still exists, and the witnesses to the marriage were neither Stricklands nor

Thompsons. However, this was of no great significance since the attendance of the Strickland brothers and sisters, and their mother, at each other's weddings turned out to be the exception rather than the rule.

Susanna in her letter to the Bird family, which is thought to have been written in January 1831 said: "You know doubtless from Katie that Tom before he went to sea married Miss Thompson. She is a lovely creature and the idol of all who see her. I feel quite proud of my gazetted sister."

Catharine later wrote that she and Tom had been particularly fond of each other, but after his marriage, his wife became jealous and the brother and sister saw little of each other thereafter. Jane later in life commented that Tom could only have married Margaretta due to her physical attractions but, generally speaking, the Strickland family records are silent about Tom's wife.

August 1830: Agnes is better and busy

Agnes had a holiday visiting friends in Norfolk for a couple of months in the summer of 1830 and returned to Reydon in reasonably good health. However, she still needed James Bird to send her pills from his pharmacy, and the family still needed to use whatever conveyance for messages and parcels they could obtain. The vicar was her go-between when she wrote to James Bird on 23rd August 1830. Agnes wrote: "Our agreeable Parson having mentioned his intention of going to Yoxford tomorrow and I immediately asked him not only to become my courier but also to call for an answer from my friend the Yoxford Bard which he apparently 'nothing down-hearted' promised to do. On Thursday morning you must if you feel so disposed have a little packet ready for Necessarious Clericus in which packet you must put a box of Dixon's pills which are much better for me than all Mr Sag's dispensary."

Agnes told James Bird that she was looking much better than when he last saw her. She wrote: "I should like to come over one of these days and surprise you with my improved appearance, positively I hardly know my own reflection in the mirror which like all ladies whether they acknowledge it or not I am in the habit of consulting as often as convenience arises. I may perhaps thank the pleasant visit

I spent in Norfolk for this improvement. I was there two months and went out almost every day either for a ramble a ride or a nice tea drinking. In short I enjoyed myself and I believe returned 'some weeks older many maxims wiser but no ducats in my pocket withal'."

Agnes was not only looking and feeling better but her work was in demand and she was happily busy. She told Mr Bird: "Saturday's post brought me a letter from the Editor of the Gem saying he hoped to be able to insert my 'Life Boat' which I hope will get on swimmingly with the public. He also sent me a pretty plate to illustrate for a juvenile annual and requested me to send him a few more verses.

"This of course was sufficient to put such an excitable subject as myself into a flustration 'but as it never rains but it pours' the other letter which arrived by the same post brought me a note from Mansel Reynolds announcing his intention of inserting my 'Captive's Dream' unless I sent him two or three scenarios to make a fresh choice. So I turned from one thing to another till I was in a real" (indecipherable word, possibly 'puzzle') "what to write or what to send but I succeeded in illustrating the plate in the first place and then made the necessary selections before completing other communications for Jordan which I noticed should go in the parcel to Marshall. I am glad no one came to interrupt my lucubrations."

While Susanna, Tom and Sam were engaged or married, Agnes in this letter to Mr Bird showed herself in no hurry to enter the married state, for she signed herself 'Agnes Strickland, spinster die gratia.'

November 1830: Susanna is house-bound

When Susanna wrote to James Bird in October 1830, she confirmed that Agnes's health was much improved. She wrote: "Agnes is looking better than I have seen her for years. Mamma is busy gardening and more interested in housing her potatoes for the winter, than the blue stocking fraternity in composing sublime odes." However, she herself was confined to a couch for some unexplained reason.

A month later Susanna was still house-bound. On 9th November 1830 when she next wrote to James Bird she said: "Katie has perhaps told you of my lameness. I have not left the house for the last six weeks" with the result that her doctor's bills "will empty entirely my purse of all Annual Profit. Two bottles of medicine, two boxes of pills and two visits regularly come to a pound."

Agnes wrote to James Bird on the same day. He had sent the family some information about the appearance of their various contributions in the 1830/1831 Christmas Annuals which were beginning to be published, but Agnes was still anxiously waiting to hear whether or not some of her offerings had been accepted. She had discovered that editors had made some unhappy decisions concerning her work and wrote: "verily friend Bird these annual argosies come slowly into port. We have only received 'Ackermans' and I was in a spot at his putting my 'Edward Prince of Wales' among the baby-ware and cashiering the best verse. Can you tell me whether my piece in the 'Iris' be verse or prose. I hope the latter on account of the cash which is sadly wanted just now.

"And at the same time have the goodness to tell me whether my 'Life Boat' and your 'Wrecks' are in. I am ready to defy the Editor if he has excluded them – and feel quite in a spite before I know whether he have or not." The uncertainty seems to have upset Agnes's constitution for she writes: "Susan in still confined to the sofa but in good spirits and very busy. All the rest well except myself rather bilious, the old story, but Dixon's infallibles will put me to rights I hope in a day or two."

February 1831: Sam makes two bad decisions

When the Canada Company was put under new management in late 1830, it set about making economies which included reducing the salary they paid to Sam, whereupon Sam decided he would be better off leaving the company and reverting to life as a farmer. He wrote later: "I however found out my mistake after I had left the Company, when it was too late."

He sold his Huron tract property for $500, double what he had spent on it, and he and his family returned in February 1830 to his parents-in-law in Otonabee. His family at this time consisted of his wife, her sister (who had been so fond of Sam's first son, Edward) and his two surviving children. Sam wrote that during the four years since he had left Otonabee: "many eventful circumstances had occurred. I had buried my eldest child, a fine boy of three years old, to my great regret, but God had replaced him with a lovely boy" (named Robert Alexander, born in 1830) "and girl" (named Maria Elizabeth, born in 1829) who met their grandparents for the first time on their return to Otonabee.

Catharine later wrote an account of the death of Sam's eldest son, Edward: "The little one under its adopted Mother's care grew and throve – till it was a lovely intelligent child of three years old – when it was attacked by a sudden illness, and died. And the grief for it was great, for it had been much loved, and his little sister often asked 'Why Eddy did not waken and come to play with me'."

Sam admitted to a second mistake. He wrote: "I committed a second blunder in being tempted by a good offer to sell my farm in Otonabee and purchase land ten miles farther back in the Bush." The result of this offer was that soon after his return, Sam exchanged his 200 acre lot in the town at Otonabee, for a lot of the same size in the township of Douro plus $600 in cash. His thinking was that if he wanted to buy further wild acres in Douro, he would be able to do so at a low price, which was no longer possible in the Otonabee area.

He knew that it would take years of hard work for the new home and farm to be as comfortable and productive as the ones he was selling, but he thought it would be worth the effort, believing the scenery in Douro to be more beautiful and the land better than at his farm in Otonabee.

April 1831: Susanna eventually marries John Moodie

Among work that Susanna did on behalf of the anti-slavery movement were two pamphlets in which she transcribed the stories and sufferings of Mary Prince and of Ashton Warner. The pamphlet 'The History of Mary Prince, a West-Indian Slave' went through at least three editions and became an important document in the debate about the abolition of slavery.

In a letter to James and Emma Bird early in 1831 Susanna wrote: "I have been writing Mr Pringle's black Mary's life from her own dictation and for her benefit, adhering to her own simple story and language without deviating to the paths of flourish or romance. It is a pathetic little history and is now printing in the form of a pamphlet to be laid before the Houses of Parliament. Of course my name does not appear. I hope the work will do much good."

At the same time, Susanna had broken off her engagement, explaining to James Bird: "Circumstances have induced me to break off my engagement with Mr Moodie. Our engagement was too hasty – I have changed my mind. I will neither marry a soldier nor leave my country for ever, and I feel happy that I am again my own mistress." This letter was written when she was staying with the Pringle family, and she had just made arrangements to rent accommodation in Middleton Square, only a few minutes walk away from where the Pringles lived. She had paid £12 10s as a quarter of a year's rent taking her up to 21st April 1831 and her accommodation consisted of "a nice back drawing room to write in" and a bedroom which she shared with a Miss Jones. Susanna wrote: "Am I not a venturesome girl!"

Susanna was supplementing her income by doing some reviewing work for Mr Pringle, which she said she enjoyed. She was also, aged 28, widening her acquaintance among the literary world, attending literary evenings and receiving visitors herself. Her career was progressing well and she wrote: "I am almost tired with compliments and sick of flattering encomiums on my genius. How these London men do talk. I learn daily to laugh at their fine love speeches."

While in London Susanna heard the celebrated Edward Irving preach. Edward Irving (1792-1834) was a Scottish minister and a strong advocate for a Scottish national church. His extraordinary abilities in the pulpit and his unusual appearance (tall, gaunt and with a squint) drew Londoners of all classes and persuasions to his chapel of the Caledonian Church in Hatton Garden. Susanna declared: "It was worth enduring a state of suffocation to see and hear him. I never took my eyes off this strange apparition. Methought that Legion before he was restored to his right mind had taken possession of the pulpit.

"If you never saw him, imagine a tall man with high aquiline features and a complexion darkly brilliant with long raven love locks hanging down to his waist, his sleeves so short as to show part of his naked arms, and his person arrayed in the costume of the old reformers, and you see Edward Irving. Then his attitude! No posture master ever studied the grotesque more successfully than this extraordinary man."

Another event which Susanna saw while in London was the arrival of Henry Hunt, a Wiltshire farmer, to take his seat in parliament on 3rd February 1831. Mr Hunt was a controversial politician and not popular with the establishment. His aim was to improve the lot of the poor and to improve administration in rural areas, one of which he represented.

Susanna told Mr Bird: "I saw by accident Hunt's procession into Islington. I think my dear friend Bird you would have laughed yourself into a pleurisy. Mr Hunt upon a milk white steed most like a Farmer bold, rode foremost of the company. Then came the incomparable blacking mass filled with trumpeters who had expended all their breath before they arrived at Islington, and dirty blacking boys who with red cockades upon their hats shouted 'Hunt for ever' and 'Radical Reform' till our ears would have gladly shut themselves against their teeth jarring jargon.

"The procession stayed so long at the toll gate that I verily believe they had no money to pay. The farmers carried long poles with red streamers attached and wound about with whisps of hay. Whilst gazing upon this motley band of rag tag notoriety I discovered that MP after Henry Hunt's name signified 'mischievous person'. Do you not think I am right?"

Henry Hunt's time in parliament lasted only two years. During his time as an MP, he spoke forcefully in favour of parliamentary reform, including campaigning for the introduction of a secret ballot and for universal male suffrage. Susanna may have been enlightened as far as abolition of slavery was concerned, but her political ideas were clearly conservative if her description of Henry Hunt and his entourage is anything to go by.

After only a brief break in her engagement, Susanna married John Moodie in the early spring of 1831. Catharine wrote from Mrs Leverton's home in Bedford Square on 6th April 1831 telling the Birds: "Our dear Susanna was married last Monday the 4th of April to J Wedderburn Dunbar Moodie of His Majesty's 21st regiment of fusiliers. What do you think now of the vagaries of woman-kind? I was a witness of the marriage. Papa Pringle gave away the bride and I suppose Mrs Pringle would have given the bride groom had she been asked."

This was a time when marriages could only legally be performed before midday and in an Anglican church. Catharine wrote: "We all breakfasted at Pringles and then proceeded in a coach to St Pancras church where the knot was tied. We parted with the kind Pringles at the church door and Dunbar, Susie and I proceeded to Newman St where we dined and spent a quiet day with our cousin Cheesman and Miss Steppen" (Thomas Cheesman's niece).

Catharine continued: "I feel assured that they stand as good a chance for domestic happiness as any two persons I know of. You will not however see the nice dears so soon as was at first expected as they are quietly domiciled in comfortable apartments at Mrs Burman's, 9 Myddleton St Pentonville near Chadwell St."

Catharine asked Mr Bird if he would arrange for a notice of the marriage to be inserted in the local papers and a notice duly appeared which read: "4th April 1831. Married. At St Pancras Church, by the Rev Mr Hannam, John Wedderburn Dunbar Moodie, Esq., of the 21st Fusiliers, son of the late Major Jas Moodie, to Susanna Strickland, youngest daughter of the late Thomas Strickland, Esq., of Reydon House, Suffolk." (The change in name from 'Reydon House' to 'Reydon Hall' seems to have happened gradually over a number of years.)

Catharine had given the news to the Birds on 6th April and Susanna herself wrote to James Bird on 9th April 1831 saying: "Tell dearest Emma, a piece of now old news, that I was on the 4th instant at St Pancras Church made the happiest girl on earth, in being united to the beloved being in whom I had long centred all my affections. Mr Pringle gave me away, and Black Mary, who had treated herself with a complete new suit upon the occasion, went on the coach box to see her dear Missie and Biographer wed. I assure you, that instead of feeling the least regret at the step I was taking, if a tear trembled on my eyes, it was one of joy. My blue stockings, since I became a wife, have turned so pale that I think they will soon be quite white, or at least only tinged with a hue of London smoke. We are settled in very pleasant lodgings, only a few minutes walk from Mr Pringle's."

While Susanna was living in London in July 1831, her book of poems entitled 'Enthusiasm and other poems' was published and, whatever reservations she sometimes claimed to have about fame and about her own abilities, she did her best to ensure that she always had outlets for her work. When Mr Harral lost control of 'La Belle Assemblee' later in 1831 Susanna was already beginning to publish in the 'Athenaeum.' Her work was also appearing in the 'Lady's Magazine' where her sister Eliza had some editorial control.

July 1831: Catharine breaks off an engagement

Catharine was more modest in her literary ambitions than Agnes and Susanna. She was content to build up her reputation as a children's writer, and Mr Harral, the family friend who had moved from Ipswich to London, had contacts in London which were useful to her. Catharine and Mr Harral's son Francis had grown very fond of each other, and Catharine spent as much time as she could in London to be near him.

Early in 1831 Catharine arrived in London to stay with Mrs Leverton, by which stage she and Francis were hoping to marry, even though neither of them had much in the way of prospects, and Mr Harral's second wife was interfering in their relationship in an irrational and troublesome way.

Catharine remained in London after Susanna's marriage. With her calm and placid nature, and family connections, she was not short of invitations to be a house guest. She told the Birds: "Mrs Leverton with whom I am at present staying has renewed the invitation to me, and Lady Littledale also claims me as her guest. I go to Newman Street next week – I am quite at home in Newman St. The old gentleman makes quite a pet of me and that you know suits your Katie who always was a spoilt child."

By the time of Susanna's marriage, Catharine's courtship with Francis Harral had run into severe difficulties. Her letter on 6th April 1831 to the Birds said: "I am expecting Frank to call in every minute. I dined in Newman St yesterday with him. He had just returned from Southgate fagged to death and out of spirits. He is dearer to me, my dear friends, than ever. I wish that fortune were less adverse to us both."

Catharine told James and Emma Bird about Francis Harral's step-mother: "Mrs Harral has been annoying Susan and I. She is ten times worse than I imagined. Francis' account of her is a moderate one. Mr H is most kind to me. I am much pleased with his gentlemanly manners; he treats me with kindness. I am convinced that any reasonable person might be happy with such a man. Mrs H has twice attempted to see me but I will not meet her. I pity her and bear no malice against her."

Susanna referred to the same situation when she wrote to the Birds a few days later: "My dear Katy was with me today, she looks but so so. Mrs Harral has been annoying her in the most unwomanly way and to shew her spite put the announcement of Katy and Frank's marriage into the 'Globe' in which she called him Thomas Harral Apothecary."

The situation became so bad that Catharine decided to end the relationship, as she told the Birds in a letter dated 17th July 1831. She wrote: "the briefness and I thought coldness of Francis's visits much pained me, and under the impression that my releasing him from his engagement would be rather a source of happiness than pain to him, I wrote to him to that effect while staying with Lady Littledale.

"At the end of 3 days he came to me full of anguish. After I removed to Mrs Leverton's house he wrote to me a letter which gave me much comfort, though it contained the substance of his resigning me as his affianced. Weeks passed and though we constantly wrote, we never saw each other till the week before last. I was then very ill. Francis called and was shocked by my altered appearance, and much sorrowed at the parting soon to take place. We are both to leave Town on Monday. He for Blandford in Dorset as assistant to Mr Harrison, who will treat him as a brother and a friend, where if the salary be small his comforts will be great. He will be absent 2 years." When she wrote this letter, Catharine was staying with Mrs Leverton at Waltham Abbey in Hertfordshire, where the late Mr Leverton had an estate.

Catharine then described her daily routine: "Mrs Leverton is very kind to me and treats me as a friend and child at the same time. I find my time is never unoccupied though I make the most of it by rising at 6, seldom so late as seven and sometimes even at 5. I go to the Dairy at 7 skim the milk and superintend what wants to be done. Then I carry up to Mrs Leverton's bedroom a tumbler full of warm new milk which she takes and sleeps till half past eight."

"I sew until she comes down, make breakfast, after breakfast I write down any orders required from the shops and if there be any arrangements to make, I do it, then I find plenty of work for myself and do anything for Mrs L that I think she requires. At 2 we go out in the carriage, dine at 4 and play back gammon or draughts til it's time to visit my dairy. After tea we walk in the garden which is most exquisitely kept.

"Mrs Leverton has a school here of her own. 'The Leverton School' was established at the demise of Mr Leverton for 25 children, 15 boys and 10 girls, to be clothed and educated. The church organ was also a donation from Mr L, one of the best human beings."

August 1831: Susanna and John move to Southwold

By the end of August 1831 when Susanna wrote to James Bird, she and her husband John Moodie (variously referred to by Susanna and the family as John or Dunbar or simply Moodie) had moved from London to Southwold, where they rented a cottage.

She said they did not plan to be in Southwold for long: "Agnes will have told you I presume that we are settled for the next nine months in this unquiet little town ... The place agrees with my dear husband's health and we are a pleasant walk from Reydon. Seldom many days intervening without a visit from some of the Girls. Even Mamma forgets her resolution of never leaving home and honors our little mansion with her presence." Mrs Strickland clearly wanted to lead a simple life, but Susanna's description of "never leaving home" should not, perhaps, be taken too literally.

Susanna told the Birds that in Southwold they were visited "by the Grandees" and were shown "the kind attention of General Darling and his wife who were staying with Lady Margaret Cameron at Southwold." Susanna reported that she and John had returned the visits "with due solemnity."

August 1831: Susanna and Agnes publish their only joint work

In January 1829 Robert Childs had asked Susanna to write a small volume of psalms and hymns. Susanna did not feel confident enough to do this alone and asked Agnes to share the task, which Agnes agreed to do. Susanna and Agnes worked on the project together over the next eighteen months but it changed as it progressed, and the final production was entitled 'Patriotic Songs'. It had been published by August 1831 when the first of a series of reviews and extracts appeared in the local Norfolk and Suffolk newspapers.

The 'Norfolk Chronicle' reviewed the volume favourably and quoted Agnes's 'Life-boat'. The 'Suffolk Chronicle' was similarly favourable in its comments and also followed their review with a quotation, acknowledging in the process the difficulty involved in selecting only one of the songs. The review said: "We must give one by way of sample; but how to do this to one fair sister without offending the other? They shall draw lots; - there! Miss Susanna has it. What song has she drawn? 'The Land of our Birth' – and a very pretty song it is."

Agnes's 'Life-boat' was included in the book. It was still remembered some years later and was read at a public meeting in March 1849 and will be quoted at that point in this narrative. Susanna's poem 'The Land of Our Birth' consisted of four verses of seven lines. The first of the verses is as follows:

> There is not a spot on this wide peopl'd earth,
> So dear to the heart as the Land of our birth;
> 'Tis the home of our childhood! The beautiful spot,
> Which memory retains when all else is forgot –
> May the blessing of God
> Ever hallow the sod,
> And its valleys and hills by our children be trod.

September 1831: Sam begins to clear his new land

Sam left Mary with her parents in Otonabee, together with their daughter Maria and son Robert, and went to his newly bought land. There, on the 21st September 1831, he began the task of clearing it with the aim of getting a house built in the two months that remained before winter would set in. Sam's aim was ambitious, for there was no saw-mill within ten miles of his lot, so all the planks for the house had to be sawn by hand from newly felled trees.

November 1831: Susanna and John Moodie plan to join Sam in Canada

While Sam was busy on his land in Douro, and his wife and children were waiting patiently at Otonabee, his father-in-law made a trip to England, including paying a visit to the Strickland family in Suffolk. In a letter written in November 1831 Susanna told Mr Bird that she and her husband "entertain serious thoughts of going next spring to join my brother in Canada. Mr Read, his father-in-law, was over last week. He promises us independence and comfort on the other side of the water, and even wealth after a few years toil. This at present he enjoys after a struggle of 12 years. You must not be surprised by our flight in the spring."

Susanna recalled many years later that there was a Canada mania in England in 1831. William Cattermole, formerly of Bungay and an agent for the Canada Company, delivered recruiting lectures in Suffolk towards the end of the year, and publicity leaflets were distributed in the area to encourage emigration to Canada. Parish officers in particular were encouraging people of pauper status to leave, believing that the prospect of work with good wages lay ahead of them. To some extent this was misleading, and life in Canada for many emigrants turned out to be very hard indeed.

Susanna and John Moodie may have underestimated the benefit Sam enjoyed in always having an established family to look after him, or his wife and children, while he concentrated on clearing land and building a house. They may also have underestimated the difference in physical capabilities of Sam who was in full health and only just turned 26, and John Moodie who was eight years older and not particularly fit.

Susanna was expecting their first child, and John Moodie was away from Southwold for much of the time during the last months of her pregnancy, either arranging affairs before their emigration or seeing to the publication of his writings. These included 'Narratives of the Campaign in Holland in 1814' and 'Memoirs of the Late War'.

When John Moodie returned to Southwold early in November 1831 Susanna told Emma Bird: "Moodie has been so far from well that he kept his bed for several days. Thank God he is much recovered, but he still looks thin, and occasionally complains of the headaches from which he often suffers severely. The weather too is growing cold upon the coast and he feels it much more than we do, after such a long residence in a burning climate." They were expecting to emigrate in the spring "directly I am recovered from my confinement which I expect some time at the latter end of February. I am so happy, so very happy now, that I fear such cannot long exist upon earth."

Susanna's letter to the Bird family gave news of her sisters: "Eliza has been staying a few days with me. She and Moodie are gone to dine at Reydon this fine day. I am far from well, and thought it wisest to stay quietly at home. The walk is too far for me now. They are all but Agnes quite well. She is nervous, ailing and looks pale, and writes more than is good for her health. Dear Katy is still in Bath. She is well and happy."

December 1831: Catharine finishes her tour

Catharine was away from home for several months in 1831, staying with Mrs Leverton and making a small tour of England with her. In the quiet domestic round and in the society of her kind relative, Catharine recovered from her broken engagement.

By December they were back in Bedford Square, and Catharine wrote to tell the Birds of her travels: "I have been a far traveller indeed for one who had scarcely been beyond her own hearth smoke." They had visited Bath and spent several weeks there, taking the waters and seeing the social life of the town.

"I have also been an inmate of one of the first boarding houses at Cheltenham" presumably meaning a top-quality and fashionable boarding house "where I passed three very pleasant weeks" and made some new friends. On their way back to London, Mrs Leverton visited Oxford where Catharine was "surprised and charmed at the magnificence of the collegiate buildings."

She intended to be back in Suffolk before the spring of 1832 and before Susanna left for Canada. Catharine told the Birds: "I could not endure the thought of parting from her at a distance and possibly for years, perhaps for life."

Of Francis Harral she told the Birds: "I have heard nothing since we parted. It is painful for me to recall his name and unless anything material occurs I shall not allude to it again. I learn today with great regret that Mr Harral has lost 'La Belle.' Good heavens what will he do and those children. Agnes wrote me word."

Catharine was unwilling to write to Mr Harral in case her letter should fall into his wife's hands, and also because he might have moved house. She asked Mr Bird: "If you write to him will you tell him my reasons for not addressing him. I deeply grieve for him. He is a clever man and a warm friend."

Catharine had done hardly any writing while she was with Mrs Leverton, and had been out of touch with the literary world. She did however write 'The Siege of Antwerp' which was published in an annual named the 'New Year's Gift' for 1832 and she planned to resume writing when she returned home. Of 'The Siege of Antwerp' she told the Birds: "It was written very hastily and is not among my best productions. However, I have seen much of men and manners and new scenes which will prove useful in future time."

January 1832: Sam's house-building timetable is very ambitious

Sam's life on his new land was hard and primitive. He described his dwelling-place as an open-slab hut, the front being formed by a pole lashed between two trees twelve feet apart and as high as he could reach, while the back was the trunk of a large felled oak tree. He put a roof on this rudimentary frame which he described as "a row of split slabs, one end resting on the oak and the other supported by the pole. The ends of my camp were stuffed with hemlock-brush to keep out the wind and rain. My bed was composed of the same material, picked fine and covered with a buffalo robe."

He lived in this hut for several months and was still there at Christmas 1831, and didn't seem to mind. He wrote: "But no matter! A good fire and plenty of stirring work kept me warm." He was not entirely alone. For company he had one man employed full-time and another employed on an occasional basis.

On New Year's Day 1832 Sam moved into his new house. He wrote: "the dimensions were only twenty feet by fourteen. Still, it was paradise compared with the open camp I had just vacated." The walls were of logs and the gaps between filled with mortar. He had made a good stone fire-place at one end: "capable of burning logs three feet in length, which warmed the house thoroughly, even in the most severe weather."

February 1832: Susanna's first child is born

Susanna described her first experience of child-birth to Emma Bird. Her pains began, she wrote: "in the Sunday evening and not abed until half past one on the Wednesday morning. The last seven hours beating all I ever imagined of mortal suffering. My dear sister Sarah was with me during my anxious moments and has taken the management of the house ever since." The baby, a daughter, was born on 14th February 1832 and was baptized at St Margaret's Church in Reydon, and was named Catharine Mary Josephine Moodie.

John Moodie had to leave Southwold for London soon after their child was born and Susanna told Mrs Bird: "Moodie is in London and promises to bring dear Katie home with him. He was forced to leave me ten days after my confinement to meet his uncle, Mr Dunbar, who after coming upwards of six hundred miles to see us, fell ill in Town and found himself incapable of travelling further."

Plans to emigrate were progressing fast though it seems doubtful that Susanna and John really understood what they were letting themselves in for. They had acquired several parcels of land in Northumberland (later Peterborough County) in Upper Canada, the area in the upper reaches of the St Lawrence and its tributaries. It also seems that some of the uncleared land in Douro, which Sam Strickland purchased in August 1831, was bought on behalf of Susanna and her husband.

Susanna told Mrs Bird they were planning to settle: "in Peterborough within a mile of my brother and two of Mr Reid." The distances given by Susanna place Sam and his father-in-law closer (only one or two miles) than the distance mentioned by Sam (ten miles). Susanna continued: "My brother has already secured for my Dunbar 146 acres of excellent land fronting a small lake which he says, when cleared, will command an enchanting view." The significance of the words 'when cleared' does not seem to have penetrated Susanna's optimism.

March 1832: Tom is promoted and Margaretta begins to sail with him

On 9th March 1832, Susanna passed on news to Emma Bird: "Catharine has, I suppose, told you that my brother Thomas is now a Captain of the East Indiaman in which he made his former voyages. She is a ship of 800 tons and he is a young man of 23. Too young, I almost fear, for such an important trust and perhaps the youngest Captain of an East Indiaman that ever sailed out of the Thames."

It is probable that the news had become a little garbled in the telling, and that Tom had been made First Mate rather than Captain. In any case, Tom seems to have reached a position where his wife could, and did travel with him. Margaretta proved herself a suitable wife for him, being willing and brave enough to share his life at sea.

April 1832: Sam's family join him in Douro

By the middle of April 1832 Sam had built an extension to his house; the initial felling of the trees on the land had been completed, and he had sown his first spring crops of Indian corn and pumpkin, potatoes and turnips, cabbages and carrots.

Sam now considered his new farm and house were in a fit state for his wife and children to join him. For her part, Mary had given birth to their third child, a daughter named Emma Susanna, while Sam was busy house-building, but had recovered sufficiently to make the journey over the rough terrain to her new home mainly on foot.

Although the distance was not great, by Sam's reckoning only ten miles, the road was so near to non-existent that the journey took two days, even with the help of Sam's full-time workman, Rowlandson, and a brother-in-law. Sam wrote: "The road was only just cut out, the width not exceeding ten feet. It followed the windings of the river all the way. The creeks were un-bridged and the swamps uncross-wayed. To travel we had a carriage of my own manufacture. Rough as it was, it was the only vehicle that had any chance of going through without breaking down. The wheels were two rings, six inches thick, cut off round an oak-tree about thirty inches in diameter. A strong pole, twelve feet long was morticed into the centre of the axle for the oxen to draw by, and a small box or rack built on top was fastened with cord to the pole. Our load consisted of a barrel of salt-pork, a barrel of flour, a keg of whisky, groceries etc.

"For the first three miles we got on famously for the road was tolerable, but as soon as we got to the newly-cut road, our troubles began. Every few minutes the axles would catch against stumps and we had to prize the wheel up high enough to slip over the obstruction. If we were fortunate to get along a few hundred yards without being brought up with a jerk by some stump or stone, we were sure to stick in a mud-hole or swamp instead. With all our exertion we were benighted within two miles of my clearing, and directly opposite the shanty of a Scotch gentleman who had just commenced operations in the bush. Of course we knew we would be welcome, for no one thinks of shutting his doors against benighted travellers in the Canadian bush.

"My dear Mary had never yet seen my location. All she knew of it had been derived from my description, which I dare say I had drawn in glowing colours. Whatever might have been her thoughts, she wisely kept them to herself; she praised everything I had done, and prepared at once to assist me in making the inside of the house as comfortable as possible."

Sam's wife, Mary Strickland had lived most, if not all her life in Canada, and knew what she was letting herself in for when she became the wife of someone with pioneering tendencies like Sam. She was tactful when she saw the reality of her new home, but would probably not have been unduly surprised.

May 1832: Catharine marries Thomas Traill and leaves for Canada

Catharine was back in Suffolk by March 1832. Visiting John and Susanna at Southwold was Thomas Traill, a close friend and fellow officer of John Moodie. Thomas Traill, born in 1793, was the eldest son of the Rev Walter Traill of 'Westove' in the Orkney Islands. He was a well-educated man who, after retiring from the army at the end of the Napoleonic wars, took over the affairs of the family estate on behalf of his father in 1818. The income of the estate came from tenant farms and kelp harvesting, and in theory provided the Rev Walter Traill with an annual income of £300, plus £100 a year for Thomas, his only surviving son. As time went by the estate did not yield sufficient to pay these annual sums, nevertheless the Rev W Traill continued to have an annuity of £300 until his death in 1846, although Thomas no longer had any income at all from this source.

In 1821 Thomas Traill had taken his first wife Anne and their two young sons to the continent for the sake of her health. They lived for a time in France and in Germany before her death in 1828. The two sons then returned to Kirkwall, the capital of the Orkney Islands, where they lived in the care of their mother's family, the Fotheringhames.

In 1832 Thomas Traill was 39 compared with Catharine's 30, and his sons in the Orkneys were teenagers. Thomas had only a half-pay pension as a retired Lieutenant, plus the notional income of £100 per annum from the family estate. Catharine had no money or income at all, apart from what little she earned by writing.

Despite the difference in their ages, his existing family responsibilities, and their combined lack of money, they very quickly decided to marry and to follow the Moodie's example of moving to Canada. So it was that, only two months after returning from her travels with Mrs Leverton, Catharine Strickland married Thomas Traill and, without any apparent previous intention to do so, emigrated to Canada.

The marriage took place at St Margaret's Church in Reydon on 13th May 1832. Catharine later wrote of the event: "I was married in our parish church at Reydon by the vicar, the Reverend Henry Birch. My sisters Agnes and Jane were my bridesmaids – my brother-in-law gave me away, his wife, my sister Susanna was also present. It was a very quiet wedding, for it was preparatory to my leaving England to accompany my husband to Canada – first going to Edinburgh and then to the Orkneys, to take leave of his friends and relatives and to see his two sons, one or both of whom we expected to accompany us to Canada. The anticipation of parting with my mother and sisters and friends – for years it might be – cast a shadow over the wedding – and the few days that ensued before our final departure." The shadow which Catharine mentioned, was caused not only by her impending departure, but by reservations felt by other members of her family about the wisdom of the entire enterprise.

On Sunday 20th May 1832, Jane and Agnes Strickland were at Southwold to see the departure of Catharine and Thomas Traill on 'The City of London' steamer. Catharine recalled later that 'The City of London' "was the only steamer save her consort 'The City of Edinburgh' that plied on the ocean at that date." These steamers travelled once a week between London and Leith, calling at the various ports and seaside towns en route.

The first small leg of the journey was made in a rowing boat, the 'Betsy' which took Agnes, Jane, Catharine and Thomas from the beach at Southwold out to the steamer. All the Traills' chests and packages were stowed into the 'Betsy' under the superintendence of Thomas Traill, whom his wife described as "a tall, military, somewhat foreign-looking gentleman." Catharine also described the trio of sisters: "one is pale with dark eyes" (this must have been Agnes) "the other two" (Jane and Catharine herself) "are fair. Few words are spoken. The day is lovely – the sea unruffled."

The bells of St Edmund's Church in Southwold began to peal for morning service, and soon afterwards the captain of the 'Betsy' saw the signal that the approaching steamer had been sighted. "And now" Catharine wrote "all is hurry." The party of four were rowed out to the steamer where Catharine, her husband and their belongings were taken on board.

The sisters waved their last farewells, the rowing boat with Agnes and Jane got clear of the steamer's paddles, and 'The City of London' resumed its voyage to Edinburgh. Catharine had said good-bye to her childhood home, her friends and her family, and was on her way to begin a new life in Canada.

June 1832: Susanna spends a month in Scotland

Susanna and John Moodie's departure from Southwold was delayed by two or three weeks for some unexplained reason, though possibly due to bad weather. In contrast with Catharine, who was seen off by sisters, Susanna and John had no family waving good-bye. Instead they had two friends, one was called Allen Ransome and the other was Mr Bird, for they took with them one of the Bird's children. This was 14-year old James Bird, who was going to live in Canada with Sam Strickland, and learn the ways of Canadian farming from him.

In addition, Susanna and John took a nursemaid with them to help with the care of their 3-month old daughter Catharine. In common with the Traills, the Moodie party headed first for Edinburgh where John Moodie wanted to see friends and relations before he emigrated.

By the end of May they had reached Edinburgh where they spent a month sight-seeing, saying farewells, and looking for a suitable ship to take them to Canada. John eventually booked their passage on the brig 'Anne,' which sailed for Quebec on 1st July 1832, with twelve passengers on board.

June 1832: Catharine meets her step-sons

Catharine and Thomas Traill, having reached Edinburgh on Tuesday morning, 22nd May 1832, stayed there until Saturday evening, sightseeing and visiting friends of Thomas. From Edinburgh's port of Leith they took the weekly packet boat, which took passengers as well as the mail to Kirkwall, the capital of the Orkney Islands. This stage of the journey made Catharine ill and she had to be lifted out of the boat into the dinghy that would take her to the shore.

In a state of near collapse, and while Thomas saw to the unloading of their luggage, Catharine was taken to the family home of Thomas's first wife, the Fotheringhames, who had been given little, if any warning that he had re-married. Despite Thomas Traill's unexpected re-marriage, Catharine was welcomed and treated with kindness.

Thomas anticipated that at least one of his sons would go to Canada with him, and would supply youthful energy and enthusiasm to the enterprise. However, the elder son, aged seventeen, had plans to study at the Medical College in Edinburgh and the younger son aged thirteen preferred to stay in Kirkwall and finish his education. Both sons having decided to remain in Scotland, Thomas and Catharine were obliged to emigrate alone or not at all.

When Catharine and Thomas had set off from Suffolk, family members had tried to dissuade them and a similar situation arose in Kirkwall, where not only Thomas's family, but also the tenant farmers and their wives tried to persuade him to give up the idea of emigration and remain in Orkney. However, Thomas had made up his mind and their words fell on deaf ears.

Setting off for Canada from Kirkwall, they first travelled by boat to Inverness, which was a relatively short journey but was enough to make Catharine ill. From Inverness they took a steam boat through the Great Glen and past Ben Nevis to Greenock. For much of this journey Catharine was able to enjoy the scenery, make acquaintances among the other passengers, and admire the Scottish flora and fauna. However, by the time they reached Greenock, Catharine had developed a fever.

They had already booked and had paid their passage on the brig 'Laurel', and cancelling their voyage would have had serious financial implications, particularly as it was the last brig that would sail to Quebec that season. During their few days in Greenock, Catharine's illness worsened and it needed careful nursing and the attendance of the local doctor to get her through the worst stages.

Thomas and Catharine decided to carry on with their plans, in the hope that the sea voyage would restore Catharine to health, but their arrival on board was not encouraging. Catharine was so ill that she had to be carried on board, and the female servant who had been engaged to accompany them did not appear. On 7th July 1832, less than two months after her marriage, Catharine set sail for Canada with her husband. She was helpless due to her illness, and there was no other female on board ship.

August 1832: Catharine reaches Canada

Thomas Traill's choice of vessel for the voyage had been a good one. Catharine wrote: "The ship was clean and well conducted with a picked crew and a sober skilful Captain, Steward and First Mate. For the next three weeks my time was spent – all night in a state of suffering – all day I lay on a sort of couch made up with cloaks, on the deck shaded by a large umbrella, where I read or sewed, and watched what was going on on the deck, or listened to some tale or poem being read aloud by my dear husband. I grew so weak at last that the Steward and the Captain hint in mysterious whispers at the chances were against my reaching Canada alive.

"Our voyage was unbroken by any storm – we passed the region of fogs – the banks of Newfoundland – without any change to mark our vicinity. My involuntary fasting for several weeks was giving way to a desire for fresh food. Delightful to me was the delicious land breeze that came, bringing health and strength back to the poor invalid voyager. Now life seemed worth living. Even our taciturn Captain, and grave thoughtful chief officer, seemed glad to see me venturing to walk the deck unsupported and taking my place at the dinner table, and share the homely ship's fare of salt meat and pea soup."

Catharine in her memoirs written many years later said that having recovered her health on the voyage across the Atlantic, she then caught cholera in Montreal. There were several outbreaks of cholera in various places in England in 1832, and the disease began to appear in Canada and North America in the same year, and was thought to have arrived in ships carrying immigrants.

The timing of Catharine's voyage overall makes it sound unlikely that her recovery from an illness that was normally fatal, could be speedy enough to fit into the given timetable of events. One would suspect that her memory was at fault, confusing the fever, possibly cholera, contracted in Scotland with a less serious illness when she arrived in Canada. However, Sam separately left a record of their first meeting in Canada which confirmed that Catharine did indeed catch and recover from cholera on arrival in Montreal.

Once Catharine had recovered sufficiently, she and Thomas proceeded on their journey up the St Lawrence, making their way by various means towards Sam and his family. The first part of the journey up-river was fondly remembered by Catharine: "That voyage up the river was delightful, the weather was serene and sunny – there was so little breeze, that we could only depend on the tide and tacking from side to side to catch any slant of wind. The singing of the sailors, when the anchor was being raised, sounded like pleasant music to my ears, and chorus of the crew – 'Ho cheerily boys, cheerily boys ho', with all the improvisations that the leader of the band – Musical Joe, indulged in the moving round of the capstan, and the final 'cheer boys' that proclaimed that the mighty anchor was raised from its briny bed. And so we progressed pleasantly, if not rapidly, in the 'Rowly' working her way up the key to the West."

August 1832: Sam goes to meet Catharine at Peterborough

News travelled slowly between England and Canada in 1832, as Sam's later account of events reveals. He wrote: "In the end of July, or the beginning of August (1832) my sister Catharine, then Mrs Traill, now so well known as the author of that popular little work the 'Backwoods of Canada', and her husband, Lieutenant Traill, emigrated to Canada West. My brother-in-law, William, came up late one evening from his father's house, a distance of eight miles, to tell me that she and her husband had just arrived in Peterborough.

"This was the first intelligence I had received of her marriage or emigration. Of course I was delighted at the thought of again seeing my sister, from whom I had been separated so many years; and although I had never attempted the passage of the Otonabee in a bark canoe, so anxious was I to welcome her, that I determined to run the rapids a distance of ten miles by the river. My readers may judge of the rapidity of the current ... when I tell them that the fall in this river between my place and Peterborough ... amounted to one hundred and forty-seven feet.

"My brother-in-law having volunteered to go with me, I was not afraid to encounter the danger, although it was nearly dark when we started ... Three times we were obliged to go on shore and empty our canoe, which had half filled whilst running down some of the roughest chutes ... we providentially escaped all dangers, and arrived safely at Peterborough.

"My sister, who had only just recovered from a severe attack of Asiatic cholera, which had laid her up at Montreal, had already retired for the night; but hearing my voice, she immediately dressed and came down to see me. I need hardly describe the joy of this meeting. Those only can fully comprehend the feeling who have been separated for years from those they love.

"It was agreed that as soon as possible they should come up to my house, and reside with me until their own house was ready. Fortunately, they were enabled to purchase the lot next to mine, which had a very pretty frontage on the lake."

September 1832: Susanna writes home

Susanna and her family group sailed from the east side of Scotland which meant they had a longer voyage than Catharine and Thomas, who had sailed from the west. In addition, Susanna's vessel was becalmed off Newfoundland for three weeks so that, one way or another, despite the Moodie party having left the British Isles six days before the Traills, they arrived in Canada some two or three weeks after them.

In the intervening period, cholera had become so rife in both Quebec and Montreal that their ship was obliged to anchor near Grosse Island, the cholera inspection centre, before they were allowed to proceed. Susanna found that as well as an outbreak of cholera, Quebec had a plague of mosquitoes, and they did not venture ashore, but went straight on to Montreal. Even there, coffins lined the quay and the family decided to stay on board, but before long sickness reached the ship and they were obliged to land.

At Montreal, Susanna wrote a letter home telling of their journey and safe arrival. Agnes passed the news on to Mr Bird in a letter dated 4th October 1832. She wrote: "My Dear Friend, I have the satisfaction of being able to communicate to you, the joyful intelligence that one party of the Dear Emigrants, Moodie, Susanna, James and Baby, have arrived safely at Montreal. By this day's post we received a letter from Mrs Moodie, dated Brig Anne off Montreal, Sept 3rd in which she says after a tedious passage of eight weeks they arrived off Quebec, where they did not land on account of the cholera which destroyed upwards of 200 people a day. Then they had quarantine to perform, a very unnecessary infliction I think in an infected place.

"James, she says, has grown stout and hearty and a head taller than he was. She sends his duty to you and his mother and his love to his brothers and sisters and says he will write from Montreal. The cholera is very bad at Montreal, but still I apprehend no particular danger for them, as they did not propose to tarry in that place, and you know I was in the midst of the pestilence in London, during the India-like heat and felt no cause for alarm.

"Baby, Susan says, has grown charmingly. Hannah was seasick all the voyage, and poor Susan very ill. They had a journey of

400 miles in perspective when she wrote, which was not very likely to act as a cordial to the mind of a naturally despondent person like her, worn out as she was.

"All's well that ends well, and well it was for all parties that the vexatious delay at Southwold prevented them from going by the ship in which they proposed sailing, as she arrived in Montreal in the first rage of the cholera, and 150 of the passengers died almost as soon as they landed of the pestilence. How mysterious, but adorable was the providence which prevented them from being of the number!"

From Montreal the Moodie party made a journey by stage-coach to Prescott. There they boarded the new steamboat 'William IV' to Cobourg which was the port of access to the backwoods country where they intended to settle.

50,000 people left England for Quebec in 1831 and the numbers peaked at 52,000 in 1832, which were the years when the Strickland sisters and their men-folk made and carried out their plans to emigrate to Canada. By 1833, news had filtered back to England that life in Canada was not so easy, nor so sure of a good outcome, as publicity had claimed, and there was a substantial drop in emigration figures. However, in 1832, while Susanna and Catharine were about to wake up to the reality of life as a settler in the backwoods of Canada, their family in England still believed the favourable propaganda that had persuaded them to go.

September 1832: Sam, Catharine and Susanna are reunited but not for long

Susanna, her baby, the servant, the younger James Bird and John Moodie, having followed in the footsteps of Catharine and Thomas Traill, arrived at Sam's new home and clearing in Douro in September 1832. Young James Bird was transferred from the care of Susanna to that of Sam Strickland, with Catharine making sure that news of the youngster's progress was sent to his parents on a regular basis.

The families soon parted company again. Catharine and Thomas decided to remain with Sam and his family, and began work on their own uncleared land adjoining Sam's property. Susanna and

John, with baby and nurse, decided to buy a farm that had already been cleared, in preference to starting work on their land in Douro. The farm they bought was in Hamilton Township, about 35 miles away from Sam and Catharine, but they felt that the advantage of having a cleared farm more than made up for the disadvantage of separation.

Part 2: Life patterns form and fame begins

Commanding a ship; success and failure as settlers; 'Lives of the Queens of England' and fame for Agnes Strickland; Sheriff of Belleville; more marriages

February 1833: Susanna writes a tactless letter

Even before she arrived in Canada, Susanna had begun laying the foundations for writing commercially in Canada. Some of her poems are said to have appeared anonymously in Canada while she was still living in England, and between mid-September 1832 and the end of the year, a local paper, the 'Coburg Star' had in separate issues printed five of Susanna's poems and an article by John Moodie entitled 'The Elephant Hunt'.

In February 1833 Susanna wrote to the editor of the 'Albion', one of the most literate and reliable weekly newspapers in North America, hoping to gain publicity from appearing therein. The 'Albion' specialised in reporting up-to-date news from Britain, literature and political news. Susanna's letter began: "Sir, - The pleasure I derived from the perusal of several of the last numbers of your clever and interesting paper, has made me ambitious of the honor of contributing to its pages; and if the assistance of a pen, deemed not unworthy of public notice in my native land, when held by Susanna Strickland, can in any way be acceptable to you, and your readers, it will afford me much pleasure."

Susanna enclosed with her letter, a poem entitled 'The Sleigh-bells' the first of its four verses being as follows:

'Tis merry to hear at ev'ning time,
By the blazing hearth the sleigh-bells chime;
To know each bound of the steed brings near,
The form of him to our bosoms dear;
Lightly we spring the fire to raise,
Till the rafters glow with the ruddy blaze.

The poem and the entirety of Susanna's letter were published in the 'Albion' and were then reprinted in a local paper, the 'Kingston Upper Canada Herald' on Wednesday 13th March 1833 after a very welcoming preliminary which read: "Susanna Strickland. We have been agreeably surprised, in receiving the following communication from this lady. We had no idea that she had left the happy shores of England, and much less that she had become so near a neighbour to us."

Unfortunately, the second part of Susanna's letter, which was also published, implied criticism of the people of Canada. She continued: "I now enclose the first flight of my muse on Canadian shores. But this chilly atmosphere, at present, is little favourable to the spirit of Poesy. The minds of the inhabitants being too much engrossed in providing for their families the necessaries of life, to pay much attention to the cultivation of literature. However mortifying to the vanity of an Author, this indifference may be, it would be unjust to censure my fellow settlers for suffering more urgent and important duties to render them deaf to the voice of the syren, whose wild flights and vagaries have charmed me from my youth upwards. The close confinement of a log cabin, and the cares of a family, though they engross much of my time, have not been able to chill these inspirations ... The little sympathy which such feelings can meet with, in a new colony, where every energy of mind is employed to accumulate wealth, has made me anxious to seek a more liberal channel of communication ... which finds its way into the study of every respectable family on this side of the Atlantic, and is not inferior in literary merit, to any publication of the same class in Great Britain."

A separate item in the same edition of the 'Kingston Upper Canada Herald' noted and responded to Susanna's criticism. The article, after a preliminary which praised Susanna's work, added: "We think, nevertheless, that the fair author might have spared the implied censure ... on the want of sympathy and taste among the inhabitants of this Province" assuring Susanna that there were papers in Canada (the 'Albion' was an American publication) "who will at all times be happy to convey the 'spirit of Poesy' to the remotest townships, many of which are filling up with persons who are capable of duly appreciating literary merit."

Susanna's statement that "every energy of mind is employed to accumulate wealth" might also have raised an eye-brow. Susanna either had not realised, or chose to ignore the fact that many of those around her were struggling to survive, not accumulating wealth.

Several more of Susanna's poems appeared in various newspapers over the next few years and with the launch of the 'Canadian Literary Magazine' in April 1833, Susanna also had an outlet for prose pieces. Meanwhile, Susanna's family duties increased when her second child, Agnes Dunbar Moodie, was born on 9th June 1833.

1833: Sam is well established in his new lot

Sam's life in 1833 (aged 28) was, according to his later account of the same period, progressing nicely with no hint of any problems. After his wife Mary's arrival in Douro with their children, and after he had cleared another area of trees, he built a second house in a better situation than the first. The first house had been built on a ridge about 30 feet above the river while the second one was built on a gentle slope leading to the water's edge with a good view across both river and lake.

Sam was also busy cultivating his cleared land. He wrote that he had sowed a bed in his garden with apple pips: "This was in 1833, and as soon as the young stocks were large enough, I grafted them with the choicest fruit I could obtain – about one hundred – which I planted the following year in an orchard to the south of my house. A year or two afterwards, I planted a hundred and fifty trees in a second orchard, north of the house, besides a great variety of plums and greengages."

1833: Tom's first child is born at sea

Margaretta joined Tom in his life on board ship, and their first child was born at sea in 1833. She was given the same Christian names as her mother, but had to wait for the ship to return to London before being baptised on 15th May 1834 at St Dunstan & All Saints Church in Stepney. (To avoid confusion, Tom's wife will be referred to hereafter as Margaretta, and their daughter will be referred to as Adela. This conforms with family practice.)

1833: Agnes tries her hand at writing fiction

Throughout the 1820s and 1830s a miscellany of short articles in Christmas annuals, and poems printed in local papers, had earned Agnes some money and had brought her name into public view, albeit in a low key way and mainly in Norfolk and Suffolk.

The end of Agnes's attempts to earn a living by poetry came in 1833 with the publication of an epic poem about Greece. The background was remembered by Catharine: "It was about the year 1820 or 1821 that the cause of the Greek patriots striving to throw off the galling and merciless yoke of the Turks began to be agitated in London, especially among the literary people. Agnes was introduced to some Greek gentlemen trying to raise a loan in aid of the oppressed Greeks.

"Agnes entered with all the enthusiasm that belonged to her nature. The cause was a noble one. She threw all her poetic fervour into the subject. Her verses were indeed heart stirring and were gratefully approved by the Greek patriots, but the Greek cause was not a popular one with the English at large. The taste for poetry was already much on the wane." The poem, 'Demetrius', was not actually published until 1833, by which time it was out of date in subject matter as well as in form, the taste for epic poems being past. It was badly received by the critics.

Agnes next turned her attention to writing full length works of fiction. Her first work was entitled 'The Pilgrims of Walsingham.' The basic idea involved pilgrims recounting stories to their fellow travellers, a situation which had already been famously used by Geoffrey Chaucer in his 'Canterbury Tales.' The detail of Agnes's narrative differed from Geoffrey Chaucer's work in that Agnes had the pilgrims going to the shrine at Walsingham, not Canterbury, and the pilgrims included Henry VIII and other notable personages travelling with him incognito.

This idea had some basis in fact, as every medieval king from Henry III to Henry VIII is said to have visited the shrine at Little Walsingham in Norfolk, in some cases walking the last mile barefoot. Agnes's book was eventually published in 1835 and was successful enough to cover its costs, and Agnes retained the copyright, but she was a slow writer in fiction and she recognised that it was not her forte.

1833: The notion of female royal biographies is born

Eliza had written some biographies of female sovereigns, which were published while she was working as an editor for the 'Court Journal', and they had been very popular. The combination of Agnes's 'Pilgrim's of Walsingham' and Eliza's biographies gave rise to the idea of their working together to produce full and thoroughly researched biographies of the Queens of England.

They decided their biographies would start at the Norman Conquest and end with the last of the Stuart Monarchs. This meant they were to begin with a biography of Matilda of Flanders, the wife of William the Conqueror, who was born about 1031. Their final biography was to be that of Queen Anne who died in 1714. Their biographies would therefore cover a period of nearly seven hundred years and, given the state of public records at the time, the task they set themselves was astonishingly difficult. However, they were determined to do the job properly, and adopted the motto 'fact not fiction' thereby defining themselves as historians not novelists.

A little research told them that they were opening up a new field of biographical study. The only work that had previously been published on the subject was contained in 'History of England' by Dr Lingard, a Catholic priest whose writing was unusual in being from the Catholic point of view.

Eliza and Agnes were optimistic that they could make a decent living from their project, and Eliza gave up her work at the 'Court Journal' in 1833 to work on it full-time. She stipulated at the outset that her name should not appear on the title page of any ensuing books, and that only Agnes should be acknowledged as the author of their joint works. She maintained this determination to remain anonymous throughout her life, allowing herself occasionally to be described as assistant to Agnes, but never more than that. This meant that Agnes had to be the public face of the duo, dealing with all correspondence, publicity and legal matters. She had to be fully conversant with everything Eliza wrote, and had to be careful at all times not to reveal the truth about their working relationship.

As they were obliged to go back to primary sources, they started their research in the British Museum, and the first hurdle they had to cross was to understand the museum's cataloguing system, and the meaning of the various abbreviations used in the documents. Both of them could read printed Latin, and with the help of museum staff they learnt how to decipher medieval script. Of great use to them was a book published in 1831 by Harris Nicolas entitled 'Description of the Various Works Printed by the Authority of the Record Commission'. This contained, among many other useful things, a list of the contractions used in records, complete with an explanation of what they meant.

January 1834: Catharine is in her new house

Catharine recorded that after staying with Sam and his family for a few weeks, she and Thomas occupied "a forsaken log cabin" for much of 1833. This may well have been the first of the houses which Sam built on his Douro land, and which became redundant when he built another house in a better location. It was in this log cabin that Catharine's first child, James George Traill was born on 7th June 1833, two days before the birth of Susanna's second daughter.

With the birth of James, a nursemaid named Isabella Gordan joined the family. She had arrived in Canada from Ireland in 1832 and became a valued as well as a useful member of the household. By December 1833 enough of the Traill's land had been cleared for a house to have been built and to be ready for occupation.

Catharine wrote to Mr and Mrs Bird on 7th January 1834 to give news of their son James Bird and a description of his life with Sam. In doing so she gave a picture of a settler's life in general, and of her own home in particular. She wrote that young James Bird: "is becoming intimately acquainted with the customary work of a Canadian farm – chopping, under-brushing, logging, making brush heaps and log heaps, burning the fallow; sowing and harrowing wheat and rye, planting corn i.e. Indian corn, setting pumpkin seeds and turnips, raising potato hills etc – Discuss the merits of Buck and Bright, the orthodox names for Canadian oxen, go through the logging exercise with stentorian lungs."

Catharine drew a comparison between fishing in Suffolk and in Canada: "How the quiet little anglers of the ponds and tiny streams about his native village would stare to hear fishing by torch light on big lakes in a canoe made of the bark of birch trees, and instead of a little hook a trident or a hook big enough to haul in a whale." She said that young James "grows tall and will make a fine lad. Just now he is at an awkward age, I mean for looks as all boys are when growing into men."

She sounded cheerful and content in her new house, which they named 'Westove' in memory of Thomas's family estate in the Orkneys. Catharine wrote: "We are now comfortably settled. We moved into it on the 8th December (1833). Its situation is fronting Katchawanook Lake. The inside of the building gives us a nice parlour with glass door opening towards the lake. A window looks south towards my brother's clearing. We have a small but pleasant bedroom opening from the parlour and a kitchen, pantry and store closet. A cellar below the kitchen, and an upper floor which can be divided into three bedrooms. In the parlour we are kept warm and cheerful by a Franklin stove." This was metal lined and had a particular structure which gave more heat, less smoke and used less wood than an open fireplace would have done.

From the description she gave of her home, it was an attractive place and Catharine had made friends among the local people: "The floor is covered with an Indian mat plaited by my friends the squaws from the inner bark of the cedar. We have a handsome sofa with a brass railing which also serves as a bed. I have made blinds for the windows of green cambric, and white muslin draperies which have a light and pretty effect. These with the painted white chairs, a stained table, book case and some large maps and prints of General Lafayette, Kosciusco, Fox and Brougham form the tout ensemble of our log sitting room. I hope you will say that we keep good company for Backwoods men, though it be somewhat radical of its kind." Both the Marquis of Lafayette (1757-1834) and Tadeusz Kosciuszko (1746-1817) were adventurers and revolutionaries. Charles James

Fox (1749-1806) and Henry Brougham (1778-1869) were British statesmen, the latter also being a philanthropist whose name will crop up several times in the lives of Catharine Parr Traill and Agnes Strickland.

Of her own 7-month old son James, Catharine wrote: "He is the joy of my heart. He is sitting at this moment on his doting nurse Isabella Gordan's knee with half closed sleepy blue eyes. My little James grows bravely and governs the house." She also asked: "How is my friend Mr Harral and Francis. Do not be surprized at my naming the latter. We have never been less than friends. I believe he is generous enough to rejoice that I am happy. It is my ardent wish that he should be so."

February 1834: Susanna and John return to Douro

Susanna and John Moodie's neighbours in Hamilton Township had been there long enough to have learnt how to live in the backwoods. They were mainly American and Irish people whose loyalty to Britain was questionable, and they were a sharp contrast to the literary people that Susanna had lived amongst in England. Susanna and John found their new life and their new neighbours difficult. Rightly or wrongly, Susanna felt that she was being taunted, and that her neighbours were being deliberately unhelpful.

By the autumn of 1833, and after barely a year living on the cleared farm they had bought in Hamilton Township, Susanna and John were so unhappy with their neighbours and surroundings that they decided they would prefer to live near Sam and Catharine in Douro, even if it meant facing the challenge of working uncleared land. They sold their Hamilton farm back to the land-jobber from whom they bought it, and in February 1834 moved to their land-holding in Douro.

1834: Rebecca Leverton and Thomas Cheesman die

The two relatives of Thomas Strickland who had done so much in different ways to help his daughters, both died in 1834. Susanna mentioned receiving legacy money of £700 at about this time, and it is probable that the six sisters were each bequeathed the same sum either by Rebecca Leverton alone, or in combination with Thomas Cheesman. Mrs Leverton is known to have been wealthy, and neither she nor Mr Leverton had any surviving children, but there were charitable causes needing financial support for their continuation. Mr Cheesman left provision for the niece who had shared his life and looked after his home. He also left instructions for the use of his property and investments after the death of his niece which would, in due course, benefit some of Thomas Strickland's grand-children. The exact source of the Strickland sisters' legacy money in 1834 is not known, but all of the six sisters were in need of the money.

With the deaths of Mrs Leverton and Mr Cheesman, Agnes lost the two homes in London where she could live free of charge. Eliza was accustomed to paying for lodgings in London, but had given up her job to concentrate on research. Agnes continued to write for Christmas Annuals and Eliza continued to write reviews for magazines but for these two sisters, the legacy money gave them the financial cushion which they needed while researching and writing the early volumes of their royal biographies.

In Canada, both Catharine and Susanna were producing children without the means to support them. Their husbands were using up limited resources by employing labour to clear their land and build their houses, to a far greater extent than the younger and more robust Sam had done. These two sisters needed their legacy money to cover costs until their farms became productive enough to feed and support their families.

Jane and Sarah were both living at Reydon House, and any money they received was needed either to invest for their future needs, to pay for day to day living, or to help maintain the house, which was far bigger than needed, but which could not be sold during their mother's lifetime.

1834: Agnes and Eliza settle into their new lives in London

Although Agnes had found friends with whom she could stay for short periods, for much of the time when she was in London, she needed to be based near the British Museum and in peaceful surroundings, so that she could both study and write without interruption. Eliza lived full time in lodgings, sometimes she and Agnes shared London accommodation, and sometimes they lodged separately.

Agnes's social life changed after Mrs Leverton died. With her concentration on historical writing, Agnes no longer spent time in the literary salons of the day. Instead she began to make social contacts among historians and antiquarians, which included members of aristocratic families whose properties and family papers were a valuable source of information for herself and Eliza.

December 1834: Susanna is building her reputation as a poet

Susanna continued to write and to have her work published. The 'Canadian Literary Magazine', whose aim was to improve literary tastes in Canada, included in its issue dated December 1834 a review entitled 'Mrs Moodie's Poems.' The review was written by the editor and praised Susanna in glowing terms, describing her as a poet whose: "genius and feeling are of no ordinary kind."

Three examples of her poetry were appended to the article, and it is said that the magazine printed eleven of Susanna's poems before there was a change of editor late in November 1836. However, while Susanna's poetry was adding to her fame, it was not bringing much in the way of payment.

October 1835: Sarah marries into the Childs family

On 15th October 1835 Sarah was married to Robert Childs at Reydon Parish Church. Despite being the beauty of the family and having a personality which ensured that all the family loved her, she remained single until she was 37 years old. The husband she chose was 12 years her senior. J Ewing Ritchie, son of the Wrentham Congregationalist minister, wrote: "Uncle Robert as I used to hear him called ... had a nice house" said to have been named 'The Chase', "and lived comfortably marrying after a long courtship, the only one of the Stricklands who was not a writer."

The family into which Sarah married was one of some fame or notoriety. The Childs printing firm had been set up in Bungay in 1795 by Robert's grand-father. Robert's father had subsequently taken over, and by 1835 it was run as a partnership between John, Robert and Charles Childs. 'The History of Printing' reports that "Robert Childs and his elder brother John had the merit of converting a business for the publication of very common works in numbers, into one of the best stereotype and printing establishments in the kingdom." They were a major employer in Bungay, employing in the region of a hundred men.

As well as being successful business men, sociable and interested in phrenology, the menfolk in the Childs family did not accept situations with which they disagreed. Robert and his elder brother John were vocal opponents of printers' patents granted by the King. They were especially opposed to the Crown having a printing monopoly of the Bible, and in 1831 they had both given evidence to a parliamentary enquiry into the matter.

The Childs were also staunch dissenters and were among many who objected to paying a church rate which benefited only the parish church when they worshipped elsewhere. In May 1835, only a few months before Sarah married his younger brother, John Childs decided to refuse to pay the church rates, knowing what the consequence would be, and was duly sent to prison. Theoretically the imprisonment could have lasted indefinitely, and at least until he paid the required rate. Despite his determination to continue with his protest, John Childs' health quickly began to deteriorate inside jail, and after a few days his supporters realised that as a matter of urgency they had to resolve the situation to everyone's satisfaction. As the Church also did not want John Childs to die in prison, the two sides managed to negotiate terms for his release which were acceptable all round.

The imprisonment may only have been brief but it gained the publicity required. John Childs was the first Englishman, other than a member of the Society of Friends (also known as Quakers) to be sent to prison on a matter of conscience. The Establishment had little sympathy for the case and Robert Peel, when the case was discussed in parliament, referred to John Childs disparagingly as 'The Bungay Martyr'. 'The Times' newspaper also carried a lengthy report of the case which consisted almost entirely of outrageous abuse.

Whatever eminent politicians in Westminster and writers for London newspapers thought of him, John Childs was a hero in East Anglia. When he was released from prison, a procession welcomed him back to Bungay, and the 'Suffolk Chronicle' described the event in great detail. The procession was headed by 80 horsemen riding two abreast followed by a large crown made of flowers; then came flags and banners followed by a band in a van drawn by two horses; more flags and banners; 200 children from the local school; carriages carrying Mr Childs and his family; more flags and banners; then about 100 carriages and other vehicles bringing up the rear, the whole procession being watched by thousands of local people.

The local papers also reported the public dinner which was held at the end of June 1835 in the theatre in Bungay in honour of John Childs. 170 gentlemen sat down to the meal (the ladies were spectators in the gallery and upper boxes) and there were many speeches and toasts in support of his action.

The setting and collection of the Church Rate struggled on for a few more years as a bone of contention, not only in Bungay but also in many other parts of the country, before being abolished and Sarah's husband, Robert Childs was among those who continued to refuse to pay it. Although these events mainly happened before Sarah and Robert Childs were married, she would have been fully aware of the strength and the nature of the political and religious views of the family into which she married.

Unlike Susanna and Catharine, Sarah was marrying a prosperous man with the prospect of financial comfort and, given her age at marriage, the likelihood of fewer children than her married brothers and sisters.

1835: Catharine and Thomas decide to move from Douro

By making their first home in Douro near to Sam and his family, Catharine and Thomas immediately had relatives to whom they could turn for advice and help, and they joined the social net-work of Sam and Mary Strickland's friends in the area. Catharine enjoyed the social freedom of Canada which allowed her to make friends with any and all of the people she met, including the indigenous Canadian peoples whom she referred to as the 'Hiawatha' people.

An important and long-lasting friendship which Catharine formed early in her life in Canada, was with Frances Stewart, who had arrived from Ireland with her husband Thomas Stewart in 1823. The two women were both well-educated, genteel in manners and shared deeply-held religious beliefs. Frances was eight years older than Catharine. She and her husband had a farm named 'Auburn' in Douro Township. They had settled successfully and were able to help Catharine and Thomas Traill with practical advice as well as moral support.

Despite having some good reasons for remaining near Sam, it soon became apparent that Thomas Traill was not suited to farming in the backwoods of Canada. He had been responsible for the family estate in the Orkneys and had been an officer in the army, but neither of these prepared him for the hard physical labour of cutting down trees, clearing the land and building a house in the backwoods. Without the help which the presence of his teenage sons might have provided, it was necessary to have hired help, and Catharine's legacy money had to be used towards the cost.

Catharine was continuing to earn some money by writing for English and Canadian journals, and she was also writing a book based on notes in her diary. It was partly auto-biographical and based on letters which she had written home to England soon after her arrival. It used descriptions of her own journey to Canada, the routine of her new life, and the details of her new surroundings in terms of climate, seasons and wild-life. It was mainly written before financial troubles befell the family and contains much in the way of cheerful optimism. She wrote: "I must freely confess to you that I do prize and enjoy my present liberty in this country exceedingly ... we do what we like; we dress as we find most suitable and convenient" and, unlike in England, they could take no notice of what the neighbours might think: "We are totally without the fear of any Mr or Mrs Grundy; and having shaken off the trammels of Grundyism, we laugh at the absurdity of those who voluntarily forge afresh and hug their chains."

Catharine intended her book to be used as a reference guide for emigrating gentlewomen, and included much practical and essential information such as describing an alternative to yeast for bread-making, how to make sugar from maple syrup and much else besides. The title given to the book was 'The Backwoods of Canada' and her completed manuscript was sent to England at the beginning of 1835.

It was accepted by Charles Knight in early June 1835 and was printed as one of the 'Library of Entertaining Knowledge' publications of 1836. The book was a success and was re-issued over the following ten years. Catharine, however, had made the mistake of selling the copyright outright for £100, without ensuring that she would receive any additional payment based on sales. The success of the publication was therefore of no financial benefit to her.

When Thomas's £100 annual allowance from the Orkney estate failed to materialise, his half-pay lieutenant's pension was their only reliable source of income. Catharine's earnings from writing and her legacy money helped, but funds soon began to run low. Susanna and John Moodie having returned to Douro to try their hand on an uncleared farm, Thomas and Catharine began to make plans to do the opposite. In 1835 they decided to sell their farm in Douro, and move to a more settled part of the country, hoping that this would be better suited to Thomas's capability.

December 1835 : Tom and Margaretta have three small children

Tom and Margaretta's daughter Adela had been born in 1833 and they had two sons in 1835 which seem to have been close pregnancies rather than twins. The sons were named John Arthur Strickland and Thomas Strickland and both were born at sea. This meant that Margaretta had three very young children to look after, whilst living at sea, by the end of 1835.

February 1836: Burglars break into Reydon Hall

With the marriage of Sarah in 1835, the only full time residents at Reydon House, or Reydon Hall as it was becoming known, were Mrs Strickland and Jane. Agnes lived there when she did not need to be in London but Sarah and Eliza, as well as Tom when on land, were now only visitors.

The spring of 1836 was a memorable one for Mrs Strickland and Jane containing, as it did, a break-in of their home and the trial of the culprits. The burglary happened early in the morning on 18th February 1836 and the subsequent court case at the Suffolk Lent Assizes was reported in the local papers on 26th March the same year.

The family had two live-in servants, one of whom was named Ursula, who had made sure all the doors and windows were shut and fastened before going to bed on 17th February 1836. When she came down next morning at half past six, she found that a sash window in the drawing-room had been broken, and two drawers of the sideboard in the dining-room were open, one having been forced.

Eliza was staying at Reydon at the time, and had to give evidence at the trial. Consequently her name appeared in the papers, something she otherwise managed to avoid. At the trial Eliza said that the upper part of the shutter in the parlour had been broken into and the sash window had been pulled down. The shutter of the store-room had also been cut and forced open, and there were matches and tinder on the store-room table.

News of the event travelled fast, for a local man named Jonathan Mills had heard about the robbery by 7.30am, at which time he saw William and Ezra Cotton, the two brothers who were accused of the burglary, at a field in Henham, about 1½ miles from Reydon. Jonathan Mills said that when he saw the men, they each had a parcel wrapped in a cotton hand-kerchief under his arm, the contents seeming to be hard with bits of metal protruding. They were walking away from Reydon and Mr Mills saw them go on to the road to Yarmouth, which was a port some 23 miles away. Jonathan Mills not only knew the brothers, but had spoken to them when he saw them.

Thomas Freeman, steward to Lord Stradbroke, a neighbour of the Strickland family, went to Reydon Hall at about 11.30 on the morning of the robbery. He saw three distinct sets of footmarks on a flower bed under the store-room window, but could not follow them because they went on to the hard gravel road. However, the steward took the measures of the foot-marks and noted any distinguishing features. The third person on trial was Sarah Cotton, the wife of James Cotton. He and she were both 34 and Ezra was 31 years old. The shoe sizes of the three defendants were found to correspond with the measurements taken by the steward.

At a quarter to six that evening, Ezra Cotton went into a silversmith's shop in Yarmouth with some silver plate that he wanted to sell. The silversmith was suspicious and, saying that he would send for someone who understood the value of the articles better than he did, actually sent for the constable. Ezra Cotton was taken into custody and, having given one false name when he was arrested, gave a different false name the following morning.

When James Cotton's home was searched, a bunch of keys was found hanging behind a post which Eliza identified as a bunch of keys from Reydon Hall. Two days after the robbery, two young boys found in a rabbit burrow near the Cotton's home, a parcel containing a silver cream jug, sugar tongs and tea-pot, which were identified as belonging to Mrs Strickland. They also found five pick-lock keys in another hole nearby. Her silverware was returned to Mrs Strickland, but it had been damaged by the robbers, and through lack of money was never replaced.

At their trial James and Ezra Cotton pleaded not guilty to the charge and Sarah Cotton initially pleaded guilty. However, the judge advised her to change her plea to not guilty and take her chance in a trial, which she did. In the face of all the evidence, James and Ezra Cotton made no defence and were found guilty and sentenced to death (which seems a bit harsh and hopefully was commuted to something less drastic). The judge told the jury that Sarah Cotton, being in company with her husband, was supposed by law to be under his coercion, and that she must be acquitted, which she was.

(1836: Literary context - Charles Dickens becomes famous)

Charles Dickens' work 'The Pickwick Papers' was published in 1836/1837, initially in serialised form and then as a book. It marked the start of Charles Dickens' life as a famous author.

1836: Agnes notes the life of Princess Victoria

Agnes while living in London resolved to see as many noteworthy events as possible, particularly ones involving female royalty. She followed her family tradition of being an ardent royalist and her attention naturally focussed on Princess Victoria who was next in line to the throne, and would succeed to the monarchy unless one of the Royal Dukes produced a legitimate son, which was becoming increasingly unlikely as the years went by.

In 1836 Agnes saw Princess Victoria returning from a Drawing-room, a regular Court event where members of the Royal Family mingled with distinguished visitors, and Agnes described her as "a sweet smiling girl, the idol of the multitude."

1837: Agnes opens negotiations with Henry Colburn

As part of their agreement that Agnes was the public face of both herself and Eliza, it was Agnes who had to find a publisher for their work and negotiate terms. She had already dealt with a number of small publishers, but in 1836 she went to Henry Colburn to see if he would be interested in publishing the series of royal biographies that she and Eliza were writing.

Henry Colburn was a fashionable publisher and had some famous authors on his books, but his business methods were not admired and he was known as the 'Prince of Puffers.' By this was meant that he was very good at having favourable reviews printed, for books which he was publishing, in the several journals which he owned. He was also in a general way very good at advertising his own wares.

While all this was good reason for Agnes to look on Henry Colburn as a potential publisher, she does not seem to have appreciated the nature of the man. Eliza, who had worked for him when on the staff of the 'Court Journal' ought to have had some idea of the dangers of getting entangled with him. An example of his ruthlessness in business matters is that Henry Colburn had bought the 'London Weekly Review' in 1828 from David Lester Richardson who had set it up the previous year. The two men had an agreement that Mr Colburn would take over the running of the established publication. In return Mr Richardson would receive a share of the profits. However, as soon as Henry Colburn was in control of the magazine, he simply changed its title from 'London Weekly Review' to the 'Court Journal,' thus putting an immediate end to Mr Richardson's right to any share in the profit.

Henry Colburn had made a name for himself by printing so-called 'Silver Fork Novels', light weight literature based on the lifestyles of rich and aristocratic families. In 1830 he decided he needed a partner in his business – some say this was because he was in serious debt and needed the cash, though there is no proof; others say his health was poor and he had decided to retire and live by the sea. At that time, the Bentley family were printers and Henry Colburn's business with them was substantial. Richard Bentley heard that the partnership was on offer, tried but failed to persuade one of his brothers to take it, and finally went into the partnership himself for the sake of the Bentley printing business. The agreement was that the partnership would last three years, after which Henry Colburn would retire and Richard Bentley, who was ten years younger than Henry Colburn would take over.

However, the personalities of Henry Colburn and Richard Bentley were so incompatible that their partnership ran into trouble before the three years were up. Henry Colburn as well as having an unscrupulous nature, was not good at keeping the business books in order. Richard Bentley was punctilious in his book-keeping and fair in his business dealings. The mismatch soon developed into a battle, and lawyers became involved. In September 1832 the original partnership was dissolved and a new agreement was drawn up which tried to ensure that Henry Colburn kept his word, and at least semi-retired. It included the stipulation that he would not set up a new business within twenty miles of London or Edinburgh, with a penalty of £5,000 if he did so.

Mr Colburn immediately set up a new business in Windsor, 21 miles from London, and soon began to ignore the geographical prohibition. By 1836 his business had moved to Great Marlborough Street, in central London, and Richard Bentley's lawyer told him that it was impossible to devise a restrictive agreement from which Henry Colburn would not escape. In June 1836 Colburn paid Bentley £3,500 and both men signed a formal Deed of Release. Richard Bentley was no longer involved with Henry Colburn but the ending of the business relationship had been acrimonious.

Susanna's husband might have heard warnings about Henry Colburn when he had a book published in 1835 by Richard Bentley, but if he heard warnings either he did not pass them on, or Agnes was not worried by them.

July 1837: Agnes signs a contract

On 20th June 1837 King William IV died and Agnes was among the crowds at St James's Palace the following day to see and hear Victoria being proclaimed queen. On becoming queen, Victoria moved from St James's Palace to Buckingham Palace, and from there on 17th July 1837, she drove in state to dissolve parliament. Again Agnes was in the crowds and wrote home that she had seen the new queen "in her diadem go in state to dissolve Parliament, and a sweet lovely creature she looked, all smiles and animation. It was a pleasure to see her apparently so happy."

Henry Colburn probably sensed that the arrival of a young female monarch would increase interest in Agnes's projected books, and they began to discuss the details of their contract. Agnes, in an act of astonishing naiveté, allowed herself to be persuaded to write the contract herself and signed it, in the belief that she was making a good deal with the publisher.

As soon as the deal had been signed, Henry Colburn began to advertise the proposed work in a number of his periodicals. The advertisements stated that the 'Historical Memoirs of the Queens of England' would be published in the autumn of 1837. Agnes, whether of her own initiative or at the suggestion of Henry Colburn, requested of Queen Victoria that the books she was writing be allowed to carry a dedication to the new monarch, and permission was granted.

Hardly had all this been done than another author, Miss Lawrence used for her own book the title that Henry Colburn was advertising. Agnes was so annoyed by this that she was inclined to give up the project altogether and Eliza had to persuade her that another title would do just as well, and that the reason for the change could be explained.

December 1837: Sam starts a brief military career

Sam's happy and prosperous life continued its steady pattern with little excitement to report, apart from a brief episode due to a rebellion in 1837. Sam described it as: "an event of vast importance in the history of Canada. For several years preceding the rebellion, the country had been agitated by the inflammatory speeches and writings of William Lyon Mackenzie."

William Lyon Mackenzie was a journalist and politician. He had been mayor of Toronto several times and was highly critical of the way the colony was being run. He was particularly critical of corruption in government, and consequently had refused several government positions. An economic depression in Canada boosted the number of his supporters, and frustrations came to a head in December 1837, when Mackenzie assembled 800 followers outside Toronto. He planned to seize the Governor appointed by the British, and set up an alternative provisional government.

The unexpected news of this rebellion reached Sam on 4th December 1837 at about 4 o'clock in the afternoon. A neighbour came to tell him that a body of rebels under the leadership of Mackenzie was in arms and marching on Toronto. The neighbour brought a printed order for as many volunteers as possible to be mustered and to march for Toronto early next morning.

Sam immediately prepared to join the volunteers by "cleaning my double-barrelled gun and running a quantity of balls." His neighbour did likewise and a few hours later they set off for Peterborough together, on foot and through a snowstorm "only halting at my father-in-law's house for a few hours rest."

Sam said that next morning nearly 400 volunteers left Peterborough to assist in putting down the rebellion. Although Sam was a Lieutenant in "the 2nd Regiment of Durham Militia the distance to join them was great and I thought best to march with the volunteers." Sam showed his views in respect of the rebellion, by noting that the volunteers "would have been less active, could they ever have imagined that the Rebels would, at the end of the Rebellion, have been compensated for the losses they had themselves occasioned."

Sam wrote that along the way the volunteer army grew to over a thousand men, and the first news they received was that Toronto had been burnt and the loyalists were in full retreat. This was soon followed by a Proclamation of "action at Montgomery's Tavern – Gallows-hill as it is generally called – and the dispersion of the rebels" which meant they were no longer required. When they got back to Peterborough, the volunteers received orders to intercept some fleeing rebels, but they found "the country was perfectly quiet" and they all went home.

1837: Thomas Traill has difficulty selling his land

Thomas Traill also answered the call for volunteers when the news of the rebellion arrived. He got as far as Cobourg when, as Catharine later wrote: "by the time the men there were enrolled, orders countermanding their march came from Toronto, and, after some weeks of vexatious delay and uncertainty, they were disbanded and returned to their homes."

At the time of the rebellion, Catharine and Thomas Traill were still trying to sell their farm in Douro to raise the money to buy another farm on cleared land, but the rebellion caused land prices to fall at just the wrong time for them. Sam noted "For a long time the Upper Province suffered from the effects of the Rebellion; money was everywhere scarce, and the value of land much depreciated." Not only did Thomas want to sell his Douro farm, he also needed to sell some land which he had bought as a speculative investment near the Otonabee River. He believed the land would increase in value when the navigational systems of the area improved, which in the long-term could well have been the case. Unfortunately, at the time when he needed to sell, the land was worth less than he paid for it.

December 1837: Sarah becomes a widow

After marrying Robert Childs in October 1835, Sarah had little more than a year of married life in Bungay before her husband's mental health became a cause for concern. Robert Childs was dead by the end of 1837 and the subsequent inquest was reported in the 'Bury and Norwich Post' on 3rd January 1838.

Robert Childs had been subject to periodical bilious attacks for some time but his doctor only began to notice his declining mental health when he was called in to see Robert in February 1837, at which point he found Robert Childs "in a state bordering on idiocy, but in a few days he had resumed his normal health."

Charles Childs, Robert's nephew, said that by November 1837 Robert's mental health had declined drastically and he was in such a serious state of depression that he was placed with Dr Dalrymple, of Norwich, who said that the problem was "exceeding debility of his nervous system."

When he was sufficiently recovered to return home from Norwich, Robert Childs asked to have a private conversation with Charles Childs. Charles said that Robert: "was suffering under the misapprehension that he had mismanaged an estate, of which he was trustee, and wasted the whole of the property." Charles knew that there were no grounds for this concern, and explained this to his uncle who, Charles said, "seemed to yield to his explanation" but during the following week Robert Childs was in "a most agonising despondency," and on the Saturday Charles Childs "sent an express to Dr Dalrymple, who declared that it was a case of insanity, as distinctly marked as any he had ever witnessed." There was no cause for the state of anxiety, the whole was mental delusion.

The papers reported: "Every precaution was taken to prevent any act of self-destruction." However, "Hannah Silverstone, servant of the deceased" at "about nine o'clock in the morning on 17th December 1837, having left the room for half a minute, she found Robert Childs gone. Jonathan Fenn, servant to the deceased stated that he was at work in the wash-house, and alarmed by hearing a noise, followed by groans, proceeded to the garden, where he saw his master lying on the ground and saw one of the upper back-room windows open." The doctor was called and said he found Robert Childs covered with dirt, and very much bruised. The lower half of his body had entirely lost sensation and motion.

On Tuesday 19th December and on several occasions after, Robert Childs had said to the doctor that throwing himself from the window was the act of a madman – that he had been mad, and nothing could prevent him being so in future. His insanity was the cause of his throwing himself out of the window, not a result of it.

Robert Childs (1786-1837) died at about 9 o'clock on the morning of Christmas Day, 25th December 1837 and was buried on 29th December at Bungay, Suffolk. He was buried in the Childs vault in the churchyard of the Independent Congregational Church.

Sarah Strickland Childs, having been married at the age of 37, was a widow before she was forty. An obituary in the local paper included the question: "In the domestic relations of life, who was more beloved, or who by his wit, social disposition, hospitality, and intelligence more thoroughly won the affection of those around him?" than Robert Childs.

1838: Mrs Strickland has 19 grand-children, mostly in Canada

All three of Thomas and Elizabeth Strickland's children who had emigrated to Canada were producing children quite regularly, regardless of the state of their finances. Sam, the only one of the three who was prospering, had three children when Susanna and Catharine arrived in Canada, and three more children were born over the next few years, George William Ross in 1833 and Henry Thomas in 1835 and Francis Arthur in 1838. At this point, Sam and Mary Strickland had two daughters and four sons living, Sam then being 33 years old.

Susanna and John's family grew with the arrival of three sons in the early years after they began to farm near Sam in Douro. John Alexander Dunbar (known as Dunbar) was born in 1834, Donald in 1836 and John in 1838. So by 1838 Susanna and John Moodie had two daughters and three sons, Susanna then being 35 years old.

James Traill was an only child until he was three years old. Catharine and Thomas then had three more children in quick succession, Katharine Agnes in 1836, Thomas Henry Strickland in 1837 and Anne Fotheringhame in 1838. So by 1838 they had two sons and two daughters, Catharine then being 36 years old.

The Canadian branches of the Strickland family by 1838 therefore had fifteen children between them. The four sisters in England were either unmarried or, in the case of Sarah, a childless widow. Tom and Margaretta Strickland had a fourth child born at sea, Julia Lily born in 1837, giving them two sons and two daughters by 1838, Tom being about 30 years old.

4th January 1838: Robert Childs' Will is accepted

Although Robert Childs had written a Last Will and Testament which had been duly witnessed and authorised when he was in good health, it was realised on 19th December 1837, two days after he had jumped from the window, that this Will had somehow been destroyed and needed to be rewritten as a matter of urgency.

The rewritten Will specified that Robert Childs' watch, seal and chain were bequeathed to Charles Childs; that all the furniture of Robert Childs' house, together with his other personal effects were bequeathed to Sarah; and that Robert Childs' share in the family printing business would pass to John Childs.

This share of the family business had been valued at £1,000, and John Childs was entrusted to provide for Sarah's future with this amount of money. He was to pay £200 to Sarah within three months of Robert's death, and was either to pay Sarah interest on the remaining £800 at the rate of 5% every year for the rest of her life, or to buy an annuity to the value of £800, the income to be for Sarah's benefit.

This rewritten Will had been read to Robert Childs item by item on 19th December 1837, and he had agreed that each item was correct. This had been done in the presence of witnesses including Sarah, and witness signatures were attached accordingly. By this time Robert was just about able to make his mark, but was no longer able to sign his name.

Robert Childs' rewritten Will was accepted and authorised for implementation on 4th January 1838. His executors were his brother John Childs and his nephew Charles Childs.

June 1838: Agnes attends Queen Victoria's coronation

Somehow, though it was not explained how, Agnes Strickland was able to attend by invitation the coronation of Queen Victoria at Westminster Abbey on 28th June 1838. In the account of it that she wrote in a letter to Jane and her mother, Agnes said of the Queen: "her fair hair, in plaits, was neatly folded and arranged at the back of her head. She wore a garland-shaped diadem resembling a wreath of hawthorn blossoms covered with dewdrops. She appeared serene and composed when she seated herself in her recognition chair, round which her train-bearers were grouped in costumes of white satin and garlands of blush-roses. The pause before the crowned queen was presented to the people by the Archbishop of Canterbury was broken by the Westminster scholars with the chorus of 'vivat Victoria Regina'." Agnes said her seat gave her "a fine view of her Majesty on her return and progress through the choir in her purple robe, the crown-royal on her head, in her right hand the sceptre, in her left the orb."

While the coronation was going on in Westminster Abbey, hot-air balloonists Mrs Graham and Captain Currie, were preparing to rise and sail over London. They took as their signal to launch, the sound of the first gun fired in salute of the coronation. Weather conditions were good, and they rose successfully from Green Park, and controlled their balloon so as to descend not far away, in Marylebone Lane.

In the evening of Coronation Day, Agnes walked to the place where the balloon had taken off in Green Park, and where "Mr Gaffin's novel and interesting fireworks" were in full swing. To round off her day, Agnes walked through the main thoroughfares of London where, despite feeling a little nervous, she found the crowds "in high good humour" and the illuminations "like constellations." Agnes being full of excitement about the entire experience, recounted it all to Henry Colburn.

July 1838: Sam has to build another house

Sam was called-up a couple more times during the course of the 1837 rebellion, and received his commission as Captain of the local militia before the rebellion was completely over. On neither occasion was Sam involved in any military action. He was attached to a regiment which was stationed at Peterborough, and continued to serve until it was disbanded in May 1839.

In July 1838, in the midst of Sam's time with the militia, his family had an excitement of a different kind when their house was struck by lightening. Sam wrote that it: "shattered the whole gable end. I had left a cross-cut saw leaning against the chimney in the garret, which saved the lives of my wife and several members of my family, the lightning splitting the chimney till it came to the saw, which it took as a better conductor, knocking down part of the parlour ceiling in its passage to the earth.

"My little boy Arthur, who was then a baby in its mother's arms, was stunned by the explosion, and my eldest daughter, who was reading in the open verandah, had her arm burnt. The house was filled with soot from the chimney and a great many stones were hurled down by the shock."

It was fortunate that no-one had been seriously hurt, but the house was so damaged that Sam decided to build a new house rather than try and restore the old one. Sam described the next house that he built, and which lasted for the rest of his life, saying that it was: "of frame-work on a stone foundation, lathed and plastered inside, and rough-cast without." Originally it was 38 feet by 26 feet, to which he added a wing 40 feet by 20 feet and it had a verandah, nine feet wide, running along the front and one end, which helped keep the house cool in summer. Sam wrote that: "In very hot weather we often dined and drank tea in the open verandah in order to enjoy the coolness of the air." The house was named 'Homestead'.

October 1838: Susanna and John benefit from the rebellion

John Moodie, like Sam, was a member of the local militia with the rank of Captain. Mostly this was an unpaid role but if they were called to arms, members of the militia were paid at the same rate as their equivalent in the regular army. This made the brief period of the 1837 rebellion a source of much-needed income for John Moodie.

Susanna's writing career also benefited from the rebellion. Like Sam, her views were on the side of the establishment, and her patriotic poems were published in January and the early spring of 1838. Some of these poems were included in a book published in 1852, for example 'The Oath of the Canadian Volunteers.' This poem had three verses, the first of which gives a flavour of the voice Susanna used in her 'Rebellion' poetry:

> Huzza for England! – May she claim
>   Our fond devotion ever;
> And, by the glory of her name,
> Our brave forefathers honest fame,
>   We swear – no foe shall sever
> Her children from their parent's side;
>   Though parted by the wave,
> In weal or woe, whate'er betide,
>   We swear to die, or save
> Her honour from the rebel band
> Whose crimes pollute our injured land!

Susanna also used the rebellion and her pen in another way. In the summer of 1838 she wrote to Sir George Arthur who was

Lieutenant-Governor of Upper Canada from 1838 to 1841. She described the harsh conditions of her life in colourful detail, and asked him to keep her husband in the pay of the militia services so that they could clear their debts. Although Susanna received no direct reply, it is thought that her letter was effective, because in October 1838 John Moodie was appointed paymaster to the militia in the Victoria District.

This was a great relief financially but the post was only temporary, and had the disadvantage that John was away from home while it lasted, leaving Susanna lonely, albeit located near to Sam, and with the stressful responsibility of running the farm.

11th January 1839: Susanna passes on family news to John

On 11th January 1839 Susanna wrote to John passing on news from England. She said: "Kate had a letter from Agnes this week, dated Oct. They are all well at home. Agnes has backed out from the old man, she says so discreetly that she hopes that he will leave her a legacy after all, and she is going to marry a Mr Kirby, sometime during the winter, who is much attached to her and is only 55, is very rich, and promises to make very handsome settlements upon her." Whether this is an accurate account, or one coloured by Susanna's imagination is impossible to say but it does show that there were some romantic entanglements in Agnes's life. At this time Agnes was 42 years old.

Susanna continued: "Sarah has left Reydon, and is living opposite to where the Wales's lived in Southwold, is visited by all the genteel families near, and is slowly but surely recovering her health and spirits." Suffolk Archives have a paper which shows a Sarah Child being the tenant renting 'Honeysuckle House' at 17 Park Lane in Southwold in 1841.

Other comments show that Agnes was keeping a watchful eye on things in England on Susanna's behalf, for Susanna told John: "Some Mr Turner, has set a song of mi[ne] to music, and A wanted him to make me some remuneration, but this he declined ... She wishes me to try him with Canadian songs, as it might, 'perhaps bring my poetry a little into notice.' I don't think it worth the trial and would rather now, be popular in the country of my adoption than at home."

February 1839: Catharine and Thomas manage to sell their farm

Catharine's literary career was faring less well than Susanna's, and she was regretting having sold the copyright of her book 'The Backwoods of Canada' with no additional benefit from sales. On 19th February 1838 she sent a complimentary copy to Sir Francis Bond Head, Lieutenant-Governor of Upper Canada from 1835 to 1838, though to what purpose is not recorded. Thus Catharine had made an attempt to gain help from a Lieutenant-Governor who was at the end of his time in Upper Canada, while Susanna had made the more sensible move of writing to the man who arrived to replace him.

Catharine's complimentary book having had no effect, Susanna wrote to Sir George Arthur on her behalf. In a letter dated 18th December 1838 Susanna wrote: " 'The Backwoods of Canada' which has brought great emolument to the publishers has done little towards administering to the wants of the poor Author; who is struggling in the Backwoods on a limited income, with four infant children and contending with difficulties which would scarce be credited by Your Excellency." Susanna's letter did no good, and Catharine and Thomas had to struggle on in a near penniless state.

Thomas and Catharine eventually managed to sell their backwoods farm in February 1839 for £400, and moved into 'Mill House' on the farm of their friends Frances and Thomas Stewart, until they found somewhere more permanent to live.

March 1839: Mr James Bird, poet and friend, dies

Mr James Bird, whose correspondence with the Strickland sisters has been a valuable source of information about their lives, died in March 1839 at the age of 50 after a long illness. His widow, Emma Bird continued to run the shop in Yoxford with the help of their eldest son, George, but the death of James Bird more or less marks the end of the surviving correspondence between the Bird and the Strickland families.

The only remaining correspondence after James Bird's death is that in which Agnes ensured that she had paid Emma all that was due for stationery and medicines, and that Emma had the financial benefit of a biographical article Agnes had written after the poet's death.

The younger James Bird, who had emigrated with Susanna to live with Sam, settled in Canada and was still in contact with the Canadian members of the Strickland family when he died many years later.

May 1839: Susanna starts writing for the 'Literary Garland'

In May 1839 the 'Literary Garland' published one of Susanna's poems for the first time. The magazine had been launched as a quality literary magazine and its editor, John Lovell, gave priority to work written locally. His views were similar to Susanna's and he paid his contributors, which was not the case with many magazines. Susanna and John Lovell got on well together and developed a good working relationship. She became a regular contributor to the 'Literary Garland' during the time that John Lovell was its editor.

In a letter written many years later (1865) to Richard Bentley, Susanna showed the importance of the articles which appeared first in this magazine, forming the basis of many of her subsequent books. She wrote: "I contributed for seven years, to the 'Literary Garland' published by Mr Lovell of Montreal. 'Roughing It in the Bush,' appeared in its pages, as 'Canadian Sketches', 'Mark Hurdlestone' as the 'Miser and his Son', 'Geoffrey Moncton, The Memoirs of a poor Relation' ('The First Debt') the MS you returned to me, was the most popular story I wrote for it. 'Jane Redgrave', 'Mildred Rosier', and 'Monica, or Witchcraft', three novels, have never been republished."

This quote implies that Susanna had a steady stream of money coming in from her writing in the seven or twelve years following 1839 because, although Susanna always pleaded poverty in Canada, she told an aspiring author, Louisa May Murray in a letter written on 13th January 1851: "I have found the five pounds per sheet that I have received from Mr Lovell for articles contributed to the 'Garland' for the last twelve years, no inconsiderable help in bringing up a large family." Susanna in a letter written to Catharine in December 1853, defined a sheet in the 'Literary Garland' as consisting of 16 pages.

July 1839: Tom takes command of the 'Enmore'

A fifth child was added to Tom's family with the birth of Mary in 1839. Mary may have been born at sea, or at Cowes on the Isle of Wight. Up to this point, all of Tom's children, as well as his wife, were sailing the world with him which might explain a comment made by Jane Margaret Strickland some years later that Tom's children had been strangely brought up. However, this seems to have changed in 1839 when there is the first identifiable mention of Tom Strickland being in command of a ship.

In June 1839 the ship 'Enmore', under the command of Captain Nash, was reported as preparing in London Docks for a voyage to Ceylon. Captain Nash had been commander of the 'Enmore' for several years, but by the time preparations had been completed, command had passed to Tom.

The advertisement for the next voyage of the 'Enmore' was conventional in style, giving in simple words all the key facts and appearing in the relevant specialist newspapers. The advertisement declared: "The fine and remarkably fast-sailing barque 'Enmore' A1, burden 350 tons, coppered and copper-fastened. Commander Thomas Strickland. 'Enmore' for Ceylon direct. For terms of passage only apply to Henry and Calvert Toulmin, Lombard Street."

A barque is a sailing-ship with at least three masts, and a voyage to Ceylon required the captain to be skilled in many areas, particularly navigation. However at 350 tons the 'Enmore' was relatively small, and the advertisement implies that it was mainly, if not only, a passenger vessel. Therefore it seems reasonable to suppose that Tom in recent years had been working his way up the command structure on a larger vessel, or vessels, and the 'Enmore' marked his first command. This might explain it being the first voyage where Tom's wife and children remained in London, leaving him free to concentrate on the responsibilities of being in command of his ship.

The 'Enmore' under Tom's command passed Gravesend on 28th July 1839 at the start of the voyage to Ceylon (now named Sri Lanka).

August 1839: Catharine suggests opening a school

By August 1839 Thomas and Catharine had moved to a house in Ashburnham, roughly 10 miles south of their first farm, which had adjoined Sam's land. Here they lived for the next few years in very precarious circumstances.

Catharine thought of opening a boarding school with pupils from the nearby township of Peterborough and wrote on 20th August 1839 to explain her idea to Barbara Fotheringhame, Thomas Traill's former sister-in-law. Catharine suggested that Barbara move to Canada and become the teacher in the school, while Catharine took care of the domestic arrangements. Nothing came of this suggestion, but Catharine opened a school by herself for a short time, having to give it up when her health almost failed her.

At the same time Catharine was also busy writing, and trying to build on the success of 'Backwoods of Canada' by writing a sequel. Agnes tried to find a publisher in England but, despite her best efforts, was unable to do so. However, some of Catharine's sketches seem to have appeared in Chamber's 'Edinburgh Journal' over the next few years and this may have been thanks to Agnes's efforts. Sketches which are said to have appeared in this way are 'The Mill of the Rapids: A Canadian Sketch' and 'Canadian Lumberers'.

December 1839: 'Lives of the Queens of England' begin to appear

Agnes went through a period of ill health towards the end of 1837 but by early in 1838 she was fully recovered and back in London working with Eliza on their 'Lives of the Queens of England'. While the first two volumes were being written, Agnes and Eliza developed contacts and friendships with antiquaries and scholars. The work of Sir Nicholas Harris Nicolas (1799-1848) had provided them with valuable guidance when they began their research among British Museum collections, and he became a close friend who they consulted on any difficult historical point.

For some time Sir Harris Nicolas had been making great efforts to get a wider range of information available for study. He objected to the inactivity of the Commission of Public Records which was accused of charging substantial fees for permission to study the documents in its care. Sir Harris Nicolas thought they should follow the example of the British Museum and allow access to their papers free of charge.

Agnes's illness delayed the appearance of the first volume of the female royal biographies until late in 1839. It was launched with the title 'Lives of the Queens of England'. Agnes explained both the change of title and that illness had caused the delay in a preface to the first volume. Her preface was dated 16th December 1839 and was addressed from 'Reydon Hall, Suffolk'.

The first volume contained five biographies and covered almost 200 years of turbulent history. It began with a biography of Matilda of Flanders, born about 1031, and ended with controversial Eleanora of Aquitaine, who died in 1204 and was the wife of Henry II. Of these five biographies, Jane recorded that Agnes wrote three (Matilda of Flanders, Matilda of Scotland and Matilda of Boulogne) and Eliza two (Adelicia of Luvaine and Eleanora of Aquitaine).

The first volume sold very quickly and Henry Colburn put great pressure on Agnes for the next book in the series. The second volume contained eight biographies again stretching over 200 years. The first biography was of Berengaria of Navarre (born about 1160 and wife of Richard I) and the last was Anne of Bohemia (who died in 1394 and was the wife of Richard II). Because of Henry Colburn's insistence, it was produced so quickly that it too had a publication date of 1839, with Agnes writing two of the biographies (Eleanora of Provence and Isabella of France) and Eliza the other six (Berengaria of Navarre, Isabella of Angouleme, Marguerite of France, Philippa of Hainault, Anne of Bohemia and Eleanora of Castile).

On top of this, when the engagement of Queen Victoria to Prince Albert of Saxe-Coburg and Gotha was announced in November 1839, Henry Colburn remembered the vivid account that Agnes had given to him of the events on Coronation Day in 1838, and asked her to write a book entitled 'Queen Victoria from her Birth to her Bridal'. He promised to provide all the necessary material, including anecdotes and press cuttings, so that the work involved for Agnes would be relatively light. Agnes agreed and, even though she had more than enough to do in relation to 'Lives of the Queens of England', got on with the task enthusiastically.

December 1839: Tom reaches Ceylon

Available information about Tom's life at this time is sparse, mainly being extracted from the specialist newspapers of the time, which carried details of shipping movements worldwide, such as the 'Shipping and Mercantile Gazette' but these are enough to show how far his voyages took him, and how long he was away from home each time.

Tom, having left England at the end of July 1839, arrived safely in Ceylon in the 'Enmore' five months later, on 29th December 1839.

1839: Sam has another son

Sam and Mary Strickland's seventh child, John Percy Strickland was born in 1839.

1st January 1840: Susanna escapes from life as a farmer's wife

Towards the end of his time as lieutenant-governor of Upper Canada, Sir George Arthur granted to Susanna's husband the much coveted, newly created office of Sheriff of Hastings County. In his letter to John Moodie he wrote: "I hope it is agreeable to you; and as to your loyalty and attachment to British institutions, I took it for granted that you must possess both, or you would not have been the husband of Mrs Moodie." He had noted their circumstances and wrote: "I was quite mortified it was not earlier in my power to confirm some appointment upon you."

John Moodie went in advance of his family to Belleville, the main town in Hastings County and about 70 miles south-east from their farm and Sam in Douro, to find their next family home. Susanna and their children left the backwoods of Canada on New Year's Day 1840 to join him. Their new surroundings were more comfortable, and the town environment more to their taste, than their previous homes in Canada had been.

10th February 1840: Agnes attends the Royal Wedding

The marriage of Queen Victoria took place on the 10th February 1840 in the Chapel Royal in St James's Palace and Agnes managed to get a ticket for the colonnade of St James Palace. The ticket was obtained with the help of Lady Stradbroke, whose family estate adjoined Reydon Hall. From her place in the colonnade, Agnes saw guests and the bridal procession on their way to and from the Chapel Royal.

Jane wrote that after the marriage service was over and the Chapel Royal was empty of the wedding party, Agnes and others went into the chapel and saw the 'Attestation Book' with the signatures of the royal couple. Agnes also came across the room in which choristers "were being regaled with sherry and bride-cake" and was invited to drink her Majesty's health.

Agnes, by following people she thought were on their way out, happened upon the banqueting-room "by the entrance of which" Jane said "stood the lord-in-waiting, who permitted each party a brief view of the glories therein." When Agnes reached the door and asked to look into the room, he replied "that he would open the door with great pleasure if she had a ticket." Having no such thing, she managed to persuade the official that it would do him "no harm to give her a sight, though she had no documentary claim to it." He agreed and said that if she came up with the next group who had a ticket, he would ask her no questions. By this means Agnes saw the magnificent banqueting room, the table covered with glittering gold plate "while the royal bride-cake, with its banners and blazonry, occupied a separate table."

Agnes's publisher, Henry Colburn had been very keen for Agnes to attend the wedding and took advantage of the occasion to promote 'Lives of the Queens of England'. He had advertisements placed in a number of newspapers including 'John Bull' and 'The Sun'. The latter added a very positive review of the book in a column headed 'Literature' which said: "Authentic Memoirs of our English Queens is a work that has been much wanted; and the present appears likely to supply the deficiency. It is the production of Miss Agnes Strickland, who states in a very brief introductory notice, that she has dedicated many years to the task, and spared neither labour nor research, to complete it in an efficient manner.

"A careful perusal of the first volume – the only one yet published – convinces us that this lady has done herself no more than bare justice when she speaks of the pains she has taken with the work, for it shows in every chapter marks of extensive reading – especially among the old Norman Chronicles, and the monkish Latin authors

– and of that patient and persevering spirit of inquiry, and skill in comparing, sifting, and drawing likely inferences from conflicting authorities, without which no history, worthy of its name, ever was, or ever will be, written.

"When the work has made more progress – for we perceive that it is to be issued in monthly volumes – we shall be better able to make an estimate of its pretensions; but in the meantime, we may say of the present volume, that instead of being a mere dry chronicle of facts, it is penned in an eloquent and attractive style, and shows a talent for description by no means of an ordinary character. The Life of 'Matilda of Flanders,' the wife of William the Conqueror, possesses – like the last four volumes of Gibbon's immortal history – all the interest of romance."

15th February 1840: Agnes meets the Howard family

While Eliza and Agnes were carrying out research for the early volumes of their work, they were on a similar footing with their scholarly contacts, and were equally comfortable with them, but the publication of the first two volumes of 'Lives of the Queens of England' changed the situation.

Agnes was becoming famous through their joint work and Eliza, of her own choice, was not. As a result, and no doubt helped by her presence at the Coronation and at the Royal Wedding, Agnes began to have contacts among members of titled families whose archives contained important information for future research. Agnes's very useful, but also sincere friendship with the Howard family started in this way.

In a letter dated 16th February 1840, Agnes wrote to her mother: "Yesterday I returned the call of Mr Howard of Corby and was received like a princess by that beautiful and queenly old lady Mrs Howard, Mr Howard and the charming Philip. They kept me two hours and invited me to dine with them there today at seven. Philip took me to the carriage on his arm and when he saw Eliza had been waiting made many apologies for not having shown her up and Mrs Howard wrote in the morning to include Pye" (Eliza's nickname) "in the invite. They are princely people and of such lofty courtesy that I felt as if in company with the Plantagenets.

Mr Howard promises me great personal assistance with the succeeding Lives."

Both Henry Howard and his son Philip were historians and antiquarians. They gave Agnes access to many documents in their own family collection, and on her behalf requested information from their similarly-minded contacts in France. For example, Philip Howard's contact the Count de Montalembert, in response to a request for information, wrote to Agnes: "I have consulted several persons with regard to the will of Margaret of Anjou. I have requested a member of our House of Commons, Monsieur Leprecost, renowned for his anti-quarian lore, to search on the General Record Office. As soon as I hear something favourable on this subject, I shall hasten to transmit the information to you."

19th February 1840: Tom sails from Ceylon

Tom having arrived at Ceylon at the end of 1839, remained there for seven weeks. He began his return voyage to London in the 'Enmore' on 19th February 1840.

March 1840: Agnes receives a 'thank-you' letter from Queen Victoria

When each volume of 'Lives of the Queens of England' appeared, a few special copies of the first edition were bound in crimson silk and stamped with the Royal Coat of Arms. Early in 1840, Agnes took one of these special copies of Volume I of the series to Mr Glover, who was in charge of the Royal Library, and asked him to present it to the Queen. Mr Glover wrote a letter of thanks on behalf of the Queen saying that: "her Majesty received it very graciously, and was pleased to honour me with her commands to express to you how very sensible her Majesty is of your attention in presenting it for her perusal."

Agnes also sent one of the special copies to Queen Adelaide, the Queen Dowager (widow of King William IV). Lord Howe wrote a shorter note of thanks, dated 23rd March 1840 from Marlborough House, on behalf of the Queen Dowager, saying that she had: "received it with great satisfaction."

March 1840: Agnes realises her mistake

Henry Colburn was both persuasive and domineering, and the contract that Agnes signed, specified that the work would be published under a share account, which she understood meant that she had no risk and that the profit from the work would be divided equally between them. The agreement that she had drawn up herself, in ignorance of the technicalities required had, she thought, (as Jane Strickland put it) made "a good and binding agreement for herself as well as for her publisher."

Agnes was kept very busy by Henry Colburn writing 'Queen Victoria from her Birth to her Bridal' as well as working on future volumes of 'Lives of the Queens of England'. She did not initially worry that she had received no payment as her share of the profits. When eventually Agnes did manage to pin him down about money, Colburn (Jane reported) showed that "from the share account of the most popular work he ever published" Agnes would receive "a paltry and inadequate remuneration" while Henry Colburn reaped the benefit.

This was beyond the limit of what Agnes could stand physically and mentally. Not only had she been over-working, she now realised that she had committed herself and Eliza to years of hard work in return for practically nothing. Agnes became seriously ill and Henry Colburn fully illustrated the ruthlessness of his character by sending her a lawyer's letter telling her to fulfil her obligations immediately or suffer financial penalty. When a medical certificate was sent to him to verify Agnes's inability to work, Henry Colburn's attitude did not change.

April 1840: Eliza renegotiates the contract

Eliza took over the situation at this stage. Firstly, she consulted an eminent barrister, Mr Archibald Stephens, who was also a family friend. On this, and on subsequent occasions when they needed his help and advice, usually when they were in combat with Henry Colburn, he gave his help free of charge. Eliza asked whether the document which Agnes had signed was legally binding, and he confirmed that Agnes was obliged to carry out the work as specified. Eliza, however, was under no such obligation, as her name did not appear in the document. Archibald Stephens also assured Eliza that while Agnes was ill, she could not be compelled to work.

Henry Colburn had believed Agnes to be the sole author of 'Lives of the Queens of England' but when he learnt that Eliza, previously one of his employees, was joint author, he requested an interview with her. He began by assuring her that as Agnes was ill, he would be satisfied if she would do the work instead. Eliza pointed out that she was not mentioned in the contract and she refused to do the work, saying that her contribution was merely to help her sister in, as Jane recorded "the arduous labour that had injured her health and left her in her present precarious position."

The publisher wanted the next volumes written, and knew that he would only get them by offering additional payment, which he then did. Eliza replied that she would not refuse her help if, when Agnes recovered, she was satisfied with the new arrangement. However, she repeated her stipulation that her own name was not to appear on the title page. Jane Strickland wrote that Eliza "had no real reason for her aversion, for her talents were equal to her sister's, and her industry greater, but she hated notoriety, and never courted it in any shape."

As a result, a new agreement was drawn up by Mr Stephens which gave the sisters £150 per volume, Eliza having explained to Henry Colburn how matters really stood. Agnes accepted the new agreement, and the sisters added the proviso that no amendment was to be made to their work by anyone other than themselves. Although the newly agreed payment was far better than they would have received under Agnes's original contract, Jane said it was "a poor remuneration for a work so eminently important and successful as the 'Lives of the Queens of England'."

Agnes recovered at Reydon Hall from what Jane described as "nervous depression" quite quickly, but it took some time for her to recover from the "sore throat and fever" which also beset her, and during her convalescence she occupied herself with needlework. Jane wrote that Agnes made "a fine batiste handkerchief," an elaborate piece of embroidery which she designed herself which was "a very delicate and beautiful imitation of point-lace, wrought in the cambric itself, and would have been greatly valued and probably framed, if it had not been stolen by an ungrateful maid some years afterwards, to the great mortification of the artiste."

April 1840: Tom reaches Mauritius

Tom and the 'Enmore' had a short break in their journey back to England from Ceylon, reaching Mauritius, a small island to the east of Madagascar on 5th April 1840. Tom left Mauritius on 14th April, sailing south towards the Cape of Good Hope.

May 1840: Agnes cultivates influential contacts

One of the most eminent people who was helping Agnes and Eliza with their research was the French historian and government minister Monsieur Guizot. While he had been Minister of Education in 1832 in the government of King Louis Philippe, he had ensured that the French state provided adequate funds to care for and publish medieval documents and chronicles. He, as an historian, had written 'The History of the Revolution in England from Charles I to Charles II', a book which Agnes knew well.

In 1840 M Guizot was French Ambassador in London for a few months, and then he returned to France where he became Foreign Minister. While he was in London, Agnes sent him a copy of the first two volumes of 'Lives of the Queens of England' as a token of gratitude for the help he had given. In May 1840 he wrote a letter of thanks in which he said he found the work "charming, studied from the source, and presented singularly exempt from dryness" and he said he had sent the books to his daughters because he thought they also would enjoy reading them. Not only did M. Guizot write this very gracious letter of thanks, he allowed Agnes to quote from it, which she did as part of the introduction to Volume III in the series.

May 1840: Agnes is presented at Court

Eliza and Agnes had to spend much of their time living in lodgings in London with the associated expense. An additional expense for Agnes arose because she had to dress appropriately for her numerous social engagements, particularly when she began to attend Court events. She had a busy social life, partly for her own pleasure but also to build up contacts for future research. With the success of 'Lives of the Queens of England' she needed to look the part of a successful authoress, despite the fact that the books were making Henry Colburn rich, and that what little money he paid, had to be shared equally with Eliza.

In May 1840 Agnes was presented at Court. This had been arranged through the Howard family, and Agnes described it in a letter to her friend Miss Porter. She wrote that Mrs Howard had asked "her venerable friend Lady Stourton" to present Agnes to the Sovereign. Agnes found it "an agitating but gratifying day. When my name was announced, her Majesty smiled and looked most kindly. Prince Albert returned my curtsey with a very courteous bow."

A few days later, Agnes was again at Court, this time attending a Birthday Drawing-room. She told Miss Porter it was "a brilliant scene. The Queen gave me a nod and smile of friendly recognition when the lord-in-waiting pronounced my name." Agnes had worn a dress of "violet velvet lined with primrose over Brussels lace and white satin" and with a lengthy train. On a note of economy she added "from the absence of trimming and frippery, my dress cost less than many of the butterfly costumes around me. It was very suitable for the occasion, and will be useful."

June 1840: Eliza and Agnes publish Volume III of 'Lives of the Queens of England'

Work on Volume III of 'Lives of the Queens of England' had been well in hand when Agnes became ill in April 1840, and Eliza carried the volume through to completion. It contained six biographies beginning with that of Isabella of Valois (second Queen of Richard II; born 1387) and ending with Anne of Warwick (Queen of Richard III; died 1485) and was published in June 1840. Agnes had written two of these biographies (Joanna of Navarre and Margaret of Anjou) and Eliza wrote the other four (Isabella of Valois, Katharine of Valois, Elizabeth Woodville and Anne of Warwick). Even with two hard-working and speedy authors, it is hard to see how they could have managed this rate of production. For Agnes to have achieved it on her own would have required a super-human effort, yet no-one seems to have questioned the fact that she alone was the author, even though no secret was made of her period of illness.

In June 1840 when the publication of the third volume was announced, the 'Norfolk Chronicle,' a paper well used to publishing Agnes's poems, and to noting her contribution of articles in Christmas annuals, admitted: "When we first learnt of the intention to become an historian of our Queens, it required confidence in her unwearied industry, to divest ourselves of certain misgivings as to originality of information from authentic sources. Miss Agnes Strickland has, however, triumphantly proved her perfect competency to execute this arduous and important task, uniting a strict fidelity to historic records with a most fascinating indulgence in anecdotal narrative. These 'Lives of the Queens of England' are indeed worthy of the graciously accorded permission, under which they are inscribed to our Sovereign Lady, Queen Victoria."

July 1840: Susanna has a sad time in Belleville

When Susanna arrived at her new home in Belleville, she was pregnant with her sixth child. She gave birth to a son on 19th July 1840 who was named George Arthur Moodie, after the family benefactor, but baby George died within a month of his birth.

Soon after this, the family home was destroyed by fire and they lost much of their furniture, clothing and winter stores. During the fire their two year old son, John Strickland Moodie, became temporarily lost in the confusion.

Susanna later wrote: "The agony I endured for about half an hour I shall never forget. The roaring flames, the impending misfortune which hung over us, was forgotten in the terror that shook my mind lest he had become a victim of the flames."

Summer 1840: Agnes annoys Queen Victoria

Sometime after Agnes was presented at Court, her book 'Queen Victoria from her Birth to her Bridal' was published in two volumes. Agnes intended to show Queen Victoria in a very favourable light being upright, just and considerate. She said, for example, that the Queen had paid off her parents' debts from her personal savings.

Unfortunately, Agnes had written the book in great haste, and without checking the information she had been given.

Agnes and Eliza had adopted the motto 'Fact not Fiction' for their historical biographies of the queens of England, but Agnes had written a partial biography of the current monarch based entirely on information given to her by Henry Colburn, which she assumed to be true, but which turned out to be mainly hearsay.

The work was well received by the press, but Queen Victoria objected strongly to it, and went through the entire two volumes writing robust comments such as 'absurd' and 'not true', and making corrections. She then gave the two volumes to a lady-in-waiting who copied the queen's comments neatly and with some slight tactful amendments, into another set of the books.

One or other of these pairs of books was then given to George Anson, Prince Albert's private secretary, who wrote to Agnes inviting her to collect the books because: "Mr Anson is sorry to tell Miss Strickland that there are a great many inaccuracies in it, which in the Event of another Edition appearing, he feels sure Miss Strickland would be glad to correct."

Agnes had unwittingly offended the queen and was suitably horrified. Henry Colburn owned the copyright and refused to reprint, saying he would rather simply scrap the book. Sale of the books was stopped, and as many as possible were retrieved and destroyed.

August 1840: Tom has a letter published

Tom completed his voyage in the 'Enmore,' sailing past Gravesend into London Docks on 12th August 1840, having been away from England and his family for just over a year. It was the only voyage he made in the 'Enmore' and he spent a few months in England while he found a new command.

During his time at home Tom wrote to a newspaper, the only known piece of writing by him, for no other correspondence seems to have survived, either letters exchanged with the family or otherwise.

On 24th September 1840, a letter had been printed in the 'Globe' evening paper. The writer asked if any-one could identify a strange-looking large fish that had been caught and which was described in some detail. Tom's reply showed him to be not only skilled at navigation and seamanship, but also an educated man of inquiring scientific mind.

His response was printed in the 'Globe' on 10th October 1840 under the head-line 'The Great Unknown' and in summary was as follows: "A correspondent calling himself 'Thomas Strickland, Master Mariner,' says the fish described is commonly called the sun-fish, and he proceeds 'I presume it has obtained this name in consequence of its being round, and generally keeping on the surface of the water when it takes its food, which consists of medusae and the nautilus, commonly called the Portuguese man-of-war.

'They are frequently seen near the edge of soundings on the English bank off Cape Finisterre and the Azores. I have taken them off the Cape of Good Hope from three to seven cwt. The skin you mention will, if thrown down on the deck of a ship, rebound to an amazing height. I have cooked the inside part, which is white and flaky, but do not consider it whole-some; the liver alone appears to be of use. It makes a red-coloured oil, which is said to have the property of curing rheumatism. This oil is generally made in the heat of the sun, and is very much prized by seamen. However, I cannot vouch for this, having frequently seen it used without success'."

Tom's next command was of the ship 'Diana,' which at 600 tons burden was almost twice that of the 'Enmore'. On 17th December 1840, Tom set sail, not from London Docks, but from Liverpool. His destination was New Orleans, and this was the first recorded voyage where he sailed west to America rather than south then east to India.

1840: Agnes has celebrity status and Eliza retains her anonymity

The Royal Wedding in 1840 had increased interest in royalty, and a very large edition of the third volume of 'Lives of the Queens of England' sold so quickly that a reprint was needed before the fourth volume could be published. The second edition of Volume III contained some amendments and additions, and also gave Agnes the opportunity to widen her thanks to those who had helped in the work. By this means she managed to include a mention which hinted at, but did not state Eliza's fundamental involvement in the writing of the histories. Agnes wrote that she thanked "my fellow labourer and faithful assistant, my sister Elizabeth."

The agreement that granted Eliza anonymity meant that only Agnes received begging letters, requests for her autograph, questions relating to the books, and letters from people studying their own family history who wanted free information from her. All of these put a burden on Agnes which reduced the time she had available for studying and for writing future biographies.

The final annoyance associated with the success of 'Lives of the Queens of England' was plagiarism, which required constant vigilance. Other authors emerged who not only took the same subject as 'Lives of the Queens of England' but even took whole sections from the work without acknowledgement. When caught and challenged, this sometimes helped the finances of Agnes and Eliza, but was an annoyance nonetheless. One firm, Jane reported, "had to pay a considerable sum" when their magazine used the work "without the slightest attempt at alteration."

A positive effect of the fame of the work, and of the name of Agnes Strickland, was that Agnes found it increasingly easy to gain access to information kept in private and family archives. Supporters of the project, and her widening number of friends, would sometimes refer her to obscure works that might otherwise have been overlooked.

February 1841: John Moodie is Returning Officer at elections

The Belleville into which Susanna and John Moodie moved in 1840, although only a few decades old, was already a town where the politics were strongly Tory, reflecting the views of the majority of the families living there, who were both British and Loyalists. Around this core was an expanding group of people who were sympathetic to the idea that some kind of political reform was needed.

One of John Moodie's duties was to be the Returning Officer at elections and as such he should have been, and should have appeared to be, politically neutral. In July 1840 the Act of Union had been passed by the British Government which created the Province of Canada. Upper Canada became Canada West, Lower Canada became Canada East, and a general election was held in Canada when the Act of Union was proclaimed on 10th February 1841.

In Hastings County, where John Moodie was the Returning Officer, the candidate for the Tories was the incumbent, Edward Murney. The candidate for the Reform group was Robert Baldwin, Solicitor General when the election was called, and a rallying figure in re-building the Reform opposition. Robert Baldwin won the seat by a narrow margin and the local Tories accused John Moodie of political favouritism.

Robert Baldwin was appointed a minister under a new administration and as a result had to seek re-election. He stood in two places, one was a safe seat which he won, and the other was his seat in Hastings, which he correctly expected to lose. At the Hastings election there was so much violence and intimidation that John Moodie, as Returning Officer, had to close the polls and call in troops and the militia to stop the riots. The election was re-run with a different Returning Officer and Edmund Murney re-gained his seat.

1841: Eliza has a home in Bayswater

Eliza by 1841 no longer lived in central London. Instead she had taken the lease of 'Avenue Lodge', which was described as a pretty cottage in Bayswater set among orchards, and which was to be her home for the next fifteen years.

In the early years of Eliza's working partnership with Agnes, she had reluctantly accompanied Agnes to social events, but as time went by she refused, preferring to live a quiet and studious life in Bayswater.

June 1841: Tom returns from New Orleans

Tom in command of the 'Diana' arrived in New Orleans on 7th February 1841, less than eight weeks after sailing from Liverpool. His stay there must have been brief because he had returned to England, and his ship was being hauled in to London Docks by 2nd June 1841.

He spent the next few months at home with his family, and had arrived back in time to be recorded in the first census of the population, which was taken on the night of the 6th/7th June 1841. Tom and Margaretta, with their four children and a servant girl, are recorded as living in the Ratcliff area of Stepney, not far from London Docks. Their children Adela, John Arthur, Julia Lilly (known as Julia) and Mary were aged 8, 6, 4 and 2 years old respectively. There was no mention of their son Thomas Strickland, who had been born in the same year as his brother John.

1841: Agnes and Eliza struggle to get a pass to the State Paper Office

Agnes and Eliza were working on Volume IV of the 'Lives of the Queens of England,' which would be published in April 1842, and would contain the biographies of Elizabeth of York (wife of Henry VII) and the first five wives of Henry VIII. By this stage in their research, they needed access to the relevant State Papers.

When Robert Lemon had been appointed deputy keeper of the State Papers earlier in the 19th century he had found them in a chaotic state and barely protected from decay. In 1818 he had begun to sort out and arrange royal letters, Irish and Scottish correspondence and papers connected with the gunpowder plot. In 1823 he had come across a manuscript 'De Doctrina Christiana' which was thought to have been written by Milton about 150 years beforehand.

Although there is now some controversy about the authorship of this manuscript, its discovery and the original attribution prompted Robert Peel, then Home Secretary, to improve the storage and publication of records of historical importance. George IV also supported Robert Lemon by issuing him with a command to undertake the project.

In 1841 when Agnes wrote to the Home Secretary, then Lord John Russell asking for access, he refused to grant it. Jane reports that Agnes was "surprised, and somewhat indignant, but was determined not to give the matter up, as she must examine legal documents before commencing biographies of Anne Boleyn and Catharine Howard – delicate and difficult tasks, requiring great research and considerable tact."

Agnes asked Mr Howard if he would help her and, together with Sir George Strickland, he applied to Lord Normanby for the pass that had been refused by Lord Russell. Sir George Strickland was a Member of Parliament and, despite their surname in common, he and Agnes were not related, although it seems likely that their ancestry was linked in some unknown and distant way.

Lord Normanby was a novelist who had contributed to some of the same Christmas Annuals as Agnes, and he was very willing to help. By this route Agnes and Eliza were each provided with orders of admission to the State Paper Office, which they could use at any hour or on any day they pleased.

By this time the State Papers had been transferred to the safety of a fire-proof building in Duke Street, St James, London. But although the storage and organisation of the State Papers had, in general, improved a great deal since Robert Lemon started his work, papers for the period of interest to Agnes and Eliza were still being worked on, which made their task far more difficult than for historians following even twenty years later.

Agnes and Eliza later found that the French had taken better care of their national records than the British. The French papers, Jane reported: "had been preserved throughout the age of anarchy and terror, and were beautifully and methodically arranged" whereas organisation of British papers had not happened until "an immense collection had been destroyed by rats or used for waste-paper."

August 1841: Tom prepares to sail to India

The ship 'Diana' was chartered by the Honourable East India Company to sail to Bombay (now named Mumbai), and at the end of August 1841 it entered the Custom House at London Docks for inspection before loading. The ship was to carry passengers as well as cargo, and in September 1841 advertisements appeared in newspapers offering passengers on 'Diana': "very superior poop and other cabin accommodation."

Tom's wife Margaretta had been pregnant when Tom began his voyage to New Orleans, and the baby, a daughter, was born on 8th September 1841. She was known as Diana, but her full registered name was Agnes Diana Strickland, honouring her famous aunt as well as her father's ship. By the time Tom got round to registering the birth, it was 8th October, and he was almost ready to set off on his travels again.

On 26th October 1841 the ship 'Diana,' under the command of Captain Thomas Strickland, was hauled out of London Docks and set sail for India.

September 1841: Agnes and Eliza go on a tour

Another phase of life and research was opening up to Eliza and, more particularly to Agnes who was arranging for them to make a tour of the country, staying as guests at relevant places en route. Agnes was now regarded by the world at large as a successful authoress while Eliza continued to behave as though she was merely Agnes's assistant and travelling companion. In these roles, both the apparent and the real, the two sisters set off at the beginning of September 1841.

Their first destination was 'Middle Hill' in Broadway, Worcestershire, the home of Sir Thomas Phillips (1792-1872) who had begun collecting books and manuscripts when still at school, and continued thereafter to the point of obsession and near bankruptcy. His collection eventually contained some 40,000 printed books and 60,000 manuscripts, making it the largest collection of privately-owned books in the world. Sir Thomas Phillips had often invited Agnes to visit his famous library, had transcribed articles from it for her, and he had also given her references to relevant manuscripts in other libraries.

Agnes in a letter to her mother described the journey: "We took train to Slough – a place well deserving of its name. At five o'clock we reached an antique stone wayside house, where an old woman was on the look-out to take care of us till a post chaise would arrive. Our vehicle soon drove up, and we were rattled up and down such precipitous hills that Eliza would fain have got down and walked. 'Middle Hill' is a fine old place on elevated ground. We were met by our learned host and his three pretty daughters, and just had time to dress for dinner. We study, dear mama, from breakfast to luncheon-time; after which we walk or write letters. In the evening we work, or hear music, or look at fine illuminated manuscripts." Philip

Howard joined them at 'Middle Hill' and "has been of great use to us in transcribing some of the treasures to be found in Sir Thomas's noble library."

The gratitude and pleasure of Agnes and Eliza, in being given such hospitable access to Sir Thomas Phillips' library, was charmingly reciprocated, for in reply to Agnes's letter of thanks, Sir Thomas wrote: "my daughters and myself have been fighting for your letters and we are jealous of each other's possessing such literary diamonds."

When they had finished their research at 'Middle Hill', Eliza and Agnes travelled on to Sizergh Castle in Westmorland, the family home of the ancient Strickland family, to which they believed themselves to be in some way distantly connected. Katharine Parr, Henry VIII's sixth wife, had been brought up in Sizergh Castle, and Agnes had been invited to examine relevant documents there.

The journey was a slow one as Agnes described in another letter to her mother. An accident on the line delayed their train and after sitting in "the dismal dark" for two hours without refreshment "a lad went to some houses and brought us two slices of bread and butter, which we ate very gladly." Their train made five attempts to proceed and five times reversed back to the station "our engines howling all the way." After four hours the train had only got them as far as "Minshul, a dismal, swampy place" where the stoppage had occurred. Agnes wrote: "We then had to walk in the dark with a deep stream on one side and rugged ground on the other. I was in mortal terror, and besought the guard to allow me to take hold of the tail of his coat, upon which he offered me his arm, to which I clung."

After a walk of half a mile they reached Warrington at one o'clock in the morning and in order to get beds for the rest of the night, the staff in the hotel had to be woken up. All this was sufficient to give Agnes a cold and sore throat which lasted for several days. From Warrington they made their way to Preston and from there, the roads being in a poor condition, they travelled slowly northwards by canal to within a mile of Sizergh Castle.

Agnes and Eliza walked the rest of the way, leaving their luggage to be brought on after them, and enjoyed the experience of a slow approach to the castle with which they felt themselves distantly connected. Agnes's letter home said that they "at last stood before the venerable pile and heard the musical old clock strike seven."

They were greeted by the steward Mr Ellison and his wife. "We went to bed early in two stately chambers but my cold was troublesome." Although Agnes was enthusiastic about Sizergh Castle, she had to admit in a letter to Jane that it was "rather cold and damp."

The sisters had permission to search through the muniment chests at Sizergh Castle and to copy anything of relevance which they found. The papers were not in order and in searching for the information they wanted about Katharine Parr, Eliza and Agnes found papers relating to the court of the Stuarts when in exile in France, which would be useful to them at a later stage in their project.

The next stop on their long tour was at Corby Castle near Carlisle, the home of their friends the Howard family. The castle had been rebuilt in Georgian times and was not of interest, but its contents included Stuart relics and portraits, plus the Corby family papers. Throughout the tour, Agnes and Eliza generally kept to their daily routine of studying and writing in the morning, and sightseeing in the afternoon.

The last visit on their tour was to be at Sunderland with Sir Cuthbert Sharpe, an admiral and an enthusiastic antiquarian. Mr Henry Howard arranged that on their journey from Corby Castle to Sir Cuthbert, Agnes and Eliza would be given breakfast by the monks at Hexham where they explored the battleground and saw the cave where Margaret of Anjou and her son had sheltered. Agnes writing to Sarah said: "Our monks treated us royally, and after breakfast preached us a sermon on the vanity of beauty, bidding us think of ourselves not as we were then, but of what we should be ten years hence." This seemed to imply a compliment which Agnes thought "was better fitted to excite vanity than to repress it."

Sir Cuthbert Sharpe welcomed the sisters and took them sightseeing in Durham for a few days. They then opted to return to Southwold on the London packet (mail-boat) which was scheduled to stop at Southwold on its journey. The plan went awry when a fierce gale blew up while they were at sea, making a stop at Southwold impractical, and the captain had to make straight for the shelter of the Thames Estuary and London, where Agnes and Eliza arrived in a dishevelled and exhausted state.

Another passenger on board, a mother with a young family, very kindly gave Agnes and Eliza a bed for the night, and time to recover before they finished their journey home to Suffolk the following day. When they arrived at Reydon they found their mother in fear and trembling that her two daughters had both been shipwrecked and drowned.

This was the first of Agnes and Eliza's country house tours in search of information. For Agnes it became an annual event, repeated with various itineraries for a number of years. For Eliza the pastime was only occasional. She usually remained in Bayswater, partly from personal preference but also because one of the sisters had to be within easy reach when any of their books was going through the press. Agnes developed the annual routine of living at home at Reydon and writing up her findings during the winter months; spending April to July in London, then undertaking her series of visits during the late summer and autumn before returning once more to winter at Reydon Hall.

1841: Catharine's family grows

Catharine gave birth to two daughters in the two years following the move from the farm in Douro to the property at Ashburnham. The first daughter, Mary Helen Bridges Traill, was born on 30th October 1840 but Catharine had the sadness of this baby dying before she reached her first birthday.

Soon after the death of baby Mary Helen, another baby was born and was also christened Mary. Mary Elizabeth Jane Traill was born on 7th November 1841.

1841: Agnes samples life in a convent

Agnes sometimes felt that research should go beyond the mere study of documents. In 1841, in order to help her understand the options available to ladies associated with royalty in pre-Reformation England, she decided to experience life in a convent. She knew that Lady Bedingfeld, a Woman of the Bedchamber to the Dowager Queen Adelaide, had rooms in a convent in Hammersmith to the west of London. Lady Bedingfeld was from an old Suffolk family and with her letters of introduction, Agnes obtained permission to spend two weeks at the convent, living in a cell and observing convent life.

In a letter to her sister Sarah, Agnes gave an account of her arrival: "We rang at a bell attached to a grated door, which was opened by the porteress who ushered us into a shabby, ugly parlour, hung with prints and paintings of saints. After a time the lady abbess came in, wearing her Benedictine dress, black veil and gold cross. She took us to see her chapel and burying ground. Then Dame Selby, the abbess, claimed kindred with me from the Stricklands of Sizergh Castle, and we became excellent friends."

Jane Strickland in a commentary of the visit wrote: "Agnes was then introduced to a novice and shown her cell. It had nowhere to keep clothes and Agnes questioned this. The novice replied that she had no clothes of her own, that her vestments were furnished from the conventual wardrobe. Although acknowledging that this was an excellent regulation in a religious community it gave Agnes, who was rather fond of rich attire, a melancholy view of conventual life."

During Agnes's time at the convent she witnessed a novice nun taking her final vows. The nun was calm and firm, while Agnes was moved to tears – the soulful music which accompanied the service highlighted the solemnity of the occasion and was a marked contrast to the cheerful shouting of hymns that Agnes was used to at Reydon Church and Sunday School.

Lady Bedingfeld was seventy at the time, and after Agnes had visited Lady Bedingfeld in her rooms at the convent, Agnes told Sarah: "they are beautifully arranged, and contain fine paintings and many curiosities. She will give me a letter that was written to Queen Mary Beatrice when she returns my visit, which she means to do the first time she comes to Town." Lady Bedingfeld was very kind to Agnes and also gave her letters of introduction to Costessey and Oxburgh, both important Catholic houses in East Anglia which were likely to have objects of importance to Agnes' research.

Agnes had written an Almanack of verses, which she dedicated to the Queen Dowager, and asked Lady Bedingfeld if she would take a copy to Queen Adelaide. Lady Bedingfeld did so but, according to Jane's account, Queen Adelaide smiled, and "described the book as a bribe by which she would not be influenced. However, she also said that if she was subsequently sent one by the publisher, she would buy it."

On 30th October 1841 an advertisement appeared in the 'Norfolk Chronicle' for 'Pawsey's Ladies Fashionable Repository for 1842' stating that "the Queen Dowager has been graciously pleased to express her approbation of the Literary Contributions to Pawsey's Suffolk Repository, by Miss Agnes Strickland, and has ordered a copy for the ensuing year." This, presumably, was the almanack brought to Queen Adelaide's attention via Agnes and Lady Bedingfeld.

Queen Adelaide must have liked, or at least been sympathetic to Pawsey's Repository. It was a local East Anglian publication, which evolved over the years, but with Agnes always among the contributors, and with Queen Adelaide and subsequently Queen Victoria being named in advertisements as annual subscribers. For example, the advertisement for the 1851 'Pawsey's Ladies' Fashionable Repository' said that it was "Embellished with six highly finished engravings ... original contributions from Miss Strickland ... and other talented writers, with upwards of 100 Enigmas, Charades &c."

January 1842: Tom stops en route

Having been hauled out of London Docks on 26th October 1841, by 21st January 1842 the ship 'Diana' had rounded the Cape of Good Hope and got as far as Mauritius. Tom spent four days there before he set off to complete his journey to Bombay.

March 1842: Catharine asks Lord Brougham for help

In March 1842 Catharine made another attempt to get more financial benefit from her book 'Backwoods of Canada'. She wrote to Lord Brougham, the British reform politician whose picture had been one of those on the wall of her home in Douro. She explained that her family, like many in her class of settler, was struggling in poverty. They had five small children; her husband had applied unsuccessfully for civil and for military employment; and she was managing to earn only a small amount by her writing.

She told him that her efforts had included a journal which covered many aspects of natural history in the Canadian forest, but her sister (Agnes) had been unable to find a publisher for it in England.

Catharine's letter had some success. She received, through Agnes who acted as her agent, a further £15 from the 'Society for the Diffusion of Useful Knowledge' of which Lord Brougham was chairman. Whilst this does not seem generous, it was better than nothing.

April 1842: The auction at Strawberry Hill is convenient

In the spring of 1842, the possessions which Horace Walpole had amassed in his summer house at Strawberry Hill, near Twickenham, were put up for auction with public viewing days from 28th March to 4th April. Horace Walpole had been a writer, a politician and was the son of Sir Robert Walpole, Britain's first Prime Minister. He had also been a very determined collector. Work on building Strawberry Hill began in 1748, and it had become filled with his collection of pictures, furniture, sculpture and artefacts. Many of these items were of interest to Agnes and Eliza.

The public viewing days gave an excellent opportunity to examine in one place, portraits and items which would soon be widely dispersed, and Agnes was sufficiently famous that she was given special treatment at her visit, which was remembered many years later when J & P Wharton were describing some miniature portraits at Strawberry Hill in their book 'Wits and Beaux of Society 1860.' They wrote: "How sadly, in referring to these invaluable pictures, does one's mind revert to the day when, before the hammer of" (the auctioneer) "had resounded in these rooms – Agnes Strickland, followed by all eyes, pondered over that group of portraits: how, as she slowly withdrew, we of the commonalty scarce worthy to look, gathered round the spot again, and wondered at the perfect life, the perfect colouring, proportion, and keeping of those tiny vestiges of a bygone generation."

26th May 1842: Agnes attends a Birthday Drawing-room

Agnes, despite her heavy work-load, continued to find time for social and court life. On 26th May 1842 she attended a particularly notable Drawing-room at St James's Palace, held to celebrate Queen Victoria's birthday. Newspapers reported that the Archbishops of Canterbury and of York were there, together with fourteen Bishops. They had a brief audience in private with Queen Victoria and, having paid their respects, retired. The people who remained were members of the diplomatic, ministerial and household corps, all dressed in their respective full-dress uniforms with medals. The other attendees included a long list of the nobility of the day and, among the names of untitled persons present, was 'Miss Agnes Strickland'.

July 1842: Catharine briefly has another child

A third daughter to be born to Catharine in quick succession was baptized Eleanor Stewart Traill on 11th July 1842, but her life was very short, and baby Eleanor died aged only three months. By the end of 1842 then, after seven pregnancies, Catharine had five surviving children. Sons James and Harry were nine and five years old while daughters Kate, Anne and Mary were aged six, four and one.

The family do not seem to have had much land at Ashburnham, and had only Thomas's half-pay pension for a regular income. Catharine's writing and any money remaining from her legacies were the only additions to the family finances. The Strickland and Traill families in England and Scotland were not in a position to give financial help, but boxes began to be sent from Reydon Hall which contained clothing, other necessities and books, all of which were gratefully received.

September 1842: Tom is home but not for long

The 'Shipping and Mercantile Gazette' reported the arrival of the 'Diana' at Mauritius on 21st January 1842 and its departure on 25th January, but no other mention has been found of Tom's voyage to Bombay nor of his return voyage to London.

However, he was back in London and his next voyage was being advertised by 13th September 1842. The advertisement was in a fairly standard format and appeared five times before the end of September:

"For Bombay. To sail 10th October. The well-known fine fast-sailing British-built Barque Diana; A1, 600 tons, coppered and copper-fastened; Thomas Strickland, Commander; lying in St Katharine Docks.

This ship has a very superior poop and other cabin accommodation for passengers, and will carry a surgeon; and, for the accommodation of passengers, will call at Portsmouth.

For terms of freight or passage apply to the Commander, on board; at the Jerusalem Coffee-house; to Messrs Forbes, Forbes and Co., 9, King William-street; or to Phillipps and Tiplady, Sworn Brokers 3, George-yard, Lombard-street."

October 1842: Agnes and Eliza publish two books

Before they began to write 'Lives of the Queens of England,' Agnes and Eliza had begun collating the letters of Mary Stuart, also known as Mary Queen of Scots. These they translated from old French, with the idea that they might one day write an account of her life. Agnes's friend Jane Porter, while living in St Petersburg with her brother Sir Robert Ker Porter, discovered that there were some un-translated letters by Mary Stuart in the Imperial Russian Archives and set herself the task of getting access to them, and of getting them translated for Agnes to use.

With this help, October 1842 saw not only the publication of the fifth volume of 'Lives of the Queens of England', which gave biographies of Henry VIIIs last wife Katharine Parr and of his daughter Queen Mary, but also a two volume work containing the letters of Mary Queen of Scots which had not previously been published, and to which Agnes added an introduction.

November 1842: Tom gets caught in a gale

Despite the advertised departure date of 10th October, it was 5th November 1842 before all preparations were complete and the ship 'Diana' with Tom in command, set off from London Docks for

Bombay. The ship had not got very far when it lost its anchor in a gale, and had to return to Deal for a replacement.

Second time lucky, Tom got the 'Diana' to Portsmouth only a week behind schedule, and set sail onwards on 18th November 1842. There were no further mishaps or delays and the 'Diana' arrived at Madeira, off the coast of north-west Africa on 3rd December 1842.

November 1842: Susanna buys a piano

With the help of John Lovell, editor of the 'Literary Garland' Susanna bought a piano, and on 26th November 1842 wrote to him to acknowledge its safe arrival. She also sent him her account for the year, and mentioned that Agnes's fame would help in the sale of her own work. All this implies that Susanna was an astute business woman and financially quite comfortable.

She was also not ashamed to praise her own daughter. She wrote: "My dear Sir, The piano arrived quite safe two days ago and sustained no injury from the stormy passage up. I am quite satisfied with it in every respect, and feel extremely grateful to you for the care and trouble you have taken about it. My girls will I hope profit by it. Poor dears they have both been seriously ill and I much fear my beautiful Addy will go into a decline. We have prized too highly the surpassingly fair face which few pictures could rival, when the dear child was in health, and I have been too proud of the universal praise bestowed upon her by all, and now I fear my Lily of the Lake, as an old friend used to call her, is doomed to an early grave. She has excellent talents too, and promised so fair."

On the business side Susanna wrote: "Now for pounds, shillings and pence – I find our account" which she then detailed, came to "a total of forty pounds, ten shillings. This I hope you will put to your account against me for the piano."

Susanna was thinking of turning the stories printed in serial form in John Lovell's 'Literary Garland' into books for sale in England. She wrote: "If I had time, I would try Moodie's publisher, Bentley of London." Whatever reservations or sense of rivalry, or possibly jealousy, she had from time to time felt about Agnes, Susanna believed that her sister's fame could be of benefit to herself. She added: "My sister Agnes's name would be a great help to me now in selling a book of my own. I am reading the Queens, and am greatly delighted with the work."

It is not known whether or not the three Strickland siblings in Canada were at this stage aware of Eliza's share in the work which was published under the name of Agnes Strickland. The writing partnership between Eliza and Agnes did not begin until Sam, Susanna and Catharine had emigrated. No letter has been found which mentions Eliza's involvement in the work while both Agnes and Eliza were alive, and their siblings in Canada may have been kept in ignorance for the sake of protecting the secret.

End 1842: Agnes and Eliza realise the difficulty of joint authorship

For the fifth volume of 'Lives of the Queens of England', Agnes wrote the biography of the protestant queen Katharine Parr, while Eliza wrote the biography of Queen Mary, a staunch catholic. When it was published in October 1842, this volume caused a furore which was partly caused by both Agnes and Eliza departing somewhat from their intention of 'facts not opinion' and by both of them putting a favourable slant on the life of their subject.

Jane described Agnes as portraying Katharine Parr, the first Protestant queen-consort, as "the truly Christian wife of the cruel Henry, who helped to mould the beautiful character of Henry's young successor – the pious, charitable and learned Edward VI." In the same volume, Jane said that Eliza strove to show Mary "as she was, an able ruler, and but for her bigotry, a just one" thereby expressing a sympathetic view of Queen Mary, the Catholic Queen whose treatment of Protestants earned her the nickname 'Bloody Mary.'

Thus these two queens were widely different in their religious views, and the enthusiasms of Agnes for Katharine Parr, and of Eliza for Queen Mary, highlighted the difference. A letter to Agnes from a Mr C W Lucy summed the situation up neatly. He wrote: "Hang me! If you have not made out Bloody Mary a better woman than your Protégée Kate. Why they will dub you a Papist in disguise!" He was right, for it became suspected that Agnes had converted to Catholicism in between writing the two biographies, this being the only explanation the public could come up with for both biographies being sympathetic to the subject, the truth of two authors having to remain secret.

Agnes had to cope with the situation alone because Eliza was still determined to remain anonymous. Although the two sisters obviously worked together, Eliza was always presented as merely assisting Agnes. It is said that the only person who suspected the truth was Queen Victoria who, having read the whole of Volume V carefully, said to a lady-in-waiting "These two lives are by different authors."

In addition to the sympathetic telling of Queen Mary's life story, Agnes's friendships with prominent Catholic families, and the fortnight that she had spent in a convent, all seemed to point towards her conversion, and the rumour caused a sharp decline in sales of the series. Agnes had to offset the rumours by attending church more often, and by making greater efforts in teaching at the Sunday School in Reydon.

Another potential source of embarrassment for Agnes was in talking with acquaintances about a biography which they thought she had written, but which had really been written by Eliza. Agnes was from time to time complimented on the biography of Mary Tudor, and in a conversation with her friend the historian Mr Alison, she talked at some length about Queen Mary's high character and nobility of mind.

Mr Alison referred to the conversation in his autobiography. He wrote: "to which I replied: "That may be all very true, Miss Strickland; but unfortunately she had an awkward habit of burning people – she brought 239 men, women and children to the stake, in a reign which did not extend beyond a few years." "Oh yes," she said "it was terrible, dreadful, but it was the fault of the age, the temper of the times: Mary herself was everything that is noble and heroic."

After this awkward conversation with Mr Alison, Agnes learnt to be wary and simply acquiesced by silence to be the author of Queen Mary's biography. However, when Lady Hayter, a Catholic, congratulated Agnes on writing a biography that was more sympathetic than most to the queen who is often called 'Bloody Mary,' Agnes is said to have made the rare confession that the author of this particular biography was her sister and not herself.

July 1843: Tom has another son

Tom's previous voyages had been simple out-and-return journeys, but the one he began on 5th November 1842 was to be more complicated, and when he left home Margaretta had recently become pregnant.

The first leg of his voyage was completed when Tom arrived at Bombay on 1st May 1843. After remaining there for a few weeks he set sail for China, and it was while he was on this leg of his journey that Margaretta gave birth to a son. The baby was born on 7th July 1843 at the family home in Arbour Square, Mile End Old Town, slightly to the west of their previous address in Ratcliffe.

Tom and the 'Diana' arrived in China on 15th August 1843. Margaretta took their son to be baptised with the name Walter Strickland on 23rd August 1843, at the church of St Dunstan and All Saints in Stepney, London. Tom and the 'Diana' remained in China for several months.

July 1843: Agnes and Eliza publish two more books

The life of Queen Mary having been covered in volume V of 'Lives of the Queens of England', the next queen in the sequence was Queen Elizabeth which Agnes undertook. This was a very large topic and occupied Agnes for much of 1842 plus part of 1843. The resulting biography formed all of volume VI and half of volume VII in the original twelve volume series.

Jane recounted an incident which happened at about this time. Agnes and Eliza, having spent an evening with the Howard family, returned to their lodgings. Jane wrote: "Their maid, after she had relieved them of their gala dresses and ornaments, went to bed, leaving a lighted candle in an open drawer filled with pieces of muslin and cotton ... While they were arranging their hair for the night, their attention was attracted by the smell of smoke, which, upon opening the door, filled the room, leaving no doubt respecting its cause. The house was on fire.

"Elizabeth, always prompt and energetic, hastened to find from whence it proceeded, while Agnes ran up-stairs to arouse the sleeping occupants of the house, eleven persons in number. She found this no easy matter. The master of the lodging-house was blind, too, which seemed to make the preservation of his large family and property more difficult.

"Elizabeth, who had discovered that the fire was in the kitchen, opened the door, calling "Fire!" while Agnes, half dressed, took her manuscript life of Elizabeth in one hand and her sister's Bramah-desk in the other, and ran to Lady Brooke's, who received her frightened friend very kindly, wrapped her up in a blanket, and made her lie down on the sofa.

"Two policemen and fire-engines were soon on the spot, and the flames were speedily got under; the blind man, with much presence of mind, keeping the doors and windows closed to exclude currents of air – the loss of the kitchen furniture and boarded floor being the amount of the injury he sustained."

When it was published, the biography of Queen Elizabeth was very popular and overcame the religious difficulties that the previous volume had caused. Queen Elizabeth was a more popular topic than her predecessors, and her biography had a wider audience of readers than previous volumes. The entire edition was sold as soon as it was in print and, as Jane put it: "added greatly to the fame of Agnes Strickland, and very much to Mr Colburn's profits."

One of the reasons why Agnes and Eliza's work was so popular was that they had a different approach to history from other historians. They gave details of everyday life which made them more readable than the customary approach which centred on battles and treaties. This was one of the reasons why their contemporary, the traditional historian Thomas Babington Macaulay, disliked their work.

As well as the mammoth task of researching and writing the first part of a biography of Queen Elizabeth, a new edition of the 'Letters of Mary Queen of Scots' was being prepared. This second edition had some amendments and additions, and was issued in binding to match 'Lives of the Queens of England'. The second edition of 'Letters of Mary Queen of Scots' must have been the work of Eliza, because it was published in July 1843 at the same time as the sixth volume of 'Lives of the Queens of England', written by Agnes.

July 1843: Susanna has her last child

Although the Canadian politician Robert Baldwin had spent only a small amount of time in Hastings County, a friendship had developed between him and the Moodies which continued after he was no longer connected with the area.

Susanna had another son, born on 8th July 1843, the day after Tom's wife had given birth to Walter Strickland. He was named Robert Baldwin Moodie as a reflection of his parents' friendship with the politician, and was Susanna's last child.

1843: Sam's family is also increasing in numbers

Sam and Mary Strickland's family was continuing to grow. A son named Walter Reginald was born in 1841 and a daughter Jane in 1843. This brought their family to nine children, three daughters and six sons.

August 1843: Sarah and Agnes go on holiday together

By the time it got to the late summer of 1843, Agnes needed a rest from writing and Sarah accompanied her on a holiday tour. The first stop on their tour was in Lancashire. They then visited the Lake District, progressed through Carlisle and ended their holiday in Scotland. At this stage Sarah was 45 years old, had been a widow for more than five years and was still the family beauty. Agnes was aged 47 and was a famous historian-cum-authoress.

After spending a few days with friends in Lancaster, they took a coach across the treacherous Duddon Sands, accompanied by two guides to ensure they avoided the sinking sands. Jane recorded that these guides were cheery characters "mounted on strong Flemish horses. The men had round rosy cheeks and broad grins, their ragged frieze-coats were girt with strong leather belts. When the dangerous part of the journey was past, the guides came grinning on each side of the coach, holding out their hats for what the passengers chose to bestow – such hats as only men of their calling ever do wear – their gratulatory grins were well worth, Agnes thought, the gratuity she gave. If science has banished these guides" Jane added "it would be a loss to be lamented."

Agnes and Jane might have been pleased to know that despite the advent of a railway replacing the coach as the main means of crossing the sands, there is still a royally appointed guide, the 'Queen's Guide to the Sands' who will take people across the treacherous sands, which is a popular challenge for walkers and charity fund-raisers. Although the route is marked on some maps as a highway, the former Queen's Guide, Cedric Robinson, described it as "the most dangerous highway in Britain."

Agnes and Sarah's next stop was at the town of Ulverston in Lancashire, where they arranged to stay at the Sun Hotel for a few days. This was Sarah's first visit to the Lake District and she enjoyed the contrast of the scenery with that of East Anglia. On arriving in Ulverston they booked in at the Sun Hotel then went to explore the town, calling in at the shop of Mr Soulby, the local stationer, for Agnes to buy some paper.

While she was waiting for Agnes to be served, Sarah looked through the books and annuals that were for sale and, coming across a juvenile book written by Agnes, pointed it out to her sister. Both Mr Soulby and a clergyman who was waiting in the shop noticed the sisters smiling over the book, and realised Agnes's identity. Gallantries and introductions ensued and the clergyman called on them the same evening at their hotel.

The clergyman was the local vicar, Richard Gwillym, and he invited Agnes and Sarah to stay with himself and his sister at his home, Stockbridge House, during their stay in Ulverston. Agnes was accustomed to being invited to stay in the homes of respectable strangers, and the invitation was accepted.

Over the next few days, Agnes and Sarah went on several excursions to see the main sights of the locality which included Furness Abbey and Conishead Priory. They also went to Cockermouth and Whitehaven, for although Agnes was having a rest from writing, she was still working, and these were all places of relevance to her historical studies as well as being of interest to Sarah as a tourist.

One of the visits made by Agnes and Sarah was to William Wordsworth at his home, Rydal Mount on 25th September 1843. William Wordsworth was the greatest poet of the time and had become poet laureate at the beginning of April 1843, soon after the death of Robert Southey. When he became poet laureate William Wordsworth was 73 years old, and he only accepted the post when told that it would not require him to write any poetry, and he produced no official poems during the seven years that he held the post up to his death in April 1850.

Jane wrote: "Agnes Strickland was delighted with the Lake country, for she and her sister were frequent visitors at Rydal Mount, a perfect home for a poet, and redolent with the remembrance of Wordsworth." In 1843, Agnes and Sarah did not have time to become "frequent visitors" and William Wordsworth was still alive. The phrase "redolent with the remembrance of Wordsworth" indicates that Jane was referring to visits which would be made in the future.

September 1843: Sarah accepts a proposal

Richard Gwillym was a bachelor and was well-thought of locally. In Jane's words: "Before the termination of the short visit, he proposed, and was accepted by Sarah, whose charms of person and mind had gained at once his affections. This brief courtship terminated after a few months in a long and very happy union."

Leaving Ulverston and Richard Gwillym, Agnes and Sarah spent a few days at Corby Castle near Carlisle, followed by a month in and around Edinburgh before returning to Reydon Hall.

September 1843: Susanna doesn't help matters

By 1843 John Moodie had been Sheriff of Hastings County for three years. He had arrived as a stranger and a non-Tory, and it is said that a local determination had grown to make his life difficult. His job did not carry a salary, his income being derived from fees received for serving writs and making court appearances, and for administering the sale of impounded goods. When it was realised that he had no independent means, the local Tory lawyers and public officials are said to have delayed payments to him on the flimsiest of excuses, launched nuisance suits against him and generally did all they could to thwart his efforts. Despite all these obstructions, John Moodie was said (by academics in 1985) to have earned in the region of £250 a year from being sheriff, and it was a role that he could not afford to give up.

Susanna's anger at the way her husband was treated in Belleville was intense, and resulted in a four-part story entitled 'Richard Redpath' appearing in the 'Literary Garland' from September to December 1843. The story is said to have been set in Jamaica and was about the abolition of slavery. Wisely or otherwise, Susanna included a merciless portrait of the villainous editor of the 'Jamaica Observer', whose physical appearance was such that it was unmistakably a description of the editor of the local paper in Belleville which criticised John Moodie.

Although Susanna detested this man, this opinion was not shared by everyone and he has been described as "a vigorous and imaginative politician who worked hard for his Belleville voters."

1843: Queen Victoria asks for Agnes's autograph

Agnes's place at Court functions by 1843 was both accepted and acceptable. Indeed in 1843 Agnes was informed that Queen Victoria would like to add Agnes's autograph to her collection. Jane recorded that Agnes "was gratified by a request that did her so much honour."

October 1843: Catharine is busy with domestic matters

Catharine's domestic life was too busy to allow much time for writing as was shown in a letter she wrote at the end of October 1843 to Ellen, daughter of Frances Stewart. Catharine was about to send some home-spun wool for Ellen to knit into socks for Catharine's children while Catharine herself was busy sewing children's dresses and trousers, and bonnets for the girls.

November 1843: Life is busy at Reydon Hall

Agnes and Sarah returned to Reydon Hall in the late autumn of 1843. Agnes returned reinvigorated and ready to spend the winter completing her biography of Queen Elizabeth, which was her share of volume VII of 'Lives of the Queens of England. She also had to produce a revised version of the existing work on Queen Elizabeth for a new edition of volume VI.

Her visit to Scotland also determined Agnes to write a biography of Mary Queen of Scots, and she was in the process of collecting material for it in what she called "My Stuart Album", which contained memorabilia and sketches of relevance, as well as written notes.

Sarah on her return to Reydon prepared for Richard Gwillym to make his first visit to her family home, during which they made plans for their ensuing wedding and life together.

January 1844: Mrs Strickland parts with another daughter

Of Mrs Elizabeth Strickland's eight children, three had emigrated to Canada. Her son Tom was away from England for long periods living a dangerous life at sea, and his family home was near London Docks. Eliza had her own home in Bayswater and Agnes spent much of each year either in London or visiting friends. Therefore Sarah's marriage to Richard Gwillym would result in another of her children moving away from Suffolk, leaving only Jane as a full-time resident to keep her company at Reydon Hall. Mrs Strickland was 71 years old, and had been a widow living on very limited resources for over twenty five years. Jane was 44 years old and suffered from chronic bronchitis.

Jane in her 'Life of Agnes Strickland' wrote "to spare the feelings of her mother, who, though pleased with the match, was reluctant to part with her daughter, Mrs Strickland's separation from her two youngest girls, Catharine and Susanna, had caused her so much sorrow that it was thought better that the parting with Sarah should take place before the marriage." Sarah accordingly left Reydon Hall and went to London early in 1844 to be married.

January 1844: Tom is on his way home

On 3rd January 1844, Tom set sail back to London from Canton. He arrived at St Helena in the South Atlantic Ocean off the coast of West Africa on 21st March 1844. St Helena was one of the remote but strategically important islands dotted round the world, where British sailing ships on long voyages could re-victual and carry out any necessary repairs.

1st February 1844: Sarah marries well

Richard Gwillym's history was given in local papers after he died, but is more usefully related at this happier point in his life. The papers said: "He was the only son of Richard Gwillym Esq. of Bewsey and Jane Elizabeth, his wife, and was born on the 29th August 1802" which made him four years younger than Sarah. "Both Mr Gwillym's parents were descended from ancient Lancashire families. His mother was sister to, and co-heiress with, the late Mrs Earle, of Speaklands, near Liverpool."

The report continued: "He studied at Brasenose College, Oxford obtained BA in 1825, MA in 1827, was ordained deacon in 1827 and priest in 1829 by the Bishop of Chester. He was appointed curate of West Derby, Liverpool in 1827; St Stephen's, Exeter in 1833, and domestic chaplain to Lord Harrowby in 1836. On the death of the Rev John Sutherland, Mr Gwillym was appointed to succeed him as incumbent of the Parish Church of St Mary, Ulverston, in October 1837."

Ulverston was therefore Richard Gwillym's first parish and he had been there for seven years, with his sister Henrietta looking after domestic arrangements in their joint home. When he had arrived at Ulverston in 1837, the parishioners had money available to build a vicarage. However, the parish church had no bells, and Richard insisted that the money be spent on a peal of bells for the church rather than on a house for himself. He rented or leased his home, Stockbridge House in Ulverston rather than owning it.

That Richard Gwillym had influential contacts within the Anglican Church is shown by the people who attended and officiated at his marriage. Whether sparing her mother's feelings was the real reason for Sarah marrying in London, or a tactful reason given by Jane, Sarah's second wedding was in marked contrast to her first. When she had married Robert Childs, the service had been conducted, as was customary, in her parish church with the local vicar officiating. When she married Richard Gwillym on 1st February 1844, the marriage took place in the highly fashionable church of St George's in Hanover Square, London.

Eliza and Agnes were at the wedding, but Jane was with their mother in Reydon Hall, and an account of the proceedings was sent home by Agnes. It was a cold but sunny morning with a thin layer of snow on the roof-tops which Agnes described as "a glorious day and the bride came forth fair as the day, though her modiste employed so much time and pains upon her dress that nothing but the announcement that the Dean of Carlisle was waiting could induce her to conclude the bridal toilet, which flurried the bride a little."

Sarah wore a dress of white satin trimmed with swans' down, with a white lace scarf looped over one shoulder and a white camellia as a corsage. She arrived at the back door of the church in Mill Street where about twenty guests were waiting to greet her in the vestry. Sarah walked down the aisle on the arm of Johnson Lawson, son of the Dean of Bath and a friend of Richard Gwillym, past the sightseers at the back of the church, and the guests at the front.

Agnes recorded: "I stood next to her and held her bouquet, and Marianne Skinner her gloves. The church was full and the bridal party filled the chancel." The Rev Mr Tufnell, who would later be the Bishop of Brisbane, was the best man. "The Dean, dear old gentleman, behaved like an apostle, and never did I hear anything half so beautiful as his reading of the marriage-service."

After the service, the register was signed by seven witnesses rather than the usual two. The witnesses included Agnes Strickland and Richard's sister Henrietta Gwillym. Eliza Strickland was at the wedding, but despite being the eldest of the sisters, she acted true to form and was not among those whose names appear in the register. The service and formalities finished, the couple left the church through the high portico just as the church clock struck twelve.

Agnes continued: "We then had a splendid breakfast. It was a gala day, all the bells rang in honour of the Queen, who went in state to open Parliament." Sarah changed into her going away outfit – a purple damask dress, velvet mantle and bonnet "and looked charmingly in her elegant travelling parure." A parure is a matching set of jewellery which Agnes reported that "everyone admired" but unfortunately did not describe.

Sarah and her new husband had a week for their honeymoon, first staying in accommodation at Hampton Court Palace, which had been opened to the public a few years earlier and was a great tourist attraction. They then made a brief visit to Windsor before starting their new life together in Lancashire.

1st February 1844: Eliza and Agnes hear the Queen's Speech

The Opening of Parliament in 1844 took place in its traditional location of the Painted Chamber at Westminster, despite the chamber having been gutted by fire in 1834. It had been re-roofed and re-furbished, and continued to be the House of Lords on a temporary basis until the new Palace of Westminster was ready. Unfortunately, it was demolished in 1851 and has been described as a very great treasure lost to the nation.

Queen Victoria arrived at the Painted Chamber precisely on schedule at 2 o'clock and entered the House of Lords on the arm of Prince Albert. The body of the Chamber was already full of Peers plus wives and daughters, with members of the public including Eliza and Agnes filling the galleries. The traditional procedure of Black Rod being sent to summons the members of the House of Commons was performed, and after the members of the House of Commons had arrived and crowded into the remaining available space, Queen Victoria read the 'Queen's Speech'. This gave the Government's planned programme for the session ahead, with the annexing of Scinde in India being the first item announced.

February 1844: Ulverston celebrates Sarah and Richard's wedding

Whilst Richard Gwillym was being married in London, his parishioners in Ulverston were marking the occasion in a number of ways, including ringing the bells of St Mary's Church while the marriage ceremony was taking place in London. The local papers reported that the bells: "sent forth a merry peal to celebrate the event, and on Sunday white rosettes and gloves, bridal favours, were sported by the churchwardens and others, to show the estimation in which the worthy vicar is held."

Also on the wedding day, and probably paid for by Richard, a ball was held which was reported in the papers: "A tradesman's ball in honour of the marriage was held at the Assembly Rooms in the evening" of 1st February 1844 "and was attended by upwards of 80 persons. The ball was opened with the good old English contra-dance 'Haste to the Wedding'. Quadrilles and contra-dances alternately were kept up with much spirit until the company separated, well pleased with their evening's entertainment, and wishing health and happiness to the reverend gentleman and his fair lady. The refreshments supplied by Mrs Parker, of the Sun Hotel, were of the best quality and most numerous." So the Sun Hotel, having lost their two lady guests to Richard Gwillym the previous September, had the compensating business of catering for his tradesman's ball a few months later.

The following Friday, 9th February 1844, when the vicar and his bride made their first appearance together in Ulverston, they were greeted in style. The local papers recorded: "A number of parishioners arranged to meet and welcome them. Accordingly, the carriage was met in Morecombe Road, a little below the Gas Works, between four and five o'clock in the afternoon, by a procession composed of a great number of the respectable inhabitants, accompanied by two bands of music.

"The carriage was stopped by the churchwardens, who told them that it was the wish of many to take the horses from the carriage, and draw them into the town and they hoped they would not object to it. The rev gentleman was deeply affected, but consented to leave himself in the hands of his friends. The four horses being taken from the carriage, a number of men proceeded to harness themselves and drew, with great good will through the Ellers, Market-street, Market-place, Duke-street, and to Stockbridge House, the residence of Mr Gwillym, the distance being upwards of a mile. We may remark, that in the progress up Duke-street, such was the energy exerted by those who had taken charge of the carriage that a drummer and a flag-carrier had nearly been run down, which caused much merriment.

"All the schools had a holiday for the occasion and before reaching Stockbridge the crowd had increased immensely, but the greatest order was observed throughout. The principal inns, the National School, and many private houses, had banners displayed from their windows. Hundreds of people were assembled in the Market-place, independent of the crowds which followed the procession, and which had with it two bands of music, with banners flying.

"In the grounds adjoining his house, a triumphal arch had been erected, decorated with evergreens and artificial flowers, and in the centre of the arch was the word 'Welcome!' When the bride and groom alighted from their carriage, cheers, loud and long, rent the air, whilst the bells of St Mary's Church sent forth their musical and enlivening notes. The rev gentleman then addressed the assembled throng; but his manner was a language more forcible than any eloquence. His feelings were depicted on his countenance. Refreshments were provided for all who wished to partake, and many availed themselves of the opportunity."

By Sunday 11th February 1844, life had still not quite settled into its new pattern. The local paper said: "The happy couple attended church, where Mr Gwillym preached. The churchwardens and other officers wore white gloves with bridal favours; and the choir (Mr Daniel at the organ) gave, in fine style, the anthem sung at the marriage of our gracious Queen."

The next day, 12th February 1844: "Mr Gwillym gave an entertainment to celebrate the auspicious event of his marriage when 110 individuals all enjoyed themselves to the utmost, in the way best suited to their various fancies. It was 'liberty hall', most of the rooms having been thrown open for the accommodation of the guests. The evening was spent in the most agreeable manner, in music, singing and dancing. On the bride and bridegroom making their appearance, attended by Miss Gwillym, the whole company stood to receive them."

As well as celebrating their marriage, the event provided a means by which Sarah could be introduced to all the principal members of the community. It was also a farewell party for Richard's sister Henrietta who shortly afterwards moved away. The papers reported that speeches were made, thanks given, introductions made, healths drunk and: "Tea was served at 7 o'clock and supper at half-past 11. Each was excellent; the supper fit for the table of the most hospitable nobleman, whilst the tea might have graced the table of a queen. All were delighted with the hospitable manner in which they had been treated; and as they left the roof of their worthy host and hostess, they wished them every happiness that Heaven could bestow." The marriage was to be a happy one with Sarah supporting Richard in his many future endeavours in the parish.

March 1844: Eliza recognises Southwold

Eliza and Agnes remained in London after Sarah's wedding to be on hand if needed while volume VII of 'Lives of the Queens of England,' was going through the presses. It completed the life of Queen Elizabeth (written by Agnes) and also contained the life of Anne of Denmark, wife of James I (written by Eliza) and was issued in April 1844.

The first edition of 'Lives of the Queens of England' included pictures of all of the queens involved, which in some cases were difficult to obtain. When a portrait was needed of Anne of Denmark, wife of James I to complete volume VII, Eliza went to view the one at Hampton Court and took with her an engraver to make a copy of it.

While he was at work, Eliza was shown attics and other rooms of particular interest and among the things she saw were the Sole Bay Tapestries, a series of tapestries commissioned by James II from William van de Velde. The Battle of Solebay had been fought in Southwold Bay (also named Sole Bay) on 28th May 1672 and had been the first naval battle in the Anglo-Dutch War.

The English fleet was assembled at Southwold for a re-fit under the joint command of James, Duke of York (who later became King James II) and the Earl of Sandwich, when news arrived that the Dutch fleet had been sighted and was expected to arrive soon after dawn. The English fleet had 71 ships, each with 40 guns, plus frigates and fire-ships, bringing the number of vessels to 90 in total, while the Dutch fleet had 61 warships. The battle went on all day, ending inconclusively at sunset with both sides claiming victory and both sides having lost two ships.

In the course of the battle, casualties were in the region of 1,800 dead on the Dutch side and 2,000 on the English side. This was a very memorable event in the history of Southwold, which had about 800 injured sailors to cope with after the battle, as well as the many bodies which eventually washed up along the shore-line.

The tapestries were therefore of local as well as historical interest to Eliza. Having examined them carefully, she is said to have come to the view that they gave an accurate and valuable depiction of the battle because they contained so many sights that were familiar to her. These included a familiar stretch of coast, the square tower of St Edmund's Church in Southwold, the rough pier and black posts at the entrance to the river Blyth, and even the trees round Reydon Hall itself.

March 1844: Agnes and Eliza have special access in Westminster Abbey

Eliza and Agnes were busy collecting material for biographies still to be written, and noting information which might form additions and amendments if any past volumes were re-issued. Their network of contacts and the fame of their work allowed them to obtain access to historical places and materials not available to the population at large. When they visited Westminster Abbey they were shown all the royal tombs in the Abbey, not only those of the queens whose lives they were studying.

The fifteen tombs of royal queens included five Annes, three Elizabeths, two Katharines, one Eleanor and one Philippa. They are said to have varied widely with, at one extreme, a tomb bearing a bright effigy of a Spanish queen, and at the other extreme there was a dull chest tomb of a German queen decorated with a skull and cross-bones. Even the crypt of Henry VII's Chapel was opened for them, which was such a rare event that the vergers took the opportunity to look inside it as well.

3rd April 1844: Eliza and Agnes travel to France

Agnes and Eliza's research continued at break-neck speed and they were working on volume VIII before volume VII had been printed. They had reached the life of Mary Beatrice, wife of James II, who went into exile in France with her husband and died there. Although the sisters had found some information on the exiled queen when at Sizergh Castle, and had received some help by means of correspondence, they needed to search French archives and see French sites first-hand.

Neither of them had any experience of foreign travel, but they set about organising their itinerary, making good use of their established contacts. The main and initial contact in obtaining access to French Archives was Monsieur Guizot, who had helped them considerably in the past and was now French Foreign Minister. They also obtained letters of introduction from their English friends and acquaintances, such as Lady Braye and Lord Strangford, which were addressed to distinguished individuals in Paris.

The trip began on the 3rd April 1844. Eliza left her home in Bayswater with her maid Harriet, to meet Agnes at Waterloo Station where they caught a train to Southampton. At Southampton they were met by Sir John Eustace of Sandford Hall in Norfolk, who kindly took charge of them and their luggage.

Their first task was to find the steamer in which they had booked an over-night passage to Le Havre, and then to get their luggage safely on board. That done, they had a look round Southampton and dined with Sir John at the Dolphin Hotel. At half past eight that evening they boarded the steamer ready to depart. Sir John knew the captain of the steamer, the 'Lady Saumarez', and asked him to keep an eye on Agnes, Eliza and Harriet until they were safely installed in a hotel in Le Havre.

The overnight journey was uncomfortable. They had black sofas to lie on which Agnes described as "prickly as a gooseberry and narrower than my coffin will be." They were below decks and were kept awake, partly by the sound of men tramping about overhead but also, as Agnes wrote home, by "a pretty Norman baby called Paul, who disapproved of the discomforts he met with on board, and testified his displeasure by loud squalls during half the night."

At nine the next morning Agnes and Eliza were on deck and, Agnes "saw the cliffs of Havre stretched like a wall before us, and enjoyed the fresh air. At eleven we made the quay." Eliza also sent home an account of the voyage. The Ness of Havre and its cliffs looked to her very similar to the cliffs of Dunwich, near their home in Suffolk "and, like them, seemingly disposed to crumble into the sea." Agnes's impression of the port was that every building "seemed to wear an antique aspect, even to the hotels on the quay."

Arriving at Le Havre they had a number of formalities to go through. The first of these, Agnes found both amusing and pleasant: "a very smart Monsieur in a white and blue uniform placed his hand on his heart and chausseed in front of our seat and said 'Votre passeport Madame.' He was rather a picturesque figure, in a light-blue uniform, cocked hat and white feather, bearing a ludicrous resemblance to the portrait of Napoleon. He received our documents with an air of theatrical homage" which made them laugh and begin to enjoy their adventure.

This was followed by the customs official who was not so pleasant. While he examined their luggage, the ladies had to be checked in person for contraband. He led them to the 'Hotel de Londres' where a female customs officer took them into "a small glazed room like an inn parlour, but very shabby and dirty." Here she generally prodded and poked them about to see if they were carrying anything they should not. Agnes was for safety wearing under her dress a bag, which contained not only money and documents, but the precious letters of introduction.

The douaniere on feeling this bundle in Agnes's clothes: "pinched it a little and then said 'cette a rien' with a knowing look intended to convey a contradiction to her words. We offered her three francs for her civility, which she rejected with a look of horror until perceiving that we were about to take her at her word, she gave a suspicious look around the room, and extended her hand with a satisfied grin."

After this they went to the 'Bains de Frascati', a bath barracks where travellers could wash. Eliza wrote: "We felt a wish for a warm bath, our taste would have been for fresh, but a proper regard for health led us to order salt water baths." These cost two Francs each, plus the cost of attendance, cloths and soap. They thought this was expensive compared with similar facilities in Southwold, though Agnes said "it was the cleanest and prettiest establishment imaginable."

Feeling brighter and fresher, they went to get their baggage cleared through customs. Eliza had taken import duties into consideration in advance and "prudently settled her conscience with Louis Philippe" by wearing her new Shetland shawl, by lacing her feet into new boots, and by instructing her maid Harriet "to trot ashore" in a pair of her mistress's new shoes. Agnes and Harriet decided on a more honest route, so Agnes declared a piece of new flannel and Harriet a new flannel petticoat. The reward for their honesty was to have both items confiscated.

The Captain of the steamer, having finished his arrival duties, honoured his promise to Sir John Eustace by escorting them on a stroll round the town. Eliza described the town as having "little to see and a great deal to smell. Agnes, whose olfactory nerves were remarkably acute, was disgusted with the odour from the stagnant ditches, and displayed by sundry gestures her dislike to La Belle Promenade."

After a night in an hotel, Eliza and Agnes were up early next morning to get all their luggage stowed on board the boat that would take them up the Seine to Rouen, their next destination. Eliza wrote: "We had an excellent breakfast, and went on board the Seine steamer at nine, when all our plagues about customs being over, we began to think about Henry V's march and the route he took."

4th April 1844: Eliza and Agnes reach Rouen

On their journey along the Seine, Eliza and Agnes tried to pick out the places they knew from history. A priest overheard them and introduced himself, then pointed out some of the sights as they passed. By the time they reached Rouen soon after mid-day the priest, Abbe l'Angloise, had volunteered to be their guide in Rouen, and had recommended to them a suitable hotel, well placed near the main places of interest.

On arriving at Rouen they were harassed by another set of fierce-looking customs officials who, Eliza explained: "were not searching for contraband cottons and muslins, but for joints of meat, bottles of wine and other eatables and drinkables which are subject to the octroi, an ancient and very unpopular imposition upon natives as well as strangers."

They had arrived in Rouen on Good Friday 1844 and, Eliza wrote: "after an excellent lunch-dinner, consisting of stewed eels, half a fowl and a preserved grape tart" they met Abbe l'Anglois at Rouen's Notre Dame and attended a Tenebrae service, held on the days leading up to Easter. It involved the gradual extinguishing of the candles then a sudden loud noise in the total darkness near the end of the service. Eliza wrote "We entered and for the first time heard the Catholic service in one of the majestic temples reared by Catholic piety. We paid for chairs and witnessed this really imposing service. This gave me more pleasure than any opera or oratorio ever afforded me. The voices ringing through the ancient arches of Notre Dame was worth them all."

The Abbe had brought with him a lady who could speak some English, to help if interpretation was needed, and after the service they went to see the various tombs which were on Agnes and Eliza's list.

As it grew dark the Abbe insisted that they also visit the church of St Ouen which he said was finer than Notre Dame or Westminster Abbey. After having seen it, Eliza was inclined to agree with him: "the glorious view of the side aisles not being cut up in divisions with nave and choir. It was utterly unlike all we had seen in worship before." The Abbe and the interpreter then put Eliza and Agnes a little to shame. Eliza wrote: "Down knelt our Norman lady. Down knelt our Abbe and they continued to pray in the gloaming, while we stood and seemed somewhat heathenish by contrast. It reminded me of Southey 'It would not hurt thee George to join that evening prayer'."

April 1844: Agnes and Eliza reach Paris then St Germain

Next morning Agnes and Eliza travelled on to Paris and to a Pension, where a young friend from Suffolk lived. They attended at Notre Dame a service which included a procession round the ambulatory at the east end of the cathedral. Eliza and Agnes had not previously understood the purpose of this part of the building, English cathedrals tending to have pews and general bits and pieces filling up their east end. For their historical researches, Agnes was thinking of it as the building where Mary Stuart was married to Francis, eldest son of Henry II of France, whilst to Eliza it was the place where the proxy wedding of Henrietta Maria to Charles I of England took place.

On Easter Monday they travelled on to St Germain-en-Laye for the next phase of their studies, researching the lives of the Stuarts in exile. They arrived at Chatou, about a mile from their destination and needed transport for the remainder of the journey. In a letter home Agnes wrote: "a sturdy old man with a flat leather cap much the worse for wear, seized our carpet bags and trotted off with them at so brisk a pace that we had much ado to keep him in sight, nor did we come up with him till he had tossed our luggage up into a sort of go-cart of the rudest construction with a wooden canopy and ragged leather curtains, which he requested us to enter.

"We assured him that it did not suit us but as he had stowed away our bags, we, remembering the caution of an experienced traveller 'Whatever you do, never lose sight of your baggage' entered the vehicle." The driver kept reassuring them by saying "Bon, bon." Agnes wrote: "Our maid Harriet who was infinitely more disgusted than ourselves and did not understand French, said 'If the old man's buns are not better than this ramshackle old shay, they won't be worth eating'." This amused Agnes so much "that I never left off laughing as long as I remained" in the vehicle.

Agnes continued: "we formed the rear of a very extraordinary procession of holiday-keepers which crossed the magnificent bridge over the Seine, and wound slowly round the lofty hill crowned by the royal chateau of St Germains. The sun shone, everybody looked so full of holiday spirits, that I never enjoyed a drive more in my life" until, that is, a fierce customs officer demanded to see their passports and "instead of opening our bags, swore at our old man who, it seems, was addicted to smuggling in wine, brandy, legs of mutton and other excisable items without the formality of paying duty on them."

The sisters wanted to visit the Chateau which had been the residence of the court of Louis XIV until Versailles was built, and part of which was then given to the exiled James II and his court to occupy, but it was mainly being used as a military prison, and they were refused permission to enter. However, their second application was successful and they were shown round by a Commandant, wearing the Legion of Honour, who gave his arm to the celebrated English author, Agnes Strickland, thereby conveniently leaving Eliza free to make notes about the surroundings.

By the time they returned to Paris, Agnes and Eliza were receiving a great deal of attention, and received so many visits which they were expected to return, that they had little time left for their studies. Other than this social draw-back, everything was going well until Agnes began to pine for home. She disliked French food and French sanitation, and became ill with a fever and sore throat.

Agnes was to have been presented at the Tuileries and had ordered a very fashionable and expensive brown striped silk dress for the occasion, but was too ill to go. An English doctor was called in, and while Eliza and Harriet nursed Agnes back to health, some cheerful English schoolgirls at the Pension were delighted to escape compulsory French conversation classes by keeping Agnes company.

May 1844: Agnes and Eliza meet Monsieur Guizot

When Agnes was partly recovered, she and Eliza returned to Saint-Germain for Agnes to convalesce. Although this was an unwelcome delay to their plans, it gave them time for further exploration and to some extent catch up on their writing.

When Agnes was fully recovered, they returned to Paris and stayed with a Mme Colmache who was an educated lady with useful social and literary contacts. She acted as their interpreter and accompanied Eliza and Agnes on visits to ministries, archives and museums because, although Eliza and Agnes could read French easily, they could not hold a conversation in French.

Mme Colmarche was astonished that M Guizot, despite being a very eminent politician, found time to see her visitors. The meeting was a great excitement for Agnes who described M Guizot to her mother: "He is the most delightful and amiable person with beautiful eyes beaming with intelligence and kindness. He is about 55 years of age, rather below middle height, with a pale clear complexion, grand forehead, and small features but decidedly handsome. He speaks English beautifully, and has the sweetest voice in the world. I should lose my heart if I were to see much of him; but he is at this time overwhelmed with business and, I daresay, would be much happier as an author among his old chronicles than as a Minister of State."

M Guizot gave them letters of introduction to people in charge of the various state archives, and with the influence and help of this powerful statesman Agnes and Eliza were able to search, or have searched on their behalf, the well-organised Archives de Royaume de France and the Archives des Affaires Etrangeres. To speed up the process, they employed two transcribers to produce for them full copies of selected documents.

Agnes recovered from her home-sickness as well as her illness, but never grew to like French food, sanitation, brick floors and beds in alcoves. Eliza grew to detest France and wanted no delay over their return to England. As far as society in Paris went, Agnes told her mother: "All the English in Paris make much of us – who, by the by, congregate together like a flock of sheep. As for the French society, I know little of that."

Although Agnes had no qualms about mixing with all layers of society, she was timid in matters of personal safety, and was terrified by the traffic in Paris. Crossing the road was so nerve-wracking for her that she took a fiacre, the horse-drawn equivalent of a taxi, for even short journeys. She once allowed herself to be persuaded by an English friend to go on foot to a particularly beautiful church, but was nearly paralysed with fear on the walk home, and vowed never to go out on foot again.

Eliza went to public entertainments and on sight-seeing trips with Agnes, but rarely accompanied her to social events. Instead she attended a few seances which were all the rage in London, and were even more so in Paris. Eliza was not sure whether or not to believe the Paris seances but when she got back to London, she allowed herself to be put into a trance by a medium, and from that time on was no longer sceptical.

By the end of the three months which they had allotted for the trip, Agnes and Eliza had a great deal of material for their future biographies and knew their visit had been well worthwhile, but they were both pleased when the time came for Harriet to pack their bags ready for the journey home.

Part 3: Return to Lancashire and difficulties

A return to Lancashire; a financial disaster; running aground; end of a smooth patch

Mid-June 1844: Tom meets his youngest son

Tom spent five days at St Helena and then on 26th March 1844 he continued his voyage home. He arrived at Gravesend on 10th June 1844 and by 14th June the 'Diana' had been cleared by the Custom House and unloaded.

Tom Strickland, having been away for more than a year and a half, was back in London in time to meet his newest son, only a couple of weeks before his first birthday.

25th June 1844: Sarah meets the Bishop of Chester

Richard Gwillym's sister, Henrietta left Ulverston soon after her brother's marriage, and in so doing passed on to Sarah the domestic duties of running a substantial household plus the parochial duties of a vicar's wife. Sarah left little record of her life as Mrs Gwillym, but items which appeared in the local newspapers give an indication of what it entailed.

Her new home, Stockbridge House is now a Grade II listed building set in extensive grounds. Recent pictures of it show a flat-fronted detached house, built of grey stone with a slate roof, and symmetrical on each side of the front door. Built on two floors with eight bedrooms, it was only a few years old when Richard first arrived.

At the end of June 1844 Richard's bishop, the Bishop of Chester visited the area. There were many places that he could have chosen to stay, but it was Richard and Sarah who accommodated him and his entourage, giving Sarah an early test of her capabilities as a hostess.

The newspapers reported: "On Tuesday evening (25th June 1844) the Right Rev the Bishop of Chester, with Chancellor Raikes, arrived on his triennial visit to Ulverstone. On Wednesday morning he performed the rite of confirmation in the parish church, Ulverston, to nearly 200 young people, in the presence of a numerous congregation. The prayers were read by the Rev Richard Gwillym, vicar of the church. In the afternoon his lordship proceeded to Dalton to perform the rite of confirmation in the parish church and in the evening he returned to Ulverston. On the following day, he delivered his charge to the clergy of the district in the parish church."

The Bishop of Chester at this time was John Bird Sumner. He had held the Bishopric since 1829 and would become Archbishop of Canterbury in 1848. He was also a prolific author, producing over 40 books during his lifetime. His Chancellor, Henry Raikes, was a philanthropist and an antiquarian, and nephew of the founder of the Sunday School Movement. Both these men had been educated at Eton and Cambridge and had been close friends since their university days.

When he became Bishop of Chester, John Sumner appointed Henry Raikes to the post of Chancellor which meant that Chancellor Raikes was Bishop Sumner's right hand man. Together they had recently founded the University of Chester as a teacher-training establishment, the first such institution to be set up. The other four founders were all notable figures, and included two future prime ministers in the persons of Lord Stanley (who became the Earl of Derby and prime minister three times) and William Gladstone (already a privy councillor in 1844 and prime minister four times during his long lifetime).

Having such men as guests for two nights must have been quite daunting for Sarah, only four months into her marriage, but the visit was also more than a trivial task for the Bishop. 'Delivering his Charge' of 1844 involved giving a speech which, when printed, ran to 44 pages plus explanatory appendices. It gave his view of the progress being made in strategic matters in his diocese, and pointed out the areas where he wanted his clergy to concentrate effort. It also covered some liturgical points which were controversial at the time. It provided guide-lines for Richard and his fellow clergy to follow for the next three years.

The Church of England by 1844 was distinctly different from the Anglican Church of Sarah's childhood in Suffolk. As Catharine wrote in her memoirs, the hunting and riding clergy of the Georgian period had given way in Queen Victoria's reign to a more worthy set of men.

The Bishopric of Chester included much of north-west England with towns that had grown up in the industrial revolution. The population had grown substantially and quickly, and Bishop Sumner reported that 196 new churches had been built since his arrival fifteen years previously; that 100 more curates were being employed, and that 50 new parishes were being endowed. His aim was to limit the maximum population size per parish to 3,000 people.

He reported that only between three and six per cent of the population had received any school education and then only for an average of 2 years. The Sunday School Movement had helped, but attendance at school for one day a week, where the teachers were untrained, and on a day which should also contain leisure and religious observance, had been a start but much more was needed. National Schools had been set up by the Church of England and at first encountered doubt and antagonism, but parents were realising that their children benefited from attending school, and the demand for places was growing.

Bishop Sumner commented on the existence of Dissenting Churches. He acknowledged that they had good cause to come into existence when the Church of England was failing in its duty, but that his Clergy should aim to render Dissenting Churches unnecessary, and so to combat their expansion.

He also referred to the great difference between the wealthy and the impoverished in the country, and expressed his view that those with wealth and leisure had the duty to use both these God-given gifts to help those less fortunate than themselves. Judging by Richard's subsequent activities in his parish, he accepted the Bishop's

Charge of 1844 and, with Sarah's support, did his best to follow its guidelines.

25th June 1844: Susanna loses another son

On the same day that Sarah was dealing with the visit of the Bishop of Chester, Susanna was experiencing the tragic loss of her son John. The local paper dated Tuesday 2nd July 1844 reported what happened. It said: "Melancholy Accident – On the afternoon of Tuesday last, John Strickland Moodie, aged about six years, third son of our respected and esteemed Sheriff, was found drowned, near the wharf of Billa Flint, Esq. The poor little fellow was fishing, and it is supposed, in his eagerness to secure a prize, which he had caught (since found on his line) the accident occurred. He was a fine, sprightly boy, and his sudden death has plunged the family into the deepest affliction, and with them, the public, we doubt not, sincerely sympathise."

This was the child who had briefly gone missing when their house caught fire four years earlier, after which Susanna had described the agony she had endured until the child was found.

26th July 1844: Catharine's next child is born

Catharine was very familiar with child-birth, not only through her own experiences but also in her role as an unofficial midwife for her neighbours. She herself had another child in 1844 when William Edward Traill was born on 26th July, bringing her family to three sons and three surviving daughters.

August 1844: Sarah is entertained and entertains

Someone who was an important member of Ulverston life, and a friend of Richard Gwillym, was Mr Daniel. He was generally at the centre of any musical activity in the town and was organist at Richard's church of St Mary.

Ulverston Choral Society had been formed in 1843 and gave its first concert on 15th August 1844. The concert was held in the upper room of the Ulverston National School and Mr Daniel accompanied the choir on a grand piano.

The papers noted that at the end of the performance: "the Rev Richard Gwillym MA, one of the vice-presidents of the society, rose to thank members" and to encourage them to give another concert in the near future. The audience was "numerous and highly respectable" and no doubt included Sarah because "the society ranks among its patrons, several of the leading gentry and clergy of the town and neighbourhood."

A social event was held at Stockbridge House less than a fortnight later, on the evening of Tuesday 27th August 1844 which would have involved Sarah and her housekeeper in considerable work. The papers noted: "The Rev Richard Gwillym gave his annual entertainment to the singers of the church and the children taught at the National School. A considerable number of the gentleman's friends were present, and the evening was spent very pleasantly and harmoniously."

August 1844: Tom takes command of the 'Scotia'

Almost before Tom had arrived home, advertisements for the next voyage of the 'Diana' were appearing in the press. Captain Thomas Strickland was named as the Commander, and the destination was to be Bombay (Mumbai). After some delay and changes, the last shipping date was eventually fixed for 20th August 1844 and the destination was changed to Madras (Chennai).

However, Tom's career was on an upward trajectory and during the few months when he was in London in 1844, he took command of a larger vessel. The 'Diana' had been a ship of 600 tons, but his next ship, the 'Scotia' weighed 778 tons. His change of command lengthened Tom's stay in London, but only by a few days.

Advertising for the 'Scotia' declared it to be a "splendid passenger ship lying in the East India Docks under engagement to the Honourable East India Company." The ship was about to leave for "Madras and Calcutta, will embark passengers at Portsmouth and will carry a surgeon". It carried freight as well as passengers and it was scheduled "to sail from Gravesend 31st August, last shipping day 26th August 1844."

Tom, having arrived home in mid-June, had two months to finish his duties with his old ship, find his new command on the 'Scotia', and familiarise himself with it before embarking on another long and dangerous voyage.

1844: Agnes has a new home-from-home in London

By 1844 Agnes had found, at the home of the Mackinnon family in Hyde Park Place, somewhere in London where she could stay whenever she wanted. Alexander Mackinnon had been Member of Parliament for Dunwich in the neighbourhood of Southwold and Reydon. When the seat was abolished, Dunwich having all but disappeared due to coastal erosion, he became MP for Lymington.

Mr Mackinnon was involved with the RSPCA (Royal Society for the Prevention of Cruelty to Animals) which was founded in 1824 and gained its Royal status in 1840. Together with another MP, he was responsible for the 'cruelty to animals act of 1835' which made public baiting and fighting of animals illegal. As well as being an MP and a Quaker (member of the Society of Friends), he was also an active member of the Royal Society and of the Society of Antiquities. His wife, mother of his three sons and three daughters, had died in 1835.

He and Agnes had met when he had been a Suffolk MP, but their continuing friendship was based on his literary and antiquarian interests. He was a naturally sociable man, and his home became something of a meeting place for high-ranking political exiles. Among the people Agnes met at Mr Mackinnon's home were King Charles X of France, and the ex-Kings of Spain and Portugal.

Agnes formed friendships easily, and whilst the people she contacted or was introduced to were of use to her research, they were also the kind of people whose company she enjoyed, and these friendships often lasted for many years. Her friends were of all ages and both sexes. Emma Mackinnon (born in 1811) was as much Agnes's friend as was her father, Alexander Mackinnon. Similarly, Philip Howard was as much a friend as his father, Henry Howard.

In addition to Agnes's friendliness, her celebrity status opened to her the doors of some of the most exclusive houses in Britain, including the homes of the Duke of Devonshire. The Duke had sent Agnes and Eliza a letter from his family archives about the first Court held by King William and Queen Mary. He subsequently invited them (in Jane's words): "to visit him at his villa at Chiswick, and examine some archives that might be useful to them.

"The Duke came from Brighton to receive them, and opened his stores for their examination. He gave them a delicate French dinner; but he dispensed with the attendance of his servants in the dining-room, summoning them when requisite by striking upon a tumbler. Notwithstanding his deafness they found him a pleasant companion – amiable, manly, and unassuming, though surrounded with splendour on every side."

The Duke maybe wanted to satisfy himself that Agnes and her sister were honest and trustworthy before he gave them any further access to his treasures. He must have been reassured by meeting them because, as Jane continued: "He invited them to visit Chatsworth and Hardwicke, to examine his family archives, and gave them tickets for these remarkable places, assuring them that his housekeepers should pay them every attention. He gave them an order to see Devonshire House, of which they were delighted to avail themselves."

Agnes's meetings with famous people often seemed to be a two-way pleasure. When the Duke of Wellington was presented to Agnes at a grand party, it is said that he shook hands with her warmly and thanked his hostess, Emma Mackinnon, for having introduced him to such a celebrated lady. Agnes described this evening, at a party with 800 guests, as one of almost perfect happiness. The party did not end until four o'clock in the morning, but that did not prevent Agnes, aged 48, from maintaining her normal routine and starting work at the British Museum before ten o'clock the same morning.

Agnes's London routine consisted of beginning work immediately after breakfast, either in the Reading Room at the British Museum, or at Eliza's study at Avenue Lodge in Bayswater. After a full morning's work, she had a rest in the afternoon and by tea-time was ready for her social life to begin. Her appearance at the British Museum after that particular party was partly due to habit, but was also because Henry Colburn was urging Agnes and Eliza to finish the next volume of 'Lives of the Queens of England'.

September 1844: Tom is 'spoken to'

Tom Strickland having set sail from London on 30th August 1844 must have sailed through bad weather, because on 22nd September 1844 the newspaper 'Lloyd's List' felt it necessary to report that the 'Scotia' had been spoken to at Lat 16N Long 25W. This is about two hundred miles to the west of Gambia, off the far west point of Africa. The phrase 'spoken to' gave reassurance that Tom and his vessel had not been lost or seriously damaged, and were proceeding safely on their way.

November 1844: Catharine is working hard

Catharine and Thomas had settled into their new home at Ashburnham but it was somewhat isolated. When Catharine wrote to her friend Frances Stewart in November 1844 she said: "There is no privation I feel more than not having the means of going to church – I regret this for my little ones as well as for myself. When the roads are well packed with snow and hard the elder children may be able to attend church – but I doubt even for Kate the walk will prove too far – for myself I fear I should hardly accomplish it on foot." Kate was 8 years old. A neighbour had offered occasional help: "Mr Best has a horse now – and he very kindly offered me the loan of him in sleighing time occasionally which offer I gladly accepted."

There was some illness in the family, both with three year old daughter Mary and with Catharine herself. Mary was having trouble with her eyes and her ears, which had to be syringed daily. Catharine thought that cutting teeth had caused more problems than usual and said: "yet the dear child is fat and florid – but the wilfulness and perverseness of her temper is dreadful. I am at times in despair how to manage her."

Catharine's own trouble was with her eyes: "I find it is more painful by candle-light than in the day time – this hinders me from getting on with my work though I am obliged to sit very late, seldom am I in bed before one and even later – and this I dare say also affects my eyes."

19th December 1844: Tom reaches Madras

Tom and the 'Scotia' having been spoken to in September 1844 were not mentioned again until it was reported that they had arrived in Madras on 19th December 1844.

February 1845: John Moodie despairs of politics

John Moodie had already discovered that expressing his political views had caused him difficulty with the majority of the population of Belleville who were Tories, but he became completely disillusioned with politics when he found that local people who agreed with his politics were indifferent to his plight. When he wrote to Robert Baldwin in February 1845 he said that some of them were even, as he put it: "eagerly watching an opportunity to supplant me" in his office as Sheriff.

The main purpose of John's letter was to explain that he was abstaining from politics to such as extent that he did not even vote, in an "endeavour at last to take some care of myself. At the age of nearly 50 with a large family entirely dependent on this paltry office I hold for bread, and unable to clothe them as well as respectable mechanics do – I think you can hardly blame me."

Susanna and John had five surviving children, ranging in age from thirteen year old Catharine down to eighteen month old Robert Baldwin. It was not until he wrote this letter that John Moodie told Robert Baldwin his youngest son had been named after him because, John wrote: "I would not tell you while you were in office."

April 1845: Financial disaster hits Thomas and Catharine

In March 1845, Catharine replied to a letter from her new brother-in-law, Richard Gwillym and described how fishing differed in Canada from in England. Catharine said there was no need for subtlety in Canada because "with ease the silly fish are caught, but this is well, where they form an article of subsistence, not luxury."

Richard had praised Catharine's book 'Backwoods of Canada' and Catharine thanked him adding "my work was not written with the design of inducing anyone to leave their own fair homes in Britain to seek a wooden hut in Canada, rather to cheer and advise such as were compelled to emigrate to make the best of a bad bargain." She told him that misfortune meant that she and Thomas had become less prosperous and hopeful than when she wrote her book, but that the country as a whole was prospering and she hoped that is due course her children would do likewise.

Catharine's interest in, and study of botany and wild life was already well established. She told Richard: "I often wish I had time to arrange into proper form a mass of material that I have collected on various subjects connected with this province, especially as regards to its natural productions both vegetable and animal, but I fear I must now wait till my Kate grows up to take a part of the household duties off my hands but then I shall have grown old and dull and unfit for literary labours."

Soon after this letter was written, a Scottish friend of Thomas, George Hay MacDougall drowned. He had taken out a loan to build a mill on the Otonabee River and Thomas Traill had guaranteed the loan. Catharine later in life wrote the following note to explain the family's financial problems: "My dear husband was by nature, open generous and not anticipating the trials that afterwards befell us, he gave his name to the notes of a friend, a fellow countryman and a man of high connections among the nobles of Scotland, but a person of small means. The notes were coming due and the amount was large when sudden death seized upon the gentleman for whom my husband had endorsed.

"There were no assets to meet the notes and of course the creditors came upon the endorser. To add to his loss, my husband had made purchase of a cleared – or partly cleared farm, on which he paid a portion of the purchase money. This was seized and sold to meet the debts and we found ourselves deprived of all that had been acquired during the years of outlay and labour since we emigrated to Canada. Thus with an increasing family we found ourselves poorer than when we began life in the backwoods. Still, we had the yearly income of a Lieutenant's half pay, but it was insufficient to meet our daily needs."

Catharine and Thomas were in desperate circumstances and during the winter months the family was confined to the house because of lack of outdoor clothing. As they also lacked firewood to heat their home properly, the result was general ill health. They survived on gifts of food and small amounts of money from various friends and relations.

Her daughter Annie wrote later "in all these years my Mother had not very good health, but she was always able to get servants, and generally good ones, from among the settlers' families, and then $3 a month was all they asked. I remember many of her old servants coming back to see her at different times, and saying how good she had been to them."

1845: Agnes entertains with her paper cutting

At about this time Queen Victoria held a fancy dress ball, and Agnes was asked for advice about some of the costumes to be worn. Lady Katharine Jermyn dressed as Berengaria, the queen of Richard Coeur de Lion. Her husband, Lord Jermyn, the treasurer of her Majesty's household, dressed in the style of Edward III. Agnes was invited, together with other notable people, to the Earl of Bristol's house in St James's Square, to see Lord and Lady Jermyn in their costumes.

Lord Jermyn, Agnes wrote: "wore a tight cote hardi of crimson velvet, embroidered with gold, and trousers of different colours – one being red, the other blue – a crimson velvet hood, and gold checkered boots, which he complained pinched him. His throat was bare, his hair curled down each side of his face; he had on his head a red and blue beret cap. And he seemed greatly annoyed with his finery." His annoyance probably wasn't helped by his reception. Agnes wrote in a letter to Sarah: "When he came forth ... the children laughed so immoderately that I unluckily caught the infection, and laughed as much as they did, instead of making a solemn curtsey when he was presented to me.

"When he was gone we finished our tea, and spent a most delightful evening. How you would have doted on Lady Georgina's sweet little girl, a lamb only three years old, but so engaging and well-behaved! I made a paper boat for her, and cut her out some sailors, which the ladies considered a wonderful performance."

1845: Eliza is 5' 8" tall; Jane is taller

When Agnes and Eliza were in France, Eliza went to the Observatoire where she encountered a dog named Dragon which she described as "an immense animal spotted like a Danish one, but as tall as a donkey. As it was the canine law in Paris that all dogs should be muzzled, Dragon had a little basket attached to his neck, which did not, of course, cover his mouth. This noble creature took a great fancy to me, rubbing his head against my shoulder, which his height permitted him to do without any inconvenience to himself or me, and I am a stately five feet eight, though my shoulders are low."

Agnes, in describing Lady Katharine Jermyn in her Berengaria outfit in 1845, said to Sarah: "Lady Katharine is very tall – taller than our sister Jane." The clear implication is that Jane was the tallest of the sisters and therefore must have been noticeably taller than Eliza. That being the case, Jane would have been something like five feet ten inches in height.

As there are no known pictures in existence of Jane Margaret Strickland, it seems worth adding at this point the two other pieces of information mentioned about her appearance. Catharine described herself and Jane as fair, compared with Agnes being dark, when the three sisters were on the beach at Southwold waiting for the steamer which would take Catharine away to Canada in 1832. An obituary, in due course (June 1888), will reveal that Jane had blue eyes, which must have been unusually attractive to have been mentioned in such a context.

Finally, Jane had been a very attractive child and therefore was presumably an attractive adult. Catharine in writing her memoirs had recorded this fact when she described how, as children, they had enjoyed May Day when they lived at Bungay. Catharine wrote: "Our greatest most longed for holiday was May day – early in the morning we were all up and lively, the maids and my sisters seeking for blossoms on the hedgerows for the first May flowers and begging others from the gardeners with which to make the May Queens' Crown and Sceptre and I was the happy chosen Queen – and year after year was chosen to wear the floral crown – I do not know why it was conferred on me instead of Jane, who was older and a very beautiful child she was – I fancy my historical name of Katharine had something to do with the choice – After leaving the banks of the

Waveney we never kept this holiday again, a change had taken place – and Reydon Hall was not Stowe House – there were no flowers like those of the meadow on its banks – the sea breezes were not so soft and sweet ..." Jane was two years older than Catharine, who was nearing her seventh birthday when the Strickland family moved from Bungay to Reydon.

25th June 1845: Susanna remembers her son

On 25th June 1845, the first anniversary of her son John's death, Susanna wrote a poem to commemorate him. The poem appeared in full in Susanna's later work 'Life In the Clearings'. Two of its central verses show the sorrow which Susanna still felt for the loss of this son:

> Long weary months have pass'd since that sad day,
>   But naught beguiles my bosom of its sorrow;
> Since the cold waters took thee for their prey,
>   No smiling hope looks forward to the morrow –
>   My boy – my boy!

> The voice of mirth is silenced in my heart,
>   Thou wert so dearly loved – so fondly cherish'd;
> I cannot yet believe that we must part, -
>   That all, save thine immortal soul, has perish'd –
>   My boy! – my boy!

11th July 1845: Sarah hosts a children's tea party

Before his marriage Richard Gwillym had given entertainments to his parishioners but in such a way that they received very little mention in the papers. After his marriage they began to escalate and become newsworthy.

In July 1845, local papers reported an event of unspecified size, but which involved Sarah ensuring the catering was adequate, and having large numbers of children running loose in the garden. The papers said: "On Friday 11th July, the Rev R Gwillym MA, of the Parish Church, Ulverston, gave a treat to the children taught at the

National School. They assembled at the reverend gentleman's house, at Stockbridge, in the afternoon, where they were provided with tea and cake by Mrs Gwillym, who at all times has manifested a spirit of kindness to the little children. After partaking of tea, they were allowed to play on the green, where they enjoyed themselves until evening, when they had supper served up to them, and then departed to their respective homes, highly gratified with the entertainment.

"In the evening, the rev gentleman entertained the singers of the Parish Church, and others, as usual, who spent the evening in a very agreeable manner. The health of Mr and Mrs Gwillym were drunk, and heartily responded to by the company."

July 1845: Agnes dances a reel

In 1845, Agnes's visits to country houses began in Scotland at Craufurdland Castle in Ayrshire where her friend Elizabeth Constance Howison Craufurd married James Ogilvy Fairlie on 22nd July. Miss Craufurd's father was the hereditary cup-bearer of the kings of Scotland and the wedding was suitably grand. There were two wedding services to reflect the different religions of the bride and groom. The first service, the Church of Scotland (Presbyterian), was the bride's church and took place in the drawing-room. The second service, with an Episcopalian minister for the Church of England, Mr Fairlee's religion, took place in the Library. The laws in England which specified that marriages could only be conducted in an Anglican church, and must be performed before mid-day, obviously did not apply in Scotland.

Agnes must have been a close family friend because she helped prepare the rooms for the services. She told Jane that at the weddings she wore a "blue satin dress with white lace robings." A dinner in the banqueting hall followed the services and the newly married couple set off on their honeymoon in the evening. The day was concluded with a ball held in the great barn, suitably decorated and lighted, for the tenants and servants and at which all the wedding guests were expected to dance.

Agnes described her partner as "an old man who insisted I should dance a reel with him, giving me an encouraging pat on the shoulder and telling me I 'was a bonnie lassie, and should do as well as any o' them.' My partner was so elated with having got me, that he chose to turn the reel into a polka by turning me round and round until I was out of breath laughing."

16th September 1845: Tom has a complicated itinerary

Having arrived at Madras on 19th December 1844, Tom spent much of 1845 on supplementary voyages in command of the 'Scotia' and far from home. From Madras and Bombay there were trips to Aden, to Singapore and to Hong Kong.

These voyages completed, Tom in command of the 'Scotia' set off homewards from Hong Kong on 16th September 1845.

1845: Sam's family and business interests continue to grow

Sam's life had been proceeding busily and peacefully during the 1840s. His family was large with a new baby arriving every year or two; his farm and business life were prospering, and his role in the local community was well established.

His son Roland Clement Strickland had been born in 1844, and in 1845 Sam and Mary Strickland had their eleventh child. This was their eighth son, was named Richard Strickland and Sarah was his godmother.

When writing in 1852, Sam explained the genesis of some of his business interests around Lakefield. First he detailed the location of his own farm: "At the foot of the lake" which Sam said was "called by the Indians Kawchewahnoonk" and "just where the Nine Mile rapids commence, my farm is situated."

He then wrote, referring to 1845: "Seven years ago, immediately below my farm, my brother-in-law and myself" and here he must be referring to a brother of his wife "constructed a dam across the Otonabee river, opposite the village of Lakefield. We built it on a new principle, and were our own engineers. The work has stood the spring-floods well, although the river is subject to a perpendicular rise of six feet. A few yards below the dam, we erected a saw-mill, which is in full operation, and is calculated to cut logs from one foot to four in diameter, and up to twenty-six feet in length."

September 1845: Another volume of 'Lives of the Queens of England' is published

Volume VIII of 'Lives of the Queens of England' was published in September 1845. It contained the lives of Henrietta Maria (wife of Charles I) written by Eliza, and Catharine of Braganza (wife of Charles II) written by Agnes.

26th December 1845: Richard Gwillym holds a Christmas party

The second social event of 1845 to be held at Stockbridge House was much as it had been in previous years, and was reported as such in the local paper: "On Friday 26th December 1845, the Rev R Gwillym MA vicar of the Parish Church, Ulverston, gave his annual entertainment to a select party of friends in Ulverston and to the singers in the Parish Church. The evening was spent in a very harmonious manner."

24th February 1846: Tom returns home

Captain Thomas Strickland in command of the 'Scotia' rounded the Cape of Good Hope in time to reach St Helena on Christmas Day 1845. He completed his voyage and arrived back at Gravesend on 24th February 1846 having been away from home for eighteen months.

March 1846: Thomas Traill is suffering from depression

Catharine's situation was still in a poor way when she wrote to Susanna in March 1846. Her eldest son James, aged thirteen, was attending the Colbourne District Grammar School in Peterborough, but her daughters were receiving little education. Catharine wrote: "Much of their precious time is spent in household drudgery – and little has been done for them since we came here owing to illness, depression of spirits and work."

She was expecting a visit from Dr Lister, a kind and skilled local doctor. "I fear Dr Lister if he comes in will think but little of me and my poor bairns. Our house is uncarpeted and shabby, nay hardly clean, for I have been suffering from weakness in my back which prevents me from stooping, and my best help Kate has a severe unhealed burn on her hand and elbow which baffles all my skill and that of others." The children's clothes were a problem: "We can barely keep them decent – hardly that – and as to diet they fare hardly and often scantily."

Catharine had continued her efforts to earn money from her writing. She was in the process of sending some of her work to John Lovell, editor of the 'Literary Garland' to which Susanna was a regular contributor. Catharine told Susanna that she had: "a great mind to ask £5 for what I have sent, as at present the money would be most essential in helping to pay for a yoke of oxen or paying off small annoying debts that we cannot leave unsettled. The harassing state of uncertainty in which we are kept about our future plans is preying dreadfully on Traill's mind, nor can I rouse him from it."

March and April 1846: The evils of drink are illustrated in Ulverston

Sarah and Richard might have been amused by the coincidence of two events which took place in the spring of 1846. On Monday 10th March, Richard chaired a teetotal meeting where: "Mr G Noscoe addressed a crowded audience in the Theatre, Ulverston, on the benefits of total abstinence" at the conclusion of which "several persons took the pledge."

A month later, on 14th April 1846 at Ulverston Petty Session: "Charles Walkingshaw, of Ulverston, brush-maker, was charged with having stolen a large hand bell, from the premises of Rev R Gwillym." The papers reported that: "Walkingshaw was at the time he committed the offence, very drunk. This circumstance, coupled with the very good character given him by his master Mr Taylor, the magistrate was of the opinion the bell was not taken with a felonious intent. At the same time telling the prisoner 'larks' were very dangerous, he fined Walkingshaw 5s with costs for being drunk."

April 1846: Catharine and Thomas are offered 'Wolf Tower'

Catharine and Thomas's circumstances improved in April 1846 when they were offered a home rent-free for a year. It was an unusual property on the south shore of Rice Lake which required them to move about 30 miles southwards. The house had a wooden tower which Catharine is said to have named 'Wolf Tower' when they visited the owner, the Rev GW Bridges, in 1838. He was an Anglican clergyman who had come to Canada from Jamaica, but after a few years he returned to England, his homeland in 1841.

The offer of Wolf Tower brought Thomas out of his depression, and in early April 1846 he set off with 8 year old Harry to their new home. They went by wagon, with supplies for themselves and tools for the spring planting. The adjoining lot had recently been purchased by George Lee, 26 years old and Oxford educated.

Catharine wrote to Susanna: "Traill has got possession of the old grey tower and left me this day week in high spirits for Traill, with brave Hal seated beside him full of boyish glee." They had taken with them "the bedding with axe, hoe, rake & spade. All this was well and he was going too not as a hermit but to a house of plenty. Our nearest neighbour is a young Oxonian with full purse and free heart, and he gave Traill and Hal a warm invitation to stay with him until we join him which will now be soon for the 'Forester' is making a few small trips for trial on our little lake previous to the regular voyage down." The 'Forester' was a paddle-steamer.

Catharine continued: "Traill is to get his nine acres of wheat sown and the garden prepared for seeds and then come for us. Mr Lee who has no land ready wants to go shares with us for spring crops and as he has horses and seed and we have none, and can hardly manage to get them this year, we think a good arrangement may be made."

April 1846: Sarah loses her godson

Sam's son Richard Strickland had only a short life, as Catharine told Susanna in a letter written in April 1846: "You will be sorry to learn that Sam and Mary have lost their youngest, little Richard,

Sarah's godson a fine lively boy of fifteen months – measles or scarlet fever, but it is not known which, she is ill and Sam much distressed."

28th April 1846: Tom sets off for Bermuda

Tom's second voyage in command of the 'Scotia' was relatively straightforward. He had two months at home after his return from the Far East, and then set off to Bermuda on 28th April 1846 with the prospect of a simple out-and-return voyage.

May 1846: Catharine arrives at 'Wolf Tower'

While Thomas was preparing 'Wolf Tower', a letter arrived with the news that Thomas's father, the Rev Walter Traill had died. In theory he left everything to his widow, but as he died insolvent, his creditors had seized what they could to repay debts. Catharine told Susanna: "The creditors mean to apply to Traill to give up his right to some annuity which falls to him."

The letter had been written by the Rev Traill's curate and Catharine wrote: "Now the curate pleads in behalf of the destitute widow so movingly – I think it will be prudent first to ascertain what the sum is." The widow was presumably step-mother rather than mother to Thomas Traill and has not been mentioned elsewhere.

The news had not yet reached Thomas, as Catharine had read the letter in his absence. Catharine thought Thomas would take nothing "if it reduces her to distress, nor do I think he ought." Nevertheless Catharine, rather wistfully, hoped to gain a little "even £10 per ann. with the farm and what I have from dear Sarah would be a help and enable us to live comfortably – if we could but buy a milking cow and a horse we should not want." This is the first mention that Sarah was sending money to Catharine and, judging by these words used by Catharine, money was being sent on a regular basis.

In Thomas's absence, Catharine and her children had been living on a poor diet. She told Susanna: "bread, a few potatoes, given to us by dear good Mr Stewart, and a few small fishes from day to day and week to week have been our fare – baby and I have grown so thin – I have a few small hams but these we reserve for the 'Tower' as James and his father will need meat to work upon. We were afraid of our supplies of flour being cut off but good Mr Stewart sent us nearly a barrel and Nicholls is really most kind. This very day he came across and lent me five dollars for fear I should be distressed during T's absence and not like to ask for it."

In May 1846 'Wolf Tower' was ready to receive Catharine and the rest of the children. Catharine regretted moving further away from her friends in Peterborough and Sam's family in Lakefield, but she was hopeful that the life of her family was about to improve.

1846: EH Baily sculpts Agnes and remembers Sarah

Agnes sat on two occasions to the sculptor Edward Hodges Baily (sometimes misspelled as Bailey). EH Baily RA FRS (1788-1867) is most famous for being the sculptor of the statue of Admiral Lord Nelson which stands on top of Nelson's Column in Trafalgar Square. Among the many other and illustrious people he sculpted were Lord Byron, Sir Robert Peel, George Stephenson and Michael Faraday.

He was unfortunate in being declared bankrupt on two occasions, firstly in 1831 and again in 1838. The first bankruptcy was partly caused by delayed payment for work done for Buckingham Palace, and questions were asked in Parliament on his behalf. In the 1830s he asked for, and received financial help from the Royal Academy. They again helped him in the 1860s when he was awarded a pension of £200 per annum as an honorary retired Royal Academician.

His first bust of Agnes was not finished due to bankruptcy or, to use Jane's words: "circumstances occurring to the great sculptor had prevented him from finishing" it. When Agnes visited his studio in the mid 1840's, it was located in Newman Street where Thomas Cheesman had lived many years previously.

Agnes wrote to Sarah: "the moment Bailey saw me he said 'I hope you will come and sit to me. We were very unfortunate in losing that bust, but I will make something better of you now.' I am to sit to him this morning, though nothing can restore to my person the long years gone by when I was in my prime." Agnes was 50 years old.

Jane's comment on the bust when finished was: "Bailey made a fine bust and excellent likeness of Agnes Strickland which was duly exhibited the following year." However, Jane may have misremembered, or been referring to an exhibition other than that of the Royal Academy as no record has been found of the bust having been exhibited there at this time.

The sculptor also remembered Sarah, as Agnes reported in her letter: "He asked 'How is your pretty sister Miss Sarah Strickland?' I told him you were quite well, and very happily married. Replied he 'What a beautiful creature she was! I had a great wish to model her, only I was too busy at the time'."

30th June 1846: Richard and Sarah make sure the children enjoy their annual treat

On 30th June 1846, Richard was taking note of his bishop's charge to his clergy and was ensuring the local school was being run properly. Local papers reported: "The children taught at the Ulverston National School were examined (previous to the midsummer holidays) by the Rev R Gwillym MA Vicar of the Parish Church, in the presence of a number of patrons and supporters of the institution. The children were examined as to their proficiency in reading, geography, arithmetic &c and shewed that they were well grounded in their studies. The rev gentleman expressed himself highly pleased, and complimented Mr and Mrs Daniels on the satisfactory manner in which they had conducted the school and on the proficiency of the pupils."

Having gone through the task of their examination, the same children were given their annual treat which was held in a slightly more elaborate style than in the previous year. The papers recorded: "The Rev R Gwillym, Ulverston, gave his annual entertainment on Tuesday evening, 30th June 1846 to the children of the National School, and the singers of the parish church &c and a number of friends in Ulverston. The children were regaled with tea, and the smile of joy depicted on their young countenances and gratitude was expressed on every lip to Mr and Mrs Gwillym, who take great interest in the welfare of the children.

"The treat was given in the grounds adjoining the mansion of the rev gentleman. The children sang in excellent style, and Mr Thomas Salmon senior, added much to the hilarity of the evening by his comic songs &c. The children danced on the green till eight o'clock and then retired, after which the friends of the rev gentleman spent the remainder of the evening in the pleasantest harmony."

July and August 1846: Tom returns from Bermuda and sails for Bombay

Tom's return voyage to Bermuda took two and a half months and on 14th July 1846 the 'Scotia' was recorded as back in London Docks, but preparations were soon in hand for his next voyage, which was to be to another long voyage to India.

After a turn-around time of just under six weeks, the 'Scotia' under Captain Thomas Strickland was reported on the 23rd August 1846 sailing out of the River Thames and passing Deal on the way to the Cape of Good Hope and Bombay. Tom's wife, Margaretta Strickland was left in London to look after their six children, ranging in age from Adela aged thirteen to Walter aged three.

September 1846: Agnes is annoyed by Lord Campbell

Agnes had grown accustomed to her work being copied by other writers and most of these she ignored but (as Jane wrote): "when the highest law officer in the empire was guilty of the same offence, she did not let it pass without notice."

Lord Campbell (who was to become Lord Chief Justice in 1850) published between 1845 and 1847 his 'Lives of the Lord Chancellors' about which it was said that Lord Campbell had felt free to tell lies about all Chancellors, whether living or dead. This general inaccuracy did not worry Agnes, but when she found that he had taken passages from 'Lives of the Queens of England' without acknowledging the source, she was irritated and in September 1846 she wrote a letter of complaint to the 'Times'.

The 'Suffolk Chronicle' summarised the event under the heading "Charge of Piracy against a Cabinet Minister!" following this with a report that "Miss Agnes Strickland has preferred a serious charge against Lord Campbell, one of her Majesty's Cabinet Ministers. She accuses him of having pilfered her property, and appropriated it to his own use!".

"Writing to the Times, she says: 'I am sending you the second volume of my 'Lives of the Queens' with a request that you will do me the favour of comparing my Life of Eleanor of Provence at page 70 with Lord Campbell's biography of the same princess in his 'Lives of the Chancellors' volume 1 and you will see that his Lordship has published an abridgement of that which has now been before the public six years. He has transposed the language a little to disguise the fact, and discreetly transferred the references which I honestly gave to his own margins; but he has not put forth a single fact in addition to those which I had previously put forth merely curtailing my matter and adding a coarse joke of his own'.

"After some further observations she says 'I should have been proud that anything from my pen had been of such use to a learned dignitary of the law, and regarded his abridgement of my Life of Queen Eleanor as one of the highest compliments that had been paid to my work, if his Lordship had candidly referred to the source from whence his information was derived; but he has carefully abstained from even alluding to the existence of a previously published Life of that Queen.'

"The lady then goes on to rate the lawyer in rare style – Lord Brougham could not have done it better – for his want of gallantry!" Lord Brougham, among his other activities was a famous orator of the day and a former Lord Chancellor.

1846: Lord Campbell apologises to Agnes

Not long after Agnes's complaint had appeared in the press, Lord Campbell had the opportunity to apologise, as Agnes told Jane in a letter. Agnes wrote: "The scene of explanation took place in a corner of the House of Lords ... It was arranged by" (Lady Willoughby) "and Lord Clare that Elizabeth and I were to hear a debate in the House of Lords; so we had tea with her before we set off. We were duly admitted into Sir Augustus Clifford's box, below the bar. Lord Brougham was pouring forth a storm of eloquence when we entered, and by-and-by Lord Campbell rose and made a long speech too. We rather admired his appearance, and were amused by his manner and delivery.

"After a time he crossed the House and joined a coterie, of which Lord Clare was one, who with a smile pointed me out to his attention. Whereupon Lord Campbell came to the place where Eliza and I were standing, and said 'Miss Agnes Strickland, I have long been desirous of the opportunity of apologising to you for having given you cause for complaint, but I mean to say something about it in the book.'

"I had then to apologise to him for the annoyance my letter must have caused him. He made a very kind reply, praised the 'Queens', and inquired after the forthcoming volume – which, by the by, is not yet forthcoming – and asked me to shake hands with him, which I did with hearty goodwill, assuring him that he was the most amiable man in the world for not having answered me in an unpleasant way. He certainly behaved like a wise one. This little scene below the bar caused some excitement. But our conference was broken up by an order for the House to be cleared for the division."

1846 or 1847: Agnes and Eliza visit the new House of Lords

Agnes's friend Lady Willoughby d'Eresby was the wife of Lord Willoughby who, Jane recorded, was: "the hereditary grand chamberlain of England." Lady Willoughby invited Agnes to join her when she was shown round the new House of Lords by her husband. Agnes was delighted to accept, took Eliza with her, and wore a new dress for the occasion.

As with many of the invitations which Agnes accepted, the purpose was as much in the interests of research as in straightforward pleasure. Agnes reported that they were shown: "many beautiful miniatures and interesting relics of the Stuarts." The new Houses of Parliament were: "a mass of gold and blazonings in the florid Gothic style, but truly imposing. We went everywhere, even into a sly gold cage over the throne, where the Queen can hear debates perdue if she wishes. We poked about the unfinished building and hurt our feet among the loose stones, to the no small injury of my new drab satin dress. Lady Willoughby's black damask was half a yard deep in dust. Fortunately, mine being dust-coloured, did not show it so much."

29th November 1846: Tom leaves the Cape of Good Hope

Tom must have encountered bad weather on the way south and, while the 'Scotia' was undamaged, he came across another ship that had not been so fortunate. 'Lloyds List' reported that the 'Scotia' spoke to the 'Braema' which was on its way to Calcutta, and supplied it with provisions at the Cape of Good Hope.

Tom and the 'Scotia' having had a short break in their voyage, left the Cape of Good Hope for Bombay on 29th November 1846.

December 1846: Richard and Sarah expand their hospitality

Richard's regular Christmas treat, in common with his summer treat to children, was expanding with Sarah's help and involvement. According to the local papers: "30th December 1846 – the Rev R Gwillym, of Stockbridge House, Ulverston, gave on Wednesday last, his annual treat of tea and supper to the singers &c belonging to the parish church, and a numerous company of friends. All were highly delighted and say it was the most delightful party they had attended at Stock Bridge House."

January 1847: Agnes is denounced

Some clergy within the Church of England were moving towards Catholicism in what was termed the Oxford Movement, causing concern among the more Protestant wing of the church. Such concern might explain a verbal attack made on Agnes and 'Lives of the Queens of England', at a well attended meeting of the Ipswich and East Suffolk Protestant Society in January 1847.

Rev JC Ryle had the task of bringing the meeting to an end, and he included in his closing remarks some damning comments about 'Lives of the Queens of England'. The local paper quoted him as saying: "I warn everybody solemnly not to read that book. She may not be a Jesuit; she may be a professing Protestant. But if ever a book was written to serve the cause of Romanism and to write down the cause of Protestantism, it was that book. That book is doing more harm to the minds of the women of England than any book that has come out for a long time. It is a book that should be expelled from every house, and kept out of the hands of every woman and child." Unfortunately he does not specify which particular volume in the series had offended him or maybe his injunction was intended to apply to the whole series.

Agnes was reassured that Rev Ryle was not expressing a generally held view when she received a message, sent via Jane, from Dr Stanley, then Bishop of Norwich and later Dean of Westminster. The message, Jane wrote, was: "expressive of regret that one of his clergy should have made such a remark, which he described as unchristian, unprovoked and uncalled for." He thought that Agnes had handled a difficult task "very ably, delicately, and with a great regard to the truth."

January 1847: Tom reaches Bombay

Having left the Cape of Good Hope on 29th November 1846, two months later Tom and the 'Scotia' had completed the journey to Bombay, arriving on 26th January 1847.

1847: Agnes finishes her 'Lives of the Queens of England'

Volume IX of 'Lives of the Queens of England' was scheduled for publication in 1846, but was delayed because of the amount of information that Agnes and Eliza had discovered in France with the help of M Guizot's contacts. The volume was to contain the first biography ever to be written of Mary Beatrice of Modena, the wife of James II.

Agnes had more material than could be included in one volume and the remainder had to be carried over to Volume X. She portrayed Mary of Modena as a saintly queen, whose husband caused her much suffering, and the partial biography in Volume IX caused a sensation, but Eliza had to nag Agnes for the final part of the biography, which showed signs of delaying Volume X which Eliza had otherwise completed.

Agnes in a letter to Jane and her mother at Reydon Hall, said she was wearied by all the rush and bustle, by continual interruptions from people wanting to see her, and by the sheer volume of correspondence that she had to read and write. Agnes almost, but not quite, envied the route of anonymity that Eliza had chosen, and her consequently quieter life.

However, once Agnes had completed the biography of Mary of Modena, she had finished her share of 'Lives of the Queens of England' and could relax. Eliza's biographies of Queen Mary II and of Queen Anne, both of which had to be split between two volumes because of the over-running of Mary of Modena's biography, completed the original twelve-volume series.

February 1847: Sarah helps provide soup kitchens

The winter of 1846/1847 was particularly severe and on 25th January 1847 the local papers in Ulverston carried a report: "Detention of the mail – During the latter part of last week, there was a heavier fall of snow between Ulverston and Whitehaven than has been for many years. In many places the snow-drifts were several yards thick" and as a result of the bad weather, steps were being taken to open a soup kitchen for the benefit of the poor in Ulverston.

However, people were also struggling in other parts of the country. Queen Victoria issued a letter on behalf of the poor of Ireland, which was to be read out in all the churches in the country on Sunday 31st January 1847, and there was also a great deal of poverty and distress in the north of Scotland. A committee was set up in Ulverston, of which Richard Gwillym was a member, with the task of organising the carrying out of two door-to-door collections, one for the benefit of the poor in Ireland and the north of Scotland, and the other for the benefit of the poor of Ulverston.

Within a week the two collections had been made, raising £50 for the Irish and Scottish poor, and a slightly larger amount for local people. Not only had the money been collected but a soup kitchen was up and running. The local paper announced: "A soup kitchen has been opened, and soup is intended to be given out on Saturdays and Wednesdays. On Saturday 6th February, 261 families were supplied with soup by the committee and on Wednesday 10th February 240 families were also supplied." Richard Gwillym was named as one of those: "taking an active part in this work of benevolence who, by their kind smiles and sympathising looks, encouraged the recipients of their bounty to 'come again' and partake of the nutritious food given to them, which consists of the following ingredients for making 60 gallons – beef, 50lb; Scotch barley, 30lb; groats, 15lb; peas, 25lb; onions, 5lb; salt, 5oz; pepper, 5 oz." People were also given an allowance of bread to go with the soup.

Sarah was still working at this project in March. The local papers on 27th March 1847 recorded: "Irish Distress – Amongst the contributions for the distressed Irish sent from Ulverston, was seven pounds collected by Mrs Gwillym, which would be distributed at Strangford, County Down, amongst 150 children, who receive daily a pint of soup and a roll of bread."

May 1847: Catharine moves from 'Wolf Tower' to 'Mount Ararat'

After their year of farming and living rent-free at 'Wolf Tower', Catharine and Thomas Traill moved in mid-1847 to their second temporary home near Rice Lake, which Catharine named 'Mount Ararat'. St George's Anglican Church was built nearby in Gore's Landing in 1847 which enabled Catharine with Thomas and their children to attend church services regularly again.

May 1847: Tom sails back round the south of Africa

Tom's sojourn in Bombay on this voyage was relatively brief, and he had completed the return journey in the 'Scotia' as far as Simon's Bay, Cape of Good Hope by 28th May 1847.

June 1847: Agnes has her portrait displayed

In 1846 Agnes had her portrait painted by John Hayes of Frith Street, Soho. Examples of his work were displayed at the Royal Academy Summer Exhibitions in most of the years from 1814 until 1851. In 1847 his three-quarter length, oil on canvas portrait of Agnes was included in the exhibition.

The Royal Academy Summer Exhibition has long been a major event, and in the mid-1840s attracted around a quarter of a million visitors each year. The exhibition in 1847 ran from 3rd May to 24th July. These exhibitions were renowned for their densely packed array of exhibits, with the top artists of the day, even Turner and Constable, having to compete for the best positions.

Agnes's portrait was on display as one of 173 pictures in the West Room. The total number of displayed items, including sculptures and miniatures, was 1,451 and the number of artists displaying work was 800. So, although it was flattering and no doubt gratifying for Agnes to have her portrait exhibited, she was very far from having a unique experience.

Jane put into context the painting of this portrait. She wrote: "Agnes, in spite of the influenza and its consequent debility, lived a very gay life in Hyde Park Place – going much into society with her friend Miss Mackinnon. While with this young lady, she had her portrait taken by Hayes ... At the time it was painted the likeness was very striking, for she was thinner than at any other time in her life. After she became stouter, a half-length in water-colours by Cruikshank represents more truly the Agnes Strickland of latter days." When Jane's biography of Agnes was published many years later, it contained a half-length picture of Agnes in mature middle-life with no artist named. It seems likely that this is the portrait by Cruikshank to which Jane here refers, but the famous Cruikshank artists of the time were two brothers, both mainly caricaturists and cartoonists, therefore unlikely to have painted a portrait of Agnes Strickland.

July 1847: Sarah has a large number of mouths to feed at Stockbridge House

Sarah and her staff had a major event to cater for early in July 1847, which needed dry weather to be successful. The local papers reported: "The Rev R Gwillym, of the parish church of Ulverston, gave his annual treat to the Sunday scholars taught at Townbank, and at the National Schools, and also to the church-wardens, singers and a number of friends, on Wednesday 7th July.

"The children assembled at an early hour at the National School, and from thence walked in order to the Rev Gentleman's residence at Stock Bridge, accompanied by their teachers. They were allowed to play in the pleasure grounds and were supplied with a profusion of fruit, also with tea, cake, &c and supper, indeed the rev gentleman and his worthy wife exerted themselves to the utmost in order to please the children. Before leaving they sang the evening hymn, and afterwards gave three hearty cheers for Mr and Mrs Gwillym.

"After the departure of the children the whole of the rev gentleman's friends, amounting to seventy, sat down to an excellent supper, after which the evening was spent dancing and other innocent recreations upon the soft green sward in front of the house. The whole proceedings were conducted with much hilarity and propriety, and the company separated at a seasonable hour after three cheers had been given to the worthy gentleman and his lady."

1847: Sam and Mary have another son named Richard

In 1847, the year after the death of their baby son Richard, Sam and Mary had another son. They named this little boy Richard, but added the middle name Gwillym, with Sam's brother-in-law Richard Gwillym being his godfather whereas Sarah had been godmother to the child they had lost. Sarah and Richard Gwillym had no children of their own.

July 1847: Agnes and Macaulay cross swords

In an exchange of correspondence in the press, Thomas Babington Macaulay challenged Agnes's interpretation of the character of Mary of Modena, and said that the queen had sold prisoners from the Monmouth campaign to the West Indies. Agnes maintained that this was untrue and challenged Macaulay to produce evidence for his accusation, to which he did not reply.

An amused observer of the exchange of letters is said to have noted: "Agnes's is a very grand performance. It has only one fault. It does not get rid of the letter of Sutherland to Jeffreys" which recorded "'The Queen hath asked for a thousand' of these prisoners."

Although Macaulay did not respond to Agnes's challenge, he probably thought that he had the final word, for there appeared in the 'Edinburgh Review' in July 1847 a very lengthy article which was a sustained attack on the section of the 'Lives of the Queens of England' which covered the Stuart period. The beginning and the end of the article were written in the usual editorial style of the publication, but most of it was written in a different style and was generally believed to have been written by Macaulay. The article described 'Lives of the Queens of England' as lacking impartiality and said that the treatment of James I and James II was too favourable, while the treatment of William III was too unfavourable.

The 'Edinburgh Review' was a supporter of the Whig party and one of its contributors was known to be TB Macaulay. A competing Edinburgh publication, 'Blackwood's Magazine' supported the Tories, and therefore shared Agnes's political views, in opposition to the 'Edinburgh Review'.

Agnes was not too concerned. In a letter to Sarah she wrote: "There is a great attack on the 'Lives of the Queens' in the 'Edinburgh Review', but I do not care about it. It is merely a tirade of contradictions. He sets out with attacking female authors and then says of me 'This lady is a staunch adherent of the Church of England.' That is of far more value to me than praise. It may serve to disprove the false charge of Romanism brought against me."

August 1847: Tom is back home

Having left Simon's Bay, Cape of Good Hope at the end of May after only a two day break, Captain Thomas Strickland had brought the 'Scotia' safely back to the Custom House at London Docks by 9th August 1847, having been away from home for slightly less than a year.

August 1847: Agnes sets off in the steps of Mary Queen of Scots

Agnes, having completed her share of the 'Lives of the Queens of England' for Henry Colburn said she felt "like a bird released from a cage." Although Eliza still had work to do on the final two volumes, Agnes had time for a brief rest before she carried on collecting material for the biography of Mary Queen of Scots, which she intended to write without Eliza's help. Agnes decided to visit every place which had associations with Mary Stuart, and with this in mind she undertook an extensive round of country house visits in Scotland in 1847.

Most 15th and 16th century houses in Scotland had a Queen's Chamber, or a portrait, or some trinket or memento of Mary Stuart, which had become a treasured family heirloom regardless of the religion of the current owner. There was no catalogue of these portraits and relics, and Agnes recorded each one which was shown to her. She enjoyed this activity, and her high-ranking friends were equally enthusiastic about showing her their Mary Stuart treasures.

Agnes made a complicated series of visits, criss-crossing Scotland from the home of one titled personage to another. For much of her 1847 tour she had a friend, Miss Harriet Home to keep her company, and to help with sketching and recording the items they were shown. Harriet's father was Sheriff of Edinburgh and her family lived at 'Avontoun House' not far from Edinburgh, where Agnes was a regular guest.

One of the most important places for Agnes to visit on this tour was Stirling Castle. When she arrived in Stirling, Agnes sent in her card at the governor's house by way of introduction, whereupon she and Harriet were invited in by the governor's daughters and were shown around the castle, including (Agnes told her family in a letter home): "the closet where the Douglas was stabbed and thrown out of the window."

Harriet and Agnes were then invited to tea but, Agnes wrote: "when the dear old veteran governor, Sir Archibald Christie, came in" he insisted they must stay and dine, regardless of their travelling dresses. "The old dear cared not to eat his dinner for talking to me. He engaged me to dine with them on the 20th to meet a grand dinner-party, and the ladies made me promise to stay with them during the races and go to the ball."

As arranged, Agnes returned to Stirling in August 1847 for the races and ball. She wrote to Sarah describing how Sir Archibald Christie had taken her for a drive to call on Lady Seton Steuart, hereditary armour-bearer to the kings of Scotland. "It was quite a sensation driving through all those old royal courts, and embattled gateways, and wherever we came the soldiers presented arms to his excellency.

"On Friday I went to the ball, and wore my white satin dress, lace tunic and pearl tiara. We did not get home till the sun was rising over the mountains. It seems a complete romance being here. Every one makes so much of me as if I were a queen; and I sit in Queen Mary's chair, and am in close conversation with one of her descendents, who looks like Charles I come to life again, he resembles him so much."

September 1847: Susanna and John Moodie launch a magazine

In September 1847, Susanna and John tried their hand at editing a magazine which was called the 'Victoria Magazine'. Their local paper, the 'Kingston Upper Canada Herald' on 8th September 1847 announced: "Mr and Mrs Moodie are about to become the Editors of a monthly Literary Magazine, to be published in Belleville, by Mr Joseph Wilson, at the low rate of 5$ per annum. The literary reputation of Mrs M has long since been established. The Canadian public, we are sure, will hail with pleasure the appearance of a work which is to be conducted by two of our own most popular writers. We wish them every success."

September 1847: Agnes and Sarah hear Jenny Lind, the 'Swedish Nightingale', sing

Towards the end of her tour of Scotland in 1847, Agnes went to Pollok House, Glasgow, to stay with Lady Matilda and Sir John Maxwell, who had become her friends during a previous visit. Sarah and Richard Gwillym were also invited, and the visit included going to hear Jenny Lind, the famous and very popular Swedish opera singer, perform in Glasgow City Hall on Friday 17th September 1847. The 'Stirling Observer' said: "The assembly of rank, beauty and fashion which congregated to hear Jenny Lind was the greatest and gayest which ever met in this city on any occasion."

Not all Agnes's visits were for pleasure, she also saw some of the realities of life. On one such occasion she wrote: "On our way home

I had to pay the penance of going over a factory, where £1,000 are disbursed in weekly wages. I saw the whole process of cotton-dressing, but I would rather pick stones at three-pence a day than exist in the hot, stifling, noisy den of machinery for any consideration. All the people work barefoot. One of the young masters gave me his arm and showed me everything, very courteous; but a factory is a horrid bore to see, and I was glad to get into the delicious air again."

After her tour in Scotland with Harriet Home, Agnes travelled to Ulverston and there spent a few weeks with Sarah and Richard.

December 1847: Eliza has work published at the same time as Charlotte Bronte

Volume X and Volume XI of 'Lives of the Queens of England' were published in 1847. Of these, Volume XI was published in December 1847 and was being advertised at the same time as a new novel, 'Jane Eyre' by Charlotte Bronte.

21st December 1847: Tom has been at home for longer than expected

After Tom and the 'Scotia' had returned to London from Bombay in August 1847, the ship went to the West India Dock to await its next commission. Advertisements were soon appearing, offering room for passengers or freight, destination Bombay and sailing date 30th September 1847. With this plan in progress, the 'Scotia' got as far as having a preliminary clearing through the Custom House and beginning to load.

However for some reason, the plan changed and the 'Scotia' was moved from the West India Dock to the East India Dock while it again waited for its next commission. There continued to be uncertainty with advertisements appearing in October 1847 which offered room for freight or passengers, the destinations of Madras and Calcutta, and the departure was to be some time unspecified in December.

By November 1847, the voyage was settled as an emigration mission and was advertised accordingly: "Free emigration to the

Cape of Good Hope under the Authority of her Majesty's Colonial Land & Emigration commissioners. The splendid first class Ship Scotia with a poop & most superior cabin & steerage accommodation will embark passengers on the 14th December, and at Plymouth on the 24th December direct for Cape Town and Algoa Bay."

Terms and conditions were listed: "Poop Cabin passengers will be taken at £25 each to Table Bay. Steerage passengers not eligible for a free passage will be charged £14 to Table Bay & £16 to Algoa Bay, which will include new bedding and mess utensils. An experienced surgeon appointed by the government will be aboard. All particulars as to classes eligible for free passage, dietary on the voyage etc on application" Tom had been in London for four months before the 'Scotia' sailed, leaving Gravesend on 21st December 1847.

29th January 1848: Ulverston is to get an Athenaeum

Richard was taking seriously the need to provide education for the poorer people of Ulverston, and with this in mind he supported the suggestion of an Athenaeum in the town, which would provide an educational facility for young people who had received little or no school education.

A meeting was set up and the event was reported in the local papers: "On Saturday 29th January 1848, a meeting was held at the National School, Ulverston, to establish an Athenaeum, comprising a library, reading rooms, and lecture and class rooms, for the promotion of general literature and the useful branches of education, more especially among the youth of the town and the vicinity." There would also be concerts with admission charged at a very low rate.

A committee of twelve was set up and Richard was voted chairman. Premises in Theatre-street, Ulverston had been advertised as 'To Let' and it was agreed they might be suitable. The paper wished the institution every success, commenting: "We regard this as one of the most important and valuable movements that has been made in the spirited little town of Ulverston which sets an example to places of larger size and more fancied importance."

24th March 1848: Tom reaches South Africa then sails on to Madras

After a voyage lasting three months, Tom and the 'Scotia' arrived at the Cape of Good Hope with their emigrant passengers on 24th March 1848. Tom may well have known that he would have further to sail before he headed home. After a couple of weeks, on 7th April 1848 the 'Scotia' headed east and north towards Madras.

5th April 1848: Hoad Hill in Ulverston is to be improved

Ulverston was brimming with community ideas in 1848, and Richard Gwillym was present at a public meeting held at the Savings Bank on Wednesday 5th April 1848, where plans were discussed to improve Hoad Hill, which overlooks the town and reaches a height of 436 feet.

Local papers reported that suggestions were made to improve the hill by adding: "walks, seats and grottoes, and by partial planting; and thus render a more inviting promenade and enjoyment of all classes of the population, and of tourists, with expenses from £40 to £100." This was proposed and passed.

Richard, perhaps beginning to fear that plans were getting over-ambitious, moved an amendment. He said: "as for himself, he was an ardent admirer of nature in her wildness. It was not his intention to oppose the plans, but his own opinion was that improving the walks and seats was sufficient, without arbours, grottoes etc." and a resolution omitting the arbours and grottoes was then comfortably carried.

A third resolution followed which drew the matter to a close with a compromise. It was agreed that: "If sufficient funds, certain plots of the Hill be planted with shrubs and trees and, should subscriptions permit, a summer house be erected." A committee was then set up to solicit subscriptions. Richard, who was about to embark on a major project himself, did not volunteer to join the fund-raisers.

1848: Macaulay publishes his 'History of England'

1848 saw the completion of the publication of 'The History of England from the Accession of James the Second' by TB Macaulay. Published in five volumes, it is generally known as Macaulay's 'History of England' although it only covers seventeen years from the accession of James II in 1685 to the death of William III, Macaulay's hero, in 1702. Macaulay was a Whig politician as well as an author and reviewer. His work has been criticised for lack of accuracy and for giving a one-sided view of events in the period covered. His politics and his bias were therefore directly contrary to the politics and enthusiasm of Agnes.

6th May 1848: Ulverston Athenaeum gets its premises

The premises in Theatre-street, Ulverston were found to be suitable for an Athenaeum, and on 6th May 1848, Richard and his committee agreed to take a seven year lease on the property which included a Theatre and an Assembly Room.

17th May 1848: Tom reaches Madras and then travels onwards

Having left the Cape of Good Hope on 7th April 1848, Tom arrived at Madras on the east coast of India on 17th May 1848. He then had another commission to fulfil, and after a six week stay in Madras, at the end of June 1848, the 'Scotia' set out on a relatively short voyage south to Pondicherry.

19th June 1848: Sarah's husband starts an Infant School

By the middle of 1848, Richard had committed himself to provide an infant school in Ulverston, despite there being little support for this idea in the town. He took the gamble of paying all costs and expenses for the first year, hoping that the value of the school would by then be appreciated, and that other benefactors would share the financial burden with him.

As with the founding of the Athenaeum, matters once under way, moved swiftly. The papers reported: "A new school, for infants under six years of age, was opened in James-street on 19th June 1848, in a large and commodious room expressly fitted up for the object. The school is intended as an auxiliary to the National School, and will be under the sole superintendence of the Rev Richard Gwillym MA, the incumbent of the Parish Church who, for the first year, takes all the liabilities upon himself. After that time he anticipates that it will be firmly established. The charge is one penny a week. Miss Lawrence has been appointed mistress. We trust the project will succeed, and instruction be thus advanced among the children of the labouring poor."

28th June 1848: Sam fulfils his role as a Major in the Militia

Sam recounted in his autobiography that: "in 1847 a new Militia Bill was prepared which required all able-bodied men from sixteen to sixty to enrol, and all those aged sixteen to forty had to attend a training day each year on the 28th June. In the county of Peterborough" where Sam lived "the Peterborough regiment was formed, consisting of seven battalions, each commanded by a lieutenant-colonel." Sam (by this time aged 43) was appointed Major in the 2nd battalion of this regiment, a role that was unpaid except in times of active service, if such should arise.

Sam in his book explains his title of Major and the ridicule attached to it: "The township of Douro and half the township of Dummer form the 2nd battalion of the Peterborough regiment, of which I have the honour to be major ... Under the present law the Militia training is apt to excite the ridicule of regular soldiers. After an hour or two of hard work, when you have at length succeeded in forming your men into line, the appearance they make would agonize a martinet. Let my military readers fancy seven or eight hundred men, of all heights and sizes from four feet six to six feet four, clad in white linen coats, black coats, blue coats, grey coats, and some, indeed, with no coats at all; while straw hats, black hats, cloth caps, Scotch caps, or the bonnet rouge, form their various head-coverings, and you have a slight picture of the figure and appearance of the men on a training day. However, Napoleon would have thought nothing of the dress and everything of the men, and as for our loyalty and activity they at least will pass muster." Sam was also running an agricultural school where newly arrived immigrants were taught such farming skills as would prepare them to run their own farms in due course.

Sam in his autobiography gave a useful explanation of the Halifax currency, whose existence somewhat complicates understanding of costs and wages at the time. His explanation was as follows: "Halifax currency is less than sterling: the bank value of the sovereign" which had a face value of £1, or twenty shillings sterling "is twenty-four shillings and four-pence half-penny" in Halifax currency. "In payment of store-debts the merchant generally allows five dollars." One pound sterling was therefore roughly equal to five Canadian dollars while a Halifax pound equalled four Canadian dollars. Sovereigns were made with gold and any that exist today are worth very much more than originally intended.

28th June 1848: Sarah joins in the fun

The anniversary of Queen Victoria ascending the throne on 28th June was not only the regular date for Sam in Canada to be involved in militia training, in 1848 it was also the chosen date for the Ulverston children's summer treat. These events at Stockbridge house (also spelt Stock Bridge House, with variations) continued to grow each year and in 1848 involved a bit more pomp than usual, with Sarah joining in the fun.

The papers reported that on Wednesday 28th June 1848: "the scholars assembled at the National School, and marched through the town with banners flying, accompanied by Mr and Mrs Gwillym, with teachers, and the Ulverston brass band. At the Market Cross the national anthem was played, and hearty cheers given for the Queen, and though the day was not so favourable as might have been wished, the sports at Stockbridge were carried on with great spirit; the running, leaping, &c, &c was joined in by many gentlemen who were present, much to the satisfaction and delight of the young ones. Three hundred children had coffee and cake; the quantity drunk being sixty gallons.

"Two hundred ladies and gentlemen also had tea, supper and refreshments. The table on which the supper was served on the lawn was 90 feet long. Dancing on the green was kept up long after the 'witching time of night'. The party was a very pleasant and agreeable one. Mr Gwillym was here there and everywhere; had he been some highland chief, and this the gathering of his clan, he could not have been more stirring – his amiable lady was quite as much so, kind and affable to all. Previous to the children leaving they had a pie each. Several songs and hymns were sung, and three cheers for Mr Gwillym, three cheers for Mrs Gwillym, and though absent not forgot, three cheers for Miss Gwillym."

The event had now become so large that it had to be split into two separate occasions but with hardly time to draw breath between them. The following day, Thursday 29th June 1848, the papers added: "seventy of the infants belonging to the Infant School, and 26 children from the Town Bank School, had a similar treat, and like the others, much enjoyed themselves."

Richard was clearly taking seriously his bishop's view that those who have been given the gift of wealth, should use it for the benefit of others. Richard's salary as vicar of Ulverston was only in the region of £100 a year. The rest of the money required for all his activities came out of his own resources.

9th August 1848: Catharine's last child is born

On 9th August 1848 Walter John Strickland Traill was born. He was Catharine's seventh surviving child with her oldest child, James, being aged fifteen. Catharine was 46 and Thomas was 56 years old, and Walter was the last of their children.

August 1848: Susanna and John's magazine comes to an end

The monthly magazine founded and edited by Susanna and John Moodie in September 1847 was intended to have an educational tone and was aimed at farmers. Although they tried to find contributors, Susanna and John had to write most of it themselves and after twelve months, publication ceased.

During the year that they were co-editing the 'Victoria Magazine', Susanna was continuing to contribute to the 'Literary Garland' and other magazines, and John was continuing in his role as Sheriff of Hastings County.

August 1848: Tom returns to Madras

From Pondicherry, Tom returned with the 'Scotia' to Madras early in August 1848. He was there for almost four weeks and on 31st August 1848, sailed out of Madras to begin his voyage back to London.

September 1848: Agnes makes a second Scottish tour

In the late summer of 1848, on her second tour of Scotland, Agnes was still collecting information about Mary Stuart, and was focussing on her domestic life and arrangements. Agnes had as her companion Emily Norton, a 27 year old grand-daughter of Sir Charles Blois, of Cockfield Hall in Yoxford, Suffolk. Emily's sister had died recently, and she was depressed and in poor health herself. Her tour with Agnes gave her change of air and activity, and she also on occasions acted as Agnes's assistant.

Among the notable new acquaintances that Agnes made on this tour were Lord Ashley and Archibald Alison. Lord Ashley was a champion of factory reform, and legislation to protect children who were employed in factories. He had recently joined the Whigs while Agnes remained a confirmed Tory. When they walked together to visit the Falls of Clyde, Agnes found conversation unusually difficult and they could not find a topic on which they agreed. However, Agnes described the man himself in very flattering terms when she wrote home, saying he was: "one of the handsomest and grandest persons you ever saw – a man eminently fitted to cope with the powers of darkness. He is a magnificent specimen of the aristocracy."

Her other new acquaintance was more congenial. Archibald Alison was an historian and a diehard Tory politician, and he and Agnes became firm friends. In his autobiography he told how he had met Agnes and gave a description of her. He wrote: "Our intimacy with Sir John and Lady Matilda Maxwell, among other valuable acquaintances to which it led, brought on one of an interesting kind – Miss Agnes Strickland – who was a frequent guest for weeks together at Pollok House. This able and learned lady was then writing the latter volumes of her highly interesting 'Lives of the Queens of England', and making researches connected with the work, which she progressed and afterwards completed, of her 'Biography of the Queens of Scotland'.

"The vast extent of varied reading and research in printed books, ancient records, family papers, and manuscript correspondence which the composition of such books necessarily required, rendered her conversation at once original and entertaining. She had strong talents, rather of a masculine than of a feminine character, indefatigable perseverance, and that ardour in whatever pursuit she was engaged, without which no one could undergo similar fatigue. But if her powers of thought and composition were those of a man, her heart and feelings were those of a woman. She was impulsive in her disposition, and had to the fullest extent that tendency to exaggerate the merits of her favourites and indulge in the luxury of hero-worship, which is so common in women of cultivated minds ...

"Miss Strickland had great powers of expression and disquisition – too great, indeed, for when she got on one of her favourite subjects she descanted with such animation, that in the intensity of her own thoughts she came to forget that those of her auditors were by no means wrought up to a similar point. Like Macaulay, she poured out without mercy whatever at the moment was occupying her own mind, without ever recollecting that those she addressed were probably interested in totally different subjects. On this account, what she required above all things was a good listener and the presence of that quality almost compensated for the want of any other. She did not even require an answer or a sign of mutual intelligence; it was enough if the one she was addressing simply remained passive.

"One day when I was laid up at Possil on my library sofa, from a wound in the knee, she was kind enough to sit with me for two hours, and was really very entertaining, from the number of anecdotes she recounted of queens in the olden times. When she left the room she expressed herself kindly to Mrs Alison, as to the agreeable time she had spent; and the latter said to me on coming in:

"What did you get to say to Miss Strickland all this time? She says you were so agreeable." "Say," I replied; "with truth I assure you I did not say six words to her the whole time."

21st October 1848: Sarah and Richard's garden produces a monster

Saturday 21st October 1848 would probably have seen Sarah and her husband attending the North Lonsdale Agricultural Society annual show, held in a field at Lightburne, not far from Ulverston, where there was shown a cabbage of remarkable size from their own garden.

The report of the show in the local papers included the comment: "Some splendid specimens of mangle wurzel, also a few fine turnips, were displayed; but the greatest vegetable monstrosity exhibited was a cabbage, of the drumhead kind, grown in the garden of the worthy vicar, the Rev Richard Gwillym; it weighed 32lb., and had been produced without any extraordinary application of manure; when growing it covered a space of more than five yards in circumference." What they did with it after the show has not been recorded.

October 1848: Agnes visits the Duke of Devonshire's libraries and archives

Following her 1848 tour of Scotland, Agnes took up the Duke of Devonshire's offer of access to his properties, in her quest for information about Mary Queen of Scots. Agnes made these visits on her own.

She was looked after at Chatsworth House by the housekeeper, Mrs Hastie, the house being only occupied by staff at the time. Unfortunately, the curator of the Chatsworth library and archives was not there, but the housekeeper showed Agnes into the famous library and left her to get on with her work as she pleased. During her stay at Chatsworth the Head Gardener, Mr Paxton, showed a delighted Agnes round the grounds, including the lighted waterfalls and cascades that had been built to his design, for the visit of Queen Victoria and Prince Albert in 1843.

When Agnes was ready to leave Chatsworth House, she was provided with transport to her next destination which was Stubbing Court, Wingerworth, home of Agnes's friend Mrs Thompson. Agnes gave a light-hearted description of the journey in a letter to Jane. She wrote: "I was sent in an elegant open carriage drawn by the Duke's pretty grey ponies, driven by his own coachman. We descended such hills as I never travelled down before, and I felt rather afraid. My driver missed his way, and alighted to enquire of some men at work in the fields – leaving me, O Mistress Jane, to hold his spirited steeds!

"I do not know what you would have thought if you had seen your Agg, as you sometimes presumptuously call me, in such a predicament. The gallant greys, nowise tired by their twelve miles trot, looked inclined to race after coachie. He, seeing their intention, blocked up the wheels with large stones. I sat in fear, though the pretty dears were as quiet as lambs while he was gone." Jane in her biography of Agnes added that when she and Agnes went on a daily drive in a pony-carriage, Jane had to manage the horse and if Agnes had to hold the reins for any reason, she would get into a terrible fright until relieved of the responsibility.

Agnes's short stay with Mrs Thompson gave them time to take a picnic to Wingfield Manor, one of the places where Mary Stuart was imprisoned. From there Agnes told Jane: "Mrs Thompson carted me to Hardwick, and we lunched in the Duke's private dining-room." Agnes stayed working at Hardwick Hall for a few days and wrote to Jane: "It is all like a chapter of romance – a dream – these lonely tapestried halls, and Tudor windows that look out over the lovely wild valleys of Scarsdale." After Hardwick Hall, Agnes went to Bolsover Castle, another of the Duke's houses, as she pursued the thread of Mary Stuart's life. She then returned to Reydon Hall for the winter.

November 1848: Richard uses his sisters-in-law's expertise

The winter course of lectures at Ulverston Athenaeum began on 29th November 1848 with an audience of over 200 people. Richard was named as one of the lecturers in the programme for the season. His talk had the title 'Manners and Customs of the time of William the Conqueror' and Agnes, possibly also Eliza, no doubt helped their brother-in-law by supplying him with plenty of facts and anecdotes.

November 1848: Jane and Agnes face a busy winter

While her brothers and sisters were leading more noteworthy lives, Jane Margaret Strickland had been quietly carrying on her literary activities such as editing and writing for Christmas Annuals, at the same time as helping Mrs Strickland with the various duties and tasks involved in living in a large, old and badly-maintained house on very limited means. In the autumn of 1848 Agnes agreed to work with Jane on the 'Fisher's Juvenile Scrapbook', which would be on sale for the Christmas season that year, on condition that Jane (according to Jane herself) should contribute: "the larger portion of the work and also edit it" while Agnes found the poetry.

Agnes was also producing a book for the 1848-1849 Christmas season entitled 'Historical Tales of Illustrious British Children' which was described as "a series of moral and instructive tales, each founded on some striking authentic fact in the annals of our own country, in which royal or distinguished children were engaged."

Agnes and Eliza were continuing their task of reducing the original twelve volumes of 'Lives of the Queens of England' to an eight volume version. This was going to take some time, indeed it was not published until 1852, and Henry Colburn wanted something written by Agnes to maintain interest in her in the meantime. To this end he offered Agnes £100 for a 350 page volume of work which began with a few anecdotes about royal personages, but which mainly consisted of a compilation of previously published poems, together with some original work. Jane acted as editor of the book which was entitled 'Historic Scenes and Poetic Fancies'.

Under this pressure of work, Agnes became ill, not with the bilious attacks of her youth but with tic doloureux, which resulted in sudden and very sharp stabbing pains in the side of her face. Jane took some of the load from her sisters' shoulders by helping with the final proof-reading for the revised 'Lives of the Queens of England', and checking that no inconsistencies or errors of fact had crept into the work.

18th December 1848: Sarah is a regular visitor to the Infant School

A long-term and serious duty for Sarah had established itself with the opening of the Infant School in James Street, Ulverston in June 1848. Six months later, on Monday 18th December its first public examination was carried out, and the local paper gave a very full report, starting with a description of the school-room and an outline of the examination.

A summary of the report is as follows: "The room was tastefully decorated with evergreens, banners &c and the healthy and cleanly appearance of the children with their orderly conduct gave a fascination to the scene before us. The examination began with a manual exercise, questions from the first chapter of Genesis followed, which the children answered very correctly. They then sang the song of the clock, and of the shoemaker. A boy, only five years old was called from the gallery, in which the children were arranged, and any of the company present were requested to mention a letter from the alphabet. The boy repeated, by rote, a text from the Scripture, the first word of which began with the letter named. This was done to a nicety. Five or six girls then sang a little song, beginning 'Here We Stand'. Then a different manual exercise, and another song by the whole number ... the national anthem ... Scriptural questions from the History of Joseph were answered without hesitation.

"The Rev R Gwillym then addressed these words to those who were assembled 'Ladies and gentlemen, and kind friends, I hope this examination has answered your expectations, and that you will think with me, that the manner in which the dear children have gone through it, reflects great credit on the teacher. The school has only been opened six months ... many have been admitted within this month. They are all under five years of age except one who is two months older.

'I believe you are aware that I have taken all the expenses of the school upon myself for this half year. This has cost us a very considerable pecuniary sacrifice, but we made it most cheerfully for the good of others. Indeed, whenever Mrs Gwillym and I have visited the school, we have always left it expressing our pleasure that we had been able to provide for the instruction of these young ones. In future, I shall be glad of any kind of aid towards the support of the school; but if none is given, we shall cheerfully go on as we have done.' The Rev RG then thanked them for their attendance, and hoped to see them at the next examination in the summer."

That was not the end of the day's event and the paper reported the children being given a treat and the local teachers arrived for a cup of tea and a chat. The papers said "A bun was then given to the children (who) looked happy, and seemed pleased to go through the various exercises. The room was so crowded by the parents, and by the principal ladies and gentlemen of the town, that many could not gain admission. Four little garments were given to the four best children. The teacher and her little sister, who acts as her assistant, afterwards drank tea in the room, and were joined by the teachers from the Town Bank and National Schools. Upwards of 300 persons were present and the 90 little children."

The paper then put in a plea for funding: "We would appeal to the inhabitants of Ulverston to assist the reverend gentleman in this laudable undertaking. Many a child may, by being thus early instructed, be kept from error and vice and, for aught we can tell, may fill high and important stations in life ... a word of praise for Miss Lawrence, the teacher, for the very great efficiency shown."

15th January 1849: Tom is home from Madras

Tom, having sailed in the 'Scotia' outward past Gravesend on 21st December 1847, returned safely from his travels to India thirteen months later, reaching Gravesend on 15th January 1849.

29th March 1849: Agnes's 'Life-boat' gets a public reading

One of Agnes's old poems was read at a public meeting within a lecture delivered at Southwold Town Hall on 29th March 1849. The speaker was FW Ellis Esq., RN and his subject was the 'Life Boat, and other means used for the preservation of life from shipwreck.' Agnes's poem had first been published in the volume 'Patriotic Songs' which she and Susanna had written together in 1831.

The local paper reported the event: "The room was appropriately decorated with flags of all nations, and some beautiful models of naval architecture were displayed. The hall was crowded and many went away disappointed, finding it impossible to make their way through the crowd on the stairs and landing. The object was twofold – to deliver a lecture and to present a medal to John Fish, of the Southwold Life Boat, for his bravery in rescuing two men from the wreck of the 'Ury' in December last.

"The lecture was listened to in the most attentive manner and was enlivened by various quotations and anecdotes. Some spirited lines on the Life-Boat, which the lecturer repeated, written by Miss Agnes Strickland, who was present, were received with a burst of applause highly flattering to the fair authoress." The poem in full is as follows:

> The Life-boat! – the Life-boat! – when tempests are dark,
> She's the beacon of hope of the foundering bark!
> When midst the wild roar of a hurricane sweep
> The minute-guns boom like a knell o'er the deep,
>
> The Life-boat! – the Life-boat! – the whirlwind and rain,
> And white-crested breakers approach her in vain:
> Her crew are resolved, and her timbers are staunch –
> She's the vessel of mercy – God speed her to launch.
>
> The Life-boat! – the Life-boat! – how fearless and free
> She wins her bold course o'er the wide rolling sea!
> She bounds o'er the surge with gallant disdain,
> She has stemmed them before, and she'll stem them again,
>
> The Life-boat! – the Life-boat! she's manned by the brave,
> In the noblest of causes, commission'd to save;
> What heart but has thrill'd in the seaman's distress,
> At the Life-boat's endeavours – the Life-boat's success?
>
> The Life-boat! – the Life-boat! – no vessel that sails
> Has stemmed such rough billows, and weather'd such gales.
> Not e'en Nelson's proud ship, when his death-strife was won
> Such glory achiev'd as the Life-boat has done.

March 1849: Tom gets his Third Class Certificate and leaves for Australia

While Tom was in London early in 1849, and despite having been a captain for many years, he applied for and was granted a Third Class Certificate, a necessity caused by new regulations.

He was not home for long and within three weeks of his arrival back in London Docks from India, advertisements were appearing for another major voyage. This one was to be to Australia, according to the advertisements: "under engagement to her Majesty's Colonisation Commissioners, for Sydney direct, to sail 4th March 1849" with a stop to pick up passengers at Plymouth. The voyage was delayed a few days, but on 13th March 1849 the 'Scotia' was on its way from London to Plymouth, and from Plymouth set sail for Australia on 24th March 1849.

March 1849: Richard continues his support of the Athenaeum

In 1849 the various projects begun in 1848 became established, and Richard's expenditure on worthwhile local activities in Ulverston continued to expand. Sarah's husband gave two lectures at the Ulverston Athenaeum, both of which probably had the help of Agnes and her anecdotes. In March 1849 he gave his advertised lecture on the 'Life and Character of William Rufus, and the principal events which occurred during his reign' and in April 1849 he gave another lecture which had a similar title but the king was 'Henry the First, surnamed Beauclerc.'

Richard was not entirely financially separate from the Athenaeum, for after its first AGM the local paper recorded: "Various officers were elected, and the report was read, which was of a most satisfactory character ... The Rev R Gwillym in order to manifest his anxiety for the welfare of the Athenaeum, intends giving, at his own expense, a soiree, to the members of the institution." Presumably this took place, and maybe at Stockbridge House with Sarah's involvement, but the newspapers carried no further mention of it.

May 1849: Catharine and Thomas buy a farm but sell his pension

When the owner of Catharine and Thomas's second temporary home in Rice Lake Plains sold the property early in 1849, they bought a nearby farm called 'Oaklands' in the township of Cobourg, and moved there in May the same year. In order to raise some of the $200 needed to buy the property, Thomas somehow managed to sell his half-pay officer's pension which was the family's only regular source of income. The rest of the money was raised by means of a mortgage with the help of Sam Strickland and John Moodie.

1849: Sam's life continues on its smooth path

Sam wrote in his auto-biography that his life during the ten year period from the end of the rebellion in 1839 to 1849 had: "presented too little variation to be worthy of record ... happily married and a large family had been growing up" around him. In fact he had become a successful man with several businesses as well as a prospering farm, and he had become a prominent citizen in the growing community of Lakefield and a magistrate. Sam had been involved in local politics in Douro Township for a number of years, and for a time was appointed Reeve for the town and was thereby a member of Peterborough County Council.

With the birth of Richard Gwillym Strickland in 1847, he and Mary had eleven children living. In 1848 their eldest daughter, Maria married Benjamin Beresford, a local man. Sam wrote: "The marriage of my eldest girl did not break up our cheerful family circle for she was located within a mile's walk, so we had gained an affectionate son without losing a daughter."

20th June 1849: Sarah and Richard head a procession to their own home

The 'Sunday School Annual Treat' in Ulverston, despite having become a major local event, continued to be held at Stockbridge House requiring a good deal of work and responsibility on Sarah's part.

In 1849 the event was held on 20th June, and the newspapers gave a description: "the Sunday Scholars belonging to the National Town Bank and Broughton Beck Sunday Schools, near 400 in number, neatly attired, assembled in the National School and marched in procession through the town, preceded by the Ulverston brass band and banners, and headed by Mr and Mrs Gwillym.

"They stopped at the Market-place, where the national anthem was sung and played, on the way to Stock Bridge House where the children were fed and amused until eight o'clock" after which the "church wardens and singers of the parish church and several of the tradesmen &c of the town who were invited, sat down to an excellent supper provided by Mr and Mrs Gwillym on the lawn in front of the dwelling house, after which a dance was held and the company separated about midnight."

1849: Eliza tours incognito

The completion of the original twelve volumes of the 'Lives of the Queens of England' was far from being the end of the work involved in the project, and both Agnes and Eliza, with help from Jane, continued to be working on various editions of the series for the rest of their lives.

The first amended edition of 'Lives of the Queens of England' not only reduced the volumes from twelve to eight, it tidied up the arrangement of the series, so that no biography was split between two volumes. An additional intended change was to include a range of illustrations that were not present in the original series. Eliza took on the task of finding the illustrations, and in 1849 she toured the country finding scenes to illustrate important locations which were to be used, in addition to pictures of the queens themselves. Henry Colburn, true to form, offered some pictures of various queens which Eliza rejected on the grounds, as Jane put it, that "they were not, in fact, pictures of the queen as named."

Eliza was very studious and very thorough. She had studied female costume so carefully that she could, it is said, date an historic outfit to within a decade. She believed it was more important for the illustration of a queen to be wearing the correct style of headgear, than for the features to be a supposed likeness of the queen. In all this work, Eliza continued to take great care to preserve her anonymity. When giving her many instructions to artists and printers, and in all correspondence on these matters, she always used Agnes's name, not her own.

July 1849: Catharine receives boxes from England

In 1849 Catharine had several pieces of work published, which brought a small amount of money into the household. She also received in July 1849 four boxes from England, two for herself and one each for Susanna and Samuel. Three of the boxes had originated in Reydon. The extra box for Catharine came from the Rev Mr Wood. According to Catharine's daughter Annie, the Rev Mr Wood: "took a great fancy to my mother" and sent a yearly parcel until he died suddenly in 1858.

Catharine in a letter to Susanna listed the contents of her boxes as the freight charge of £2.13s.9p had to be divided between the recipients. The list of the contents of her own box from Reydon Hall showed the nature and extent of the help being sent from the family in Suffolk whose own resources were limited.

Catharine wrote: "Agnes sent me a very excellent Scotch plaid winter gown of her own which I was very glad of as it was ready made and fits me well; 16 yards of pale blue calico for frocks for the girls; 12 checked muslin de laine; 14 good grass cloth; about 18 yards white cotton; 12 blue check shirting very useful for the boys; some flannel; about 10 yards red chinzam; a dress which I shall endeavour to pay old Zinney some washing arrears with; some plain cap net; two chimizettes from Agnes, always valuable to poor me; some cap ribbons from Agnes; 6 pairs of white stockings; some yards of clean striped muslin; a good pair of boots for myself, most acceptable as I was literally shoeless and bootless; two small pairs for Will and Walter who were ditto; the fourth vol. of Queen's and a copy of the new Scrapbook; some half pound of cotton, a few tapes, and pins and needles, are the contents of our box – and very acceptable the things will be for I was beginning to wonder how I should find clothing for these poor children now reduced to worse than bareness."

Catharine's news in her letter to Susanna with regard to health and farming matters was not so good. There had been whooping cough in the family, as well as other ailments which Catharine puts down to poor nourishment, as the harvest had been poor, the milk yield from the cow had been low and they had no money to buy extra provisions.

18th August 1849: Sarah has a new bishop as a house guest

In August 1849, Sarah had a new bishop as a house guest for a few days. Bishop Sumner, who had stayed at Stockbridge House in the past, had become Archbishop of Canterbury in 1848. His replacement was Rev John Graham, who would continue to be Bishop of Chester until his death in 1865.

On Saturday 18th August 1849, Bishop Graham confirmed 533 young people at Dalton-in-Furness then, the local paper reported: "his Lordship paid a visit to the picturesque ruins of Furness Abbey, and proceeded thence to Ulverston, where he became the guest of the respected vicar, the Rev R Gwillym.

"On Sunday morning he preached to a crowded congregation in the parish church. On Tuesday 21st August 1849 his Lordship held a confirmation at Ulverston."

August 1849: Tom reaches Australia

Tom Strickland having left Plymouth in the 'Scotia' in March 1849, arrived at Sydney early in August 1849, but as with his previous carriage of emigrants, he had tasks to perform other than depositing his passengers, before returning home. After a three-week stay in Sydney, the 'Scotia' left Sydney for Calcutta on 25th August 1849.

September 1849: Jane, Catharine and Agnes's names appear together

In 1849, four of the Strickland sisters were earning money by writing for magazines. Susanna's efforts seem to have been confined to Canada, Agnes and Jane's to England and Scotland, while

Catharine's work, with the help of her sisters in England, was printed on both sides of the Atlantic.

In England, on 22nd September 1849, a review was given of a new weekly publication 'The Home Circle'. It was the brain-child of one Pierce Egan, jun., who was based in St Martin's Lane in London. The reviewer wrote: "We have frequently called attention to the state of our 'cheap literature' and to the want of work inculcating good principles, and really useful knowledge, at a low price. The work before us supplies, in part, the desideratum required. It is a weekly publication containing 16 large pages – and when we name Miss Agnes Strickland, and her sister Mrs Traill and Miss Jane Strickland" and three others "as contributors, we think there is guarantee, that the matter will be not only good in a literary point of view, but unexceptionable, in point of principle. There are patterns and enigmas for the ladies, a column for boys, every class of reader may find something to interest and amuse."

October 1849: Agnes and Jane visit Norfolk

In 1849 and before autumn turned to winter, Jane had a short holiday in Norfolk with Agnes, and this is one of the few mentions of Jane having any life further away from Reydon Hall than Southwold.

She and Agnes spent a few days in Norwich, where Agnes was treated as a local celebrity when she went shopping. Jane wrote: "the customers crowded round her to get a look at the author of the 'Queens of England'." This had its compensations for when: "She chose a shawl at the most fashionable depot in Norwich for such articles," the vendor refused to take any money for it. In return Agnes agreed to go round his factory, but instead she was taken to a place where orphan girls were employed making Lisle lace collars.

Jane wrote: "A benevolent lady had gone abroad purposely to learn this beautiful art in order to teach the orphans." The lace school was under the patronage of Bishop Stanley's eldest daughter and "her Majesty Queen Victoria and Queen Adelaide had given ample orders for their lace."

The two sisters on this holiday visited friends from their youth, Mary and Katharine Rackham, who lived in Aylsham, several miles north of Norwich, whom they had not met for several years. They also visited: "their cousin Admiral Hawtayne and his daughter Elizabeth, at Catton" near Norwich.

November 1849: Tom has run aground

Having left Sydney for Calcutta on 25th August 1849 Tom and the 'Scotia' set sail northwards along the east coast of Australia. He then sailed through the Torres Straits which separate Australia and New Guinea before making his way west through, or south of, the many large islands in the South China Sea such as Java and Sumatra, before turning north past Burma to reach Calcutta at the north east corner of India.

Unfortunately on this journey Tom had a major mishap when the 'Scotia' ran aground on the Torres Straits. The 'Scotia' continued to be sea-worthy and Tom managed to reach Calcutta on 1st November 1849, but there he had to remain while substantial repair work was carried out on his vessel.

December 1849: An expensive year ends for Sarah and Richard

Richard and Sarah's Infant School in Ulverston was firmly established by the end of 1849. Some financial help may have been given to reduce the burden on Richard, but he had expanded his expenditure in another direction by providing Christmas dinners and clothing for some of Ulverston's poor residents.

The local papers were supportive of Richard's efforts and reported the various events, starting with the third Public Examination of the children at the Ulverston Infant School on Tuesday 14th December 1849. The papers recorded: "About eighteen months ago, the Rev R Gwillym opened an infant school in Ulverston. The school had been established, fitted up and the expense incurred for teaching &c had been borne by Mr Gwillym. We trusted some benevolent individuals would lighten the expenses by contributions of a valuable nature ... such has been the case, but the burden is still somewhat heavy.

"The school room was crowded with visitors. The children, about 120 in number, from two to seven years of age, looked the picture of health and happiness, and answered the questions of Miss Lawrence (their teacher) in a manner that would have done credit to older heads. At the conclusion, the children gave three cheers for the Queen, three cheers for Mr and Mrs Gwillym, and three cheers for the visitors – and were then each presented with a cake.

"Boys and girls at this school are also taught to knit, and to sew. Pinafores, handkerchiefs, &c were also presented to the children who made them, Mr Gwillym finding the material of which they are made. A very suitable address from the Reverand Gentleman wound up the afternoon's proceedings. We were highly delighted, and deeply sensible of the usefulness of such schools."

The expanded Christmas 1849 and New Year 1850 treats were also noted: "During the Christmas week, the Rev R Gwillym, with his usual liberality and kindness, presented 60 poor families meat sufficient for their Christmas dinners. The same charitable gentleman, on New Year's Day, gave a dinner in the infant school room to 60 poor old men and women who had been constant attendants at Church. Their united age amounted to upwards of 4,000 years, averaging 70 years each. The dinner which was served to them by Mr and Mrs Gwillym, assisted by several active young ladies, consisted of roast beef, veal, pies, plum-pudding &c. After dinner, a cup of port wine negus and a cake were given to each person, and the party, after returning thanks, separated, highly delighted with their entertainment. Seven of the number were too feeble to walk so far, and had their dinners sent to them."

Another act of winter charity was reported: "On Monday 11th February 1850, the Rev R Gwillym, with his usual liberality, gave his annual donation of clothing to 90 poor persons belonging to Ulverston, consisting of shirts, flannels, petticoats and gowns."

14th January 1850: Tom sets sail homewards

Tom spent November and December 1849 in Calcutta while the 'Scotia' was being repaired, and while he dealt with the business that had taken him there originally. Whether the repairs or the business dealings took longest is not known but, either way, it was not until 14th January 1850 that he set sail back to London.

1850: Jane helps with Agnes's correspondence

By 1850 Jane's role in Agnes's literary life expanded further when she began to answer some of Agnes's letters. Jane described her role as: "being very useful by answering such correspondence as, though trivial, required replies; but Agnes had an immense number of important letters as well. Besides these, she wrote frequently to the large circle of her friends. Her buoyant spirits enabled her to perform an immense deal of work in a brief period, a walk or drive seemingly restoring her."

1850: There are three deaths in Sam's family

Sam's life, after running more or less smoothly for many years, suddenly hit a very unhappy period which began with the death of his youngest son, Samuel, who had been born in 1849. Sam wrote of his son: "He was a sweet and promising little boy" who was just at an age when he was beginning to talk.

Sam's son-in-law Benjamin Beresford, despite being fit and healthy, was struck down by cholera while away on a business trip. Sam wrote: "My son-in-law died next, in a distant city, of cholera, leaving my poor young daughter a widow on the eve of her first confinement, scarcely in her twentieth year."

Maria returned to her family home but "her health was so broken up that we never expected her to survive her approaching trial." She survived child-birth, but was still far from strong, when the third family tragedy struck and her baby died, aged only a few weeks.

15th May 1850: Agnes substitutes for William Wordsworth

One of the few famous people to have come from Ulverston was Sir John Barrow. He had been born in a small cottage in a hamlet near the town. His father was a tanner, and he had attended Town Bank School in Ulverston. From these humble beginnings John Barrow had become one of an elite team who, among much else, charted large areas of the Arctic, and discovered the North Magnetic

Pole. He was Second Secretary to the Admiralty for forty years, a Fellow of the Royal Society, a writer and a statesman. Among his writings was the first account of the mutiny on the 'Bounty' which was the basis of the famous book and film which had the title 'Mutiny on the Bounty'.

When Sir John Barrow died, it was decided to build a monument in his memory, and over £1,000 was raised, with many of the nobility and senior officers of the Royal Navy being among the subscribers. It was also decided that the most suitable place for the monument would be on the top of Hoad Hill in Ulverston.

Wednesday 15th May 1850 was chosen as the day for laying the foundation stone of the Barrow Monument. This was a major event in Ulverston and was described in great detail in the local papers, with Richard Gwillym, Sarah and Agnes each having a part to play. Richard's parish church of St Mary flew flags and he officiated at the ceremony; Sarah had over 100 small children to feed and entertain after the ceremony was over, and Agnes had to write a memorial poem.

An edited version of the newspaper report of the day's events is as follows: "The weather was fine. At an early hour the bells of St Mary's Church sent forth glad peals, and the Ulverston Brass Band gave joyous strains from the Market-place. The Town Bank School, associated with the early life of the distinguished individual whose memory was about to be perpetuated was wreathed in evergreens, with the flag of England, sent from the Admiralty for the occasion, waving over its roof; and streamers stretching from the belfry to the field adjoining, appeared glorifying the one humble scholar it had sent forth into the world to gather reputation and renown.

"At the foot of the bank, a triumphal arch, decorated with evergreens and flags, had been erected, displaying the arms of the Barrow family. Flags were also seen on the site of the Monument – on the steeple of St Mary's Church – on the vessels in the port – upon the straw-roofed cot in which the late Baronet first saw light. Indeed, King-street, Market-street, Upper Brook-street &c appeared one continuous display of flags and banners.

"As early as eight o'clock some hundreds of inhabitants congregated in groups in every quarter. As the day advanced thousands more flocked in from the surrounding neighbourhood to wait the procession. It began to move at one o'clock, under the direction of Sergeant-major Bates, of the Duke of Lancaster's Own Yeomanry Cavalry."

The procession included three bands, school-children and teachers, local and other dignitaries, with the general population bringing up the rear. It set off from the Market-place and stopped outside the Town Bank School "whilst some verses, written by Miss Agnes Strickland for the occasion, was sung by the children of the infant school."

The poet who had been due to contribute to the occasion was William Wordsworth, poet laureate, but he had died on 23rd April 1850 and his successor, Alfred Lord Tennyson had not yet been appointed. Agnes's offering was the only poetic one of the day, and she may have been asked to contribute at short notice due to Wordsworth's demise. Her poem has thirty lines of which the following is a selection:

> Rise votive column to attest the worth
> Of Nature's Noble man "of lowly birth,"
> Who naught inherited, but bravely won,
> Wealth, fame, and honours, as the people's son ...
>
> ... God gave him talents and the spirit, too,
> To show his compeers, what a man may do, ...
>
> ... And midst his well-earned honours ne'er forgot,
> His humble Alma Mater, nor the cot,
> At Dragley Beck, whose lowly roof beneath
> He drew, in poverty, his earliest breath.

Having heard Agnes's poem sung, the procession went on its way, reaching the site of the monument at two o'clock where, the papers reported: "Mr Smith, the builder, presented a beautifully wrought silver trowel, with ivory handle to Sir George Barrow" who was son of Sir John Barrow "together with a bottle containing several current coins of the realm, and a copy of the 'Ulverston Advertiser'. These were deposited by the son of Sir George Barrow in the cavity prepared for its reception. Sir George Barrow then laid the foundation stone assisted by his brother Mr John Barrow. The stone with the following inscription having been lowered, received several strikes with the mallet (one prepared for the occasion, wrought in mahogany) and Sir George's son having applied the level, Sir George Barrow declared the stone properly laid." The inscription reads "on the 15th May AD 1850 in the 14th year of the reign of her most Gracious majesty Queen Victoria, Sir George Barrow, Bart and John Barrow, Esq FRS deposited this stone to record the commemoration of the testimonial to the late Sir John Barrow, Bart. Andrew Trimen, Architect."

A speech was made explaining that Sir John Barrow had risen: "from the position of a poor man, by his own integrity and perseverance, to the high position which he held in the Admiralty." Sir George Barrow then made a speech explaining that the monument was intended as a beacon for shipping in the bay. Rev Richard Gwillym said prayers and "Sir George Barrow next called for three cheers for the Rev R Gwillym which he acknowledged in a very suitable address." The ceremony was: "concluded by the Regimental Band playing the National Anthem. This band, 24 in number, was certainly one of the great attractions of the day."

The beautifying works which had recently been carried out on Hoad Hill resulted in a pleasing visual effect, as the papers described: "In returning from the ceremony, the procession, as it wound round the head of Hoad, formed one of the most imposing spectacles, as the serpentine walks became gradually filled, until from top to bottom, an apparently endless chain of humans appeared to have been set in motion, the effect heightened by the numerous flags." It was estimated that 8,000 people had congregated at the top of the hill to take part in the ceremony.

When the procession got back to town, it broke up into various groups each of which went to its allotted place for dinner. Sarah and Richard Gwillym had the children of the infant school to cater for and entertain at Stockbridge House, the older school children had a meal at the National School, and the workhouse children were fed and entertained for the rest of the day at the cottage where Sir John Barrow was born. The day was rounded off by a sumptuous dinner for eighty people held at the Athenaeum Assembly Room. Among the many speeches and toasts was one given by Richard Gwillym.

11th July 1850: Tom's ship is put up for auction

Having left Calcutta on 14th January 1850, the 'Scotia' had short breaks in Madras and at St Helena on the homeward journey and Tom was back at Gravesend on 2nd June 1850 having been away from home for fourteen months.

Running aground on the Torres Straights seems to mark the turning point in Tom's career and in any case, steam ships were taking over from sailing ships in the merchant navy. Although it had been fully repaired at Calcutta, the 'Scotia' seems no longer to have been the desirable ship that it had been before it ran aground. Tom's return to London was followed by the 'Scotia' being put up for sale.

The advertisements for the sale gave details of the ship. It was 132 feet long, 26 feet wide and 22 feet deep and had been built in Newcastle in 1836 by Messrs T & W Smith. It was described as a frigate-built ship, which meant it had three main masts carrying an array of square sails, and had been classified as A1 from the time it was built until 1848.

The advertisement reassured potential buyers by saying that the 'Scotia' had had "most thorough and searching repairs in 1849" and "is now ready for sea." Even though the advertisement claims "the sailing and carrying qualities of this ship cannot be excelled by any other ship afloat" its suggested use was "adaptation for troops, emigrants or convicts" which sounds a rung or two lower on the ladder of uses than those it had previously enjoyed.

It was announced that the 'Scotia' was to be sold by auction on 11th July 1850 "unless previously disposed of by private contract." The private contract must have come about, for by 12th July the 'Scotia' had entered the Custom House of London Docks as a preliminary to sailing for Sydney. The owner was now W Phillips; the commander was still Thomas Strickland; and the 'Scotia' had become one of a regular schedule of ships that would leave London for Sydney on the 15th of each month.

Summer 1850: Sarah has a ball to attend and a party to organise

A ball was held on 6th June 1850 in the Assembly Room in Ulverston to celebrate the first anniversary of the Athenaeum. Sarah was one of the named patronesses as well as being listed with Richard among the attendees at the ball.

The annual summer treat for the children of Ulverston continued to grow. Scholars from the Workhouse School were now included in the event and nearly 500 children paraded through the town, preceded by the town brass band on their way to Stockbridge House on 10th July 1850 where they were fed and entertained until 8.30pm

After the children had left, the supper and dance which traditionally followed had also expanded. It now included teachers and trades-people as well as many of the ladies and gentlemen of the town.

21st August 1850: Susanna's younger daughter marries

Five of Susanna's children lived to adulthood, her daughters Katie and Agnes, and her sons Dunbar, Donald and Robert. The first of them to marry was Susanna's younger daughter Agnes who, on 21st August 1850, married at the age of only 17. Her husband was Charles Thomas Fitzgibbon, a son of Colonel James Fitzgibbon who in some accounts was credited with having saved Toronto from the rebel forces in 1837.

After her marriage, Agnes Fitzgibbon moved from Belleville to live in Toronto with her husband, who was a lawyer. She was prone to ill-health and her husband was prone to risk his money by speculating. Both of these were aspects of her daughter's life that worried Susanna.

1850: Sam's family tragedies continue

Sam's wife Mary had nursed her daughter Maria through the traumas of widowhood, child-birth and loss of a baby, regardless of the fact that she herself was heavily pregnant. Having previously survived thirteen child-births without serious problem, the combination of events was too much for Mary, and she died within half an hour of giving birth to her fourteenth child, her fourth daughter, who was given the names Mary Agnes Strickland.

Sam recounted: "My widowed daughter received from her dying mother the charge of the little infant, whose birth had cost us so much. This precious treasure seemed to replace her own in her heart, and we anticipated for her long years of life." But this child "so beloved and treasured was seized with a complaint indigenous to the country, and fatal to infants, which cut off our little Agnes at the engaging age of five months to the infinite grief of her sister-mother."

After all these family bereavements, Sam decided that both he and his daughter needed a long holiday, and that a visit to England would be a good idea. Not only did he want to visit his family in England, but the English family of his daughter Maria's late husband wanted to meet her. He began to make plans which would enable him to be away from Canada for a full year.

1850: Agnes and Eliza choose a different publisher

Having finished 'Lives of the Queens of England', Eliza and Agnes set out on a similar project entitled 'Lives of the Queens of Scotland'. Agnes had wanted to start at the earliest point of Scottish regal history, but Eliza foresaw two problems with this. The first problem was the difficulty and quantity of research that would have been needed. The second problem was that one of the earlier Scottish Queens, Margaret Atheling had been canonised, and her biography might have renewed the outcry against Agnes from the anti-Catholics of the day. Eliza persuaded Agnes that it would be better to begin with Margaret Tudor, consort of James IV, and therefore an ancestress of the royal family of Great Britain.

They planned to conclude with the princesses connected with the royal succession to the British throne. On account of Agnes's research into the life of Mary Queen of Scots, she already had contacts for studying the lives of other Queens of Scotland.

When the first volume was ready for publication, Agnes and Eliza went to Henry Colburn to negotiate terms for the series. Henry Colburn had made a great deal of money out of 'Lives of the Queens of England' and no doubt wanted to strike a similarly beneficial deal for the biographies of Scottish Queens, but Agnes and Eliza did not intend to be caught a second time. Henry Colburn and Eliza were barely on speaking terms, but Agnes sometimes got on reasonably well with him. However, on this occasion even Agnes was offended by the abrupt manner in which he refused the terms they suggested. As Jane put it: "Agnes, who was even-tempered only smiled; while her sister, whose temper was irritable, was offended by the brusquerie of the wealthy and consequential publisher, and showed that she was so."

Agnes and Eliza's contract with Henry Colburn only covered 'Lives of the Queens of England' and they were free to find an alternative publisher for their work on the queens of Scotland. William Blackwood, a well-known Edinburgh publisher seemed suitable for the work, but before offering 'Lives of the Queens of Scotland' to him, Agnes asked her friend Mr Home, Sheriff of Edinburgh, for his opinion. He wrote: "I do not think they give very high prices or are what is called dashing booksellers. But they are fair ones. They deal fairly with you and expect you to do the same by them."

This sounded like a refreshing change after Henry Colburn's trickiness and they offered their new work to William Blackwood who, Jane reported: "instantly agreed to their terms, and nothing could have been more honourable than their conduct with the authors."

September 1850: Tom's eldest daughter marries twice

Tom was scheduled to leave for Australia in the 'Scotia' on the 15th September 1850. Advertising for the voyage gave particulars of the accommodation available and the associated costs. It stated that the 'Scotia': "has superior accommodation for cabin, intermediate and steerage passengers having a full poop and will carry an experienced surgeon. Cabin 60 – 80 guineas; intermediate £30; steerage £15 including a liberal dietary scale and enclosed cabins." The poop is the cabin accommodation built on the superstructure at the rear of the ship.

The voyage would take Tom away from home for many months and his eldest daughter, Adela although aged only 16 or 17, wanted to get married. If she did not marry before Tom sailed for Australia, presumably she would have had to wait until he returned, or until she became old enough to marry without his permission. She chose to marry before her father set sail and on the 10th September 1850 married Gent Wigg, eldest son of George Wigg Esq of Acle in Norfolk, by licence at the Church of Allhallows, London Wall.

Tom would have been unable to leave his ship for any length of time so close to his departure date, hence necessitating a London marriage for his daughter. Tom, having attended his daughter's wedding, sailed for Australia from London Docks on the 18th September 1850, only slightly behind the published schedule.

Adela, having married of necessity in haste in London on 10th September 1850, married Gent Wigg a second time, in a more leisurely manner, at the Parish Church in her new home of Acle in Norfolk, on 30th September 1850.

August and September 1850: 'Lives of the Queens of Scotland' begin to appear

Having an Edinburgh-based publisher for 'Lives of the Queens of Scotland,' necessitated Agnes being on hand in the Scottish capital while the books were being printed. The first two volumes were published in 1850 and Agnes set to work on the third volume which began the life of Mary Stuart.

Agnes could stay with her friend, Miss Helen Walker in Edinburgh when she wanted to get on with work quietly. Agnes's other friends in Scotland kept an eye on her so that if and when her health showed signs of suffering, they swung into action to smooth her path. In a letter to Eliza, Agnes wrote: "Helen Walker has been very good to me. I had meals at my own hours too; but the publication of the two works, letters and toilets, as well as travelling, are rather too much for me. My journey here was only forty minutes, and Lady Morton sent her carriage for Fisher and me. I have thirty letters to write, and must send one to Muz, or she will fret." Muz was a pet name for their mother and Fisher was Agnes's ladies-maid.

Agnes told Eliza about the progress of the first volume of 'Queens of Scotland': "Three thousand were printed, of which 250 sold immediately. Everyone here is delighted with the volume. The publishers are in high spirits. They wish to have the volume revised for the reprint, in case it should be immediately required."

While Agnes was in Edinburgh checking proofs and collecting information for further volumes, Prince Albert arrived to lay the foundation stone of the National Gallery Scotland on 30th August 1850, and Agnes was given a ticket to attend when Queen Victoria arrived at Holyrood for the occasion. Agnes was standing next to Lady Belhaven, wife of the Lord High Commissioner, with whom the Queen shook hands. Agnes made a curtsey and felt that she received a smile of recognition. She also saw Prince Albert lay the stone: "with a gilt mallet. The Scots Archer Guard were in attendance with their long bows, which made a grand historical spectacle."

Although Agnes enjoyed the occasion, she caught a serious cold and developed a sore throat. Her doctor said the air of Edinburgh was too cold for her, and one of Agnes's friends came to the rescue. Jane wrote: "Lady Lucy Grant came to see her, took her to Kilgraston" a few miles south of Perth "where the climate was milder, and nursed her with care till she was able to return to Miss Walker's and her literary labours."

Agnes met in Edinburgh some of the relatives of her Scottish brothers-in-law John Moodie and Thomas Traill. Agnes wrote home: "I dined yesterday with Moodie's aunt, Mrs General Macgregor, a dear old lady. She sent for her sister-in-law, Lady Charlotte Macgregor, who told me that Moodie was her cousin. There was another relative of his – the Hon Mrs Sinclair – and they all wished to claim me as a near connection through him."

Jane recorded: "This was very gratifying to Agnes, who soon after was invited to visit St Margaret's Convent to meet an eccentric old lady, Miss Traill, the sub-prioress, a relation of Thomas Traill. This lady had become, from a rigid Presbyterian, an equally austere Catholic." This had happened when Miss Traill went to Rome to persuade the Pope of the errors of his belief, and was herself persuaded into Catholicism by a chaplain of the Pope.

Agnes drank tea with this Miss Traill and looked at pictures which Miss Traill had painted, feeling that her skill as a painter was greater than her skill at making converts. Agnes visited her again the following year but Miss Traill had risen to become Superior at the convent and was so enthusiastic in her endeavours to convert Agnes to Catholicism, that Agnes felt it better not to visit her again.

28th September 1850: Catharine is struggling on

Catharine earned what she could by writing, and Agnes in England did what she could to place Catharine's items. On

28th September 1850 Catharine told Ellen Dunlop, the married daughter of her friend Frances Stewart, that she had: "yesterday finished my arduous and fatiguing task of copying the MS of the 'Canadian Crusoes'. I suffered great pain in the muscles of my right shoulder and arm during the last week's work. I wrote latterly 20 close pages a day – besides much needle work and many letters. I must now give my arm a holiday in the writing way."

Apart from her writing, Catharine was busy making and mending family clothes, accumulating rags which could be made into a carpet, and doing quilting for petticoats and bedding. Her eldest daughter Kate was busy learning to spin and knit from carded wool, and the wet weather was hampering the men-folk who wanted to get on with ploughing and with sowing the autumn wheat. Catharine's daughter Annie went to live in Peterborough with Frances Stewart for part of 1850 and 1851 in order to attend a school run by Frances's niece.

November 1850: Agnes, Eliza and Jane are busy with various 'Queens'

During the winter months of 1850/1851 the three unmarried Strickland sisters were hard at work on regal biographies. Agnes and Eliza were using the documents and notes which Agnes had accumulated in Scotland, and were writing further volumes of 'Lives of the Queens of Scotland', as well as continuing with their seemingly never-ending task of producing an eight-volume edition of 'Lives of the Queens of England' from the original twelve volumes. Jane continued with her tasks of proof-reading and fact-checking prior to printing, and of helping Agnes with mundane correspondence.

3rd January 1851: Richard Gwillym nearly resigns

An upset to the usual pattern of life occurred in Ulverston in January 1851 when Richard Gwillym was so incensed by an accusation that he was a Puseyite, that he said he would resign. Edward Pusey and the Oxford Movement aimed to move the Church of England nearer to the Catholic Church, and the movement was the cause of a great deal of controversy in the 1830s to 1850s.

There was dismay in Ulverston as a result of the intended resignation. The local papers reported: "It being understood that the Reverend R Gwillym MA contemplated resigning, the inhabitants anxious to retain him hastily got up a petition" which speedily grew. "A petition got up on Wednesday 8th January 1851, earnestly desiring him to continue his present ministration, had on Thursday 9th January, the day following, received upwards of two thousand signatures. We trust, therefore, that when the rev gentleman sees how highly his efforts are appreciated, he will forego his present resolution and bide amongst us."

The petition was very soon presented to Sarah's husband. The following week the newspapers reported: "On Friday 10th January 1851, a deputation waited on the Rev R Gwillym requesting him to reconsider his resignation. He said he could not do otherwise than accede to the request and he could most gladly continue" as their vicar.

The paper explained: "since the contemplated resignation was announced, it has become known that it was in consequence of his being accused of Puseyism. The only ground for such an accusation being his curate, Mr Parker" had given a sermon which "savoured strongly of Puseyite doctrine." Richard, by his reaction against the suggestion that he held High Church views, positioned himself very firmly among moderate and mainstream Anglican ministers.

10th January 1851: Tom reaches Australia

Tom, having sailed from London on 18th September 1850, made good time to Sydney, arriving within four months of departure on 10th January 1851.

17th January 1851: Catharine's new home is not ideal

Catharine recounted, in a letter written to Frances Stewart in January 1851, that her home 'Oaklands' was cold and in an exposed location. She wrote: "Owing to the depth of snow, the wood was nearly done before we could get more which obliged us to economize the fires. The cold exposure of our situation on the top of the high hill above the woods renders this a difficult house to keep warmed – we sit in the small parlour and keep but two fires – consequently the bedrooms are cold." Another disadvantage of the hill top location was the long uphill walk when anything had to be carried to the house.

Catharine said she could not reach Sam to ask for his help, and although she had hinted to Agnes about the bad state of her family finances, she had done no more than hint. In a letter to Frances Stewart later in 1851 Catharine wrote: "I dared not tell her how pressing it really was for my dear old mother would be so distressed and agitated that it would hurry her and make her ill – besides – I knew it would be useless – she has it not in her power to help us."

January 1851: Susanna leaps to Agnes's defence

From time to time during her early life at Reydon, Susanna had hinted at a feeling of rivalry with Agnes, though Agnes never expressed any such feeling about Susanna. Whatever reservations Susanna may have had, she was a great admirer of Agnes's work and defended her if the need arose.

In their book 'Susanna Moodie – Letters of a Lifetime' edited by Carl Ballstadt, Elizabeth Hopkins and Michael Peterman it is reported that an article based on a series of letters had been published in the 'Toronto Patriot' in January 1851, which Susanna summarised in a letter of rebuttal thus: "Miss Strickland is represented as being a very dear and intimate friend of the Southey family" which, the article said, was "denied by Mrs Southey, who said that Miss Strickland intruded herself at a moment of great distress for the purpose of manufacturing literary capital to suit her own purpose."

Susanna had written to Agnes about this, and Agnes had in turn written to Mrs Southey, widow of the poet laureate Robert Southey. Mrs Southey replied that she had never met Agnes but was an admirer of her work. At Susanna's instigation this correspondence is said to have been printed in the 'Albion' on 6th May 1851 and so Susanna achieved her objective of clearing her sister's name. However, if the names of the publications have been correctly recorded for posterity, and there is no reason to suppose otherwise, it leaves the question of why the refutation appeared in the New York publication, the 'Albion' when the original slur had been published in the 'Toronto Patriot.'

The closing lines of Susanna's letter to the 'Albion' describe Agnes as having "a reputation of unsullied integrity; and who is more prized by her family for her high moral qualities, her truth and faithfulness, than even those great mental attainments, that have made her one of the most remarkable women of her age and country."

Reydon Hall, Suffolk

Susanna by Thomas Cheesman

Sarah by Thomas Cheesman

Agnes Strickland by John Hayes 1846
© National Portrait Gallery, London

Agnes (or Eliza?) Strickland by Charles Gow 1844
© National Portrait Gallery, London

Susanna Moodie circa 1850

Part 4: Authors galore

*Trans-Atlantic visits and marriages;
'Roughing It in the Bush' and fame for Susanna
Moodie; 'Twenty-Seven Years in Canada West' by
Samuel Strickland; family support for Catharine;
'Rome; Regal and Republican' by Jane Margaret
Strickland; 'The Canadian Settler's Guide'
by Catharine Parr Traill; 'Life of Mary Queen
of Scots' by Agnes Strickland; a fire*

1851: Sam mentions his Civic duties

The details given of Sam's political and community life are sparse, but occasional hints and mentions give some clues. In his autobiographical account of his life in Canada, as context for an account of the after-effects of a thunder storm, Sam wrote: "I remember that, not more than two years since, I had occasion to go out into the township of Douro to attend the sitting of the Council, of which I was then a member." This implies that in 1851 he was a local councillor, but when he wrote this account in 1853 he was not.

The story he was relating continued: "I had, on my way, to pass through a small clearing" which contained "several large hemlock trees" that "had been dead for some years ... The day before, there had been a terrific thunder-storm which struck the largest, which was fully four feet in diameter, shivering it from top to bottom, and throwing the pieces around for upwards of sixty yards in every direction. If a barrel of gunpowder had been placed under the tree, greater devastation could not have been made."

1851: Sam says that Thomas Traill had civic duties in the 1830s

In mentioning his own civic duties, Sam also revealed that Thomas Traill had carried out some similar duties. Sam wrote: "During the administration of Sir John Colborne" from 1828 to 1839 "I was appointed one of the new commissioners for holding the Court of Requests for the townships of Douro and Dumner, which I continued to hold until the court was abolished, and the Division Court instituted in its place. Under the old Court of Requests, a suit could be instituted for any sum above ten pounds. The commissioners were generally appointed from the magistracy or from the most influential persons in the division.

"Messrs Traill, Thompson, and myself used to hold a court once a month for our division. The average number of cases did not exceed fifteen, and the amount sued for seldom exceeded two pounds upon each summons. The commissioners were entitled to one shilling each for every case decided by them. This court was in reality a Court of Equity: not being clogged by the technicalities of the law, we gave our judgement according to the weight of evidence laid before us, without prejudice or partiality."

Sam gave as an example of the kind of case involved, one in which a woman was being sued by a carpenter. She refused to pay his bill of six shillings for constructing a spinning-wheel from parts which she had supplied, on the basis that it was impossible to spin a thread from the spinning-wheel. She argued that as it did not do its job, it was not a spinning-wheel and as no-one in the court-room could manage to make the wheel spin thread, she won her case.

30th March 1851: The English census seems incomplete

The first of the regular ten-yearly censuses had been fairly basic and had been taken in 1841. The second census, carried out on the night of 30th/31st March 1851 was intended to be more informative.

The only member of the Strickland family who declared herself as residing at Reydon Hall that night was (Mrs) Elizabeth Strickland. She was recorded as 76 years old, a widowed gentlewoman and head of the household. She had four live-in servants with her. One was

Enid Fisher, the ladies maid who had been with Agnes during her tour in Scotland the previous summer, and who was aged 19 on census night. The other three live-in staff were also young. They were a cook aged 22, a general maid aged 18 and a 15 year old errand boy. Eliza, Agnes and Jane Margaret Strickland have not been found on the census.

Sarah appears in the 1851 census, though with a slight adjustment to her age. She and Richard Gwillym are both recorded at Stockbridge House, Ulverston, and both are said to be 48 years old, although Sarah was actually 52. Like her mother, Sarah had a staff of four live-in servants. In Sarah's case the staff consisted of a housekeeper, a butler, a housemaid and a kitchen-maid. The housekeeper, Mary Daniel, was aged 54 and so was contemporary with Sarah. The butler and house-maid were both 27 years old and the kitchen-maid was 17. The surname Daniel crops up in three contexts in this narrative. Mr Daniel as the church organist with other musical talents; Mr and Mrs Daniels being mentioned in relation to the National School, and here Mary Daniel as Sarah's live-in housekeeper. Whether this is coincidence, or whether the various Daniels were related in some way is not known.

Tom Strickland, being in Australia on census night was not included in the census returns, but his family appear in the records. They were living at Balaclava Terrace, West Ham, Plaistow and consisted of Margaretta, recorded as a Master Mariner's wife, and four of her children, all said to have been born at sea. The four children were Thomas, aged 16 and a builder's clerk; together with Julia, Mary and Diana, aged 14, 11 and 9 years old respectively. A servant girl, aged 20, completed the household. Their eldest son John Arthur Strickland was not mentioned, nor was their youngest son, Walter. From later information, John seems at some point to have emigrated to Australia, possibly on the trip that Tom has just made. Walter being 8 years old may have been away at school.

Tom's eldest daughter, now Adela Wigg, was 18 years old and living on a farm in Old Road, Acle, Norfolk with her husband's family. Her father-in-law was a 55 year old farmer with a 300-acre farm employing ten men, and her mother-in-law was 51. Her husband Gent was 27 and, like his 25 year old brother, was described as a farmer's son. The final family member living in

Adela's new home was another brother of her husband, aged 23 and a ship's agent.

12th April 1851: Sarah's husband continues his benevolent expenditure

Richard Gwillym's gifts and treats to the poor over Christmas and New Year of 1851 may have suffered due to the upset over his possible resignation. Alternatively, his resignation and the resulting petition may have been a more interesting story for the papers than his customary gifts.

Therefore his action in April could have been a replacement or an addition to winter gifts. The local paper recorded that on 12th April 1851: "The Rev R Gwillym with his wonted liberality, has given to the poor of Ulverston, during the past week, no less than 110 articles of wearing apparel, consisting of gowns, shirts, flannel petticoats and flannel waistcoats. These are both seasonable and serviceable gifts" and the recipients felt "sincere gratitude."

26th April 1851: Tom leaves Australia but not for home

Having arrived in Sydney on 10th January 1851, Tom and the 'Scotia' remained there until 26th April 1851. He then began a complicated series of voyages between Sydney, Madras, Singapore and Bombay which lasted for the rest of 1851 and nearly all of 1852.

3rd May 1851: Agnes visits the Great Exhibition

Agnes had a widening array of people who became her friends, and who invited her to stay with them, sometimes on a regular or prolonged basis. Among these were Mr and Mrs Kirby with whom Agnes stayed on several occasions at their home in Devonshire Street, Portland Place in London. Together they visited the Great Exhibition in the Crystal Palace on 3rd May 1851, just two days after the State Opening.

The Crystal Palace covered 18 acres and had been erected in Hyde Park over the winter of 1850/1851. Many people doubted whether it could be built at all, yet alone in the short time allowed for it, but Agnes, having seen Mr Paxton's work at Chatsworth never had any such doubts.

8th July 1851: Sam with Maria begin their journey to England

By 8th July 1851, Sam's plans for a long absence from home were all in place, and he set off with his daughter Maria for England. The first day of their journey, Sam later wrote: "lay through the Indian village of Rice Lake" and they visited the Nogun family of Indians (to use Sam's description). Sam and Maria knew the Nogun family well, and they were welcomed and given a meal of fried venison, bacon and hot shanty-bread "and a good cup of tea" served with "a clean cloth on the table" and everything nice and clean.

Sam said: "We had often given them flour and pork, and many a dinner and tea" as well as including them in the family Sunday service at times, but, he wrote: "this was the first opportunity they had of showing their hospitality and gratitude." In the evening Sam and his daughter crossed Rice Lake and "stopped all night at the pretty village of Gore's Landing" near to where Catharine and her family lived.

Next day they continued their journey by boat to Rochester, then by omnibus to Buffalo and, after making the final leg of the journey by train, reached Albany that evening. From Albany, Sam wrote, they took: "the 'Hendric Hudson', one of the largest of those floating steam-palaces which ply upon the Hudson. We left Albany about nine o'clock in the evening, and were safely moored at her wharf, in New York, between five and six o'clock in the morning." They had travelled "the whole distance from Rochester, five hundred miles, in twenty hours, for which we paid the reasonable charge of something like £1.5s" (£1.25) "per head."

Sam and Maria spent five days sight-seeing in New York then, Sam wrote: "On the 16th of July, we sailed in the 'Hungarian', 1300 tons burthen, Captain Patterson, and had a remarkably pleasant passage of twenty-two days" to Liverpool from New York.

July 1851: Sarah and Richard split their summer treat into two

By 1851, the number of school children eligible for Richard and Sarah's summer treat had grown very great, and they divided the event into two separate occasions. The first children to have their treat were the infants who had their party at Stockbridge House on 10th July 1851, a week before their school examination.

The school examination was held, the papers said: "in the presence of their patron, the Rev R Gwillym, and lady, Sir Geo Barrow and party, and a numerous assemblage." The teacher seems to have been a kindly lady: "Miss Lawrence, and the complete ascendancy which, by gentle means, she had gained over children so very young, elicited the admiration of all present."

After the stress of the examination was over: "the children were invited to tea at the residence of the Rev R Gwillym, at Stockbridge, and indulged afterwards with a lengthened and merry romp in the pleasure grounds of the mansion."

Sarah and Richard then had a break before the older children in the National School had their party at Stockbridge where they: "mustered to a large number" a month later, on 21st August 1851.

July 1851: Agnes spends the summer at Reydon Hall

In 1851 Agnes spent more of the year at Reydon Hall than usual, in order to be on hand to supervise some building work that she was financing. She was therefore unusually at Reydon, rather than in London or on one of her late summer tours, when Sam and Maria arrived unexpectedly.

8th August 1851: Sam arrives home without warning

Twenty two days after leaving New York, Sam and his daughter Maria landed at Liverpool. The next day, 8th August 1851, Sam was back at Reydon Hall, over twenty-six years since he had left. When Sam Strickland had left England to travel to Canada in 1825, the journey had taken him over two months. On his return journey, transport systems had improved so much that it took only a month, including five days spent sight-seeing in New York.

Sam had not told the family in England about his intended visit. Why he chose to arrive suddenly, denying them the pleasure of anticipation, and also the opportunity to make preparations is not explained. When she wrote a biography of Agnes, Jane wrote: "Agnes was still engaged in her improvements and alterations when two unexpected visitors enlivened the family group at Reydon Hall – her brother, Major Strickland, came as a widower, having lately lost his pious and amiable Irish wife. His eldest daughter, Mrs Beresford, a widow of nineteen was with him."

Sam wrote of his arrival "It would have been a still more delightful reunion could the whole eight have once more met beneath the parental roof. This, however, was impossible, as I had left two sisters in Canada, and my brother was on his way to Calcutta."

Agnes described Sam to Sarah in a letter: "He is very like our dear father, but not quite so tall or handsome. The loss of his beautiful light brown curls has taken from his height. He has a military air, and is so frank, good-natured and intelligent, and so full of sense and sensibility, that you must love him."

1851/1852: Sam gets engaged

Sam and Agnes took a little tour of Norfolk together, including a visit to Aylsham where Sam had apparently finished his education with the Rev Mr Jervis, though this was not mentioned earlier or elsewhere.

In Aylsham, Agnes's friends the Rackhams were former acquaintances of Sam and he (in Jane's version): "renewed his schoolboy acquaintance with Miss Catherine Rackham, for whom he had an old liking, which ended in their engagement – though, as her widowed mother refused to part with her daughter, the marriage did not take place till after the old lady's death."

Catharine's version of events was: "at Aylsham, the schoolboy had been forgotten, except by a widow lady and her family, who had always been kind to the young student, and it was there that he met one whom he even as a boy had admired – I will not say loved – but in her found all that was charming, though no longer the lovely girl, for she was but a few years his junior – but still lovely, and lovable. An engagement took place – but they were not married until later as she would not leave her mother who was old and infirm." Sam was 46 years old.

Sam was not only busily occupied visiting his fiancee in Aylsham, he also set to work to write an autobiography which told of his journey from England as a young man and his subsequent life and adventures in Canada.

His daughter Maria went to Kent to spend some time with her late husband's family.

Catharine in a letter to Ellen Dunlop in 1852 passed on some news from England. Of Maria Beresford's activities Catharine wrote: "Maria is at Tunbridge Wells or Hastings – her grand-mother Beresford has given her a splendid piano and she is taking lessons in music drawing and other things. I am very glad for her sake for she is a worthy girl and deserves any good fortune that may befall her – I heard this through the Browns."

Autumn 1851: Agnes crosses swords with Macaulay again

Agnes left Sam and Reydon Hall while she saw to the launch of the next volume of (to give the full title) 'Lives of the Queens of Scotland; and English Princesses connected with the Regal Succession of Great Britain' and to work on subsequent volumes.

In London Agnes again stayed with Mr and Mrs Kirby in Devonshire Street, and together they visited various large houses which contained portraits or items of relevance to Agnes's current project. In this way the Kirbys introduced Agnes to the Duke and Duchess of Somerset who took a liking to Agnes, and invited her to routs and dinners at their home. The Duke of Somerset was himself a writer and studied various topics. The Duchess was his second wife and a very able society hostess.

On one evening in 1851, Agnes met all the new Tory ministers and ambassadors with the exception of Lord Derby. Among these were Disraeli and his wife. Disraeli, himself an author, complimented Agnes on 'Lives of the Queens of England'. She must subsequently have sent him some books, because an elaborately worded 'thank you' letter in Disraeli's handwriting was found among Agnes's papers after her death.

On another occasion, the Duchess of Somerset seated Agnes and Macaulay together at dinner, thinking that the two famous historians of the day would enjoy each other's company. As Jane wryly commented, they should have had the sense to talk on subjects about which they could agree, but unfortunately they didn't, and the Duchess of Somerset had not taken into account that they both liked to talk rather than listen. Maybe also they were conscious of the long and critical review of Agnes's writing in the 'Edinburgh Review' in 1847 which was commonly believed to have been written by Macaulay.

Jane wrote: "A very handsome quiet young man, who faced them, apparently afforded Mr Macaulay a topic for conversation, for he looked pointedly at him, and commenced a tirade of invective on the stupidity of handsome men, by which the Adonis of the party evidently was embarrassed and annoyed. Agnes thought the attack unfair, and replied, 'It was a consolation for ugly men to consider them so.' He became sulky, and they had no further conversation together."

Agnes thought Macaulay "vulgar, pompous and unprepossessing" and was no doubt pleased when his writing was accused in a review of containing its "usual inaccuracy."

2nd November 1851: Catharine is worrying about her sons and the bailiffs

Life for Thomas and Catharine was still a struggle two years after the purchase of 'Oaklands'. In addition to their financial troubles, their older sons, James (aged 18) and Harry (aged 14) did not understand, and were not able to sympathise with Thomas's bouts of depression.

In a postscript to a letter to Susanna dated 2nd November 1851, Catharine was candid about the relationship between Thomas and his two older sons, and asked for Susanna's help. She said: "One thing grieves me both with James and his brother Harry, a want of respectfulness and deference of manner to their father. When you see James my dear sister, impress this duty upon him for my sake. I know that James does not intend to offend and cannot see that his want of respect and courtesy to one whose situation as the father of the family and a person of advanced years demands every attention. On this subject I have said much and may also have suffered much." Thomas was 58 years old.

Just how bad things were at 'Oaklands' became clear early in 1852 when Catharine wrote to Susanna to ask for John Moodie's advice about the power of bailiffs to seize goods. She wrote: "I have many questions to put to Moodie. Can the bailiffs seize the flour and pork that are in the house – I think you said they could not. Can they seize the crops on the ground for the ensuing year? What check have we upon the Sheriff's officers in the disposal of the proceeds of the sale of the stove, watch, gun, books? In short dear, I am so ignorant in these matters. My husband cannot bear to discuss them and indeed I believe he knows as little as I do myself – he is so utterly cast down, unable to think for his own benefit and a prey to everyone."

However, the situation was beginning to improve. James was now bringing some money into the household. Catharine told Susanna that James "is busy on the road carting in hay and grain for some of our neighbours. The hay is paying for rail timber for the new wheat fallow. The wheat is to earn money to buy shoes and boots of which there has been a melancholy deficiency in the family for some months past, also to renew some parts of the harness which was utterly worn out and not fit for going on a long journey."

9th January 1852: Susanna's book 'Roughing It in the Bush' is published in England

Late in 1851 both Susanna and Catharine were trying to get a book published in England. Catharine sent her manuscript to Agnes, who took it round various publishers in London until she found one who would offer a decent deal. When a deal had been agreed Jane, Agnes and Eliza between them did the proof-reading and other such necessary work to get Catharine's work from manuscript stage to publication.

Susanna took a different approach from Catharine and, instead of involving her sisters, asked a friend in London, John Bruce to find and deal with a publisher for her. John Bruce had wide experience of publishing and editing, including having been one of the founding members of the Camden Society when it was set up in 1838. The

Camden Society had been named after William Camden, a 16th century antiquary and historian, and its purpose was to publish early historical materials, such as previously unpublished manuscripts and new editions of rare printed books.

John Bruce offered Susanna's book to Richard Bentley, who had published a book for John Moodie many years earlier. Richard Bentley's first offer was £50 for the copyright of the work, but John Bruce improved on this offer to ensure that Susanna would also receive half of any profit which her book might make, and that on the day of publication she would receive an advance of £20 on such profits. This deal was agreed, and on 9th January 1852 Susanna's book 'Roughing It in the Bush' was published in London, and Susanna was immediately sent £20 advance on profits, as well as £50 for the copyright.

'Roughing It in the Bush' purports to tell the story of Susanna's life in Canada, beginning on 30th August 1832 when she arrived at Grosse Island at the time of the cholera epidemic, and ending with her journey to join John Moodie in Belleville at the beginning of 1840. The book consists of a series of sketches interspersed with poems and gives an unflattering account of her life and of the people she encountered. Her concluding paragraph made grim reading. She wrote: "If these sketches should prove the means of deterring one family from sinking their property, and shipwrecking all their hopes, by going to reside in the backwoods of Canada, I shall consider myself amply repaid for revealing the secrets of the prison-house, and feel that I have not toiled and suffered in the wilderness in vain."

The book carried a dedication: "To Agnes Strickland, author of the 'Lives of the Queens of England'. This simple tribute of affection is dedicated by her sister Susanna Moodie." Agnes was familiar with the benefit of dedications and had herself dedicated 'Lives of the Queens of England' to Queen Victoria, but whereas Agnes had first obtained permission from the Queen, Susanna may have made her dedication without consulting Agnes.

February 1852: Catharine's book 'Canadian Crusoes' finds a publisher in London

The book for which Agnes had found a publisher was Catharine's story 'Canadian Crusoes: A Tale of the Rice Lake Plains'. It was primarily an adventure story in which three children get lost in the Canadian Backwoods, but it also contained practical information on living in the backwoods which enabled the children to survive for three years before being found. George Virtue of Hall, Virtue and Company agreed to pay £50 for the right to print 2,000 copies.

Catharine told the good news when writing to her friend Ellen Dunlop on 12th February 1852. She was looking forward to receiving the money even though it was all needed to pay debts. Catharine said that clearing some debts would be "a comfort" even if there would not be "a penny to spend on household matters, however necessary, for the children."

Her eldest son James had had enough of the situation. He had developed lung problems when still quite young, and had received little by way of education. In a letter to his aunt Susanna in 1852 he said: "I am heartily tired of remaining at home, droning out my existence on an uncultivated farm, merely doing work that a common Irish labourer can do much better."

March 1852: 'Blackwood's Magazine' reviews Susanna's book

Susanna may be said to have been thoughtlessly cashing in on Agnes's literary reputation with a book which featured her own poverty, at the time when Agnes was spending much of her time among wealthy and titled people in Britain, and with the world at large wrongly assuming that Agnes was rich.

To make matters worse, it is said that a review in 'Blackwood's Magazine' in March 1852 included the following contrast between Susanna as the heroine of the book, and wealthy ladies in England, of whom Agnes might be thought an example: "deftly embroidering in carpeted saloon, gracefully bending over easel or harp. Suspend for a moment your silken pursuits, and look forth into the desert of your sister's sufferings! May you never, from stern experience, learn fully to appreciate them. Transport yourself in imagination's car, to Canada's backwoods, and behold one, gently nurtured as yourselves, cheerfully condescending to rudest toils. Not to such hardships was she born, nor educated for them. The comforts of an English home, the endearments of sisterly affection, the refinement of literary tastes but ill prepared the emigrant's wife to work in the rugged and inclement wilderness, harder than the meanest domestic, whom, in her own country, she was used to command."

It is not clear if this quote was written by the reviewer or was an extract from 'Roughing It in the Bush'. If the latter, it has not been found in an edition published in 1986 (which has an introduction by Margaret Atwood). If the former, the comparison was either accidental or inexplicable, as Blackwood was the publisher of 'Lives of the Queens of Scotland' and their reviewer should not have been implying anything negative about one of their currently successful authors. If the extract or review was speaking to Agnes, then Susanna was conveniently forgetting the reality of struggling to make ends meet at Reydon Hall, or the reviewer was unaware of it.

Early 1852: Agnes accompanies the Countess of Newburgh

After a period of hard literary work at Reydon Hall, Agnes made a trip to London early in 1852. She was, Jane wrote: "suffering much from pain in the face nearly as bad as tic doloureux." Her doctor said she needed a break with some relaxation, having been busy with proofs and revisions during the printing of her 'Life of Mary Stuart' within the series 'Lives of the Queens of Scotland'.

Agnes had been attending Drawing-rooms at St James's Palace for some years. When Lady Dorothy Leslie became Countess of Newburgh on the death of her younger brother, and was presented to Queen Victoria as was customary, Jane wrote: "upon the accession of rank" she "wished to take Agnes with her – an arrangement that was agreeable to both."

1st April 1852: Agnes helps out while Catharine waits to be paid

Unlike Susanna who received substantial payment in advance, Catharine had to wait for her money. Two months after hearing that she was to be paid £50 for 'Canadian Crusoes', Catharine, when she wrote to Ellen Dunlop on 1st April 1852 had received nothing, and most of her family were ill either with mumps or with eye or throat infections, all of which were widespread in the region.

Finances were less dire than when Catharine had last written to her friend, but she was still having to watch every penny, even "finding paper on which to write needs to be taken into consideration." Agnes had come to the rescue, having sent Catharine some money for "a new piece in Sharpe's Mag with a little from herself additional."

Mid 1852: Sam and Maria return to Canada

Sam, during his year in England, achieved three things of lasting effect. The first and most important was that he became engaged to be married, and when he and Maria returned to Canada in mid 1852, it was agreed that he would return at an appropriate time, to marry Katharine Rackham.

Secondly, he had completed the manuscript of his book which would have the title 'Twenty-Seven Years in Canada West; or, The Experience of an Early Settler' and which contained a mixture of his personal life-story and indications on what to expect and how to cope with being a settler in Canada.

Sam in his book described the evolution of the district of Canada in which he lived. As more immigrants arrived, so administration districts were sub-divided and new town plots were laid out. He said the town-plot of Lakefield had recently been surveyed and named, and was within half a mile of his home which was in the township of Douro. He thought Lakefield would become a place of some importance in due course, particularly if a bridge were to be built across the river at that point. References to where Sam and his family had established their home, gradually changed from Douro to Lakefield.

Sam's third achievement of lasting effect while he was in England, was to raise money towards building an Anglican church in Canada. Non-conformist chapels of various denominations in and around Douro/Lakefield greatly outnumbered Anglican churches, and Sam wanted to help redress the balance. He took sufficient money back to Canada to construct the walls of the church, and to change this project from an idea to a reality.

14th July 1852: Agnes writes to her lawyer friend

After all the work that Eliza and Agnes had done to create an eight volume version of 'Lives of the Queens of England', Henry Colburn made the task unnecessarily difficult.

On 14th July 1852 Agnes had to ask Archibald Stephens for legal help. She wrote: "You were kind enough to renew your offer of professional chivalry. My sister and Colburn have had a notable skirmish on the following grounds. We were pledged to superintend the adaptation of the illustrations of both plates and woodcuts for the revised edition. After we selected the woodcuts, he refused to have them in, and demands us to go over our work again, choosing to impose a deal of trouble upon us. High words took place between him and Eliza, she gave her testimonial to his conduct in the matter of the 'Queens of England' in not very flattering terms.

"He wrote to me to come and confer, and tried to coax and bully your humble servant into signing a paper, engaging to work in the rejected woodcuts for nothing. I told him I had performed my contract according to his own instructions, and called upon him to pay the balance due. He walked out of the room in a huff, but soon returned and said he would pay us for what we had done, but would send us a notice to put in his woodcuts, and compel us to do so by legal means. Then he spoke of the abridgement which he now wants, but I referred him to you."

20th July 1852: 'Roughing It in the Bush' crosses the Atlantic

Whilst Agnes and Eliza were having trouble with Henry Colburn, Susanna was beginning a friendly correspondence with Richard Bentley. She first wrote to him on 16th April 1852, when John Bruce was ill and there was some business matter to communicate. When she wrote to him again on 20th July 1852, she had received from him £50 for the copyright of 'Roughing It in the Bush'.

Whereas the £50 promised to Catharine was all ear-marked to pay off debts, Susanna seemed to have no such matters to consider. She told Richard Bentley that the money would be used to fulfil a promise she had made to her second son, Donald aged sixteen. He wanted to emigrate from Canada to Australia "to which Eldorado"

Susanna wrote "all his thoughts at present tend." Gold had been found in Australia in February 1851, and the Australian Gold Rush officially started three months later.

The first edition of 'Roughing It in the Bush' sold in England for a guinea a copy. In North America there was very little copyright protection and a cheaply produced version was soon being sold in New York for 50 cents a copy. Indeed, extracts from 'Roughing It in the Bush' had appeared in newspapers in North America before Susanna had even received payment for the copyright. The first extract that has been found, occupied all the left hand column on the front page of the 'Brooklyn Daily Eagle' on 9th July 1852 with extracts appearing in other papers during the remainder of the year. Susanna hoped that familiarity with her name would benefit her future work in North America, even if she made no money from 'Roughing It in the Bush'.

Before the end of July 1852, imported copies of 'Roughing It in the Bush' were being advertised in Canada, and on 20th July 1852 the 'Halifax British Colonist' was advertising "New Books per Steamer Albatross" followed by a list of seventeen books. The first book on the list was "'Roughing It in the Bush; or Life in Canada' by Mrs Moodie."

September 1852: Catharine expresses her botanical views

Catharine had long been accustomed to writing children's books, but her letter written to a publication called the 'Genesee Farmer', probably in September 1852, illustrated the extent of her interest in, and knowledge of Canadian flora. She wrote: "I am a great admirer of the indigenous flowers of the forest, and it is with regret that I see them fade away from the face of the earth. Many families, containing blossoms of the greatest beauty and fragrance are fast disappearing before the chopper's axe, fire and plow. They flee from the face of men and are lost, like the aborigines of the country, and the place that knew them once, now knows them no more. I look for the lovely children of the forest, those flowers that first attracted my attention, but they have passed away, and I seek them in vain – another race of plants has filled their place. Man has altered the face of the soil – the mighty giants of the forest are gone, and the lowly shrub, the lovely flower, the ferns and mosses that flourished beneath their shade have departed with them." She goes on to encourage others to do the work that she wished she could do herself: "I cannot help regretting that none of our Botanical societies have made any effort to preserve correct representations of these rare and evanescent beauties of the woods."

Catharine despite all her domestic duties, managed to find time to continue writing, albeit her work was speculative. She described herself to friends as "writing things for some American and Canadian periodicals which I hope will sell." In 1852 and 1853 she wrote a series of sketches on backwoods life and the Rice Lake Plains which she offered for sale to various magazines under the title 'Forest Gleanings'. Some of the sketches were published and in some cases more than once.

September 1852: Agnes wisely loses her nerve

Agnes paid a long visit to Lady Newburgh at Hassop Hall in Derbyshire in 1852. This was a working holiday and Agnes wrote to her mother: "We are perched upon the High Peak four miles from Chatsworth. We are very quiet here so I am able to correct my proofs and revises."

Agnes was still in the process of visiting all the places with which Mary Stuart was associated, and from Lady Newburgh's home she visited other friends with this purpose in mind. One of the places she visited was Peak's Hole, a cave Mary Stuart had entered and had explored as far inside as a pillar which subsequently bore her name. Agnes was less brave than her heroine. Jane wrote: "Her guide gave her a naked candle wrapped in a cabbage leaf, and being dressed in muslin, Agnes trembled lest a gust of wind should cause her flowing draperies to take fire."

Despite her previous determination to be brave: "a very few steps settled the matter, and she ingloriously returned." Jane commented that for Agnes "to be personally brave was impossible to her. Those who had known her from girlhood were surprised she had overcome her constitutional timidity as much as she had done." This timidity seems to have been a lasting legacy of her mental health difficulties in her teenage years, and contrasts with the tree-climbing exploits of her childhood.

Jane wrote: "The first two volumes of the 'Queens of Scotland' had made a great sensation in Scotland; but the third, containing the early life of Mary Stuart exceeded them in popularity. Agnes had to bestow immense research on this complex biography to ensure her account was accurate." This work kept Agnes in Scotland longer than usual, and although she stayed much of the time with her friend Helen Walker, and with Helen's relative the Dowager Lady Drummond, she also stayed for some of the time with the Blackwoods "with whom" Jane said "she was on friendly as well as professional terms."

25th November 1852: Susanna is recovering from illness

Immediately after writing to Richard Bentley in July 1852 Susanna was taken ill, as she told him in her next letter, written four months later on 25th November. She wrote: "That very night I was taken alarmingly ill and have been confined to my bed until a few days ago. I am a sort of living skeleton." She had been attended by two surgeons but "nature has thrown off, without the aid of their dreadful knives, one of those painful internal complaints that are generally fatal" but much of the money from 'Roughing It in the Bush' had been needed to pay her medical bills, and her son Donald did not go to Australia.

November 1852: Two of Agnes's friends die

Lady Newburgh had been in poor health when Agnes stayed at her home in Derbyshire, which was one of the reasons why the visit had been a quiet one, and she died only a few weeks later, in November 1852. Agnes was very saddened by the death, and wrote a letter of condolence to Lady Newburgh's husband. She told Sarah: "He has sent me a beautiful brooch – one, he said, she wore often – as a little memorial of one who loved and valued me so much. I shall miss her, indeed, more than I can express." Agnes was 56 and Lady Newburgh had been only eight years older.

Not long afterwards, another of Agnes's friends died. This was Dr Monk, Bishop of Gloucester. As with Lady Newburgh, Agnes had not known him long, but during their friendship she had stayed several times at the bishop's palace, visiting and exploring the locality with him and his wife, and the friendship had become quite strong.

The loss of these friends concentrated Agnes's attention on finishing the remaining volumes of the 'Queens of Scotland' and, more importantly, her 'Life of Mary Stuart'. But, Jane said, the library at Reydon Hall, whose shelves of books now contained eight blue volumes of the revised edition of the 'Lives of the Queens of England', gave Agnes comfort and revived her spirits.

29th December 1852: Tom is on his way home at long last

Tom, having completed all that he needed to do since arriving in Australia on 10th January 1851, set off homewards in the 'Scotia' from Bombay on 29th December 1852.

11th January 1853: Ulverston shows its appreciation

In Ulverston, the generosity and hard work of Richard and Sarah Gwillym in respect of the Infant School was widely recognised, and the parents decided it was time to give something in return to show their appreciation.

On 11th January 1853, Richard was presented with a gift as the local papers reported: "a tribute of highly deserved respect was made to Rev R Gwillym, in the presentation of a time-piece of the most elaborate workmanship, and to the value of twenty pounds as a slight acknowledgement of the rev gentleman's benevolent zeal in the establishment of the Infant School at Ulverston."

The paper added: "The subscription was got up chiefly by the parents of the scholars, aided by friends and admirers of the institution. The presentation was made in the school-room, in the presence of a wide assemblage. Mr Gwillym said the school was by far too small, and it was his desire to erect a larger one. He hoped his richer neighbours would come to his assistance" as it would involve a considerable expense. He concluded "by again expressing his sincere thanks on behalf of himself and Mrs Gwillym."

By making this speech, Richard had taken a step towards committing himself to providing a larger building for the infant school. It was a substantial commitment, both in financial terms and in terms of the energy required to carry it through.

22nd January 1853: Jane and Agnes experience one happy and two sad events

On 22nd January 1853 Jane and Agnes were among the guests at a grand house-warming party at Benacre Hall, the home of the Gooch family. For Agnes this event might have been nothing out of the ordinary, but there seem to have been very few such events in Jane's life.

The local paper reported that Benacre Hall was: "the scene of extraordinary festivity. Sir Edward and Lady Gooch entertained a numerous and select party of friends in a style of magnificence which the county of Suffolk had not witnessed during the present century. Nothing that could increase the splendour of the reception, or the comfort of the guests, was omitted. More than 300 invitations were issued, and the fortunate recipients began to arrive even before nine o'clock and continued to flow in until nearly midnight.

"The visitors passed through the spacious hall, beautifully carpeted, in which a roaring fire betokened the warmth of the welcome, into the gorgeous reception-room where the host and hostess greeted their friends. At ten the spacious saloon was thrown open, and dancing was commenced and continued until supper at a quarter past one. At two the votaries of Terpsichore resumed their delightful occupation until morning."

On a less cheerful note the winter was very severe and there were deaths among their acquaintances. Jane told how each day she and Agnes walked "half a mile in deep snow to visit and comfort Ann Rowe, their Sunday school teacher" who was "slowly passing away." They had known Anne Rowe "an excellent and amiable woman" for many years. She had attended the school since she was eight years old. Jane continued: "The Lady Francis Hotham was very kind to the sufferer, and liberally contributed to her comforts

– though, like poor Anne Rowe, she also passed away." Both died early in 1853.

12th February 1853: Sarah and Richard have an evening out

Richard and Sarah's life was not all work, and one of the social events they attended was the anniversary meeting of the Barrow Mechanics Institute at which the formalities of the occasion were followed by something more lively.

In 1853 the event took place on 12th February in the ball room of the Furness Abbey Hotel, Barrow-in-Furness. After the formal meeting, there was tea, followed by speeches, then a musical entertainment, and the evening's proceedings ended with a ball.

1853: Sam's book 'Twenty-Seven Years in Canada West' is published

Sam's partial autobiography entitled 'Twenty-seven Years in Canada West', which he wrote when in England in 1851 to 1852, was published in London in two volumes in 1853. It had the same publisher, Richard Bentley, as Susanna's 1852 book 'Roughing It in the Bush'.

Whereas Susanna's book highlighted the difficulties of emigrant life in Canada and gave some portraits of characters who were often less than ideal, Sam's book had quite the opposite attitude. It was full of successful achievement, albeit needing hard work, and was written in a style which was hearty, energetic and cheerful.

Agnes's comment on her brother's book, according to Jane, was that it would be "very useful to emigrants, or persons desirous of becoming so" containing a lot of useful advice "and one, too, that will not injure the literary reputation of the family." This may have been a veiled criticism of Susanna's book, but was more likely to be an acknowledgement that their brother Sam was also a capable author.

Sam in his book, with the wisdom of hindsight and without mentioning names, clarified why he had succeeded as a farmer in

Canada while John Moodie and Thomas Traill had not. He said that the life of an emigrant in the backwoods of Canada, even in the 1850s when the country was much more developed than when he had first arrived, was not suitable for army officers on half-pay pensions who were generally gentlemen unused to physical labour. He recommended Canada to those in England who were used to hard work, such as farm labourers, or those with practical skills who, he said, could prosper in Canada through their own endeavours, which would have been almost impossible in England with its layers of class consciousness. These were points that Susanna also made in 'Roughing It in the Bush'.

28th February 1853: Richard plans some fund-raising

On 28th February 1853, Richard Gwillym chaired the annual meeting of the Town Bank Sunday School. One of the items discussed was the inadequacy of the present building to accommodate the increasing number of children attending.

Richard, in his role as chairman, suggested (as the papers reported): "they should raise a suitable building for the Infant's School, which he had had a long time in contemplation, and it might be adapted for both purposes."

A committee was appointed to find a suitable site. "The Rev Gentleman said he would himself contribute and he would make an appeal to his friends and the public for donations, and hold a bazaar."

April 1853: Catharine manages to get payment for pirated work

'Canadian Crusoes' having been printed in London in February 1852, quickly found its way to America, where a pirate copy was published in November the same year. Although Catharine had no copyright protection for her work in North America, she managed to get $50 from the publisher CS Francis in April 1853, which he described as "conscience money."

When Catharine wrote to Frances Stewart in April 1853, two of her younger children were attending school, but it required much effort on their part. Mary aged 11, and William aged 9, had to set off from home at seven in the morning and walked the two miles to school, not getting home again until nearly seven in the evening. Catharine told Ellen: "It is very hard upon them and sadly wears out shoes but Mary is anxious to go and the good she derives from the teaching makes me loth to keep her back."

Catharine having achieved some fame with her writing, was hoping soon to have paid off all their debts, but life was still a struggle with money in short supply. She had tried to manage without a servant but she and Kate were not strong enough to cope, and they had a widow, Mrs Butler acting as a housekeeper. Mrs Butler's small daughter, Topsy was also helping and in return the little girl was taught to read, knit and sew, as well as receiving a small wage.

Catharine managed to subscribe to four magazines for which she either contributed articles or hoped to do so. One was the 'Horticulturalist' and Catharine's interest in botany was apparent in her letter to Frances. She wrote: "I am going to try and get specimens of the milk white violets that used to grow in the park among the rotten logs. I very much want to get some Spring Beauty we have none here. There is a tiny white flower that grows on the roadside next the river. It is a saxifrage I think." These flowers were destined to be preserved by being pressed.

When Catharine wrote to Ellen Dunlop a couple of months later, she gave a picture of home activities. Kate aged 17 had been busy in the flower garden, including planting some seeds received from England. Annie aged 12 was helping Catharine attend to the vegetables while Walter aged 5 and Topsy were weeding between the rows.

1853: Susanna is irritated by Sam's book

Although Susanna's own book had been successful, her reaction to Sam's book, which seems to have been less successful, was not particularly gracious. She mentioned Sam's book when she wrote to Richard Bentley in the late spring of 1853, at which point she had apparently not seen a copy. Susanna wrote: "I am really sorry that my brother's book has had such little success at present. He is a dear good fellow, and if my sisters would have allowed him to write in his own way, in his own frank natural language with the great experience he has had of the Colony, his book must have been a very amusing clever one." Whether or not any of the sisters in England had played any part in the text of Sam's book is unknown. Only Susanna mentioned it, and she tended to depart from the truth when roused.

"But he told me that Jane who edited it for him insisted on taking out everything that she considered vulgar, and this must have shorn the work of its identity. Rough Canadians don't use the fine language of an English drawing room; to make people talk like a book would be ridiculous. I shall be delighted to see the copy for which I thank you very much." Sam used the title Major, obtained through his service with the militia, but it had involved him in little in the way of military service, and Susanna mocked the fact that Sam was referred to as Major Strickland in his book.

The fly-leaf of Sam's book gave a great deal of prominence to Agnes Strickland as the editor of the work. No mention has been found in any surviving correspondence in paper form in England, or available to read on line from Canada, of Agnes's reaction to Susanna's dedication, nor is there any mention of any dispute on the subject between the sisters. However, Susanna had requested Richard Bentley to remove the dedication from editions of 'Roughing It in the Bush' after the first, saying that Agnes had "wounded my feelings so severely about this dedication that it is to me a perfect eye sore in front of my unfortunate book."

Susanna's irritation with Agnes was increased when she learnt, that with the involvement of Agnes as negotiator on behalf of Sam, he had received £100 per thousand copies of his book, which Susanna thought was considerably more than she had received for her book. However, Susanna had already used much of her material in the 'Literary Garland' whereas Sam's book was nearly all newly written, which could explain the speed with which extracts from 'Roughing It in the Bush' appeared in American newspapers.

In her letter to Richard Bentley, Susanna described the financial situation of her family, which sounds less favourable than in the previous year. She wrote: "We contrive with rigid economy to make both ends meet but it is hard pinching. The money earned by the two works you have published has paid off a mortgage on our little estate of 18 acres, and that alone saves the interest of £15 per annum on a small mortgage of £150. Userers thrive here. This is 10% but I have known 20% given upon loans." This property was known as 'Moodie Cottage' and was their second home in Belleville, the first having been destroyed by fire.

She also commented on her husband's job: "The Shrievalty is so reduced of late years by handing over all writs once served by the Sheriff to the smaller courts, that the income is very small. The lawyers never pay their fees. Some have owed us for twelve years and will until the day of doom, and in this country, you cannot get one of them to sue another."

1853: Susanna and Sam's books have something in common

One of the later chapters in Susanna's book 'Roughing It in the Bush' is entitled 'The Whirlwind'. Like all the chapters, it begins with a poem. In this case, the author of the poem was acknowledged in a footnote: "for the poem that heads this chapter, I am indebted to my brother, Mr Strickland, of Douro, Canada West."

The chapter contains an account of a whirlwind in the context of Susanna and her Irish servant preparing to move to Belleville, and the introductory poem is as follows:

Dark, heavy clouds were gathering in the west,
   Wrapping the forest in funereal gloom;
Onward they roll'd, and rear'd each livid crest,
   Like Death's murk shadows frowning o'er earth's tomb.
From out the inky womb of that deep night
   Burst livid flashes of electric flame.
Whirling and circling with terrific might,
   In wild confusion on the tempest came.
Nature, awakening from her still repose,
   Shudders responsive to the whirlwind's shock,
Feels at her mighty heart convulsive throes,
   And all her groaning forests to earth's bosom rock.

But hark! – What means that hollow, rushing sound,
  That breaks the death-like stillness of the morn?
Red forked lightnings fiercely glare around,
  Sharp, crashing thunders on the winds are borne,
And see yon spiral column, black as night,
  Rearing triumphantly its wreathing form;
Ruin's abroad, and through the murky light, -
  Drear desolation marks the spirit of the storm

This same poem appears towards the end of the first volume of the book that Sam was writing in England, but with the following four additional lines, separated from the rest by a row of asterisks:

How changed the scene; the awful tempest 's o'er;
  From dread array and elemental war
The lightning's flash hath ceas'd, the thunder's roar –
  The glorious sun resumes his golden car."

Sam used this poem to end a chapter and added a footnote of his own, which reads: "My description of this whirlwind, and the accompanying lines, have already appeared in the 'Victoria Magazine', published in Canada West, under the signature of 'Pioneer'."

Sam therefore was more of a writer and poet than simply his autobiography, and despite her comments about Sam, Susanna had been happy to include some of his work in her own book, and in the magazine of which she and John Moodie had briefly been joint editors.

10th May 1853: Tom arrives home and his ship is for sale again

Tom, having set sail for London from Bombay on 29th December 1852, was back in Gravesend on 10th May 1853 having been away for over two and a half years.

As soon as he arrived back in London Docks, the 'Scotia' was again advertised as 'for sale'. It was lying in the East India Dock and Captain Thomas Strickland was named as in command.

July 1853: Susanna's 'Life in the Clearings' and 'Mark Hurdlestone' appear

With the success of 'Roughing It in the Bush', Susanna and Richard Bentley wanted a follow-up as soon as possible. Two books were published in England in 1853, 'Life in the Clearings Versus the Bush' which was a follow-up to 'Roughing It in the Bush', and a novel entitled 'Mark Hurdlestone; or, the Two Brothers'. Susanna received, as became normal with Richard Bentley, £50 as an advance share of the profits of 'Mark Hurdlestone'.

By 30th July 1853 Susanna's novel 'Mark Hurdlestone' was being advertised and reviewed in the 'Nyack Rockland County Journal' in New York State. Under the headline 'Our Book Table' the article said: "'Mark Hurdlestone' by Mrs Moodie, author of 'Roughing It in the Bush'. The first work of Mrs Moodie, which is a delineation of pioneer life in Canada, contained so much vigorous originality and graphic power of description, that it created a sensation in the literary world scarcely inferior to 'Jane Eyre'. It had an immense run, and everybody has since been on the tip-toe of expectation for the next work that should appear from her pen, 'Mark Hurdlestone' has not disappointed the expectations aroused." The paper then gave an outline of the plot.

On 11th August 1853 the 'New York Daily Times' was advertising a pirated version: "'Mark Hurdlestone; or, the Two Brothers' at a price of 75 cents in cloth and 50 cents in paper covers." The paper then printed an anecdote, which incorrectly said that Susanna had lived near Rice Lake, but which managed to include Agnes's name twice. A shortened version of the anecdote, appeared under the heading 'Opinion of the Press' as follows: "Mrs Moodie is an English lady, and the sister of Agnes Strickland, also distinguished as a writer, though better known in England than here. She settled in a retired part of Canada West, near the Rice Lake.

"Before her first work came out, we heard from Dr Bethune, of Brooklyn, a description of an accidental visit made by him to Mrs Moodie's new home. He was taking a summer fishing vacation when he came upon a retired English settlement" containing "persons of thorough education and refinement ... In taking up a volume from the parlor table, he noticed it was one of Miss Strickland's works, and on the fly-leaf saw the inscribed words 'Mrs Moodie, from her sister, Agnes Strickland.' Dr Bethune passed several days at this new found and hospitable home in the wilds of Canada. Here Mrs Moodie has been using her pen with industry, and certainly in a most attractive way. 'Mark Hurdlestone' is far more dramatic than its predecessor, and is, in fact, a regularly developed romance."

The anecdote was followed by favourable quotations for reviews in ten different newspapers and ended: "We could multiply our notices to any length, but the above will suffice. Dewitt & Davenport, publisher." It seems that the 'puffery' of which Henry Colburn was accused in England was also practised abroad.

Summer 1853: Catharine and Thomas have a visitor

In 1853 Catharine's story 'The Governor's Daughter; or, Rambles in the Canadian Forest' is said to have appeared in twelve instalments in a Canadian publication called the 'Maple Leaf'. It was a story for juveniles and was also published in London by Arthur, Hall and Virtue in a single volume under the title 'Lady Mary and Her Nurse; or, a Peep into the Canadian Forest'. This was quickly followed up by firms in Boston and New York, but with the more egalitarian title 'Stories of the Canadian Forest; or, Little Mary and her Nurse'.

At about this time, in the summer of 1853, a Scottish gentleman named George Leith, met Catharine and Thomas Traill while visiting the Rice Lake Plain looking for good farmland and he gave his impression of them both in a letter to his wife, which has previously been quoted by C Ballstadt, E Hopkins and MA Peterman in 'I Bless You in My Heart, selected correspondence of Catharine Parr Traill' published by University of Toronto Press in 1996. He wrote: "Fancy a tall thin-faced man about 50 with a long kind of loose great coat of grey cloth a great deal faded and stained – a shawl around his neck that one would not have picked out of the gutter and that had not been washed for a month – a nose very much smeared with snuff; hands and face evidently in want of soap and water, yet with all this unprepossessing exterior, a kind hearted and well informed man.

"He has not been fortunate in his farming operations being evidently unfitted both mentally and physically for anything of the kind, and to add to his misfortunes, he endorsed a bill for a friend who of course left him to pay the amount, which nearly exhausted his funds, and has given his family a very hard struggle for a livelihood."

This was at a time when Susanna's book 'Roughing It in the Bush' had achieved its fame. Mr Leith continued: "We went up to see Mrs Traill and found her an invalid on the sofa busy with manuscript leaves of some new book she is to publish soon. She is a pleasant enough woman, elderly, stout with a slight blue tinge" as in blue stocking or female intellectual "but very frank and made no secret of their having had a great struggle for the bare necessities – indeed she and her husband both said they could have published another and more melancholy story than Mrs Moodie who, they seemed to say, had rather drawn upon her imagination for some of her facts."

2nd August 1853: Sarah helps run a bazaar

The fund-raising bazaar which Richard Gwillym mentioned in February 1853 was held on Tuesday 2nd and Wednesday 3rd August 1853 in the Concert Hall, Ulverston and entailed "the sale of useful and fancy articles" also of paintings and drawings.

Sarah was one of the dozen or so ladies named as being in charge of the stalls. The bazaar was a great success, raising £470 by the end of the second day, and with further donations expected.

26th August 1853: Tom gets his Master Mariner Certificate

On 26th August 1853 Tom was issued with his Master Mariner Certificate in exchange for the Third Class Certificate granted to him four years earlier. He now had the certificates required by recent maritime regulations, to match the job that he had been doing for many years.

The 'Scotia' despite being put up for sale in May, and whether or not it had a new owner, entered the Custom House on 3rd September 1853 as a preliminary to loading for departure. Its next destination was given as Sydney. However, the 'Scotia' was far from being alone. On 20th September 1853, 286 ships were listed as being loaded in the Port of London and 38 of them were said to be destined for Sydney, New South Wales.

3rd September 1853: Susanna's 'Flora Lyndsay' is ready for the publisher

Susanna Moodie on 3rd September 1853 sent the manuscript for her novel 'Flora Lyndsay' to Richard Bentley with a covering letter in which she offered him the copyright for £300, adding that if this was more than he was willing to pay, she would accept the same terms as for her previous books. 'Flora Lyndsay' was very loosely auto-biographical, beginning when Susanna was newly married, living in Southwold and expecting her first child, and ending with her arrival in Canada.

Susanna told Richard Bentley that she still had doctors' bills to settle, and needed to pay Donald's expenses at medical college in Montreal, all the money she received in June having been used to pay past nursing bills.

September 1853: Agnes and Sarah take the waters in Harrogate

After the London social season of 1853, Agnes went to visit Sarah and Richard Gwillym in Ulverston and with them went to the spa town of Harrogate to take the waters. There she became friends with a lawyer, Mr Greaves and his wife, and afterwards stayed with them a number of times when in London.

From Harrogate, Agnes went to Scotland to visit the Dowager Lady Blantyne and her daughter Georgina at Lennoxlove, East Lothian, to the east of Edinburgh. This was another of the places where she could spend much of her time working, appearing for exercise and social life in the evenings. 'Lives of the Queens of Scotland' was still dealing with the life of Mary Queen of Scots and Agnes told Jane: "Blackwoods have ten compositors at work on 'Mary Stuart'." As a result she was kept busy for some weeks "working through the proofs and revises." She had assistance from the family of her hostess, which was often the case. Agnes told Jane: "The beloved Georgina Stuart as usual being a very efficient help in the corrections."

1853: Mrs Strickland reaches her 80th birthday

Mrs Strickland reached her 80th birthday in 1853 and, as the years went by, Jane's task of being her carer and of looking after family affairs increased. Jane's continued residence at Reydon Hall was partly because her health was not good as she suffered from chronic asthma and bronchitis. As well as helping Agnes and Eliza, Jane Margaret Strickland continued to be an author in her own right. She had some moral tales for children published in book form, but most of her literary work was in magazines and in annuals, both writing and editing.

8th October 1853: Susanna is spiteful about her family

Dewitt & Davenport, who had organised such fulsome praise for their pirated edition of Susanna's novel 'Mark Hurdlestone', wanted to formalise the arrangement and offered Susanna $200 to re-publish her next book. Susanna wrote to Richard Bentley on 8th October 1853 for his permission to accept the offer.

By this time she and Richard Bentley's letters included family news and other matters as well as business. Despite Susanna considering herself somewhat radical in her views, she was very far from being a feminist. She wrote: "Is not the woman's Rights movement, the most preposterous absurdity of the present day? If they would only let these ambitious masculines in petticoats, have their own way, the disease would soon cure itself. Imagine a refined woman holding the plough, or knocking down an ox. Faugh the idea is disgusting."

She was scathing about her brother Samuel: "I'm afraid I am not very sorry for the non-success of the Major's book. Between ourselves, the thing has no vitality, is in fact a humbug. But it has got him a good berth in the Canada Company's service and the instruction of four hapless young Englishmen, in the mysteries of Canadian Agriculture, at the sum of £100 each per annum. I wish I could give you a picture of the education in progress at the Agricultural College and the gallant Major C(anadian) M(ilitia)'s method of tuition. It would shock all thinking people."

Susanna also made some sharp comments about her sister Eliza. "My eldest sister is an extensive reviewer, and for many years followed it as a means of increasing her income. Hers is a ready and clever pen. It is more than probable that to her both my brother and I are indebted, he for the good and I for the bad reviews of our respective works. Could this be ascertained, and made known to the public, through some indifferent party, it would turn the tables upon the malevolent authors. It is however on a piece with all their conduct to me. My brother's book being entirely one-sided has met less favour than 'Roughing It'. I have never heard from Reydon since the publication of the latter work."

She told Richard Bentley that hers had been an unhappy childhood but her marriage was a happy one: "As a wife and mother, I have been so blessed, that one day spent in the company of my dear white-haired husband, is worth all the joys and sorrows of those sad years at home."

2nd December 1853: Tom and Margaretta sail away together

The next role of the 'Scotia' was to be part of the regular rota of packet ships carrying mail between London and Sydney. The 'Scotia' left London on 2nd December 1853, called briefly at Plymouth on 5th December and then sailed straight for Sydney.

The difference for Tom and his family with this voyage, compared with those in the recent past, was that his wife Margaretta accompanied him. They had five unmarried children in England ranging in age from 18-year old Thomas, through Julia, Mary and Diana aged 17, 15 and 12, down to 10-year old Walter.

Their son Thomas had a job and remained living in the family home in Plaistow, while the four younger children seem to have been placed in the care of various boarding schools.

25th December 1853: Susanna is looking after Mary Traill

On Christmas Day 1853 Susanna wrote to Catharine about Mary Traill who was staying with her aunt Susanna and attending school in Belleville. Susanna said that Mary "learns fast and is a darling good child."

Mary and her cousin Robert were great playmates, and Susanna told Catharine about their Christmas preparations. Of Mary she wrote: "the little woman attended me like a familiar sprite watching me make mince pies and Christmas cake and pudding talking all the while, of her own household Gods, and wondering what Mamma and Papa, and all the brotherhood and sisterhood of home were about – while Rob was wondering what old St Claus would bring for them – Poor dears! It was little Aunt had to give, but such as the good old Patron of childhood brought, was received this morning, with extatic delight, and Papa and I chatted a full hour over our bedroom fire last night, Laughing as we filled the socks left very diffidently by our stove pipe, and wondering what the children would say in the morning – what a little swells to overflowing the gay glad heart of Childhood. On Christmas morning Papa went" to church "with the little ones and after dinner, took them a long sleigh drive. They have now walked hand in hand to church and I sit down to scribble to you."

Susanna also mentioned financial matters. She told Catharine: "I was indignant at McClear wanting to cheat you out of your hard earned rights – 16 pages is a sheet of the 'Anglo-American' – as any book or magazine of that size. Bentley's 'Miscellany' is not so large, and I receive 10 guineas sterling for every such sheet I write. Don't put up with such a base fraud – for such it is. Your Mr Hope has just written to Moodie to dun him for contributions from me – but really – I can't afford to write for the old twadler for nothing. He is going to publish a pamphlet containing Lord Ellsmere's and your contributions and wants me to add my mite. As this is solely for his own benefit I shall do no such thing."

Susanna also told Catharine about her son Donald and the cost of his medical studies. She had heard that he was "studying hard to pass his Latin examinations in January and he hopes with success ... Donald makes friends wherever he goes. He seems one of those beings born for popularity, and is a fine hearted noble boy ... It will cost us one hundred pounds his seven months at college, and this for four succeeding years. But I will work with more zeal in the hope of serving my darling boy."

Susanna told Catharine that her communications with the family in England were slight. She wrote: "from Reydon, I never hear, and suppose I never shall, as my correspondence is confined to the poor Mamma, whose will to write is perhaps beyond her power" and she made scathing comments about Sam's educational college. She wrote that her daughter Katie "had been up to Douro – Rather – I should say deeply disgusted with the education in progress to the poor lads at the Agricultural College."

6th January 1854: Eliza and Agnes are helping Catharine

Catharine wrote to Susanna on 6th January 1854 saying she had not been well and had to stay in bed despite her bedroom being very cold and difficult to heat. She had received a small parcel from Agnes including "a kind letter and a few friendly words from Eliza" urging her to finish a little book started long ago "on the same plan as the Downy book which she will edit for me and sell" and encouraging her with her work on the 'Female Emigrant's Manual' which Catharine intended to be a book of instruction, recipes and hints "such as I should have been glad to have had myself when I came out."

Thus both Agnes and Eliza were working on Catharine's behalf in England, with advice and practical help towards publication. In 1854 Catharine finished 'The Female Emigrant's Guide and Hints on Canadian Housekeeping' and it was published in Canada in 1855.

20th January 1854: Richard and Sarah go to Barrow

Life for the Gwillyms in Ulverston was still hectic and full of responsibilities. On the fun (with duty) side, Richard and Sarah Gwillym attended the annual meeting of the Barrow Mechanics Institute on 20th January 1854 in the large room of the Furness Abbey Hotel.

The event was described in the local papers: "The attendance was very numerous and Ulverston Philharmonic Society added to the entertainment. After interesting speeches" with Rev R Gwillym being one of the four speakers "Several glees and songs were sung, and songs were sung at intervals" then "the room was cleared for a ball" which was "a gay and happy affair."

26th February 1854: 'Roughing It in the Bush' goes to a third edition

The success of 'Roughing It in the Bush' continued, and a third edition was needed as soon as 1854. Although none of Susanna's subsequent books were able to reach the same levels of popularity, she is said to have earned over £350 by her writing between 1852 and 1856. The money was mainly used for the education of her sons and to pay medical bills.

Despite her own success, Susanna still felt the need to be unpleasant about Sam when writing to the man who had published books for both of them. On 26th February 1854 Susanna's letter to Richard Bentley, in mentioning Sam said: "The Major has been staying with me for the past week. He is very sulky about his book. His literary honours have sadly spoilt a naturally frank, good natured, but vain man, and made him pompous and arrogant."

No other member of the Strickland family ever wrote a bad word about Sam, rather the reverse. In later years the population of Lakefield included a number of families which were formed when students from Sam's Agricultural College subsequently made their homes in the area, referring to Sam affectionately, it is said, as 'the Major'.

March 1854: Richard needs a new curate

Richard had for some time been employing one or two curates to help with the duties of the parish. In March 1854, he had to advertise for a replacement, his previous curate having obtained a living elsewhere.

The wording of the advertisement shows that Richard was bearing the cost, for the advertisement ended by saying: "the appointment being in the gift of the Rev Richard Gwillym, MA, rural dean."

5th April 1854: Agnes is short of money

Catharine was discovering that her style of writing was considered old-fashioned in England, for when Agnes wrote to her on 5th April 1854 she referred to Catharine's book 'The Governor's Daughter' which was in some situations called 'Lady Mary and Her Nurse' and told Catharine bluntly: "it is in the stiff old mould style of children's books of the last century" and "No one attends" to that kind of story any longer.

Agnes warned Catharine of the danger of publishing in magazines in Canada anything which might be published as a book in England, something which had not worried Susanna. Agnes told Catharine that "any English pirate may re-publish" and it was important for Catharine to protect the copyrights.

Catharine may have felt that this advice ran contrary to the way that Susanna had achieved financial success. Almost all that Susanna had published in England and America in the 1850s had previously appeared, albeit she made amendments, in the 'Literary Garland', which explains how she was able to produce so many books in such a short time period in the 1850s. However, there was a difference in timing and when Susanna's work had first appeared between 1839 and 1846 in North America, it had done so in serial form, which would presumably have removed the feeling of direct comparison when published in England several years later.

On a more positive note, Agnes had taken Catharine's work referred to as "your Squirrel Family" to Virtue and Hall, publishers, "who seem disposed to regard" the possibility of publishing it but, Agnes wrote: "you will not get much poor dear."

Agnes was almost as short of money as Catharine, to the extent that the cost of postage on manuscripts was a matter of concern. Agnes and Eliza had invested money in property which was costing them more in maintenance than they were getting back in rent. At the same time Reydon Hall was draining Agnes's resources, Agnes seemingly the only member of the family trying to maintain it. She told Catharine: "I have spent a great deal of money in repairs, for the house was ruinous and it wants a great deal more which I cannot afford just now."

Despite this, Agnes had put together a box of things that she hoped Catharine would find useful and which a friend was going to transport to Canada for her. Among the contents were: "A nice pretty muslin dress with blue edged flounces, the blue ribbons to match, some black ribbon with brown edges – a cashmere jacket trimmed with military braid, a sort of knitted woollen petticoat and two remnants of print – one blue with shaded spots and the other a pale pink with blue figure. The blue print is but eight yards but I thought it would make a dress for Mary."

There were health problems on both sides of the Atlantic. Agnes's health was poor, as was often the case, and she was working too hard. She told Catharine: "my doctor tells me I must go to Harrogate and drink the waters for congestion of the liver and erysipelas in the face, the result of intense hard work." She was still working on the life of Mary Stuart and she had to consider very carefully what she wrote: "My work is very slow on a subject so much contested."

Of the health of Catharine's family, Agnes said she was: "sorry to hear so poor an account of your dear James whom we all esteem very highly on account of his dutiful conduct." Mrs Strickland was doing well for her age but: "The dear Mother is very deaf and feeble. She is very sorry not to have more to send to her children."

The Crimean War was in progress and prices had risen as a result. Agnes's view of the situation was: "our ministers have rushed in to help the infidel Turks whose day for falling is come."

23rd April 1854: Susanna's son Dunbar has mixed success prospecting

Susanna told Catharine in a letter written on 23rd April 1854 that her eldest son Dunbar, who had been prospecting successfully near San Francisco, had gone through a bad patch. Susanna wrote: "The poor fellow, has lost all the money he had made, and has to work hard to pay up the Company's debts, to which he belongs, they having sunk in their last mining speculation, all their savings, and run into debt to the amount of 500$. He seems rather dejected and talks of leaving the hill mines, and going to Oregon. It seems, that one of their company, got a hint, from some quarter, that gold was to be found in large quantities there."

22nd May 1854: Tom and Margaretta reach Australia

Having left England on 5th December 1853, the 'Scotia' with Tom in command, and Margaretta accompanying him, reached Sydney on 22nd May 1854.

24th May 1854: A foundation stone is laid in Ulverston

The various projects under way in Ulverston were thriving, with the Athenaeum reaching its sixth anniversary on the same day that Tom and Margaretta arrived at Sydney.

The local paper reported the Ulverston Athenaeum AGM on 22nd May 1854, where Richard Gwillym was in the chair: "The directors' report was encouraging as regards the accomplishments of the Institution. The Museum was rich in valuable deposits, and were continually receiving new accessions" and the library had "upwards of 2,000 volumes."

The project for a new school building was proceeding apace. On 24th May 1854 local papers gave an account of the laying of the foundation stone. The report said: "Infant, Day and Town Bank Schools – The first stone of the proposed building for these schools, in Ulverstone, was laid on Wednesday, by Master HH Askew, of Conishead Priory. The spot is a plot of ground on the south side of the Church Walk, and close adjoining the Old Church.

"The rain fell at intervals during the morning, but not heavily. At twelve o'clock the procession of the scholars carrying flags, banners, and garlands of flowers commenced through the town. Soon after HW Askew, Esq., of Conishead Priory, his lady and family and numerous friends arrived which was a signal for cheering. The Revd R Gwillym presented a silver trowel to the young master mason, a prayer was said and the stone was laid with all due formality. Mr Gwillym made an appropriate address as also did Mr Askew.

"The funds have been obtained through the unwearied solicitations of Mr and Mrs Gwillym, assisted by the committee, Mr Gwillym himself being a liberal contributor. The architects are Messrs Thompson and Webster, of Kendal. It will be built primarily of lime-stone in a neat but finished style. The length of the school-room will be 40 feet. The contractors are Messrs M Tyson and J Wearing of Ulverstone. The cost is estimated at about £760."

14th June 1854: Susanna's 'Flora Lyndsay' is launched

The publication of Susanna's book entitled 'Flora Lyndsay; or, Passages in an Eventful Life' was announced by Dewitt & Davenport in the 'New York Daily Times' on 14th June 1854. The article said that: "By an arrangement with Mrs Moodie ... The work is issued here at the same time as in England. So confident are the Publishers of the great popularity ... they have issued a first edition of 10,000 copies."

The article then quoted positive extracts from seven different newspapers. Further reviews and advertisements followed over the next couple of months. 'Matrimonial Speculation' was also published by Richard Bentley in 1854 in England but did not appear in America.

20th June 1854: Catharine's home becomes more isolated

Early in 1854 the steam boat that had called at Gore's Landing near Catharine's home, changed its stopping point to Harwood about five miles away. The Traill family had no wagon and Catharine told Ellen Dunlop, in a letter post-marked 20th June 1854, that the walk was too much for them so they "cannot get parcels to and fro as formerly."

Other news in Catharine's letter to Ellen mainly related to family ill-health, of which there had been a good deal. The first one to fall ill had been her eldest son: "James had one of his very worst attacks of erysipelas which laid him up for a week blind and helpless and alarmingly ill." Annie then had a slight dose of the same illness, which is normally an acute skin rash.

Catharine had a severe fever and sore throat, followed by Kate with the same problems. In Catharine's opinion all the illnesses had been caused by the sultry weather, plus overwork, by getting chilled in the morning when milking cows, or by nursing other family members.

Mary Traill had returned from her stay with her aunt Susanna, where she had been well looked after and happy. Catharine was slightly anxious for the child and told Ellen that Mary: "must feel the change from a house of plenty and every comfort to ours which is not so – but she never murmurs and is as kind to everyone as she can be."

Thus Catharine's view was that Susanna and her family were living in relatively comfortable circumstances. No record has been found of Susanna giving any help to Catharine apart from sometimes caring for one or other of Catharine's children.

17th June 1854: Katharine Rackham's mother has died

Sam had returned to Canada from England in 1852, engaged to be married to Katharine Rackham, with the marriage delayed by Katharine's need to care for and be a companion to her mother.

The following notice appeared in the 'Deaths' column of the 'Norfolk Chronicle' on Saturday 17th June 1854: "Died Wednesday last at her residence" in Aylsham "after a short illness, Martha relict of the late Thomas Rackham aged 81."

12th August 1854: Tom and Margaretta arrive in Madras

Having reached Australia on 22nd May 1854, the 'Scotia' remained in Sydney for a few weeks. If Tom and Margaretta's eldest son had emigrated to Australia, possibly travelling with his father on a previous trip, then Margaretta's journey would have had more purpose than merely being a sight-seeing voyage. From Sydney, the 'Scotia' sailed to Madras, arriving there on 12th August 1854.

August 1854: Agnes, Sarah and Richard take the waters at Harrogate

Agnes followed her doctor's advice in 1854 and went to Harrogate to drink the waters for their health benefits. The town was less busy than usual because of cholera outbreaks, which were occurring and causing anxiety in both Canada and Great Britain.

Agnes wrote to Catharine in the summer of 1854: "I left Harrogate which had been at half business on the 19th August." From Harrogate, Agnes went to Scotland.

There is no record of an annual treat for the children of Ulverston in the summer of 1854, and both Richard and Sarah needed to go to Harrogate for a while for the sake of their health. At least part of their visit coincided with that of Agnes.

1854: Jane Margaret Strickland publishes a very learned book

Jane had been studying Tacitus, Plutarch and other books on Roman history for many years. Her studies included trying to fit together historical references in the New Testament with the history of the Roman Empire.

With all this background work and knowledge, she wrote a history of Rome which she thought would be suitable for use in schools and for family reading. The first volume was published in 1854, with Agnes named as the editor, and with the title 'Rome; Regal and Republican; a Family History of Rome'.

This first volume needed over 600 pages to cover the period from BC 753 to BC 121 and was published in London by Arthur Hall, Virtue & Co of 25 Paternoster Row. Although described as a family history, any family tackling the book would have needed to be similar in taste and ability to Jane's generation of the Strickland family. It was a long way from being simplistic, and showed Jane to have intellectual capability and application of the kind displayed by Eliza and Agnes.

September 1854: Sarah and Richard join Agnes in Scotland

Agnes wrote to Catharine on 17th September 1854 with family news. She said: "I have had a charming sojourn with the sister of Lady Matilda Maxwell of Polloc. She asked the dear Gwillyms at the same time which increased the pleasure."

Agnes told Catharine: "Sarah is decidedly better for Scotland" and she too was improving: "I am better but not yet strong." In their different ways Agnes, Richard and Sarah were overdoing things and suffering the consequences. Agnes told Catharine: "I am very busy with proofs and must continue so for the month to come or more and I expect it will be published at the end of October."

September 1854: Sam's son Robert visits Reydon Hall

With the death of her mother, Katharine Rackham was free to marry Sam after a suitable period of mourning. It was maybe thought more respectful if Sam did not immediately visit England, and it was his eldest son Robert whose presence in England was commented on when Agnes wrote to Catharine in September 1854, although the timing of his visit may have been a coincidence.

Agnes wrote: "Robert came and slept the night and came to a nice party with me. He was very much liked by every one and is a fine young man." It sounds as though Robert was meeting the family at Reydon Hall for the first time, and if that was the case, he became engaged after a very short courtship, for Agnes continued: "He is to marry Caroline Ellis, so there will be two brides coming out and will contribute to the general happiness of my brother and his household I am sure." Caroline Ellis was the daughter of Captain Ellis, who had read Agnes's poem 'Life Boat' during a lecture he gave in Southwold in 1849.

October 1854: Agnes seeks a publisher for Catharine

Agnes and Eliza were much happier working with the publisher William Blackwood than they had been with Henry Colburn, but that did not mean Agnes had an easy task when she tried to persuade them to publish Catharine's work. Agnes in her September 1854 letter told Catharine: "I would not be in Edinburgh till October to confer with Mr Blackwood when I will try and induce them to agree for your work but they are shy creatures, and difficult to deal with. However, I go home through London, and if I fail with Blackwoods, will try others and hope to make some arrangement."

A parcel that Agnes had got ready to go to Canada was still in Reydon: "I am sorry to say poor Mamma forgot to give the little box I had packed and directed for you, but never mind you will have it next time a parcel goes."

Agnes was too busy to write to Sam but asked Catharine to pass on a message regarding a new edition of Sam's book: "Tell him I have begun several letters to him" to tell him "that Bentley is cheating – the infant is only the old edition bound in one volume and reduced in price but I think" there "is no help for it" and she ended hastily: "I have just a dozen letters to write and a sheet to correct so no more at present from your loving sister Agnes Strickland. Kind regards to Mr Traill."

November 1854: Susanna's 'Life in the Clearings' reaches America

'Life in the Clearings Versus the Bush' had been published in England in 1853 in the same year as 'Mark Hurdlestone', but in America the order of publication was different with 'Life in the Clearings' not appearing until November 1854, after the publication of 'Flora Lyndsay'. It seems to have received relatively little by way of review.

13th December 1854: A contentious volume is published

In the event, despite advertisements which announced that the fifth volume of the 'Lives of the Queens of Scotland' would be published in September, it was not until 13th December 1854 that the papers could say: "This day is published the fifth volume of 'Lives of the Queens of Scotland' containing the continuation of the life of Mary Stuart." One of the controversies within this volume, which Agnes had written with great care, was whether or not Queen Elizabeth intended the execution of Mary Queen of Scots.

17th December 1854: Tom and Margaretta set off back to Australia

Tom's ship the 'Scotia', having arrived in Madras on 12th August 1854, remained there for four months, setting sail back to Sydney on 17th December 1854, by which time Margaretta was heavily pregnant with their last child.

25th December 1854: Sam's church has its first service

The money which Sam raised in England towards building an Anglican church in Lakefield had been sufficient to fund the basic structure. A young local architect, Kivas Tully was employed and the rest of the funds were raised. Sam's widowed daughter Maria Beresford married the architect, and became Maria Tully. The first service was held in the new church on Christmas Day 1854.

January 1855: The Crimean War effort reaches Ulverston

Christmas 1854 and New Year 1855 were again a time of increasing charitable giving and events for Richard and Ulverston. Local papers reported that on Saturday 23rd December 1854: "upwards of 70 families received from the Rev R Gwillym a piece of meat for their dinner on the Monday following."

New Year's Day was a particularly busy day and the papers reported that on the 1st January 1855: "two long tables were spread in the upper room of the National School, at which 73 poor aged people sat down to dinner, provided by Mr Gwillym, consisting of two large rounds of boiled beef, two forecrops roasted, leg of mutton, and eleven veal pies, with mashed potato, pea pudding, &c. More than 40 others, unable to attend either through sickness, infirmity, or the stormy weather, had a supply of meat and potatoes sent to their homes."

The day continued with another major event in the same location: "The annual treat to the children attending the National Schools was given them on Monday 1st January 1855, when upwards of 200 boys and girls were regaled with coffee and buns. The parents afterwards sat down to an excellent tea in the upper room after which they listened to recitations, songs and rounds sung by the children" but this time the financial burden did not lie entirely on Richard's shoulders. "The funds providing this treat for the children were raised by sums subscribed for this purpose by friends in the town and neighbourhood."

There was also fund-raising in the district to help the Crimean War effort. Richard and Sarah attended an associated event in

January which the papers reported: "Banquet at Conishead Priory of the Ulverstone District Patriotic fund – HW Askew, of Conishead Priory, who has so prominently exerted himself establishing committees for the district, entertained the Ulverston Committee at dinner on Tuesday 9th January 1855.

"The large dining-room of the mansion was gracefully and appropriately decorated for the occasion. At the head, in large letters, neatly worked in sprigs of boxwood, by Mr Stead of London, were the words 'Inkermann', 'Alma', 'Balaklava', 'Success to the Patriotic Fund'.

"The display of the table was superbly rich – the dinner recherchee. Covers were laid for 26. The company consisted of HW Askew, Esq., his lady and daughter; Mrs Askew of Wimpole Street, London; the Rev R Gwillym and Mrs Gwillym, Stockbridge; John P Machell, Hollow Oak" followed by other names of local notables and their houses. "A band was in attendance during the evening, and many of Mr Askew's trades-people were also liberally entertained."

January 1855: Eliza upsets Catharine

On 21st January 1855 Agnes wrote to Catharine, firstly explaining that she has been too busy to write and that her eyes were suffering from so much writing in winter time: "I have had more to do than I could get through" and was finding it hard: "to bear the glare of white paper, especially by candle-light, which curtails several hours from my working time, and makes every letter I write a perilous addition to my toils. You must not therefore impute my silence to unkindness, but inability to write."

Agnes then comforted Catharine for any harshness from Eliza: "I am very sorry Eliza has written to you but it is her way." The phrase 'but it is her way' seems to be the gentle means by which this generation of the Strickland family excused each other, and served to put to one side behaviour which might otherwise have caused offence.

Agnes continued: "We have many such trials to put up with now she has returned with her irritable and tyrannical temper, to embitter the peace of the home." It sounds as though Eliza was now living at

Reydon Hall, even though she still held the lease of the cottage in Bayswater where she had lived for many years.

However, Agnes then went on in a more gentle tone than that apparently used by Eliza, to chide Catharine for an arrangement she had made for her work in Canada, which Eliza and Agnes thought unwise: "For regards to your book, my dear Catharine, I can only say that if your friends in Canada can manage so that you derive a remunerative profit, it will be well, and I hope it may be so, but you have I fear spoiled your English market by the arrangement." Despite all the work that Agnes had to do on her own and Eliza's account, she had made great efforts with booksellers and publishers on Catharine's behalf, but with little success.

Part of the problem was the continuing Crimean War, but Hall & Virtue were working on some of Catharine's writings. Agnes reported: "they told me the 'Canadian Squirrel' was not ready yet, and I fear from what they said will not be published till the midsummer holiday approaches, on account of the bad state of literature in the time of war.

"This I fear will be a sad disappointment, as the money will not be paid till the day of publication. They say the 'Crusoes' has sold well and they hope ere long to come to a reprint if we have peace, which is now ardently desired, and hoped. I called on Bentley but did not see him. I fancied he was after publishing a little work of yours for I saw the annuals mention 'A Peep into a Canadian Forest' by Mrs Traill but could find nothing more about it. I have been unable to do anything with the sketches I hold but think from what Virtue & Hall said they are likely to take them with time. But nothing sells now but newspapers."

The Strickland family at this time was waiting to hear about a legacy from a relative of their mother. Agnes told Catharine: "I had hoped to be able to tell you something comfortable about the residues of the legacies, but alas the lawyers and executors have given in accounts so nefarious that very small indeed is the portion that is to fall to our lot. Their calculation is that we are not to have more than from thirty five to thirty seven pounds each. And there is a chancery suit with old Linder who is not worth a sous. It rests in suspense at present."

Agnes's own finances were not in a good state either: "I have had very heavy expenses with my last winter's illness and my journey to Harrogate and Scotland, so that I am myself straightened not a little and a heavy lawyer's bill to pay of which I, as yet, know not the amount." This seems to have been some litigation over a property freehold in which she and Eliza had become embroiled though the reason is not explained.

Agnes closed her letter with a summary of other family news: "I grieve to hear you have been suffering so much anxiety about your good James and Walter and poor Catharine, and your own sickness poor dear, but cheer up there may be good time coming. I saw Barbara Fotheringhame" (Thomas Traill's sister-in-law who had brought up his children and grandchildren from his first marriage) "in Edinburgh looking bright and handsome. She enquired affectionately after you all, and sent her love. The Ellis's are all well. You will like Caroline" (Robert Strickland's fiancee) "and love Kate Rackham."

19th February 1855: Catharine gives news of her family

In a letter written on 19th February 1855, Catharine told Ellen Dunlop of the difficulty they had in their supply of firewood. She wrote: "This year has kept James busy drawing firewood and cutting for the stoves. The snow lies so deeply drifted and our supply of wood is a mile off with oxen only to draw."

Her son Harry had found a way to further his education with minimum cost. Since the New Year: "he goes for 4 hours in the early part of the day to Mr Hudspith's school" where classics were taught "then works for Gideon Page for his board for the rest of the day. The arrangement suits both parties and I hope my dear boy will feel the benefit of his assiduity."

Harry Traill had been very anxious about "his deficiency in those useful branches which he should have acquired while he was labouring so hard for us. Our little boys go to common school" but the snow had obliged them to stay at home recently.

Catharine's daughters shared the housework. Kate "has all the kitchen work to do, Annie and Mary share the other housework between them" but their house was such "that their really hard work does not show much." Catharine did the family sewing, and wrote if and when she could "see any good end in view."

There was some positive news for Catharine to pass on, as she had been asked to take management of the Ladies Department of the 'Canadian Agriculturalist', a new magazine published in Hamilton. Catharine was developing a speciality as a writer on natural sciences, a subject whose popularity was helped by the fashion for, and fascination with ferns. This had reached the point where the term pteridiomania had been coined.

Catharine said of her new role: "The emolument is not great but will be easily earned, and rather falls in with my desire to write useful articles. The time may come when my name will be associated in the literary history of this new country, and I am more ambitious of its being recorded for the useful than the amusing only." Catharine is said to have provided monthly articles to this magazine from February to June 1855.

25th February 1855: Tom, Margaretta and baby arrive back in Australia

Tom and Margaretta's last child, a daughter named Elizabeth Marina, was born on the Indian Ocean in January 1855, and the 'Scotia' arrived back at Sydney with the month-old baby as an additional passenger on 25th February.

1st March 1855: Jane is ill and Sam turns up unexpectedly

Jane had been sorting out the complications of a legacy which was to be divided between herself and her seven brothers and sisters, but had become too ill to write during January and February 1855. She told Catharine in a letter dated 4th April 1855: "I have had dreadful rheumatic fever attended with inflammation of the right kidney and was only just able to creep down for an hour or two when dear Sam came in on the 1st of March quite unexpectedly in the midst of one of the longest coldest winters this country has ever known."

Jane had better news than anticipated about the family legacies: "At last my dear sister I have the pleasure of forwarding to you on the Canadian Company's Bank £75 17s 3d which I hope will reach you safely, being at least £25 more than I had hoped for. Of course the executor account was a complicated piece of villainy but the lawyer said there was no means of righting that." Catharine and Thomas had originally hoped to receive a substantial legacy which would get them out of their difficulties, but in this they were disappointed.

Mrs Strickland had not recovered completely from an illness which is not specified, but she had one ailment in common with her grandson James Traill. Jane told Catharine: "Mamma has not been strong since her bad illness and was so poorly we sent for Rackham." (presumably their doctor but maybe also a relation of Katharine Rackham) "She is charmingly now for her, if it pleases God to keep her so." Mrs Strickland sent her love to Catharine but, Jane said "Nothing troubles her so much as writing as it brings out the eryisepelas into her poor face" but "her love for her children in Canada is not contingent upon her writing to them. I think that you know that."

Early 1855: Tom's daughters are abandoned

Two of the children that Tom and Margaretta had left in England, got into an unforeseeable difficulty while their parents were away. Jane told Catharine in her letter written in April 1855 that "Julia and Mary poor things were in a fix from which Eliza sent money to extricate them. They were at school you know near Exeter when their schoolmistress ran away for debt to the Continent leaving her young people to shift for themselves.

"We dared not have them here but they went to their father's house in Plaistow to their brother who wished to send them to the school to which Walter and Diana are. They chose to stay with him – it is an awkward business that indeed they have been so strangely brought up that we dare not be responsible for them.

"I am told they are handsome clever and good natured but though fond of their brother do not mind him – How should they – I wish Tom would send them out to Canada to farm where they would marry and get better protection than they have now."

(31st March 1855: Literary context – The last of the Bronte sisters dies)

By 1855, the eight Strickland children who had survived babyhood, all continued to be reasonably hale and hearty, despite poor living conditions in Reydon Hall and, for Catharine, in Canada. Eliza, the oldest was 61 and Tom, the youngest was 47.

A far less fortunate family health-wise, was the other literary family of the day, the Brontes. In 1855 Charlotte Bronte, the last and longest surviving member of the Bronte siblings, died on 31st March, three weeks before her 39th birthday. Her sisters had all died of consumption and Bramwell died of alcoholism probably combined with consumption. Charlotte's death was due to an extreme form of morning sickness in the early stages of her first pregnancy.

18th April 1855: Sam marries for the third time

Jane passed on to Catharine news of Sam's forthcoming wedding in a second letter written in April 1855: "Sam is to be married April 18. If I am well Agnes and I are to go to Whatfield in Suffolk with Leigh to the wedding, at least 50 miles off being near Essex – I am sure you will love Kate who has been staying with us a few days. She is a slender and graceful person lively and obliging, pious and sensible. I think my Strickland a happy man – Only think he has bought me a silver grey Moiree antique and it is a perfect beauty." Moiree antique was a process applied to fabrics, for example silk or satin, which gave a distinctive watermark pattern and could be very expensive.

"He is a dear generous amiable creature and Kate is a happy woman to get him. She has had many offers far more eligible but has been faithful to her first affection. Her character is very high and many presents are sent her from all quarters. She has a pretty fortune but nothing in comparison to her own worth." So Sam, prosperous as he was, would be taking back to Canada a wife who was comfortably off in her own right, in marked contrast to Susanna and Catharine, who had both been poor and had been taken to Canada by husbands with very limited means.

Jane did not, after all, manage to go to the wedding. The only one of Sam's sisters present was Agnes, who gave an account of the event when she wrote to her mother the same day. She said that the wedding had taken place at 9.30am "this lovely morning. We all took breakfast in our own rooms, that we might be ready in time. The bride looked young and lovely in her white bonnet and veil, and exquisitely neat morning dress. She went in a clarence" (a four-wheeled closed horse-drawn carriage with a projecting glass front, and seats inside for four passengers) "with her sister and sister-in-law, Mrs Fowler and Mrs Rackham; the bridegroom in an open carriage with Mrs Wickes and myself. The other gentlemen walked – the distance from the church not being much."

The wedding was a family affair with the vicar being the bride's brother-in-law. Agnes wrote: "Mr Fowler performed the service, and the brother of the bride gave her away. I was bride's-maid and Mr Leigh groomsman. All went off beautifully. We had an excellent dejeuner a la fourchette at the rectory, and a profusion of flowers. They leave here at four for London, and I start tomorrow for Blandford Square. All sent their love to you, Eliza and Jane." The couple spent their honeymoon at Avenue Lodge, lent to them by Eliza, before leaving England to begin their lives together in Canada.

The notice inserted in the local papers in Suffolk read: "April 18th 1855. Married at Whatfield, by the Rev FC Fowler, Major Strickland of Douro, Canada West, to Katharine, youngest daughter of the late Thomas Rackham, Esq., of Aylsham."

June 1855: Catharine's book sells well but makes her little money

Catharine's book 'The Canadian Settler's Guide' was published in 1855 and many copies were sold, but with her usual financial misfortune or mismanagement, Catharine made less money from it than she should have done. The respectable-sounding Rev Hope published it for her in Canada in 1855, and in 1859 the 'Old Countryman' magazine of which he was editor, is said to have been advertising the tenth edition. The £100 that he was paid in advance by the Department of Agriculture for 600 copies, apparently did not reach Catharine, nor does she seem to have received any money from the bulk purchase of copies which the British government made in the late 1850s to distribute to potential emigrants.

Agnes had tried to find a publisher or bookseller for it in England but had no luck. She told Catharine in a letter written on 2nd June 1855: "I got Mr Savill, Routledge printer to offer your Emigrants Guide to Routledge's but he said it had been offered him and he had rejected it before and indeed nothing that is first published in Canada will sell in England so never deceive yourself again with the idea that it will."

Richard Bentley's publishing business and magazines were in considerable difficulty in 1855 but did manage to recover. He was holding some of Catharine's work at the time and Agnes's letter told Catharine: "I will not return your sketches till Robert comes for his bride because it is possible that I may get them into a magazine. Bentley's failure has frightened all the life out of publishing for he was reported a very rich man. He had some of your sketches, for which I have asked him but I hope I may get them yet." Agnes was continuing to send clothes to Catharine and her family. She added: "I have sent you a black spot net, very little the worse for wear, and various things which may be useful to you and your girls. I am sorry I had nothing better for you this time."

Although Agnes and Eliza in England had been unable to prevent Catharine making unfortunate arrangements with publishers of her work in Canada, Agnes did succeed in getting her an offer of work. In August 1855 Agnes's publisher in Edinburgh, John Blackwood, asked Catharine to write for 'Blackwood's Magazine' and offered her a good rate of pay.

Her sisters managed to get her book 'Little Downy' published in England in 1855 by Dean and Son, albeit wrongly attributed to Susanna. They also managed to get 'Lady Mary and her Nurse; or, A Peep into the Canadian Forest', published in London by Hall, Virtue in 1856 even though it had previously appeared in Canada in serial form.

20<u>th</u> July 1855: Agnes develops a belief in homeopathy

After Sam's wedding Agnes went to London and stayed in Blandford Square with Mr and Mrs Charles Greaves whom she had met in Harrogate in 1853. Jane described Agnes as "quite at home" when staying in Blandford Square, and Charles Greaves seems to have read Agnes's 'Life of Mary Stuart' for her when it was at proof stage.

In 1855 Agnes was again accused of having become a Roman Catholic. The accusation came in a letter in the 'St James's Chronicle' when the controversial end to the life of Mary Stuart was reached in the series 'Lives of the Queens of Scotland'. Agnes insisted on an apology or, as she put it in a letter home: "I have made the editor apologise for allowing me to be called a Jesuitess in the letter of a lucubrator of the Dogberry variety."

On 20th July 1855, Agnes wrote a long letter to her sister Catharine, necessitated by the need to report on her extensive efforts on Catharine's behalf with publishers, mainly without success. Of her own news, Agnes told of her new-found faith in homeopathic medicine: "I have put myself under Homeopathic treatment with excellent effects and hope never to have to pay a doctor's bill again."

Apart from her health, she has been distracted from her work on Mary Queen of Scots by Henry Colburn: "I am in litigation with Colburn which must be settled by arbitration but of course it is a great worry and has unsettled me from finishing my work." She was also having to cut down on unnecessary correspondence: "I have made up my mind not to write any letter to distract my attention till I have finished my work. There is a sad expenditure of time and a good outlay of money in useless correspondence. I must cease to answer troublesome people who land me with letters on their own affairs."

Agnes only took a short summer holiday in 1855. She spent a few days with friends near Leeds and, she told Catharine: "I then crossed the country to Ulverstone and spent a happy fortnight with dear Sarah and her excellent husband, and had some excursions to Windermere and Coniston Lake, Furness Abbey etc." The railway net-work in England had advanced, and Agnes could travel a good deal of the way back to Reydon Hall by train. She told Catharine: "I returned home July 17th, Eliza and Mamma came to the terminus at Lowestoft to meet me. We drank tea together at the Royal Hotel and came home at 9 in the evening."

Soon after this, on 15th August 1855, came the death of another of Agnes's friends, the Duke of Somerset. Agnes wrote to Jane: "I called yesterday upon the widowed Duchess of Somerset. She kissed me, reproached me for not coming to see her before. Her eyes were swollen with weeping for her poor old Duke." Agnes's friendship with the Duchess of Somerset seems to have been a great consolation to the Duchess during the first year of her widowhood, and they exchanged letters a number of times. When the Duchess began to entertain again after the Duke's death, Agnes was often invited and continued to meet nobles and notables on these occasions.

July 1855: Agnes visits Tom's children

Agnes in writing to Catharine on 20th July 1855 passed on some news about the children Tom and Margaretta had left in England. Agnes wrote: "I went to see Tom's children at their school in Gravesend and was much pleased with them." This would have been Diana aged 13 and Walter aged 12, as the three older unmarried children were living at the family home in Plaistow.

28th July 1855: Ulverston's new Infant School building is in use

By the summer of 1855 the new Infant School building in Ulverston had been built and brought into use. It is first mentioned in the local paper in connection with one of the year's summer treats: "On Saturday 28th July 1855, the children attending the Infant School were mustered in the new room, which is now completed, and marched in procession to the residence of the Rev R Gwillym for their treat. The weather was very favourable, and the children indulged in the usual juvenile games on the grass and were refreshed with buns, pastry and coffee. There were upwards of 100 present, many of the parents also attended, and expressed their satisfaction with the manner in which the school is conducted. The room is found admirably adapted to the purpose for which it was designed, and we hope it will soon be placed out of debt. We are given to understand a concert of local talent will be given some evening during the next month, which it is hoped will be well supported by those residing in the town and neighbourhood."

1st August 1855: Susanna's elder daughter becomes Katie Vickers

On 1st August 1855 Susanna's elder daughter Catharine, known as Katie, married John Vickers and went with him to live in Toronto.

John Vickers had emigrated from Dublin in 1849 to New York where he started working for a steamship company. He then decided to become a farmer and moved to the Belleville area where he met the Moodie family.

Before long he realised that he was not cut out for the farming life and became an employee of the American Express Company, followed by setting up a successful express business of his own in Toronto. Katie Vickers lived her married life in financial security.

After Susanna's daughter Katie had married and moved to Toronto, Annie Traill went to live for a while with her Aunt Moodie in Belleville.

1st August 1855: Sarah gets drenched

In Ulverston a more adventurous treat than usual was planned for the older children, but the weather brought it to an abrupt end. The papers reported: "On Wednesday 1st August 1855, the annual treat of buns and coffee was given to the children attending the National Schools by Mr and Mrs Gwillym. The morning was wet and unpromising, but it cleared up at noon, and the children assembled about two o'clock to the number of 250 or upwards, and went down to the sea shore near Conishead Priory. There were provided 90 gallons of coffee, and 530 buns.

"The usual games were proceeding much to the enjoyment of those present, when distant thunder was heard, and we regret to say, the storm approached so rapidly, that before the happy group could be arranged in order for their return, the rain poured down in such torrents as to drench the scholars and teachers and the lady visitors who had accompanied them. We have not heard that any colds or severe illnesses were contracted as a consequence."

A quieter newsworthy item in Sarah and Richard's life in the autumn of 1855 was at the Annual Exhibition of the Ulverston Horticultural Society where one of the awarded Cards of Merit was to: "four choice fruit trees in pots, the property of Rev R Gwillym, which were in full bearing."

August 1855: Agnes loses a friend but also loses a foe

In August 1855, Agnes's friend, Henry Lawson died. He and Agnes were both interested in Tudor history and both believed themselves to be somehow descended from Katharine Parr, the sixth wife of Henry VIII. They therefore felt linked by relationship as well as by friendship. Henry Lawson had written to Agnes saying he wished to put her "in possession of the relics of our progenitor Queen Catharine" and asked where he should send them.

When his gifts arrived carriage-paid at Reydon Hall, Agnes knew they were items with which he would not have parted unless he believed himself to be near his end. They included a wooden dish with a royal coat of arms in bronze, and a napkin which had belonged to Catharine of Aragon, plus various portraits and prints. Henry Lawson died the week after Agnes received the gifts, having survived his wife by only a few days. He also left Agnes a legacy of £50. It is said that he gave the bulk of his fortune, a sum of £20,000 to the Observatory at Bath.

Probably less lamented by Agnes was Henry Colburn who died within a day or two of Henry Lawson, on 16th August 1855. No-one knew Henry Colburn's age but he had been in the publishing business for so long that he was thought to have been in his seventies.

Henry Colburn had retired in 1852 and had sold his business in Great Marlborough Street, but he had kept a few of his most valuable copyrights. These included the copyright of 'Lives of the Queens of England' as well as the copyrights of published versions of the diaries of Samuel Pepys and John Evelyn, Burke's Peerage and some novels by Benjamin Disraeli.

Summer 1855: Trainee farmers are boarding at 'Oaklands'

Thomas Traill had followed Sam's example, and gave tuition in farming to young men who boarded at 'Oaklands'. In the summer of 1855 James Parr Clinton Atwood aged 19 emigrated to Canada from Gloucestershire where his father was a clergyman. He initially boarded at 'Oaklands' and when he was ready to run his own farm, he bought a property nearby named 'Thorndale'.

The development of photography was beginning to alter the way people kept in touch. For Thomas Traill this meant that he was sent pictures of his grand-children in Scotland. Thomas's son John had eloped with Eliza Dunbar Heddle in 1841, and the couple had two children before Eliza died in 1844. John Traill died in 1847, and the two children went to live with Barbara Fotheringhame, sister to Thomas Traill's first wife, who had previously brought up Thomas's two sons. In 1855 Barbara sent Thomas photographs of his grandchildren, Catharine's step-grandchildren, Henrietta and William then aged 14 and 13 respectively.

September 1855: Susanna is investigating spiritualism

Susanna was intrigued by spiritualism and read many of the books which were published in the 1850s, nearly all of which had as their starting point the experience of the Fox sisters, Margaret and Kate. They had been brought up on the American side of Lake Ontario and in 1848, when the girls were aged 12 and 13, mysterious rappings had been heard in the old house in which they lived. A means of interpreting the noises was found, and tests were carried out to validate the idea that these were communications from the spirit world.

The Fox family had at one time lived in Belleville, and an older sister remained living in a nearby village. When Kate Fox, and maybe her mother and sister Margaret Fox, visited the third sister, John Moodie and Susanna not only met them, but invited Kate Fox to their home.

When Susanna wrote to Richard Bentley in about September 1855, she gave details of the visit, and said that she and John had tested Kate Fox's powers in a number of ways. They had found her convincing to the point where Susanna believed Kate Fox was remarkable, but she was sceptical about her being able to communicate with the spirit world.

Susanna had heard of the death of Henry Colburn, who had been an adversary of Richard Bentley after a break-up of their business partnership many years before. The historical contest between Bentley and Colburn as publishers seemed still to be in existence in 1855 because Susanna, when commenting on a book by Mr Doran published by Bentley, said that Mr Doran's other book "is not out yet in America." This "other book" seems to have been a book entitled 'Lives of the Queens of England of the House of Hanover' which was published in two volumes by Richard Bentley in 1855. This was the extension to the 'Lives of the Queens of England' which Agnes and Eliza had refused to write for Henry Colburn, on the grounds that these lives were too close in date to Queen Victoria and would have covered areas of some difficulty, including the conflicts between George IV and his estranged wife, Queen Caroline.

Mid-October 1855: Tom and Margaretta return safely to England

Having arrived in Sydney in February 1855, Tom and Margaretta set sail back to London in time to be safely back to London Docks and re-united with their children in October 1855.

On 11th November 1855 Jane wrote a letter to Catharine which contained a reminder of the dangerous life that their brother Tom lived. She wrote: "Only think of seven ships being total wrecks on the beach at Southwold, two at Easton, and more than thirty on the coasts of Norfolk and Suffolk. No lives were lost. The life boat apparatus brought off all. I think the gale of 1st and 2nd November 1855 will be long remembered.

"The return of Tom a fortnight before the heavy storms saved us much anxiety. He with Margaretta and Elizabeth Marina, his daughter born on the Indian Ocean, came safely to land in the middle of October. Tom speaks in his letter of his mermaid Marina with more affection than of any child he has ever had." Jane added: "She is fair with blue eyes but a tiny baby and though ten months old has not yet cut a tooth."

Jane told Catharine that Tom: "talks of settling with all his family in Australia if he can get the situation of Harbour Master at Sydney. I think it would be wise in him for the poor unprotected girls would marry well there and to leave them as he did was most careless and unpaternal." Jane added, in referring to Tom's eldest daughter, Adela Wigg: "The Wiggs I am told are in difficulty" but she gave no further details.

Tom maybe knew, although Jane did not mention it, that his time as captain of the 'Scotia' was near its end, which might have been another reason why Margaretta had accompanied him on his last voyage. After two previous journeys the 'Scotia' had been put up for sale, but this time the ship's fate seemed final. By 5th December 1855, the 'Scotia' had been moored in the West India Dock prior to being laid up.

November 1855: There are troubles in the Moodie household

1855 ended for Susanna on a difficult note for two reasons. The problem of the most urgent kind was that Susanna's second son Donald, then aged nineteen, became seriously ill with typhus fever. Susanna had to nurse him constantly, and it took seven weeks before he was well enough to get out of bed, and sit in a nearby chair for a little while each day.

While Susanna was nursing Donald, John was being sued for damages. In his role as sheriff, he had seized and sold a property which he believed to be the joint property of two brothers, in order to satisfy the creditors of one of them. However, they had managed to pass ownership to the brother who was not in debt, and he sued John as a result. The case, which John lost, was heard in November 1855 and he had to pay damages of over £36.

11th November 1855: Jane's book on Rome has moderate sales

The first volume of Jane's work 'Rome; Regal and Republican' having been published in 1854, Jane continued working on the second volume, but by November 1855 she knew that the first volume had not been as successful as she had hoped. She had finished writing and told Catharine that she was: "preparing my second volume for the press in case it should be required. I do not lose hope – but my publisher is not enterprising. However nearly a thousand copies have been sold so it has not done badly after all."

Jane's letter to Catharine, written on a Sunday 11th November 1855, showed that she as well as Agnes and Eliza, was working on Catharine's behalf in England. Agnes had managed to find an English publisher for 'Lady Mary and her Nurse', but it was Jane who did the necessary proof-reading and other things needed to turn the manuscript into a book.

Timing was such that Jane had to break one of the Ten Commandments by working on the Sabbath. She eased her conscience by saying to Catharine: "However there is some good and no harm in little Lady Mary's sayings and doings, so I will not stop the press and as you are anxious, add the naughtiness of this note to the other sin, for of course you will want the money very much."

Jane had been going through a spell of bad health. She wrote: "I have suffered very much with spasms in my right side which affects the muscles in my arm so that writing is often painful. I have had a great plaister all over the liver which has reduced it a little. I am better but not strong, the swelled liver makes me stouter than I should be, and I wear a quantity of flannel, a great expense and no pleasure."

Sarah had been on a visit to Reydon and Jane made a telling comment about the lasting effect on Sarah of her first marriage. Jane wrote: "The dear Gwillyms have just left us. Both looked well though he like me is always ailing – any sudden change for cold or damp making him indisposed. Sarah looked more like herself than she has done since her first woeful marriage and was cheerful and seemed happy. Mamma recovered her health in time to enjoy their visit but the weather was dreadfully wet and stormy. Poor Gwillym was much affected to see a ship in distress in the Bay with the waves washing over her decks for no help could be given her – not even a lifeboat could live in such a sea.

"Agnes has been suffering from a crushed toe but is mending. Eliza is at her own house and quite well. I lost my visit to St Margarets by the Gwillyms not keeping their set time." This last sentence is also a telling one. Mrs Strickland was 82 years old and, by implication, Jane as carer was very restricted in what she could do, having to be on hand to look after things when there were visitors, even family members.

December 1855: Reydon Hall has too many potential visitors

From the long and chatty letter that Jane wrote to Catharine in November 1855, it is evident that a number of Mrs Strickland's

Canadian grand-children and their friends had visited England and stayed at Reydon Hall, and they generally seemed to be young unmarried men.

Jane told Catharine: "We are looking forward to seeing Robert Strickland with pleasure but Mamma's health and spirits are unequal to receiving any companion with him. Susan leads us to expect her son Alexander" (Susanna's eldest son, aged 21, and usually referred to as Dunbar) "and indeed, dear Kate, he will be a welcome visitor."

However, the bachelor status of the visitors sometimes caused difficulty. Jane wrote: "It would not be pleasant for Mr Leigh to meet the Ellises." Mr Leigh had been best man at Sam's wedding a few months earlier and might also have been Mr Lee, the 'young Oxonian of full purse and free heart' who had been the nearest neighbour of the Traill family during their year at 'Wolf Tower'.

Whoever he was, Mr Leigh had got himself into mischief on his trips to England. Jane continued: "His proposing for Miss Hawker after his marked attention to Charlotte will make him unwelcome there. Of course his conduct excited surprise and it was necessary to tell her what she was sure to hear, that he was the lover of Miss Hawker. We like Mr Leigh much as a clever amiable and accomplished young man, and appreciate his talents and pleasant company – However, he is a dangerous companion for young ladies with the Atlantic between him and them."

Jane continued with the list of intending visitors: "Mamma will be happy to see George Strickland" who was Sam's second son and fourth child and born in 1833 "at some future time – five young men in the house at once would be too much for her." The identity of some of the five was not revealed. Jane asked Catharine to sort out the problem: "Will you dear Kate make her wishes known. It is an awkward task for you but Sam is so free from affront-taking that I am sure you can manage it with him."

Charlotte Ellis, sister of Caroline, although she did not marry Mr Leigh, apparently married a relative of Catharine's friend Frances Stewart in 1860, and with him went to live in Ontario. Given that divorce was almost unheard of, English women in the mid-19th century seem willing to take great risks with their futures by marrying men they hardly knew.

December 1855: Susanna's 'Geoffrey Moncton' appears in America

Susanna's book 'Roughing It in the Bush', first published in 1852, having been a success in England, Canada and the United States, was followed by a swift succession of other books on both sides of the Atlantic. However, fashions in literature in England and in North America were drifting apart so that the trend in sales of Susanna's books in England was downwards, while her popularity as an author in North America was increasing.

As a consequence the main publisher of Susanna's work changed, and whereas in 1853 it had been necessary for Richard Bentley in London to give his permission before De Witt could publish Susanna's work in North America, by 1856 the American firm had become Susanna's main publisher and Richard Bentley's business relationship with Susanna had ended, although their friendly exchange of letters continued.

This change was noted in reviews of 'Geoffrey Moncton'. An American press report on 19th December 1855 noted: "The talented author of 'Roughing It in the Bush', has thrown all her power into this work, which is by far the best of the many excellent ones that have issued from her pen; and we think it will make a sensation both here and in England, as the most brilliant novel of the day. By special arrangement with Mrs Moodie, and by a liberal outlay, this work is printed first in this country, and the proof-sheets sent to Bentley, and published in England simultaneously with the issue here."

A touch of ungraciousness crept into references to Agnes at this time, with the 'New York Daily Times' a few months later (26th April 1856) saying: "'Geoffrey Moncton', by Mrs Moodie (sister of, but a much better writer than, Agnes Strickland, the historian) is a very readable fiction, not inferior to the same author's 'Mark Hurdlestone'." Advertisements for new books available in Canada and America sometimes included 'Lives of the Queens of England' or 'Lives of the Queens of Scotland' as new volumes or editions were issued.

18th December 1855: Sarah deputises for Richard

Life for Sarah followed its usual path for much of 1855, but Richard's ill-health meant that she had to stand in for him at the

Infant School examination in December. The local paper reported: "Infant School – The annual examination of this school took place on Tuesday 18th December 1855 in the noble structure in the Church-walk, lately erected, in the presence of the Rev G Procter MA, Rev S Robertson, Mrs Gwillym (the Rev R Gwillym, the respected patron being, by indisposition, prevented from attending) and a numerous attendance of other ladies and the parents of the children. At the conclusion there was the usual distribution of presents. We would take this opportunity of reminding our readers that the soiree in aid of liquidating the remnant of debt upon the building, takes place on the 28th December 1855."

22nd January 1856: Susanna has high praise for her own son

While Susanna's letters to Richard Bentley sometimes contained criticism of her brother Sam and her sisters Agnes, Eliza and Jane in England, she was fulsome in praise of her own children, particularly her son Donald. Having recovered from typhus fever, he had returned to his medical studies at McGill College, and Susanna told Richard Bentley in a letter dated 22nd January 1856 that she hoped Donald will "be somewhat in his native land. With great personal beauty he unites that winning frankness of manner, which reaches all hearts." She added "My only fear arises, from the attention and flattery he meets with everywhere, which is enough to turn wiser heads than belongs to a boy of nineteen." She had been similarly shameless in describing her daughter Agnes when she wrote to John Lovell, editor of the 'Literary Garland' in November 1842.

Of her relatives in England she told Richard Bentley in the same letter: "I never hear from Reydon now. They have ignored me and my books." This conflicts with Jane in November 1855 telling Catharine that they were expecting a visit from Susanna's son Dunbar, and asking Catharine to give Susanna their love and thanks for her letters. However, Richard Bentley had probably had enough dealings with the various members of the Strickland family to accept Susanna's use of language as a reflection of her volatility, rather than as exact depictions of the truth.

Susanna added a couple of dashes of vinegar to her letter: "My sister Traill, is publishing a juvenile work, with Hall and Virtue's establishment, for which she receives £25." This referred to 'Lady Mary and Her Nurse' being published in London. "This is not much, with Agnes's weight in literature to back her. How does the Major's book sell now? If fine reviews could sell a work, his should have brought a fortune." Unfortunately no record has been found of whether Sam's book sold well or badly, apart from Agnes's mention of a second edition.

In a postscript, Susanna gives a clear illustration of her tendency to prefer drama to truth when relating her own past experiences. She told Richard Bentley: "My first attempts at authorship, were all tragedies. One of these, Mr Young, the tragedian, pronounced a very high opinion, though I was but a child of 14. I was persuaded by foolish fanaticks, with whom I got entangled, to burn these MSS, it being they said unworthy of a christian to write for the stage. 'Henrie', 'The Bride of Brittany', and 'Bourbon' were, perhaps, the best things I ever wrote that perished in this auto da fe. The little headings in blank verse, that often occur in my books are snatches that memory retains of these tragedies. Nature certainly meant me for a dramatic writer, and having outlived my folly, I really regret the martyrdom of these vigourous children of my young brain.

"Don't laugh at me. That portion of my life, would make a strange revelation of sectarianism. But it may rest with my poor tragedies in oblivion. I do not wish it to meet with their fiery dooms or the ridicule of the world."

Susanna here seems to be confusing the story told by Catharine in which Susanna threw a manuscript into the fire at Reydon Hall after Eliza had criticised it severely, with her brief time as a member of the Congregational Church in Wrentham. The Congregational Church is a moderate non-conformist church, and there is no evidence whatsoever to support Susanna's claim that the church had any objection to her writing, or made her burn any of her work.

25th April 1856: Sam's son Robert marries in Southwold

Judging from Jane's letters to Catharine, Robert Strickland arrived in England in November or December 1855 and presumably remained until after his marriage which took place on Tuesday 25th April 1856. This was the same day that the Earl of Stradbroke laid the foundation stone of the new infant school-room in Southwold and the two events were linked in a report in the local papers.

The report, referring to Southwold began: "This pretty little town has been enlivened by events of no ordinary interest" and then gave details of the laying of the foundation stone. The report then detailed the wedding by saying: "On the same day was celebrated the marriage of Miss Ellis, the eldest daughter of Captain FW Ellis, RN, to Robert Alexander Strickland, Esq., the eldest son of Major Strickland, and nephew of the well-known Miss Agnes Strickland, of Raydon Hall, Suffolk.

"A wedding is always an animating pageant at Southwold, from the hearty feelings which prompts the nautical population to indicate their good will by hoisting colours on the cliffs, and vessels in the harbour; but on this occasion the demonstrations were more than ordinary, every inhabitant seemed anxious to mark with respect an event of such interest to families long known in the neighbourhood.

"Every quarter of town, Gun-hill, and cliffs, seemed one arcade of banners and garlands. The bridal party was complemented by a large assemblage of personal friends and relatives, and the church" (the Southwold parish church of St Edmund) "was crowded with a congregation of voluntary witnesses, who had come to offer their prayers and good wishes for the young townswoman, whom they had seen grow up among them from infancy.

"After the ceremony upwards of forty friends sat down to a dejeuner at Hill-house, the residence of Captain Ellis."

Caroline's father, Captain Francis Wilson Ellis RN was the local Harbour Master and his home was on Constitution Hill in Southwold. The couple left for Canada soon after the wedding.

1856: Jane's 'Adonijah' is published

In 1856, Jane had a romantic adventure story published entitled 'Adonijah: a tale of the Jewish Dispersion', which she had written many years earlier. For this novel Jane told Catharine: "I am to have thirty pounds for the use of the copyright for seven years – a low price but may lead to better things."

It was about this time that Jane bought Park Lane Cottage in Southwold as an investment, intending to let it out each year during the summer holiday season.

1856: Eliza moves to Surrey and has a day out with Agnes

By 1856 London had expanded as far as Eliza's cottage in Bayswater. The orchards and countryside around it had gone, and the land on which the cottage was standing was wanted for development. Eliza had in any case been living much of the time recently at Reydon Hall. In 1856 she bought what was described as a small villa, called 'Abbot's Lodge', at Tilford, near Farnham in Surrey.

When Agnes visited Eliza in Tilford to plan and progress their joint work, they sometimes went on excursions together, an early one of which Agnes described in a letter to her mother. It was a visit to Winchester Cathedral in connection with their writing, and they travelled via Aldershot so they could see the army camp that was being built there.

The camp was to be Britain's first permanent army training camp and needed sufficient open land to carry out large-scale military exercises. Aldershot having been a small village, set in open heath-land almost devoid of buildings, roads and trees, was ideal. Construction began in 1854 with the soldiers living in tents until they had built lines of wooden huts, each of which could accommodate 22 men or 8 officers. In 1856 the Royal Pavilion was built for Queen Victoria and the royal family to use when they visited the developing camp, and work on the camp was completed by 1859.

Agnes in describing her outing with Eliza wrote: "We had an open carriage to take us to Farnborough station, which made our excursion very pleasant. The view of the camp, partly in tents and partly in barracks, with hotels springing up like mushrooms, is curious enough in the midst of a vast barren heath. It was very pretty when, on our return, we saw it all lighted up.

"We got to Winchester in time to lunch with Mr and Mrs Heathcote and to attend service in the beautiful cathedral, after which we went all over it. We saw the tombs of many worthies and unworthies, all packed together like giblets in a pie. Then we drove down to St Cross, a grand hospital foundation. Here, following the rules, we wayfarers were offered white bread and a horn of beer at the buttery hatch. As I was very hot and tired, I ate the bread and drank the beer. We did not get back to Tilford till eleven at night."

Jane recorded that both Agnes and Eliza enjoyed "the examination of ecclesiastical antiquities. Elizabeth especially took infinite delight in these existing relics of the past, and sometimes would have rendered the royal biographies too erudite for general readers if Agnes had been of the same mind as herself." However, from Agnes's point of view Eliza's temper could spoil a visit. On one occasion, Agnes wrote home that she was "not in health for her hurricanes" and had been obliged to leave after a quarrel on the third day of her visit.

June 1856: Catharine receives some of Thomas's relatives from Scotland

The flow of visitors and relatives between Canada and Great Britain in 1856 included some relatives of Thomas Traill arriving in Canada. The first was Francis Traill, illegitimate son of Thomas's unmarried elder son who had been brought up in the Orkneys. He stayed at 'Oaklands' until he found a job as a clerk in Cobourg.

Two other relatives of Thomas arrived to stay with Catharine and family in June 1856. One was only a temporary visitor until he could find work; the other became a boarder with the aim of learning about farming. This arrangement seemed to work well and Catharine considered taking two or three small boys as pupil lodgers but Susanna warned her against it.

30th July 1856: John Moodie is at the seaside

When Susanna wrote to Catharine on the 30th July 1856, her husband was away. Susanna wrote: "He had been so worn and worried with business, that I prevailed upon him to take a little trip for the benefit of his health" but while he was away, Susanna missed him. She told Catharine: "Time lengthens to ages when he is away. He is as dear to me after five and twenty years as when we first met."

John's trip had taken him to New York then Boston, returning by sea steamer to Portland. He did much of the journey by train and this was the first time he had seen the sea since arriving in Canada in 1832. Susanna said: "Everybody here is taking trips to Portland to the sea side. Ah don't I envy them but I cannot afford to go."

26th August 1856: Jane helps with fund-raising

The laying of the foundation stone for a new infant school-room in Southwold shows that Richard Gwillym was not alone in his championing of education for children. In Southwold a fund-raising bazaar was held on 26th and 27th August 1856 with Jane and Agnes being among those mentioned in the papers which reported: "Southwold – The Bazaar. The charming Gun-hill was the scene of the charity. There were four large stalls; at the first presided Mrs Saville Onley, with several other ladies, including Miss Jane Strickland. Here we bought the autograph of that world-known lady, Miss Agnes Strickland, and a beautiful book of poems written by the same gifted authoress as a 'Seaside Offering'.

"At night there was a ball. The next day the scene was repeated, terminating with an auction, at which the remnants of the refreshments were sold. During the two days of the bazaar Howlett's band from Norwich enlivened the scene. The charity has cleared £300, for which much is due to the liberality of Miss Sheriffe, and the exertion of the Rev Mr Crowfoot, the Vicar."

September 1856: Church of England reorganisation affects Richard and Sarah

In 1856 in Ulverston, there was no mention in the local papers of a summer treat for the children. There was, however, reorganisation of the Church of England, and Richard's parish was one of several that were transferred from the Bishopric of Chester to that of Carlisle. Summer treats for the children seem to have occurred on a less regular basis after this reorganisation, which came at about the same time as cracks were beginning to appear in the health of both Richard and Sarah.

The only other item in the local papers which adds to the picture of Sarah's home-life was in regard to the Ulverston Horticultural Society where a fruit tree from Stockbridge House got a special mention. It was reported that: "The autumn show of this society took place on Tuesday 2nd September 1856, and as a whole was considered a success." Among the items mentioned was the comment: "nor must we pass unnoticed the Pitmason Orange Nectarine with 31 fruit on it, from the Rev R Gwillym."

October 1856: Harry Traill has taken over the management of 'Oaklands'

In 1856 Catharine's eldest son, James married Amelia Muchall, and they bought a small parcel of land on Rice Lake Plains intending to farm near Catharine and Thomas. However James's health was not good, and they soon moved to Belleville where, with help from Susanna and John Moodie, James Traill became a trader, buying and selling goods across the border with the United States.

After James had left 'Oaklands', Catharine's second son Harry, at the age of 19, successfully took over running the farm for his ailing father. The situation for the Traill family had improved with the establishment of the farm, and the labour which the two older sons had supplied, but the family still needed outside financial support.

Agnes did what she could to help. In a letter to Catharine written on 22nd October 1856, Agnes said: "My dearest Catharine, I send you a letter of credit to enable you to receive with benefit of currency the sum of £5 8s 3d, being the balance of the proceeds of three of my Canada Land Shares which I sold the other day and transferred the cash into Canada Land and Loan shares. I thought this little sum would be particularly acceptable to you now."

Sam's wife Katharine Strickland and Catharine Traill had become close friends, despite the distance between their homes in Lakefield and Rice Lake Plains. Agnes wrote in her October 1856 letter to Catharine: "I am so glad you appreciate Sam's sweet Katharine and that she is so kind to you. She promised me she would be."

November 1856: Susanna sees her first steam train

The Grand Trunk Railway reached Belleville when the first train arrived on 27th October 1856, and it became possible for Susanna to reach Toronto and Montreal in only a few hours. Susanna described her first impressions of a steam train to Richard Bentley in a letter written on 27th November 1856: "The Grand Trunk Railway has been opened now a month. The traffic upon it is immense. I never saw a Locomotive engine at work before. The sight filled me with awe. The spirit of man seemed to work in the wondrous machine, as the spirit of God in us. I have not ventured into one of the cars yet."

Susanna, like Catharine, was having relatives of her husband arriving from Scotland, as their first home after emigrating to Canada. Susanna told Richard Bentley: "A nephew of Moodie's has come out to us with his wife and child, intending to buy land and settle in Upper Canada." The visit was expected to last all winter, but the nephew and the Moodies did not get on, and the stay was not as long as anticipated.

8th December 1856: Ulverston plans to join the national rail network

The railway network was expanding in England as well as in Canada. Ulverston already had a railway station to mark the terminus of a short local stretch of railway but, at the end of 1856, the town took the first steps towards being more widely connected by rail.

The papers recorded: "The South Durham and Lancashire Union Railway – On Monday evening last, 8th December 1856, a public meeting was held at Ulverstone, under the presidency of the Earl of Burlington" to consider a proposal for a railway line which would connect the coalfields of Durham, the ironstone of Cleveland and the local mineral wealth. The papers observed: "The meeting was numerously attended. The deputation from the promoters consisted of the Mayor of Kendal; H Pearce, Esq., Darlington; and J Wilson, Esq. (ironmaster). Amongst those of Ulverstone and neighbourhood were the Rev R Gwillym" whose name was followed by about 30 other names "and principal tradesmen of Ulverstone."

Forty four miles of railway were needed to make the connection, at an estimated cost of £8,500 per mile. Some of the money had already been raised with £15,000 coming from the town of Kirby Stephen and £25,000 from Darlington. The meeting heard the details of the proposed scheme and discussed the various objections that had been raised. At the end of the meeting: "Resolutions were then passed highly approving of the scheme" which moved swiftly forward, and the line was opened in August 1857.

9th May 1857: Tom's baby daughter dies

Tom's command of the 'Scotia' ended in 1855 even though the ship survived its laying up, and became a packet ship to Australia. For the next few years it is not possible to establish whether Tom became captain of another vessel, or whether he retired, because the movements of several ships were reported in the papers where the captain had the surname Strickland but with no Christian name given. Any or none of these Captain Stricklands might have been Tom.

Elizabeth Marina Strickland, the baby born on the Indian Ocean, did not have a long life. She died at the family home in Plaistow, Essex on 9th May 1857 aged 2 years and 4 months.

26th May 1857: The copyright of 'Lives of the Queens of England' is sold

Following Henry Colburn's death, the copyrights which he owned were put up for auction on Tuesday 26th May 1857. Among the items in the sale catalogue was 'The Lives of the Queens of England' described as 'fourth edition in 8 vols., 1854, embellished with portraits of every queen; copyrights, stereotype, steel plates and remaining stock of 96 complete sets and 1,050 of the later vols., also an abridgement executed by Miss Strickland for schools, ready for press, price to be settled by Mr Charles Dickens named as umpire.' Bidding on this Lot was delayed while Agnes mounted a legal challenge to the sale but she lost and 'Lives of the Queens of England' became the final item in the auction.

The Lot was offered for sale at £1,000 but the copyright of 'Lives of the Queens of England' was still a valuable property and several bidders contended for the Lot. The copyright was eventually sold for £6,900 while the new stock was sold for £227 5s. The exact part played in the proceedings by Charles Dickens was not explained.

27th May 1857: Agnes attends a society wedding

One of Agnes's younger friends, Georgina Eliza Stuart of Lennoxlove married Andrew Buchanan, grandson to the Earl of Caithness, and she became the Hon Mrs Buchanan, on Wednesday 27th May 1857. The wedding took place at St George's Church in Hanover Square, the same church where Sarah and Richard had been married in February 1844.

The banquet which followed Georgina Stuart's wedding was held in Hill Street. Agnes was one of the guests and said it was "by far the grandest wedding at which I have ever been present and the pleasantest." She wore a white embroidered tunic skirt over a primrose silk foundation with a matching jacket, and a transparent bonnet trimmed with flowers. As a wedding gift, Agnes gave a copy of 'Lives of the Queens of Scotland'.

The bridegroom was the Minister to Denmark, and during her married life Georgina Buchanan lived with her diplomat husband in many of the courts of Europe. Before her marriage she had often helped Agnes with her research and writing in Scotland, and her friendship with Agnes continued by letter, and lasted until Agnes's death.

June 1857: Susanna receives a spirit message from Thomas Pringle

John Moodie had become very enthusiastic about spiritualism, and Susanna recounted some of their experiments and experiences in her letters to Richard Bentley. She told him on 22nd June 1857 that she believed she had had a spiritual communication from Thomas Pringle, the abolitionist from whose house she had married.

The message came via the spiritoscope that John had made. Susanna described it as: "A board running upon two smooth brass rods with an index that pointed to the alphabet" which allowed a spirit to spell out messages by moving the pointer. Thomas Pringle's message told Susanna that she would not live to see the abolition of slavery in the United States. "It will end in blood and great political changes must take place. A long struggle between the North and South will set the poor Negro free, but this will take years to accomplish."

The American Civil War began in April 1861 and ended in April 1865. The message supposedly from Thomas Pringle could therefore be interpreted as correct, though why or how someone in the spirit world would foretell the future might need an explanation. This message from Thomas Pringle was only one of a series of events that changed Susanna from being a sceptic, to sharing John's belief in spiritualism.

19th July 1857: Agnes has said farewell to Lady Maxwell

Deaths among Agnes's friends had become far more numerous than weddings. In July 1857 Agnes set off for Scotland to continue her working holidays there. Jane, with a slight error in her dating, wrote: "On her way to visit Lady Seafield at Balmacaan in the Highlands, Agnes stayed some days at Pollok House with Lady Matilda Maxwell. This was in the autumn of 1857 and when Agnes arrived, Lady Matilda was apparently in good health. In the course of three days her ladyship seemed poorly." Her condition deteriorated so rapidly that her sister, Lady Lucy Grant, and the medical man thought it best to clear the house of visitors.

Jane continued: "Lady Matilda insisted on seeing Agnes, who perceived the hand of death upon her friend. Upon her sad journey Agnes received the intelligence of the death of this friend, by a note from Lady Lucy Grant, which grieved but did not surprise her."

The 'Perthshire Advertiser' printed the news: "Death. The Dowager Lady Maxwell ... died suddenly at Kilduff, East Lothian on the 19th July 1857 ... aged 76."

July 1857: Susanna has a holiday in America

Susanna Moodie did little writing for publication in 1857. She had already admitted to Richard Bentley: "I have grown weary of writing idle tales, and the public seem weary of them too and I begin to feel a mortifying certainty that my style does not suit the generality of readers. It belongs like me to the past."

Susanna also had other preoccupations, one of which was that her daughter, Katie Vickers suffered from chronic bronchitis. Hoping that a change of air might help, Katie and John Vickers took a month-long holiday in July 1857, and Susanna and John went with them. Susanna described the event in a letter written to Richard Bentley on 2nd December 1857, including the excitement she felt on her first train journey. She wrote: "I felt very much inclined to shout with joy at the wondrous speed. The harmony of their motion is beautiful."

The start of their journey re-traced the route taken by the Moodies when they first arrived in Canada. The countryside had not changed in Susanna's opinion, but the journey had. On this trip "what was never dreamed of in '32, we shot those glorious rapids, as the natives call passing through them. The Lachine rapids, the grandest, most formidable and exciting, we passed through at sunset. The boat was crowded with lads from the Toronto Colleges, going to spend their holidays. When the great vessel was tossed like a feather on top of these boiling surges, the boys flung up their caps and hurrah'd and I could have joined in that glad wild cry. But the soul is always young. It is only the mortal that grows weary."

The next day they went by train to Portland. Susanna wrote that they: "travelled all day, through splendid country" and Susanna saw the sea again for the first time in many years. She told Richard Bentley: "There was the sea again. The dear, old familiar sea, by whose side I had been bred and born, with whose every tone and phrase I was familiar in my English days. How I enjoyed the long-forgotten smell of the salt brine, and the far off years rose up from the grave of time to stare me in the face." This illustrates Susanna's tendency to exaggerate when in an enthusiastic frame of mind. She had been born in Bungay, which is an inland town at least fifteen miles from the sea, and her family did not move to Reydon until she was five years old. Even then her home was two miles inland from Southwold, albeit the sea could be glimpsed from some of the top floor windows.

After an overnight stop in Portland, they went on to Port Elizabeth where they stayed in the Ocean House Hotel: "our quarters for the next month. A large solitary Hotel, which stands alone in its glory, on that rocky coast." By the end of the journey Katie Vickers was exhausted, but Susanna had enjoyed the scenery and the journey too much to feel tired. Life in the Ocean House Hotel was more egalitarian than Susanna had expected: "The servants were all ladies and gentlemen, and really one of the female waiters was more lady-like than many of the visitors from the Canadian side. If music and singing were going on in the drawing-room the servants came in, as a matter of course, and formed part of the audience, at which no one took umbrage."

25th August 1857: Catharine's home burns down

Disaster struck again for Catharine and Thomas when their house at 'Oaklands' burnt to the ground early in the morning of 25th August 1857. Thomas recorded the event in his journal: "At 3 o'clock this morning Mrs T awoke me, saying the house was on fire. I had barely time to awake the sleepers upstairs, and we got out a part of our bedding, wearing apparel, a few of our books, 3 chairs and 3 tables before the whole house was in a blaze. I am so thankful that our lives were saved, particularly our dear Walter, whose room was full of smoke when we called him, that I hardly regret what is lost. Thanks to God for all his mercies." Catharine's notes on Canadian wild flowers were among the few items saved from the blaze.

In the immediate aftermath, the family moved in with their neighbour, Clinton Atwood while they looked for somewhere suitable to rent. Sam and his family helped as did other friends in Canada, although there is no mention of any help coming from Susanna's direction. The news was sent to England to obtain help from the family there.

10th September 1857: Relatives and friends in Canada rally round

On 10th September 1857 Catharine told Ellen: "My kind brother has given me an order on Nicholls for £10 which will replace some of our household goods – and we have now many new clothes, thanks to our kind friends – our flour and potatoes and some meat and other things will be kept in hand for the first year's stores, and when we are settled we are to have R Strickland to teach," (presumably Sam's youngest son Richard, aged 9) "and so we shall not be destitute. The great weight on my mind is getting a house for a tenant to put up; and selling off all we have to pay the debts before we quit this place."

Catharine told her friend that she hoped "to be able to redeem the losses by the work I am writing – and if we let our farm we can live at a small expense and earn something in a quiet way by needle-work and knitting, pressing flowers and other matters." The family was still staying with Clinton Atwood, where the men-folk could carry on farming on their 'Oaklands' land, while Catharine was busily doing what she could to prepare for a new home. She told Ellen: "I want very much to get our carpet woven. I can get warp (coloured would be best from Nicholl's) but I do not know how the rags are to be got down to the Weaver's without troubling someone to take them there. We shall want it wherever we are and we shall have money in from our Dried Plants directly to pay for the weaving. We have more rags here as there are many old things at Clinton's useless but for that purpose."

12th September 1857: Jane suffers a loss, emotional and financial

Admiral Charles Sipthorpe John Hawtayne was (by some unknown connection) a cousin of the Strickland family in Suffolk, and was another of their relatives who was famous in their own sphere. From Jane's letter it is apparent that he had once been her suitor, but she had sad news of him to pass on to Catharine when she wrote a letter dated 27th September 1857.

Jane wrote: "We sustained a severe shock in the sad accident at Lowestoft which deprived Admiral Hawtayne of life. He was coming over to Reydon to take my house" ('Park Lane Cottage' in Southwold) "by the year for a sort of box for his family. He went to Norwich and brought back with him to Lowestoft Mr Hart, the rector of his parish, his wife and the little daughter Alice to dine and spend the day.

"On their way to the train, the parents went to the reading room which was lighted up, the September evening being dark, and the admiral went on the chain pier in the dark that Alice might hear the band. There is no railing round the edge and the child said she took both his hands and turned him round to dance to the music, lost her balance, and went over, drawing him with her. He was small in person and very slender. She was precipitated into the mud but he struck his head against the piles – They fell seventeen and a half feet. The water was not in but the fall was enough. The little girl's face was bruised, but the admiral never spoke again. The daughter of the Admiral was telegraphed for in haste, but he had been dead for half an hour before she could reach him."

Jane added: "He was an affectionate friend and to me would have been more had I not been fearful of his state of mind. He liked to confide to me his cares and troubles and he had many real ones and far more imaginary ones. I soothed the first and laughed at the rest. The death of our warm-hearted and affectionate kinsman has made us heavy hearted at Reydon."

Charles Hawtayne had been born in 1782 and Jane in 1800. Jane's account of the accident is confirmed by a short entry in the 'Suffolk Chronicle' on Saturday 12th September 1857 which noted: "Death of Admiral Hawtayne – We have received the following message by electric telegraph from Norwich – Admiral Hawtayne fell off the South Pier, Lowestoft, last evening and sustained a concussion of the brain which proved fatal."

September 1857: Relatives in England also rally round

Agnes was the first of the family in England to be told of the burning of 'Oaklands' and she immediately sent some money and passed the news on to the rest of the family in England. Jane was limited in what she could to help, but in her letter to Catharine on 27th September 1857 said: "Agnes told us what she had done for you adding 'Neither you nor Mamma can do anything in it I know' – Alas her words are too true we cannot as far as money goes but I will see whether I cannot find you something useful in the shape of linen and furnishing. I have five Holland chemises as good as new – and I can spare a pair of sheets and a quilt and with such help my poor means must end."

Jane's purchase of 'Park Lane Cottage' in Southwold had been intended to give her a source of income, but it had so far been more of a liability than an asset. Jane wrote: "I have been deeply engaged in furnishing my house which I have done in a cheap neat style as if for myself. Everybody admired it – but I have not been fortunate in letting – indeed it was finished late and will not bring in more than thirteen pounds instead of thirty and I feel anxious about my liabilities. I sold half my Trust and Loan Shares at I fear a sad loss to do this, and could I sell the rest should be clear again, but they are far below that low marker now."

September 1857: Catharine tries to publish her wild flower work in England

One of Catharine's plans for rebuilding her finances was to have published in England a book on the wild flowers of Canada, and John Murray had been approached as a potential publisher. As always Catharine needed someone in England to check what she had written, and to proof-read prior to publication.

Eliza had substantial knowledge of botany and although Jane was by no means ignorant on the subject, Catharine had hoped for help from Eliza. In this she was unlucky as Jane told Catharine in her letter of September 1857. Jane wrote: "Eliza is here looking well and I thought it best to mention the editing of your work, but she says her finishing the lives of the queens of Scotland, building her house and the prospect of an abridgement of the Queens of England will leave her no iota of time – This is quite true dear Kate, but you need not be anxious about that for Murray is a scientific man with celebrated men at his command, for Hugh Murray of his own name would see your work through."

Jane then showed her own botanical knowledge in her advice to Catharine about the book: "You will have to class your flowers and forest trees by the Linnean system if you wish it to proceed. Murray is not an ignorant person like Colburn but an accomplished and learned man" but then Jane confirmed Agnes's view of the market for books, while also showing that Catharine had a following in England for her work. Jane wrote: "Literature is at a total stand. I do nothing in it – but you are a popular author and so may find a publisher at this crisis."

October 1857: Agnes and Sam have come to the rescue

In October 1857, with the end of the farming season and the approach of winter, Catharine's family left Clinton Atwood and the vicinity of 'Oaklands' and split up. Catharine and Thomas with their youngest son, Walter went to live with Sam and Katharine Strickland in Lakefield. James and Amelia Traill undertook to look after James's two other brothers, Harry and William for a few months until the baby they were expecting in February 1858 was due. The three girls in the family, Kate, Annie and Mary stayed with various friends in the Rice Lake area.

Agnes sent £20 and this, together with help from Sam, funded Catharine and Thomas in a new land holding. When writing to Mary in October 1857, Catharine was able to tell her that with Agnes's gift she had bought "a lovely bit of ground three lots – from Mr John Reid – on the village plot but not among the present houses. It has some charming trees that will make it most ornamental. Your uncle will also allow us the use of two plots adjoining, all will be enclosed with one fence; so that we can have ground for potatoes and a grass paddock for a cow and a good garden." John Reid was the eldest son of Sam's second father-in-law. The many links by marriage of the various families in the locality is illustrated by John Reid. He, as well as being Sam's brother-in-law was apparently also a brother-in-law of Thomas Stewart, husband of Catharine's close friend, Frances Stewart.

Plans were being put in hand to build a new home. Catharine was hopeful of further help from England, adding a foot-note to her letter to Mary: "Dear aunt Agnes thinks that when the Gwillyms and your aunt Eliza meet at Reydon this month they will send us something to help us, and if not we may be able to sell 'Oaklands' and take as much as will build us a small house by contract" but all this would take time and the winter was closing in and the family would have to continue in temporary accommodation for a few months longer. Catharine wrote: "We cannot get a house up till the Spring I fear."

By this stage, the Strickland family decided that some legal precautions were needed to prevent Thomas's creditors being able to take away the house they were planning to provide. Catharine told Mary: "We shall have the deed in trust so that nothing can deprive us of it."

Part 5: Life changes

Catharine moves to Lakefield; John Moodie gives away their home; Reydon Hall is sold; Jane and Agnes move to Southwold; a widow and a widower

January 1858: Catharine is ready to act as midwife

In January 1858, with the approaching arrival of Amelia and James Traill's first child, the family had a bit of a move round. Catharine and Kate went to stay with James to look after Amelia, with Catharine ready to act as midwife if necessary.

The other main move was by Annie Traill who had gone to live with Robert and Caroline Strickland while Clinton Atwood returned to England to ask for his father's approval to marry her. Approval was obtained and the couple married on 5th May 1858, Clinton continuing to farm on Rice Lake Plains.

20th February 1858: Sarah is living in an ambitious town

Ulverston, having improved its connection with the rail network, was ambitious to become more noteworthy. On 20th February 1858 the local papers reported: "Royal North Lancashire Agricultural Society – a public meeting was held in the Victoria Hall, Ulverston, his Grace the Duke of Devonshire in the chair, to consider soliciting the Council of the Royal North Lancashire Agricultural

Society to hold the next meeting at Ulverston." The Duke of Devonshire was, and still is, a major land owner in the north-west of England.

"The meeting was a highly successful one, and besides the noble chairman, the platform was occupied by the Rev R Gwillym, incumbent of St Mary's Ulverston; the Rev J Macaulay, rector of Aldingham; HW Askew, Esq., Conishead Priory" and five others. "Railway communication was no longer a stumbling block. The Council had named three places, at one of which their next exhibition would be held: - Blackburn, Chorley or Ulverston. The town would reap considerable benefit ... The Ulverstone and Lancaster Railway Company were prepared to offer every facility for the transit of cattle."

February 1858: Susanna is convinced and Catharine is a Medium

A friend of the Moodies had a Scottish servant who was a medium, and Susanna described to Richard Bentley in a letter dated 2nd May 1858 some of the physical events that had occurred during seances with this woman. Susanna wrote: "I have seen a large heavy English dining table rise in the air repeatedly, without contact, have seen the leaf of the said table, fly up, and strike the snuffers out of my husband's hand, and put out the candles." Despite witnessing these events, Susanna had remained sceptical.

She continued: "My husband had become an enthusiastic spiritualist and was much hurt by my obstinacy." After a disagreement with him on the subject, Susanna said she went upstairs and wept bitterly: "I was sitting alone by a little table, and feeling very angry, I said tauntingly enough 'If there be any truth in this doctrine, let the so called spirits move my hand against my will from this table, and lay it down on my lap!' You would have laughed to have seen the determined energy with which I held my hand on the table. You may therefore guess my surprise, not to say terror, when my hand became paralized, and the fingers were slowly wrenched up from the table, and the whole hand lifted and laid down in my lap." Susanna asked the spirit to spell its name and it spelled Thomas Harral.

Susanna from this and other events accepted that a spirit world exists and that there can be communication with it. She told Richard Bentley that Catharine was of the same opinion: "My sister, Mrs Traill, is a very powerful medium for these communications. She, who was quite as sceptical as me, has been rendered happy" by communicating with her dead children "which has quite overcome the fears of death that she till lately entertained."

This was probably while Catharine was staying with James and Amelia near Belleville in January and February 1858, as Susanna and Catharine had not lived close enough to visit each other while Catharine was at Rice Lake Plains. Catharine confirmed her ability to act as a medium in a letter to her friend Ellen Dunlop written many years later, but she noted that this period had not lasted long and she had "had the mental courage to abandon all that sort of thing" because she found it difficult to reconcile with her Christian beliefs.

15th May 1858: A fund-raising bazaar is planned in Ulverston

In 1858 there was still money owing for the construction of the larger school-room in Ulverston and fund-raising efforts were being made to clear the debt. The local papers announced on 15th May 1858: "Bazaar – It is intended to hold a bazaar in the Infant Day and Town Bank School room, Church Walk, Ulverston, for the purpose of greatly reducing, if not altogether paying off the debt, which is still owing on this beautiful erection."

Although not bearing the cost himself, Richard Gwillym was ensuring that the size of the remaining debt was not increased by bank charges. The papers noted: "It is not perhaps generally known that an annual rent is paid for its use, by the Rev R Gwillym – to the amount of £25 – to prevent the interest on the money borrowed from the bank of Messrs Petty and Postlethwaite, adding to the principal. We sincerely hope the inhabitants of the town will give strenuous support to set the building free from debt, that the expense of maintaining the Infant School in its present state of efficiency may not fall so heavily as it hitherto has done on our Incumbent."

(Literary context: Mr Postlethwaite and Mr Soulby provide a slight link between the Bronte and Strickland families)

Almost twenty years earlier, in December 1839, a Mr Postlethwaite (of Petty and Postlethwaite Bank in Ulverston) had advertised for a tutor for his two sons, then aged ten and eleven. Replies to the advertisement were to be sent to Mr Stephen Soulby, Bookseller of Ulverston. This was presumably the same Mr Soulby of Ulverston, in whose stationery shop Agnes and Sarah had first met Richard Gwillym in late summer 1843.

Branwell Bronte got the job and passed through Ulverston on his way to work for Mr Postlethwaite, who lived in Broughton-in-Furness, about ten miles north-west of Ulverston. Sarah never had the opportunity of meeting Branwell Bronte, as his stay in Lancashire only lasted six months.

Branwell Bronte returned to the Bronte family home in Haworth, Yorkshire in mid-summer 1840. He had been dismissed very abruptly, possibly having fathered an illegitimate child soon after his arrival.

June and July 1858: Sarah and the Bishop of Carlisle help fund-raise

The Bishop of Carlisle did his bit to help reduce the debt on the new school building in Ulverston, as reported in the local papers: "A sermon was preached on Wednesday 30th June 1858 in the Parish Church, Ulverston, by the Right Rev the Lord Bishop of Carlisle, in aid of the funds for liquidating the debt remaining on the Infant Day and Town Bank Sunday school. Prayers were read by Rev R Gwillym, incumbent, to a large congregation.

"The rev prelate took occasion to observe that the building was the handsomest of its character in the diocese, and he warmly eulogised the unwearied exertion of our incumbent in the cause of education, and the great zeal he evinced in the discharge of his sacred duties, as also the large amount of good he dispensed among the poor parishioners. The sermon occupied nearly an hour. The collection amounted to £33 0s 7d and contributions already received were £20."

Soon after the Bishop's sermon, the date for the Ulverston Bazaar was announced in the papers with Sarah getting a mention: "Ulverston Bazaar – We beg to remind our readers that the bazaar to raise funds to liquidate the debt remaining on the building – the Infant Day and Town Bank Sunday Schools – will be held in the School-room on Wednesday 7th and Thursday 8th July 1858. Any contributions towards this object will be thankfully received by Mrs Gwillym, or any of the committee of the Town Bank School.

"There will be a large collection of useful articles made by the children of the Infant and National Schools, as well as other things of an ornamental character. The doors will be opened at 10 o'clock, at the charge of 2s 6d for each person; the admission at 12 o'clock will be reduced to 1s; children under 12 years of age half price. Arrangements have been made for serving visitors with refreshments."

The report of the bazaar noted seven stalls. Five of them were general stalls, one of which was run by Sarah, while the school mistresses of the Infant School and of the National School ran the other two stalls which sold articles made by their respective pupils. The bazaar raised £163 9s 2d.

Summer 1858: Agnes visits the West Country and North Wales

The concluding volume of the 'Life of Mary Stuart' was published at Easter 1858, by which time Agnes was ready for a long break from writing, and a holiday somewhere other than Scotland. She first went on a tour of the West Country where she met and became friends with the bishop of London, Bishop Tait and his wife.

Agnes then went to Chester and spent a few days with Mary Kilner, a friend of the Strickland family whose husband was the chaplain of Chester Gaol. Agnes visited Chester Gaol and attended services both there and in Chester Cathedral before setting off on a tour of North Wales in company with the Kilners.

Her itinerary shows how much faster travel had become compared with the early days of her travels. From Chester, she and her friends caught a train to Conway and had time to look round the castle, see a Welsh fair and still, as Agnes wrote to Eliza: "got to Bangor the same evening, where we had nice quarters. Saw the old castle and the Menai Bridge and started next day for Caernarvon." Thomas Telford's Menai Suspension Bridge had been open since 1826 while the Britannia Bridge had opened more recently, in 1850.

Although she was theoretically on holiday, the historian in Agnes was never far away. She told Eliza: "On Tuesday we walked on the ramparts of Caernarvon Castle. The room where Queen Eleanor brought forth her unfortunate son is in good preservation. But of course it was not in such a mere closet, as Queens delivered in public, and this is in the back-stairs nest of apartments." From there they went to Llanberis: "I had a fine view of Dine-Brun Castle, which Lady Spencer defended against the troops of Mortimer and Queen Isabella. We dined luxuriously on trout and chickens at the pretty inn by Snowdon Lake. Went to see a waterfall. Three pretty Welsh children sang hymns to us in their native tongue. We started at five for the Pass of Llanberis, for the first miles some boys running after us and holding up pieces of crystal" of which Agnes bought a few pieces.

From Llanberis they went to Llanwrst, saw Gwydr Chapel and the coffin of Llewellyn the Great. They also visited Gwydr Castle "a beautiful old castle mansion of Lord Willoughby's" before catching a steamer for "a glorious two hour passage" reaching Conway at sunset. Agnes reported that they "had a nice tea at the Temperance Hotel, and at eight o'clock took the train for Chester, and had a glorious moon, and the comet with its beautiful tail to delight us on our journey." They were home in Chester by ten o'clock.

The comet referred to would have been Donati's Comet which was one of a number of spectacular comets seen in the 19th century. Apart from the Great Comet of 1811, Donati's has been rated the most spectacular. It was visible with the naked eye from June 1858 until April 1859 and had lengthy tails both of gas and of dust, and was the first comet to be photographed. There was a period of three weeks when it is said to have thrown off the haze surrounding itself at the rate of once every four and a half hours, which was described as the comet appearing to be casting off a series of veils.

In her letter Agnes revealed a little about Eliza's skills and interests other than those associated with history or spiritualism. Agnes wrote: "Mary showed me a pincushion with a butterfly painted for her by you, which she values very much" and "I have only seen three goats in Taffyland, one like your Jet."

August 1858: Sarah's duties as hostess have diminished

The Bishop of Carlisle returned to Ulverston on 18th August 1858 but with less work for Sarah than the visits of the Bishop of Chester had required in earlier years. The Bishop of Carlisle seemed to manage day trips to Ulverston now that communications were easier, so there was no need for him to stay at Stockbridge House. Indeed, Sarah and her housekeeper escaped having even to provide lunch as the various parts of the party ate in two local hotels.

The clergy of the area and the church wardens of Ulverston were involved, and the report in the papers noted: "The bishop's first visitation of the clergy of that deanery, in the Parish Church of Ulverston. Prayers were read by the Rev R Gwillym. Afterwards the Bishop and Clergy adjourned to the infant school, where luncheon was supplied by the 'Sun Hotel'. The church wardens were treated by the Rev R Gwillym to an excellent dinner at the 'Hope and Anchor'." So the church wardens got a small treat by way of lunch, but with Richard's increasing age and declining health, the large parties held by the Gwillyms were now a thing of the past.

There was a more substantial event for the people of Ulverston to experience in August 1858. The town had been successful in pitching for the Royal North Lancashire Agricultural Show and it took place over two days – the 24th and 25th August 1858. The papers reported that there was a very large exhibition, that there was an immense concourse of visitors and that the town was suitably decorated. To end the proceedings: "Dinner was served up in the Victoria Concert Hall, by Mr Smith of the 'Sun Hotel'." The chairman was again "His Grace the Duke of Devonshire KG." Rev R Gwillym was among the list of attendees and "the meeting did not break up until about 8 o'clock."

October 1858: Agnes and Eliza write a couple of time-fillers

As a bit of light relief after all her work on Mary Stuart, Agnes compiled a volume of her past contributions from annuals, together with a few new short stories based on rural life in Suffolk. The idea had been suggested by an Ipswich publisher, Mr Burton together with the title 'Old Friends and New Acquaintances'. The book was published before the end of 1858.

Mr Burton also suggested that Agnes write biographies of the kings of England who had never married. There were only three of them, and these were William Rufus (who was killed in a hunting accident in the New Forest aged 44 in 1100), Edward V (who was murdered in the Tower of London aged 13 in 1483) and Edward VI (who died from tuberculosis at the age of 15 in 1553).

As these kings had nothing in common apart from dying unmarried, and as only one of them lived to be an adult, their lives made a very flimsy subject for a book. It did however give Agnes and Eliza a reason to fill gaps in history which had been left by their 'Lives of the Queens of England', and something to do until they had a better idea. Therefore Agnes accepted Mr Burton's offer and the work was portioned out with Agnes agreeing to write biographies of William Rufus and Edward VI while Eliza wrote a biography of Edward V and found suitable illustrations.

December 1858: Sam's son George is to marry

Sam's fourth surviving child and second son, George Strickland married Frances Rothwell in 1858 when George was 25 years old. Susanna had commented on the proposed marriage when writing to Catharine on 12th December 1858. She wrote: "I received my Nephew George's wedding cards and I wish him and the young bride much joy. By all accounts he has made a wise choice and therefore stands a fair chance of much domestic happiness. Pray give him Aunt Susannas love and kind wishes for their future welfare – and congratulate my dear brother on the settlement of another son. He is very fortunate to have them living so near him."

December 1858: Susanna advises Catharine against taking female boarders

One of Catharine's ideas for re-establishing independence and continuing to farm, was to rent a house near their former home of 'Oaklands', and pay the rent with the help of taking in two girls as boarders. Susanna when she wrote to Catharine in December 1858 advised against such a plan, on the grounds that the plains were cold and comfortless, and that the work involved in having female boarders would be too great for the enterprise to be worthwhile. More specifically, Susanna said: "Your husband is not a likely person to agree with any boarder. Do you know anything about these girls, if they are likely to put up with any inconvenience, or any irritability in the temper of others."

December 1858: John Moodie is in financial difficulties

When Susanna wrote to Catharine on 12th December 1858, John was in legal difficulties again. The case which they thought had been dealt with when John had to pay damages in November 1855, was known as the Cinque Mars case and had begun afresh. Susanna wrote: "There is an execution against lands and tenements on that score. And no time to be given – and no mercy shown to the kind benevolent old man who has had mercy on so many. He feels it very bitterly."

There was a second similar problem. Susanna told Catharine: "There is likewise an execution of £50 for some failure of security in the parties of the suit of another case, and where the money is to come from I know not. Moodie has been obliged to recall Donald from Montreal, because he cannot raise the money to keep him there. Poor Aggie is penniless, and I have not the means to help her, even with clothes of my own, for I am literally in rags."

She wanted to sell their house: "I wish Moodie would consent to board, either at one of the respectable hotels, or with some private family. It would save us hundreds." She had one servant girl, but she was not much help: "Yet I pity the girl so much that I don't know how to tell her to go." Her father had been a wealthy farmer and his daughters had been well educated but, like Thomas Traill, the father had endorsed for others and had been ruined as a consequence.

Susanna said the girl was unhappy and lazy, and also so timid that she could not be left alone in the house. She wrote: "If poor Joanne would only submit to unavoidable circumstances, she might be very comfortable here – but pride will not let her be at peace, while ghastly nervous fear robs her of sleep. I have to do half her work, and as I am very lame, it is not done as it should be."

Susanna was expecting her sons Donald and Robert home for Christmas. She hoped that it would be possible to keep 15-year old Robert at school for another year. Her eldest son Dunbar, who had gone to the goldfields of California in the hope of making a fortune, had written to Susanna in good health and: "making with 5 others, 200 dollars per diem (among them) – which he says, if it only lasts, will soon make him independent. I think we are as far off seeing him as ever now." She and John wanted to leave Belleville. "If Dunbar should settle in the Western States, we have pretty much made up our minds to join him there with Robert."

Both Susanna's daughters had forgotten or ignored their mother's birthday on 6th December in 1858 and Susanna told Catharine: "I was quite alone that day, Papa being at Montreal, and it passed so sadly and slowly away, that I almost wished it might be the last." Despite her loneliness and lack of home help, and the fact that Catharine's family was still scattered about, Susanna said she could not help: "I am sorry dear Catharine that I cannot ask Kate just now to stay with me. But Moodie in his present troubles would not tolerate visitors."

11th January 1859: Catharine has done herself more harm than good

On 11th January 1859 Agnes wrote to Catharine while staying at Hampton Court Palace. She wrote: "I am here for a few days dear Cath with the dear Gwillyms" then after a few preliminaries such as: "I left mamma quite well" she gave Catharine a telling off which started quite gently but showed considerable irritation as the letter progressed.

The details are lost among some illegible hand-writing, but the meaning is clear: "Now dearest I fear you have sold interest in the 'Canadian Crusoes' or fallen into the snares of men ... I took infinite pains to guard your interest and make them keep to their agreement which was fifty pounds per 2,000 copies ... but as they had printed more than the past edition of 2,000, having fixed too high a price, it was not till this summer they talked of reprinting it. Then they wanted to shirk from the agreement but I would not yield, and when at last they desired ... to print 6,000 copies for the 50£ I told them not, but knowing your need of money to build your house, I offered to sell the copyright, as your agent, for one hundred pounds or else they must abide by the original bargain."

So far so good but Catharine in the meantime had messed things up by writing to the publishers herself, and when Agnes went to collect either the £50 or the £100 on the 6th January 1859 she said: "Virtue pretended he knew nothing about it, as it was Arthur Hall's private speculation ... I was so deeply mortified that you must not expect me to take any more fruitless troubles on your behalf but manage your own literary affairs for the future. I assure you I have taken ten times more pains on your behalf than I should for myself ... I left all your MSs published and unpublished in Jane's hands ... You must not suppose I am angry with you, but I grieve that you should have fallen into the toils of so designing a knave who has I am sure taken advantage of your wants and inexperience to break the agreement and cheat you."

February 1859: Queen Victoria chooses Ottawa

In a letter to Richard Bentley dated 12th February 1859, Susanna said the Canadian economy was in a very poor state. She wrote: "The rail roads do not pay. Numbers of people are out of employment. The Colony is bankrupt" and the decision of Queen Victoria to fix the seat of Government in Ottawa "has put Toronto, Montreal and Quebec, into the sulks."

However, Susanna thought the unexpected decision would work out well: "In natural beauty it far surpasses all its more wealthy rivals" and "the difficulty of deciding between the three great rivals" may have been "one main object in her decision."

February 1859: Thomas Traill's health deteriorates

Catharine and Thomas gave up the idea of returning to their farm on Rice Lake Plains, and after staying with Sam until early 1859, they moved into a cottage which was lent to them by Frances Stewart and her husband. They planned to remain there until the new house being built for them in Lakefield was ready.

Although Thomas had seemed to accept the fire philosophically, it turned out to be one too many misfortunes for him to bear.

In biographical notes written many years later by Susanna's granddaughter Maime Fitzgibbon, the situation when they were burnt out at 'Oaklands' was thus: "owing to some cause or accident never ascertained, the crowning misfortune of all the losses in the bush happened. They were burnt out and lost absolutely everything – all the treasures they had striven so hard to save, books, manuscripts and other valuables, the family barely escaping with their lives. Mr Traill felt the loss very much, especially of his books. He never quite recovered from the shock and sorrow of seeing his family thrown thus homeless on the world." Thomas's physical health deteriorated and he was already prone to periods of depression.

March 1859: Agnes tries again for Catharine

Although in her letter written in January 1859, Agnes sounded as though she had washed her hands of Catharine and her affairs, this was not the case. On 5th March 1859, Agnes wrote to Catharine (again with some unreadable bits) and said: "My poor unlucky Catharine, I cannot say how annoyed I am at the cold blooded villainy of that wretched man; and the worst of it is that I cannot do you any good because you have invalidated my agency by taking the matter into your own hands and writing to him yourself ... and countered all I had exerted to secure to you the benefit of your own work. Can ... Hall's letter and send it to me? For as he has ... falsehood of me, I shall endeavour to intimidate him by threatening him with Chancery proceedings."

Agnes had calmed down sufficiently to include some news and family chat which had been missing in her previous letter. She wrote: "I have not yet thanked you for the elegant book of ferns you sent me. I thought Eliza would like to give it to her neighbour the Bishop of Winchester who is a great fern fancier, and has several conservatories full of South African ferns so I transported it to her. They are beautifully got up and I admired the collection very much and did not see any specimens like them in the Bishop of Winchester's fern houses (at) Farnham Castle when Eliza and I lunched last summer, and the Bishop took us all over his gardens and to the top of the fine old tower built by Cardinal Henry Blois, Bishop of Winchester.

"It is now late so I must say farewell with love and best wishes to you and yours that there may be a good time coming, believe me my dearest Catharine your faithful attached sister, Agnes Strickland"

The final surviving letter on the subject of dealings with Virtue and Hall is dated 21st March 1859 and is from Agnes to Catharine: "My dearest Catharine, I went this morning into the city and visited my friend Mr Stephens on the subject of the cruel advantage Arthur Hall has taken of your application to him. He says if you can send the letter Hall wrote to you with the false statement of my having mitigated the terms of the agreement, and a copy of your own letters, he doubts not, if it is as you say, he shall get them to fulfil their terms of the agreement, but if you have not preserved these documents it will be useless.

"I visited Hall myself and asked him to pay what was due according to the terms of the agreement. Oh said he 'I am in correspondence with Mrs Traill herself, and she is perfectly satisfied.' 'She writes differently to me' replied I 'for she complains that you have sent only the 25£ instead of fulfilling your agreement made with me which I hold.' I then asked how many copies he had printed, he said 2000. Now if he told you 4000 and you can send me his letter to prove" (and then the writing becomes unclear) "He said at last 'Well if Mrs Triall will write to me to request the other 25£ to be paid perhaps I may do it.'

"I said of course you are bound by your agreement to pay 50£ for 2000 copies. 'Well' said he 'so I will when the other 1000 copies are all sold.' You are bound I replied to pay that sum on publication. He then retorted that if you wrote to him signing it ... Don't, dearest, you must enclose that letter to me, for fear of committing yourself ... write 'Dear Gentleman I shall be obliged by your ... completion of the payment for the second edition of the 'Canadian Crusoes' according to the conditions covenanted in the agreement executed by you and my sister Miss Agnes Strickland in my behalf ...

"They are now selling the books for 5s and pretend they have only printed 2000 copies but if you can ... mentioning 4000 we can compel them to pay for them also. You must now prepay all letters from Canada or they will be taxed six pence and double postage which of course vexes the recipient."

Agnes added a little family news before she returned to the main topic: "The dear Gwillyms are perfectly restored to health. They have now returned to Ulverston. Be sure not to reply to any letter Hall may write to you without sending it first to me or you may commit yourself unreasonably, they are such artful men."

Of her own health she wrote: "I am not very well, the noise of London and great anxiety about the dispute with Colburn's executors, which is a constant source of expenses, annoys and worries me. With love and best wishes ..."

19th April 1859: Tom's daughter Julia marries

There were signs that Tom's eldest daughter, Adela had made an unfortunate choice of husband and that the family upbringing had been unconventional, but Tom's second daughter Julia married, on 19th April 1859, a very distinguished-sounding man.

The notice in the papers read: "Married at the parish church of West Ham, Essex, Joseph Hutton Dupuis, Esq., her Britannic Majesty's Vice-Consul at Naples (son of Joseph Dupuis Olim of the Consular Service in Ashantee and the Mediterranean States in Africa) to Julia Lilly, the second daughter of Capt Thomas Strickland, of Plaistow, Essex, granddaughter of Mrs Strickland of Reydon Hall, Suffolk, and niece of Miss Strickland, the authoress."

June 1859: Agnes has her watch stolen

In London in June 1859, Agnes was robbed of her watch, her father's gold repeater, when she was walking in Hill Street on her way to visit Lady Blantyre. She had been stopped by a young couple who asked for directions to Sloane Street.

Agnes in a letter to a friend in Suffolk wrote: "The young man had his arm bandaged and looked very ill. I thought he was a student and the young woman who was respectably dressed his elder sister, so I took great pains in directing them. I knew this was the watch snatcher's dodge; but could not suspect them. They pretended to be very stupid, which was only to gain time, for my watch was well secured, as I imagined, but when I came in and took off my cloak, I found that it was gone. The chain was neither cut nor broken but the watch, key and ring to which they were attached were gone. This they must have cut in two or they could not have got it off the chain." She reported the theft to the police but the watch was never recovered.

21st June 1859: Thomas Traill dies

Thomas Traill's health was clearly in decline, and Catharine spent much time with him during May and June 1859 writing their reminiscences and his account of the history of 'Westove', the Traill family estate which had nominally been under his control since the 1820s. It was a group of properties centred on the island of Sanday, and Thomas had retained some hope of future financial security if the debts on the property could be repaid and the estate sold, but early in 1859 when it had been for sale for several years, he gave up these hopes and accepted that 'Westove' was so heavily mortgaged and encumbered with debt that no profitable buyer would ever be found for it.

On 21st June 1859 Thomas Traill died, and he was buried in the cemetery attached to the church in Lakefield which Sam had been instrumental in building. Catharine wore widow's black for some fifteen years after Thomas died as a mark of her love and respect for him.

Catharine wished to preserve a positive record of her husband's life, and in a journal entry after Thomas's death, she wrote: "let me as a wife, and now a widow, bear testimony to my husband's worth. With some foreign eccentricities of manner, and some faults of nervous irritability of constitution, he was a true hearted loyal gentleman, faithful in deed and word – a kind and benevolent disposition, a loving father, husband and friend – a scholar and a true gentleman, whose virtues will be remembered long after his faults have been forgotten."

June 1859: Agnes gets her own back on Macaulay

The weekly newspaper the 'Suffolk Chronicle' had a supplement entitled 'Suffolk Worthies and Persons of Note in East Anglia'. Agnes was the subject at the end of June 1859.

It included a partial clarification of the term 'blue-stocking' which was used by and about the Strickland sisters. The article recorded: "At the commencement of the present century literary ladies as a class suffered greatly from blue-stocking imposters. The public, in the treatment of female authors received the specimens nearest at hand as characteristic of the whole class, and made the body politic suffer for the vices or frailties of an individual.

"If a professed blue-stocking failed to witch the world with authorship, the check she experienced was chuckled over as the destruction of petticoat presumption, and formed a never failing source of congratulation to those who think blue stockings and blue devils synonymous –

'Who wondered much what little knavish sprite
Had put it first in woman's head to write'

– and deny to the whole sex the honours attendant on intellectual cultivation, just as the Mahomedan denies them the privilege of a soul, and on no better foundation."

Having got that intended witticism out of the way, the article gave a long account of Agnes's life and the Strickland family history. It also told the story of Lord Campbell using Agnes's work in his own writings and said that others had done the same.

The only other plagiarist mentioned by name in the article was Macaulay, who had become Lord Macaulay. The article was specific in its accusation saying: "The amusing little anecdotes of costume in the two first volumes of 'Macaulay's History', which contributed greatly to the popularity of his book with the ladies, may be traced to the lives of Mary Beatrice of Modena, Mary II, and another in the 'Lives of the Queens'; and it is obvious that Lord Macaulay's time as a statesman was too importantly occupied to allow him to search for such feminine details. Other authors have availed themselves, unacknowledged, of Miss Agnes Strickland's labours, and abused her at the same time!" The article included a reference to Mrs Strickland, aged 85, reporting: "The venerable lady is a great reader, and is still able to enjoy a daily newspaper."

These quoted extracts are near enough a word for word repetition of a letter written by Agnes from Reydon Hall on 22nd December 1858. The surviving part of the letter was addressed only by opening

'Dear Sir', the end of the letter and the envelope having been lost, but it is reasonable to assume that Agnes was contributing to the 'Suffolk Worthies' biography of herself, and therefore that Agnes engineered this bit of retaliation against Macaulay.

The letter was part of a continuing exchange, and Agnes revealed something about the legal dispute in which she was embroiled when she wrote: "I am obliged by the caution you recommend in regard to the conduct of the late Mr Colburn which though true was imprudent, inasmuch as his widow and executrix is now married to Mr Forster, of the 'Examiner' a formidable limb of the law, with whom I am still at issue, about the conditions of the said agreement, which I was induced by Mr Colburn in" (illegible) "for myself to sign."

August 1859: Catharine's life as a widow begins

The sale of 'Oaklands' was put on hold following Thomas's death, and in order to obtain some immediate income Catharine rented the farm to a neighbour. This is said to have continued until 1867, when an old friend of Thomas bought the property for $130.

Catharine rented three rooms in Lakefield West as the family home, so that Mary Traill could begin teaching at a school in the village, which she did in July 1859 at the age of seventeen. Mary not only wanted to earn some money towards family house-keeping, she also wanted to obtain her second-class teaching certificate and improve her future employment prospects.

Catharine received a letter dated 10th August 1859 which told her the debts against 'Westove' had totalled £56,500 as of 31st December 1858, and that the bank seeking to sell it expected at best £26,000 on the open market. The letter concluded that there was: "not the slightest prospect of any benefit to Mr Traill's family from the estate."

Harry Traill had more cause to regret the fire at 'Oaklands' than his brothers and sisters, for with the loss of the house, he lost his job as the farm manager as well as his home. He had to look for alternative employment but in August 1859 he was kicked by a horse which caused serious rib and internal injuries, and it took him months to recover.

Catharine kept herself busy in various ways aimed at raising money, both for the family upkeep and to pay for the new house. She made and mended trousers, worked on her manuscripts (even when she had little prospect of selling them) and she prepared flower, fern and moss albums as gifts or for sale. As well as her own small contributions towards the cost, the cottage was being built by means of donations from family and friends. Sam provided the timber and organised the builders, and the walls had been raised by September 1859.

Catharine knew that her two elder sons had suffered both in health and education due to family circumstances when they were young, and she wanted her two younger sons to have a better start in life. William was 14 and Walter was 9 when their father died. William received some tutoring in Lakefield and then enrolled in the school of William Tully near Peterborough. Mr Tully is said to have been a kindly man who helped William a great deal by way of training, advice and general support.

18th September 1859: Richard's church has a re-furbished organ

September 1859 saw the church organ in St Mary's Church in Ulverston back in use after having been re-furbished and improved. The local paper noted: "The Re-opening of Ulverston Parish Church Organ – Sunday 18th September 1859" was marked by "elegant discourses, in the morning by Rev R Gwillym and in the evening by Rev AV Hadley. The organist Mr Daniel did full justice to the renovations and additions carried out which fully succeeded in restoring the tone of the organ to its original quality. It was built in 1812 by GP England, the most eminent organ builder of that period."

14th to 21st September 1859: Agnes attends the British Association meeting in Aberdeen

Agnes went to Aberdeen to attend the annual meeting of the British Association held there from the 14th to the 21st September 1859. As well as being interested in the work of the British Association for the Advancement of Science founded in 1831, Agnes was also interested in the work of the British Archaeological Society. This had been founded in 1843 to encourage the recording, preservation and publication of archaeological discoveries. It was her interest in these associations which began to take her on courses of lectures, and to annual meetings in various parts of the country.

Prince Albert was staying at the royal estate of Balmoral when the 1859 annual meeting of the British Association was held, and he took part in the proceedings. Agnes told Jane: "Prince Albert is to come in on Wednesday, and the British Association are invited to lunch at Balmoral; but I do not hear that any ladies are asked. To-night Prince Albert and all the grandees arrive, and the ladies, including myself, go to the Music Hall to hear his address. All the Scotch antiquaries are entreating me to write the lives of the early Queens of Scotland" an idea which Eliza had already vetoed.

Agnes had lent an item to the Exhibition in the Aberdeen Music Hall. She told Jane: "I have been to see the portraits in the Music Hall, preparing for exhibition. The Darnley cuff is in a case lined with white satin made to fit it, and is exhibited by Sir Patrick Threipland. I could not help laughing at the droll manner in which my maid begrudged it to him; but I am glad I had it in my power to add to the collection. We have glorious weather, and the town is dressed with flags. The air, too, is brisk and pleasant, and enlivens every one."

Of Prince Albert's address Agnes said: "On Wednesday evening he gave the address, or rather I should say read it, which he did most beautifully. His voice is very sweet and pleasant, and he has no trace of a foreign accent. He spoke for nearly an hour, and was excessively cheered and applauded.

"Prince Albert made his appearance yesterday at the morning section, and passed close to me. He went first to the Archaeological Exhibition, but every one was kept out. Elphinstone Dalrymple related to him some of my remarks on Mary Stuart's portraits. Mr Dalrymple told me that if I had only sent in my card, he would have admitted me and presented me to his Royal Highness. Tonight there is to be a very interesting lecture on the Geology of the Northern Highlands by Sir Roderick Murchison."

Agnes also visited friends while she was in Scotland, during which visits she was driven to Loch Leven and was rowed across to have another look at the castle there. The boatman had read Agnes's 'Life of Mary Stuart' and had cleared away the rubble and the undergrowth, so that the castle would be easier for her to explore than on her previous visit. He refused to take any money for his trouble and Agnes told Jane that he treated her "with as much reverence as if I had been Mary and he her Lord Chamberlin."

Agnes promised to send him an inscribed copy of the 'Life of Mary Stuart'. In return he cut her a piece of wood from Queen Mary's Thorn that Agnes later had made into a snuff box for her sister Jane. Queen Mary's Thorn was a hawthorn tree which was believed to have been standing when Mary Queen of Scots was imprisoned in Loch Leven Castle from 1567 to 1568.

26th October 1859: 'The Great Storm of 1859' affects Ulverston

'The Great Storm of 1859', sometimes known as the 'Royal Charter' storm, was the most ferocious storm of the 19th century. It claimed over 800 lives and the loss of 133 ships over the night of 25th/26th October 1859. The storm derived its name from its most famous casualty, which was the steam sailing-ship the 'Royal Charter' which, having travelled from Australia, was lost within a short distance of land near Ynys Mon (Anglesey), but 60-foot high waves pounded it to pieces and no help could reach it. The loss of life in this storm was so terrible that Captain Robert Fitzroy, who had been studying weather patterns for some time, set about developing a warning system, which has developed into the shipping forecast, in order that ships could be forewarned and take shelter when necessary.

Ulverston had its share of casualties due to the 'Great Storm', and the local papers noted: "Sermons were preached in all the places of worship in Ulverston on Sunday 27th November 1859, in aid of the widows and orphans of the shipwrecked mariners belonging to Ulverston, who were lost in the late gales. At the Parish Church on Sunday afternoon, after a sermon by the Rev R Gwillym, the amount collected was £7 15s." Similar services at the other churches in the town – Trinity Church, the Wesleyan Chapel and the Independent Chapel raised £37 18s 1d.

(24th November 1859: Literary context – Charles Darwin publishes 'Origins of Species')

Charles Darwin's book 'On the Origin of Species' was published on 24th November 1859, which marked the point at which it became hard to sustain belief in the literal truth of the biblical account of the beginning of the world.

December 1859: The value of money in England is illustrated

The amount of money collected in Ulverston in response to the 'Great Storm' sounds like a small amount, but the value of money at the time is indicated by charitable donations at Christmas 1859. Local papers reported: "Ulverston Seasonable Benevolence – HW Askew has forwarded to the Rev R Gwillym £10 for the purchase of blankets and coal for the deserving poor of Ulverston. Mr Huddlestone gave, as usual, a large quantity of provisions and money to nearly 100 poor families, amounting in all to £10."

Sarah and Richard were involved in Christmas activity as the papers recorded: "The Rev R Gwillym on the 23rd December 1859 gave meat to upwards of 80 persons for their dinner on Christmas-day" and the people of Ulverston in 1859 showed their appreciation of the Gwillyms' activities with a gift in return. The local paper recorded: "Treat to School Children – On Thursday 29th December 1859, the children of the national schools had their annual treat of currant buns and coffee in the Infant School. A large number of the parents and teachers also partook of tea, after which Mr Clark, the master, presented the Rev R Gwillym with a papier machee inkstand, pen-holder, paper knife and a written address, from the scholars and teachers, as a token of their gratitude and esteem for the kind interest manifested as a friend and manager of these schools. The rev gentleman replied in a very feeling speech. At the close the children gave hearty cheers for their kind patron, and after singing the national anthem, separated, all evidently highly pleased."

December 1859: John Moodie is found guilty

When John Moodie was finding his work-load too heavy in 1856, he hired a deputy and an employment agreement was draw up between them and signed. Unfortunately the agreement did not specify how the deputy would be paid for his services. A very important phrase 'out of fees' was omitted.

This omission passed unnoticed for a while but in 1858 John Moodie was accused of the 'farming of offices' which meant holding more than one office, and selling one to someone else for a profit. The accusation was made by Mr Dougall, a nephew of a former political enemy. The government refused to support the accusation but Mr Dougall decided to fund the case himself. It was brought to court in October 1859, and in December at the Belleville Assizes, John Moodie was found guilty. This verdict was upheld in the Court of the Queen's Bench in Toronto in the spring of 1860.

While John Moodie accepted that he was technically guilty, he felt that his only misdeed was not noticing the flaw in the wording of a legal document, and he appointed a new lawyer to appeal against the verdict.

9th February 1860: Agnes and Macaulay are compared again

Lord Macaulay died a wealthy man, aged 59, on 28th December 1859. Despite his death, he came in for another mention in connection with Agnes when her book 'Old Friends and New Acquaintances' was reviewed on 9th February 1860.

The review said: "Lord Macaulay turned aside from his history to write articles for an Encyclopaedia, and here we have the historian of the 'Queens of England' seeking by a series of tales to amuse the people.

"The name of Agnes Strickland is alone a tower of strength, and the volume needs but little commendation at our hands, but in justice we must say that the subject was well selected, the scenes cleverly sketched, and the characters truthfully portrayed. These tales will most assuredly become popular."

The book was successful, and during 1860 Agnes wrote a second volume, as well as completing her share of the writing of the 'Bachelor Kings of England'. Even allowing for the fact that Eliza was doing a good half of the writing of their joint royal biographical books, this has to be balanced out by Agnes undertaking all official correspondence on their joint behalf, meaning that Agnes's output was continuing to be extraordinary.

April 1860: Stockbridge House tests a washing machine

Richard Gwillym had a long period of ill health in 1860 and there were only two items in the local papers which mention the Gwillyms, neither of which required much effort on Richard's part. The first event was on 22nd April 1860 when he and Sarah were among the guests listed as attending a very grand wedding at Cartmel Priory. The bridal procession consisted of 13 carriages and the day finished with a ball after the newly married couple had left by train for their honeymoon in Devon.

The other mention is in a number of advertisements for a washing machine which proclaimed: "Lyon's Universal Washing Machine – Has now been fairly tested and approved by the following among other persons in Ulverstone and the neighbourhood: - The laundress of the Rev R Gwillym, where it washed 8 bed sheets in 10 minutes, and 60 bed-room napkins in 20 minutes without rubbing; Mr Robinson, draper; Mr Town, draper; Mr Atkinson, Lane House; Mr Soulby; Mr Ripley, grocer" and three more names. The machines were available in several models which ranged in price from £2 2s for the most basic model up to £3 12s for the most de luxe version.

23rd May 1860: Catharine's new home is nearly ready

Catharine in writing to Ellen Dunlop on 23rd May 1860 told of the progress of her new home. She said: "The plasterers are at work now. By the end of next week it will be fit for us to move in. I doubt our poor furnishing will do little credit to the nice new house, nevertheless I dare not lay out any money to buy anything for it, yet a large portion of dear Mary's earnings will have to go to pay carpenter's bills. Kate has got as much as will make a decent rag rug for the floors. I hope to get it soon to the weavers. Harry dear boy is now busy fencing in the lot for us – the back part ready for planting potatoes."

She sent some seeds to Ellen and discussed her plans for the new garden: "I shall beg from you my dear when you can give it a sweet violet and a slip of scarlet geranium, if any of those we stuck in boxes have struck. My dear lavender is alive and some slips seem growing too. All Mrs Strickland's scarlet geraniums were killed by the frost which she greatly regrets, being very fond of them."

Catharine was still earning some money by selling dried flowers and ferns, and was about to send two sets to Ellen whose friends had agreed to buy them: "I have been preparing the sets of dried ferns and flowers. I hope they will not think the price too great, but they do cost me a great deal of time and close attention to gather, press and put them down, besides naming them, which indeed is sometimes the most laborious part of the work. Yet $5 does seem a great deal to give for wild plants, does it not?"

Catharine and her children named their new cottage in Lakefield 'Westove' in memory of their first family home in Canada, and of Thomas's family estate in Orkney. The legal arrangement made by Sam and his family prevented the possibility of Catharine losing her home to creditors, by making it the property of her three daughters but with Catharine having the right to live in it during her lifetime. Catharine was now firmly settled in Lakefield, living near to Sam with his large family and their successful businesses.

September 1860: Agnes meets John Clare, the pastoral poet

During September 1860 Agnes was one of many guests invited by Lord and Lady Spencer to witness a grand rifle meeting. Tents and food were provided for the 500 volunteer riflemen who were to compete for trophies and cash prizes. Jane wrote that rallies of volunteers were being held in many counties, motivated by a combination of pleasure, patriotism and dislike of the French, who were suspected of preparing an invasion attempt.

Unfortunately the weather was very wet and very windy when the Northamptonshire rally was held. The accommodation tents for the volunteers were blown down, and when the ladies, including Agnes, went out to watch the riflemen compete, the weather was so bad that they soon returned to the house.

The meeting was held at Althorp (where Diana Princess of Wales was buried in 1997) and Agnes was, as usual, combining work with pleasure. When Lady Spencer took her guests to Burleigh House, Agnes spent her time examining the relevant pictures and other treasures which were shown to her. At Althorp itself there was a collection of portraits for her to study, plus the Library with one of the greatest collections of books in the country. Agnes described her stay in a letter to Jane. She wrote: "I am not idle at Althorp, I examine many books. I am aided by Lady Sarah, who looks them out for me. We have the great rifle-meeting today and the house is full of company to witness it. We have had such floods of rain that Lord Spencer's trenches have become unwelcome canals. After, there is to be an archery-meeting for the ladies."

In a letter to Catharine, Agnes described her time in Althorp Library more fully: "I had the finest library and three librarians at my command, besides Lord Spencer and his sweet sister Lady Sarah who were indefatigable in digging out books such as I required."

Lord Spencer invited Agnes to visit the Northampton Lunatic Asylum where she met the pastoral poet, John Clare who had been an inmate there for twenty years. Agnes described the meeting to Jane: "I saw poor Clare, the celebrated Northamptonshire peasant. He is sullen and sad, but not violent. He told me he was much happier when he worked with his hands, for then he was strong and healthy. It was literature that had turned his brain, and he put his hand to his head. His remark and action gave me the heartache."

14th September 1860: Jane gives Catharine family news, especially of Tom

Jane wrote a chatty family letter to Catharine dated 14th September 1860. Of herself and Mrs Strickland, she wrote: "all mother and visiting falls upon me and business of every kind for which my own is generally neglected. I have been better this year than for several preceding. I know not what would happen if I were to fall ill – Mamma is infirm as to moving, requiring my arm and the use of a stick – Mind of uncertain power sometimes bright as ever, sometimes dull." Mrs Strickland was 87 years old and Jane had turned 60.

Jane mentioned that an old family friend was staying at Reydon Hall: "dear Maria Garnham. She is deaf – nearly blind and very infirm for her time of life – seventy one next month. She and poor Louisa have only thirty pounds to exist on and were sick all winter. She often spoke of you – each and every one of us dear to her – I am sorry she could hold but little conversation with Mamma whom she could not hear at all."

Tom and his son had also been visiting Reydon Hall. Jane wrote: "Tom came down with Walter, whom I had not seen since he was a plain but most fascinating fellow of a year old – well he is just seventeen, very dark, very small but handsome and intelligent. He is very reserved, not shy, and is in a great bill broker's house – nature intended him for a barrister but whatever he is – I think he will rise – I wish his intellect was less acute – hard and dry."

Of Tom, Jane observed: "Tom very strict, very flustering and very vain – He is to have a ship I am happy to say – for he loses on land what he gets at sea. Speculation requires more head and less openness to flattery." This implies that Tom had been at home since his command of the 'Scotia' had ended four or five years previously. Jane continued: "He seemed pleased to meet Maria but all her old kindness to him in childhood and manhood failed to draw a coin from him."

September 1860: Tom's daughter Julia comes to a sad end

Jane in her September 1860 letter to Catharine, gave news of Tom's daughter Julia Dupuis. Her husband had been 'her Britannic Majesty's Vice-Consul at Naples' when they married in April 1859 but had been given a new appointment, which meant that Julia had to move home just as her first child was due. Jane told Catharine: "Julia near her first confinement has sailed for Constantinople and will there, if God permit, give birth to her first born – a trial for her, though as Naples will soon be besieged perhaps it is for the best."

In the event, Naples was not besieged. When Garibaldi, who was fighting for the unification of Italy, arrived there with his army he was welcomed rather than resisted. Garibaldi entered Naples on 7th September 1860. News of Julia arrived in time to form a postscript to Jane's letter written on 14th September. The baby had arrived safely, and the new father: "in his praise of his babe forgot to say if boy or girl but being large and like Tom no doubt boy" and had been born on 2nd September 1860.

When Jane next wrote to Catharine she told the whole sad story. Jane wrote: "Julia poor thing got her death by an anxious maternity – She had a Moldavian nurse whose language was unknown to her and who did not speak English – There was no help for it. She had a clever German doctor who spoke English and she had some English ladies who took it by turns to watch her during the day.

"She had a safe time and did well for a week – the fifth night the Consul was roused by her frantic calling upon him. When he came she told him the nurse had been poisoning the baby as she had seen her putting something into her mouth. He opened her mouth but found only a lump of sugar which he said seems to be the way of settling babies there – She however could not get over her maternal grief and terror, became delirious and died with puerperal fever at the end of a few days.

"The little girl lives and is a fine child. A sad close to Dupuis' year and a half of perfect happiness – She we hope is in a better world where such partings are unknown." The baby was named Julia in memory of her mother, who had died at the age of 23.

November 1860: The Gwillyms have to stay in Southwold

Jane told Catharine in her September 1860 letter: "The Gwillyms talk of coming to Reydon in November – He has been very much ill." In the event, when Sarah and Richard visited Suffolk, they stayed in Southwold and not at Reydon Hall.

When Agnes wrote to Catharine in December 1860 she said: "The dear Gwillyms have been staying at Southwold for poor Mamma can no longer bear the fatigue and excitement of having any alteration to her domestic routine."

November 1860: Susanna plans for the worst

John Moodie's appeal dragged on for almost two years, with the intervening period being a drain on both his health and the family finances. When Susanna wrote to Catharine on 28th November 1860, she thought the judgement on John's case was imminent and was prepared for the worst. She told Catharine: "If all is lost, we shall in all probability collect the debts due to the office, which involves large sums, and emigrate with Robert and Dunbar to some distant land – California or the Western States, to begin life afresh on the verge of the grave.

"Here I do not wish to stay, and the change in our circumstances can be better borne among strangers. I have not ties to bind me to Belleville, beyond the dear home that has sheltered us for so many years, and the trees I have planted, and last, but not least the graves of my poor boys. So do not grieve for me my sister, my dear tried friend. Fortunately, Papa settled two years ago, the house and ten acres of land upon me. This cannot be touched so, let the worst come, I shall still have a home."

In writing to Catharine about her sons' reactions to the family's financial uncertainty, Susanna showed she had given up believing Donald would make a success of his life. She wrote "Dunbar says we shall never want while he has hands to work for us, and he is firm and true, and he will keep his promise. I feel most for Donald. He is deficient in that energy which alone ensures success and will be left to struggle for his living. It may, however, be the best thing that ever happened to him."

Her letter also reported the healing of an unexplained rift between two of her children. Susanna said: "As soon as Katie heard of the issue of the trial she came down to see us, and her shrewd sense, and hopeful disposition, did much to inspire her father with fresh courage to battle with his persecutors." Also: "It brought about a meeting, and a friendly one, between Donald and his sister, an event for which I have prayed for years, so you see dearest, there are some bright spots. Rob has behaved like the darling he is. He carries on the whole business of the office during his father's absence, with a judgement and decision, you could hardly expect from a boy of 17."

Despite having advised Catharine against taking in female lodgers in December 1858, Susanna had done so herself. Boarding with her were Elizabeth and Julia Russell, daughters of the Hon Robert Russell, a colonial administrator in Jamaica who wanted them to grow up in a more English environment than the West Indies could provide. Susanna wrote of them: "I find my boarders a great comfort to me. If only I could procure more on the same terms, we might yet live comfortably. Dear Lizzie is a daughter to me in my trouble and dear little Julia does her best with her angelic voice to drive away care."

25th December 1860: Agnes is despondent

When Agnes was in London late in 1860, Eliza was also there, as Agnes told Catharine in a letter written on Christmas Day that year: "I spent a week in London, studying in the British Museum. Eliza was staying with friends and I was lodging at a private hotel in Montague Street, close to the museum, so we met every day. She is much altered, but is very fond of her own domain at Tilford near Farnham in Surrey, and much happier than when she was living at Reydon as she has everything her own way."

Returning to Reydon for the winter had not helped Agnes's health: "I have had a serious attack of bronchitis and inflammation of the mucus membrane, which pulled me down very much, directly I returned home. This confined me a great part of the day to my bed, and thrown me back with my present undertaking 'Lives of the Bachelor Kings of England'. I am now almost stifled in proof sheets and have still to write the life of Edward VI.

"I have just published my second series of Suffolk tales, under the title of 'Old Friends and New Acquaintances' and it has been very favourably received, but whether it will prove lucrative depends on the honesty of my publisher. But in truth, the cheap reprints have so completely injured literature that it is impossible for the profits to be really great of any class of literature, more especially works of fiction. Then in regard to history, the expense of getting up the material devour all the profits leaving the empty bubble of fame, to repay the sacrifice of years of toil and loss of health and spirits, and it is so painful a stress on the brain, it perfectly unfits anyone for the active duties of life."

Agnes told Catharine that not only had her own health been poor, but the needs of Mrs Strickland were increasing. She wrote: "my eyes now begin to weary of pen, ink and paper, so that I rather shrink from letter writing. Dear Mamma requires one to devote some time to her now the infirmities of her great age are confining her much to her chair, and she is now so intensely deaf, that nothing seems to amuse or rouse her except cards; so that I have to spend an hour or two in that way, which much abridges my time for letters. She is thank God still a great reader and enjoys a new book. I take a daily and a weekly paper for her use."

Agnes added: "This Christmas day brings you, Susan and my dear brother Sam all to my mother's memory, and she sends her love and blessing to her beloved absentees. We are a diminished circle, only the poor old mother, Jane and I. Miss Martin our tenant's pretty niece drank tea with us and I have stolen away to perform the long delayed duty of writing to you and expressing the affection that still cleaves to you. I regret the impossibility of corresponding with more than you and Sam, and I am a very poor correspondent to you and him.

"I hope my 'Bachelor Kings' will prove a remunerative undertaking, for I have toiled much for very little. I feel this when I would like to help others. I have a parcel for you dear when I can get a conveyance for it."

March 1861: Tom sets sail for America twice

Tom took command of the ship 'Julia' in February 1861. Whether the name is a coincidence, or whether it was a new ship and Tom was able to influence its name to commemorate his daughter is unknown. He set sail for America in March 1861 but soon ran into a storm as Jane told Catharine in a letter written a couple of months later.

Tom seems to have been well accustomed to encountering storms at sea for Jane told Catharine: "Well he has had his old weather luck tossing about in the heavy March storm in the Downs and then after he did get out was run into by a Swede off Dungeness – down went the Swede like a stone but the crew were saved."

The incident was reported in Lloyds List on 11th March 1861. It recorded: "The 'Julia' has arrived in the Downs and reports having been in collision with a Swedish brig last night off Dungeness, that the brig sunk, with a cargo of coals; crew saved, the 'Julia' has sustained damage, and returned to the River for repairs." There were many incidents of ships in trouble that night; Tom was far from being alone in having to put back for repairs.

He set off again from Gravesend on 20th March 1861. Jane said to Catharine: "You will be glad to hear that Tom has got a ship – but the events of the Civil War in America changed her destination from India to New Orleans." The American Civil War did not begin officially until 12th April 1861, but the direction that the situation was taking was already clear in March.

In her letter written in May 1861 Jane wrote: "In case he could not carry out his owner's intentions he would return northwards and try to see you all, but the necessity would be bad for him and his owner. I fancy the Southern States will not disoblige England and that the anticipated visit will not take place."

7th April 1861: The census finds only some of the Strickland family

When the 1861 census was taken on the night of 7th/8th April 1861, the only member of the Strickland family recorded as living at Reydon Hall was Mrs Elizabeth Strickland. The record shows her as an 86 year old widow, a land holder and deaf. Jane and Agnes, and also Eliza, again seem to have escaped inclusion on the census though there is no mention in any found correspondence of them having any objection to it.

In 1861, as in 1851, there were three staff living-in at Reydon Hall, all of them young and therefore inexperienced. There was an 18-year old cook, a 15-year old housemaid and a 13-year old foot boy.

Tom was out of the country on the 1861 census night, but his family was recorded in Milton Road, Milton, Gravesend. The household consisted of Margaretta, described as a 50 year old master mariner's wife, together with daughters Mary and Agnes Diana, aged 22 and 14 respectively, and Walter who was aged 17 and whose occupation was recorded as a Commercial Clerk for a Discount Broker. The elder son Thomas, aged 26 and a builder's clerk in 1851, was not recorded in Milton Road, and has not been found anywhere else in England.

The other member of Tom's family who appeared in the 1861 census was their eldest daughter Adela Wigg, who was still living with her parents-in-law at their farm in Acle in Norfolk but the farm had shrunk. In 1851 it had consisted of 300 acres and employed 10 men. In 1861 it had reduced to 166 acres and employed only 6 men. Two sons were living on the farm, George Wigg, aged 36 and unmarried, and Gent Wigg aged 39, together with Adela and their six children. These consisted of four sons and two daughters ranging in age from 1 to 8 years; Adela was 28 years old.

The 1861 census records Sarah living at Stockbridge House in Ulverston with her husband Richard both of whom are recorded as 58 years old. They had five living-in members of staff. These were a 42-year old housekeeper and a 38-year old male house servant together with a lady's maid, a housemaid and a kitchen maid, aged 27, 19 and 18 respectively.

11th May 1861: Tom reaches New Orleans

Tom was able to travel to his original destination despite the American Civil War, and having left Gravesend successfully on 20th March, he arrived in New Orleans with the 'Julia' just over seven weeks later on 11th May 1861.

12th May 1861: Jane is in debt

Jane's house in Southwold was still costing her money instead of being a source of income, and this resulted in her getting slightly into debt. In her letter to Catharine dated 12th May 1861 Jane explained: "My house did not let last year and five pounds taxes and keeping up has left me ten pounds worse than the world, a rare thing for me. I am in want of everything but hope. I think I may be more lucky this summer but shall not if the season is cold as it is now."

Jane listed the contents of a parcel that would soon be taken to Canada for Catharine, with Agnes as usual being the main contributor but Jane showing that she also sent items to Canada on a regular basis. Jane wrote: "Agnes left a nice dress and cloak, a scarf and other nice pretty things in my charge which are packed up and sent. Mamma put in a silken gown I bought her some years ago. It may be useful to you – It is the first time in my life I have sent you no remembrance."

Of family in England, Jane told Catharine: "Eliza is in Tilford and has a goat which interests her a good deal – Sarah Gwillym and Richard are at Harrogate for the renovation of their health. Tom's family at Gravesend. Agnes is staying at the Red House, Ipswich with Mrs Edgar en route for London and Hampton Court – She will leave Ipswich this week."

27th June 1861: Agnes wears Court mourning

The Queen's Drawing-room was a regular social event in Agnes's calendar. The death of the Duchess of Kent, the mother of Queen Victoria, on 16th March 1861, meant that mourning had to be worn at the Drawing-room which Agnes attended that year. Having sent her condolences to her friend Lady Augusta Bruce, a Lady-in-Waiting to the deceased Duchess, Agnes asked for advice about what jewellery should be worn to the Drawing-room.

Lady Augusta replied that jet would be best, but that diamonds and pearls would be acceptable. As well as pearls Agnes told Jane that she "wore a black velvet train, black silk under-dress, and a black velvet tiara, lappets and plume. I fear that the head-dress must have given me the look of Bellona." Bellona was an ancient Roman goddess of war always depicted wearing a military helmet. Agnes continued: "However, as everybody wore the same style of head-gear, it did not much signify. There was an immense crowd; and but for the assistance of Lord Talbot de Malahide, who got the carriage up for me, I should never have got through the crush."

The papers announced: "Her Majesty the Queen held a Drawing-room on Thursday afternoon 27th June 1861 in St James's Palace." It described the queen's outfit including: "Her Majesty's head-dress was formed of black feathers and black crape veil" and Agnes Strickland was included in the list of people mentioned as present at the event.

2nd July 1861: Richard gives a school treat

Sarah and Richard returned from Harrogate in time for the children at the Ulverston Infant School to have a summer treat, albeit more simple than in some previous years. The event was held on 2nd July 1861 and was reported in the local papers: "Ulverston. Treat of

School Children – the children, to the number of 240 attending the infant school, have received their annual treat from the Rev R Gwillym. They were liberally regaled with buns, coffee, nuts, oranges, &c and seemed highly delighted with the liberality of the reverend benefactor. There were present, besides a number of the parents of the children, the Venerable Archdeacon Evans, the Revs T Carter and W Townson, and other influential inhabitants of the town. The Venerable Archdeacon delivered a suitable address to the pupil teachers."

27th July 1861: Susanna is rather abrupt

In July 1861 a list of 'Canadian Celebrities' was being compiled by Henry Morgan who asked Susanna for permission to include her name in the list. Rather than being flattered or honoured, Susanna was annoyed and when writing to him on 27th July 1861 was hardly even polite.

She wrote: "Any ambition I once had for literary distinction is so completely obliterated, by the sterner cares and trials of life that I feel no wish to see my name placed among your list of Canadian worthies. By birth and education I cannot have the least claim to the honour you intend me. Wishing your undertaking all success, Susanna Moodie."

In Susanna's defence, she may have felt some slight indication of what was about to happen, for on the following day, 28th July 1861 John Moodie had a stroke which left him paralysed down his left side. Although he recovered some use and feeling in the affected area, he remained partially disabled for the rest of his life.

Susanna attributed the stroke to his anxiety over the situation surrounding his position as Sheriff but John was said to be rather less specific when listing the possible causes of the stroke. He had just organised the local elections and thought that the stress of that activity may have been the trigger. He also thought there may have been a deeper and longer-standing cause, stemming from living in South Africa many years before.

July 1861: Agnes makes a helpful suggestion

Agnes in writing to Catharine in July 1861 showed that she was still doing her best to help her sister earn money by writing.

Catharine's book 'The Female Emigrants Guide', of which she had sold the copyright, was still being widely sold without benefit to the author. One relatively easy option which Agnes suggested was for Catharine to write a revised version with her name prominently printed on the cover and making clear that it was an improved and up-dated version.

Summer 1861: Tom spends a few weeks in England

Having reached New Orleans on 11th May, Tom stayed in America only a short time and was back in London by 20th July 1861.

Although there is no record of any contact between Tom's wife and Reydon Hall, the children seem to have made visits when they were no longer young children. Jane told Catharine in her letter dated 12th May 1861: "Walter and Dye will run down for a few days in the summer. I owe a letter there – but I have oft times as much to do as any other person which leaves me no time at all for writing letters."

On 13th September 1861 Tom in the 'Julia' laden with ballast, set sail for a very long voyage which would necessitate him navigating round Cape Horn, probably for the first time. His destination was Callao, the principle port of Peru, and very close to Peru's capital of Lima, where he was to collect a load of guano.

Guano is the accumulated droppings of sea birds whose diet of fish made guano a very effective, but smelly fertilizer. The best guano was found on the Chincha Islands off the coast of Peru. Mining and transporting guano were both dangerous and unpleasant activities, but commercially very worthwhile.

11th September 1861: Agnes attends a ball in Ireland

When the 'Bachelor Kings' was published, Agnes had a presentation copy sent to the Prince of Wales who at that time was unmarried. It reached him when he was at the Curragh Racecourse in Ireland, and as a result the Mayor of Dublin invited Agnes to attend the ball to be held on 11th September 1861 in honour of the prince. The invitation reached Agnes when she was in Manchester early in September to attend a meeting of the British Association.

Agnes assumed it would be an exclusive event and deserved priority over the British Association. She hurriedly altered her plans and set off for Ireland. Unfortunately it was all such a rush, and Agnes managed to get in such a fluster, that she boarded the boat to Ireland without noticing that her maid was absent.

It was not until she was standing on the deck of the departing boat, watching the land disappear, that Agnes realised that both her maid and her luggage had been left behind, and that she had not even an over-night bag with her.

Luckily she came across her friend and some-time lawyer, Archibald Stephens as she was making her way to the Gresham Hotel and he came to her rescue. He calmed her down and managed to sort things out so that both maid and luggage arrived in time for the ball. Jane in relating this story added: "Agnes could have managed without her maid, but her ball gown, accessories and jewels were essential."

At the ball Agnes was presented to the Prince of Wales whom she described as: "really a very pretty fellow, small in stature, but very well-shaped and dignified in appearance, though timid in manner. His eyes, eyebrows and hair are really beautiful; he has a handsome, well-cut aquiline nose, full lips, beautiful teeth and an agreeable smile. He danced unwearedly and very elegantly, though the height and fulness of some of his partners nearly eclipsed him."

Agnes had been flattered to receive an invitation, but in the region of 2,000 such invitations had been issued, and it was far from a select affair. Her beautiful Honiton lace dress was badly torn, and she had to cling to the arm of Lord Brougham on the way to the supper room, where manners were decidedly lacking. Glasses of champagne, bottles of whisky and plates of dressed crab were scrambled for and grabbed. Agnes described people as behaving like gorillas, but it was some comfort to her that when she remained in Dublin after the ball, the Mayor and the Viceroy, Lord Carlisle, looked after her.

October 1861: Sarah and Richard plan to be away at Christmas

At the beginning of October 1861, the Ulverston children had a school treat which regained the excitement of former events.

The local paper reported: "School Festivities – On Wednesday 2nd October 1861, the children attending the National Schools were treated to a half-holiday, and spent the afternoon in the Tarnside meadow, each receiving a bun, the gift of the Rev R Gwillym, whose kindness to them is already proverbial. Games of different descriptions, to suit both sexes, such as foot-ball, cricket, races, scrambling for half-pence &c &c were entered into and kept up with great spirit, under the superintendence of Mr and Mrs Gwillym, the Rev T Carter, the Rev W Townson, and many of the lady visitors and teachers. The number of children to whom buns were distributed amounted to 394, viz 245 boys and 149 girls.

At the end of October the school examination was held, earlier in the year than usual, as the papers explained: "Examination of Infant Schools – What is usually the Christmas examination of the scholars attending the Infant School took place on Wednesday 25th October 1861, in consequence of the contemplated absence of the Rev R Gwillym at the ordinary time. Miss Lawrence conducted the examination. The Rev R Gwillym remarked that the school had always been considered one of the first, and he was glad to see that it kept up its character. The children were regaled with buns, sweetmeats, &c, and before dispersing gave three hearty cheers for Mr and Mrs Gwillym. There were upwards of 200 present."

November 1861: Agnes returns to Reydon Hall

Agnes remained in Ireland for over a month after the ball. She was looked after, treated as a 'personage' and visited friends, all of which she much enjoyed. She returned to England at the end of October 1861 and went to stay with the Gwillyms for a while. Here, Jane reported: "she took a pleasant tour with a party of friends to Ullswater and Patterdale, driven by Mr Askew of Bardsea Priory."

From Lancashire, Agnes returned to Reydon Hall to end the year quietly, and had a bit of financial good fortune to make up for some of the disappointments she had suffered over the years. Twenty four years earlier, Agnes had written a book of poems for young people entitled 'Floral Sketches'. It was to have been published by Effingham

Wilson, but his business had failed and Agnes had never been paid. Despite the lapse of time, Mr Wilson wrote to Agnes when he realised that her work was being pirated, having been published by Webb & Millington of Leeds, who also had an establishment in Fleet Street.

Archibald Stephens sent one of his clerks to Fleet Street to buy a copy as evidence, but there was none available, whereupon Agnes told Sarah that her 'Floral Sketches' was: "now very handsomely got up, and full of pictures" and asked if Richard could "get someone to buy two copies in Leeds. The purchaser must write on the title-page 'I purchased this book at such a shop at Leeds and for such a sum' and sign his name to it and the date." The copies were obtained as requested and, Jane reported, Webb & Millington "paid the compensation for the copyright demanded by the author, to avoid the threatened lawsuit."

1861: Catharine gets help from Lady Greville

Not only her brothers and sisters, but even some people she had never met were doing their best to help Catharine manage financially. In England, Lady Charlotte Greville had, through a mutual friend, become interested in Catharine's botanical work and knew of her lack of money. She had sent a gift of a flower press to Catharine in the summer of 1859 which helped Catharine prepare flower and fern albums for sale.

Lady Greville also tried to get Catharine a pension by being added to the Queen's List. She was unsuccessful, but did manage to persuade Lord Palmerston, then Prime Minister, to provide Catharine with a grant of £100 which Catharine received, probably in 1861.

(14th December 1861: Historical context – Prince Albert dies)

Prince Albert, husband of Queen Victoria, died on 14th December 1861. The bright clothing that Queen Victoria had worn for the first half of her reign disappeared, and she dressed in black for the remainder of her life.

5th January 1862: Agnes tries Catharine's ideas on publishers

In a letter dated 5th January 1862 Agnes reported having tried out an idea of Catharine's: "When I was in London I spoke to Murray the great publisher about your projected work 'The Hand Book of a Young Canadian Settler' by James Traill and he thought if it were well done it would take and he would be happy to look at it." Nothing came of this idea as neither Catharine nor James had the knowledge to write it without considerable research and effort.

Catharine's other idea fared less well, as Agnes wrote: "In respect to your book on Forest Trees my dear Kate, I fear that no London publisher could undertake it on account of the expense of bringing out such a work and without the scientific names."

29th January 1862: Sarah and Richard are at Hampton Court

Sarah wrote to Catharine on 29th January 1862 from Hampton Court Palace where they were on holiday, and where she and Richard had spent their honeymoon eighteen years earlier. Agnes also from time to time stayed at Hampton Court Palace with no explanation of the circumstances of her stay given, nor presumably needed.

By 1862 Hampton Court Palace was no longer a Royal Palace, but rooms within the palace and its confines were lent by the Crown as Grace and Favour dwellings, often to widows whose husbands had served the Crown in some senior role. Some of these dwellings were allocated by the Lord Chamberlain as he thought fit. It may be that there was accommodation put aside for the use of Anglican clergy on a short term basis, and Agnes may have had friends she could visit among the long-term residents.

Sarah told Catharine that she and Richard had been at Hampton Court Palace all winter but would soon be returning home. She wrote, as far as can be deciphered due to much cross-writing on flimsy paper: "next week is our last at the Palace as our leave of absence from our Bishop expires. We have enjoyed our sojourn here very much. All the Ladies have made so much of us ... a magnificent old palace and full of ... pictures ... and some of the State Rooms ... it is a fine historical palace and we can ... few get admittance to ..."

Her talk of the weather shows that the residents in Hampton Court Palace were on friendly terms with the soldiers stationed in the adjoining barracks: "I don't know what it has been in Canada but here it is a warm ... winter. We have had two days of hard frost during the whole winter in the Home Park – amid sport lamentations of the 5th Lancers stationed here when all ice disappeared."

1861-1862: Crinolines cause complications for Agnes

When crinolines were in fashion, the transportation of luggage was by no means simple and had to be planned in advance. Just before Christmas 1861, Agnes was invited to a house-party at the Chantry House in Ipswich. Her host, Sir Fitzroy Kelly, wrote to her with travelling instructions including supplementary arrangements for crinolines. A closed carriage was to meet her from the 1.30 train at Ipswich Station, together with a cart for the crinolines, so that all would arrive safely at the Chantry House by two in the afternoon.

As well as being inconvenient luggage, having a hoop to her dress could be a dangerous thing, as Agnes discovered in the early spring of 1862, when she went for a walk alone in the grounds of Reydon Hall. She described the incident in a letter to Sarah: "I walked through the plantation; but when I got to the gate opening into the free meadow, finding it locked, I attempted to climb over it, when my hoop caught on the top bar, and I was thrown backwards onto the ground, striking my head with great violence.

"Fortunately the grass was soft – no stones in the way. After a few minutes I was able to sit up, put on my crushed hat, and walk home. If I had fractured a limb, I might have lain there all day as no-one knew in what direction I had walked – and this part of the grounds is so unfrequented." After this mishap, Agnes always took her maid or Jane with her when she went for a walk.

29th January 1862: Percy Strickland visits England

In 1862 Sam's seventh child and fifth son, Percy Strickland travelled to England with his bride as part of their honeymoon.

Sarah in the bits of her letter which can be deciphered, and written to Catharine on 29th January 1862, gave some news of Percy's itinerary. Sarah wrote: "I have just got a note from Percy Strickland saying he will be with us on Monday the 3rd February. He is now at Southwold. I fear from what he says that he is about to leave England. I hope we return north ... I shall be very sorry ... have liked much to have seen him and his Bride at Ulverston and to have shown him some of our pretty country."

Sarah added: "I am sure they will not be able to receive Percy at Reydon for dear Mamma is not left night or day for a moment. They could not receive Richard and me as the least excitement would be fatal, and all the maids ... with attention to dear Mamma." Also, Reydon Hall had deteriorated. Sarah wrote: "Agnes is very poorly I am sorry to say but Reydon is ... no one can be well there."

The visit of Percy Strickland to England gave an opportunity for having parcels taken to Canada for Catharine. Sarah mentioned that she had things for Catharine which she would give to Percy if he visited Ulverston and in the meantime she sent some money. She said: "My dear husband has given me £5 to share between you and young Richard Strickland. We think that you might take £3 of it with the rate of exchange, and give him £2 with his godfather's love and best wishes. My dear husband sends it as a mark of his love to you and thinks that the money will be of more use to you than laying it out by way of a present and I know you will receive it with the same kind spirit in which it is sent."

3rd February 1862: Agnes sends a box to Catharine

Agnes took advantage of Percy's visit to England to send a letter, dated 3rd February 1862 together with a parcel to Catharine. The parcel contained, Agnes wrote: "such things as I had, and thought might be useful to you and your girls. The blue mohair is quite new and I have only worn it two or three times, and the blue mixture silk would do for yourself with the black net over it, for I think you ought now to leave off your widow dress, which makes you look older than poor mamma, and must be very hot and uncomfortable, and is always expensive. You will of course divide the ribbons and dresses as may seem good to you. There is a white net and double skirt which has never been washed, and lots of ribbons, which are as good as new, if ironed out. Some are nice and expensive ones. There was neither time nor opportunity to buy anything, so I sent you all I had by me."

Other news in the letter was of family health and financial matters, where Agnes seemed to be almost as unfortunate as Catharine: "The best news I have is dear mamma's recovery from her long dangerous illness, which made us so uneasy, but I think now she may go on again. I had hoped to dispose of your fables to Webb and Millington, but they are men of straw. The bill for 25£ I took of them in part payment for the edition they pirated of my 'Floral Sketches' was dishonoured. I will have nothing more to do with them."

The following day Agnes added to her letter: "I am happy to add that the dear mother continues to amend. She came down stairs yesterday, and is lively and amused this morning. Eliza complains of ill health. Tom is at Lima and does not return until June."

Catharine seems to have been requesting family photographs at this time. Sarah had written in her letter of 29th January 1862: "I sent you my Richard's photograph in my last letter which I hope you got quite safely." Agnes in her letter dated a few days later, 3rd February 1862 wrote: "I send you a photograph a hideous caricature, as indeed they all are."

10th June 1862: Tom reaches Ascension Island on his return journey

Tom ran into trouble on his return from Peru in the early part of 1862. He was reported to have stopped at Ascension Island on 10th June 1862: "to make good defects" and had to stay there for nearly three weeks. It sounds as though he had run into bad weather, as three other ships also had to stop at Ascension Island for repairs.

Tom and the 'Julia' with a load of guano were ready and able to leave Ascension on 30th June 1862. He did not, however, sail for London which seems to have been his original destination, but instead headed for Spain.

August 1862: Eliza and Agnes set to work on Bishops' Lives

Eliza and Agnes had exhausted all the options for writing biographies of British royalty, and other authors had capitalised on the success of 'Lives of the Queens of England' by writing books with titles beginning 'Lives of ...' As a result the Strickland sisters had some difficulty in finding topics for future work.

After a fallow period they managed to find one other suitable subject for study, and they set to work on the 'Lives of the Seven Bishops' sent to the Tower of London by James II in 1688. These lives spanned the period 1617 to 1720, and involved a certain amount of ecclesiastical complexity. Eliza began work on the lives of Bishop Lloyd of St Asaph and Bishop Trelawney of Bristol, while Agnes began to work her way through the lives of the other five.

Since Agnes had become famous, unknown distant cousins had introduced themselves to her and, in some cases, invited her to visit them. Among these were Mr and Mrs Cottrell Dormer who lived at Rousham House in Oxfordshire. One of Mr Dormer's forbears was linked by marriage to the Cottrell family who were also among the ancestors of Agnes and her family. Mrs Dormer had been a Strickland before her marriage and was cousin to Sir George Strickland MP, who had become a friend of Agnes after helping obtain entry permits to the State Record Office for Agnes and Eliza twenty years previously.

With these convoluted family connections, Agnes in August 1862 included a visit to Rousham House in her summer tour where she said she: "was warmly and affectionately received, though I had never seen Mrs Cottrell Dormer before." The Cottrell Dormer's home was convenient for the Bodleian Library in Oxford, and gave Agnes somewhere congenial to stay while studying there.

Agnes in a letter to Jane described her daily routine when at Rousham: "I rise at half-past six to be in time for the first train and get to the Bodleian before the Library is open, and amuse myself in the picture gallery. Mrs Cottrell Dormer gives me a fine bunch of grapes every day to take with me, and her housekeeper provides me with sandwiches for luncheon which enables me to work till past three. Then I drive to the station, and my maid meets me at Heyford with the key of the grounds. So we return through a lovely green valley by the beautiful river, cool and shady for about a mile.

We reach the hall about five, where coffee and biscuits are ready for our refreshment, then I dress for dinner and enjoy the rest of the day. On Friday I was so delighted at meeting Dean Stanley and dear Lady Augusta at the station – a great and unexpected pleasure."

Mrs Cottrell Dormer was a friend of the Duchess of Marlborough, and not only took Agnes to visit Blenheim Palace, but arranged that Agnes could see the private apartments, together with some historic relics, miniatures and portraits not normally shown. Among these was a portrait of Queen Elizabeth I which Agnes said was the finest she had seen, and which had been painted quite early in the queen's reign.

August 1862: Tom reaches Valencia

Having left Ascension on 30th June 1862, Tom and the 'Julia' laden with guano sailed to Valencia on the east coast of Spain, arriving on 11th August. There he presumably unloaded either part or all of his cargo, for he remained in Valencia until quite late in September 1862.

Autumn 1862: Agnes collects her material

Agnes had visited Sudeley Castle in her late summer tour of 1862 before going to the Cottrell Dormers at Rousham. After a spell at Rousham she continued her travels, including a visit to York where Agnes wrote: "Mrs Gordon got the historian of the cathedral, Mr Brown, to go over it with me." She also attended archaeological meetings in the summer of 1862, first at Worcester and later on at Cambridge.

It was at Cambridge that Agnes caught a cold, and became so seriously ill that Sarah and Richard Gwillym went to keep her company for a while. When partially recovered, Agnes went to stay with friends in Yorkshire to convalesce, but the air did not suit her, and she moved to stay with another friend, Lady Campden, who was herself an invalid, and the quietness did Agnes good. She told Jane: "We are quite alone; but I like it, as I shall not be obliged to dress for dinner."

Agnes had an extraordinary knack of finding useful contacts for her work, though it is probable that any famous person can obtain help when needed, and in return gives a little reflected fame in the private lives of those who have provided the help. When she needed some information about the birthplace in Fressingfield, Suffolk of William Sancroft, one of the Bishops she was studying, she was invited by the local vicar, Rev Mr Coltbeck to visit him and his family at their parsonage for the day, and during her visit he took her to nearby Ufford Hall, where Bishop Sancroft had been born.

The wife of another local vicar, Mrs Hopper, took Agnes to Gawdy Hall, the home of her mother Mrs Holmes, where she was shown a portrait of William Sancroft as a young man, also his armchair and his 'time-piece'.

Agnes had been friends with Bishop Tait, Bishop of London, since 1856 and with his help gained access to the library in Lambeth Palace. Agnes said she always enjoyed working within a building that the subjects of her research would have known, and Lambeth Palace was no exception. Lambeth Chapel had been restored by Archbishop Sancroft, and Bishop Ken, another of her subjects of study, had been consecrated bishop there. Bishop Tait was to become Archbishop of Canterbury in 1868.

So it was that Agnes, in her working life of research and in her social whirl, had an exciting, full and sociable life, but the only place she could call home was Reydon Hall, a place which was in no fit state to entertain people as she was entertained elsewhere, and here she spent the winter months turning her research notes into biographies.

At Reydon Hall her aged mother was diminishing in her capabilities, Jane was often ill and the building itself was in need of far more renovation than Agnes could afford to fund. In a letter to Catharine, written in July 1861 Agnes had described Reydon as now "a joyless place" so winter for Agnes was a difficult time of year.

11th October 1862: Tom heads off back across the Atlantic

Tom left Valencia late in September and reached Gibraltar on 2nd October 1862, but he was not homeward bound. After a few days at Gibraltar he left on the 11th October 1862, the 'Julia' having been cleared to sail to New York.

13th October 1862: St Mary's Church in Ulverston is to have new seating

The main event for Sarah and Richard Gwillym in 1862 was the initiation of work on the parish church. On 13th October 1862 the local papers reported: "Ulverston St Mary's Church – We have been informed that the Archdeacon, in company with the Rev R Gwillym and the wardens, inspected this building on Monday evening last, when it was thought desirable to re-pew the whole of the church. The estimated cost is £2,200. No doubt a vestry meeting will be called before anything is definite. Mr Paley, of Lancaster, is preparing a plan of the alterations which will be photographed and circulated among the parishioners for approval."

16th October 1862: Agnes writes biographies for magazines

Whilst working on the 'Lives of the Seven Bishops', Agnes was earning some money by writing a series of magazine articles giving the life stories of some of the minor figures she and Eliza had come across when studyng the lives of the various monarchs of England and Scotland. An advertisement for the 'Englishwoman's Domestic Magazine' on 16th October 1862 announced: "This month's number" contains "instalments of interesting series and gossipy articles. The 'Historical Female Biographies' by Agnes Strickland are continued, and we have in this number the life of Mary Livingstone, one of the maids of honour of Mary Queen of Scots."

Agnes also seems to have made some money in advance of publishing the book of bishop biographies. An advertisement for the 'Churchman's Family Magazine' dated 10th December 1864 noted: "The 'Lives of the Seven Bishops in the Tower' by Agnes Strickland is continued in this month's number of this well conducted periodical." The book itself gave 1866 as its date of publication.

November 1862: Tom arrives in New York and his daughter Mary marries

Tom having left Gibraltar on the 11th October 1862 to sail to New York, arrived at his destination on 14th November.

While Tom was heading towards New York and had not quite reached his destination, another of his daughters made a good marriage, though how his daughters came to meet these very eligible bachelors is not explained.

The marriage on 11th November 1862 of 23 year-old Mary was announced in the papers: "Marriages. Pohle – Strickland, at Milton next Gravesend, Mars Mourier Pohle, Esq., 35th Reg., only son of the late Uriel Pohle, Esq., of Babington Gardens, Madras, to Mary, third daughter of Captain T Strickland, late of Plaistow, Essex."

Mary not only married while Tom was away, she also left the country and went to India with her husband. Agnes gave news of the event when she wrote to Catharine from Reydon Hall on 23rd December 1862. Agnes wrote: "Tom's daughter Mary is married to a lieutenant Pohle, and went out to India with him on the 4th of this month."

6th December 1862: Richard's plans become more ambitious

By the time the local papers came out on 6th December 1862, the proposal to re-pew St Mary's Church in Ulverston had changed to something more ambitious, but the estimated cost, which had seemed high at £2,200 for re-pewing, barely increased with the changed plans.

The papers reported: "Ulverston Improvement of the Parish Church – The Rev R Gwillym, incumbent of Ulverston, has issued proposals for enlarging and improving Ulverston Church. The proposed alterations are to be according to designs by Mr Paley, architect, of Lancaster and are to cost £2,300."

23rd December 1862: Catharine seems to get through money fast

The £100 which Catharine had received from Lord Palmerston sometime in 1861 did not last very long and in a letter dated 23rd December 1862 Agnes wrote somewhat wearily, and possibly with a bit of advice concealed in the last phrase: "My dearest Catharine, I was very sorry and indeed surprised to receive so melancholy an account of your finances after you had received the large sum from the Queen so lately, which we all hoped would have made you comfortable for some time.

"However, I send you a letter of credit for five pounds as you see and wish it were in my power to give you more but the dividends are so shabby now from the company and I have so many demands made upon me for money that I cannot do more without leaving myself in arrears, which I will not do under any circumstances for I always pay my way as I go and limit my outlay to my means."

Christmas 1862 and January 1863: Richard distributes to the poor

Christmas 1862 saw Richard Gwillym's efforts, though more limited than in previous years, noted in the local papers: "Seasonable benevolence. The Rev R Gwillym, with his usual benevolence, is distributing meat to no less than 70 poor families in the town."

Richard was also the chosen person for distributing other money to the needy, as the local papers noted on 13th January 1863: "Ulverston Operatives – John Bather, Esq., has placed in the hands of Rev R Gwillym £10 to be distributed among the operatives of Ulverston who are out of work by the closing of the mills – being half the sum subscribed by the workmen and others, employed in the Low Wood Powder Mills ... other half to the Central Committee."

15th January 1863: John Moodie resigns

In a letter written on 28th December 1862, Susanna told Catharine that she had been ill, and had been taking large doses of aspirin to ease the pain. One doctor had told her that she had stomach ulcers, another that she had kidney disease, and family anxieties would not have helped. There had still not been a decision from the Appeal Court but the signs were not encouraging, and on 15th January 1863 John Moodie decided to resign.

His retirement took place officially in March 1863 and kind words were said, the general view was reported as being that although John had broken the law, he had done so unintentionally. It was said also that if he were given another post by government appointment, it would be welcomed by the population at large, but nothing materialised. John was in his sixties and partially disabled. Also there was a change of government, which did not help his prospects.

Although he was no longer sheriff, John was entitled to collect unpaid fines and settle accounts from his time in office. Robert Moodie had been more or less running his father's office for some time, and carried on trying to get the money that was owed to his father. Susanna's income from writing had dried up, partly because she had no publisher for her work in England, and partly because she felt that she had run out of topics for her writing.

1st January 1863: Tom's wife dies

Agnes when writing her Christmas 1862 letter to Catharine, not only mentioned the marriage of Tom's daughter Mary, she also gave some worrying news about Tom's wife. Agnes wrote: "Tom is now at New York with his ship, and will be home before you receive this. His wife is very ill."

His wife was indeed very ill and died before Tom returned home. The notice in the local paper read: "Death on 1st January 1863 at 50 Milton-road, Gravesend, Margaretta Adela, the beloved wife of Captain Thomas Strickland." She was 51 years old and the cause of her death was given as disease of the brain and apoplexy.

Tom and his ship, the 'Julia' had left London on 13th September 1861 and it was nearly a year and a half later that he arrived back at London Docks on 26th February 1863. The home he returned to was now minus his wife and another daughter. This left only his daughter Diana and his son Walter to welcome him home and console him.

1863-1864: The copyright situation of various editions of 'Lives of the Queens of England' is difficult to disentangle

Agnes and Eliza seem in 1863 to have been working on abridged versions of the 'Lives of the Queens of England' but there was some associated confusion about ownership of the various copyrights, including those which were sold at auction after Henry Colburn's death.

Henry Colburn's widow soon re-married and her new husband was John Foster. Jane recorded that Agnes paid the couple about £1,800 in 1863 for some copyrights. How this ties in with the copyrights that were auctioned is not clear and might have been the subject of the litigation between Agnes and Colburn before his death, and subsequently between Agnes and Mrs Colburn's second husband, John Foster.

Any new editions were presumably separate from past entanglements. Jane said that: "Agnes Strickland had repurchased the copyright of 'The Queens of England'. Longmans then brought out an illustrated version in eight volumes while Messrs Bell and Daldy produced a cheaper version in six volumes." Agnes was said to prefer the shorter edition "to its more showy brother" because it "contained the final additions, though the type was smaller and the portraits wanting." The type was indeed small, and it requires very good eye-sight indeed to read the footnotes or, more importantly, extracts from letters included in the text. Jane reported that "The copyrights of both editions were finally purchased by Mr Bell after the decease of the author."

8th April 1863: Richard's plans become even more ambitious

By 8th April 1863, Ulverston Church was one of several requesting funds from a diocesan building committee. The reported request was for £150: "towards proposed additional accommodation for 330 worshippers. The whole expense of enlarging, restoring and partly rebuilding the church being £2,300."

The original intention to re-pew the church, having passed through a phase of intending to enlarge and improve the building, had now added the intention of carrying out restoration work. However, the original estimated cost of £2,200 had only been increased to £2,300.

20th April 1863: Tom and Diana sail for New York

Tom Strickland having arrived home from New York at the end of February 1863, set sail on his next voyage two months later.

On 20th April 1863 and still in command of the 'Julia', he was sailing past Gravesend on his way back to New York and he had with him for company, his 20 year old daughter Diana.

28th April 1863: James Traill is visiting England

Catharine's eldest son, James Traill took a trip to England in the spring of 1863 in the hope that it would relieve his lung health problems. After he had spent a few days at Reydon Hall, Jane wrote a lengthy letter to Catharine to tell her all about it, and in so doing gave a lot of information about other members of the family, as well as an illustration of her own ability to give news in a light-hearted manner.

Jane wrote, on 28th April 1863: "My dear Kate, Your son has just left us after a few days visit. We have found him a very delightful young man. Agnes was at Fressingfeld when he arrived and was absent two days – but we got on very well and he was so kind and attentive to the feeble and infirm grandmother that she did not insist on us going to ..." (one indecipherable but important word, maybe bed, or our rooms) "... at nine or half past eight as she usually does to Walter Strickland – Her own old Tom says 'Only Mammet let me finish this gin and water' and yarns till two in the morning."

It is regrettable that no-one ever persuaded Tom to turn his yarns into an account of his life, starting with what happened after he left home at fourteen up to and through his years as a Master Mariner. Judging by the letter he wrote to the 'Globe' in October 1840, he was as capable of writing a book as the rest of the family, and he clearly had plenty of material.

Jane's letter to Catharine continued: "It was lovely weather but windy and the aunt and nephew chose to be asthmatic so neither went beyond the grounds the first day. Upon the Friday evening the Agg came home and you may suppose added much to our small home circle and we went to Wangford to return our dear Vicar's call on James and to see the shell of Wangford church for spire and side aisles are nearly down. Wangford Church hosted honey bees, for fourteen pounds of honey was taken out of the steeple besides the value of the wax. Mr Crowfoot was too generous to claim his share.

"Then we called upon Anne Wales who has hired two rooms at Wangford and is writing for a prize essay which I dare say she will not get as it is a matter of favours in most cases. Anne was not at home but called upon us yesterday but we were on a tour in Agg's carriage.

"For Monday Agnes ordered a horse for her carriage and as we were to dine at my house my little cook walked in to light my dining room fire and cook some beef steaks. While I went shopping, Agnes and James drove down to the ferry and crossed to Walberswick to see the ruins – in the mean time the table was set and James and Agnes were tired and rested while the steaks were cooking in the room as one fire was enough. We had a bottle of ale and some nice coffee after we dined, Agnes lay down on the sofa while I did the honours – Our friends had all gone off to town so we paid no visits.

"Then we went to Benacre Hall to call on our friend Mrs Johnson. She was out but James saw the interior of an English park. I had sugar to buy at Wrentham and there we saw a lot of French silks and James bought a handsome black glace for his Amelia at a better rate than he could have done in London. Home we came and found neither tea nor fire – unluckily we had a bricklayer at work and the housemaid was courting him I suppose – I scolded but the little cook came home in time to get us a comfortable tea – James had some shrimps but they were small and I think winkles or pinpatches pleased him better.

"Then I packed his books, found a box for the goods Agnes gave – A piece of warm cord for Amelia's boys, a black and mauve swiss dress for you and two elegant dresses barely worn for your single girls – and I begged Mamma's tippet to keep you warm as it is a costly thing and when you are dressed will do for outdoor wear. It was not clean when Tom put it down but Huggs washed ironed and hung it up in a warm sunny windy day and it came out quite white and new – I do not say that it has not been worn but never here – I fancy it was one used by Margaretta but being carefully mended is as good as ever."

Jane mentioned her own and Mrs Strickland's health and added more information about family customs, and about Mrs Strickland and James. Jane wrote: "I went through the winter badly with gout and asthma – and though better am still husky – I find the best mustard mixed and put in a paper my best remedy, but it is not pleasant to be helpless half one's life. Mamma has gone through the winter well and looks a pretty old dear – On Sunday while Agnes read the chapter she sat hand in hand with her dear grandson and whispered 'your dear mother little thinks how we are sitting together hand in hand' – the likeness was unmistakeable for she is a pretty old lady and he a handsome and elegant looking young man."

April 1863: Jane tries to organise a reunion for Tom and Sam

In 1863, there was a chance for family members to meet in North America. Jane's letter to Catharine written on the 28th April that year, made reference to Catharine and Margaretta's conflict over Tom in the early days of Tom's marriage. Jane wrote: "Tom is off for New York with Diana who wanted change having lost her Mother so sadly and her lover through his friends. The ship God willing will be in port in a fortnight – the Julia Captain Strickland will find her – and you might write to him leaving away bygones only expressing sympathy – I do not think him a very disconsolate widower – but such a woman could only have hold on the senses – besides he never could love more than one person – you first then his wife – now Diana and people dear Kate cannot help their natural dispositions.

"As I cannot write to Colonel Strickland you might advise him to write to Tom who cannot leave his ship and appoint a time for seeing him for it is a pity the brothers can never meet as Tom stays three months. Di might visit her cousins if any one could take charge of her. She is pretty and domestic not like you but her features are like in miniature – Tall and light in figure – She has black eyes and hair and a lovely complexion. Mary has married an officer in the 34th and is in India with her husband a splendid match. They do not expect to be long in India – as Mr Pohle's father left him a large fortune."

Jane ended with a miscellany of interesting little nuggets: "Agnes sends her love and dear Mamma her blessing. She has nothing more to send – No more have I dear Kate being poor and owing for the mourning for Margaretta to pay for – but I had nothing but a bonnet – your James does not lose his cough – but he was better when he left us.

"I am glad Percy's pretty and aristocratic bride makes such an excellent wife. I liked them both much – her particularly though he reminded me of my father. He is the handsomest of all the Stricklands I have seen. Thank you dear Kate for the photographic it is not like you – but it is like the cast – otherwise I should not have owned it. Though of course the loss of teeth and a fine head of hair have altered me out of all knowledge. I am too vain to have myself taken by a mechanical process." The cast may have been taken in the days of their friendship with the Childs family and their interest in phrenology, but has not been mentioned elsewhere.

April 1863: Jane leaves clues about the Homer family

Jane then wrote about Mrs Strickland's relations, members of the Homer family, and harked back to the financial loss sustained by their father. "I sent your James to enquire, with their sister's love, for Mrs Sinder and Aunt Martha – Sam Homer's daughter who lives with Aunt Sally received him kindly insisted on his taking tea and conducted him to Aunt Martha. Mrs Sinder he did not see. She was confined to her room and Martha told him was failing fast in mind and body. He found Martha respectable and in good health.

"Of Aunt Sarah should she die while James is in England he must go to the funeral and hear the Will read for it makes sure Mamma must, as the eldest sister, administer being with Martha her joint heir, and as Mamma's Will divides her property among her children it would be a good thing for us to get something back out of the robberies, but I have heard that the sisters settled their money upon the business when Aunt Sally married."

The Strickland family do not seem ever to have received the recompense for which Jane was hoping.

May 1863: Susanna passes on Jane's news to Catharine

At the time of James Traill's visit to Reydon Hall, Jane wrote to Susanna, as she had done to Catharine. Susanna passed on news from Jane's letter to Catharine in a letter written in May 1863: "Jane wrote kinder than is her wont to me and I felt grateful for the friendly feeling that her letter displayed. Our dear old mother was quite well – had got through the winter splendidly. Jane was complaining as usual." Susanna wrote that Jane said: "I am delighted with James Traill. He is not so handsome as his mother, but he is very like her, and his uncle Tom, but much better looking than Tom ever was."

Susanna also passed on to Catharine, not realising that Catharine had also heard from Jane, news from Jane about their brother Tom. Susanna wrote that Tom had visited Jane and his mother before setting sail for New York and that Tom: "had his daughter Diana with him, for a change of scene and air, as the breaking off of her marriage with someone whom she does not name, on account of money matters, was the cause of her Mother's death."

Diana may have been engaged before her mother died, but she had not been married and there is no suggestion elsewhere that this had any effect on her mother's health. Other notes left in Susanna's family archive are also inaccurate in relation to Tom, for example recording that his first wife had been called Anne Thompson and he had been a widower when he married Margaretta, whereas he married only once and Margaretta Adela Thompson was his wife's maiden name.

20th June 1863: Agnes attends another Drawing-room

Agnes was continuing to enjoy social life in London, including going to Court Drawing-rooms. The Prince of Wales had married Princess Alexandra of Denmark on 10th March 1863, and although Queen Victoria continued to wear mourning for Prince Albert, the rest of the court no longer did so, if the newspaper description of the Drawing-room of 1863 is anything to go by.

The report said: "The Princess of Wales held a drawing-room, on her Majesty's behalf, in St James's Palace on Saturday afternoon 20th June 1863. The presentations of ladies amounted to 223. The Princess of Wales wore a mauve petticoat, with bouffants of tulle, trimmed with handsome white Brussels lace and roses. The train of white moire, with a deep border of mauve silk, covered with handsome Brussels lace to match the petticoat. The head-dress of the Princess was formed of a diamond tiara, feathers and a tuile veil."

A few of the other outfits were also described, including that of: "Miss Agnes Strickland – Train of royal blue moire antique, lined with white grosse; skirt of rich white glace, with double tunic of Honiton point lace, decorated with blue glace, ruches to correspond with the train, and looped over with three narrow goffered flounces, ruched with blue; stomacher of pearls and pearl necklace. Head-dress of feathers, pearl tiara and point lappets

19th and 23rd June 1863: Richard gives summer treats to the children and to the teachers

After a few quiet years, 1863 saw Richard and Sarah involved in whole-hearted summer treats. Firstly the Ulverston school children had an outing with the costs shared among three of the local gentry (including Richard). This was followed by a separate treat for the teachers, which Richard alone provided.

The children's event was an enormous affair as described in the local press, with one of Richard's curates doing the organising: "Ulverston Sunday School Excursion to Coniston – On Friday 19th June 1863, the children of the Town Bank Sunday, and the Workhouse Schools, numbering with their teachers 400, assembled at the Infant School, and headed by the Ulverston Volunteer rifle band, walked in procession to the railway station, which they left about 2 o'clock, arriving in Coniston at a little after 3.

"They then formed in order and proceeded to the Watershead Hotel in front of which they amused themselves with cricket, football, racing &c &c till they were summoned to an excellent tea" after tea "the order was given to prepare for home" and the children gave "most hearty cheers for the Rev R and Mrs Gwillym, the visitors and the Rev W Townson, who had the management of the treat.

"The weather was fine" and in addition to the children and teachers "250 friends had accompanied" the party. They all got back "home by 9 o'clock, having enjoyed the trip immensely. The rifle band added very greatly by playing during the afternoon – The expenses were mainly provided by the liberality of the Rev R Gwillym, HW Schneider and HW Askew Esqrs."

The teachers' treat took place a few days later and was reported on 23rd June 1863: "Ulverston Excursion to Windermere – Last week the teachers of the National and Infant Schools had, through the liberality of the Rev R Gwillym, an excursion to Windermere. The party, numbering 32, arrived at Bowness at 12 o'clock when, after rambling about the village, they sat down to an excellent dinner at the Royal Hotel. After visiting some objects of interest, they crossed to the Ferry Hotel where tea was provided. The rain now began to fall and to some degree marred the pleasure; nevertheless" they "continued merrily and reached home at 11 o'clock and gave the reverend gentleman three hearty cheers."

15th July 1863: Sarah passes on family news

James Traill not only visited Reydon Hall but also visited the Gwillym's in Ulverston while in England. Sarah, when writing to Catharine on 15th July 1863 passed on family news from her point of view. She wrote: "I was very glad to hear from Dear James today that he had a safe and pleasant voyage home. Agnes is in London but is coming to me next week – She is to make a long visit I believe. I have Walter Strickland, Tom's son, staying with us. He is a very nice young man with the brightest black eyes I ever saw."

Of herself and Richard, she wrote: "We have just returned from spending the day at Furness Abbey with the Bishop of Carlisle and Mrs Waldegrave and their children. The weather is beyond everything lovely so hot. My dear Richard rejoices in the heat. We have a great quantity of strawberries this year but neither apples nor pears. I don't think I shall be able to go to Reydon this year for Richard is restoring his church and when once it is set about" it will "be best not to stir from home."

Tom had not managed to meet his relatives in Canada. Sarah wrote: "I am sorry that Tom could not get up to see you and your brother and all the family connections. He had Diana with him, they thought a sea voyage would do her good." Though as Tom had the responsibility of his ship and cargo to deal with, and Diana would not have been expected to travel alone, it seems more regrettable that no-one from among Sam, Susanna and Catharine and their families had made the effort to go to see Tom, rather than the other way round.

This letter contained the first surviving mention that Sam had developed diabetes. Sarah wrote: "I am glad to hear a better account of my dear brother's health. I hope it will continue to improve. I never hear from Eliza. She will neither receive nor write letters."

25th August 1863: A bazaar is held in the grounds of Reydon Hall

From London in 1863 Agnes went to Ulverston and to the Gwillyms for a restful holiday, and while she was away, two events took place in Suffolk which added some variety to Jane's life. There is no record of Jane ever visiting Ulverston or London, though she seems to have had one or two short holidays in East Anglia.

On 4th August 1863, Lord Stradbroke held a review of the Suffolk volunteers and sent invitations to a large number of the nobility and gentry of the area. Miss Jane Strickland was among those listed in the papers as attending the review and enjoying the hospitality that went with it.

In addition, Jane would have been involved in a fund-raising event reported in the local papers at the end of August. The report noted: "Reydon Bazaar – ... to build a more commodious schoolroom in the parish for the use and education of the poor children ... on Tuesday 25th August 1863, in a paddock adjoining the residence of Mrs Strickland, was held a bazaar well supplied with articles of fancy work. Entrance tickets, refreshments and articles sold amounting to £71.3s.2d which with the sum previously subscribed would nearly suffice. There was also in the grounds a cricket and archery party, which added greatly to the interest of the proceedings. The Band of the 14th Suffolk Rifles played lively airs throughout the day."

28th August 1863: Tom and Diana are back from New York

Tom, with Diana, and in command of the 'Julia' left New York and was back in London Docks with a load of guano on 28th August 1863. This would have given him perhaps two months in New York, not the three that the family mentioned in their letters.

October 1863: Agnes goes to the dentist

Agnes wrote to Catharine in October 1863 from Oxford Terrace in London, a belated letter after meeting James Traill but with other news as well: "My beloved sister, I intended to have written to you six months ago to tell you how pleased we all were with your son James but in truth I have been so much occupied and out of spirits I have not been able."

Of her own health, Agnes wrote: "I have gone through a very painful operation at Cartwrights this afternoon to a large back tooth which he is stopping having first cut out the inflamed pith and destroying the nerve. On Monday he will fill it up with gold. I shall be glad when the process is complete. I should have saved more of my teeth if I had understood homeopathy when I was young as it is astonishing what an effect that system has on neuralgic pain, I never now take anything else nor have I for 12 years. I believe I have been the instrument with God's blessing of keeping poor Mamma alive by administering suitable doses to her when attacked by eryseppelas and colds." Agnes's belief in homeopathy and Jane's adherence to traditional medication was a bone of contention between them.

The weather in the Lake District must have changed after Sarah wrote her letter to Catharine in July, for Agnes wrote: "I have just returned from Ulverston where I spent five weeks with Sarah and her good kind husband but we had such wretched weather I only went to Windermere twice. From Ulverston I went to Rousham to spend a pleasant week with the kind Cottrell Dormers and from there was asked to Loseley Park, a glorious old place, where I was much feted and caressed. I expect to be a week in town and then shall return to Reydon for the winter."

Agnes was still making efforts on Catharine's behalf with publishers, but without much success: "I vainly tried to do something for you with Virtue. Hall is out of the business, having proved himself a great rogue. I think if you could write a nice Canadian story for young ladies about 12, I might possibly meet with a publisher but it is a difficult matter."

28th October 1863: Tom sets sail with Diana for Valparaiso

Tom left London Docks on another long voyage in the 'Julia' on 28th October 1863. He again took Diana with him, and his destination was Valparaiso in Chile.

24th December 1863: Sarah catches a severe chill

In 1864, Sarah began writing on more robust paper than previously and with less cross-writing. Her letters are therefore reasonably legible and the rest of her story can partly be told in her own words (but with '...' signifying illegible parts missing) and with less reliance on news in the local papers.

When she wrote to Catharine a letter dated 13th January 1864 from Stockbridge House, her early paragraphs show that she had regularly given Catharine part or all of the dividends from her investments, which may be all that she had by way of freely disposable income.

Sarah wrote: "My Beloved Catharine, I fear the small sum I send you will be hardly worth accepting but it is the whole of my Dividends for the half year from my Canada Shares. There is two pounds for you, please transfer the other pound to my nephew Richard. I wish it was more but the dividend now is so bad that I fear the Company is not in a flourishing state."

Sarah had been unwell and the reason shows the extent of her involvement with Richard's work in the parish. She said: "I have been very ill and only came down stairs last Sunday, some inflammation of the windpipe. I had great difficulty of breathing or even speaking and the cough was very distressing. I took cold on Christmas Eve – my dear husband gave meat to a hundred poor parishioners for their Christmas dinner and I and my housekeeper cut and portion it according to the number in the family and got it all away with my own hands. The day was so cold and perishing" and the meat was taken round in an open carriage, hence her illness. Sarah said "I like to help my dear excellent husband all I can and not add to his anxiety ... there is so much to be done in the parish."

Richard was well at this time. Sarah wrote: "My dear husband is wonderfully well. We were at Harrogate all October which always does him good – he is giving many blankets and coals to our poor neighbours ... I don't know what Ulverston would do without him. I wish you knew him dear Kate how you would love him and he you."

December 1863: Catharine's daughter moves to Belleville

In December 1863, Catharine's daughter Mary married Thomas Muchall. The couple left Lakefield and moved to Belleville, where Tom Muchall and James Traill became business partners. Tom was twenty years older than Mary but seemed to be a kind and sensible man. However, before long it was realised that he was better at talking than doing, and was more of a liability than an asset.

Catharine's daughter Annie had married Clinton Atwood, who was a very hard worker and a capable farmer, but Annie had weak lungs and poor health like her brother James. Catharine worried about Annie's health in general, particularly when she was pregnant. Catharine herself had persistent attacks of such things as gout, lumbago, sciatica, neuralgia and rheumatism which caused her to be bed-ridden for quite lengthy periods, during which times her daughter Kate looked after her. Kate was another of the family members whose health was not robust.

13th January 1864: Plans for St Mary's Church are contentious

In her letter to Catharine written on 13th January 1864, Sarah gave her view of the plans to renovate the church in Ulverston: "My dear Richard ... to a great work we have undertook. He had set his heart for many years but he was not well enough to undertake it before, which is to enlarge and restore our Parish Church. He has collected all the money for it two thousand six hundred pounds. He gave two hundred ... at present room only for a hundred and twenty poor people and we have about four hundred belonging to us by adding ... and make it a beautiful church ... at the Priory gives us nothing but trouble and abuse but my Richard will not be turned from a good work by any opposition but it is an onerous task he has got before him but it is for the glory of God, there is no fear but it will grow and prosper." It seems that Mr Askew of Conishead Priory was by no means sure that the plans for the church were entirely a good idea.

The Consistory Court of the diocese of Carlisle had (and has) jurisdiction over consecrated ecclesiastical property. A few days after Sarah's letter to Catharine, Richard Gwillym together with three of his church wardens, applied for permission to make alterations to his parish church which would increase the number of free sittings from 200 to 400. This would involve a re-construction of the interior of the church and there were objections from several holders of the existing pews.

The matter was discussed on 19th January 1864 and the newspaper report said: "Some of the sittings especially of the poor people, were miserable and in the coldest part of the church. By the proposed alteration sittings would be gained and the poor people would receive the best pews, which was the point of issue for existing pew-holders who wanted to preserve their rights." The Chancellor in making his decision skirted round this tricky point by saying that the matter of allotment of pews was for later discussion, and he expected there to be a very large number of unappropriated sittings.

29th February 1864: The 'Julia' arrives in Valparaiso

Having navigated the dangerous waters of Cape Horn again, Tom with Diana and the 'Julia' arrived in Valparaiso on 29th February 1864. There were many British people in Valparaiso and it was a suitable place for Diana to be left while Tom completed his journey up the coast of Chile to Peru and the Chincha Islands, to collect another load of freshly mined guano.

8th March 1864: Plans for St Mary's Church in Ulverston are complete

By 8th March 1864, the final and full extent of the planned alterations to St Mary's Church were given in a detailed application for approval to proceed. The existing church could only seat 1,100 people while the town of Ulverston had a population of 6,000. This was part of the reason why the church alterations were needed.

The plans involved taking down the north wall and parts of the east and west walls of the church, and then rebuilding them. The east window was also to be taken down and rebuilt. The vestry and organ were to be moved to the east end of the church to allow additional pews to be put in the existing organ gallery, although the re-positioning of the organ was a subject which was debated. The church was to have pews of a uniform length (11 feet long and 2 feet 11 inches wide). It was also intended to remove the plaster ceiling in the church and leave the roof open, to put in a hot-water central heating system, and to install gas lighting.

Despite the very major additions to the project, the estimated cost had only risen by £300 from the initial estimate of £2,200 for a simple re-pewing of the church, up to £2,500 for more or less re-building the whole edifice. However, Richard may have purposely put in an initial over-estimate knowing that other changes would be needed.

Subscriptions had already amounted to £2,703 and the question of funding was not considered a problem, though presumably no-one was going to be surprised if the project ran over budget. Permission was granted and Richard, with Sarah's support, had a very major task ahead of him.

7th April 1864: Tom's daughter Diana marries

In Valparaiso Diana became engaged, and her marriage took place on 7th April 1864. The notice in the papers read: "Married. Patrickson – Strickland, at Valparaiso, Thomas Edmund Patrickson, Esq., to Agnes Diana, youngest daughter of Capt Thomas Strickland, and grand-daughter of the late Thomas Strickland, Esq., of Reydonhall, near Southwold."

Unfortunately no-one has left any information about this marriage, which apparently followed a very brief courtship, unless the couple already knew each other. Valparaiso is about as far from London as it is possible to be and Diana's marriage, unless Mr Patrickson was only in Valparaiso temporarily, meant that when Tom set sail, he might never see Diana again.

14th April 1864: Richard is made an Honorary Canon

On 14th April 1864 the papers reported: "Ecclesiastical Preferment – We have much satisfaction in announcing that the Lord Bishop of the Diocese has confirmed upon our vicar, the Rev Richard Gwillym, MA, the post of Honorary Canon of the Cathedral of Carlisle, as a recognition of the long and valued services which he has rendered to the church in the parish and deanery of Ulverston."

As it was an honorary post, Richard was not paid anything extra as a result of his new title, on the other hand it did not involve him in any extra work.

Spring 1864: Jane, Agnes and Mrs Strickland are all short of money

Jane wrote to Catharine in the spring of 1864 seemingly having lived in rented rooms in Southwold over part of the winter to be on hand while her cottage was having work done on it. Among her tasks was to give "directions to the gardener in cutting trees for opening the magnificent sea view of Dunwich – and the pier, the common and Walberswick, for being on a hill there is a fine view on every side. I used to go up to my workmen twice a day and then had a nice beach walk which I enjoyed as much as when we were little girls and used to gather shells and stones on the shore, they were our treasures and it is pleasant sometimes to recall those days."

Much of the work was to make necessary repairs following bad tenants who, Jane wrote: "bolted leaving my windows unmended and my rent unpaid ... the cottage was in the last degree of dilapidation ... All is done now but finishing the painting. Never since I had an income was I so poor and with sixty or seventy pounds of bills."

The next part of her letter hinted at the disadvantage of living at home when her mother was desperate for money and Jane received legacy money. Jane wrote: "Still dear Kate I can let rooms and eke out my livelihood for there can be little doubt that I shall lose the 350 mamma got from me on mortgage for buying Rogerson's part of the estate which has now only 7 years to run – She was cruel to urge and never behaved kindly after it was done."

Jane said that Agnes and their mother were also short of money: "Mamma is poorer than for some years past owing to the price of everything" and, unexplained, "Agnes has her Carnaby Street repairs."

28th April and 3rd May 1864: Richard and Sarah take their teachers for a day out

Richard's preferment came when he and Sarah were planning to give their teachers a special treat in the quiet period before the church alterations got under way. A couple of weeks after he was made a Canon, the local papers reported: "Treats to Teachers – On Friday 28th April 1864 the Rev Canon Gwillym, with his wonted and well-known generosity, gave his annual treat to the teachers of the Town Bank Sunday School.

"A little before 9 o'clock in the morning, the teachers, to the number of about 40, assembled at Stockbridge House, where they were kindly received by Mr and Mrs Gwillym. They were then conveyed in four carriages, one of which was drawn by four horses, to the Crown Hotel at Bowness. The day was bright and sunny, the country was lovely and all enjoyed the drive. After rambling on the banks of the lake, they all repaired to the hotel, and sat down to an excellent dinner.

"Mr Gwillym's liberality did not stop here; fresh carriages took them to Grasmere. After a time in this pretty little village and seeing the spot where Wordsworth reposes in so much greater seeming peace than our own noisy and foot-trodden grave-yard, they drove back to Bowness where an excellent tea awaited. The drive home in the grey twilight was enlivened by songs from the young ladies. As they passed through villages people could hardly have helped envying Ulverston in possessing such a benevolent and liberal vicar. At Stockbridge House, three deafening cheers were given for Mr and Mrs Gwillym."

A few days later a repetition of the event was reported: "On Tuesday 3rd May 1864 a similar excursion was given to all the teachers connected with the weekday schools, the number on this trip being 34. It thus appears that by Mr Gwillym's liberality upwards of 70 persons within the last few days have been entertained at the Crown Hotel, Bowness, and had an opportunity of seeing three lakes.

"It is impossible to speak in too high terms of such unsparing generosity. Is there another parish in the kingdom, where such treats are conducted on the same liberal scale? The object of our vicar is to give encouragement and to show how highly appreciated is the service of the teachers. It is the heartfelt wish of all who work with him he may long continue to preside."

10th May 1864: Tom arrives at Callao

Tom must have continued on his voyage in the 'Julia' soon after Diana's wedding on the 7th April 1864, sailing northwards up the west coast of South America with only the ship's crew for company, because by 10th May he had reached Callao in Peru.

21st May 1864: Eliza has been asked for her autograph

Eliza replied to a letter from a friend on 21st May 1864 in which she explained her attitude to receiving letters. It also appears from her letter that her contribution to the work published under Agnes's name was more widely known than she wished.

Eliza wrote: "It gave me great pleasure to read your letter giving me the pleasant news of your married happiness and that you had a lovely baby." However, Eliza admitted: "There was one drawback always is in a friends' letter must be answered and I do not find that writing letters is any relaxation after the mind is worn with proofs and MSs. Nay the eyes do not like it and tell me they expect rest or they will not go on."

An auto graph had been requested, and Eliza's reply showed that this was not the first such request she had received. She wrote: "And autographs are more than usually tormenting especially when I have made what the world would think some sacrifice in the hope that everybody would let my writing pass without caring a fly about it and that no one would want either my autograph or what is some degrees worse my photograph. How can I have an autograph when I have never committed my name to the public? And then instead of scribbling faster than speech one must ... write ones' copy well!!"

In response to the request for a letter with Agnes's autograph, Eliza's reply managed to protect Agnes from another chore, at the same time as giving Mrs May what she wanted, by her own efforts rather than Agnes's. Eliza wrote: "My sister is at present much teased with negotiations respecting a new stereotype edition of the Queens of England ... We must not ask her for the letter you want ... I have done what I can clipped some beginnings and endings from her almost daily letters to me which are by mutual agreement all destroyed when the memorandums they contain are acted upon. But the correspondence though often delightful is not for the world's pen – As for the little dull notes she never writes them to me at least I would think her gone delirit(?) if she did." Presumably the mystery word is "delirious" or something similar.

The remoteness of Eliza's home was another reason for her reluctance to exchange letters. She wrote: "Among my difficulties of correspondence I am here" – at 'Abbott's Lodge' in Tilford – "nearly two miles from the Post Office and have no letters three days in the week. I never stay in London only passing through to visit my mother in Reydon Hall if she is ill. I am just returned."

24th May 1864: Catharine's son William joins the Hudson's Bay Company

Having seen the health and employment difficulties that her older sons suffered as a result of the hardships of their early life, Catharine hoped her younger sons would fare better. She had a contact in the Hudson's Bay Company, through a cousin of Thomas Traill who was married to a senior employee, and Catharine did what she could to help William get a job there.

Either with Catharine's help or by his own efforts, William Traill was offered a job as an apprentice clerk with the Hudson's Bay Company and on 24th May 1864 he left Lakefield, initially for Montreal, to begin his new life. Although his job sounded safe enough when described as an apprentice clerk, it turned out to be the beginning of a dangerous life involving buffalo hunts, winter travel across the prairie to outlying posts, and occasional meetings with disgruntled traders and local communities.

11th June 1864: The teachers of Ulverston show their appreciation

The teachers of Ulverston who had been treated to a day out by Richard showed their appreciation a few weeks later. The papers noted on 11th June 1864: "The Rev Canon and Mrs Gwillym have been presented with a handsome epergne" – an elaborate centre piece for the dining table, often made of glass but sometimes made of metal – "from the teachers of the Town Bank Sunday-school, Ulverstone."

1864: Catharine is given false hope

As well as writing articles for magazines, Catharine was trying to get her book on Canadian plant life published in Canada, having accepted that she would not find a publisher in England.

In 1864, Adam Brown, a prominent businessman and president of the Hamilton Horticultural Society showed interest, and Catharine sent him her manuscript. However, it made no further progress, and Mr Brown kept the manuscript for a long time, without getting a decision from the society about its publication, and without replying to Catharine's letters about it.

August 1864: Jane is very ill and calls Agnes back to Reydon Hall

Agnes made a shorter stay in London than usual in 1864 and had gone to stay at Losely Park, near Guildford, when she received a letter from Jane reporting her own illness and calling Agnes home.

Agnes, not realising just how ill Jane was, wrote back to her and said: "I grieve to hear how much your dutiful attention to our aged mother has affected your health. You have indeed little to cheer you but the conviction that you are doing your duty nobly and will not lose your heavenly reward." To more practical purpose, Agnes cut short her visit and returned to Reydon Hall.

Still not realising quite how serious the situation was, Agnes stopped at Ipswich on her way home to keep a stall at a fund-raising bazaar for, in the blunt description of the time, and using Jane's words in her biography of Agnes: "the idiot Asylum of Ipswich, to which she had for some years been a subscriber."

Jane, when she wrote to Catharine on 10th September 1864, told of her own ill health and its effects on Mrs Strickland: "I was given over, my long sickness since December having reached its climax – Bronchitis the chronic kind, asthma and inflammation of the coats of the stomach and nerves lying under the chest.

"At that time the poor thing suddenly looked at me and became aware of my danger, and was in an agony at the idea of losing her steward and housekeeper. I know not how her faculties suddenly returned only to make her sensible of the misfortune apparently awaiting her. As soon as I was confined to my bed, she took to hers. I was willing to go but God spared her that pain, and if I get through the winter I may go on, but my breath of a night is getting noisy again."

24th August 1864: Richard is in trouble

In August 1864 work was beginning on St Mary's Church, but there was less than whole-hearted agreement with the plans, and every move was being watched critically. An article in the local paper reported: "Ulverston – Alteration at the Parish Church. Authority has been granted to Rev Richard Gwillym and" (7 named) "churchwardens and" (6 named) "committee of parishioners to make certain alterations.

"It is alleged by Henry Askew, Esq., and James Rawlinson, that the before-named, wilfully and unlawfully, and in excess of powers given, have broken the soil of the church yard to a greater extent than necessary, have disturbed certain graves and exhumed remains contrary to the law ecclesiastical. The matter was fully gone into at the Carlisle Consistory Court on Wednesday 24th August 1864. Judgement was deferred to the next court day – 21st September 1864."

Despite this hiccup and while awaiting judgement on the allegations, work proceeded to the point where it was time to arrange a ceremony for the laying of a foundation stone. The date chosen for the ceremony was Tuesday 13th September 1864.

31st August 1864: Tom sets sail back to England

Tom in command of the 'Julia' arrived at Callao on 10th May 1864 and remained there for three and a half months while the ship was loaded with guano. On 31st August 1864 all was ready and he set sail back to England.

10th September 1864: Mrs Strickland dies

Jane recorded that when Agnes got back to Reydon Hall in August 1864, Jane herself was: "so ill from bronchitis and spasmodic asthma that she was scarcely able to move." As for Mrs Strickland: "an attached old friend was watching over her. She suffered no pain, but increasing debility. She rarely showed any glimpse of consciousness, and had forgotten the faces of her friends. Her daughter Jane was the only unforgotten family link; but she had not quitted her for many years."

The old friend of Mrs Strickland, seeing that Jane's illness was worsening, helpfully told Jane that she would not survive many days. The family doctor was a little more positive: "Dr Girdlestone thought it possible that the sick daughter might recover, but the aged parent must die."

Mrs Strickland, Jane wrote: "lingered a month, but recovered her faculties a few days before her decease. She fell asleep and died without a sigh or a struggle, her daughters Agnes and Jane holding her hands as she passed away" on 10th September 1864.

Jane Strickland in her book 'Life of Agnes Strickland' added a footnote to the account of Mrs Strickland's death. In the footnote Jane wrote: "Are dying people conscious of things we know not? Are the loved and long lost actually present with them? The day before her death Mrs Strickland said to her daughter Jane, 'My dear, I have seen my father. He sat by me on the bed some time, and smiled so sweetly upon me.' 'Did he speak?' 'No my dear. But I was not dreaming, for it was day-light; and I was not afraid, but glad and happy'."

13th September 1864: Sarah has to put on a brave face

The ceremony of laying a foundation stone at Ulverston church having been fixed for Tuesday 13th September 1864, the death of Mrs Strickland on Friday 10th September, put Sarah in a difficult position.

The event went ahead and was described in the local papers: "Ulverston St Mary's Church – On Tuesday 13th September 1864 the ceremony of laying the corner-stone at the north-west angle of the Parish Church took place. The Lady Louisa Cavendish performed the ceremony, and an address was afterwards given by the Venerable Archdeacon Evans.

"The forenoon was wet and uncomfortable, and there were slight showers during the proceedings, relieved, however, by a gleam of sunshine during the remarks made by the Rev Canon Gwillym. There was a large assembly in the church, including the National and Infant scholars; and in the organ gallery, besides Mr Daniel and the choir, were a number of spectators."

"About one o'clock the bells of the church pealed forth, and soon afterwards His Grace the Duke of Devonshire, the Lady Louisa Cavendish and Lady Frederick Cavendish ascended the platform. The Venerable Archdeacon Evans followed, and on that portion of the platform where the ceremony took place were the Rev Canon Gwillym and Mrs Gwillym, the Revs T Townson and N Brady, curates of St Mary's; the Rev John Macaulay, rector of Aldingham; and John Fell, Esq., of Flan Howe, one of the members of the Building Committee." The paper then lists the other spectators on the platform which included five more ministers. There is no mention of the presence of the disapproving Mr Askew of Conishead Priory.

The papers record that: "The foundation stone bore the following inscription: – 'This corner-stone of the new north aisle of the Parish Church of St Mary, was laid by the Lady Louisa Cavendish, to the honour and glory of God, on the 13th September 1864.' Upon the trowel, made of silver by Garrard & Co of Haymarket, London was engraved 'Presented to the Lady Louisa Cavendish, by the Incumbent and the Building Committee, upon the occasion of the restoration of St Mary's Church, Ulverston, September 1864'."

17th September 1864: Mrs Strickland is buried

When Sarah wrote to Catharine on 29th September 1864 she told of the difficult position she had been in when she heard of their mother's death: "My beloved Kate, You will ere this have heard of the death of our dear Mother, most mercifully taken away without any pain or suffering – still you as much as all of us must feel the loss of our dearly loved parent and the breaking of the home of our childhood and though from the last letter from Agnes, I was led to expect that her life was near its close yet when the sad news arrived it seemed quite to overpower me and it came at a time when I was obliged to appear in public and not to bow to the sense of sorrow I was in.

"I received the sad intelligence on the Monday night by the late post" (12th September 1864) "and the next day had been fixed for Lady Louisa Cavendish to lay the corner stone of the new aisle we are adding to our church. Everything had been prepared for the ceremony, most could not be put off as nearly a hundred work people" were involved one way or another.

Sarah's role was more than that of simply being on the platform to watch: "Lady Louisa, the Duke of Devonshire and Lady Frederic Cavendish" were among those who "were to lunch with us after the ceremony and a larger party" was there "to meet them" before it was time "to go to the church in our carriage. I kept my grief to myself and no one in our home knew the sad news.

"Everything went off well, our noble guests, most friendly – but I was glad when it was all over and I could have a few quiet minutes. We started off for Reydon the next day and got to London at 10" and stayed over night "at the Euston, and got to Reydon at 9 o'clock on the Friday. Dear Eliza was there most kindly – dear Agnes and Jane and Walter Strickland. It was a melancholy meeting. Poor Jane looks dreadfully ill with a bad cough and great difficulty of breathing. Agnes quite worn out and upset poor dear."

The funeral was held on Saturday 17th September 1864, the day after Sarah and Richard had arrived. Sarah told Catharine: "Eliza, Agnes, Jane and I followed the hearse in a mourning coach, Richard and Walter in Agnes's carriage. Rev Edghill and Rev Crowfoot in Rev Edghill's carriage" then "Dr Girdleston and all the servants in Miss Sheriffe's carriage. All the cottages had their shutters closed out of respect. On the Sunday we all went to church and Rev Crowfoot, our vicar, preached a beautiful funeral sermon which was very gratifying."

The funeral took place at the parish church of St Margaret, Reydon, where Mrs Elizabeth Strickland was buried and where a monument was erected. This is a distinctive 4' square pillar shaped like a pepper pot, to the north east of the church. The inscriptions have been eroded away but it once bore the names of Thomas Strickland who had died aged 60 in 1818, Elizabeth Strickland who died in 1864 aged 91, and their last born child Ellen Strickland, who had died at the age of six months in 1811. Mention of this memorial bearing Ellen's name is the only reference that has been found of her existence.

September 1864: Mrs Strickland's Will is read

Mrs Strickland's Will had to bear in mind her husband's Will of 1818, which had specified that the Reydon property was for his widow to live in, and as a source of income during her lifetime, and that at her death the property was to be sold, and the money shared equally between his eight children.

When Mrs Strickland died her possessions consisted of the one-eighth of the Reydon Hall estate which she had bought from Sam in 1826 when he needed £300 to buy land in Canada, plus one-fourth share in a freehold estate called the Old Bull's Head in Rotherhithe, which she and her three sisters had inherited from her father, plus a leasehold property in St Giles, in Norwich.

The £300 for Sam was obtained by taking out a mortgage on his share of the property with Eliza, Agnes and Jane standing surety for the loan. The leasehold property in St Giles was bought with £350 borrowed from Jane Margaret. The mortgage of £1,400 that existed when Thomas Strickland died was unchanged, Mrs Strickland presumably having managed to pay the annual interest from rental income.

In 1848 she had of necessity to repay the loan, made in 1818 by Richard Morgan, which covered the shortfall between Thomas Strickland's liabilities and his assets when he died. This she had done by borrowing £222 from Eliza and £87.16s.0d from Jane, with a signed agreement that they would in due course be repaid, with interest added at the rate of 4% per annum.

Mrs Strickland specified in her Will that not only Reydon Hall estate should be sold (as per her husband's Will) but that everything she possessed, with no exceptions, should be sold as soon as possible after her death. The money remaining after paying the main debt on Reydon Hall, was to be used to pay her funeral expenses (which she specified were to be keep to a minimum), the costs of executing her Will, the mortgage of £300 taken out in 1826, and the money plus interest owed to Eliza and Jane since 1848. Any money left over was to be divided equally between her eight children. There was no mention of repaying Jane the £350 with which she bought the leasehold property in St Giles and Jane, so it seems, was not repaid.

27th September 1864: Harry Traill marries

Catharine was pleased when, on 27th September 1864 her son Harry Traill, aged 27, married Lilias Maclean. Catharine felt that his marriage gave to Harry's life a purpose that had previously been lacking.

After the loss of 'Oaklands' where Harry Traill had been acting as farm manager, and his recovery from being kicked by a horse, Harry worked for the Strickland lumber business in winter doing odd jobs, and worked as a thresher in late summer. William, writing later of his own delight with his life as an employee of the Hudson's Bay Company, said of his brother Harry: "I wish he had had such a chance before he ruined his strength."

29th September 1864: Sarah puts Catharine in the picture

After she had told Catharine about their mother's funeral, Sarah in her letter of 29th September 1864 went on to discuss Mrs Strickland's Will and its implications. First she reassured Catharine about the executors. She wrote: "Rev Edghill, a most excellent clergyman, the rector of Uggeshall, is joint executor with my dear Richard, and the whole family may be assured that everything that can be done will be performed by them both with great care as to expense and with the utmost conscientiousness."

Sarah than warned Catharine that there would be little in the way of inheritance for each of them: "I fear there will be little after the mortgage is paid off, which amounts to upwards of seventeen hundred pounds, to divide. There are no debts" apart from money lent by Jane, Eliza and Agnes "merely the half yearly bills which the half yearly rent of the farm" would cover "but land sells badly now that high interest is paid for money.

"The house is in good repair thanks to all that dear Agnes has expended on it. The furniture is all old and thoroughly worn out as you may believe, remembering what it was when you married and near thirty years has not improved it as you may well believe. Richard doesn't think it will sell for a hundred pounds and though the beds are good yet no one has large beds now."

Sarah's next comment shows just how poor were the conditions that Agnes lived in when at Reydon Hall, despite her great fame and the beautiful and complicated dresses she wore socially. Sarah wrote: "Of plate there is next to none as it was all stole and broken up when the house was broken into" (this was the burglary that had taken place in February 1836) "and poor mamma could never afford to buy fresh silver – I do assure you it is the more great wonder how they could go on at all with such a small income and so few things to use."

Of the rest of the family, Sarah wrote: "Agnes has helped a great deal and has all her furniture in the room where she writes. I don't know whether my dear brother will come to England or how things will be arranged but nothing can be done till at Reydon they have heard from him – and all the other members of the family – I write to you dear sister instead of to Samuel thinking that perhaps he may be on his way to England – as soon as possible after they hear, the Executors will have to sell the estate according to my father's Will. My brother Thomas was to be in England this week. His ship was telegraphed at Falmouth but Walter did not think he would land as he has to go off to another place directly with his cargo.

"We were obliged to leave Reydon early on Wednesday morning so we were only there from Friday afternoon till Wednesday. My dear Richard was obliged to return home on Church matters. I should have liked to have been another day longer with the dear sisters but I never leave my husband. We got home quite safely and now my dear Richard has lost his first cousin and has gone off to his funeral leaving me to entertain the Rector of Grasmere during his absence, who is staying here. My dear husband and his cousin were very much attached to each other and he is in deep grief at his death.

"I have now told you dearest all that I thought you would feel anxious to hear and now thank you very affectionately for your sweet letter. I am very glad you are better. I was very grieved to hear of my dear brother's suffering so kindly tell him if he is still at home – give our dear love to him and his dear wife and to all the dear relations, and with affectionate love from us both to you, S Gwillym."

28th October 1864: Sarah writes a family news letter to Catharine

When Sarah next wrote to Catharine, on 28th October 1864, she showed that Jane had needed help from Richard at a time when he was already financially stretched by the church renovations. Sarah wrote: "My Darling Kate, I enclose a post office order from my dear husband ... only sorry that he cannot send you a larger sum but restoring his church has taken so large a portion of his income that he cannot do more but he thought it might buy you ... so that you must receive it in the same affectionate manner in which it was sent.

"Our journey into Suffolk cost us more than twenty pounds and he gave dear Jane £5 to buy mourning for she had no funds to fall back upon – her house not having been let during the summer and her other money being tied ... Richard placed £20 in the Bank of Southwold for her to pay current expenses. I don't know what ... have done without it so that you may imagine that he cannot do more dearest further at this time.

"The book that you wished to have dear Kate was carried off by Tom years ago I believe for one time when I was at Reydon I wished to make some artificial flies ... and not being able to find it dear Mamma said she thought she had given it to him." This sounds as though Sarah, unconventionally but in common with Susanna and Catharine had inherited their father's fondness for fishing. The book was probably Izaac Walton's 'Compleat Angler' which is mentioned elsewhere as a particular favourite of their father, and which goes into great detail about fly making.

Sarah's family gossip also gave an insight into other members of the family: "Tom is expected in England any day I believe, but I heard from Jane yesterday and he had not then arrived. His dear son Walter was at Reydon. He came down for his grandmother's funeral. He is a very nice young man, a great favourite with us. He is very handsome, very black eyes and hair, a remarkably handsome nose and white teeth. He is tall and has ... complexion. He only staid till after the funeral. He has a very good ... and will get on well in life I dare say.

"I am so sorry for your dear son James & hope that he may get over the effects of his bad cough poor fellow it is very sad and ... his young family. I fear the cold for him and he does not look as if he ever had much strength at the best of times. I always felt so sorry that he ... not stay longer with us he got so well in the time ... I fear Harry is not much stronger from what you say. I hope your other dear ones are more healthy." Percy Strickland had managed to meet his aunt Sarah while on his honeymoon in England. Sarah wrote: "I liked Percy and his handsome wife very much."

Sarah's own news came next: "This has been such a lovely spring, summer and glorious autumn but the weather has changed now for much rain. We are going to Harrogate next week for November. Richard and I require change and rest, and the baths and drinking the water always sets us up for the winter."

She touched on the prospects for selling Reydon Hall: "I fear that Richard will have to go over to Reydon again during next month or December. It is unfortunate the great distance and the expence for he will not make any charge for his expenses – I fear there will be some trouble selling Reydon. It is such a large inconvenient house no one can really be comfortable there with the rooms opening into each other in short a thoroughfare through them ... the place looks in better order than it has done for years ... Richard has taken a great dislike to the place."

Of their sisters in England: "Agnes has taken a long lease on Jane's house in Southwold and Jane means to live in the small cottage close to Agnes. I was so glad to meet dear Elizabeth it is more than six years since I had seen her ... was so kind and nice, a great comfort to dear Jane and Agnes to bear all the matters of business ... temper got the better of her she only staid at Reydon from Friday afternoon till Wednesday morning." Eliza's fierce temper does not seem to have mellowed with age.

Sarah finished her letter with more of her home news which suffers from bits of illegibility but has valuable hints: "I fear that you will find this a ... letter for the last ten days our home had a houseful of friends ... dinner parties every day and made talking long into the morning as they cannot go out ... carriage and I am so tired that I am longing for ... Harrogate ... my dear husband ... he never for one moment doubted ... I would pledge my life on his doing all that is true and right. I am so sorry that he has been suffering so much with his leg he must ... not increase but perhaps his leg being broke ... where the constitution ... other complaints only great care must be taken not to injure it." No other information has been found about Richard Gwillym having broken his leg.

20th November 1864: John follows Susanna's example

John Moodie in his correspondence and memoirs was inclined to express the same unkind and seemingly unmerited opinions of the Strickland family as Susanna. The most notable example was in a letter he wrote to his daughter Katie Vickers on 20th November 1864, two months after his mother-in-law had died.

Referring to Sam he wrote: "I hear Strickland is gone home to get some plunder I suppose at Reydon. Mrs Gwillym is to give her share of Reydon proceeds to Strickland. I think it would have shown more benevolence to have given it to either of her *Sisters* in Canada who want it *so much more*."

There is no evidence that Sam went to England at this point, although his presence would have been very welcome. Susanna, and therefore John, must have known that Mrs Strickland's Will required everything to be sold and the money divided equally. He should also have been aware that Mrs Strickland had been living in near poverty for decades, and that there was very little in the way of "spoils" to be had. There is no mention or suggestion elsewhere that Sarah gave her share to Sam.

2nd January 1865: Tom reaches England

Sarah was optimistic when she thought Tom would be back in England early in November. Having left Callao on 31st August 1864, it was not until the 2nd January 1865 that he reached England at Falmouth, where news of his mother's death had been sent by telegraph.

He spent a week in Falmouth before setting off on 9th January 1865 on the last leg of his voyage, arriving in Glasgow on 16th January 1865 where he had to see the 'Julia' unloaded before he could think of making his way to Suffolk.

His previous long voyage had him returning home to a diminished family, his wife having been dead for several weeks, and his daughter Mary married and gone to India. From this voyage he returned to the consequences of his mother having been dead for almost four months, and his daughter Diana having married and remained in South America.

However, he still had his son Walter, his daughter Adela Wigg and her family, and four sisters living in England.

21st January 1865: Richard's parishioners plan a memorial window

January 1865 was a memorable as well as a busy month for Richard Gwillym. Having been made an Honorary Canon of the Cathedral of Carlisle in April 1864, it was not until 15th January 1865 he took his place in a formal way as announced in the local paper: "Carlisle – The Rev R Gwillym of Ulverstone will read himself in an honorary canon next Sunday 15th January 1865, but we are told that the Dean has determined not to suspend the musical services."

This implies that 'reading himself in' was not a major event but nor was his new title. If Richard had been appointed to the role of a Canon, rather than an Honorary Canon, he and Sarah would have had to live in the precinct of Carlisle Cathedral, he would have shared responsibility for the cathedral and it would have been a paid position. By contrast, the title of Honorary Canon was merely a mark of appreciation which made no practical change to Richard and Sarah's lives.

However, the people of Ulverston decided it was time to honour Richard's work in his parish in a more tangible way. The local papers reported: "Ulverston Memorial to the Rev Canon Gwillym – On the afternoon of Saturday 21st January 1865, a public meeting was held in the Infant School, Ulverston, to appoint a committee to carry out a suggestion made that a memorial be placed in the Parish Church, to mark the indefatigable exertions of the Rev Canon Gwillym, in promoting the restoration of the Parish Church.

"The chair HW Schneider, Esq., of Lightburne House stated it had been suggested a memorial window would form a beautiful ornament, an ever present testimonial of the sincere and affectionate esteem in which Mr Gwillym was held. The resolution was passed 'That in recognition of the Rev Canon Gwillym's service, in the parish of Ulverston, during the long period of 30 years, a stained glass window be placed in the Parish Church, as a mark of the esteem in which he is held by his parishioners.' The cost including the stone work would be about £100. Subscriptions were solicited and about £80 was subscribed."

22nd February 1865: Susanna's daughter Agnes Fitzgibbon becomes a widow

Susanna's second daughter, Agnes Fitzgibbon became a widow when her husband died suddenly on 22nd February 1865. She had been married for fifteen years to Charles Fitzgibbon, a barrister with political prominence and legal abilities, but whose financial position was as precarious as his health.

When her husband died, Agnes Fitzgibbon was only 31 years old. She had given birth to eight children but two of her daughters had died when only a few months old. She was left with six children to support and her own health was not good. Two of her sons, aged 6 and 4 died over the next two years leaving three daughters and one son.

14th March 1865: Reydon Hall is sold by auction

With Tom back in England in January 1865, the necessary paperwork and preliminaries could be completed, and the process of selling Reydon Hall and its contents began. Advertisements announcing the sale of Reydon Hall appeared in newspapers during February 1865 and they stated: "Suffolk – The Reydon Hall Estate, comprising 74 acres of fertile land and ancient residence, for many years occupied by the late Mrs Strickland, and eligible alike for occupation or investment. Messrs Debenham, Tewson and Farmer are instructed by the Trustees to sell by Auction, at the Guildhall Coffee-house in the city of London, on Tuesday March 14th 1865 at one o'clock precisely.

"The capital freehold and copyhold estate, comprising an interesting and moderate-sized residence of the Elizabethan period, surrounded by well timbered ornamental grounds and very rich and fertile arable and pasture land, in all about 74 acres, 48 acres being arable, of fine mixed soil, well adapted for growing barley and roots, and for sheep, the residue being pasture and meadow, capable of carrying a considerable quantity of stock.

"The property is situated in the parish of Reydon, adjoining the Estate of Lord Stradbroke, Ewin, Barns Barn and John Norris, Esq., about two miles from Southwold and the sea coast, and about eight miles from the town and railway station of Halesworth. Possession of the residence and gardens can be had on completion of the purchase, and of the farm at Michaelmas next, if wished, or the present respectable tenant would probably remain. Particulars and plan may now be had ..."

Sarah wrote to Catharine on 29th March 1865 to tell of the sale: "Dearest Catharine, You will have heard that poor old Reydon is sold to a Mr Wilmeas of Brighton for three thousand eight hundred and fifty pounds, just three hundred and fifty more than our Father paid for it when it was a far nicer place than it is now with good house and a dear old garden.

"Richard and I think it is a very good price for it ... it was all that could be got for it. My dear Richard went up for the Sale at great expense to himself for he does everything for the family at his own expense & he ... no more could be got for the property – I fear when the mortgage is paid and all other expenses that a very small sum will have to be divided. The auction of the furniture will take place in April"

March 1865: Agnes and Jane move to Southwold

While waiting for the sale of Reydon Hall, Agnes took a 99-year building-lease on Jane's house 'Park Lane Cottage' in Southwold at an annual rent of £20, while Jane seems to have purchased the neighbouring, and possibly adjoining smaller cottage.

Over the winter of 1864/1865 they made any necessary changes and improvements to their future homes, and moved into them at the end of March 1865 after Reydon Hall had been sold.

29th March 1865: Sarah gives Catharine a telling off

While Richard Gwillym was busy and harassed both with his church restoration and with sorting out his mother-in-law's affairs, Catharine took it into her head to send him a manuscript, though why, and what she thought he could do with it, goodness knows.

Sarah, in her letter dated 29th March 1865, after news about the selling of Reydon Hall, plus news of Agnes and Jane, became the third of the sisters in England to give Catharine a telling-off because of her actions with regard to publishers or manuscripts. Eliza and Agnes had been annoyed by Catharine in 1855 and ten years later Sarah was feeling much the same.

Sarah wrote: "And now dear Kate I must not close this note without saying that I have been much vexed and annoyed that you should have taken such a strange step as to send your MS to my husband who can know nothing about the disposal of such things. If you had in the first place written as you ought to have done to me about it I should have told you at once that he could do nothing but to say the least it was ill advised just at a time when he is harassed to death with Reydon affairs – and he knows nothing about publishers and can do nothing. He is vexed and I am truly mortified that such a liberty should have been taken with him.

"Agnes says he can do nothing with it. The editors of that magazine owe her £40 which she cannot get from them so she will not write any more for them – If there is any one you wish me to send the MS to I will do it but you will have to write to whoever you wish to have it sent for neither Richard nor I ... have anything to do or I will send it back to you."

The final legible, or partially legible section of this letter touches on their Mother's family where hopes of restitution for the financial problems caused to their father existed in small measure but diminished as the years went by. Sarah wrote: "Old aunt Sally is dead a few weeks back. She has left all her money the ... and Homers and the Estate to our Mother and ... to know whether will be the same when she dies ... I fear so we must reckon anything in that quarter ..."

12th April 1865: The contents of Reydon Hall are sold

Reydon Hall having been sold by auction in London in March 1865, the contents were all sold on site a month later. The newspapers gave a full list of the contents which, apart from the books in the library, were indeed modest given the number of rooms in the house. "Sale of Household Furniture, Plate and Plated Goods, Linen, China, Glass &c; also a valuable Library of upwards of 500 volumes of books, at Reydon Hall near Southwold, Suffolk. George P Freeman has received instructions from the Executors of the late Mrs Strickland to submit to public competition, without reserve, on Wednesday next, 12th April 1865.

"The furniture in the dining room and drawing rooms; comprising mahogany, centre and occasional card, and other tables, pair of pier tables, inlaid with Indian rosewood, carved mahogany-framed chairs in horse-hair, and American cloth covers; walnut-tree chairs with figured Utrecht velvet covers; sofas in Utrecht velvet and horse-hair covers; walnut-tree cheffioneer with marble top, drugget and Kidderminster carpets, easy chair in leather cover; mahogany sideboard, scarlet and crimson moreen window curtains, and cornices with poles and rings, &c. In the Hall – Mahogany table, chairs, floor-cloth, &c.

"Study – Ancient carved oak Elizabethan cabinet, curiously inlaid in rich yellow marqueterie, original date inlaid 1603; ancient carved oak portiere; ancient carved oak chest with bookcase, ancient carved oak sideboard, inlaid with bone and ebony; ancient carved oak cabinet, looking glasses in gilt frames, with gold burnt in glass; six and two elbow antique dark mahogany chairs; inlaid antique screen in gilded American cover, with four divisions; bronze dial, Dutch carpet, dining table, &c. Library contains upwards of 500 volumes of books.

"Bedrooms – Mahogany four-post tent, Alcori and other bedsteads, with rich antique embroidery and other furniture; excellent goose feather beds, wool and hair mattresses, antique carved, oak-framed, and swing looking-glasses; mahogany and painted chest of drawers, dressing tables, washing stands, toilet sets, mahogany, cane-seated and other chairs; invalid's chair, Japan linen chest, Kidderminster and Brussels carpets, and other useful items.

"Linen – Calico, hemp, and linen sheets; pillow cases, Scotch, damask, and other table cloths; dinner napkins, towels &c. Plate and Plated Goods – Silver dinner, dessert, tea and salt spoons; silver gravy ladles, silver soup ladles, silver skewer, silver cream jug, labels for spirit bottles; plated teapot, sugar bason, cake plate, butter knife, forks, spoons, sugar tongs, nutcracks and candlesticks. The Glass – consists of cut tumblers, wine glasses, good flint finger glasses, ice plates, decanters, custard and jelly glasses, &c. Kitchen & Offices – Nankeen Indian China dinner and tea services, eight-day clock in wainscot case, tables, dresser, chairs, japanned trays and mahogany voiders, and a large assortment of useful lots in each department.

"The furniture may be viewed on the morning of the sale, from 9 until 11 o'clock, at which hour the sale will commence punctually, in consequence of the great number of lots (477). Catalogues containing descriptive particulars can be obtained upon the premises, and on application ..."

Sarah in her March 1865 letter to Catharine wrote of the forthcoming sale: "The auction of the furniture will take place in April but everything is so old and shabby as you well remember and thirty years wear and tear since has not improved its appearance and there seems nothing to make use of hardly but poor Mamma's income was so small that they made shift with anything. When Richard and I used to go to see her we" stayed "at Southwold."

Agnes and Jane had been left in charge of the auction and Richard was again being thoughtful and generous. Sarah told Catharine: "Jane has been most seriously ill. I pity poor Agnes with all the worry of moving, and only she and Jane to arrange about the auction. They move this week to their new home at Southwold where if they can live, they will be far happier than at damp desolate Reydon – Richard has directed that some of the china shall be bought in for you, Samuel and Susan at the auction at his own expense, but things are so broken that I hardly know what to bid upon."

After the Reydon property and its contents had been sold, after all mortgages and debts had been repaid, and after other expenses had been taken into account, there was said to be a little over £200 for each of the eight siblings. This sounds rather higher than would be expected and possibly the £200 sent to Catharine was more than a fair share and had been added to by other members of the family. On the advice of her son James, Catharine invested £125 in mortgages in the Belleville area, to gain for herself a small annual income, with the remainder to be used for day to day living expenses.

Christ Church, Lakefield, Ontario 1925

Richard Gwillym circa 1860

Agnes Strickland by Wheeler & Day, Oxford circa 1865
© National Portrait Gallery, London

Catharine Parr Traill 1884

'Westove', Lakefield, Ontario

Canadian commemorative postage stamp 2003

Part 6: From eight to seven

Sam goes first; two more widows; Sarah moves to Haverthwaite; Susanna becomes unsettled; a murder; trans-Atlantic visits continue

25th April 1865: Susanna is offered help via the Royal Literary Fund

By early March 1865 Susanna had given up any hopes that John Moodie would be given a new government position. She sent a manuscript to Richard Bentley entitled 'The Race for Royalty and who won'. She told him that she had written it many years beforehand and added "My sisters Agnes and Elizabeth used to say it was the best thing I ever wrote. It has lain by me for many a long year. I should be glad to sell the MS out and out for whatever sum you deem it to be honestly worth."

On 25th April 1865 Susanna replied to a letter from Richard Bentley and began with effusions of gratitude. His letter was not about the manuscript she had sent him, but had contained an offer to apply on Susanna's behalf to the Royal Literary Fund, of which he had been a director for some years, and which had been set up to help impoverished or ailing authors.

Susanna wrote: "God bless you for your goodness, and reward you an hundredfold. I never imagined that any writings of mine could deserve assistance from the Government, or from any literary society." She then referred with pride to her own past fame: "One of the Canadian Government's public men, Dr Rolph used to say, that Mrs Moodie deserved a pension for the good that her patriotic songs did, during the rebellion of '37. I hold perhaps the first place among the female authors residing within the Colony. But this has not made them more ready to give my dear husband a small place under the government, to keep us from the Author's fate – A dry crust and the garret. My husband is now in Toronto to mortgage the few acres we possess to settle the law costs."

Susanna pleaded helplessness: "When he returns, we will fill in the literary fund schedule, and return it to you with the necessary documents. I am a babe in such matters. I leave it entirely to you, the memorial to the government. I am sure it will be done so much better, than I could do it." Her preference was for a pension rather than a lump sum payment from the fund. "An annual pension, however small, would be a great mercy, if it only enabled us to pay the interest (of 10 per cent) on these horrid mortgages. We are living on the few small debts that Mr Moodie now and then gets paid, for work done while in the office. Would you believe it? Lawyers, whose dues to us embraced hundreds of pounds have pleaded the 'statute of limitations' and thus escaped paying their just dues."

Susanna ended her letter by concluding: "I think I can safely say, that I never wrote anything, but in the hope of its doing some good. But I believe that I do not deserve half the credit for talent that the world, especially the American world, has bestowed upon me. The Canadians will never forgive me for disclosing secrets of that rural prison-house the Bush. I have no doubt they consider our present distress a just punishment for telling the truth."

The papers submitted to the Royal Literary Fund are in the British Library and reveal two things of relevance to Susanna's life. One item is a report from a court source which shows a weakness in John Moodie's claim to be innocent of any error apart from a missing phrase in a contract. The report stated (with two illegible words guessed and typed in brackets): "The complaint was sustained upon (evidence) that Mr Moodie had agreed to receive £300 per annum from the deputy, (who) was to have the fees accruing excepting certain specified fees which were reserved. The sum thus fixed to be paid to Mr Moodie was based upon the idea that it would be the Sheriff's half of the fees – but the contract contained no clause to shew this fact, and although such a bargain would have been perfectly legal, and is that usually made between the sheriff and their deputies, yet the sum to be paid to Mr Moodie was not contingent upon the amount received by the deputy, but a fixed sum (£300), the Court held that Mr Moodie contravened the statute and forfeited his office." This was followed by a comment that he had held the office long enough to be aware of the rules.

If the deputy was to pay £300 per annum, it implies that the post of Sheriff yielded to John Moodie something in excess of £600, substantially more than he and Susanna claimed.

The other revelation is also interesting, though perhaps less so. It was that Susanna's widowed daughter Agnes Fitzgibbon had an income of £80 per annum and so was not, as Susanna tended to claim, destitute. This ties in with a comment in a letter which Catharine is said to have written on 2nd March 1865 after she had visited Agnes Fitzgibbon in Toronto. Catharine felt that Agnes Fitzgibbon: "will not be badly off. She will have enough to live on with comfort if careful."

May 1865: Richard has to take complete rest

Sarah's most important news when she wrote to Catharine in July 1865 was about her husband Richard, whose health seems to have been broken by the accumulated strain of the burdens he was bearing. Sarah wrote: "I have been suffering the greatest possible anxiety about my beloved husband. His health quite failed him during Lent and his illness proceeds from heart complaint. After Easter we went to stay with our dear friend ... Crompton who after thorough examination confirmed what our surgeon had ... to rest at once ordered him ... from duty for May and to take entire rest but he would not allow us to leave England while he was in such a weak state."

The last two sections of Sarah's letter contain many words that are not easy to decipher, but the ones that can be read give an indication of the variety there was in Sarah's life at that time. Having been told to rest but not to go abroad, Richard and Sarah went to stay in nearby Paterdale: "for a month taking the carriage and horses with us ... with his wife and their darling children carried us there so we make a nice family party. The weather was most lovely only too hot ... the banks of the lake ... plenty of ... I think the rest did him good. After that we went to stay with Miss Gwillym at ...We often went to town and my dear Agnes came to town so we had the pleasure of seeing her. She is looking better than when we saw her at Reydon last autumn but she still has a bad cough but she writes me word that she is better now."

June 1865: Agnes is cheered at Oxford University

In 1865 Agnes took a short break from writing, and from Southwold, to attend the Commemoration at Oxford University where, to her amusement, she was recognised and cheered by the students. She told Sarah: "I enjoyed the Oxford Commemoration very much. I had a ticket for the inner semicircle, a place of honour. I breakfasted at Oriel with Rev Mr Burgon and a select party, and he escorted me to the theatre. Some of the undergraduates, whom I had met at Worcester and Merton Colleges, recognised me and named me to their compatriots, and the moment I entered I was greeted with the cry 'The Queens! The Queens! Three cheers for the Queens' with vociferous shouts following."

Many of the undergraduates wanted a photograph of her so she had a new 'likeness' taken while she was in Oxford. The National Portrait Gallery has 3 cartes de visite showing Agnes Strickland dated at about this time. In all of them she looks rather grim and not at all like previous pictures of her.

July 1865: Agnes Fitzgibbon starts working with Catharine

Susanna's daughter, Agnes Fitzgibbon had a talent for painting flowers and other still life subjects, and was determined to be active and financially productive in her widowhood. Catharine's interest in botany had developed over the years into a serious, almost academic level of knowledge, but her book on the subject of Canadian flora had made no progress towards publication. Agnes Fitzgibbon decided to take the initiative and to get the work published.

Susanna Moodie when she wrote to Richard Bentley in July 1865 told him of Catharine: "My sister Traill lives in a neat cottage, on the banks of the river Otonabee devoting herself to her favourite pursuit of botany. She has written a very interesting work on the wild plants of Canada, which my poor widowed Agnes, who paints flowers delightfully, is illustrating."

10th July 1865: Susanna sends thanks to the Royal Literary Fund

On 10th July 1865, Susanna sent to Richard Bentley a letter of thanks, to be forwarded to the Royal Literary Fund, for the £60 which had been sent to her through his kind efforts. The grant had been made very quickly after her completed application form had reached England.

13th July 1865: Sarah brings Catharine up to date

Sarah wrote to Catharine on 13th July 1865 and began by dealing with financial matters: "My beloved Catharine, I am truly sorry that I have such a small sum to send to you but the Canada Company after giving no dividend last winter only gave fifteen shillings per share this July and as I have but three shares the sum is small indeed but my kind husband has given me these cheques to add to it so that it brings it up to £5.5s ... part of it is for his godson Richard Strickland if you would kindly give it to him with his godfather's kind love."

They all had to sign papers before the sale of the Reydon estate could be completed: "I hope that the Deeds of Reydon Estate have arrived quite safe and that you will ... and that they will shortly arrive in England that no further delay may arise. It is very sad ... the small sum to divide but it is exactly what ... therefore with only the Reydon Property to divide amongst so many with a heavy mortgage and Jane to pay out of it. I hope it will all be settled – and then no more anxiety about it."

Catharine's manuscript was still in England and, as in 1855, once the dust had settled it was Agnes who did what she could to help Catharine. Sarah wrote: "My dear sister Agnes has kindly taken the MSs that you sent and is trying to get it into a Mag for you ... I hope some good may result from them."

Sarah then told Catharine about Richard's poor health, and the rest they had been taking since May. They had returned to Ulverston where life was again busy. Sarah said: "We were obliged to come home to receive her Majesty's Inspector of Schools and he is here still. I have been the whole morning with him in the Infant School of which he made a charming report, and we have had a deputation for the Lord ... staying with us ... the central African expedition with Bishop ... a most able and interesting man.

"Today there is a great bustle in the town with the election. My husband's old friend Colonel Wilson Poth ... has just been here and my husband has driven him down to ... he and the Marquis of Hartington are returned I am glad to say but there is a great ... of bells ringing and shouting. I don't know how our spirited horses will get through the crowd and noise." The Marquis of Hartington was a prominent Liberal politician who would succeed his father as Duke of Devonshire in 1891.

Sarah concluded her letter with reiterating how worried she was about Richard: "We are going to stay with Dr and Mrs Crompton upon the 25th of this month when I hope that he will say that my beloved husband is better. No words can say how anxious I was and have been. I never leave him, he is so good and kind."

26th July 1865: Jane attends a Grand Fete

Relieved from the responsibility of caring for her aged mother, and running Reydon Hall, Jane's health gradually recovered. On 26th July 1865 she was able to attend a major local social event. The local papers reported: "Grand Fete at Henham Park – One of the grandest local Fetes which it has been our lot to record took place at Henham Park, the seat of the Earl of Stradbroke, the Lord Lieutenant of Suffolk. It was in celebration of the christening of son and heir, Viscount Dunwich was of a princely character and passed off with a success commensurate with its magnificence. The gathering was quite irrespective of class, creed or party. His Lordship and the Countess having ordered invitations to be thickly scattered over a radius of 12 miles. The guests included the whole of the Suffolk Volunteers.

"Henham Park is in an out-of-the-way locality. It is about 7 miles from Ditcham station and not quite as far from Halesworth. It contains 800 acres ... company began to arrive as early as 9 o'clock. Refreshment booths had been erected, travelling round-a-bouts, swinging boats and all the paraphernalia of country fairs.

"A principal feature was the Volunteer review. Special trains carried the volunteers to Darsham and Halesworth. For their conveyance to the grounds an innumerable number of waggons had to be provided. The tenantry cheerfully provided them and their best horses. To see many hundreds of riflemen in waggons was a sight for the villagers, who declared they had 'ne'er seen the like on that afore'.

"The Luncheon took place in two monster marquees, some 2,500 invitations were issued and the guests were entertained in a style of princely magnificence. A roll on each plate was stuck with a tiny flag staff, the flag being dark blue, bearing a coronet in gold. The following is a list of those who accepted invitations." The lengthy list included "Miss Jane Strickland."

July 1865: Agnes finishes a novel

Many years earlier, Agnes had written a novel with the title: 'Althea Woodville' which was set in Lancashire and the country around Calgarth Hall near Windermere. While Agnes was visiting Sarah and Richard Gwillym in Ulverston, she had visited the places named in her novel, and so was able to correct and expand on her earlier descriptions of the area.

While settling into her new home in Southwold, Agnes finished this novel, a light-hearted and fast-moving mystery romance, set in the time of the English Civil War. It is not surprising to find, with Agnes's historical opinions, that the characters who were on the side of the Cavaliers were mostly depicted as attractive heroes or heroines, while those on the Roundhead side tended to be villainous both in appearance and in personality.

Richard Bentley renamed the story 'How Will it End?' and his firm published it in three volumes in 1865. By Jane's account, Richard Bentley paid Agnes £250 on the day it was published having "secured many orders from a curious public."

10th July 1865: Susanna describes Lakefield past and present

In 1865, Susanna and John Moodie spent a fortnight in Lakefield, which Susanna said was the first time she had been back since they moved to Belleville at the beginning of 1840. Susanna told Richard Bentley in a letter dated 10th July 1865 that in 1840: "only three houses all composed of logs and of the smallest dimensions were to be found within three miles of us. Now my brother, who may be termed the father and founder of the village of Lakefield, has a handsome commodious house and a beautiful garden, which would amply satisfy the taste of any gentleman of moderate fortune, four of his five lads are married and settled near him. A neat village of pretty, well-built houses has sprung up."

Based on the family trees given by the academics who transcribed and printed selections of Susanna and Catharine's letters, Sam had seven surviving sons. Their names were Robert, George, Henry, Percy, Walter, Roland and Richard. Either the transcription of Susanna's letter is in error, or Susanna for some reason miscounted Sam's sons. Sam's three surviving daughters had all married and became Maria Tully, Emma Barlee and Jane Blomfield.

Susanna continued her description of Lakefield: "The place already has four churches, and they are busy building a very handsome new church. The old one raised 12 years ago, is not half large enough to contain its worshippers. My brother's son, Walter Strickland, is the architect, a young man of much taste and talent." The new church, designed by Walter Reginald Strickland would be named St John the Baptist Church and was completed by October 1866. It was built just across the road from the earlier church of 1854.

Susanna told Richard Bentley that she had enjoyed her fortnight's visit to the place where she had once lived, but there was no trace of her former homestead. She did not mention Sam's state of health but said: "My brother talks of visiting England some time next month" and so he would be able to act as a courier if Richard Bentley thought there might be a market for Catharine's botanical book in England.

<u>July 1865: Agnes and Eliza visit the Tower of London</u>

After finishing the relatively light task of re-working her novel 'How will it End?' Agnes got on with finishing her part of the 'Lives of the Seven Bishops'. Since all these bishops had spent time in the

Tower of London, Agnes and Eliza felt that it was a good time to examine the place closely.

Lieutenant-Colonel Whimper was in charge of the Tower and lived there, and Agnes obtained permission for herself and Eliza to visit it. They particularly wanted to see, as Jane wrote: "the antiquities of the Lieutenant's residence at the Tower, the Wakefield and Portcullis or Bloody Tower." They made their inspection of the Tower of London and all its relevant nooks and crannies with the help of the wife of Lieutenant-Colonel Whimper, while they were both together quietly in London in the summer of 1865.

Also in 1865 Eliza and Agnes were working on an edition of 'Lives of the Queens of England' which was to be published by Longmans. Jane wrote that Agnes (presumably in common with Eliza): "was continually adding fresh matter whenever she discovered any fact or anecdote that would give more interest to her work."

In the summer of 1865 Agnes saw a great deal of Bishop Tait at Fulham Palace, and through him met Emma, ex-Queen of Hawai'i. Agnes subsequently sent the ex-queen a copy of the 'Lives of the Queens of England' and in return received a very gracious letter of thanks. It was dated 31st July 1865 and Queen Emma wrote: "To say that I have always admired and taken pleasure in your work, is only to express a feeling in common with everybody else. But these volumes coming direct from the authoress, you may be assured I shall always preserve with especial care."

Autumn 1865: Sam visits England for the last time

When Sam and his wife Katharine visited England in the autumn of 1865 they hoped he might find a doctor in London who could treat his diabetes, but the illness was too long-established and knowledge of treatment was too limited to be of any use. They remained in England until the spring of 1866

Catharine in her memoirs said that Sam and Tom only met once after they left home as teenagers, and it must have been a rather sad meeting during Sam's final visit to England, for it was the only time that Sam and Tom were both in England at the same time.

December 1865: Agnes Fitzgibbon is making good progress

By the end of 1865 Agnes Fitzgibbon was well on her way with designing all the flower drawings to be used in conjunction with her Aunt Catharine's work. She was also teaching herself lithography, believing this to be the only way in which she could ensure the high quality pictures that were needed.

She had already found a printer for the book and was undertaking the necessary business arrangements. The printer was John Lovell, the former publisher of the 'Literary Garland' to which her mother, Susanna, had been a regular contributor.

December 1865: Agnes entertains at Christmas

Agnes was enjoying having a home of her own and was beginning to think of having guests to stay. At Christmas 1865 she did some charitable entertainment as she told Richard Gwillym in a letter thanking him for his Christmas gifts "of wines and other good things." Agnes wrote: "I followed, dear Richard, your good example in asking some persons to partake of my roast-beef and plum-pudding who could not requite me, and made them very happy" and in a letter to Sarah, Agnes said she hoped Sarah "and Richard will come to me next summer, as I am getting my guest chamber nicely fitted for you."

December 1865: Susanna and John give away their home

In a letter Susanna wrote to Catharine, probably written in December 1865, Susanna was optimistic about the future of her second son Donald. She had sent him $40 so that he could travel from Toronto to New York where he had been offered a job as a Check Clerk to the Inman Steam Company.

Susanna told Catharine that the job was to be well paid: "He has $800 a year and his board, worth $500 more – and excellent fare – on board the great steamers. He checks all the parcels with the custom house officers." Donald settled in well and Susanna admitted to Catharine that this was: "a bright gleam on my dark cloud, for my anxiety about Donald was killing me."

With Donald seemingly on a better path in life, Susanna's eldest son, Dunbar, gave rise to family conflict. Having followed the gold rush to California and Nevada in the 1850s, Dunbar had returned home in 1862 at the age of 28. He subsequently married Eliza Roberts who, with her sister Julia, had lived as boarders with Susanna and John since 1860. Dunbar and Eliza set up home near Susanna in Belleville, and by 1865 they had two children.

All was going well until Susanna and John decided to make their stone cottage in Sinclair Street over to the young couple, in exchange for an understanding that Dunbar and Eliza would provide a home for John and Susanna for the rest of their lives, possibly in addition to a sum of money well below what the property was worth. Although described as a cottage, a photograph of it shows it to have been a detached house and, by modern English standards, a substantial size.

John and Susanna's son-in-law, John Vickers thought his father-in-law was acting very unwisely. He may also have been irritated because he had given financial help towards the cost of the house in the past. His annoyance was such that he refused to give any further help, and there was no contact between Katie Vickers and Susanna for several years.

After the property had been made over to Dunbar, Susanna began to resent the behaviour of Eliza Moodie, and it was not long before Susanna considered it impossible to live in the same house as her daughter-in-law. Dunbar and Eliza decided to sell the house and buy a farm in Delaware where their third child was born in 1866. They invited John and Susanna to go with them, but Susanna could not face the prospect of living with Eliza, or of emigrating again at the age of 63.

Donald Moodie was also put out by the way his parents had disposed of the family home. He added to Susanna's anguish by marrying Eliza's sister, Julia Russell in New York in February 1866 without telling his parents in advance.

1866: Another fire leads to a new 'Oaklands' on Rice Lake Plains

Early in 1866 fire destroyed much of Annie and Clinton Atwood's farmhouse in Rice Lake Plains which was near to where Catharine and Thomas Traill had lived at 'Oaklands'.

The Clintons had some insurance but not enough. However, they managed to carry on living and farming in the area and when their new home was complete, they named it 'Oaklands' in memory of Catharine's former home.

21st February 1866: Susanna has a nerve

Susanna was seriously ill during January and February 1866 with a combination of typhoid fever and inflammation of her stomach, liver and kidneys. By the end of February 1866 Susanna and John were facing the prospect of living in Belleville with no income and no home.

When Susanna wrote to Richard Bentley on 21st February 1866, she described her situation to him with characteristic lack of restraint, saying: "I never did like the idea of turning Yankee in my old age, or of living a miserable dependent, I might truly say, a servant of all work, to my son's West Indian wife. A selfish, cold hearted arrogant Quadroon, a woman of little intellect, and who despises it in others. Since Mr Moodie, gave up his little property to his son, in the hope of securing a home for us, in our old age; her conduct has been so cruel, that you would imagine we were beggars depending on her bounty, instead of the obligation being all the other way."

Susanna not only explained her situation to Richard Bentley in dramatic terms but went on: "I am now about to ask of you a very great favour. With this letter, you will receive, a small MS. It is a work for the juveniles, and I want you, to give it your powerful recommendation to some of the publishers in that line. I can hardly ask you to read such a trifling performance ... perhaps Mr Nelson might be induced to buy it. I do not expect more than 25 pounds for the copyright, and would take less, for I have a heavy Doctors bill to pay, and no funds to meet it.

"I see by the papers, that the 'Temple Bar Magazine' has passed into your hands. Could you give me any employment in that quarter?" She added: "You see what a bold beggar I have become."

Most of the manuscripts which Susanna had sent to Richard Bentley over the years, were mainly re-workings of old stories rather than anything fresh, and there is no record of Susanna having asked

Agnes, Eliza or Jane for any help in disposing of her work in England. However, on this occasion Susanna asked a man of substantial reputation as a London publisher and who had retired from business, to tout her "small MS" round lesser publishers before, as she put it herself, becoming a "bold beggar" by asking him for work on a magazine owned by his family firm. This behaviour seems, albeit in a different way, as unaccountable as Catharine's when she had sent her manuscript to Richard Gwillym.

1st April 1866: Agnes is ill again

During the cold winter months early in 1866 Agnes became ill. Dr Girdlestone, the family's doctor was called, and in Jane's opinion treated Agnes successfully. Agnes was impatient to get back to London and returned to Town as soon as she felt well enough, both to get on with her work, and for the social life she enjoyed there. When she got to London, Agnes changed from traditional medicines to the homeopathic ones she favoured and which she believed speeded up her recovery.

Agnes told the sceptical Jane that: "Dr Wilson's magical teaspoons have cured my toothache and melancholy. I begin to eat and go out, and am getting on much better" but even in London, where her social life was of itself a great tonic, Agnes took a long time to get back to full health.

On 1st April 1866 in a letter to Catharine, Sarah wrote among her family news: "dear Agnes is ill with inflammation of the liver but no danger is apprehended" and Agnes followed her liver problems with a bout of influenza.

1st April 1866: Sarah tells of family troubles in England

When Sarah wrote to Catharine on 1st April 1866, she seemed to be surrounded by ill health and family upsets. Of Richard's health and family sensibilities she wrote, again with only partial legibility: "my dear husband is much better though still requiring ... I don't know whether Dr Crompton will allow us to go to the South of France this spring ... he has ordered us to Bath upon the 9th. We can only stay 12 days and it is a long journey by rail from here but the waters and baths will do my husband a great deal of good ... you know Bath well I think ... there with Mrs Leverton ... what a bright beautiful girl you were then.

"I can tell you nothing about Jane she has taken an affront with me ... not write for which she is very silly for I am the only ... and from Elizabeth I never hear ... she hates to receive letters or to write them."

By this stage, Sam's health was very poor. Sarah told Catharine: "I have not yet seen dear Samuel and his wife. They talk of taking us upon their way to Liverpool. They are now staying at Southwold with dear Agnes – I had a letter from her the other day. She gives a very sad account of our dear Brother, she fears that he will never return to his own home again but he writes now more hopefully of himself."

Sarah sent some money to Catharine with her letter and again referred to Sam. Sarah wrote: "My beloved sister, Richard sends you ... hoping that you will accept it as a brother's gift to a dear and valued sister as it is quite uncertain when our dear brother may be able to return to Canada my husband thinks it better that you should have it at once to do what you like with."

16th June 1866: Tom is mugged

Tom was 57 when he returned from South America at the beginning of 1865. There is no mention of him making any further voyages as captain of the 'Julia' nor can he be identified as the captain of any other vessel.

There were no more mentions of Tom until the middle of 1866 when the following curious story appeared in a number of newspapers: "Accident to Capt Strickland – We regret to hear that on Saturday 16th June 1866, Captain Strickland, brother of the celebrated authoress, Miss Strickland, was attacked by a ferocious bull in the grounds belonging to A Kidder, Esq., of Plaistow, Essex. Checking the animal for a time by throwing down his overcoat, the captain reached a quickset hedge, over which he climbed with much difficulty, and fell many feet into the road on the other side.

"Captain Strickland, who is in his 87th year, was greatly injured by the fall, several of his ribs being displaced, and his right leg and lower portion of his left arm sustaining compound fractures. He is now lying at the Black Lion Tavern, Plaistow, and the medical men in attendance regard his condition with great apprehension, as they fear the lungs have been perforated."

Tom's age was a long way short of 87. The rest of the report had some kind of foundation but may have been mixed up with a malicious hoax. In either event the same newspapers reported the following correction about a month later: "We have been requested to state that a report that has been circulated in the newspapers as to Captain Strickland, brother of Miss Agnes Strickland, having met with a serious accident is not true. Captain Strickland has for some time been suffering from a severe attack of illness, and is, we are happy to hear, now progressing favourably towards recovery."

Despite this retraction being published, Tom had definitely had some kind of misadventure, but the family never found out exactly what had happened. He seems to have been beaten and robbed, and maybe chloroformed. He never recovered his memory of the event, or at least never gave a satisfactory account of it.

June 1866: Sam is back in Lakefield

Sam managed to return to Canada, and Catharine then sent news of his health back to the family in England. Early in July 1866 Agnes wrote to Catharine to say: "I will not delay acknowledging your great kindness in telling us how our dear brother is though alas the account is very sad. But he rests on the 'Rock of Ages' we must be thankful that he is in the best and surest keeping."

Catharine's kind and caring nature had always been such that Agnes could write: "You must be a great comfort to our dear suffering brother and his faithful wife at this anxious and sorrowful time. Give my tender love to them both."

7th July 1866: Agnes is temporarily short of cash

Not only was Agnes's physical health in poor shape in 1866, but by the summer of that year her finances were in a similar condition. Agnes told Catharine in her letter dated 7th July 1866: "I grieve that it is not in my power to send you anything my dearest Catharine, but my past enterprises in purchasing back the copyrights of 'Queens of England' has so crippled me to swallow up all my capital and the alterations and repairs of this cottage exceeding all the estimates and the incomings of the new editions have left me in great anxieties for the future." Two major changes made to the cottage in the summer of 1866 were described by Jane as building a coach-house and new-fronting the house.

Agnes continued: "It entirely depends on the honesty of the publisher in regards to the proceeds of the abridgement whether I shall be able to make ends meet. If they are honest and the undertaking prospers, as it ought, it may be a great thing for Elizabeth and me. I have only finished the proofs on Saturday for they have dawdled over them most provokingly at press, losing the Christmas market most recklessly for the volume ought to have been published last month." July seems very early in the year to be worrying about losing the Christmas market, but that is what Agnes wrote.

She then said: "I have been too much worried to write anything while it has been going through the press, and indeed there appears to be so complete a change in the style and fashion of literature that I have no heart to write either truth or fiction now. We shall see however how the work sells when once published."

The 'Lives of the Queens of England' continued to sell well, though in more than one edition. Agnes subsequently wrote to Eliza that she had: "seen Longmans, and he tells me the cheap edition of the 'Queens' with Bell and Daldy has not injured the sale of the library edition, which goes on well; so does the cheaper one."

After the 'Lives of the Seven Bishops' was published in July 1866, Agnes went to an 'at home' at Fulham Palace with a presentation copy to give to the Bishop of London. The Bishop of Oxford was there at the time and requested equal treatment, and a copy was duly sent to him. By this time Agnes felt well enough to attend a Drawing-room and Mr Mackinnon helped by providing his carriage, complete with coachman and footman for transport. Princess Alice was presiding, but for the first time Agnes found the proceedings rather dull. She was glad when it was all over at half past three, and felt that perhaps she wasn't quite as well as she had thought.

July 1866: Catharine's younger sons move far away

William Traill was enjoying an adventurous life with the Hudson's Bay Company, and with his help and encouragement Walter Traill followed in his brother's footsteps, joining the company as an apprentice clerk in 1866.

In July 1866 both Walter and William were sent by their employer to live and work in the Lesser Slave Lake area of the North West Territory, many hundreds of miles from Catharine and her home in Lakefield.

31st October 1866: Sarah sees Richard's parish church re-opened

When St Mary's Church in Ulverston was re-opened, the newspaper report of the event shows the extent to which the initial intention simply to re-pew it, had grown into a major re-construction. A curtailed version of the newspaper report showed that re-opening the church involved Sarah in quite a lot of entertaining. The papers said: "Re-opening of Ulverston Parish Church – This event, which was much looked for in the neighbourhood, took place on Wednesday 31st October 1866. The Lord Bishop of the Diocese arrived on Tuesday evening and was entertained by the Rev Canon Gwillym. The Committee of Management met his Lordship that evening at the Vicar's hospitable board. On removal of the cloth, a very interesting ceremony took place – the presentation, by the Committee for the Memorial Window, out of the surplus subscribed, of a very elegant Pocket Communion Service to Canon Gwillym. On Wednesday morning the clergy of the town were invited to meet his lordship at breakfast.

"The Church and Organ – the last services were held on Sunday 22nd May 1864. It was found necessary so to extend the original plans ... the tower only remained. On 13th September 1864, the corner stone was laid. The front of the church, from the church-yard, the approaches made much wider, has a very imposing appearance, built entirely of red sandstone from St Bees" which is on the north-west coast of Cumbria "... style Tudor or perpendicular. The porch is a very fine feature, the figures which grace the arch are much admired.

"In the body of the church the uniform expanse of open pews is a great improvement and accommodate 1,400 persons. The pillars of 7 arches on each side of the nave have been under-pinned, a difficult and delicate operation in consequence of an alteration in the levels of the floors. The pulpit, like the font, is of Caen stone. The magnificent organ occupies a large space at the east end of the north aisle. The pipes are not yet ... to be diapered ..." Further details of the organ were given including: "... 50 stops, and about 3,000 pipes from 16 feet to ¼ inch ... intended" to be powered by "an engine on the hydraulic principle" but there was insufficient water pressure "at present" in the meantime "2 men will ..." work the bellows "... a plate bearing the inscription 'Erected by Wilkinson and Son, Kendal 1866. R Daniel, Esq., Honorary Organist.

"Every window in the church is of stained glass" three of which being memorial windows dated 1866 were then described. "To the left of the Tudor arch ... entrance to the tower ... window dedicated '... a token of appreciation of the long and valued services of Richard Gwillym, MA, honorary canon of Carlisle, and incumbent of Ulverston ... especially ... untiring energy and zeal in promoting and accomplishing the restoration of the Parish Church ... 1866" After some of the other windows had been described in detail, the report noted: "... general comment" that the 20 or 30 stained windows in number "make the church dark and somewhat gloomy but the brilliancy of colour gives a pleasing charm on the whole.

"The entire floor is raised 10 – 12 inches by brick and stone supports" for "ventilation and drainage. For warming ... pipes of hot water give genial warmth throughout the church ... for lighting there are about 282 gas burners.

"The Opening Service – At 11 o'clock the Hon and Right Rev Dr Waldegrave, the Lord Bishop of the Diocese arrived. At the church gate the Rev Canon Gwillym, in surplice and hood ... supported by his three curates presented the petition for consecration." The papers then gave details of the procession which entered the church and of the service given: "at the close ... the preacher (Bishop of Carlisle) urged the necessity of giving cheerfully and liberally. The estimated cost of the original alterations was about £3,000 while the actual cost exceeded £8,000 and there was yet a deficit of from £1,300 to £1,500."

Sarah's heart must have sunk when Richard decided, after having worked himself into early old age and spent too much money on the church, that he had another project in mind. The papers continued by reporting (here again an edited version): "The Luncheon took place in the Victoria Concert Hall. 150 persons sat down and Rev Canon Gwillym presided." Among the speeches and toasts the Bishop: "reflected that Mr Gwillym had been in Ulverstone for nearly a third of a century, last Sunday completed the 33rd year. The motto 'if you wish to see his monument, look around' might be said of Mr Gwillym – the beautiful infant school and improvement of the church and now bringing forward another good work – a sanctuary for the working class, he proposed building ... the working men were to have a reading room and schools etc as well as the use of the building for religious services.

"There were three curates for Ulverston, the third required on account of the feeble health of Mr Gwillym, but two had long been established. When he (the Bishop) thought of the pitiful emolument of the living, he hardly thought it possible for anyone to act as Rev Gwillym has done – employing three diligent curates, building the infant school, aiding the church, and helping forward the new building in Rattenrow. He prayed God to spare Mr and Mrs Gwillym to see some of the children they had benefited becoming fathers and mothers." At the end of the speeches: "Mr Gwillym's health was drunk with hearty cheers."

Two other edited excerpts from the newspaper reports add to the picture of the situation: "... proposed the health of the architect, Mr Paley for one of his most successful efforts. Mr Paley in returning thanks said the result was an agreeable surprise. The church was really handsome and few churches in the North of England could compare with it. The collection in the morning including £50 sent by his Grace the Duke of Devonshire, was upwards of £280 (cheers).

"Mr Daniel had found very nearly the £800 for the organ. He thanked God for giving him money to spend and the will to spend it in His service. Mr Daniel alluding to the 32 years he had been connected with the music of the church, hoped that he and Mr Gwillym might be spared to work together a few years longer. At the evening service every available space was occupied."

November 1866: Susanna earns money as an artist

After Dunbar and Eliza Moodie moved to America, John and Susanna rented for £2 a year, a small cottage near the Bay of Quinte, a mile from Belleville. They bought a cow, kept chickens and had enough ground to grow vegetables including beans, cabbages and pumpkins.

Katie, Dunbar and Donald Moodie had all fallen out with their parents. This left two children, Agnes and Robert who would have helped their parents financially had they been able to do so but they both had children to support on slender means.

Susanna turned to painting pictures of flowers and selling them, and John Moodie compiled a book of his previously published essays and poems, with additional personal reminiscences. In November 1866 they went to Montreal for him to have his photograph taken for the frontispiece, to sell subscriptions for the book, and to organise its printing. The book was entitled 'Scenes and Adventures of a Soldier and Settler during Half a Century'.

Susanna took one of her water colour paintings to John's publisher in the hope that he might be able to sell it. To the surprise of the publisher it sold quickly and, as a consequence, he offered to sell for $5 each, as many as she was able to produce.

As far as the book was concerned, Jane in her letter to Catharine written in December 1866 wrote: "I got Moodie's little book from Susan last night." Being cross-written over previous news, the only legible part of her view on the book is: "it will not help them much."

2nd November 1866: Sarah's husband hosts an enormous tea party

Sarah, having entertained the Bishop of Carlisle when he visited Ulverston to re-open the church, must have been relieved that she could attend and enjoy the enormous tea parties given a couple of days later without being responsible for the catering. The papers reported: "Ulverston Treat to teachers and scholars – In connection with the re-consecration of Ulverston church, the Rev Canon Gwillym has shown his accustomed liberality in providing the scholars and teachers of the Infant and National Schools with tea and all the other et ceteras. Nearly a thousand scholars and teachers, on Friday afternoon 2nd November 1866, partook of tea by the worthy rector's generosity, the scholars being served in the Infant School and the teachers in the large room of the Sun Hotel."

17th December 1866: Tom is in a poor state

In her letter to Catharine dated 7th July 1866, Agnes had written that Sam: "rests on the 'Rock of Ages' in the best and surest keeping" and then went on to mention Tom: "I would we could feel the same confidence for our Tom but the sad habits into which he has fallen in his latter days prevents such hope until it should please the all merciful God to grant him a better light before the last long eclipse of reason. It makes us all very sad.

"Eliza offers him a home with her but he would not come. He might have lived with his rich son-in-law Captain Pohle and Mary but then he must have given up his sad propensity which he will not relinquish. He is a lost creature I fear. How very sad it is." This implies that Tom had simply taken to drink since he retired, but there may have been more to it than that, with the mysterious accident leaving Tom with some form of mild dementia or brain damage.

Jane Strickland in a letter to Catharine begun on 17th December 1866 passed on family news and gave more information about Tom's mysterious 'accident': "My dear Kate, I have been waiting to write till I could give a more satisfactory account of poor Tom or rather I hoped to do so. As he (was) unable to maintain himself Eliza most generously offered to give him a home, and it was offered that he should come to her – but though his bodily health was better, his good daughter Mary Pohle considered his state of mind would try her strength too much, and she boards him at Plaistow with Mrs Dun... whose husband attends upon him.

"His memory is gone but he is self-willed and his daughter who has provided good clothes for him cannot get him to put them on unless the old ones are taken away. There is some yet unfolded mystery about the condition in which he was found but he was probably chloroformed and his pockets had been rifled and his watch gone. He had lain all night in the pouring rain and had been bruised by his fall. His strong constitution has overcome this fall but mind and memory are gone.

"Well my dear Kate my constant prayer for him that God may give him repentance for I fear he has been a great sinner. At one time he had begun to read the Bible but his unfortunate habit has taken him captive. Still, he had lost his home, and the marriage of his favourite daughter Diana had in a manner thrust him on the world – so that there are some extenuating circumstances."

Tom had some money left, but had lost much of it. He would, however, soon begin to receive a pension so he was not faced with total destitution. Jane wrote: "He has only seven hundred pounds which includes what he had as his share in the Reydon property, for he lost in speculation what he had saved – something considerable I believe – but next year he will be as a younger brother of the Trinity entitled to sixty pounds a year. His rich and dutiful daughter Mary will never suffer him to want. I wish I could have given you better tidings of poor Tom – be guarded about these sad facts – they are not known here and we should be much annoyed if they were discussed as coming back from Canada."

Later in the same letter, which was finished on 21st December 1866, Jane added: "Eliza sent a nice note from Mary Pohle today. Tom had put on his new suit and was chatting with Walter over a glass of sherry, talking of a trip to Valparaiso, but wanderingly. Eliza fancies he is really going but it is quite clear he fancies he is going for no owner in the world would engage him now. It is however possible that a voyage might restore him."

Jane then wrote: "I always thought Lord Anson the navigator's character suited him –" and Jane may be referring to a written work by Lord Anson rather than the character of the man himself when she continued, presumably referring to Tom: "– a brave man and great navigator at sea and a fool on shore – He was always talked into some scheme by some artful rogue or another. I am glad his health is better."

This letter also mentions "Tom's eldest son" and describes him but the writing is difficult to read. It seems to say that he looked like his mother: "eyes features forehead darkly silky hair only with his father's complexion at least he was when I saw him last he has been in Australia for years." "Eldest son" strengthens the idea that Tom had three sons, two born in 1835 plus Walter born in 1843, but Walter Strickland was the only son mentioned by name in the sisters' family letters.

December 1866: The running costs of Ulverston church are considered

Richard's Christmas treats in December 1866 seem to have been relatively minor. The only one reported in the local paper followed the school examination: "The annual treat by the Rev Canon Gwillym to the scholars" of the Infant School "was given on Wednesday afternoon the 19th December 1866. The juveniles went through their examination with great credit to Miss Lawrence and the other teachers." This shows that while Miss Lawrence was still the main teacher at the Infant School, the increasing number of pupils meant that she had long since stopped relying on the help of her younger sister to teach the children, and was now the headteacher with supporting staff.

As 1866 drew to a close, the question of how to cover the running costs of the renovated church had to be addressed. Instead of being dark and cold in winter, the church was now a comfortable place to worship, but the heating and lighting had to be paid for. The papers reported: "Meeting of the Congregation of the Parish Church – On Saturday 22nd December 1866 in the Infant School Ulverston, Rev Canon Gwillym presided ... question of raising funds" to cover "the expense of maintaining the choir, and warming and lighting the Parish Church. A resolution was adopted that a monthly collection be made in the Parish Church" each person who "occupies an allotted sitting be asked to contribute one penny for each sitting for each Sunday in the year."

December 1866: Jane is contented with her simple life

Jane's letter to Catharine written in December 1866 gave news of her own daily routine in her new home in Southwold. She wrote: "I have a very quiet life here, visit little but am sought out by some of the comers and an old friend or two." Her garden helped make ends meet: "My maid hoes the potatoes. There is about 3rd of land which finds me in potatoes from midsummer to Michaelmas. I grow rhubarb, vegetable marrow and french beans. Cooper comes for a day to plant potatoes and I buy a sack of potatoes for winter consumption. I have gooseberry bushes and currants from Reydon but a dishonest family robs me for a ten foot wall is nothing to keep out boys.

"My life is very regular. I rise early if my dormouse of a maiden can be roused – have prayers and then breakfast – Arrange my affairs work read or write or manage my garden ... Walk when my health will let me on the beach, take my devotions reading have a biscuit and cup of milk. The maid reads a chapter of the New Testament to me which I explain – have prayers and to bed – she was Mamma's housemaid and is a good pious girl, a Burns of Reydon Church. This quiet life after so many trials and fatigues suits me – if my income was not so narrow and I had better health I should be very happy – as it is I am as happy as I deserve to be."

As well as telling Catharine her own news, Jane gave a summary of the rest of the family in England. She wrote: "The Gwillyms are pretty well – Eliza much the same – Agnes out of spirits and poorly."

Jane then elaborated on Agnes's situation with the implication that Agnes, like Catharine, tended to let money run through her fingers a bit. Jane wrote: "I am sorry for Agnes – she wants society – but does not like the expense and trouble of it, then she fills her house with elegant things, incurs the expense which is needless and then is nervous about the indispensable outlay of housekeeping."

3rd January 1867: Sam dies in Lakefield

When Susanna wrote to Richard Bentley in September 1866 she had said that Sam, having come back to Canada from England, had come home to die. She said that his large family were all prospering, that he was greatly loved and would be missed and said she was grateful to Sam for his kindness to their sister Catharine. Sam lived for a few more months but on the 3rd January 1867, he died at 'Homestead', his home in Lakefield, aged 63.

The news of Sam's death crossed the Atlantic in a letter from Catharine to Sarah, and was then passed on through the family in England. Sarah told Catharine: "I sent your letter on to dear Agnes and asked her to send it to Eliza to whom I wrote and asked her to let Tom see it for it might induce him to change the dreadful life he is leading and make him think seriously of his future state – he drinks fearfully and spends his time on nothing else. Eliza and his daughter Mrs Pohle try to induce him to come to them but he will not leave his bad habits but leads a most reckless and hopeless life."

Sarah's letter of condolence to Catharine, written on 23rd February 1867, told a lot about Catharine's role in family life. Sarah wrote: "Yours was indeed sad news and deeply do we sympathise with his dear wife in her deep sorrow ... great will be her consolation when the first great grief is over to look back to all she has done for him ... and you my dear Kate will feel comfort in being the help and comforter to her and your dear kind brother. It must have been a real blessing to them both to have you with them, kind tender nurse and consoler you always were when sickness or sorrow came upon those who were near and dear to you – and you have known so much trouble since you left your own home in this far away land that you can so truly sympathise with your poor sister-in-law. You have lost a good and true friend as well as a kind brother.

"From the first my dear husband said there was no hope of recovery it is a fatal complaint unless at the very first stage the diet is strictly attended to and even then Dr Crompton tells me that only one in a hundred survives the complaint."

28th January 1867: Richard is feeling his age

At the end of January 1867 an item in the Ulverston local papers contained a sombre note within a quote from Richard. It reported: "Ulverston Monday Evening Concerts – The first concert of the season was held in the Victoria Concert Hall, Ulverston, on Monday evening 28th January 1867. The attendance was fair, but not as large as, at the low prices charged for admission, might have been anticipated. The chair was occupied by the Rev Canon Gwillym, who was supported on the platform by the Revs N Brady and R Mulcaster.

"The programme was a very pleasing one. Mr W Salmon presided at the pianoforte. The Rev Canon Gwillym briefly introduced the subjects of the concerts ... At the conclusion was given a vote of thanks to the chairman. The rev gentleman expressed the pleasure it gave him to meet his flock on all occasions." He said: "He had been amongst them a long series of years, and had always received kindness ... He was now an old man, but he trusted the same kindness would ever subsist between them, till the end of his labours."

23rd February 1867: Sam's Will brings changes

After Sam's death, and in accordance with his Will, his eldest son Robert and his wife Caroline Strickland moved into 'Homestead', and the care of Sam's widow, Katharine Strickland was entrusted to them.

Catharine was still staying at the 'Homestead' on 23rd February 1867, keeping her sister-in-law company and helping her to adjust to the changes in her life, when she wrote to her daughter Kate. Catharine wrote: "I have a fire always in my room and sit there writing all the morning, and spend the afternoon reading and working in your dear aunt's room; and we go down at tea time and stay till bed time.

"On the whole I have no cause for complaint. Caroline is very kind, and I need not say what your dear aunt always is. She is more cheerful and contented in her mind now but so pale, and so thin – it is sad to see the change a few weeks has wrought."

February 1867: Catharine and the Muchalls pool resources

The business partnership in Belleville of Catharine's son-in-law Tom Muchall with her son James came to an end, due to Tom's inactivity in the business and his increasing drink problem, and James's declining health.

Mary and Tom Muchall were planning to move to Lakefield so that Mary could resume teaching after the birth of their third child. Amidst these plans and in late February 1867 James wrote a warning letter to his sister Kate in which he said: "It is my duty ... to tell you that our dear sister should not be alone any longer, her unfortunate husband has so given himself to drink, that he is seldom or never sober and he talks and raves in almost an insane manner, and though always kind to his poor wife, it is fearful for her to be in the house with a man who is actually out of his senses half the time. He drinks in the middle of the night, and what I fear is an attack of delirium tremens which might come on at the very time of her confinement."

As a result of Tom Muchall's drinking, when his family arrived in Lakefield he was put under some kind of domestic surveillance. Catharine and the Muchalls began to pool resources, thus saving money as well as keeping a general eye on each other. Sometimes the Muchalls went to stay with Catharine at 'Westove'. On other occasions Catharine and her daughter Kate went to live in houses which the Muchalls had rented, and 'Westove' was rented out. As well as Mary's teaching and Tom's occasional employment, Mary added a little to the family income by writing.

After Sam's death, his family kept an eye on Catharine, to ensure that she and her children were as comfortable as circumstances allowed. In particular, Sam's son Walter leased 'Westove' from Catharine several times. This provided Catharine with income, and relieved her of maintenance costs for a while. It seems that while Walter was a tenant, he and others in the Strickland family would take the opportunity to make improvements to the building on Catharine's behalf.

February 1867: Sarah is happy but fearful for the future

Sarah's letter to Catharine in February 1867 gave news of her own life. She wrote: "We have had a most severe winter a little snow and a very great deal of frost and ice and we have had so much to do for our poor people more than ever. My dear husband keeps tolerably well and so am I if it was not for the rheumatism in my ankles and knees. I am obliged to walk with an umbrella to help me up the steep street that leads to our home. Both my husband and I now walk very slowly he dear fellow on account of his heart and I with rheumatism.

"I have our house quite full with my husband's nephew Atherston Rawstorne and his wife and two boys and a darling little girl who dotes upon me and she is such a beauty. They all have whooping cough and our fine air will cure them of it – We are going next week to stay with the Archdeacon of Chester at Warrington and the change will do us both good for we want rest.

"We have such a beautiful church now it is all finished how I wish that I could show it to you but I fear there seems to be little chance of our ever meeting again in this world but distance cannot change the fond love that has ever existed between us, indeed every day seems to strengthen it as I look back to the days that are past, as I often do, it seems like a dream to recall our early youth and all we had to struggle through.

"Mine is now a bright life of happiness with one of the best and kindest of husbands who makes a complete idol of me but my happiness is clouded when I see how feeble he is though full of energy untiring in his various duties. He is so dearly loved by everyone his benevolence is unharnessed and ... the blessings of the poor ... one old woman of 80 said to me 'Bless him, he is Feather and Moother to me haith I hope he will live as long as I do for I cannot get on without him'."

14th April 1867: James Traill dies

All the family who had met James Traill on his visit to England had liked him, and letters to Catharine after his return to Canada always contained enquiries about his health. Jane had very similar health problems to James and she took a particular interest in him.

When she wrote to Catharine in December 1866 Jane was concerned but optimistic about James's future. She wrote: "I am deeply concerned for poor dear James. I do not consider his case hopeless – every symptom you describe as if it were relating to mine – and though I was quite given over – it has pleased God that I should recover – not my general health but in a fair state my age considered" (she was 66 years old) "and the coldness of this place and the smoke of my cottage and its aspect more north than west – Mine like his is chronic bronchitis the lung pipes stopping up with risk of suffocation.

"Poor dear James has youth – he must be quite still, rest is life to him – God help him – I do not despair of his ultimate recovery though it may take a long time. He was a very interesting young man, none of my Canadian relatives pleased me like him – I wish I could help him but I am too poor – and if Eliza did not help me should not get along. However God be praised I do somehow and am thankful."

James had a short respite from his lung problems following his visit to England, but the improvement did not last. On 14th April 1867 he died in Belleville, aged 34, leaving a widow and four children.

22nd April 1867: Sarah's husband gives his last school treat

The only annual school treat in Ulverston in 1867 was reported in April, earlier in the year than was customary and was relatively modest in format. It was made possible by the loan of the grounds of a house other than Stockbridge which could accommodate the children.

The papers noted: "Ulverston Treat to Scholars – On Monday 22nd April 1867, the Rev Canon Gwillym treated the scholars of the National Day and Sunday Schools to tea. In the afternoon the children amused themselves with different games in the park belonging to Ford House, kindly lent by Montague Ainslie, Esq. Afterwards a very excellent tea was provided for them by the kind and generous vicar." Not long after this Richard's health was known to be in a poor way, and attention turned to hopes for his recovery.

May 1867: Susanna asks for her manuscripts back

After writing to Richard Bentley in February 1866, she wrote to him again in March and in September 1866 but received no reply, which seems hardly surprising. In May 1867 Susanna wrote to Richard Bentley's son George saying she had not heard from his father since July 1865 when she received money from the Royal Literary Fund. She enquired about Richard Bentley's health, and asked George Bentley to return the manuscripts that she had sent if he had no use for them.

1st June 1867: Tom has musical children

News of Tom Strickland and his family in 1867 was sparse. However, one item which appeared in the Norfolk local press relating to his daughter Adela, gave a hint of her financially difficult situation, but also told of her musical talent. The papers noted: "Acle – report of Mrs Gent Wigg's Amateur Concert on Tuesday evening, 1st June 1867, in the Acle National School-room. This lady gave another concert which was well attended. An excellent programme of songs, duets and trios" featured "several amateurs and the Norwich Cathedral choir ... Trios Mrs Wigg, Miss Livock and Mr Strickland ... Mrs Wigg gains confidence with experience and her singing was very good ... Mr Strickland sang two songs, a duet and the trios." The Mr Strickland referred to was not specified but it seems most likely to have been Walter, although his singing abilities were not mentioned elsewhere.

Of Tom himself at this time, the news was not good. A letter from Jane to Catharine dated 5th June 1867 said: "I shall not send this away until I can tell you more of Tom. He was bed ridden when Sarah heard some weeks ago – his legs swollen with dropsy and very pale. No alteration had taken place since – but as Mrs Pohle was leaving to see Eliza I may expect to hear of amendment or increasing weakness.

"I believe he has quite lost his mind but may have recovered it if kept from his bad habit. Eliza is very fond of him and would have taken him but his children considered the trial too heavy for her. This is very sad we can only pray God to have pity."

14th June 1867: Jane has little sympathy for Agnes

In her latter to Catharine dated 14th June 1867, Jane again passed on news about the family in England. She wrote: "You will wish to hear of the family. Eliza is pretty well – Agnes nothing to boast of – but as she is now in town her spirits are better. She dislikes Southwold and the quiet life she leads here, and wishes to dispose of her house and depart."

Jane continued: "She has no cause for fretfulness if I who am so poor and having lost so much of my property can be contented – ought not she." This implies Jane did not get back the value of the £350 which her mother had used to buy a lease on a property, the repayment of which was not specified in her mother's Will.

Jane continued: "Eliza has been kind and thoughtful to me but not Agnes – and it is better for me to be as independent of her as I can be." However, Jane does not seem to have taken account of the help she was getting from Agnes with respect to her Southwold property. Agnes had taken a long lease on Jane's larger cottage, which meant Jane no longer had to worry about finding a tenant for it each year. In addition, Agnes was paying Jane an annual rent of £20 and was making improvements to the property while living there.

July 1867: Susanna has another novel published

Susanna was continuing to have work published in North America, and her novel entitled 'Dorothy Chance' is said to have been published in serial form in the 'Montreal Transcript'. In July 1867 Susanna sent it to Richard Bentley in the hope that he would publish it in England.

Despite a lengthy gap in their correspondence the novel was published by Richard Bentley's firm later in 1867 or in 1868 as a three-volume novel with the title 'The World Before Them'. The long gap in the correspondence might initially have been due to Richard Bentley being offended by Susanna's importunity but at some point in 1867 he had a serious accident which would have been an added reason for the gap. Apparently he fell off the platform at Chepstow railway station and broke his leg. He was also badly shaken and the accident aged him considerably. His son George ran the family publishing business thereafter.

July 1867: Agnes enjoys the summer away from Southwold

In 1867 Agnes was still a celebrity and still enjoyed the social whirl of her life in London and her visits to well-connected friends. In contrast, the cold and empty drabness of winter in the seaside holiday town of Southwold must have been trying, even though she now had a home of her own there.

In July 1867, while in London, she went to a soiree at the Royal Academy and enjoyed the evening, as she wrote "exceedingly," having heard all the great people announced, chatted with friends, looked at the pictures and been offered refreshments.

From London Agnes went on visits to friends in the south of England and in Wales. Then, Jane wrote, Agnes: "returned to Southwold, which she found cold after her pilgrimages to warmer parts of England, and expressed some regret that she had not chosen a milder air."

Agnes and Jane on the whole got on well together, but there were points of friction between them, and this was one, as Jane showed in her biography of Agnes by adding: "However, she had no cause of complaint, for the bracing sea breeze did her a great deal of good, and quite renovated her health."

In between her summer tour and her winter in Southwold, Agnes visited Eliza at Tilford to plan their next work. This was to be biographies of the Tudor Princesses who, under the Wills of Henry VIII and Edward VI, were in line of succession to the throne.

29th November 1867: Richard dies and his obituary appears

Although Richard's health was known to be in a poor way, the local papers were encouraging when on 22nd October 1867 they printed: "We are glad to learn that the Rev Canon Gwillym is improving in health."

Unfortunately, their optimism was misplaced and only a few weeks later they carried a report of Richard's death: "Death – The Rev Canon Gwillym of Ulverston expired on Friday evening the 29th November 1867 about 8.30 at his residence, Stockbridge House." His death certificate gives the cause of death as congestion of the lungs and continued fever for 8 weeks.

The newspapers carried a lengthy obituary summarising Richard's life and good works. The sections which add most to what has already been told are these: "Of Mr Gwillym's kindness, charity and desire to do good, it is impossible to speak too highly. He was enabled from his private resources to aid all the philanthropic improvements in the town, which he did with willingness and cheerfulness. During the earlier years, he visited personally the poor parishioners, supplying material comfort. Of late years he had not visited so much, but amply made up for this by having two and sometimes three curates, all paid by himself, the small amount of the living of Ulverstone doing so little.

"In his religious opinions he was a thoroughly moderate, sound, and loyal churchman; he loved the service rendered in a hearty, efficient, congregational manner. He had no sympathy with Calvinism on the one hand or Ritualism on the other and was wont frequently to deplore the spirit of party feeling in the Church. His life was characterised by an earnest, anxious desire to do good, and render happy the poor of his parish.

"The Infant School number of scholars is now 260. When well, he visited it every day, either alone or with Mrs Gwillym who has also taken great interest in it. Long will be remembered his kindly greetings and words of encouragement. The treats at Stockbridge House and at Christmas were in a great measure borne by himself, and looked forward to with pleasure – not only the appropriate presents given but enhanced by the cheerfulness and kindness of himself and Mrs Gwillym. The teachers, too, of the National, Infant and Sunday Schools had happy days once a year with him and Mrs Gwillym in the Lake District, both of whom added so much to the day's enjoyment by their manners.

"For more than 30 years the people of the outlying hamlet of Broughton Beck had Divine Service every alternate Sunday in the little school-house there; he is gratefully remembered by the inhabitants of Broughton Beck. In closing these few notes of his life, we express a hope that whoever is nominated to the incumbency by the patron, will carry on efficiently the good works with which Mr Gwillym has been connected."

Jane in her biography of Agnes wrote of their brother-in-law Richard Gwillym: "He had proved an affectionate relation and a warm friend."

17th December 1867: Richard's funeral has taken place

If Sarah wanted Richard's funeral to be a quiet and private affair, she did not get her wish. A newspaper cutting preserved in Barrow Archives carries the following account "The funeral, which was plain and unpretentious, took place yesterday. There was neither mourning coach nor carriages. The 37A (Ulverston) Company of the

Rifle Volunteers, of which Mr Gwillym was the chaplain, formed ... in front of Stockbridge House, the members being in uniform ... the mournful procession moved slowly along, the hearse being preceded by the volunteers, the churchwardens, and after it came the chief mourners, then many of the principal inhabitants and tradesmen ... as the cortege slowly wound its way many others joined. The shops were all closed".

When the cortege arrived at St Mary's Church, the children "of the National and Town Bank Sunday School, formed a line on each side of the road. The volunteers divided along the pathway leading from the gates to the church, and the coffin was borne into the sacred edifice, which was in mourning.

"On the body being removed to its last resting place, the churchwardens ... each carried his white wand, to which was tied a piece of crape. The grave is at the east end of the church yard, on the high side of, and not far from, the steps leading to the "Ladies Walk" ... During the service, the church was full, and, on leaving it, there must have been in the churchyard nearly the whole population of the town able to attend ... his loss will be deeply and sincerely mourned for many, many years to come."

As well as reporting the funeral, local papers also noted the several funeral sermons which were preached on the Sunday following: "The Late Rev Canon Gwillym – Funeral sermons were preached at the Parish Church Ulverston, on Sunday 8th December 1867, that in the morning by the Rev N Brady, from Revelations xiv 12; that in the evening by the Rev Mr Rawsthorne (nephew of Mr Gwillym) from John xi 25; at the latter service 'Vital Spark' was sung, accompanied by R Daniel, Esq., on the organ. A funeral sermon was also preached by the Rev F Evans in Soutergate Chapel and another in the Mission Room, Swan-street."

Although Richard's funeral was quiet and private, her husband had been such a popular figure that another means was found for local people to remember him. Papers on 14th December 1867 carried an advertisement stating: "Portraits of the late Rev Canon Gwillym MA, either framed or unframed, may be had at T Todd's Artists' Repository, King Street, Ulverston. Photographs 1s; Large Lithographs 7s.6d; Memorial Cards Framed."

A few days later Sarah attended the Infant School examination, as she would have done if Richard had been alive. The papers reported: "Infant School Ulverston – The half-yearly examination of infant scholars took place on Wednesday 17th December 1867, in the presence of many visitors and parents. There were 240 scholars present, who passed a most satisfactory examination. At the conclusion each child received a bun and an orange, and some article of clothing, through the kind liberality of Mrs Gwillym, who was present at the examination, and who intends to carry out, as far as possible, all that the late pastor would have done. We may also add that the Rev R Mulcaster has given a large portrait of the late Canon Gwillym to be placed in the school."

During the course of December 1867 both the vacancy in Ulverston and the vacancy of Honorary Canon to Carlisle Cathedral were announced. The living in Ulverston was listed as a perpetual curacy with an income of £160, with no house provided, and a parish population of 5,832.

1867-1868: Catharine's flower book is in production

Susanna's daughter Agnes Fitzgibbon was occupied from 1865 until 1868 with work on Catharine's flower book, and although Susanna worried that the costs of the project would be ruinous if it failed, Agnes Fitzgibbon ensured that costs would be covered by getting 500 subscribers signed up for the book before it was printed.

Catharine's role was mainly limited to providing a preface, plus the appropriate texts for the illustrations from her existing written material. In the preface Catharine explained that the 'Book of Canadian Wild Flowers' was described as the work of Agnes Fitzgibbon because Catharine had found it impossible to get the work published on her own.

The construction of the 500 copies took several months to complete because the illustrations were printed in black and white. Agnes Fitzgibbon, with some help from her daughters and from an art student, then hand-coloured the ten plates individually before the pages could be put together and bound.

The book was first published in 1868 and was sold at $5 per copy, being aimed at members of genteel society in Canada who were willing to pay such a relatively high price. The book was a success, though Catharine said she thought the success was due more for the plates than for "the reading part of the book," and a second edition was soon needed.

26th December 1867: Richard leaves his wealth to Sarah

The executors of Richard Gwillym's Will were Sarah and his nephew, the Rev Robert Atherton Rawstone (whose name appears with variations of spelling). The Will was proved, which meant they could start implementing it, on 26th December 1867, 30 years almost to the day since Sarah's first husband had died.

Richard in his Will ensured that Sarah was well provided for. Apart from a few bequests of books and pictures to friends, he left all his household contents and personal belongings, including two horses and carriages, to Sarah to do with as she wished.

Also, apart from some minor provision for his sister, his niece and his godson Richard Gwillym Strickland in Canada, all the income from his shares and the family estate were to go to Sarah for the remainder of her life. After Sarah's death, all his shares and property would revert to the benefit of his own family, primarily to his nephew Atherton Rawstone. As a result, Sarah would have for the rest of her life more or less the same annual income which Richard had when alive but, as far as the Strickland family was concerned, Sarah's wealth would die with her apart from any savings she generated from interest on her investments.

25th January 1868: Sarah intends to carry on with Richard's good works

Since Stockbridge House was not church property, Sarah had no need to move house if she did not wish to do so, and her early stated intention was to ensure the continuation of Richard's benevolent behaviour. How she would do this would depend to a large extent on Richard's successor because, generally speaking, there is no recognised role for a vicar's widow in her late husband's parish. Despite Sarah's stated intention, she had packed her bags and left Ulverston before 1868 came to an end, and by following the news of

Richard's replacement in the local papers, it is easy to understand why this happened.

The vacancy was soon offered to someone who sounds as though he was on the same wave-length as Richard Gwillym, and with whom Sarah might have been able to co-operate happily, but it was soon reported in the local papers that the offer was turned down. On 25th January 1868 it was reported: "The Incumbency of Ulverston – We have it on undoubted authority that the Rev Mr Sullivan has finally decided to decline the incumbency of Ulverston. For the sake of the parish this is to be regretted, since there are so many points of analogy between Mr Sullivan and the late Canon Gwillym.

"Mr Sullivan we are informed, is a gentleman of considerable wealth, and withal of a kindly and benevolent disposition. We do not know that he has expressed any special reasons to persons in this town for declining the offer of the 'living', but we give no credit to the rumour that the refusal arose from the fact of the church being encumbered with debt and that the different parties in the town were always in a bellicose state." The church did still carry a debt but no mention has been found of a bellicose state during Richard's time, apart from a little excitement at election times.

February 1868: Richard's old job is redefined

By the end of February 1868 it had still not been possible to find someone willing to take on the role made vacant by Richard's death, and two changes had been made. The first change was to split the parish into two parts making the vacant parish of Ulverston smaller. This change was in line with the Bishop of Carlisle's aim to have one parish for each 3,000 of the population, and the population within Richard's parish had been approaching 6,000.

The second change was to provide a vicarage which was again in line with the Bishop of Carlisle's intentions. The days of expecting wealthy vicars to fund themselves and their parish was giving way to a more egalitarian situation. The papers in Ulverston reported that the site for the parsonage had been chosen and: "is a plot between Town Bank and Ure Mill Lane. Mr Paley, architect of

Lancaster, has already made an inspection preparatory to making plans etc"

15th March 1868: Rev Morton holds his first service in Ulverston

Almost as soon as the changes in Ulverston had been announced, a new vicar, the Rev Morton was appointed and arrived to take up his post. He had graduated from Trinity College Dublin in 1854 and followed this with seven years as a curate in Ireland and five years as a curate in London and Middlesex. The papers noted: "He gave up the curacy of Acton December 1866 and has since been resting on physician's advice." Rev Morton held his first service in St Mary's Church, Ulverston on 15th March 1868.

28th March 1868: Rev Morton and Mr Daniel disagree

Mr Daniel, the honorary organist at St Mary's Church, had been a close friend of Richard Gwillym as well as an active member of the church. His name was associated with most of the public musical events which took place in Ulverston, and he had made sure that when St Mary's Church was renovated, the church had an organ of suitable quality, paid for mainly out of his own pocket.

However, Mr Daniel and the Rev Morton did not see eye to eye in the matter of suitable church music, and on 28th March 1868 the papers reported: "The subject of Harmony in our parish church would seem to be productive of a considerable amount of discord. This must be a source of regret to both parties ... alike to the gentlemen of ritualistic proclivities and to those who take their stand on the platform of ultra evangelicism."

The discord was not helped when the freemasons had a major ceremonial event at Ulverston which they followed by a church service. On 18th April 1868 the papers reported: "There were about 200 in the procession. Whilst passing down the nave and taking their places, Brother R Daniel Honorary Organist of the church played in glorious style Beethoven's Grand March. At one time it was intended to have a full choral service but arrangements were relinquished in consequence of the appointment of the present incumbent, who entertains a dislike to cathedral services."

By 30th May 1868, Mr Daniel had resigned. The papers reported: "It will be a source of regret to the parishioners to learn that R Daniel Esq., who is just about completing his 34th year, has felt it incumbent upon him to resign the position of honorary organist at our parish church. When it is recollected that to his exertions chiefly, and to the liberality with which he has contributed out of his own private resources that we are indebted for the noble organ which now adorns the restored church, his severance from it will be felt as all the more strange and painful.

"That this result should have arisen from personal disagreements is still more grieving when we recall the cordial, kind, nay the affectionate terms which existed between the late Canon Gwillym and Mr Daniel. We hear that his place has already been filled by a young lady, a pupil of his own, though there is a strong hope that Mr Daniel will resume the position he has so long filled."

7th April 1868: Mr Morton is confrontational to subscribers to the National School

While trouble was developing with Mr Daniel, Rev Morton was also behaving in an unfortunate way in the matter of the Ulverston National School. At what was likely to have been his first meeting, he was not reported as saying anything pleasant or encouraging. The papers noted: "A meeting of the subscribers to the National School was held on Tuesday 7th April 1868 to elect a committee of management ... The Rev Mr Morton said he had been at the bank, and was informed that £33 had been overdrawn on the school account; and he then gave a short statement on what money had been received and paid on behalf of the school – Mr Pickering wished to say he believed the schools would compare well with any in the north of England. He thought there had been some neglect in the collection of subscriptions, and if that were attended to the schools would not be much in debt. In handing them over to Mr Morton, he felt they were handing them over in an efficient state – Mr Morton observed that the schools were not handed over to him, but to himself and the other members of the proposed committee.

"Mr Pickering stated that he felt sure Mr Morton, as head and chairman of the committee would take a great interest in the schools. He was put in the place of the late Mr Gwillym whom the children were always delighted to see, and who took so much interest in the schools that he visited them even in the most unfavourable weather." If Rev Morgan made any response to this point, it was not reported.

20th May 1868: Catharine awaits a legacy

Letters from Catharine to her daughter Annie dated 20th May 1868 and 14th June 1868 refer to a legacy from Richard Gwillym. In June 1868 she wrote: "I hardly expect the legacy to be paid till next January."

There was no formal bequest in Richard Gwillym's Will to Catharine so this was either a word of mouth bequest on his part or, much more likely, a benevolent pretence on Sarah's part. Also, given the size of Richard Gwillym's estate, there would have been no reason for the executors to delay a whole year before paying.

Sarah, however, was dependent on income from Richard's shares and family estate which would have involved a certain amount of paper-work to implement, and she had many calls upon her money during the early months of her widowhood. This could explain why she might have had to delay a gift to Catharine that was disguised as a legacy from Richard.

The size of the 'legacy' was not stated, but it did lead Catharine to worry that her widowed sister might cease to send her yearly monetary gift. This was a clear statement that Sarah had been sending money to Catharine on a regular basis for a number of years and, by implication, more than the small amounts mentioned in Sarah's half legible letters.

June or July 1868: Elizabeth (no longer Eliza) and Agnes visit Tom

In a letter to Catharine dated 29th July 1868 Agnes wrote: "Next spring I shall have something for you which I shall send, God willing, but at present you must be content with love and good wishes. I have been in London about seven weeks paying dearly for lodging all the time. Elizabeth (she will NOT be called Eliza now) was with me one week, she is looking well."

(As Mrs Strickland was now dead and no confusion can arise, Eliza will hereafter be referred to, as she would have insisted, as Elizabeth, even though her family didn't always do so.) Agnes continued: "I am bringing out a second volume of 'Lives of the Tudor Princesses.' Eliza has" written "more of it than I have but I have had immense labour in preparing it for the press, and shall have more in correcting the proofs. Her portion is so incorrect. Longmans publishes it in November. I hope it will be a successful work and will send you a copy when I send my present. The frontispiece will be Catharine Gray. It will be a most interesting life. I shall be very busy and shall not be able to write again till the spring."

During the week that Agnes and Elizabeth were together in London they visited Tom. Agnes told Catharine: "We both made an expedition to Plaistow to see poor Tom who seemed to me the same as ever only he had forgotten everything. Elizabeth entreated him to come and stay with her and he would not.

"He was very affectionate and we begged him to write to his eldest son who is at Sydney and very rich and I think he might go to him. The conduct of his son Walter has cut him to the heart. This is a long story so I cannot write about it but I will never speak to Walter again, nor leave him a farthing."

There is no record of what Walter had done to cause upset but he was never forgiven by Agnes, Jane or Sarah. This is the only specific reference to Tom's son in Australia and Agnes's writing verges on indecipherable, but has probably been correctly deciphered as quoted above.

Agnes continued: "Mary, Mrs Pohle, is very good and lady like. She and her husband Captain Pohle are living in Scotland. They have been staying with dear Thay" (the family name for Sarah).

8th July 1868: Sarah gives a summer treat

Despite Rev Morton's unpleasantness to Richard's old friends and parishioners, Sarah gave a summer treat to the children attending the school which Richard had created, but it was a relatively simple event compared with those held in the recent past. The papers reported: "The Infant School – On Wednesday 8th July 1868 the children attending this school had their annual treat, provided by Mrs Gwillym. The scholars, with their teachers, assembled at Stockbridge, where coffee and buns were liberally supplied, after which they amused themselves for a few hours in an adjoining field."

15th July 1868: Agnes is introduced to more royalty

In July 1868, a notable society event was held at Holland House in London, and the papers reporting the event listed twenty-six of the many guests. The list mainly consisted of titled personages, but Agnes was famous enough for the name "Miss Agnes Strickland" to be included among those who: "with others, were at Lady Holland's afternoon party on Wednesday 15th July 1868."

Agnes told Sarah that she went: "nicely dressed for the occasion in a grey Japan silk and a new bonnet; not, however, in the absurd fashion in which bonnets are now worn, with a front and no back." Agnes's journey to Holland House was itself noteworthy. She first made her way to 33 Cumberland Place: "from whence Miss Elizabeth Powys was to convey me to Holland House. She received me very kindly, though I was personally a stranger to her."

The carriage was waiting: "and we drove to Holland House, Kensington, a beautiful old palace in a park, with the finest gardens and conservatories, of which I had often heard, but never seen. Miss Elizabeth Powys presented me to her aunt Lady Holland, and then we sat in the garden to see the company arrive. The Duchess of Cambridge, the Princess Mary of Cambridge and the Duchess of Mecklenburg were expected."

Agnes mingled happily with the other guests, some of whom were already old friends, then: "Miss Powys took me into the conservatory, where tea and ices were served; then to the lovely gardens." When the royal party arrived, Agnes: "had a wish to see them. I took a chair on the lawn near, but not within the circle. Lady Holland came and told me the Duchess of Cambridge wished me to be presented to her. So she brought me up, and I made my curtsey.

"The Duchess and sweet Princess Mary made much of me and thanked me 'for all the pleasure they had enjoyed in reading my works' and asked 'what was I then about?' I told them I was writing the lives of the Tudor princesses, and they said 'it would be a treat for everyone.' Of course I was much pleased with my reception. At eight, sweet Miss Powys took me to my lodgings, after my delightful day at Holland House was over."

Agnes was also sufficiently famous that when Victor Hugo wrote to her from Guernsey to ask her for a reference, the only address he gave was simply 'Madame Agnes Strickland, Authoress of the Lives of the Queens of England' which was sufficient, Jane recorded, for the letter to arrive correctly and without delay.

July 1868: Sarah is annoyed with Rev Morton

In her July letter to Catharine, Agnes wrote: "I am now with our beloved Sarah who has this day sent off her parcel of clothing to you by Captain Barlee. She has written in the box charging you to divide your gift among your children and Sam's sons. She lamented that she had no personal gifts for yourself enclosed." One of Sam's daughters Emma was married to Frederick Barlee whose business interests resulted in him travelling quite often between Canada and England.

Agnes described Sarah as "placid but resigned" and "looking lovely in her deep weeds." At about the same time Agnes wrote to Jane and said that Sarah had been "much annoyed by the behaviour of the new incumbent" adding "However, there is no help for that."

July 1868: Agnes plans to move to Ulverston

Of her own future plans, Agnes told Catharine: "I shall return to Southwold about the end of August, but I mean to let or sell my cottage at Southwold, and live with dear Thay. We shall be very happy together, and I dare say I shall be settled with her before Christmas."

Part of the reason for Agnes planning to move, seems to have been that the disagreement between herself and Jane about homeopathy had come to a head. Agnes told Catharine: "Jane is much better and I hope will recover, for her complaint is distressing but not dangerous though as usual when anything is the matter with her she fancies she is going to die. I hope not, but she is very poorly" Agnes then went on to give her side of the disagreement saying that Jane "has so silly a prejudice against homeopathy that she will not try one and only mocks them." Agnes's views were very clear: "I have now adhered to that system for 18 years and have a faith in the dosing system. I have had a bad attack of influenza and could not take the proper medicine, but now I have done so I am getting well, thank God."

From the finishing words of Agnes's letter to Catharine, she seems to consider herself on normal sisterly terms with Susanna as well as with Sam's family, though nothing in Susanna's correspondence reveals this. Agnes wrote: "I give my love to all your children and to dear Sam's family and to Susanna when you write. I shall try and write to her when I return to Southwold but I am so melancholy when there, it would only give you all the dismals were I to write in a general way from thence. I am now cheerful and full of hope once more."

30th July 1868: Agnes goes on visits with the Archaeological Institute

One of the reasons for Agnes to be staying in Ulverston was to attend a day out with the Archaeological Institute on 30th July 1868 which she described in a letter to Jane. Agnes said that she began the day by breakfasting: "at seven, and got to Carnforth in time for the special train from Lancaster. We started on a new line to Borwick but had to walk from the terminus to the fine ancient Elizabethan hall where we heard a lecture from Mr Sharpe. Then we started for Milnthorpe, and were all stowed into twelve carriages, waggonettes and omnibuses.

"I was packed into a large waggonette with a very agreeable party and we drove to Levens" where Agnes was welcomed by General Upton as an old friend. After the lecture, he gave her his arm and led her "to the head of the table, placed in a marquee in the beautiful garden." After lunch they went to Sizergh Castle for an hour and then moved on to Kendal, the final destination of the day.

At Kendal they went: "to see the grand old church and Archdeacon Cocker gave a lecture; then we all adjourned to the

Town Hall, where a bountiful tea was provided for us by the mayor." The weather was cold and as Agnes had to travel in an open carriage back to Ulverston, the Mayor kindly lent her a heavy rug and some of his daughter's furs. He also telegraphed Sarah to warn her that Agnes would not arrive home before 11 pm.

A couple of days later Agnes went with the same group to Skipton Castle which was more relevant to her work in hand than the earlier expedition had been, for Skipton Castle had been the home of Lady Eleanor Brandon, one of the Tudor princesses Agnes was researching. Agnes was 72 years old but clearly still full of energy, and still a personage of note.

6th September 1868: Rev Morton preaches a political sermon and Mr Daniel packs his bags

By 20th August 1868, plans for a vicarage in Ulverston were ready to be put out to tender with a closing date of 9th September 1868 and Jane's statement, in her biography of Agnes, that Sarah: "after twenty years' residence with her beloved husband was compelled to seek a new home" implies some connection between the two events. However, Stockbridge House was not in any way linked to the church and Sarah, if she had wished, could have continued living there for the rest of her life. However, Richard's successor continued to upset local people, and in September 1868 one of his sermons was very contentious.

The papers gave a report of the incident: "A Church Parade of our local volunteers took place on Sunday 6th September 1868. About 60 met at the drill room and marched to the Parish Church, Lieut Brogden being in command. There was a rather numerous congregation. A sermon was preached by the Rev G Morton ... the sermon was of a political character, the object of it being a defence of the Irish Church. A considerable amount of dissatisfaction seems to have been created by it.

"Lieutenant Brogden before dismissing the men at the drill room after the service said 'I regret, gentlemen, that on this first occasion on which we have met together at the Parish Church since the appointment of the new incumbent, he should have felt himself called upon to preach a political sermon. From the tone of his remarks he might have been addressing a number of insane men, who had neither sense nor discretion, and who were unable to exercise their own judgement.

"The sermon was not only unworthy of you as a rifle corps, but was unworthy of the place in which it was preached. Now, I beg you will put all this on one side. The time has gone past for listening to the ravings of bigoted parsons'." The paper added the comment: "From the remarks heard in the ranks there was evidence that the men endorsed Lieut Brogden's opinion."

On the same day in the same papers was a report of a presentation made to Mr Daniel. £100 had been collected from a limited group of people even though the wider community had wished to take part. This implies that the collection was taken at short notice, and that the collection being made immediately after Rev Morton's controversial sermon was not a coincidence. The paper thought that if there had been the opportunity, four times the amount would have been collected.

The report noted: "feeling that the severance was altogether unexpected and undesirable between him and the church and organ to which he was so long and affectionately attached. Mr AW Schneider, Esq., said he admired and respected Mr Daniel who had not only spent almost a lifetime in the service of God but showed how a good man used the means with which he had been endowed. The late Mr Gwillym whose friendship with Mr Daniel was well known had said that Mr Daniel was one of his best and most disinterested friends, ever ready and willing to assist him in any good work."

The following week, 19th September 1868, the papers in Ulverston carried the notice: "To be let in October – The house in Church-walk occupied by Mr Daniel."

The following week again, 26th September 1868, there were three items in the papers relating to Rev Morton. Firstly Mr Schneider, who had spoken so highly of Mr Daniel at the presentation of his farewell gift, wrote in continuation of a correspondence about the sermon preached in the presence of the rifle corps. He wrote: "To the Editor of the Ulverston Mirror. Sir – The Rev GG Morton has written a letter to your paper of the 19th inst on the subject of his late sermon. I have no hesitation in saying that abundant evidence can be found to prove what I state. I have forwarded a copy of this letter and also of Mr Morton's letters to me and to the editor of the (Ulverston) Mirror to the bishop of the diocese, asking him to institute an inquiry into the matter, both on my own account, and that of my friends, who are conscientiously annoyed by Mr Morton's proceedings. I am, sir, your obedient servant, HW Schneider, Conishead Priory, September 22nd 1868"

The other two items both referred to Mr Daniel: "Mr Robert Daniel will conduct the musical part of the service at the Parish Church on Sunday (tomorrow) when the Lord Bishop of Carlisle preaches" and also an advertisement announcing an: "Auction for Robert Daniel Esq who is leaving the town, at his residence at Church Walk Ulverston, a large quantity of household furniture."

26th September 1868: Sarah carries out her final duty

In July, Agnes and Sarah had been planning for Agnes to go and live with Sarah in Ulverston. By September Sarah's plans had changed and she was about to follow Robert Daniel's example and leave the town, but she had one more task to complete first. The papers reported: "On Sunday last, 27th September 1868, a complete set of service books was presented to the Parish Church and the donation is recorded as one of the last of many generous acts of the late lamented vicar, the Rev Canon Gwillym.

"The books were formally presented to the churchwardens by Mrs Gwillym, on Saturday 26th September 1868, and gratefully received by them on behalf of the parishioners. The following inscription is inserted in each book:- 'This book is dedicated to the glory of God and the public service of the Parish Church of St Mary Ulverston, through the liberality of the late incumbent, the Rev Richard Gwillym, MA, Honorary Canon of Carlisle, who wished that a portion of the fund subscribed by his parishioners and friends for a memorial of their regard for himself, should be thus appropriated, 1st September 1868'."

The report continued: "I beg respectfully to inform the subscribers to this fund that the sum collected and interest, amounted to £173.18s.5d. The cost of the window was £130.19.7d; the silver-gilt communion service £14.11s.6d; the church books £18.12s; leaving a balance of £9.15s.4d which Mrs Gwillym has most kindly given in aid of the churchyard railing fund. The names of the subscribers have been recorded in a book which has been presented to Mrs Gwillym. JK Hodgson, Treasurer Sept 30, 1868"

3rd October 1868: Sarah prepares to pack her bags and Rev Morton is in the papers again

On 3rd October 1868 an advertisement appeared in the Ulverston papers which read: "Mr William Middleton begs to announce that he has been honoured with positive instructions from Mrs Gwillym, who is leaving the town, to sell by public auction, upon the premises of Stockbridge House Ulverston on Monday, Tuesday, Wednesday Thursday the 2nd, 3rd, 4th and 5th November and following days if necessary, at 1 o'clock prompt a large quantity of valuable household furniture, oil paintings, engravings and other effects. The furniture will be on view on the morning of each day of sale."

The items for sale were then listed by room and included a table over 11 feet long with 16 chairs in the dining room; a piano forte with "brilliant tone" in the drawing room, and in the study a large quantity of books. The housekeeper's room was large enough that its contents included five arm chairs; similarly the butler's pantry could contain a dining table and chairs. Among the kitchen items was a washing machine, presumably the one tested and mentioned in advertisements in April 1860. Also for sale were the contents of eight bedrooms. Eight paintings and 20 engravings were of sufficient quality to be listed and sold as separate items.

As well as carrying an advertisement for Sarah's auction, the papers on 3rd October 1868 carried further mention of Rev Morton's infamous sermon in the form of a letter signed 'Yours etc. An Elector'. The letter said: "The sermon as published is not the one delivered on Sunday 6th September. I was present and heard the sermon. The sermon preached occupied at least thirty minutes in delivery; the one published would barely occupy ten minutes. The political references have been carefully expunged ... as he warms to his work, his sentiments increased in intemperance. He has already discovered himself an earnest and zealous worker ... I have every confidence that in a few years we shall be delighted to find so earnest and energetic a minister has been cast amongst us."

November 1868: Sarah moves to 'Hollow Oak' in Haverthwaite

Jane, in her biography of Agnes, reported that: "Mrs Gwillym chose 'Hollow Oak' in Lancashire for her residence, which she hired of an old friend." 'Hollow Oak' was in Haverthwaite, a few miles north-east of Ulverston, in the direction of Windermere. Exactly when the move took place is not recorded but must have been about the same time as the sale of the contents of 'Stockbridge House'. If Sarah rented or leased 'Hollow Oak' fully furnished, it would explain the auction of the contents of her former home, as well as simplifying her removal. Who moved into 'Stockbridge House' after Sarah had moved out, is not known.

Jane reported that Sarah had a narrow escape when moving house. Jane said: "Mrs Gwillym had been in great danger on her way to her new home for being blasted of the rocks of Greenodd, the swerving of her horses only saving her from being killed by the falling fragments." Limestone was quarried in the area of Greenodd.

Sarah had already lived near to Finsthwaite, mentioned as the location of the family's forbears, when she lived in Ulverston. Haverthwaite was even nearer to Finsthwaite than Ulverston. If Sarah or Agnes ever visited Finsthwaite, the visit was not recorded, or maybe they passed through it so often that it was not an event worthy of mention.

6th December 1868: Catharine is unpleasant about Jane

In a letter to Susanna dated 6th December 1868, Catharine wrote: "I have heard that our poor sister Jane is declining fast. I wrote to Agnes begging to know how she is but Agnes has been away in London and I have had no answer yet. It seems to me so sad that Jane should be passing away without any of her own kin near her. As in life so it seems in death that she is a lonely woman. Poor Jane. I sometimes reproach myself for never having loved her as I ought to have done – Hers was a strange character. With talents of no mean order, beauty of person – and religious principles – yet, from childhood to old age – she has never obtained the love, the real tender love of any human being – Perhaps there is less to regret – fewer ties to bind her earthward – And yet one pities her!"

It is not clear why Catharine, having lived in Canada for over thirty years, felt herself qualified to make such a comment on Jane's friendships and life. Jane was the sister who stayed at Reydon Hall and who, despite her own poor health, took care of their ageing mother. Jane and her mother, and to a lesser extent Agnes, were trapped in a big old house which they did not have the means to maintain, and they received little or no help from Canada – certainly none from Catharine. In due course (22nd June 1888), an obituary would give a different picture of Jane and her life.

December 1868: Susanna tells her troubles to Allen Ransome

At Christmas 1868 Susanna heard via a letter from Sarah that an old friend from Ipswich, Allen Ransome had asked Jane for Susanna's address. He and Mr Bird from Yoxford had been the two friends who were present when Susanna and John caught the steamer from Southwold on their journey to Canada in 1832. He was now widowed and wealthy, and wanted to write to Susanna after a silence of 35 years, saying he was keen to know her adventures after 'Roughing It in the Bush'.

Susanna wrote to him immediately, consoled him on the loss of his wife, and then gave him a full account of her recent troubles and woes. She wrote: "For nearly 24 years my dear and honored husband held the post of Sheriff of this County (Hastings of which Belleville is the Capital, a town containing a population of 8,000) with honor to himself and held in much esteem for his integrity. We possessed a handsome and comfortable home, and enjoyed many of the luxuries of life or such as are considered so in the Provinces."

She also told him of the trouble caused to them by antagonistic lawyers, the court case and ill health of her husband, plus a version of the sale-cum-gift of their home to their eldest son, and the hardship which had resulted. She said that John had to pay the cost of the prosecution as well as the costs of the appeal which, she wrote "involved us in irreparable loss" but that every debt was paid and that he had resigned his post.

Susanna continued: "But little remained to us when all this was done. The wreck of his property did not realise more than 2000 dollars for it was sold to great disadvantage and he gave this to his eldest son Dunbar, on the condition that he was to give us a home during the rest of our lives. D, who is a clever practical man, decided to buy a farm in the state of Delaware US, thinking that Father would prefer removing to the States, to remaining in Canada goaded by the recollection of intolerable wrong, but his wife, a proud selfish West Indian, treated us so unkindly that after everything was prepared for our journey we both concluded it was the best and wisest course to remain behind and work for our own living. D gave us 200 dollars out of the sale of the furniture, the rest of the property having been invested in the purchase of a Farm in the States, and we were left to our own mental resources."

It seems that a collection had been made in the local community to help the Moodies. Susanna wrote: "Several worthy gentlemen anonymously rendered us much kind assistance through the Agency of a generous Quaker friend." This may have been Mr Rous who reappears in Susanna's life at a later date.

Susanna continued: "But we did not wish to be burdensome to anyone. My husband wrote the little work I send with this, on which he realised about 600 dollars, I another 'The World Before Them', published by Bentley in London, the proceeds of both yielding us 40 pounds a year ... So here we are – living in a little cottage with just room enough to hold us, but beautifully situated on the edge of our lovely bay, with a fine common in front covered with noble trees through which we see the spires of Belleville about a mile distant, and for which we pay a rent of 12 pounds per annum and the rates 10 dollars.

"My servant Margaret's wages 12 pounds more for I am too old, now 65, for hard work and am able to earn the money that pays her wages ... Then I have my faithful Skye terrier who is known by the name of Quiz, very ugly and small, but full of almost human intelligence and ... love. A steel kitten Grim, who is dear M's especial pet. A perfect incarnation of mischief very common to the Maltese race. 24 hens who help furnish our larder, who come to me to be fed at the sound of a small handbell ... I have no garden – and I dearly love flowers and tending them, but I have learned like dear St Paul to be content with little."

Despite all the difficulties that Susanna related, she told Allen Ransome that she and John were happier with their simple life in their small rented cottage, than they had been for many years.

December 1868: Rev Morton continues his destructive path

It was probably best that Sarah had left Ulverston before December. That was the month when, ever since his Infant School opened and when Richard's health had permitted, he and Sarah had attended the Infant School examination, left treats and gifts for the children, and praised Miss Lawrence for the way that she ran the school, which continued to grow.

By contrast, in 1868 the occasion was marked by a presentation of farewell gifts to Miss Lawrence who had decided to leave on account of her "indifferent health." The presentation and farewell speech were made by the Rev G Morton.

In a few short months, Rev Morton had completed the hat-trick of driving away three of the key people in his parish. Firstly he had driven away Ulverston's generous and hard-working organist; secondly he had up-rooted Richard's widow who had been planning to use her wealth to continue Richard's benevolent works in the parish; thirdly the teacher who had been with the successful Infant School since its inception, had decided that she too had had enough.

28th March 1869: Rev Morton shows he is not a 'people person'

Only one more item about the Rev Morton in the Ulverston papers was of relevance to Sarah's life as wife and widow of Richard Gwillym and, although slightly out of chronological order, it is included here as the final mention of the man.

The papers reported: "Ulverston The Debt on the Parish Church – On Sunday morning and evening 28th March 1869, a special appeal was made by the Rev GG Morton, and in the afternoon by the Rev J Targett, on behalf of the debt still due on account of the restoration of the Parish Church of St Mary. Mr Morton said it was due to the memory of his respected predecessor, the late Rev R Gwillym, that the church should be freed from debt."

So far so good. Unfortunately, the report continued: "The Restoration Committee had pledged to pay £800 which left £487 still owing. Mr Morton considered the parishioners morally bound to pay the whole amount (i.e. £1,287)." The parishioners appear to have disagreed, and perhaps by the smallness of the amount given, or the smallness of the congregation, showed their view of Rev Morton at the end of his year amongst them. From the two services, it was reported that: "collections totalled £21."

1st March 1869: Catharine's book needs a second edition

When Catharine wrote to her friend Frances Stewart on 1st March 1869 she mentioned the progress of the book produced jointly by Agnes Fitzgibbon and herself. Catharine wrote: "I only wish there had been fewer errors in the printing, but as yet Canada is in its infancy as regards literary matters and must be made allowances for, but the new edition may be more satisfactory in many respects, so Mrs Fitzgibbon says; but it will be 6 instead of 5 dollars the copy.

"She has already sold all the copies of the 1st and many are bespoke of the new issue. I am afraid many copies of the 2nd have been printed so the corrections will only appear in the form of an errata – Your approval dear friend of the book cheered me not a little for I was much disappointed in my share of the work which I feel is open to criticism. Fortunately the plates will redeem it in the eyes of a great many persons who would hardly care for the reading part of the work." It was not until the third edition was published in 1870 that corrections were made and removed the many printing errors of which Catharine felt ashamed.

Catharine described the second edition to Frances by writing: "The 2nd Edition of our book of Wild Flowers is a reprint with improved colored lithographs." Despite only a short time gap between the first and second editions, mechanical colour printing seems to have made sufficient progress that there was no repetition of the need to colour each of the plates in each of the books by hand.

25th April 1869: Jane is nearly better again

In one of her long chatty letters to Catharine, dated 25th April 1869, Jane gave an account of her recent illness: "My dear sister Kate, After seven long months of confinement to my room and bed but chiefly to the last – I have by the mercy and goodness of God come down again but am not able to leave the house for my back and chest are too weak at present – The severe spasms or rather convulsions having weakened the muscular system. I do not doubt that He who has thus far restored me will enable me to regain my strength. Indeed I feel more like health than I did in the summer for I eat now with appetite. Still the air tubes may refill for I have much fever and over pulsation of the heart to be too sanguine. However I trust that the grace of God will give me patient submission to His Divine Will what ever that may be."

Jane had friends who had helped her, and more visitors than she wished for. She told Catharine: "I have had much kindness and sympathy from Miss Sheriffe and my dear Mrs Foster – many nice things so that often I could spare the poor neighbours from their bounty" but she had been too ill to receive many visitors: "Mrs Foster is very clever, very lively and tenderly kind to me, a constant visitor in my sick chamber – indeed the only one besides Agnes I admitted besides my kind minister Mr Rouse."

"I was unwilling to see Elizabeth Hawtayne in September. It was death to speak and too much to listen but I was obliged to deny seeing the Miss Goodchilds who were rather pressing. I was compelled to be firm. They are good Christian women I am told have ten thousand pounds apiece from some fortunate speculation of their grandfathers. Elizabeth is bitter against them but they were thoughtless girls then when staying with Mrs Leverton and now steady women in middle life.

"Thank you for your kind letter and sympathy. I have had you see a friend who has been more than a sister to me – My maid is handy and attentive and Agnes has been kind – Sarah and Elizabeth help in money matters for such sore sickness causes much expense in light and coals – besides medicine. I am attended by Dr Girdlestone who is cheaper than the people here and more experienced.

"I am doing a little work now for continual reading is not very good for an invalid. I have worked three or four aprons – and am finishing some silk ... for a chair cover in small hexagons with a star in the middle. I have made a table cover but not yet made it up. I am not up to writing yet – the use of a pen tries me more than anything – for it gives me pain in the side – a muscular one – When you write to Susan give my love.

"I was able on Good Friday to be dressed and receive the Holy Communion out of bed – it was rather a risk for the least movement caused me so much anguish – but I have been gradually mending and am not so bare of flesh – I was like a living skeleton – I cannot boast of my looks now being a complete scarecrow. At my age one soon is reconciled to changes of that kind unless very foolish indeed." Jane was 69 years old.

25th April 1869: Catharine is sent encouragement from England

Jane in her April 1869 letter to Catharine gave part of the family response to Catharine's published book on 'Canadian Wild Flowers' plus her own technical comments. She wrote: "sister Elizabeth has been staying with Thay some time but will be in town May 1st if God permits. She is delighted with the Book both with the letter press and plates – Thay gave her a copy with which she was much gratified – My dear the paper is beautiful and the type fair – if left in London uncorrected it would have been quite as full of mistakes – none but a good botanist could correct a work of that kind."

Jane's next remarks showed that she, in common with Catharine and Elizabeth, had studied botany: "The designs are most elegant but at the bottom there should be a dissected flower to show the Linnaean class and order – the corolla should be split. As far as it can be done the flowers too should be designed so as to show what the structure is – if the dissected flower is too minute it is magnified and referred to as such."

Jane's letter made it clear that she had been exchanging letters with Susanna and her family: "I had a sweet sensible letter from Agnes (Fitzgibbon) by the same post and it shows a fine mind – Susan says that she has helped her too – Good daughter. May God bless and reward her – Poor dear Susan seems hopeful about her three undutifuls but it is a sore trial for her, worse than all she has endured."

Catharine's book also received favourable comment from Agnes, who continued in her efforts to find publishers in England for Catharine's work. In a letter written some time during 1869, Agnes wrote: "I don't think I have written to you since I received my niece Agnes Fitzgibbon's lovely book of 'Canadian Wild Flowers'. I admired it very much and also your letterpress and I spoke to Longman about it. He said 'this was not a proper house for such publications' but gave me the name of the first house in town.

"I went and saw their present manager Mr Sauper. The original proprietors A Lovell & L Shane are both dead. Mr Sauper was very polite but told me no house in London would either buy the copyright or speculate on the work, but he should be happy to have copies and act as the agent for the sale charging ten per cent on what he sold, and advertising them gratis in his catalogue.

"I sent his catalogue to Agnes (Fitzgibbon) and told her what he said. He publishes all the great botanical authors. I saw some of his publications, quite beautiful and I would advise Agnes to risk seventy five or fifty on his terms. There is no-one else will do more and it will give importance to the work being advertised in his catalogue. Farewell dearest, ever lovingly yours, Agnes Strickland."

25th April 1869: Tom is in lodgings

Jane in her letter to Catharine dated 25th April 1869 gave news of Tom, the meaning of which is not clear: "Our Tom continues in better health but his memory is gone – Walter finds him in board – the money matter is a sort of mystery. He lives from hand to mouth as long as he is able he will maintain his father but if anything happened to him Tom would be destitute – His sister would have to maintain him – as a matter of course." This seems to conflict with an earlier statement that Tom was eligible for a pension of sufficient size that he would not be destitute.

Jane then worried about Tom's soul. She wrote: "I am more grieved for his loss of memory because he has been a very great sinner – and how can he repent for what he has forgotten and never mourned for – God however works in a way not comprehended by us – and what seems impossible to us – is possible to him." Tom's sins may only have extended as far as drinking too much and being unwise in his financial dealings and friendships, any other areas in which he might have sinned are not mentioned. He may not have gone to church much or respected the Sabbath, and these might have been important sins in Jane's opinion.

June 1869: Catharine has a new daughter-in-law

In June 1869 Catharine's son William, living in the Lesser Slave Lake area, in what is now Alberta, married Henrietta McKay. She was the daughter of William's first boss, William McKay, and his Native Indian wife, Mary Cook.

8th June 1869: Sarah is settled in her new home

Sarah had become an established resident at Haverthwaite by the time the local railway network was extended in June 1869. This is shown by the local papers which noted: "Opening of the new railway from Ulverston to Windermere. This line connecting Lake Windermere with the main lines of railway in the kingdom, was formally opened on Tuesday 8th June 1869. Previously" the link was "almost complete there being a break of about 9 miles only – between Ulverston and Newby Bridge." The article then went on to give a detailed description of the new route including "The train then passes the charming residences at Haverthwaite of Mrs Gwillym and Mrs Baldwin."

June 1869: Agnes plans research on the continent

In 1869 Agnes decided to make a study of the three daughters of Charles I plus the youngest daughter of James II. Elizabeth would have nothing to do with the project and Agnes proceeded on her own. The first biography in the series was to be that of Mary Stuart, Princess Royal, who was the mother of William III. Although her marriage and funeral had taken place in London, much of her married life was spent in Holland, and there were also aspects of her life which involved Germany.

Agnes therefore needed to visit The Hague to collect information about the character of Mary Stuart, about her relationship with her mother-in-law, the character of her husband, and the complications in her life which were caused by her husband's early death from smallpox. She also needed to visit Aix-la-Chapelle, Cologne, Dusseldorf and Frankfurt to complete the project.

Bishop Tait, who had been a friend of Agnes for some time, had now risen from being Bishop of London to become Archbishop of Canterbury. His librarian at Lambeth Palace was Mr Wayland Kershaw who could read Stuart documents easily, and he gave Agnes a great deal of help by making copies of them for her. Also he had worked in the Low Countries, and gave Agnes the names of the principal librarians in Belgium and Holland, together with a letter of introduction written by Archbishop Tait. This letter requested that "Miss Agnes Strickland, the well-known historian of the Queens of England, have access to any public library in the Hague."

Agnes still kept in friendly correspondence with Georgina Buchanan, formerly Georgina Stuart of Lennoxville, who lived much of her life abroad with her diplomat husband. From the Hon Mrs Buchanan, Agnes got advice about accommodation in Holland, Georgina reassuring Agnes that she would have no difficulty with language as English was so widely spoken there. However, Georgina warned Agnes that the Queen of Holland had been unhappy with Agnes's treatment of the Dutch hero, William III, and might not be enthusiastic for Agnes to continue that line of research.

Nonetheless by the time Agnes was ready to set off, the Queen of Holland had given permission for Agnes to have a portrait of Princess Mary photographed. Also the chargee d'affaires in the Dutch court, Admiral Harris had written to Agnes assuring her that he and his wife would do all they could to make her visit a success.

Summer 1869: Tom's daughter Adela moves to Canada

The father-in-law of Tom's eldest daughter, Adela Wigg, no longer had a farm in Acle and Adela and her husband, who had been living on the family farm since they married in 1850, had to make other arrangements. After struggling unsuccessfully for a while to make a living in Norfolk, they moved to Lakefield in 1869 to join the families of Sam and Catharine.

Catharine described the situation to William in April 1870 by writing of Adela: "she and her husband and seven children of all ages down to two years came out last Summer – They were destitute of means and he Mr W – destitute of energy to do anything for his family – They all fell ill with typhoid fever one after the other – The Stricklands did all they could to aid them and others also in the place – Now Mrs Wigg is teaching music and Agnes has some pupils" (maybe referring to Agnes Fitzgibbon) "but it is a hard thing for the females to work for so many – Adela is a very handsome foreign looking woman and very talented the children are a fine set of young folks but a little too much of the father – in their manners – wanting in polish very decidedly – Mr Wigg does nothing but murmur against the country but as he never did anything to maintain his family when he was at home – it does not seem wonderful that Canada should not suit his do-nothing habits."

9th July 1869: Agnes is ready to visit the continent

Jane was again ill while Agnes was preparing to travel to the continent, and their continuing difference of opinion about medical treatment re-surfaced. Just before setting off Agnes wrote within a letter to Jane from London dated 9th July 1869: "I am very sorry to hear that you continue so ill, notwithstanding the fine weather, but I am persuaded homeopathy would cure you, if you would but give it a try."

Jane ensured that her own view was recorded for posterity by adding a footnote to this letter when she included it in her biography of Agnes. The footnote said: "The complaint was severe spasmodic asthma, and the sufferer was under skilful treatment, and had no faith in the remedies proposed by her sister."

Agnes put her personal affairs in order before setting off, and told Jane: "If I should die abroad, I do not wish my mortal remains to be brought back to England. Where the tree falls, there let it lie; and the Lord have mercy on my soul."

Despite any misgivings Agnes might have had as the departure approached, once on board the ship with her maid Vickery and bound for Rotterdam, Agnes began to enjoy herself. She and a fellow-passenger, a gentleman called Mr Harding became acquainted. With him she visited the Cathedral in Rotterdam, and when she had seen everything she wanted and was ready to move on, he escorted her and her maid to the railway terminus and made sure she went safely on her way to her next destination which was The Hague.

At The Hague, Agnes used her letters of introduction and was immediately helped by the royal librarian, who made several relevant documents and books available to her. Mr Sypestyn, who was an historian as well as a Secretary of State, gave Agnes a copy of a document drawn up at the time of Princess Mary's marriage.

Agnes was presented to the Queen of Holland by Baroness van Doorne at the 'Huis den Bosch', the 'House in the Woods Palace' in The Hague, and their meeting lasted nearly an hour. The Queen of Holland had read the 'Lives of the Queens of England' and spoke admiringly of them. She took Agnes into her bedchamber to show her a miniature of Mary Stuart, and advised Agnes to examine the 'Annals of the House of Orange' as a good and reliable source for the life of the English princess in Holland.

Agnes was treated with respectful consideration, and enjoyed attending services at the English Church at The Hague. Writing to Sarah from Holland, Agnes said: "The Baroness van Doorne took me in her carriage to church and I sat in the Ambassadors' chapel. We had a beautiful sermon from Mr Turnour. I went again in the evening, and Mrs Harris opened their pew for me; so I sat very grandly in a velvet chair."

Mr Harding, Agnes's new friend was still on hand to look after her. Agnes told Sarah: "Mr Harding told me he would see me safe to Amsterdam if I would wait until Tuesday; so as I wanted to see a monument in Delft, I agreed to remain."

Admiral and Mrs Harris had taken a great deal of trouble to help Agnes in her research. They not only traced the whereabouts of the portraits she wanted to see, but also gave her directions for finding them at the various galleries. Mrs Harris's farewell note said how great the pleasure had been in assisting Miss Strickland to achieve the object of her visit to Amsterdam.

While much of the treatment Agnes received may have been a matter of duty or courtesy, and her literary fame made it relatively easy to find people who would help her, Agnes seems also to have been the kind of person whom people like to help. She was calm, able to see the funny side of situations and able to laugh at herself.

Agnes rounded off her adventure with a sight-seeing trip up the Rhine and then retraced her steps to Rotterdam. On Monday 26th July 1869 Agnes wrote to Sarah to say she planned to return to England on the Friday of that week. She said: "We have had lovely weather and very few mishaps, but are tired of travelling, and shall be very glad to rest with you."

After Agnes had stayed with Sarah a few days in Haverthwaite, the two sisters went together to Southwold. For Sarah it was to be a holiday, for Agnes it was a return to life in her own cottage next to Jane's. The plans that Agnes had started making the previous autumn, to sell or let her cottage and move north to live with Sarah, had been abandoned.

Summer 1869: Catharine's son Harry begins work as a prison guard

After his marriage in 1864, Harry Traill went to work in newly opened oilfields at Sarnia-Bothwell in the south west of Ontario, while his wife ran a small school. He then worked for two years as an overseer in the Frontenac Lead Mines, while his wife ran a boarding house to accommodate some of the miners.

Catharine visited Harry and his family at the Frontenac Lead Mines, and Jane commented in her letter written in April 1869: "You enjoyed no doubt your visit to dear Harry and the mine opened for you a new course of intellectual enjoyment." Catharine in later years was interested in geology which seems to have stemmed from this period of Harry's life. Jane continued: "I wish poor Susan were as happy in all her children as you are – However to be mother to Agnes Fitzgibbon is something – and poor Robert would help if he could."

In the summer of 1869 Harry applied for a job as a guard at the Kingston penitentiary, and started work as a prison officer at an annual salary of $80 for a probationary period of six months.

22nd October 1869: Susanna becomes a widow

John Moodie's health deteriorated after his retirement and the paralysis caused by his stroke got worse, so that by 1869 he was unable to get out of bed without help. On 21st October 1869 he had been cheerful and in reasonably good health when he went to bed, helped as usual by Susanna, but he was taken ill during the night and died at 6 o'clock the following morning. He was seventy two years old.

Of his five surviving children, only Agnes Fitzgibbon and Robert were at their father's funeral. Dunbar and Donald were not able, or were not willing, to make the long journey back to Belleville in time to be there. Katie Vickers was too ill to attend, but her husband John was there, which was the first contact he had had with Susanna since the disagreement over the disposal of her family home.

John Vickers not only attended the funeral, but took Susanna to stay with his family in Toronto while her belongings in Belleville were sorted out, and her next home was decided upon.

9th November 1869: Susanna is living at Seaforth with Robert

Events for Susanna moved very quickly, and within three weeks of John Moodie's death she had left the Vickers' home in Toronto, and gone to live at Seaforth with her son Robert Moodie and his family. When she wrote to Allen Ransome on 9th November 1869 she told him: "Robert is a noble honest young man, and is fully worthy of his father. His circumstances at present are but limited, but he has a dear young wife and 3 small children to maintain on a very small salary. He is a freight agent at this place on the Grand Trunk Railway."

Susanna had told Allen Ransome in a previous letter that she had taken up drawing and painting as a means of earning money, and Allen Ransome had sent her money with a request for some sketches.

Susanna thanked him and said: "Dear Allen I wish I could send you the sketches you wish but I never tried to draw a landscape in my life, but I will send you two flower sketches, one of our Wild Marsh Iris, the other is a Rose that grew at my cottage door ... Your magnificent remuneration for these trifles (in England scarcely worth a cent) came most acceptably to help pay the decent funeral expenses for my dear husband. Generous, kind friend, I take it as it was meant and thank you with my whole heart."

Susanna in a letter written on 21st December 1869 to Catharine, told the rest of the story. She wrote: "How did you hear of Allen Ransome having remembered his old friends? He wrote me a long charming letter, and sent me his photograph. He kindly sent me a draft on the Montreal bank, for 10 pounds sterling, to be paid for by two groups of flowers, which are ready, but not yet sent to him."

In her 9th November 1869 letter to Allen Ransome, Susanna asked after people who had been part of her earlier life in England: "Are the good Richies of Wrentham all gone? I have not heard from them for years and I loved the dear old man and his family passing well."

The Rev Mr Ritchie of Wrentham Chapel had been the minister who welcomed Susanna into the Congregational Church in April 1830, and his wife had given Susanna lessons in drawing and watercolour painting. Catharine had described him as "a worthy, learned and excellent man and his wife an accomplished woman." This illustrates the dramatic confusion within Susanna's memory because this same Rev Ritchie was implicated by her, when she had told Richard Bentley in January 1856: "I was persuaded by foolish fanaticks, with whom I got entangled, to burn these MSS, it being they said unworthy of a christian to write for the stage ... That portion of my life, would make a strange revelation of sectarianism."

Susanna then goes on to mention a picture of herself which had been painted many years previously. She wrote: "I wish our dear old friend Mrs Bird would allow my daughter Agnes to copy that picture you mention. It should be faithfully returned to her but my children have such a wish to see the old care-worn Mother as she looked when young that it would be a great pleasure to gratify them. Do you think you could prevail upon my dear old friend to grant my request?"

Late 1869: Tom goes to live with Elizabeth

Sometime around the end of 1869 Tom Strickland took up Elizabeth's offer to live with her, so that by the time Catharine wrote to her son William on 6th April 1870 she could say: "Your uncle Tom lives with your aunt Elizabeth or has been for some time. He is in better health."

25th November 1869: Susanna is getting used to life with Robert's family

Seaforth is about 120 miles west of Toronto and, when Susanna thanked Kate Vickers in a letter dated 25th November 1869 for help given, she described Seaforth as: "intensely new, treeless and un-picturesque. The town is built entirely of wood, and pleasantly located in a swamp full of ugly stumps." On the plus side, she said: "They have lots of fine stores here, and dry goods are cheap."

Robert's home was kept too warm for Susanna's liking and she was worried by its location: "There is only a narrow path between the station house and the railroad. The little ones could fall from the door step, under the wheels. I shall have to keep a good watch over them." Her pets: "dear dog Quiz, and Grim the Maltese cat" had settled reasonably quickly into their new home.

December 1869: Jane is ill and Agnes goes to a funeral

Jane had another bout of severe asthma from the autumn of 1869 and through the following winter which kept her confined to her bedroom, while Agnes was busy next door in 'Park Lane Cottage' writing her biography of the 'Stuart Princesses'. By the time the book got to proof stage, Jane was able to help Agnes with the corrections. Jane's comment on the finished work was that it allowed Princess Mary Stuart to be seen in a new light, because although she was the mother of William III, little had previously been known about her.

In Southwold in December 1869, Miss Sheriffe died suddenly. She had been a friend of Jane and Agnes for many years, and had been a wealthy member of Southwold society, donating widely to local good causes. Jane was not well enough to go to the funeral but Agnes went, and was among those who accompanied the coffin to Uggeshall where Miss Sheriffe was buried near other members of her family.

21st December 1869: Susanna is not entirely happy at Seaforth

On 21st December 1869, Susanna gave a frank description of her new surroundings when she wrote to Catharine. Her son Robert, Susanna said, had moved "from a handsome commodious house to one no bigger than a nutshell." She had been given the best bedroom which was: "well carpeted, but there is only room for a small iron single bed, one chair, and one table to serve me as a wash stand, drawing and writing." However, the house would soon be bigger as Robert was busy adding a kitchen, and an extra bedroom for his mother-in-law and his two little girls. Robert and his wife Nellie also had an eighteen month old son. Susanna told Catharine "You can imagine what a mess we are in. I went over and boarded at the hotel for a week, until I could get a place to sleep in."

Despite her complaints, Susanna told Catharine that Robert's new job was a promotion. He was now: "Station Agent with an increase of $200 on his salary and the house (such as it is) rent-free, and all the wood, coal, oil (don't laugh) brooms and matches found for him. The wood cut and his water brought to him, which gives him an income of about $800. This, poor dear, will set him free from many difficulties. But the dear kind fellow has a shocking cough, and is very thin and delicate." Susanna told Catharine: "I pay dear Robert $100 a year for board. It is very little, and he don't want me to pay anything, but you know I could not feel happy if I were dependent for he has a large family to support."

Susanna's discomfort in the house was not only due to its size but also to his son's mother-in-law who, Susanna said: "takes the active management of the house. She works like a tiger, but without order or economy, is alternately petting the children or punishing them with injudicious violence. The consequence is utter disobedience to her commands."

Susanna had received letters from England: "I have received most kind letters from dear Sarah, Agnes, and Jane, which were very comforting to my heart. Dear Sarah, seems a most holy excellent Christian woman, but she always was a sweet creature. Jane's letter is really charming. Time and the influence of the blessed spirit, seem to be fast ripening her for heaven."

Correspondence with her son Dunbar had not been so satisfactory: "He wrote to me very kindly, on receiving news from Donald of his father's death, and said I <u>must</u> come to him, as it was with him I had to make my home." When Susanna decided to live instead with Robert, Dunbar then wrote: "a very disagreeable letter, going over all the old troubles. It cut me to the heart, that he could write in such a strain to me, at such a time." Susanna told Catharine that Donald and Julia had also written: "very kindly, but have not replied since my reply."

Susanna referred to the rift with the Vickers that had been caused by the transfer of the family home to Dunbar and Eliza Moodie. Susanna wrote: "I hope a perfect reconciliation has taken place between Vickers and Katie and I. I never thought John was in the wrong, nor do I think so now. Katie, like her father, took deep prejudices and saw the actions of others often in a wrong light and nothing could dispossess her mind of these convictions when once formed. Katie is greatly changed. I should never have known her. The cares of the world and the deceitfulness of riches, seem to have closed up her heart to all but her own. She was kind and hospitable, but not my Katie of old."

5th January 1870: Agnes goes to a ball

On a brighter note, there were more celebrations than usual in the Southwold area to welcome in 1870, and Agnes attended a ball. In fact, two balls were held with Agnes listed as attending the one held at Henham Hall. The papers reported: "The New Year's Ball at Henham and Heveringham Halls. East Suffolk has not hitherto been proverbial for much gaiety, beyond the shooting parties of the several large landed proprietors of which it boasts, and the comparatively small, though well attended and spirited, public balls at Lowestoft and Beccles. Therefore we have much pleasure in recording the occurrence of two very successful balls, one at Henham Hall (the seat of the Earl of Stradbroke), the other at Heveringham (the demesne of Lord Huntingfield). The ball at Henham Hall took place on Wednesday, the 5th January 1870, and it was by far the most brilliant of the two, nearly 200 of the aristocracy and residents in the neighbourhood being present.

"The company began to arrive at about ten o'clock, and were received in the grand saloon by the Countess of Stradbroke and Miss Bonham and the party staying in the house. By eleven o'clock the saloon was filled, and a general movement was made to the new wing of the noble mansion, where an admirably-arranged ball-room has been erected, and which, on this occasion, was very tastefully decorated with evergreens and appropriate mottos. The room was brilliantly lighted, and presented a fairy-like effect.

"Dancing was kept up with much spirit until one o'clock, when supper was served in the elegant suite of lower rooms, but dancers were not wanted to keep the musicians employed – while many supped, many danced – without a lull in the spirit of the ball which ended with a cotillion at about half-past five o'clock. The ball was a great success, and if equalled has never been excelled in Suffolk. The ball at Heveringham Hall took place two days later."

17th February 1870: Susanna has a daily routine

Susanna was feeling more positive about her daughter Katie Vickers when she wrote to her on 17th February 1870. She wrote: "Dearest Katie, I was so glad to get your dear letter. It cheered me for I have been far from well. I love to hear all about the dear children and their ways and doings." Susanna described the routine of her day in Robert's home: "One day here is the fact simile of the last. We breakfast at seven. I put my room in order and sit down to paint, knit or write. I cannot stand the heat of the sitting-room and prefer the cool and quiet of my own room. We dine at twelve and the same routine continues till five when we take tea, and I go back to my room and read till nine or ten, when I go to bed, to think, often for hours of the dear father, and of the absent ones. Everyone is kind and good to me especially dear Robert."

March 1870: Agnes enlarges her garden

While Jane was in poor health early in 1870, Agnes was very well. She enjoyed having her own garden to look after, and set about enlarging it by buying an adjoining piece of land. Lady Stradbroke sent her some plants from Henham Hall, mainly evergreen shrubs, and Agnes returned the compliment by sending her some of her bulbs from Holland.

By March 1870 Agnes was able to write to Sarah to tell her: "I have just concluded my purchase of the piece of land adjoining my garden. It cost me £100; so I hope you will send me some of your beautiful anemones, or anything you can spare. I sent Lady Stradbroke some of my Dutch bulbs, for she had been so bountiful to me in giving me choice shrubs."

6th April 1870: Catharine gives William a round-up of family news

By the time Catharine wrote to William on 6th April 1870 there had been snow on the ground for five months and she expected another month to pass before it melted. She told William that the first snow of the winter had fallen on 17th October 1869 and that had melted, but the next snow-fall on 5th November 1869 "has never left the ground – On 15th March it fell two feet – and again on the 27th two feet more. I fear it will be May before it is gone – but we have not had any great degree of cold."

Catharine was still dependent on family members giving her money, and was having no success getting manuscripts published. Her youngest son, Walter had just sent her $100 which she said was very generous but: "it grieves me to take his hard earnings. I am not destitute just at this time and I expect your kind aunt Gwillym will send me money in August – she sent me £10 this New Year which has been a great source of help to us – I did not succeed about that MS that promised to do fairly – It went into the hands of a party who after keeping it from July to March sent it back without a word. I have not heard from England about another MS – I will not allow myself to form any hope – the chances are nine to ten that you will be either disappointed or cheated."

Of the family in England, she wrote: "your aunt Agnes goes on writing her historical works. She was in Holland last year at The Hague and went the Rhine tour afterwards. She is a wonderful woman – nearly 75 – with the energy of 27. Aunt Jane has quite recovered and is able to go about now."

Catharine said that the family businesses set up by Samuel Strickland had been going through a bad patch, but she was sure they would recover. Walter Strickland had been renting 'Westove' while Catharine was away, and when Catharine and Kate returned at the end of March 1870, Catharine found that: "Walter had made many improvements which have added to the convenience of the house besides painting and papering it – We bought their cow and some things in the house to cover the half year's rent as I know that it was a convenience to them to take it out in that way – Owing to heavy expences and pressure from without; the Stricklands failed in the Timber business – The mill has gone into other hands and all the property belonging to George and Harry – have gone to the creditors – Roland has not been so great a loser as the farm &c belonged to your aunt during her life and – Walter did not belong to the firm – Robt was involved to some extent having endorsed for his brothers but neither he nor Percy were partners.

"The failing of one of the Toronto banks was one cause of the disaster – They had laid out a great deal on repairs of the mill new machinery in promoting the railroad and telegraph and now they will not reap the advantages of their outlay and the village which has been fostered and founded by your uncle and his sons just turn against them most ungratefully such is the gratitude of the working class – against those who have been their employers – It would have grieved your poor uncle if he could have seen the result – however the Stricklands will rise again from this trouble. Robt and Roland have been working away as usual in getting timber out and have effected a good sale with the Quebec merchants. Walter has got good employment as engineer and surveyor for government jobs – One of which is surveying and draining Buckley's Lake."

Spring 1870: There is ill-health in Jane's household

While Catharine was telling William of Jane's return to health, Jane's health was actually going through another bad patch. When writing to Catharine in August 1870, Jane told her: "I was dreadfully ill from the beginning of March till the end of May. My suffering intense – but the iodide of potassium with spirit of ammonia removed the fearful spasms. It is expensive – yet I must keep it on." Jane quite often included details of her medication, sometimes given as advice to Catharine as a home remedy, sometimes just as a general item of conversation.

Jane continued: "As soon as I was out of bed my poor Anne fell dangerously ill with jaundice and inflammation of the kidneys. After a month's nursing she went home for a change of air and scene – I had to keep a girl 3s per week without board – but of course the poor thing had something – and finding my Anne with comforts cost somewhat also. Milly, Agnes's cook, did what I wanted. My house had to be cleaned too" (presumably as a necessity to prevent the spreading of infection) "so I had more outlay than usual. It was a mercy that the stirring did not bring back my complaint.

"My Anne is now back after six weeks absence – Anne was only sixteen when she was the Reydon House maid and has been with me four years. She would not do for a stirring place of work but gets on with me who am not afflicted with a scrubbing mania."

14th April 1870: Agnes brings Catharine up to date

Agnes wrote to Catharine on 14th April 1870 with bad news about their literary endeavours: "Alas there is no hope of successfully pursuing literature. I have many things I should be able to sell, but it now seems to be impossible. The fad is a new school of literature, and all we can write is out of fashion! I can do nothing now, either for myself or others. Bell & Daldy told me to write in Mrs Gathy's Magazine and when I was foolish enough to begin an historical tale, Mrs Gathy was jealous, and caused such uncivil things to be said, that I left it unfinished."

Agnes was despondent about her own finances. She told Catharine: "I have got myself into such difficulties in buying a piece of land that joined my garden and building a wall to enclose it, that how I shall ever clear myself I cannot tell, for one unforeseen expense now follows another, that I know I never can go to London this year, nor can I write for want of works of reference.

"I have never been so badly off since Mamma's death. I blame my own folly in buying this piece of land. I am deeply penitent and it has prevented me from giving to the poor and doing as I ought. Even from helping my own dear sister." The sister Agnes referred to may be Catharine, but could also be Jane.

Agnes then gave news of the rest of the family in England: "Jane is poorly at this time for it is a cruel cold east wind. Elizabeth is now with dearest Thay. She has taken care of Tom all the winter and fitted him out with new clothes and boots, and got him into decent lodgings, and he promises to do his best, and she hopes he will get some agency if he does not fall into the sad way of drinking again.

"His daughter Mary has behaved shamefully ungrateful to darling Thay, who is the good angel of the family. And dearest Thay has been ill. I tremble when I hear of it. Pray God in his mercy to spare her, blessed and kind dear, and to restore her."

Of herself Agnes wrote: "Dearest Catharine I am very sad at this time, and not well; get no sleep, and suffer between times with lumbago so that I cannot turn in bed. I am grieved dearest Catharine that I cannot give you any hope or comfort. I am not what I was. I had an author yesterday from San Francisco, sending his poems to me, and begging my aid. Alas it is useless, and breaks my heart to be importuned uselessly. I get handfuls by the post of begging letters. Everyone is in like plight."

She then ended the letter with a miscellany of items, which add little points to the picture of life among the family. These include: "I hope your cow will succour and do well like Elizabeth's nice cow and then she will be a comfort to you ... now I do not even take the Times I am so poor that I seem out of all sorts of intelligence. I shall not be able to ask my dear nieces Emma and Susan, Percy (Strickland)'s wife, to come and stay with me in my present difficulties. I am quite and deeply sorry to send you such a different answer from what I should wish."

6th May 1870: Mrs Bird lends the miniature of Susanna

Allen Ransome must have complied with Susanna's request to borrow the miniature of herself which Mrs Bird of Yoxford owned, for on 6th May 1870 Susanna told Allen Ransome that her son

Robert "is so pleased with the idea of seeing what I looked like when young. It was so kind of you dear Allen sending the picture. I will get Agnes to copy for the others."

Susanna gave some news of Catharine before ending her letter to Allen Ransome, sending with it a copy of 'Canadian Wild Flowers'. Susanna wrote: "I send you with my poor pictures my daughter's book 'The Wild Flowers of Canada'. The sketches are her own, the letter press by your old friend Catharine P Traill. Dear Kate, she has had like myself a troubled walk along the hard dusty high way of life, but has borne a severe lot with the same cheerful loveable serenity which marked her youth."

(9th June 1870: Literary context - Charles Dickens dies)

The Strickland sisters had not only outlived the Bronte family by a wide margin, and Macaulay by over ten years years, they also outlived Charles Dickens, whose style of writing did much to change the fashion in English literature when he shot to fame with the publication of the 'Pickwick Papers' in 1836. Having been born in 1812 when Agnes and Elizabeth had been 16 and 18 respectively, he died aged 58 on 9th June 1870, when Agnes was 74.

11th June 1870: Agnes writes a biography of St Edmund

In the early part of 1870, while she was still at work writing 'Lives of the Stuart Princesses', the Vicar of Southwold asked Agnes to write a biography of St Edmund, to whom his church was dedicated. This was a relatively light-weight project and Agnes agreed, with the proceeds to go to church funds.

St Edmund had been King Edmund, the last king of East Anglia, and there are said to be as many as 50 churches in East Anglia which are dedicated to or have associations with St Edmund. He was said to have been murdered by the Danes, who tied him to a tree and shot him through with arrows. Local legend had the murder taking place at King's Meadow at Hoxne (pronounced Hox'n) in Suffolk. The King's Oak, reputed to be the tree against which the king had been tied, had been felled in 1848. A Danish arrow head was found embedded in it and strengthened belief in the local legend.

Agnes's booklet on the subject, entitled 'The Royal Christian Martyr; St Edmund, the last King of East Anglia' was published in London by Harrison & Son and was mentioned in the papers on 11th June 1870. The reviewer wrote: "Southwold. 'The Royal Christian Martyr' – Under this title an interesting pamphlet, containing the life of St Edmund, the last King of East Anglia, has been lately published, by Miss Agnes Strickland, the celebrated authoress of the 'Queens of England'. The narrative is simply written, and the well-known historical learning of the authoress is a sufficient guarantee of its truth and accuracy.

"One is apt to regret that the limits of a small pamphlet have precluded a more extended narrative, and simplification of the details. The book will be interesting to every dweller in East Anglia, and more especially to those residing in parishes where the church, as in Southwold, is dedicated to St Edmund. The manuscript was most kindly presented to the Rev RCM Rouse, the vicar of Southwold, to be published for the benefit of the Church Restoration Fund."

14th June 1870: Agnes Fitzgibbon becomes Agnes Chamberlin

When Susanna wrote to Allen Ransome on 6th May 1870, she was still living at Seaforth with Robert and his family. She had recently heard that her widowed daughter, Agnes Fitzgibbon was engaged to be married to a man who, Susanna wrote, was: "an author, an editor, and president of several of our best societies, but not over rich, as such men seldom are. I am afraid she will be removed from me as Colonel Chamberlin is a lower Canadian by birth and resides in the County he represents in Parliament."

Agnes Fitzgibbon was married to Colonel Brown Chamberlin on 14th June 1870 in Toronto. Agnes Chamberlin (hereinafter referred to as Agnes Fitzgibbon Chamberlin for the sake of narrative clarity) was then 37 years old and her new husband was six years older. She had three daughters and one son surviving from her previous marriage.

While away from Seaforth to attend her daughter's wedding, Susanna visited Belleville and her husband's grave. In a letter dated

9th July 1870 Susanna told Catharine: "It appeared to me such a haven of rest, that I longed with an intense longing to lie down beside him. Poor darling, the hare bells and Ox-eyes were growing on his lowly bed, and the robins discoursed to me sweet music in that early hour, before anyone was stirring. I left Belleville with regret."

July 1870: Sarah sums up family budgeting

When Sarah wrote to Catharine in July 1870, her letter included a frank summary of the cause of Agnes's financial problems. Sarah wrote of Agnes: "You know that she bought the copyright of the 'Lives of the Queens' and had to sell her investments to be able to do so and now her income is poor and uncertain – and she is fond of buying things she does not really want and then she is out of spirits when her money gets low, and she is always improving her place which is very pretty and comfortable and she had bought a piece of land to add to her garden – but she will be able to make the two ends meet and then she will be in better spirits – and everything is so dear that housekeeping is different from what it was."

From Sarah's report, Agnes was the only one of the four sisters in England who had difficulty keeping control of her finances. Sarah's writing went through a bit of illegibility but the sense is clear from what can be deciphered: "Dear Eliza like me is very prudent so will never ... money in expenditure and so is Jane but ... to help poor Jane a great deal ..."

Only two comments have been found in family correspondence about Catharine's perpetual shortage of money. The first was when Agnes expressed irritated surprise that Catharine was again pleading poverty not long after she received £100 from a fund of Queen Victoria in 1861. The second was a comment made by Susanna in a letter written from Lakefield to her daughter Katie Vickers on 18th January 1874. Discussing the poverty in the family of Catharine's daughter Mary, Susanna wrote, referring to Catharine: "Aunt has only a few dollars in the bank. But she will entertain, and never thinks of the ..." the rest of the sentence has disappeared as the page has been torn but the next word seems likely to have been either 'cost' or 'consequences'.

By 1870 Catharine was living in Lakefield near Sam's prosperous family, her sons William and Walter were able to send her money from time to time, Sarah sent money on a regular basis, Agnes sent the occasional donation, and boxes of gifts were still being sent from England to Canada. Despite all of these sources of help and donations, Catharine continued to plead poverty. All of this implies that Catharine was more similar to Agnes than to Sarah, Elizabeth and Jane in money matters, not with any implication that she bought unnecessary goods, but that somehow she was just not good at managing her budget.

7th July 1870: Harry Traill is murdered

Catharine's son Harry, having completed his probationary period, became an established prison officer at the jail in Kingston. His duty on 7th July 1870 was to help supervise the convicts who were burning lime at a kiln on the prison farm. At lunch time, two convicts had to stay at the kiln to ensure it was kept stoked, and Harry was left alone to supervise them.

It was Harry's misfortune that the two prisoners stoking the kiln that day, had already made plans to escape should the circumstance arise that there was only one guard on watch. The men initially tried to tie Harry up, but when he resisted, he was hit over the head and killed. Although the two men made their escape, they were soon caught, charged with murder, and sent for trial.

One of several newspaper reports of the murder unwittingly reveals the relative fame in Canada of Agnes, Susanna and Catharine at that time. The 'Durham Chronicle and Grey County Advertiser' on 14th July 1870, in the midst of an account of his murder which covered a full column and a half, included a short obituary of Harry. Inaccurately saying cousin instead of nephew, the paper reported: "The deceased guard, Harry Traill, was an active and efficient officer. He leaves a wife (sister of Dr Maclean of this county) and three children to grieve at his sad fate. He belongs to a very good Scottish family, and was a cousin to Agnes Strickland, the celebrated authoress, and to Mrs Moodie, of Belleville, also of literary fame. Mr Traill was lately overseer of the Frontenac Lead Mines. His mother lives in Peterboro." Catharine was living in Lakefield.

9th July 1870: Susanna's son Donald is destitute

A few days before the murder of Harry Traill, Susanna had received from her daughter-in-law Julia, Donald's wife, a letter which Susanna described when sending condolences to Catharine on 9th July 1870. Susanna said it was: "a heart-broken letter, wailing over the death of her youngest son. In want and sorrow, her husband ill and out of employ, without a friend to help them in that vast city. I think a sadder description of human suffering was never penned." Donald's job with the Inman Steam Company had not lasted long, and by 1870 he was increasingly subject to alcoholism.

Susanna told Catharine: "I had no means at hand to help them, nor could I obtain any before October. I sent them half the contents of my purse (10 dollars) which I am glad to say they received safely. 10 dollars is but a drop in the bucket, but even a drop will moisten the lips of one dying from thirst. All my dislike of her vanished. The misery fills me with sorrow and dread. Like all excitable people, reverses plunge Donald into despair."

11th July 1870: Queen Victoria grants Agnes a pension

There was good news for Agnes in July 1870. Some among her influential friends must have realised the state of her finances and acted to help her. A letter was sent to Agnes on behalf of the Prime Minister addressed from Downing Street and dated 11th July 1870. It announced: "Madam – Mr Gladstone desires me to inform you that the Queen has been pleased to approve of the grant to you of a pension of £100 per annum on the civil list." The letter then asked for details so that payment could be made and ended: "I am, madam, your obedient servant, WB Gordon."

When the addition of Agnes to the Civil List Pensions was announced in the papers, the grant was said to be given "in recognition of the merit displayed in her historical works." There is no record of how Agnes and Elizabeth shared the proceeds of their work, which could be argued to include this pension, nor of how they sorted out their tax liabilities. There is no mention of such matters among the family writings, and only a rumour that Agnes once disputed a demand for income tax, in the belief that earnings from writing were not taxable.

Jane in her biography of Agnes said that news of the pension came: "during a period of sickness and trial, and of pecuniary loss." It was: "welcome at a trying period, and when the years were stealing on to deaden the energy of the author and weaken her powers." The grant of a pension to Agnes was reported in a few Canadian newspapers as well as in the British press.

13th July 1870: Sarah passes on family news

On 13th July 1870, unaware of the tragedy that had happened in Canada, Sarah wrote from 'Hollow Oak' to Catharine, a letter which contained financial help as well as family news. She wrote: "Beloved Kate, Very many thanks for your last dear letter which was most interesting. I send you a letter of credit for fifteen pounds which I hope you will receive quite safe and that it will be able to furnish you a few comforts."

Sarah was using more robust paper than in the past which makes her letters easier to read. She told Catharine: "I received a nice letter from Robert Strickland yesterday. He and Caroline seem to enjoy their visit very much." Sarah was still dressed in her widow's weeds and intended to continue doing so. She wrote: "I shall be glad to send out a box of things by Robert if that can be arranged, of things that I shall never again put on for I shall always wear my weeds."

Sarah continued: "Agnes goes to London tomorrow but she cannot well afford the expense." Agnes was still researching for the 'Lives of the Stuart Princesses' and her trip to London might have been necessary for work, not only for social reasons.

Sarah's next few months were to be occupied with family visits. She told Catharine: "I am expecting Agnes in about ten days to stay with me till September when I shall, if all be well, return with her for a month to Southwold to see Jane and other friends, and at the fall of the leaf it is well to be away from so many trees as I have here."

She then showed that she, like Catharine, loved flowers and plants, though perhaps for their beauty only, and not for the botanical interest shown by Elizabeth and Jane. Sarah wrote: "I wish you could see my tulip trees they are one mass of blossom so lovely. We have had a long, cold spring and at present no summer at all but plenty of rain and everything verdant and beautiful, quite different from any other place"

(Sarah was even more sparing with her punctuation marks than edited extracts imply) "my garden is far too lovely and my greenhouses rich with gay blossoms – as to the roses I never saw them so beautiful." Sarah further on in her letter mentioned without sentimentality her chickens and ducks: "I have such a nice Poultry Yard such a number of chickens and six lovely young ducks ready to kill."

Sarah gave an account of her own health, which had been in a worrying state when Agnes had written three months previously. Sarah said: "I was very ill dear Kate for a little while but I have got better. It was inflammation of the bowels and very painful at the time. I suffer much from rheumatism and the ankles and knees are very weak. I always now walk with a stick or umbrella or I should fall – they quite give way under me and my back is also weak but still I have very much to be thankful for." Sarah was 72.

15th July 1870: Catharine's son William has a narrow escape

Although unaware of Harry's death, Sarah knew that Catharine's son William was in a part of Canada where there had been trouble, and that he might be in danger. In her July 1870 letter to Catharine, Sarah wrote: "I hope that all things will be settled without fighting and that you will have no further cause for anxiety in regard to your dear sons."

The trouble had arisen when the Metis, people of mixed French and Native Indian blood, under their leader Louis Riel had (depending on your point of view) rebelled against or resisted behaviour on the part of the Canadian government, which they thought would undermine their Catholic religion and their way of life. Officials of Hudson's Bay Company were neutral, but sometimes found themselves in a difficult position, particularly in areas where followers of Louis Riel were in the ascendant.

When writing to her friend Frances Stewart on 15th July 1870 to thank her for her condolences on the death of Harry, Catharine told her that William: "was very near meeting with as sad and sadder fate at the hand of an infuriated half-breed at Fort Pitt who gave him a blow on the back of the head with an axe, knocking him senseless and inflicting a wound.

"The wretch was about to finish his dreadful work when an old Orkney man came to his rescue and struck back the uplifted axe and tried to unclasp the grip he had on Will. Ten others stood by and never lifted a finger. On this crisis, Harriette the young wife flew to her husband's help. The brave girl – William writes 'did more to save me than even the old man.' The rebellious state of men in the forts have been very great for as W says they have lost all respect for the Co and know that they will be upheld by the rebels in power."

24th August 1870: Jane sends condolences to Catharine

Susanna had read of Harry Traill's murder in Canadian newspapers very soon after it happened but the news did not reach the family in England for several weeks, and it was not until 24th August 1870 that Jane wrote to Catharine with her condolences, followed by other family news.

Firstly Jane told of news of a financial disaster in Southwold that reached her a few days before news of Harry's death. Jane wrote: "Agnes came in to break the unpleasant news of the failure of the Crown Bank. She did it in such a way that I feared the family chain had been broken by the death of my poor brother and it was a relief to find that it was only money that was lost. Yet the loss was no small matter to me as my half year's dividend of government annuity had only been paid in two days – 20£ – but I had enough to go on with – I don't know how I should have felt had I been destitute. No words can speak the distress of many small housekeepers in this town who had lost their all. There will be a dividend of 3d or 4d in the pound in about a month – Then came the letter" with the news of Harry's death "and oh how light seemed all pecuniary loss to that experienced by the poor mother, the widow and her babes, and the brothers and sisters of poor Harry."

Jane sympathised with Catharine's worry for the safety of William and Walter, given the Metis conflict where they were working. In expressing her sympathy, Jane showed how well-educated she had been, and how she continued to build on that education. She told Catharine: "I know a great deal about those Indians from the description given of them by French travellers – for I read a great deal of French literature being a fluent reader and am glad when I can to keep up the language."

Jane gave Catharine a summary of the rest of the family in England who ranged in age from the youngest, Tom aged 63, to the oldest, Elizabeth aged 76: "Agnes left us for Sarah's last week and arrived there safely with her maid and found dear Thay quite well. Eliza was with Sarah from April to the beginning of June. She settled Tom comfortably in lodgings in Town for he fancied he could do something for himself – but of course he cannot, as he has little use of his hands and no memory. Sarah maintains him in comfort – Eliza loves him – but was not sorry to be relieved from the burden – as the early time for her dinner did not suit him. He was better but had not written to either of his sisters lately – indeed to write tires both his hand and his head very much I am certain. Eliza wrote to me lately and seemed in health and spirits."

Summer 1870: Some of Sam's family visit England

After Sam died, his widow returned to England, initially as a visitor, but spending increasing amounts of time back in Norfolk among close members of her own family. She and Catharine Traill had become close friends, but Katharine Strickland was not in Canada to give consolation to Catharine when Harry was murdered, and seems still to have been in England when Susanna wrote to Catharine a letter dated 18th November 1870. Susanna wrote: "What of Mrs Strickland? Will she return to Canada? You must miss her so very much."

Several of Sam's family visited England during 1870 as well as Katharine Strickland. These included his eldest son Robert with his English wife Caroline, the wife of Sam's son Percy Strickland, and Sam's daughter Emma Barlee. Some of the next generation, Sam's grand-children, accompanied them.

Although Sam, and both males and females from the next two generations, travelled back and forth across the Atlantic several times during the 19th century, neither Susanna nor Catharine ever returned to England, and none of the four sisters in England ever ventured a visit to Canada. Nor did Tom, despite all his sea voyages, ever visit his brother, sisters and daughter in Ontario.

1st October 1870: Susanna returns to live in Belleville

By the time that Susanna had been living with her son Robert for six months, she had become so unhappy that she wanted to move, and her visit to Toronto for her daughter Agnes's second wedding marked the end of her life in Seaforth. Instead of returning, she took lodgings in Belleville and began to live independently from her children. Susanna explained her feelings when she wrote to Catharine on 18th November 1870 when she wrote: "I felt it almost impossible to go back to Seaforth, to be under Mrs Russell's control." Mrs Russell was Robert's mother-in-law and no relation to Susanna's former lodgers, Julia and Eliza Russell, now her daughters-in-law. "I determined to stay with dear Katie when Mrs Rous wrote to me, making me the offer of boarding with her. I thought it might remove any jealous feeling of preference if I boarded with friends who are independent of my family."

Susanna continued: "I came here the 1st of October, and so far, I have no reason to regret the step. I have a large, nicely furnished bedroom with a stove in it, and carpeted floor and everything comfortable and handy. I can remain in my own room or join the family when I like, and then, I am independent. My absolute mistress, and to me this is life. I am near to my dear husband. A couple of minutes walk brings me to his grave, and every fine day, I go alone to spend some time in communion with the dear spirit, who seems to meet me on the spot."

The reconciliation between Susanna and her son-in-law John Vickers, had put an end to Susanna's financial worries, although she did not always admit to other people that this was the case. She now not only had John Vickers' financial advice but also, when needed, his money to help her. Susanna told Catharine: "Mrs Rous's terms were liberal, only two dollars and a half a week, and I was to find my own bedding. Upon consulting with Vickers, he thought I would be able to pay this, and any deficiency he would make up for me, both in clothes and board."

The financial help given by John and Katie Vickers went beyond mere advice and topping up Susanna's rent. Susanna told Catharine that while she had been in Toronto: "Katie, dear soul, took every care of my outward woman and helped make up with her own hands, a suit of very handsome mourning, bought me boots and shoes enough to last me half a life, and no less than four excellent widow's caps, and told me anything I wanted just to write without scruple to her and it would be furnished."

14th November 1870: The trial of Harry's murderers takes place

Catharine, in a letter to her friend Frances Stewart dated 14th November 1870, gave news of the trial of the two men involved in the death of her son Harry Traill. Catharine wrote: "I have just seen the Kingston papers giving the trials of those unhappy men. Mann is condemned to death on the 14th of next month – Smith for 10 more years added to his term of 4 yet unexpired. God give the condemned man grace during the few short weeks left to him of life." Mann had struck the fatal blow; Smith had distracted Harry's attention.

"These things have revived our grief for our lost one – It is so painful to read the sad details – Nothing new seems to have been elicited from the prisoners only that it had long been a planned thing to silence the guard by morphine or other wise – My poor daughter-in-law had to appear in court to identify the watch and clothes – A sad trial for the poor girl – I fear that this renewal of her grief will have made her quite ill – God help her poor soul."

In her letters to Allen Ransome dated 15th December 1870 and 17th October 1871 Susanna described Catharine and her character. In the earlier letter she wrote: "The murder of her son by an escaped convict was a great blow to her, and her daughter Mrs Atwood is threatened with consumption. She bears these things with real Christian fortitude. Hers is a lovely character." In the later letter Susanna wrote: "She has worn better than I have. Her calm placid spirit can better resist the rude shock waves of thought that beat me to pieces. The murder of her son was a terrible blow but she had the moral courage to forgive the wretched murderer."

18th November 1870: Agnes Fitzgibbon Chamberlin is settled in Ottawa

Agnes Fitzgibbon Chamberlin's move to Ottawa and her busy new life, brought an end for the time being to her collaborative work with Catharine. Susanna told Catharine in a letter dated 18th November 1870: "Agnes seems comfortably settled in Ottawa among the big wigs. I am only fearful lest the company that unavoidably she must keep should involve her in difficulties. He is not a rich man, and has to provide for three old maiden sisters and though his situation is a good one, 2000 dollars salary, yet house rent and every thing is so dear there, in consequence of the great fires, that she will find it hard to live in any style."

'The great fires' to which Susanna referred, had occurred in the summer of 1870, particularly in August that year. The weather had been dry and hot for months, and fires began to break out in various parts of the countryside around Ottawa in June 1870. What became known as 'The Great Fire' was accidentally started on 17th August 1870 by men working on the track of the Canadian Central Railway. They had set fire to piles of brush wood to clear a path, when winds rose and carried sparks into the surrounding and bone-dry cedar woods. The ensuing fire quickly became unstoppable, and at its height was travelling faster than a man could run. Although a great deal of timber, property and vegetation was destroyed, the loss of life was remarkably low under the circumstances, with only about ten people being killed.

Newspaper headlines were dramatic: "Awful fires! The Whole of Central Canada in one Mass of Flame! Ottawa City in Great Danger of Destruction!" The fire was stopped, according to a local history society: "by opening the dam at Dow's Lake to create a flood down Preston Street to Nepean Bay" and by this means much, though not all of Ottawa was saved.

18th November 1870: Kate Traill nearly goes to England

Robert Strickland returned to Canada in the autumn of 1870. Susanna in writing to Catharine on 18th November wrote: "I have had no news from England since the middle of summer. But the return of Robert Strickland must have brought you tidings of the whole family and I hope, something more substantial."

There were plans, which never came to fruition, for Catharine's daughter Kate to go to Sarah in England. Kate Traill was 34 years old and, in common with Catharine's other older children, had poor health. She lived with Catharine and, despite her ill health, took care of household matters.

Susanna asked Catharine in her letter dated 18th November 1870: "When does Kate go to England? You will find it hard to part with her, but it might make her independent, if the climate should happen to agree with her. Aunt" (presumably Sarah though not specified) "seemed very much set on having her with her." Susanna then added one of her less endearing comments: "Poor dear, I daresay that she feels lonely in her old age, dependent entirely on servants."

15th December 1870: Susanna's finances are taken care of, but she misses John

In 1870 Susanna's finances got into difficulties again as she told Allen Ransome in her letter to him dated 15th December 1870. Susanna wrote: "The lawyer" in Belleville "who had charge of my little property invested it in his own name, and if my son-in-law John Vickers had not come to the rescue I should have lost the little I had. I had a better opinion of this young man and was really grieved to give up my confidence in his integrity." After this had been sorted out, John Vickers became Susanna's official representative in all business and legal dealings.

Susanna, in a letter to Catharine dated 6th January 1871 again illustrates that she was being looked after by the Vickers, by listing the Christmas gifts they had sent to her. She wrote: "My Katie sent me a box full of good things by old Santa Claus – a nice winsey dress, 6 yds of grey fine flannel very good, for bloomers, card board, paper, pens, envelopes, colors. A fine Christmas cake, 2 great Lake Superior salmon, 6 boxes of sardines, 2 of choice figs, 3 large glass jars of lemon preserve, 6 packets of Epps chocolate, 3 bottles of good wine, and a lot of packets of corn starch and arrowroot. All very nice and acceptable. The larger eatables like the salmon and cake I share with my friends in the house. The dress has made me a most warm and comfortable house gown and I have it on now. Katie has been most kind to me, and I can go to her whenever I get tired of living here."

Although John and Katie Vickers were ensuring the Susanna wanted for nothing, Susanna continued to grieve for her husband. She told Allen Ransome in her December 1870 letter that she had been: "busy looking over dear Moodie's papers and letters, a sad task that keeps my eyes weak and watery. Looking over letters that I wrote to him in the Bush, when he was away from me for two long years in the rebellion." Susanna was here referring to the time when John Moodie was paymaster to the Militia, before he became Sheriff in Belleville.

Susanna moved into lodgings with the Rous family in October 1870 and her happiness there lasted less than three months. By the time she wrote to Catharine on 6th January 1871, she had become depressed. She wrote: "I feel profoundly sad, and spend most of my time in my room, only going down for meals. I have grown a solitary silent creature, wrapping my soul up in the past. To an independent creature like me, the want of a home is terrible. I pine and sigh for liberty to do just as I please."

She was critical of the food provided saying: "I suffer so from dyspepsia. Our diet is chiefly composed of stews and hashes, fat and greasy, everything but nice. But of course, I cannot expect very good diet for three dollars per week, but I never object to them but prefer a cup of tea and a bit of toast. It is quite a misfortune to have been a good cook, but I can't help it. I don't care for luxuries. Plain food cooked well is a luxury, if only porridge."

Susanna had also taken a dislike to one of the daughters of the family, referring to her own sister Jane when describing her to Catharine. Susanna described the daughter as: "very disagreeable and not over civil. She has a horrid temper, which is trying to the whole house. A sort of Jane, without her talents. It is strange, that in most families there is one, that always is a trial to all the rest, and who get their own way merely by insisting upon it. Who are selfish, indolent and conceited, and fancy themselves the genius of the family."

There is no other evidence to support such a description of Jane, though Elizabeth's temper and tendency to be bossy are mentioned by most members of the family at one time or another, nor is there any clue as to why Susanna should feel inclined to describe Jane in such a way. As with an earlier unkind comment by Catharine, a very different picture of Jane was given, in due course (22nd June 1888), in an obituary notice.

Susanna in this letter to Catharine dated 6th January 1871, passed on what news she had received "from dear Sarah just before Christmas. Very kind, but no particular news. Agnes was better, Jane quite well, Tom failing, but steady." Susanna then went on to give a little more information about pictures painted of them in their youth, by writing that Sarah: "sent a folded paper with her letter, which she said contained her photograph taken from the likeness that Cheesman took of her. I clutched the paper. But alas, she had forgotten the photograph. How surprised she will be to find it unsent." It would probably have been sent successfully with a later letter, though not mentioned again. It is the second portrait painted by Thomas Cheesman which was mentioned as making its way to Canada, the first having been Susanna's own, lent by Mrs Bird.

Susanna was earning some money by painting flowers. Someone called Mrs Ross: "ordered two paintings of me, and sent me 12 dollars for them, besides ordering another. I now have three orders to fill. Truly my darling these pictures pay better than the pen." She had had a day out: "a very enjoyable Christmas day with Mrs Murney. She sent the sleigh for me, and sent me home at 12 at night. It is the first evening I have spent out since I was alone." Mrs Murney was the widow of Edward Murney who had been a political foe of John Moodie in the past.

Susanna then made a surprising comment about smoking, presumably a pipe: "I have left off smoking for the last three months. I miss it, but do not mean to go back. If I had a place of my own it would be all very well, but it is a nuisance to those who do not smoke themselves." In England, Jane presumably took snuff as Agnes had a snuff box made for her, out of a piece of wood she had been given from a tree associated with Mary, Queen of Scots. There is no mention of any of the other sisters smoking or snuff taking. Agnes at some point described the fashion for smoking as madness.

February 1871: Clinton Atwood visits Agnes in Suffolk

Clinton Atwood, Catharine's son-in-law returned to England in January 1871 to visit his elderly father, the rector of Ashleworth in

Gloucestershire. He made arrangements for someone to look after the farm while he was away, and during his absence Catharine and her daughter Kate returned to Rice Lake Plains to live with Annie and her children, and to keep them company.

When he was in England, Clinton visited Agnes who gave the details in a letter to Catharine dated 9th April 1871. She wrote: "Your son-in-law Clinton Atwood wrote to me nearly two months ago telling me he was with a brother at a Suffolk rectory not far from Woodbridge, and was wishing to pay me a flying visit if convenient and agreeable. Of course I replied that I should be happy to see him and his brother, but the brother did not come.

"I availed myself of Clinton's coming to provide a box for you containing a new black silk dress, for you dearest Cathy, one for Susie, and a mohair dress fit for mourning, for you, one for her, one for your Katie, and one for Mary. I also sent you a pretty shawl for summer wear, black and white, quite new, and a lovely shawl, for Annie, which I have never worn, and will last her for many years, God grant her health to wear it with much pleasure.

"I send a nice net with a fashionable navy and black silk under skirt for Kate fit for evening or dinner dress. I have not worn it many times and it will do very well for her. I also sent a pretty muslin dress for Mary and a black silk mantilla and some of my poems to fill up.

"I had sent a nice parcel of things to go with dear Thay's parcel before and a flax muslin for Mrs Chamberlin which when you have the means to send to her you can let her have. There is a black moiree dress for you not new but you can taddle it up to wear of an afternoon. It was well they were not in Clinton's box, for they would have filled it too full. There were six yards in his box I thought you would know what to do with, either to make a cloak or jackets for you and the girls."

Agnes was clearly very generous in the clothes she sent to Canada, including gifts to Susanna and Agnes Chamberlin. It sounds as though she had not been told that the Vickers were taking good care of Susanna, and Susanna's daughter Agnes Fitzgibbon Chamberlin was no longer struggling to make ends meet.

This was particularly kind of Agnes given that her own and Elizabeth's finances had received a blow. Agnes told Catharine: "I heard from Elizabeth the other day. She is in great trouble about our tenant, Carling, having taken himself off, and left more than a year's rent in arrears, and so dilapidated the house that we shall be compelled to sell it for less than we gave for it. You know she does not take such misfortunes patiently and has always something bitter to say to me about it."

4th March 1871: Susanna is in different lodgings in Belleville

In Colorado, Dunbar Moodie was living in the Greeley Colony which had got under way in 1870. The colony aimed to show that if the land was properly irrigated, it could be made suitable for farming, so that mining need not be the only means of making a living in the area. The inhabitants had to be teetotal, religious and have high moral standards. Prospective colonists paid $155 into communal funds, which were used to buy land and construct an irrigation system near the junction of two rivers in Colorado.

The colony was named after Horace Greeley, the editor of the 'New York Tribune' who promoted and gave financial backing to the idea. At its foundation, about 3,000 people responded to advertisements about the project, from whom 700 were selected. In 1871 the colony was thriving and expanding, and the Rous family in Belleville decided to become colonists.

As a result, Susanna had to find a new home, as she told Allen Ransome in a letter dated 12th July 1871. Susanna wrote: "My friend Mr Rous and his family left Belleville the 4th of March and joined my son Dunbar in Horace Greeley's New Colony in Colorado." Susanna had apparently become reconciled to her life in the Rous household and said she was sorry to part company with them. She told Allen Ransome: "The week before their departure I had to seek out another home. I found no small difficulty in obtaining suitable quarters. At length a widow lady with a single daughter consented to board me, but at a higher rate than I had paid with my dear friends. I felt low enough and sad enough in parting with them to sojourn with comparative strangers, but have had no reason to complain."

April 1871: Sarah, Tom and Robert Strickland are on the census

The 1871 census was taken on the night of 2nd/3rd April and, as usual, no trace has been found of Elizabeth, Jane or Agnes Strickland.

Sarah is recorded as having independent means, being the head of her household, and having four female members of staff living-in. They were a housekeeper aged 58; a cook aged 34; an upper housemaid aged 21 and an under housemaid aged 18. Her address was 'Hollow Oak' in Haverthwaite, and Sarah had a visitor staying with her on census night, another lady of independent means who had been born in Bombay. Sarah was 73 years old.

By contrast, Tom was boarding in Tower Hamlets in London, not far from the Thames and London Docks, and is recorded as a retired master mariner aged 63. Tom was not the only paying member of the household, there was also a lady boarder aged 74 and a 12 year old lodger. The head of household was a 46 year old ships' clerk, his wife was 35 and the household was completed by a 17 year old domestic servant girl.

Another part of the Strickland family was in England for the 1871 census. Robert Strickland and his wife Caroline, both aged 40, are recorded as visitors at a house in Acton, West London. With them were their daughters Charlotte (aged 14) and Agnes (aged 13) both born in Douro, Canada, plus their son Arthur (aged 12), who had been born in Southwold.

A few days after the census was taken, Agnes wrote to Catharine from 'Park Lane Cottage'. On Easter Sunday 9th April 1871 Agnes wrote: "I have heard from Caroline and her children, and shall probably see them when I go up to town this month, but I have not accommodation for so large a party in my cottage here, neither could I afford it, besides I am growing old and infirm now, and a little puts me out of the way." Agnes was approaching her 75th birthday.

Although the trip that Agnes was planning to London was mainly a business trip, there was potential for it to turn into quite a family gathering. Agnes told Catharine "Dearest Thay is coming to join me in London. I shall try and dispose of my Stuart writings. The last thing I shall ever write. It is now fatiguing to write letters even. This, I think, will be my last visit to London."

May 1871: Catharine visits Kingston Jail

When writing to Annie Atwood on 5th May 1871, Catharine included an account of visits she had made with Harry's widow, Lily Traill to Kingston Jail where Harry had been murdered. They had visited Harry Traill's grave and planted some flowers. Catharine wrote: "On Sunday I went to church and in the afternoon one of the (prison) officers lent a double buggy and horse to L and me to take us to the cemetery. A lovely spot where sleeps the mortal remains of our beloved Harry – I had begged some sweet violets in bloom and L and I planted them in the turf over him – A sweet but sad tribute of love to our dear lamented one – It rained while we were there – and then a most glorious rainbow came in the east – the brightest and most lovely I ever saw – It spanned the valley below us ... so you saw the shadow of the landscape through its lovely hues – It seemed a happy token of Gods promises to his believing children departed from earth to Heaven."

Catharine continued: "Yesterday I went with dear Lily and Katie to the Prison – With a few lines addressed to the Guards who had shewn such kind sympathy to L in her sorrow – The deputy met us, and was most kind – and so was the Warden Mr Crichton and altogether the visit was one of great, but sad interest."

Mrs Mann as well as her son, the convict who had been executed for Harry's murder, had been a member of a gang called the Malahide Raiders, and she was herself a prisoner in Kingston Jail. Catharine told Annie: "I have not time now to dwell on all that I saw but you will be glad to hear that I had a few minutes to converse with D Mann's mother. That she wept much when I told her who I was and then she grasped my hand and said my speaking kindly to her had been a great comfort to her.

"I could obtain nothing more as to anything of our dear H but that Mann had a great respect even affection for him that their plans were laid for escape not knowing who was to be on guard that day. That he had minded Harry's watch chain for him that very morning nor did he contemplate a fatal blow when he struck the Guard. This he maintained to every one – He believed Mr Traill to be a man of religious impressions from his way of speaking and his general good conduct among the men."

After Harry's death, his widow with her two sons went to live with her brother in Kingston, Ontario and she was eventually granted $1,000 by the government to help with the financial consequences of her loss. Her three year old daughter, Katie, went to live with Catharine and her daughter Kate, and became known as Katie 3, or Katie. Because Catharine (Traill), Kate Traill (her daughter) and Katie Traill (her grand-daughter) shared the same home for much of the time hereafter, it is important to emphasise who-was-who amongst them.

Catharine told Frances about the new arrival. She wrote: "My dear little grand child is a source of great interest yet of anxious care to her aunt and myself – She is very bright and quick but also very excitable and passionate at times, needing great care, she is so affectionate and winning in her little ways that she makes us very fond of her – as who could help being of a little one so cast upon our sympathy and affections."

29th June 1871: Susanna has a publishing offer

Susanna had the chance to earn more money from her previously published work, by having them re-published in Canada, but she needed Richard Bentley's permission before she could accept an offer made to her.

A Toronto publisher had made the offer and on 29th June 1871, Susanna wrote to Richard Bentley explaining the situation. She wrote: "I have a prospect of publishing a Canadian edition of all my works. You most kindly restored to me all the copyrights but that of 'Roughing It in the Bush' and 'The World Before Them' but these are just the ones required. I feel it is too much to ask of you. Yet, the proceeds which we expect from the intended publication would place me beyond the chilling grasp of poverty."

Susanna wrote the letter while staying with the Vickers in Toronto, and had already been comfortably placed 'beyond the chilling grasp of poverty' but Susanna in her writing does not seem to feel the need, or is unable, to stick to the facts. For this reason, her work 'Roughing It in the Bush', which she to some extent claimed was a biography, has not been taken as such in trying to reconstruct Susanna's life. There may well have been elements of truth in her stories but it is impossible to separate them from dramatic elaborations.

12th July 1871: Susanna's daughter-in-law suffers abreakdown

In the letter which Susanna wrote to Allen Ransome from Toronto on 12th July 1871, she wrote about her daughter-in-law Nellie, wife of Robert Moodie who had been unwell since the birth of a son in May that year. Susanna wrote: "Her illness has culminated in raving madness, and her afflicted husband had to bring her here last week to place her in the Asylum. I promised I would go as often as I could to see her and I have been twice since he left and spent a good part of both days with her. With me she is as gentle as a lamb."

In her letter to Richard Bentley dated 10th August 1871, Susanna wrote on the same subject. She wrote: "Dr Workman says, that at her age 24, she may get over it, but I doubt it very much. She has every care and comfort in that 'paradise of the lost' as she calls that beautiful place."

Part 7: From seven to four

The end for Agnes; contentious Will;
Tom follows; Elizabeth next; work on a biography;
moves from Canada to England

10th August 1871: Susanna's works are re-printed in Canada

Richard Bentley quickly gave his permission for Susanna to use his copyrights, and Susanna wrote to him on 10th August 1871 to thank him and to send condolences to him on the recent death of his wife. However, Richard Bentley himself died on 10th September 1871, possibly before he had received Susanna's letter.

On the same day that she wrote to Richard Bentley, Susanna also wrote to Allen Ransome and told him of the deal which John Vickers had negotiated on her behalf. Referring to the republishing of 'Roughing It in the Bush', Susanna wrote: "Rose and Hunter of Toronto gave me 200 dollars for the publication of 2,500 copies and a Royalty of 4 cents on every copy required above that number. I have written an introductory chapter contrasting Canada as it was 40 years ago and what it is now. When I came to Belleville in the year '40 it was on the very edge of the wilderness" whereas by 1871 it had become "a fine handsome town full of fine buildings."

Susanna felt that her republished book was better received in Canada in 1872 than when it originally appeared twenty years earlier. This was helped by the 'Canadian Monthly and National Review' (which had the same publisher as Susanna's book) which is said to have described 'Roughing It in the Bush' as: "an extremely lively book, full of incident and character. Although its primary objective was to give warning by means of example, it is by no means a jeremiad. On the contrary, we almost lose sight of the immigrant's troubles in the ludicrous phases of human character which present themselves in rapid succession."

August 1871: Agnes attends the Scott Centenary

Agnes was sent a ticket and a personal invitation to a celebration in Edinburgh worded as follows: "Mr Usher, Secretary of the Scott Celebration, begs leave, at the request of the Committee, respectfully to enclose a ticket for the Festival to Miss Agnes Strickland, and trusts that she will do them the honour of being present." The festival would be held in Edinburgh in August 1871 to celebrate the 100th anniversary of the birth of Sir Walter Scott.

Despite some reservations about such a long journey, Agnes decided to accept the invitation and to stay with her friend the Sheriff of Edinburgh, Mr Home and his family. In a letter to Sarah written shortly before the event Agnes wrote: "The Sheriff has a ticket for the Commemoration, not far from my place, and will see me in and take care of me. Nothing is talked of in Edinburgh but the Commemoration."

Afterwards, Agnes told Sarah: "The great day, my dear Thay, is over. We lunched at Miss Craig's, in George Street, where I was to dress; but the Sheriff was in a great hurry, and wanted me to start before my maid, ticket, and gloves arrived. As soon as my arrangements were completed, the Sheriff took me and Miss Craig in a fly; but the fly broke down, and we had to get down while the Sheriff went in search of a cab, and my Indian burnoose was too smart for the crowded street. However, an open carriage was procured, and, in spite of the accident, we were much too early.

"We were very near the speakers, and after waiting more than an hour, they came in. Sir William Stirling-Maxwell of Keir spoke for an hour very well. The Dean of Westminster made a speech, which the noise unfortunately prevented me from hearing. There was a refection of cake, wine and fruit set out on the long narrow tables. The Hall was crowded, and the heat so great that I was forced to leave before it was half over. I saw no one that I knew, and upon the whole it was very disappointing." Agnes spent a fortnight in Scotland visiting friends before heading back to England, visiting Sarah en route to Southwold.

December 1871: Sarah's income drops for a while

In a letter carrying season's greetings for Christmas 1871 and New Year 1872, Susanna passed on to Catharine, family news from Sarah. Susanna wrote: "Sarah is well, as are all my sisters and poor Tom, but Sarah, poor dear seems to have met with a great pecuniary loss by the burning of Chicago."

The Great Fire of Chicago is said to be the most famous fire in American history. Much of the city was built of wood, and there had been no rain for months when the fire started in the evening of 8th October 1871. How the fire started is not known but, having begun in the west of the city, a steady south west wind carried it from building to building northwards and eastwards. The fire had become out of control after only a few minutes, and it continued through the night and all the next day.

By the morning of 10th October the fire reached undeveloped areas of the city and the banks of Lake Michigan where the fire began to die down. At the same time some rain fell and the fire was extinguished, but not before a third of the city had been destroyed and 100,000 people made homeless. The cost of the damage was estimated at 200 million dollars, or about £50 million.

Susanna wrote to Catharine: "It seems strange that it should affect her in any way, but she says 'I draw the greater part of my income from 1000 shares in the London and Liverpool Royal Insurance Company and they are the greatest sufferers in the Chicago fire, having already paid upwards of £400,000 to it. I shall not be able to draw any income this year or perhaps next either. My instalment to be paid next March was £584. I do not fret about it. I have suffered so much deeper sorrow. I only regret that it will shorten my hand to help others. However, I have not anticipated my income and with economy have enough to live upon for a year and to give Tom his usual allowance'." Susanna added the comment: "What a noble woman she is – a real Christian. No literary reputation is equal to this."

Susanna was still reasonably happy in her new lodgings in Belleville, but her room was hard to keep warm in cold weather. Susanna described her accommodation to Catharine as: "a very large cold bedroom with 3 cranky windows and 3 cold drafty doors, and though I keep a good fire, I can scarcely keep myself warm. I have had to buy wood at $8 per cord and give $1 more for having it cut and piled." A cord of wood is defined as equivalent to 128 cubic feet of well-stacked cut wood; which would be a pile of wood just over 5 feet high, wide and long, and not far short of a cubic metre.

News of Robert Moodie and of his wife was not good. Nellie was still in a mental hospital and, Susanna told Catharine, Robert's: "old cough has returned, and he seems ill and dejected. Poor hapless Nell is no better. When her mother went to take her new winter clothes last week, she kicked them about the floor, and would have torn them to pieces, if the keepers and nurses had not interfered."

January 1872: Susanna mentions the Cheesman miniature of herself.

In writing to Catharine a letter thought to date from January 1872, Susanna wrote: "I enclose a photo, of the picture cousin Cheesman took of me. Is it not like all your girls, especially Kate. I was astonished at the resemblance. I sent one to dear sister Sarah, who seems so pleased with it." By this point then Susanna has mentioned their father's cousin, Thomas Cheesman having painted a likeness of herself and Sarah (reference 6th January 1871). The only other mention found of family paintings by Thomas Cheesman is the comment made by Jane and already reported (ref 1820s) where Jane said: "Her cousin painted a fine miniature of Agnes during one of his visits to Reydon, which is now in the possession of her sister, Mrs Gwillym." No mention has been found in family correspondence or records of Thomas Cheesman having painted a portrait of Catharine, Jane or Elizabeth.

The family had a picture of Tom, date unknown, which Catharine at some point enquired about. Jane told her that it was hanging on a wall in Agnes's home. What happened to it thereafter is unknown.

3rd March 1872: Catharine writes an obituary of Frances Stewart

On 24th February 1872 Catharine's friend Frances Stewart died, and her daughter Ellen Dunlop asked Catharine to write an obituary to appear in the local paper. When sending her condolences to Ellen and confirming that the obituary had been written, Catharine in a letter dated 3rd March 1872 gave news of her own household. Her daughter Kate, who normally took care of the housework: "is quite crippled and suffering much pain from a swelling on one of the fingers of her right hand which makes her unable for her household work." Catharine had carried out the necessary household chores, she told Ellen: "certain things have to be done – and I weary so soon that it is little I can do." Catharine was 70 years old.

Although Catharine was physically in a weak state, her finances were satisfactory as she told Ellen a couple of weeks later. She wrote: "You will be glad to learn that I received a cheque for $60 from the Gov't at Toronto for MS pamphlet and have the prospect of $50 from Ottawa shortly for the MS in Mr Lowe's hands there. This addition to my funds will relieve me from want for this year. See dear friend how God does provide for me and mine – and that kind nephew Robt S not only had sent me two cords of wood, but sent down a man to cut and pile it in the shed for me this very day. Truly I have much cause to be very grateful for I have many kind friends and many blessings are showered upon my unworthy head."

March 1872: Agnes makes a faux pas

Agnes's 'Lives of the Stuart Princesses' was published in March 1872 by Bell & Daldy, and Agnes sent copies to the Queen of Holland, to Baroness van Doorne and to Mrs Harrison in Amsterdam, with expressions of thanks for their help.

Unfortunately, and inexplicably, when Agnes sent out complimentary copies in England, she forgot the help given to her by Mr Wayland Kershaw, the librarian of Archbishop Tait, and did not send a copy to the Library of Lambeth Palace. She made this oversight worse by transposing the Librarian's names when she included him among her written acknowledgements within the book. He had given her a very large amount of help and Agnes's oversight and mix-up with his name were quite out of character.

When he wrote to point out the error in his name, Mr Wayland Kershaw's letter was very cleverly and carefully worded. Headed 'The Library, Lambeth Palace' he wrote: "My Dear Madam, – Allow me with much gratitude to thank you for mentioning my name in your book just published, 'Lives of the Stuart Princesses'. There is, however, one mistake – viz., 'Kershaw Wayland' for 'Wayland Kershaw'. In a future edition may I ask you kindly to see that this palpable error is corrected.

"The Archbishop and Mrs Tait are here, and I told Mrs Tait last Friday that your work was published. It rejoices me to see that so many of your extracts were from our MSS., which just makes the use of the library the Archbishop would desire.

"I would, should circumstances permit, beg the honour of a copy, which I can place in the library for a time, and afterwards perhaps keep for my own use. We have obtained the book from Mudie's Library. – I beg to remain, dear madam, with grateful respect, faithfully yours, S Wayland Kershaw."

Mudie's Library was the precursor of the Public Lending Library.

April 1872: John Vickers has a stroke

When Mr and Mrs Rous moved to Colorado, their eldest daughter Maggie, with whom Susanna got on well, remained in Belleville and they began to exchange letters. When Susanna wrote to Maggie Rous on 22nd June 1872 she apologised for not writing sooner, explaining that: "Mr Vickers' dangerous illness, which was expected to end fatally; and from which he is only now slowly recovering, put everything else out of my head."

The illness sounds like a stroke, for Susanna told Maggie: "The second attack of paralysis was more dangerous than the first, and he was unable for several weeks to move his left arm and leg, during the last few days, he has been able to sit up and move them a little, and the medical men consider that all danger is over for the present."

This misfortune for John Vickers led to an improvement in the life of Robert Moodie. Susanna said: "One good thing has resulted from this domestic trouble. Mr V has induced Robert to give up the station at Seaforth, and take the situation of Superintendent of his office, on a salary of 100 dollars per month. This will place Robert in a very comfortable position, and he will be near his poor wife, and good schools for the children, and will enjoy the society of friends who truly love him and wish him well."

4th May 1872: Catharine expresses her religious feelings

Catharine wrote again to Ellen Dunlop on 4th May 1872 to thank her for some books sent as a remembrance of Frances Stewart. They were religious works and Catharine expressed her own deeply held religious feelings and also her self-doubt when she wrote: "The little manual of devotions, McDuffs 'Morning and Night Watches' are daily food, and very precious for her dear sake whose eye so often rested on its pages, and whose hand marked its most striking truths. But Nelly dearest I have hardly yet begun to realize the Christian life. I seem so far away from my Saviour. I would cry 'I believe Lord, help thou mine unbelief'."

On a more pragmatic level, Catharine told Ellen Dunlop of her own health. She wrote: "I have had a bad spell of sore throat again and the old pain in my back too, which makes writing always a painful thing for me. I fear I shall have to lay aside my pen soon – my vocation you see is leaving me and I it."

Kate, however, was well again, and Catharine told Ellen Dunlop they were about to have an addition to their household: "We are busy preparing for my dear sister Moodie to be an inmate with us, and Kate has much to do, and I can do little to assist. I cannot tend my garden as I used to; I weary so at the least exertion. We have not got (what will be) the spare room furnished as yet and shall hardly be settled until we know what arrangements will be required for my sister's accommodation." Susanna, after just over a year and a half living in lodgings in Belleville, was ready for a change.

May 1872: Agnes nears the end of her literary endeavours

Agnes wrote to Catharine in the spring of 1872 with news of herself and the family in England. She wrote: "My own beloved Catharine, I have let some time pass without acknowledging your last letter but I was so busy in correcting the proofs of my last volume and then I had many letters to write, and was so much fatigued that I was fain to wait till a quiet hour succeeded in order to write, dearest Catharine, to you."

"The shabby publishers have only sent me 4 copies" of the 'Stuart Princesses' "but I send one to you, as you 'asked me' to spare you one. I am sure you will like it as well as the Queens of England. Alas I have no hope that it will be so popular. I have not sold the copyright of this, and it is possible I may get something more from future editions. But no second edition has been called for 'The Tudor Princesses' although Lady Jane Gray and her sisters were among them and I expected the sale would have been far greater than the publishers think fit to acknowledge. But this is the last work I shall publish; although I shall miss the cash, for I am much poorer than I was. But it is now time to finish, for my days cannot be long in this world." Agnes's remaining literary task was to finish abridging her 'Life of Mary Stuart' from five volumes down to two.

Of her plans for the coming year, Agnes told Catharine: "I do not go to London till after Whitsuntide" which was 20th May in 1872 "and to dear Thay at the end of June. I should like to pay a last visit to Scotland this summer, but almost all my dear friends who used to welcome me, are in the 'Land of the Dead'."

Agnes's life when she was living at 'Park Lane Cottage' was quiet and orderly, with time set aside each day for work and letter-writing, for gardening, for exercise and for company.

Unlike when she lived at Reydon Hall, there were near neighbours with whom she could socialise. As well as enjoying her garden and walking, Agnes spent more time than formerly sitting quietly on Gun Hill, the green in Southwold overlooking the beach, named after the six 18-pounder guns placed there to commemorate the Battle of Sole Bay of 1672.

Of the rest of the family in England, Agnes told Catharine: "Jane has got very well. Her asthma is cured and her house nicely altered through the bounty of dearest Thay. Elizabeth is well. She is very angry if any one addresses her as Eliza in the old fashion. I have just received a very kind letter from her. She has been ill, but now is better, indeed well."

22nd June 1872: Susanna's life is more sociable in Lakefield

By 22nd June 1872 Susanna was staying with Catharine and, in a letter to Maggie Rous, described Catharine's home. She wrote: "My sister's cottage is very charming. It stands on the banks of a beautiful river. The green slope to the water is a natural grove of forest trees, and her garden is full of flowers and flowering shrubs. We are about ten minutes walk from the village." A picture of Catharine's cottage, taken at an unknown date, shows a substantial dwelling seeming to deserve the description of a house rather than a cottage, a comment also applicable to Susanna and John's former 'stone cottage'.

Life for Susanna in Lakefield was more sociable than it had been recently in Belleville. She told Maggie Rous: "All my nephews and their wives come to see me. We had a grand party last week up to Julian's Landing in Stoney lake." (subsequently re-named Kawartha Lake) "We went up in a small steamer, the Chippewa, that starts from here, landing on just the opposite side of the river. The sail was quite enjoyable, and the wild rocky islands of Stoney lake still in the wilderness, very beautiful. 1200 of these islands have been surveyed, without counting numbers of bare granite rocks that rear their red heads above the water, that look like the bare bones of some former world. We reached our destination about 3 o'clock and dined on board. A capital picnic dinner. After dinner, we all went ashore to look for flowers in the woods, but the sun was so hot and the paths so steep, and the moskitoes and black flies so savage that we were glad to return to the boat."

There had been seventeen people in the party and Susanna listed them. Ten of the participants were related to her. These were: "Mr and Mrs Robert Strickland, and their two pretty daughters, of 15 and 16, who look like twins, Mrs Traill and my niece Kate, Mrs Roland S and her husband, Mr George and Percy S" as well as "Auld Mistress Moodie."

Susanna also mentioned to Maggie Rous, the other members of Catharine's household: "my dear niece Kate is at all times very delicate. She is an excellent girl and we get on splendidly together" also "wee Katie, poor Harry's little orphan. A clever, amusing little elf, who adds a good deal to the comfort of the house, by her merry ways."

Susanna in the same letter also wrote: "I often amuse myself by fishing in the evening and have been tolerably successful. But the black flies have prevented me this week. But they will soon leave us now. My face has been in a state approaching to inflammation from their venomous bites." One of Catharine's grandsons, Hargreave Muchall is said to have recorded his memories of Susanna's visits to Lakefield, in an item which appeared in the 'Toronto Telegram' on 17th May 1952. He wrote: "We grew to be great friends and she always came to my rescue when I happened to be in trouble, which was often enough. Aunt Moodie liked to fish, so in the summer-time on many occasions she would take her fishing-tackle and go down to the banks of the Otonabee River hard by, and I always went with her to put the worms on the hook. She had a horror of doing this, due to her aversion to worms which grew to an enormous size in and about Lakefield and to her, were repulsive. This assistance on my part cemented our friendship to such a degree that I became her favourite grand-nephew."

June 1872: Agnes breaks her leg in Crouch End

When the condensation of 'Mary Stuart' was complete, Agnes went to London and arranged for its publication by Messrs Bell & Daldy. These arrangements made, and the manuscript safely in the hands of the publishers, Agnes went to stay for a few days with the Rev and Mrs Fleming at Crouch End on the northern outskirts of London.

On the Sunday morning, dressed ready for church, Agnes was going down the stairs when someone upstairs spoke to her. Agnes had let go of the banister when she turned her head to reply, missed the last step and fell with her right leg doubled up beneath her. Although Agnes did not feel any pain, she could not get up and Vickery, her maid ran to fetch the family doctor. He and Mr Fleming carried Agnes upstairs to bed and it was found that Agnes had broken both the bones in her right leg, just above the ankle. The following day the leg was set and bound up in splints, but Agnes was obliged to stay where she was and in bed, until the bones knit back together again.

Knowing what an inconvenience this was going to be to her hosts, who were due to move to another parish very soon, Agnes begged to be moved into lodgings, but the Flemings insisted that she stay where she was, and looked after her until her leg was mended.

When Elizabeth heard what had happened, she went to Crouch End taking with her Vickery's sister Jessie who was a trained nurse, and offered that they both stay and help with the task of caring for Agnes. This would have increased the already considerable inconvenience to the Flemings, and Agnes's maid said she could manage without help, so Elizabeth with Jessie returned to Tilford.

Jane in her biography of Agnes wrote that she herself was: "too weak from her long illness to attend her suffering sister" and Sarah was also "not well enough to come to her" though both were "in constant attendance upon" Agnes after she returned to Southwold. The unfortunate Flemings took good care of Agnes although "she was compelled to make such a long and inconvenient sojourn" and the weather "was intensely hot, and the poor prisoner was used to take a great deal of daily walking exercise."

Agnes worded the situation succinctly in a letter which she wrote to Elizabeth. She gave her address and the date as "Still in my bed, June 22, 1872" and after detailing some request from the publisher about 'Mary Stuart', ended the letter by writing: "The doctor says I am going on well, but I am sick of bed."

25th July 1872: Agnes returns to Southwold and has a stroke

After Agnes had been in Crouch End for six weeks she, and probably the Flemings, had had enough. Agnes wrote to Sarah a letter headed 'Still in bed, July 24, 1872' saying: "My own beloved Thay, – Though I cannot put my foot to the ground, it has been arranged for me, at my own earnest request, to travel to-morrow. Mr Fleming and Dr Hall accompany me to Shoreditch, and put me and my maid into an invalid carriage, which has been ordered for me.

"Jane has arranged that Mr Virtue, the surgeon who is to attend me, meets me at Darsham Station, to see me transferred to the carriage he comes in, and I am to sleep on the sofa in the dining-room till I can get up-stairs. So, as I cannot come to you dearest, I hope you will come to see me hopping on my crutches – Ever, dearest, your affectionate and grateful, Agnes Strickland." Sarah, despite her own temporary financial difficulties, had asked Agnes if she needed some money. Agnes, now with a regular pension, was glad of the offer but was able to manage without such help.

Agnes arrived back in Southwold at the end of July 1872 with her leg well on the way to being fully healed, but from Jane's account the whole episode had affected Agnes mentally as well as physically. In her biography of Agnes, Jane described Agnes's arrival home thus: "When she arrived at her cottage she looked up sweetly and brightly as she was welcomed once more to her own loved home. Yet how unlike the Agnes who had quitted it in health and strength! As far as the accident was concerned, nothing could do better than the fractured limb; but the shock to the system, the length of the journey, and its consequent fatigue, produced in the course of a few days a sad reaction. Agnes was able to sit up, and nothing but timidity, the surgeon thought, prevented her from making use of her right leg, for the bones were not only united but firm."

Not long after Agnes had returned home, the situation became much more serious. Jane recorded that Agnes: "appeared unusually dull one morning, answered her sister Jane's inquiries quite at random, or did not speak at all" whereupon Jane "sent for the medical man, who found that Agnes was suffering from the effects of a paralytic and apoplectic seizure. He thought it had occurred during her sleep." So whereas Agnes had originally planned to visit Sarah in Haverthwaite in June, it was Sarah who visited Agnes in August. Sarah stayed for many weeks helping Jane and Vickery to look after the invalid.

Initially, the appearance of the left side of Agnes's face was affected, particularly her mouth and eye. These were only temporary effects of her stroke, but Agnes could no longer speak clearly, and this disability was permanent. As the autumn months of 1872 passed by, and Sarah returned to her own home, Agnes slowly recovered the ability to walk, but only with the help of a stick on one side and someone to help support her on the other side. She was no longer able to do any literary work and her writing was difficult to decipher. Agnes's thought processes were still functioning but her means of communication were faulty.

Although Agnes regained the ability to manage her own personal correspondence, Jane had to take charge of progressing the abridged version of 'Mary Stuart' through the press, with occasional references to Elizabeth to check that dates had been given correctly. Also, Jane with the help of Agnes's maid, Marianne Vickery kept an eye on Agnes's financial affairs. Jane reported that the faithful maid, Vickery: "never quitted her beloved mistress night or day" and that after her stroke, Agnes was "more amiable and contented" than previously and no longer wished for the social whirl of her previous life.

Neighbours in Southwold also kept a friendly eye on Agnes, as she managed to tell Sarah in the autumn of 1872 when she wrote: "Our friend Mr Gooch sometimes comes in for a chat, and he praises you very much, and says you are the most perfect of gentlewomen. The good old gentleman is very kind to me, and often comes in to see how I am getting on."

November 1872: Susanna is treated as a celebrity

When Susanna wrote to Maggie Rous on 30th December 1872, she was still staying in Lakefield with Catharine, but she had recently been on a trip to Toronto, and her letter showed that she was something of a celebrity in Canada. Susanna wrote: "The last week in November, I went up to Toronto, with Mr and Mrs Robert Strickland and their two dear girls.

"We left Lakefield by train at 2pm and got to Port Hope at 6 but were delayed by the non-arrival of the train west, till 12pm, when Robert voted a good supper and bed. Oh, Maggie, you would have laughed, at the grand oration the Hotel Keeper made me. I wish people would hold their tongues and let me and my book slide into oblivion. I am afraid, that I received all the fine compliments very ungraciously. I dared not look at Robert for fear I should laugh out."

December 1872: Agnes is partially recovered

On 24th December 1872 to Sarah, Agnes wrote: "I am much as I have been for the last two months, and walk every fine day with my staff and the help of Vickery's shoulder. Millie goes to London for a fortnight's holiday. She has been so attentive to me during the last five months that I could not refuse her the holiday." Millie was the other member of Agnes's household in Southwold. "Dear Mrs Lillingston wished me to dine with her; but I do not visit at present, though I am getting better of my lameness but the weather is too stormy for me to walk out as usual. I am in comfortable circumstances, having a quarter untouched in hand."

19th May 1873: Another of Tom's daughters dies prematurely

Mary Pohle was the third of Tom's daughters to die a tragic death, following Marina who died aged two and Julia who died after her first baby was born. At the age of only 33, Mary Pohle caught typhoid fever and died on 19th May 1873 at 26 New Cavendish Street in London. Her occupation was described as 'wife of John Pohle adjutant of volunteers at Aberdeen.' They had no children.

Summer 1873: Richard Gwillym Strickland visits England

Sam's youngest surviving son, Richard Gwillym Strickland had a period of ill health in 1873 and made a trip to England to convalesce. He was godson to the late Richard Gwillym, and his first destination in England was Sarah's home, 'Hollow Oak' in Lancashire. He then went to Suffolk and met his aunts Agnes and Jane.

Agnes had made further recovery by the time Richard arrived, and she wrote to Sarah saying: "He is so like you, and, though dark-complexioned, resembles his poor father. I am really glad of his company. I have taken him to see Blythborough church and Covehithe, and he has been to a dinner party with Jane, and seems to enjoy his visit and to be very grateful to you for your cherishing care of him." He was 26 years old and married with three children.

In a letter from Catharine to her daughter Annie dated 10th October 1873, Catharine wrote: "I hear that Richard Strickland has sailed for Canada and is expected about the end of the month or sooner. He seems to have won golden opinions at Aunt Gwillym's and Aunt Agnes's; but your aunt Elizabeth declined to see him."

Elizabeth, having had her offer of help to Agnes rejected, is said never to have offered again, and to have remained in Tilford while Agnes was convalescing from her stroke. In refusing to receive a visit from Richard Strickland, she may have been showing her customary unsociable character. However, at some point Tom moved back from London to live with her, and if this happened before Richard Strickland's possible visit, Elizabeth might have been less able and less willing to cope with an additional visitor.

October 1873: Sarah visits Agnes

Although many of Agnes's older friends and correspondents had died, two of the younger ones living abroad continued to write to her regularly. One was the Hon Mrs Buchanan (formerly Georgina Stuart) and the other was the Duchess de Gramont (formerly Emma Mackinnon).

In the spring of 1873, before the visit of Richard Strickland had been arranged, and when Agnes was continuing on the road to recovery, Agnes wrote to Sarah with news and to make plans. She said to Sarah: "I was expecting a letter from Emma de Gramont, but was surprised at the arrival of a box from Paris containing a splendid china vase, a real Sevres, very beautiful and costly, so nicely packed, not a chip. I hope, darling Thay, you will come and stay all the autumn with me, and then you will see it."

Jane's biography of Agnes, having quoted this letter, continued: "And so Sarah did, cheering with her company her poor invalid sister so different from what she had been – the imperfect utterance, the enfeebled mind. There was, however, much to love in the patience with which she bore her confinement to the house and sofa. Nothing could exceed the care with which her sister, and the faithful (Marianne) Vickery and Milly watched over her. The marriage of the last was a trial to her, Amelia Fenn having lived with her mother and herself all her young life."

The two volume version of 'Life of Mary Stuart' by Agnes Strickland was, with Jane's help, published by George Bell and Sons in October 1873. The printer of Agnes's last work was, either by chance, by design, or due to Jane's geographical limitations, the firm of John Childs and Son, Bungay, the family of printers which had been so closely connected with the Strickland sisters many years earlier.

10th October 1873: Catharine sends family news to Annie

There are mixed and unclear reports of the continuing prosperity or otherwise of the businesses set up by Sam Strickland, and run by his sons after his death. His family home in Lakefield, named 'Homestead' or 'The Homestead', is said to have been severely damaged by fire in the early 1870s.

Sam's widow, Katharine Strickland had returned to Canada and was staying in Peterborough when Catharine wrote to Annie Atwood on 10th October 1873. Catharine wrote: "Aunt Strickland is still in Peterborough but talks of returning soon. I miss her so very much and shall be glad to see the dear old face again popping in so quietly."

This 'Aunt Strickland' had sent Catharine $10 for Mary Muchall which Catharine was ensuring was spent wisely. Catharine told Annie: "I gave her five to pay her rent and have the rest laid by for next month. Mary is engaged with tailor work at $2 a pair of trousers. She has already made several pairs but I fear she will hurt herself. She will work too hard and lives poorly and poor baby is ill."

Catharine continued "Tom (Muchall) has started on his agency work but truly I have small trust in his steadiness. He delays and vapours about what he can do and what he will do, and does nothing at all but talk, talk, talk, and I get out of patience with him seeing her working herself to death, and he relying upon her to maintain him, and those poor children – Ah my poor girl, my heart is sore for her."

By October 1873, Susanna had been living with Catharine, Kate and Katie at 'Westove' in Lakefield for over a year, albeit with breaks while she visited her children in Ottawa and Toronto. Catharine in her letter to Annie did not complain or criticise Susanna, but it is clear that Susanna was not an easy house guest. Catharine wrote: "I had made up my mind to go down to town tomorrow but the weather is so uncertain that I am not sure it will be all right, for I must return at night as I cannot leave your aunt. She will not stay at Robert's or Roland's for the night and is marvellously afraid of robbery or worse if she were alone, though we have a girl now in the house – you see how impossible it would be for me to leave home for more than a few hours." Catharine went on to ask her daughter to visit her, and added: "Aunt M is in good humour and not cranky now and you must turn a deaf ear to criticism of the little ones – it is just her way you know – We have got on very smoothly now for the last two months."

Of her health and circumstances Catharine wrote: "I have been a good deal better since I got the girl to do the kitchen work but I find it makes more than the difference in the expences of the household – She has grown so fat since she came, and not upon nothing I assure you but is quiet and on the whole does the work as well as I could expect. I give her at the rate of $4 per month – she is nearly sixteen – When she leaves I can get Anne Watson (that was) our nearest neighbour to come two half days in the week and that costs only 50 cts the week and that is much less than Charlottes wages, besides the saving in food, light, and firewood which is a serious item now as of course she keeps more fire than we ever do when by ourselves."

Catharine also mentioned Tom's daughter Adela Wigg who, like Mary Muchall, seems to have been the main bread-winner in her household. Catharine wrote: "I have had Mrs Wigg's melodeon here for a long time and really do enjoy having the use of it, though I play only by ear, old airs and tunes. Mrs Wigg is agent for the sale of pianos and melodeons but this one is her own." Adela was teaching music in Lakefield and also organised an occasional concert as an additional source of income.

Susanna mentioned a concert that Adela was arranging, when she wrote from Lakefield to Katie Vickers on 18th January 1874. The village postmaster was very ill and his death was expected at any time. Susanna wrote: "This is very unlucky for poor Mrs Wigg who was with us since Friday, getting out the placards for her concert, which is to come off on Wednesday. If Casement dies tonight, no-one in the village will go, and it will be a great loss to her, with whom it is a matter of necessity."

13th July 1874: Agnes Strickland dies

As 1874 progressed, so did Agnes's recovery. She began to go out for a walk each day with the aid of her stick and her maid, and was often taken out for a drive in her carriage. She began to think of going to church services again and in June 1874 told Sarah: "I have walked four times round the garden, and go about the house all alone by myself. I have been upstairs with considerable help, yet the change was pleasant. Lady Dillon has invited me to stay with her. I know not yet how that can be, but I certainly feel stronger every day."

Agnes and Jane had their own separate homes in Southwold but their houses were adjoining and in 1874 Jane normally called in to see Agnes twice a day. One July morning in 1874 on Jane's first visit of the day, Agnes seemed more than usually well, but this changed dramatically during the day, and when Jane returned for her evening visit, Agnes was so ill that they both knew she had not long to live.

Agnes gave directions about her Will and asked Jane to read aloud to her the prayers for the dying. Agnes, Jane recorded, said her farewells to her sister and maid, became unconscious, and died on Monday 13th July 1874, six days before what would have been her 78th birthday.

Jane wrote of her own actions and feelings immediately after Agnes had died. Referring to herself she wrote: "Her sister closed those beautiful dark eyes she was to see no more in this life. She retired to her own house, not to give way to her grief for her sudden bereavement, but to send the necessary but sad tidings of her sister's decease to her family at home and abroad. To telegraph to Mrs Gwillym, who loved Agnes so dearly, gave her intense pain, as well as to give directions for the funeral and orders for the mourning.

"At nine she saw again what had lately been Agnes Strickland; but a change had again taken place – a strange and wonderful one. The dark shadow of death had disappeared. It was her sister as she had often seen her, sleeping, calm, serene, and more beautiful than she had ever beheld her in life. Years and years had been cast off. It was indeed the realisation of those exquisite lines: –

"He who hath bent him o'er the dead
Ere the first day of death hath fled,
And marked the mild angelic air,
The rapture of repose that's there,
Some moments – ay, one treacherous hour –
He might still doubt the tyrant's power,
So fair, so calm, so softly sealed,
The first last look by death revealed."

Jane concluded her description of the day that Agnes died by writing of herself: "In the evening of that sad day her sister had another painful duty to perform – that of choosing the last resting place for the beloved remains. A kind female friend lent her a supporting arm, that she might choose the spot in the parish churchyard."

17th July 1874: Agnes is buried

Jane was not alone for long in dealing with making arrangements for Agnes's funeral. She wrote of herself: "Her sister, who had received the kindest offers of assistance from various friends, and from her kinsman the Rev William Hawtayne, was soon joined by her sisters and fellow-mourners; and the Friday following they attended the funeral, and saw the remains of Agnes Strickland consigned to their last earthly resting-place. She had nearly completed her seventy-eighth year."

The funeral took place only four days after Agnes's death and was reported in the local papers. Agnes had led a simple life when in Reydon and Southwold, due to financial necessity. The very different life that she had formerly led, visiting wealthy friends in their country mansions, and her social life in London, either were not known locally or were forgotten in the report which said: "The funeral of Miss Agnes Strickland – The funeral of this lamented lady took place on Friday 17th July 1874 in Southwold Churchyard. A very large number would have done homage to her memory, but it was requested that the simplicity which surrounded her life should accompany her to the tomb. The shops and windows of houses on the route to the Churchyard were closed, and flags were hoisted half-mast high.

"The vicar, the Rev BC Thornton; one of his curates, the Rev Scott; the medical attendant, Mr FH Vertue; and Messrs Wigg, Allen, Jellicoe and Denny, the tradesmen in charge, preceded the hearse. The sisters and servants of the deceased lady were the sole occupants of the mourning coaches.

"The accession of private carriages was courteously declined, but this did not stop the assembling of those who knew Miss Agnes Strickland, less as an authoress than as a kind, benevolent lady. They who valued her friendship and they who had partaken of her charity, formed a large and mournful concourse near the grave.

"The coffin was covered with black cloth and furniture. The plate merely indicated name, date of birth and decease. Upon the coffin rested two wreaths, one of lilies and ivy leaves, the other lilies, pink geraniums and jasmine. The ceremonial in the Church was simple, as was the service at the grave."

The family put on her grave in St Edmund's Churchyard, a monument in the form of a large curled scroll, partially unfurled, on a Carrera marble base. Inscribed upon the scroll was the name 'Agnes Strickland' followed by the proud achievement 'Historian of the Queens of England'. Elizabeth's share in writing 'Lives of the Queens of England' was forgotten in death, as well as being hidden in life.

19th and 21st July 1874: Condolences are sent and Obituaries to Agnes are printed

Following Agnes's death, obituaries appeared in many newspapers, listing her literary works, the involvement of Elizabeth in some of them, and the granting of a pension to her in 1871. The obituary that appeared in the 'Ipswich Journal' on 21st July 1874, gave its view of Agnes's style of writing. It said: "The deceased lady had that rich imaginative faculty, which enables the historian to see between the dim lines of musty parchment and rare old chronicles, the form and manners of men and women of past times. Without this faculty the historian becomes a mere analyst and his works dull and wearisome. This was never a fault with Miss Strickland's works. Her books are eminently readable, her pictures of the past, vivid and life-like.

"That the deceased lady lacked the judicial calmness and impartiality which makes the perfect historian is only too plainly to be seen in her writings; but where do we find the ideal historian? Miss Strickland moreover never used any art to conceal her partiality, she used her facts to prove a thesis as openly as a logician might marshal his arguments. Her foregone conclusions were always paraded so openly that even when we differed from her we respected her motives, and were instructed by her vivacious and industrious method.

"The deceased lady was as highly respected by the little circle of personal friends in her own neighbourhood, as she was as a worker by the literary men and women of her time. She carried the same lively interest in her neighbours into everyday life that she evinced in regard to the affairs of the great personages whom she marshalled so ably in her pages."

On a more personal note were the letters of condolence which were sent to Jane as news of Agnes's death reached those of her friends who were still alive. Lady Georgina Buchanan's letter is addressed from 'British Legation, Vienna' and dated 19th July 1874. She wrote: "With sad surprise I read yesterday in the paper the death of my dear kind old friend Agnes Strickland ... I had not seen her for many years, but we always wrote, and she never failed to send me her valuable works and to think of me. Our last communication was when I was in Scotland last December. I wrote as usual to tell her all about myself, and to ask the same from her. Her answer struck me painfully; it was short, and made no complaint of ill health, yet was difficult to read ... a painful dread that her sight was failing seized me, and I wrote to beg her maid would write and give me all particulars of her health, as I feared the exertion of writing must be bad for her.

"She nevertheless wrote a few affectionate lines ... and I have heard no more, till now I find the affectionate heart is cold for ever. She was a true affectionate friend, and every year the number of such companions diminishes ... I must offer you my deep and heartfelt sympathy."

Jane replied giving, as requested, details of Agnes's illness and death. Lady Buchanan wrote again to Jane from Vienna on 29th July 1874 adding more to her remembrance of Agnes: "She only spoke of her accident, and was always so uncomplaining, so busied and absorbed in her useful works, that there was no space left in her heart or letters for self-pity ... I shall send your precious letter to my mother and sister Mrs Ferrand, for I know their deep interest in the dear Agnes. Please give my affectionate sympathy to Mrs Gwillym, of whom Agnes used to speak so often that I feel as if I knew her well ..."

In Canada, an obituary notice in the 'Globe', Toronto contained some inaccuracies including under-estimating her age by ten years.

Susanna wrote to correct this error and followed with a lengthy description of Agnes and her character. Much of the content of Susanna's letter is covered elsewhere but it is interesting to read the affectionate character description which Susanna gave. Of Agnes, Susanna wrote: "Her conversational powers were as great as her literary ones. Possessed of an excellent temper, great flow of natural eloquence, and playful repartee; her descriptive powers never seemed to flag. Whether in her grave or gay moments she knew how to charm her listeners."

Ending her long letter, Susanna wrote: "Space will not permit me to say more of this truly great woman. Her genius is too well appreciated to need it. But I cannot close this brief notice without a slight sketch of her private and domestic character ... An affectionate, loving daughter, a faithful sister and friend, kind and benevolent to the poor, and possessing warm sympathies for the sick; she never let the adulation of the world interfere with the blessed domestic charities. A sincere Protestant, and a firm adherent to the Church of England; nothing but illness ever prevented her from joining in the Sabbath duties, and partaking of the sacred Communion. For years she conducted the first Sabbath-school in our parish church, instituted by herself, and her literary labours were never allowed to interfere with what she considered sacred obligations.

"Her long useful life is at an end and she has descended to the grave, full of years and honours. We have lost a beloved sister, but it is a great comfort to know how wide felt is the sympathy with us in our bereavement. (Signed) Susanna Moodie" and dated 19th July 1874.

July 1874: Agnes's Will is going to cause trouble

Behind the scenes while Agnes was being buried and mourned, a storm was brewing over the contents of her Will. Agnes had signed and dated the main part of her Will on 29th June 1871 by which time she had found a publisher for her last work, the 'Lives of the last four Princesses of the royal house of Stuart' and she was still in good health. She added two signed codicils on 18th November 1872 when she was slowly but apparently steadily recovering from her stroke. At the time she wrote her Will, Agnes was living in 'Park Lane Cottage', Park Lane in Southwold, which she had leased from Jane, and Jane was living next door at 'West Cottage', Lorne Road in Southwold.

The first item in Agnes's Will was to Jane's benefit, Agnes having taken a 99-year lease on Jane's freehold cottage six years beforehand in 1865. Agnes's Will stated: "This lease with all the improvements and additions I have made in the property I give and bequeath to my sister Jane Margaret and with all the furniture and fittings-up in the same including my Brougham carriage to be her own property."

A Brougham (pronounced Broom) was a very popular form of carriage. It could carry two people, was enclosed with glass windows at the front and sides, had a low step entry and was pulled by one horse or a pair of horses.

The second item was the one which was about to upset Elizabeth: "I have repurchased the copyright with the stereotypes engravings and all other stock belonging to the 'Lives of the Queens of England' now publishing on my account in eight volumes by Messrs Longmans Green. These I give and bequeath to my sister Mrs Catharine Parr Traill and my nephew John Percy Strickland son of my late brother Samuel Strickland for their mutual benefit also the abridgement of the 'Lives of the Queens of England' in six volumes by Messrs Bell and Daldy to hold both and receive the profits arising from both for as long a time as is secured by the Copyright Act."

The next beneficiary mentioned is Elizabeth. Agnes wrote: "I hereby distinctly specify that the abridged volume of the 'Lives of the Queens of England' in one volume prepared by my sister Elizabeth with my assistance for the use of schools and families is her own joint property and I give my own part in the same work to be her own exclusive property with the copyrights of the 'Lives of the Queens of Scotland' the 'Tudor Princesses' and the 'Seven Bishops of the Tower.'

Agnes owned fifty two shares in the Vancouver Land and Coal Mining Company for which she had paid £10 per share. Ten of these shares she left to Susanna and the remainder, plus her jewellery and other such items, she shared out between various of her nieces. The portrait of herself, painted by John Hayes in 1846 and which had been displayed at the Royal Academy, she left to the Kensington Museum, the fore-runner of the National Portrait Gallery.

By the time the first codicil was added to her Will, Agnes had sold two freehold properties whose address is difficult to read but looks like 49 and 49a Carnaby Market, which sounds as though they may have been in London, and she bequeathed the proceeds of "upwards of three hundred pounds" to be divided equally between the daughters of Samuel Strickland.

The second codicil dealt with a number of items such as books and china which were to be given to various family members. The main items in this codicil were two cottages in what looks like Hobury Street, Barrow-in-Furness, which Agnes left to Sarah, together with the bust of herself sculpted by Baily in 1846. Agnes's estate was given a valuation of less than £3,000.

The miniature of Agnes which Thomas Cheesman had painted when Agnes was young, was not specifically mentioned in Agnes's Will, but at some point went to Sarah, and Jane reported it being hung on Sarah's wall. From this and from Jane's reported distress at having to send Sarah the news of Agnes's death, it seems that whilst Elizabeth and Agnes were closest in terms of their working lives, and Jane and Agnes for most of their lives shared the same home, it was Sarah and Agnes who were emotionally the closest of the four sisters in England.

21st July 1874: Elizabeth writes a letter

Among the telegrams which Jane sent as soon as Agnes had died, was one to Elizabeth asking her to go to Southwold as soon as possible. Jane sent the telegram first and read Agnes's Will second, and then rather regretted her haste, but the trouble lay ahead and was just as well dealt with sooner rather than later.

Elizabeth very soon gave her side of the story in a letter which she wrote to Catharine dated 21st July 1874. She wrote: "My dear sister, I had just crossed my garden and entered Captain Tom's sitting room to see how the gout was dealing with him our brother when the Telegram followed me to announce the death of our sister Agnes that morning, 'come quickly' was added. I was suffering with a severe cough but I contrived to travel to Southwold on Wednesday – I received a letter from Jane requesting me to stay away hinting vexation was awaiting me.

"Agnes and I each possessed in equal shares the copyright of our far-famed Queens of England – strongly selling now equal shares.

We had each entered into an engagement with the other to leave in a Will our property therein to each other lest the work should be ruined by being in hands unacquainted with the peculiar management of stereotypes, besides the little we had made was dearly earned, as I who have lived a life of labour and self-denial know full well.

"I determined to proceed onward and see what had occurred. I guessed that Agnes had broken her promise and that she had left <u>her half</u> of the Copyright to someone else. I did not feel anger nor did it lessen one tender feeling of regret for her loss. Agnes' half was Agnes' own – I could live (little as I required) – free from debt and can until the blessed time of relief arrives, if I had my own property.

"Unfortunately the Will was read before the burial – and grief changed to horror when I found that she had bequeathed the whole of the copyright containing half of which was <u>my property</u> the fruits of my life long labours to you my dear sister Catharine, with reversion to a young gentleman of my late brother's family whom I never beheld. This must not be dear Kate – I would not touch on or even give an unkind thought concerning the legacy of her <u>own</u> share of the Biographies of Queens of England but wrongly appropriated possessions never do any good.

"Do not dear Kate wish to obtain my property. I can in two letters guard it by my legal man – but oh dear sister how the world will ring with the evil doings which must then become public. I have arranged a plan which will benefit you far more than carrying off to your nest my hard earned property. Dear Thay will help me and then I shall be able to settle it legally according to the Act of Parliament for many years – The number I will not quote from memory. God bless my dear Kate and guide her in time of temptation to take the right way. Thine, Elizabeth Strickland."

22nd September 1874: Tom Strickland dies

Elizabeth, having had to deal with the loss of her sister Agnes and the aggravation caused by Agnes's Will in July 1874, very soon afterwards had to deal with the final illness and the death of Thomas Strickland, the brother whom she loved very dearly.

Tom was living with Elizabeth when he died on 22nd September 1874, surviving Agnes by only ten weeks. On his death certificate his cause of death was recorded as 'delirium tremens, 2 weeks' his age was given as 64, although he was probably 67 having been born in 1807 or 1808. His occupation was recorded simply as 'gentleman'.

Tom's death was announced by means of a very simple statement in the death notices of one Surrey newspaper on Saturday 26th September 1874. His funeral took place in Tilford's parish church of All Saints where his grave is one of the oldest in the churchyard.

Delirium tremens is said to be caused by giving up alcohol suddenly with symptoms which may only last for a few days, but older people plus those who are ill or have had a head injury, and people who have been drinking heavily for many years, can also show the symptoms of delirium tremens but with fatal effect. Tom had been drinking heavily since Margaretta died early in 1863. He had lost his memory due to being mugged, and he was no longer young. Perhaps his death was caused by something a little more complicated than simply his drinking, but be that as it may, it was Elizabeth who had the responsibility of caring for him in the last weeks of his life with the attendant anxiety, strain and sorrow, and at the same time that she was dealing with the sorrow and upset associated with Agnes's demise.

There must have been family correspondence on the matter, but the only remaining trace that has been found is within the letter written by Catharine to Sarah dated 19th October 1874. Catharine wrote: "How sad I felt at the tidings of death and sorrow conveyed by Elizabeth's letter enclosed in dear Jane's and your note. My poor brother – it was indeed a sudden summons from life to death. God be merciful to his soul.

"Elizabeth seems to be satisfied that his end was peace. This sad bereavement to her as great as the loss of a husband or child to others may prove a blessing to soften down all evil passions – God of his goodness hallow this loss to her. Poor dear sister. I am afraid that she would despise my pity – yet I do feel for her deep compassion."

October 1874: Agnes's clothes and jewellery go to Canada

Although Agnes's Will was not Proven, and therefore could not officially be implemented until 4th December 1874, the task of sorting out and distributing Agnes's belongings had begun long before that.

By 19th October 1874 Sarah had sent, and Catharine had received and was sending thanks for boxes of Agnes's belongings. Catharine wrote: "It is so many years since I looked upon articles so rich and costly, the very sight of the beautiful fabrics was most interesting. Those lovely laces made me think of all the weary hours that must have passed with those that wrought them – what taste and skill in the heads that devised the elegant patterns – of laces and brocades." These would be passed on or sold to relatives who would appreciate their family value and use them themselves. The boxes also contained clothes of more practical use which Catharine's daughters would share and use.

There were garments which Catharine herself would wear. She told Sarah: "The black silks will come to my share for I wear widow's dress though fifteen years have passed – I never cared for gay clothing since – sometimes I wear grey – or purple – but your kind gifts have always supplied me with comfortable and handsome apparel and I have never wanted and never bought any garments – unless some print for morning wear from time to time."

Of Agnes's jewellery which Sarah had sent, Catharine wrote: "I have taken the cross to myself – I think Susan would prefer the brooch and bracelet – the latter is very beautiful – the ribbon – jasper is so handsome itself – and the brooch is very beautiful. I was tempted at first by it but then I could leave the cross as an heirloom to one of my dear children."

Having thanked Sarah for sending Agnes's belongings to her, Catharine moved on to other matters in her letter, but in passing acknowledged the trouble that Sarah was taking and the length of time that she had been in Southwold and away from home. Catharine wrote: "I hope dearest Thay that ere this you may be settled again at home in your own lovely place and that the vexatious troubles will soon be at an end."

October 1874: Percy Strickland is also upset

Although Elizabeth objected strongly to Agnes bequeathing all the benefit of the recent eight volume edition of 'Lives of the Queens of England', when Agnes had only done half the work, this complaint might not have been valid. Agnes on several occasions said that she had spent a lot of money in buying back the copyrights of 'Lives of the Queens of England', the implication being that she had done so at entirely her own expense, but there is the possibility that the copyrights were purchased jointly with Elizabeth, but maintaining Elizabeth's anonymity.

Another complicating factor when trying to understand the rights and wrongs of the situation is that over the years there had been several versions of the 'Lives of the Queens of England' and the relative importance of the two editions under dispute is not easily apparent. However, Elizabeth might well be thought right to have been offended at the unexpected bequest to Percy Strickland, whatever the circumstances.

Percy Strickland, not knowing much about Agnes and Elizabeth's real working partnership, nor about the intricacies of copyright and publishing, took as much exception to Elizabeth's objection, as Elizabeth had taken at the bequest, and seems to have told Catharine so quite bluntly. Catharine, perhaps lacking diplomacy, seems to have passed on to Sarah an account of Percy's reaction, and then regretted having done so.

Catharine in her letter to Sarah dated 19th October 1874 tried to sort out the ill-feelings that had arisen. She wrote to Sarah: "You must not judge Percy too hard, dearest, because he really does not know what claim his aunt has, brought up in the woods, having no taste for literature – he has had to make a living for himself and large family. A few days ago he was here and talked very nicely – indeed he is a truly kind-hearted young man but sometimes he gets sadly worn and worried and then says all sorts of things that are really foreign to his nature – He would gladly sell his right for an immediate sum – The only fear that I have is that he might let it go into hands that might prove troublesome to Elizabeth and myself."

This sounds like a tactfully different description of Percy from that given when he visited England at least twice, including having a lengthy honeymoon with an aristocratic, or aristocratic-looking wife. On one at least of these visits he met Agnes who, for some unexplained reason, decided to choose him to be a beneficiary of the copyrights when there were a number of other relatives she might have chosen, with Elizabeth obviously having the greatest claim.

Catharine went on to tell Sarah the current state of things, and to ask Sarah to help resolve the issue. Catharine wrote: "What I advised was for him to join with me in giving to Elizabeth for her life half the proceeds of the copyright to ensure her management of the business but this he did not understand – knowing nothing of the difficulties of managing such a business and not knowing anything of his aunt. I think he would soon see things in a clear light if they were explained by yourself. Pray dearest do not think hardly of him because I do not think he deserves it – and I would not forgive myself were I to have injured him in your estimation."

November 1874: Agnes is still being remembered for her kindness

Every year since 1838 had appeared 'Pawsey's Ladies Fashionable Repository'. This was the publication to which Agnes had influenced Queen Adelaide, the widow of King William IV, to subscribe. The Dowager Queen Adelaide had bought a copy in October 1841 and allowed this to be stated in the advertising. In October 1842 she allowed the advertising to report her intention of becoming an annual subscriber. Queen Victoria subsequently also became a regular subscriber and allowed the fact to be advertised, which would have been a major coup for the provincial press from which Pawsey's emanated.

Every year Agnes had contributed something to 'Pawsey's Ladies Fashionable Repository' in the way of a poem, a short story or a description to accompany an illlustration. In the advertisements for the 1875 edition, Agnes's role in the lasting success of the publication was noted. The 'Ipswich Journal' on 7th November 1874 wrote: "Pawsey's Ladies Fashionable Repository for 1875 – Regularly as winter comes round does Mr Haddock prepare for a new year this charming little annual ... In this we find not pleasure merely, but solid instruction ... It is a marvel of condensation. The Pocket-book is so small that a ladies pocket or bag will hardly be affected by its presence, yet it contains an almanac for 1875, blank pages for memoranda and cash account, Post Office regulations, original poetry, translation of last year's French poem, and French poem for translation next year ... Tales, enigmas, charades, with the answers to those given last year. Yet this book ... is a pretty little gilt edged volume, five inches by three, and by no means of clumsy thickness.

"The illustrations for 1875" were listed and included Southwold Church. The 'Ipswich Journal' continued: "Of each of these there is a few lines of description, and in reference to the latter, the loss sustained by the literary world in general, and the Pocket Book, in particular, by the death of Miss Agnes Strickland, is mentioned in terms of deep and graceful feeling ... The editor also adds his tribute to the memory of one who 'for many years, took such a kindly interest in our little annual.' We commend 'our little annual' to the notice of our readers as the best Ladies Pocket Book in print."

December 1874: Walter Traill visits Catharine

Catharine's youngest son, Walter Traill returned to Lakefield on a visit in December 1874 and Catharine had looked forward to the visit, expecting there to be a happy family reunion and to hear all about his life and adventures. Unfortunately Walter had developed the depressive nature of his father, and was in a restless but uncommunicative condition during his time at home with Catharine, leaving Catharine disappointed in the visit and unhappy for her son.

1st January 1875: Sarah is getting fed up with Jane

On 1st January 1875, Sarah had returned to her home in Haverthwaite, but still had a lot of paper-work to do in connection with Agnes's Will. The splitting of Agnes's fifty-two Vancouver Land and Coal Mining Company shares among five legatees was almost complete, and Sarah asked Catharine to pass on advice to Susanna and the relevant nieces. Sarah wrote: "I would advise them to receive the dividend which is due for the half year about the 8th of May – and sell them afterwards, they pay ten per cent."

The situation with regard to 'Lives of the Queens of England' was still not clear. Sarah said: "I will write to Mr Longman and ask what number of copys have been sold from the 14th of last July up to the 4th of December which is the time he makes up his accounts and pays yearly – of course he had to pay up to the day of dear Agnes's death. I will write to him to know if anything is coming to you and I will ask him to state the terms upon which he publishes the work and I will send his answers to you, so that after that you and Percy will arrange everything with him as I hope in a few days to have settled everything of the executorship."

At this point Sarah had an uncharacteristic moan. She wrote: "Jane has never acted, it all falls upon me." However, Jane might still have an important part to play and considerable work to do of a different kind from Sarah who wrote: "you will have to consider about correcting proofs – Jane did it and Eliza gave her £5 and Agnes gave her £5 but that did not include postage – I don't know whether she would do it now." It is not clear what proofs Sarah meant.

The publisher of the other copyright that had been left to Catharine and Percy had also involved Sarah in correspondence. Sarah wrote: "Bell and Sons publish the abridged Edition in 6 vols left to you. He pays half yearly Feby and August so half a year will be due to you next month. I will write to him to know what agreement there is between him and dear Agnes and let you know. It is only last week I got the Probate of the Will and I could do nothing till it had passed – I have to let all the Parties see it before I can demand anything." In the days before photocopying this was a time consuming task. Sarah explained: "It has now gone to London for the Secretary of the Vancouver Coal Co to see – and I will send it to Bell when it comes back – likewise to Longman."

When Sarah had written to Catharine on 1st January 1875 she had been at her home in Haverthwaite, but only three weeks later when she next wrote to Catharine, she was at Elizabeth's home in Tilford. When Catharine replied, she began her letter by apologising for not having written sooner but she had been ill, she then sent thanks for: "your precious letter of January 20th 1875 with its most acceptable contents" which probably means that Sarah had sent some money with the letter.

Sarah's visit to Elizabeth had, it seems, already been proving difficult when she wrote to Catharine in January and when Catharine replied on 10th March 1875, she was concerned by the continuing strain being put upon Sarah. Catharine wrote: "God help and support you. Poor Eliza. I think she is quite unaccountable for what she says – at her great age and infirmity." Catharine's view was that the situation:

"is likely to impose more trouble upon you dear – than will be good for you."

That may have been the case, but Jane wouldn't or couldn't leave Southwold, while Tom's children had all either died, moved abroad or fallen out with their aunts. This left Sarah (aged 77) as the only family member capable of looking after Elizabeth, now aged 81. Sarah did not have to manage entirely on her own as Mary Ann Vickery, who had been such a faithful maid to Agnes, had gone to live with and work for Elizabeth after Agnes died. Mary Ann's sister, Jessie Vickery had already been with Elizabeth in Tilford.

Catharine having asked Sarah to placate Percy and explain the situation to him, Sarah's role had evolved to the point where she needed authorisation to deal with the publishers on behalf of Percy and Catharine, a role which they had hoped Elizabeth would fulfil but which was no longer feasible. Sarah was still acting as executor for Agnes when she went to stay with Elizabeth, and had sent to Catharine for signature a document which would authorise her to deal with publishers on behalf of Catharine and Percy.

Sarah's involvement in an authorised capacity was needed because the publishers, Longman's, as had been the case with so many publishers that the Strickland sisters had dealt with, were being difficult. They were avoiding paying Catharine and Percy their share of any profit generated by a new edition of the 'Lives of the Queens of England' by insisting, rightly or wrongly, that they pay part of the printing costs.

29th April 1875: Elizabeth Strickland dies

Sarah's responsibility for the care of Elizabeth lasted a little over three months, for on Thursday 29th April 1875 Elizabeth died at her home, 'Abbott's Lodge' in Tilford. As when Tom had died, the event was marked by an entry in the death announcements of only one newspaper. Whereas the local Surrey paper had been selected for Tom's death notice, Elizabeth's appeared in the London Evening Standard. It appeared on Monday 3rd May 1875 and stated simply: "Strickland – April 29, at Abbot's Lodge, Tilford, Elizabeth Strickland, daughter of the late Thomas Strickland, Esq., of Reydon Hall Suffolk."

Mary Ann Vickery, registered the death and gave Elizabeth's occupation as gentlewoman. The cause of death was given as chronic bronchitis (6 months) and exhaustion (1 month). Mary Ann, perhaps not expecting the question and not knowing the real answer, underestimated Elizabeth's age by quite a margin. Elizabeth's age is recorded as 70 when she was actually 81.

Elizabeth's funeral followed the usual pattern of funerals where Sarah was in charge of arrangements, and is recorded neither in newspapers nor in family letters. She was buried in the churchyard of her parish church – All Saints Church in Tilford, Surrey in a double grave on top of her brother Tom.

Jane, in a letter to Catharine dated 18th June 1875, referred to Elizabeth's last months, and revealed that there had been a second cause for Elizabeth to be angry with the contents of Agnes's Will. Jane wrote: "My dear Kate, You have no cause for self reproach. You acted nobly by Eliza in fact beyond what as a Mother you ought to have done – She knew that Agnes intended to leave you her part – the real fault was done in leaving to Percy what in justice should have been left to her sister. While her" (Elizabeth's) "mind was in a balanced state she said 'you have behaved justly and handsomely' – but her brother's death, and Agnes's neglect in not having her name put in the lease of premises for which she had paid her just share, combined with the seeds of death in her frame" seem "to have overpowered her great intellect."

Remembering Agnes's unaccountable forgetfulness towards the Lambeth Palace librarian, Mr Wayland Kershaw, and these two uncharacteristic financial misdemeanours towards Elizabeth, it looks as though Agnes's mental powers may have been beginning to fade at the end of her life, pre-dating her stroke by perhaps a year.

Elizabeth's notoriously bad temper had stayed with her into 1875. Jane's letter to Catharine, referring to Elizabeth, continued: "I offended her deeply so that she would not hear my name without malediction – She complained of illness but wrote so firmly that I expressed a hope of her recovery from the characters being so strong. She wrote me a furious letter saying that I mocked her sufferings and ordered the return of the papers about Agnes's falling out with Colburn.

"I sent them back without a word but waited a week for her to cool when I reasoned with her – reminded her of the kindness she had shown me since her mother's death, and of my attention even to sick and bad servants as well as every member of my own family.

"She made no reply but continued to speak ill of me, but Sarah said she was not herself and that the words were on her lips, not in her heart, as her Will three months afterwards proved. God be merciful to her poor dear – Be satisfied that she did not know what she said and did, from the time she came here with a bad cough" (when Agnes died) "till her decease."

April 1875: Elizabeth looks after Jane and Sarah in her Will

Elizabeth had written a new Will after the deaths of Agnes and Tom, which was witnessed and signed on 28th February 1875, two months before she died, with Sarah as the sole executrix. Her estate was valued as under £3,000, the same value which had been given to Agnes's estate, indicating that the two sisters had somehow managed to share the proceeds of their work evenly despite all the complications that Elizabeth's insistence on anonymity must have caused.

Although apparently angry with Jane during the last months of her life, Elizabeth was generous to Jane in her Will. She left to Jane any rights and income from the books which she had written with Agnes plus: "the leasehold premises called the Lower Raglan Music Hall (formerly the Golden Horse) situated in Theobalds Row" and £100 plus: "such of my plate not otherwise disposed of by this my Will and also my books and such of my dresses and clothing as she may please to select and accept."

Agnes, by giving back to Jane the lease of 'Park Lane Cottage', had left to Jane in her Will a home to live in as well as one to rent out. Elizabeth left Jane money, income from published books, and a property which was generating rental income. Both sisters therefore recognised the important part that Jane had played in family life while she was living at Reydon Hall, and caring for their mother in her later years, and both sisters ensured that Jane was provided for in their Wills.

The other main beneficiary of Elizabeth's Will was Sarah, to whom Elizabeth left her property in Tilford, which consisted of: "Abbot's Lodge, where I now live, secondly the Gardener's Cottage sited on that part of my land which lies across the Haslemere Road and thirdly the cottage called Southbank Cottage at the south extremity of the estate." By this bequest, Elizabeth gave Sarah a property of her own to live in, something which Sarah had previously lacked, 'Hollow Oak' being only rented.

Susanna, Robert Strickland, Adela Wigg, and Tom's granddaughter Julia Dupuis were all minor beneficiaries in Elizabeth's Will but Catharine, understandably, was not mentioned.

June 1875: Sarah gives Agnes's portrait to the nation

Agnes had bequeathed her portrait to the nation and this was noted in newspapers on 12th June 1875. The notice read: "The Late Miss Agnes Strickland – A portrait of this esteemed and talented lady, by Mr J Hayes, has been presented, by her sister, to the National Portrait Gallery, in accordance with the Will of the deceased lady. The trustees of the Gallery have also made purchases of portraits of Lord Chancellor Thurlow and Miss Mitford to place amongst their collection."

June was the time of year when the National Portrait Gallery gave an annual report, and an item appeared in the papers on 14th June 1875 which puts Agnes's bequest into context. The article reported that: "The Trustees of the National Portrait Gallery are 18 in number" – and included the Whig Prime Minister Gladstone and the Tory Prime Minister Disraeli. During the past twelve months they had received six donations, including Agnes's, and made ten purchases.

The National Portrait Gallery had existed for eighteen years but was still evolving. The newspaper report said: "As the gallery increases in the number of works exhibited so does its popularity. The number of visitors in 1859 was 5,305, and the greatest number during the time the gallery was in Great George Street, Westminster, was 25,344. But as soon as it removed to South Kensington the visitors more than doubled. Last year however, the number was not quite so large as in 1872 when it was 67,039. The trustees complain terribly of want of room."

The National Portrait Gallery now holds many thousands of portraits and has long been situated near Trafalgar Square. Agnes Strickland's portrait was on display in the same room as portraits of TB Macaulay, Jenny Lind and the Bronte sisters when the gallery was closed in March 2020 with a scheduled re-opening date in 2023 after a major overhaul.

18th June 1875: Jane sets to work on a biography of Agnes

When Jane wrote to Catharine on 18th June 1875, she gave news of Sarah. Jane wrote: "Our dear Sarah is in her own home and rather better not well – Her trial with poor Eliza was a very heavy one – However she writes cheerfully and found everything in nice order. Her horses in fine condition, poultry yard well stocked, and fruit and flower gardens flourishing – if ever anyone deserved to be rich it is dear kind Sarah."

With Sarah's financial help, Jane had moved from her small cottage in Southwold into her neighbouring larger property, 'Park Lane Cottage', to which Agnes had added a coach-house, and had enlarged the garden while it had been in her care.

Jane had undertaken the task of writing a biography of Agnes and answered a question from Catharine as to the progress she had made. Jane wrote: "You ask about my life of Agnes – I find more difficulty in it than I had looked for. The home letters all I have unfortunately are so full of self praise, not of her talents but of her personal charms, that it is not easy to separate the author from the mere woman." Jane knew very well the part of Agnes's life that had been lived in Suffolk, but her knowledge of Agnes's life when away from home was based only on conversation and letters. Jane had never met Agnes's non-Suffolk friends, and had never visited any of the places, or experienced any of the social pastimes that Agnes had enjoyed. It seems a bit hard of Jane to have described Agnes's letters as full of self-praise. Certainly they were full of self-news, but then what else could she write when expected to send letters home to her mother at frequent intervals.

Jane was finding it difficult to recover from the sad events of the previous twelve months. She told Catharine: "I have been hindered by tendency to asthma – Not very ill but incapable of mental exertion – Poor Eliza's state caused me great anxiety and indeed though induced by her disease I could think of nothing else – I have begun again but do not feel well – giddy and feverish – there is thunder in the air." Jane at the age of 75 and in poor health, had begun to realise that in writing Agnes's biography, she had a hard task in front of her.

Jane's letter implied that Catharine was thinking of selling her share of the copyrights, which Agnes had bequeathed to her and Percy Strickland less than a year previously. Jane wrote: "I would not sell your rights on the Queens – Longman at the end of five years – one year since the death of the author is nearly gone can print it for himself – Now the sale has lately been on the increase and will bring in from forty to fifty pounds per annum – He would not give more than a hundred pounds if that – for Percy has his part – You should buy his of him not sell yours to Longman. Keeping the copyright is more in your favour than it would be for him as a purchaser."

Jane added: "Agnes would not have left it to you if she thought you would sell it. 'It will make poor Kate' she said 'a pretty income for years to come.' If you died your children would enjoy it to the end of the term – You will not hear from Longman till after August – or possibly Christmas – but he is safe and sure."

Jane may have been physically distant from Canadian members of the family but she obviously exchanged letters with several of them. She told Catharine: "I had a sweet letter from dear Suze which I must leave unanswered this post though I was much pleased with it – also I heard from Agnes Chamberlin and Jane Blomfield – these alas not replied to — My love to dear Suzy if with you." Her closing sentence was a long farewell typical of the letters exchanged by the Strickland family: "With love to you, your Kate and all my known and unknown relatives and wishes for your health and happiness, I remain my dear Kate, your affectionate sister Jane Margaret Strickland."

18th June 1875: Jane gives tantalising glimpses of the past and present

Jane's letter to Catharine, written in June 1875, hints at events in the past which Catharine did not reveal in her family memoirs. From

Jane it seems that there had been another suitor for Catharine's hand, who had given her the opportunity of making a comfortable marriage in England, instead of emigrating to Canada. Jane wrote: "From my dear friend Miss Holmes I can give you news of your old friend Mrs Freestone – George, Anthony and Edward are all dead and in one year – Edward left seventy thousand pounds among his nieces and nephews, a numerous people – He never married. No one could realise to him Catharine Strickland the first and last object of his love – Ah, he was a true lover if ever a man was – and he had my wishes for success and my deep sympathy, for he did not hide from me his disappointment and grief."

Jane then gives small clues to posterity about Mrs Garnham and Homer relatives which she mentioned, but unfortunately did not need to explain to Catharine. Jane wrote: "Susan Freestone is well and Mrs Homer speaks well of her. Mr Homer is vicar of that parish. Her neglect of poor dear Maria Garnham made me think ill of her."

Jane passed on news of Robert Strickland and family: "The Stricklands all arrived safely, at present they are near Charlotte at Acton by London. They are to visit our dear Sarah at Hollow Oak and then come perhaps to Southwold but their plans are not formed yet."

30<u>th</u> December 1875: Jane throws a bit of light on the family finances

Jane added new family information when she wrote to Catharine a letter dated 30<u>th</u> December 1875. Jane wrote: "Adela (Wigg) wrote to Sarah about Cheesman's legacy – poor Miss Stephens (Standen?) is dead I know not where or how – I believe that the unborn children at the time of the Testator's death have nothing to do with it – if they have Marina's share will be divided to the legatees – I suppose Julia Dupuis will have her mother's share and Capt Pohle his dead wife's. If it was left with benefit of survivorship then only the living can come in for it. I am sorry Walter has anything to do with it as he is not fit to be trusted with money. I have written to a legal friend to hear how the matter stands."

Diana is not mentioned and can therefore be considered alive and still in contact with the family after her marriage in Valparaiso.

It also shows that in whatever way Tom's son Walter had blotted his copybook, and whatever his side of the story, he had not been forgiven.

This puts a new light, albeit shaded, on the role of Thomas Cheesman in the life of the Strickland siblings. Whether or not he left any money to the Strickland sisters when he died in 1834, it seems that the first priority in his Will was to provide for the niece who lived with him and took charge of household affairs.

However, it looks as though his bequest to his unmarried niece gave her a lifetime interest in some assets but that he made provision for the passing on of these assets after her death. When Thomas Cheesman died in 1834, Tom Strickland was long established in his career in the merchant navy. He survived to retire safely aged over 60, but shipwreck and death by drowning were a common fate for sailors, and he might well have gone to the bottom of the sea leaving a destitute family behind him. Under this set of circumstances, it would make sense for Thomas Cheesman to specify that when his niece died, there would be some kind of legacy for Tom's children, possibly only his daughters, and that is what seems, from Jane's letter, to have been the case.

(Tom's son, Walter Strickland married on 4th March 1876. He was then 32 years old, a bill broker and living in Leytonstone in North East London. His bride was 23, daughter of a surgeon and lived at West Ham, where they married in the parish church.

Walter and his wife subsequently had at least three daughters and one son. The eldest daughter, born in 1878, was christened Agnes, so Walter ensured the name Agnes Strickland was carried forward another generation, even if his famous aunt had fallen out with him.)

30th December 1875: Katharine Strickland has left Canada for the last time

Jane in her letter to Catharine dated 18th June 1875 mentioned the third child of Robert and Caroline Strickland, their 16 year old son Arthur. Jane wrote: "I had a nice letter from Arthur Strickland to Sarah. He says that you will be sorry to hear that your friend, Sam's widow, has kept her bed ever since she has gone down to

Norfolk – This looks rather serious, for her constitution was very strong by nature."

When Jane next wrote to Catharine, on 30th December 1875, Robert was still in Acton and Katharine Strickland, Sam's widow was still ill in England. She seems never to have returned to Canada, remaining in Aylsham, her home before marrying Sam. Katharine Strickland had been comfortably off in her own right and although Sam had left the Strickland home in Lakefield, the 'Homestead' to Katharine during her life, he had also specified that it was in the care of Robert and Caroline Strickland rather than his widow. This makes it probable that both Sam and Katharine expected her to return to England after his death, either part or full time, and would neither need, nor want responsibility for the 'Homestead'.

December 1875: Jane is missing her sisters

In December 1875, Jane was feeling the loss of Agnes, Eliza and Tom. Sarah seems to have been travelling to Suffolk less than previously, but Jane's financial position was satisfactory. Jane wrote: "I missed dear Sarah's company this summer very much and feel sad when I think of poor Eliza. She was very kind and thoughtful for me. She left me the 'Lord Raglan' for which the Metropolitan Board of Works are now in treaty.

"There is to be a fine street made from Holborn to Oxford Street and the Shoreditch Station, a great gain to the cities east and west and to all people travelling from Suffolk. There is no choice in the matter as there is an act of parliament for the improvements and indeed my morale is gained" (presumably she meant strained) "by the possession of such a property and I shall be happy to part with it. My man of business asks 700£ and will do well to get it – however there will be to pay the surveyor and the Lawyer will be something considerable."

The site of Jane's 'Lord Raglan' pub was needed when Clerkenwell Road and Theobalds Road were built between 1874 and 1878 by the Metropolitan Board of Works as part of a main route across central London.

Jane was making slow progress, or none, with her biography of Agnes. Jane told Catharine: "About the life of Agnes I am copying her correspondence and stop till that is done. I ought to have done that first. It tires my eyes and my feelings but it must be done."

17th April 1877: Catharine still needs money from Sarah

When Catharine wrote to William Traill on 17th April 1877, money from Agnes's bequest of a copyright to herself and Percy Strickland, was not coming easily and complications abounded. Catharine had hoped to buy for $200 a cottage behind her own, as a home for her daughter Mary and family. However, she had to abandon the idea as the money she had received had only been enough to pay off some debts, incurred for painting and roofing repairs to 'Westove'.

This meant that despite Agnes's good intentions and the upset it caused Elizabeth, Catharine still needed the money which Sarah sent her. Catharine told William she was expecting to receive something from Sarah in July 1877, and that some money would come from the publisher Bell's in September 1877 and that, with care, these would give her enough money to manage on for the time being.

She asked William, if he had any money to spare, to send it to help the Muchalls rather than herself, which he did.

17th April 1877: Sam's grand-daughter Charlotte Strickland is an evangelist

When writing to William Traill in April 1877, Catharine gave news of Robert Strickland's daughter Charlotte Strickland who had become an evangelist. William was himself spreading the gospel among the people he met in the farther parts of Canada when working for the Hudson's Bay Company. Catharine wrote: "The meetings" at Lakefield "have continued every Tuesday evening at the Hall steadily and well attended but it is your cousin Charlotte that attracts hundreds to the afternoon meetings on Sundays.

"She has been in Toronto for the past fortnight. She needed change and rest but during her absence there has been erected a large building near the upper-mills – Which has been built by subscription purposely for her to speak in and for any religious purpose as well. Mrs Robert S gave the lot but the workmen came nobly forward to give time and labour – When the dear girl returns it will be a joyful surprize to her as I believe she is not to know of the work till it is ready – Quietly and sweetly she has gone forward speaking to the crowds that fill the Music hall – and the Spirit of Love and peace seems to move her when she pleads so earnestly in the Masters cause.

"There were two lady Evangelists in Peterboro who attracted many persons but" (one of them) "fell ill and they sent an entreaty up for Charlotte to take her place which she was at last prevailed upon to do and great was the astonishment and delight of the hearers – entreating her to remain and continue her service in Peterboro."

When Catharine continued her letter a week later she told William: "The new building is going on rapidly and is to be opened on your cousin Roberts birthday the 2nd of May – It is to be called 'The Christian Association' – It is a good thing for our village such an institution. I will send you a paper with the account of the laying of the foundation stone."

The link between Robert Strickland's family life in Acton near London, and in Lakefield in Ontario was never explained, but some clarification emerges and becomes of more relevance at a later date.

27th December 1877: Susanna's grand-daughter is to marry a Moodie

With the dramatic decrease in numbers of senior members of the Strickland family in England, relatives in Canada became more involved in ensuring that care was being taken of Sarah and of Jane. The three daughters of Agnes Fitzgibbon Chamberlin from her first marriage, all travelled to England to spend time living with Sarah, and visiting or living with Jane. The first to make the journey was Geraldine Fitzgibbon, sometimes referred to as Cherry or Georgie, and the middle in age of the three daughters. She arrived in England during 1877 at the age of 23, but for some reason the visit was not entirely successful. Whether this was because of some failing in Geraldine, or because she soon found a marriage partner is not clear.

Sarah, having been left 'Abbot's Lodge' in Elizabeth's Will, had moved her home from Lancashire to Surrey by the time that Geraldine arrived, but she still had friends in Lancashire, and there were also relatives of Richard Gwillym whom she visited from time to time.

Jane, in a letter to Catharine dated 27th December 1877, mentioned Geraldine's visit and her engagement. Jane wrote: "Our dear Sarah will soon have to part with Geraldine and to part with her in the best way – The son of a neighbour of mine admired her very much for being an elegant and pretty girl with good manners. Sarah was rather disappointed – she expected perhaps too much from a person so much younger, however she will fit her out for her bridal trousseau and give her a hundred pounds – at least so she proposes at present."

Jane continued: "The young man pleases Sarah very much and said very handsomely when informed she had no fortune 'that it was herself alone he sought not fortune' so I hope all things may be propitious for the young couple – I found the young lady very nice as far as I was concerned – I dare say in the uncertainty of a first attachment her mind was wholly occupied and taken up."

Geraldine's future husband was John Douglas Moodie and his forbears, in common with Susanna's late husband, had originated in the Orkneys. How his father came to be a neighbour of Jane in Southwold is not explained. At some time in the past the Moodie family had split into two branches with Geraldine's future husband belonging to one branch of the family while Susanna's late husband, John Moodie had belonged to the other. Susanna is said to have been particularly pleased that the marriage would reunite the two branches of the Moodie family.

It seems that after the situation had gone through a shaky patch, Sarah grew fond of her great-niece. Jane reported that: "She and her aunt are now very happy together. Douglas Moodie comes every Saturday and stays till Monday. Our Thay got a new piano and plays herself and Geraldine plays and sings so it is a source of pleasure to them both."

27th December 1877: Jane is busy writing

In her December 1877 letter to Catharine, Jane described her life and health. She wrote: "My life is so quiet and unvaried that I have little to write about" the main purpose of her letter being to send season's greetings to her sister and family in Canada. Jane told of Sarah's continuing and widespread generosity: "Dear Thay is very generous to me or I could not live in the house. My old cottage however was very nice I had made it so by degrees and the tiny flower garden was neat and a little female work and arrangement will always make a humble room look nice – of course the larger house is more capable of improvement.

"I am well at this time for me thank God though my chest is more musical than is well or safe for me – I feel the tubes are filling again by these sounds – I do not much mind the sharp cold it is the damp that hurts me – I hope I shall not have six months hindrance as I had last winter and Spring as I want to finish my literary tasks." One of these tasks was her slowly progressing 'Life of Agnes Strickland'. She said "I am still engaged with my sister's correspondence which is extensive and interesting till that is done I cannot put the work together. It cannot be I think in less than three volumes." Jane had owed Catharine a letter for some time and said: "My only yet true excuse being my long illness in the summer and the pain long after in the chest which made writing painful. To write a letter is now to me a serious undertaking."

Jane mentioned to Catharine, one of her long-standing friends. Jane wrote: "I was afraid I should have lost my dear friend Mrs Charles Foster with inflammation of the lungs she is better now and will be able to return on Friday to her Norfolk home – she is one of the dear friends God gave me when I lost dear familiar ones of my youth." Georgina Foster was 27 years old in 1877. Her husband, Charles Foster was a solicitor with a practice in Norwich. They had a summer home in Southwold and Mrs Foster was one of Jane's seasonal friends.

Another aspect of this letter implies that Catharine had asked Jane to send a photograph of herself, and Jane was not willing to comply. However, she compensated to some extent for the lack of a picture by commenting on the appearances of family members, and any similarities to either their father or mother (whose maiden name had been Homer).

Jane wrote: "I grow much like my father and when my cap is off Sarah says I have the same form of head – That form of head was all that was wanting for likeness between Sam and his father. Tom in all things was a Homer altogether – I never will have my photograph taken I would rather my distant friends should think of me as I was – than as I am."

2nd April 1878: Susanna has a room with a view in Toronto

Susanna lived in Lakefield for much of the time between 1872 and 1877, either staying with Catharine or lodging somewhere nearby. From this base she visited her children in Toronto and Ottawa. Nellie Moodie, wife of Susanna's son Robert recovered from her mental breakdown and returned to her family, and Nelllie's mother went to live with another of her children.

After these changes in Robert Moodie's household had taken place, Susanna's permanent home was with him and his family in Toronto. From there she paid short visits to her daughters and continued to pay lengthy visits to Catharine. Robert Moodie's life when Susanna returned to live with him, was much improved from that which he had led in Seaforth. He was a capable and hard-working man, and had a successful career in Toronto which had begun with the help of his brother-in-law, John Vickers.

In 1878 Robert and his family moved house in Toronto, their new address being in Caer Howell Place, The Avenue. In writing to Catharine, Susanna apologised for the long silence which she said was caused by the muddle during the removal process. Susanna described their new home, telling Catharine in a letter dated 2nd April 1878: "We have a very nice house in the Avenue, close to the Park, and surrounded by lovely trees, in which the birds salute the morn. My room looks directly up and down the broad avenue and is very bright and cheerful. All the fashionable idlers come here for walking and riding, and babies in their cabriolars, and pretty well-dressed children. Nellie is enchanted with the place and hopes this may be the last move." Nellie was to be disappointed in the last respect, for the family moved within Toronto several times over the next few years.

In a letter to Catharine dated 29th July 1878 Susanna was still professing shortage of money and wrote: "I wish I were with you, but I do not think I shall be able to command the funds to come down for a month. Mrs H Traill may be able to pay me the four dollars she owes me which would be a help." Susanna was presumably referring to the widow of Harry Traill, but one would have expected Susanna to have had less need of four dollars than Harry Traill's widow, and to have known this to be the case.

Among Susanna's children, it was Donald whose life had become most difficult, due to his alcoholism. In a letter from Susanna to Catharine dated 13th October 1878, Susanna in referring to Donald wrote: "he is steady as long as he has no money. Malcolm" (person unknown) "says 'it is a disease and he cannot help it'." Susanna then added information about Tom's drinking. She wrote: "But it cannot be hereditary as Moodie never drank, nor any of my people but poor Tom, and that not until the death of his wife."

8th June 1878: Sarah hosts a wedding

On 8th June 1878, Geraldine Fitzgibbon and John Douglas Moodie were married at the parish church of All Saints in Tilford, and Sarah Strickland Gwillym signed the register as one of the witnesses to the marriage.

Susanna in a letter to Catharine dated 29th July 1878 gave a more enthusiastic account of Sarah's feelings towards Geraldine than Jane had done six months earlier. Susanna wrote: "Georgie seems to be a great favourite with dear Sarah who says in her letter to me, that she is a girl after her own heart. She cannot bear to part with her. She gave her a magnificent set of pearls, beautiful exceedingly – tiara, necklace, brooch, earrings, bracelet and hair pins. I fancy that they must have cost a lot of money, but had belonged to either Agnes or Eliza."

Agnes had owned some pearl jewellery, but in her Will she divided it between various nieces and was specific about who should have what. There was no mention of a complete set of pearl jewellery such as Susanna described. Eliza made no mention of any jewellery in her Will and, given her attitudes and mode of living, was unlikely to have owned any worth mentioning. The present to Geraldine from Sarah was more likely to have been her own jewellery, worn when Richard Gwillym was alive, but no longer used.

Susanna continued, referring to gifts from Sarah: "She sent me a black shawl like my best one, and a nice pair of gloves which was very kind. Mr Vickers forwarded a box to you. I have no doubt that you will find in it lots of nice things."

July 1878: Catharine and Percy sell their copyright

By 1878 Catharine and Percy had given up trying to get income from Agnes's copyrights and, despite Jane saying Agnes would not have left the copyrights to them if she had thought they would sell them, they decided to accept the publishers' offers to buy them out. Catharine received almost $2,500 from the sale, with part of which she bought a house for the Muchall family near her own home. She followed the advice of her lawyers and bought shares in the Peterborough Land Company with most of the remaining money.

So it was that at the age of 77, Catharine was in a better financial position than ever before, thanks to the bequest from Agnes and (indirectly) Elizabeth, together with continuing support from Sarah, her own sons and the families of Sam's children. Despite less need to do so, Catharine continued to write, and her work continued to appear in print. Susanna in a letter to Catharine dated 29th July 1878 wrote: "Your 'Forest Trees of Canada' is in this month's 'Canadian' – to my mind a capital article – The best in the new issue."

December 1878: Jane describes her Christmas

In her letter dated 23rd December1877 and probably misdated and written in December 1878, Jane again mentioned her friend Mrs Foster. Jane wrote: "My dear friend Mrs Charles Foster has just left Southwold certainly looking better yet not so well as I could wish. My dear friend is the kindest of the kind to the sick. Never shall I forget what she did for me. It would be a bitter grief to lose her – I have good neighbours in the town but my treasured ones are birds of passage. Mrs Foster having the Marine Cottage I am sure to see her some part of the year. She always makes something warm for me Shawls or mitts of her own work."

Of her way of spending Christmas, Jane said: "I always keep my Christmas the day before which enables my maidens to see their own friends and to go to church – I usually dine with Mrs Gemper in the evening – she lives close by and her sweet daughter and her boys are very fond of me – If well enough to go to church I meet a party there – a home one, only Mrs Blois and her family to be there."

3rd March 1879: Susanna becomes a great-grandmother

After her wedding in Tilford, Geraldine Moodie, formerly Geraldine Fitzgibbon moved with her husband to Deptford near London. Their first child was Susanna's first great grand-child, and was a daughter born on 3rd March 1879 and named Melville Mary Moodie.

During Geraldine's pregnancy, her younger sister Alice Fitzgibbon arrived in England. Alice was staying with Geraldine when baby Melville was born and registered the birth. From Deptford, Alice went to Tilford to begin a long visit with Sarah in place of Geraldine. Alice was 22 years old when she arrived with Sarah, being three years younger than Geraldine.

Geraldine Moodie returned to Canada with her baby, husband and elderly father-in-law later in 1879. (In 1881 she and her family moved to Manitoba to join Walter Traill and other members of the extended Strickland family in Canada. Her husband joined the North West Mounted Police.)

30th April 1879: Tom's grand-son marries Sam's grand-daughter

Two branches of the Strickland family were united when Philip Wigg, Tom's grandson via Adela Wigg, married Agnes Strickland, Sam's granddaughter via Robert Strickland. They were married in Lakefield on 30th April 1879 when Agnes was 20 and Philip 26 years old.

After their wedding, Agnes and Philip Wigg went to Toronto where Susanna met them, as she told Catharine in a letter dated 19th May 1879. She wrote: "Dear Maria Tully came for me to spend a few days with her, and meet the bride and bridegroom. But I could only stay three days, and did not meet them there, but Walter S came for me in a cab on saturday and they came to lunch on the Monday following. They both looked very happy, and Agnes very pretty. As to Philip, he is about the handsomest young man I ever saw in Canada. Isabel Murney was quite right when she said he was beautiful. His noble features and frank bright face would make a charming picture. I hope he will turn out as good as he looks."

11th November 1879: Charlotte Strickland marries in England

Soon after the marriage of Robert Strickland's daughter Agnes in Canada, his other daughter married in England. The wedding took place on 11th November 1879 when Charlotte Katharine Strickland married John Charles Taylor at the parish church of Holy Trinity in Richmond, Surrey. She was 22 years old while the groom, a clerk in Holy Orders, was 27.

Where Charlotte and John Taylor met is not stated, but Charlotte had in the past spent time in England with her parents, brother and sister, while John Taylor had been in Lakefield, Ontario when Susanna wrote letters in 1878. In her letters to Catharine in Lakefield, Susanna in Toronto mentioned Charlotte on three different occasions. Firstly, in July 1878 Susanna wrote: "I did not see dear Charlotte until last week, she having only just returned from Brantford. The darling girl looked as sweet as usual. The light of Heaven on the dear face ... I hope your new parson will turn out a good one and not persecute dear Charlotte."

In October 1878 Susanna wrote: "I saw so little of the darling Charlotte while she was here, and it would have done me a world of good to have heard one of her sweet lectures and her prayers."

The final mention came in a short letter thought also to have been written in October 1878, Susanna wrote: "I was sorely puzzled by the card enclosed in your letter. It was a long time before I found out who the nephew John was who had sent it ... At last, I thought of the dear John Taylor, and the mystery disappeared. He had heard me say, that I could not positively say, that I was forgiven and was certain of salvation – and he sent me the card to cheer and strengthen my faith. The dear noble loving creature, what a darling he is. Tell dear Charlotte to thank him much for Aunt Susie."

23rd December 1879: Sarah and Alice have visited Jane

In her Christmas letter to Catharine in 1879 Jane wrote: "I enjoyed the visit of my dear sister in September and was happy to see her looking so well and handsome."

Alice Fitzgibbon was still living with Sarah when the letter was written on 23rd December 1879, and Jane told Catharine: "Sarah I heard from this day. She and Alice spent a very happy week with Lady Jephson and Lady Banes in Portland Place – Nothing but thick fogs in town – frost and fog just as we have here." Her own health had been lingeringly poor. Jane wrote: "I was still weak from my summer illness and had a bad fit of asthma which kept me indoors till Sunday last when I managed to go to church and yesterday for the Christmas purchases and gifts – My charitable ones are a delight but I must give to a host of officials which I do not heartily – obeying the law of custom."

Jane gave Catharine her opinion of the two Fitzgibbon sisters saying: "I must write to dear Susan – Her grand daughters are pretty elegant girls but I like her Alice best though she is not so lovely in person or so finished in manners as her sister – The baby was a sweet bright child and very good tempered – too forward I was afraid for long life – Our Sarah with Alice is going on the 29th to Broughton Park near Manchester – I am afraid Surrey does not suit her. She seems better anywhere else."

5th January 1880: Sarah sends Christmas presents to Susanna

When Susanna wrote to Catharine on 5th January 1880, she had just returned to Robert Moodie's household after a visit to Katie Vickers. Susanna had been ill but wrote: "the quiet and good nursing set me up once more. Old Santa Claus brought me several nice presents. A black dress from dear Aunt Thay a pair of black silk and fur trimmed gloves and a breakfast shawl and better than all a very affectionate letter."

1880: Catharine and Agnes Fitzgibbon Chamberlin start a new project

Agnes Fitzgibbon Chamberlin, who had helped Catharine with the production of her plant book in 1868, was herself interested in botany.

She became actively involved in the Ottawa Field Naturalists' Club soon after it was founded in 1879.

After her children began to marry and leave home, Agnes Fitzgibbon Chamberlin suggested to Catharine that they work together again, with the aim of getting more of Catharine's botanical and natural history material published. Catharine spent the early years of the 1880s doing preliminary work to get her collection of material into a form suitable for publication.

1880: Agnes (Strickland) Wigg dies

Robert and Caroline Strickland's younger daughter, Agnes Wigg became pregnant soon after her marriage to Philip Wigg and gave birth to a daughter in 1880, dying as a consequence. Her daughter was named in her memory Agnes Wigg, and was brought up almost from birth by her grand-parents, Robert and Caroline Strickland.

Robert and Caroline Strickland's elder daughter, Charlotte Taylor, also gave birth to a daughter fairly soon after her marriage. The baby was named Agnes Ethel Strickland Taylor, carrying forward the Christian name of her aunt who had died so young, and also carrying forward the full name of her famous great-aunt.

20th December 1880: Jane has a social legacy from Agnes

Jane had a relatively busy social life during the year preceding her letter to Catharine dated 20th December, and probably referring to 1880. Southwold, being a seaside town, had summer visitors and part-time residents, as well as the full-time inhabitants of the town The widespread social custom of paying visits meant that Jane was far from lonely. She told Catharine: "I never call upon the occasional visitors but many call upon me – Some highly placed persons have called and I had two invitations from Lady Constance Barne but was only well enough to go to one – This young lady was loved of Agnes who stayed with the present Marchioness of Hertford when Emily Seymour. She seemed to have won the hearts of the children since grown up.

"Lady Constance a youthful matron with four sweet children travels all over the world with her husband. She is a charming hostess and the park of Sotterly Hall has ancient trees as old as England nearly and one terrific legend. The old hall fell down in King William's time so the house is a modern antique." Sotterley is about 9 miles from Southwold and Jane's letter continued in a manner that showed her interest in, and knowledge of antiquities was considerable. She wrote: "As friends conveyed me – I enjoyed my visit very much and being Saturday went into the old church which stands in the park shadowed with trees – and filled with the monuments of the Playters, the former possessors of the lands and castellated low laid hall – One was so magnificent that on examining it I forgot my intention of looking for that of Sir John Playter the barbarous British knight, whose victim is said to haunt the spot where he was slowly murdered by his feudal lord.

"The monument that attracted my eyes is of James the first time and consists of groups of figures in alabaster in high relief from the base of the Chancel to the roof – First the Knight kneeling before the altar in plate armour, at some distance and in a separate compartment two finely sculpted figures ecclesiastics or saints – Our knight being fat and stuffy and fore-shortened too much does not appear to advantage – Then below we see him again kneeling in the same ungraceful attitude with a train in procession of his wife and two and twenty children – This very magnificent tomb could not be the work of English artists. The family were Catholics and the last of the line died a Nun in Flanders. It was probably the work of an Italian artist but is a noble and most beautiful monument."

Jane's letter to Catharine gave more news of Sarah and Alice. Jane wrote: "Of the dear Sarah I cannot speak too highly and her visit in November gave me the greatest pleasure I can hope to have on this side the grave. The company of the lively good-tempered niece was very pleasant to me. She was like a sunbeam in my cottage home.

"Happily for her she was not confined to the society of the aged Aunts for there were some nice young ladies in the town and amiable girls for walking companions – with whom she spent pleasant evenings with or without us – My friends have made much of my dear Sarah and Alice – Southwold affords a pleasant and intellectual society not like those who formed its old inhabitants.

"The only drawback of dear Sarah's visit was a fierce attack of gout in my right knee – I am still lame with it – and her attack of lumbago – However our confinement to the house was softened by our enjoyment of each other's society. She worked her new chair back and I at my flannel garments and so we got on as well as could be expected and had had some pleasant visits before – Oh my back and – Oh my knee – came on.

"Tilford does not agree well with dear Sarah and she leaves today for a long stay in Lancashire. Of course Alice goes nothing loth with her and the faithful Vickery attends her mistress. Dear Sarah's visit is no expense to me. She always gives me ample funds so that I am able to provide handsomely for my beloved guests."

3rd January 1881: Susanna is reading the latest novels

During 1880, Robert Moodie moved to a new job with an increase in salary. Susanna in her letter to Catharine dated 3rd January 1881 wrote: "It is a government appointment as General Freight agent of the intercolonial railroad but his residence is to be here in Toronto." Of her means of earning money she wrote: "We may give up flower painting altogether now it will soon be a thing of the past" and of her reading, Susanna wrote: "I have read 'Endymion' by Lord Beaconsfield. I was much disappointed, it is the poorest of all his works that I have read."

Benjamin Disraeli, now titled Lord Beaconsfield had been prime minister, but when his government fell in April 1880 he returned to writing and finished his final novel, entitled 'Endymion'. It was first published in London late in November 1880. For Susanna to have read it within two months of its publication, shows her to have good access to newly published books.

4th April 1881: Jane makes her first appearance on a census

The 1881 census was taken on the night of 3rd/4th April and Jane Margaret Strickland appears for the first time. Her address was 'Park Lane Cottage', Southwold and her census record shows her to have been 80 years old, living on funds plus an annuity, with one live-in domestic servant, Emma Howard, aged 22.

The same census records Sarah Strickland Gwillym living at 'Abbot's Lodge', Tilford. She was recorded as the head of household, a widow aged 70 and an annuitant. However, as she was born in 1798, her real age was 82 or 83. This is the same wrong age that was given on Elizabeth Strickland's death certificate which suggests more than coincidence. Whether due to Sarah's vanity, or intended as 70+ by someone who filled in the form on Sarah's behalf, or as an alternative to either 'mind your own business' or 'I don't know and don't want to ask' remains unknown.

Recorded with Sarah were Charlotte A(lice) Fitzgibbon (aged 23 and described as Sarah's niece and companion) and four live-in servants. The first was Mary A Vickery (aged 40, ladies maid) whose role in the lives of the Strickland sisters made her more than a mere servant, and who may have been the person who provided the answers for the census form. Two of the other servants were female (a cook aged 24 and a housemaid aged 18) and there was also a 15 year old pageboy.

Sam's grand-daughter, Charlotte Taylor, aged 24, was living at 14 Adelaide Villas in Adelaide Road, Richmond in Surrey. Her husband, John Taylor, aged 27 and born in Kensington, was a curate at Holy Trinity Church in Richmond. Their first child, Agnes Ethel Strickland Taylor was 6 months old and had been born in Richmond. There were two live-in servants – a 35 year-old cook and a 17 year-old nurse. John Taylor's birthplace of Kensington gives a signal that he may have come from a well-to-do English family.

23rd June 1881: Susanna passes on family news

By 23rd June 1881 when Susanna wrote to Catharine, she and Robert Moodie's family had made another of their several changes of address in Toronto. Their latest home was resulting in Susanna becoming housebound as there was no public transport available, and it was too far for her to walk to pay visits. This, plus Robert often being away from home due to his new job, was resulting in Susanna becoming despondent. She told Catharine: "We are very pleasantly situated here but it is awfully dull and my eyes have grown too weak for painting or even much reading."

Susanna had family news from England to pass on. She wrote: "I had kind letters from both Sarah and Jane. Sarah's cough was better and Jane writes in good spirits a really charming letter." Susanna continued, though whether referring to Jane or Sarah is not always clear: "She seems very fond of Alice whom she thinks if not as handsome as Cherrie far more interesting. Aunt and Alice were going to spend the summer in Sutherlandshire on the moors with the Rawstones who have a hunting box there – young Rawstone a barrister goes with them – a good chance for Alice."

Sarah and Alice must have enjoyed their 1881 summer in Sutherland with the Rawstorne (or Rawstone) family, but may have found the journey to the north of Scotland too much, for Sarah was among those listed in May 1882 as having taken a 'Scotch Moor and Forest', and the place she had taken was in Argyllshire. While Argyllshire was still a long journey from Tilford, or even from Lancashire, the journey was considerably shorter than to Sutherland.

The third of Susanna's grand-children via Agnes Fitzgibbon Chamberlin was Mary Agnes Fitzgibbon. She was the eldest, aged 30 in 1881, was known as Maime and was a writer. In June 1881 Susanna told Catharine: "Maime's book has been splendidly received in London and Bentley thinks it will be a success. He sent her £30 as the first fruits of her share and hopes to send her more soon."

This book had the title 'A Trip to Manitoba or Roughing It on the Line' and had been published in London in 1880 by the firm originally set up by Richard Bentley, and subsequently run by his son and other members of Richard Bentley's family.

1882: Catharine worries about Walter

When Catharine's grand-daughter Katie Traill was 12 years old, her uncle Walter Traill undertook to pay for her continued education, and she attended a school in Peterborough. In 1882 Walter also sent Catharine sufficient money, as she told William, that she: "was able to have my garden put in order."

This was pleasing for Catharine, but she rarely had letters from Walter, and the letters she did receive never said anything about his home and family life. He had two step-children, of whom he was very fond, but the only child his wife bore him before her health became poor, had subsequently died. Catharine feared that he was increasingly suffering from depression.

1882: Susanna remembers life in Suffolk

In Toronto, Susanna met many of the people in the literary and academic community of the city, and when James Ewing Ritchie visited Canada in 1882 he brought back to Susanna memories of her early life in Suffolk.

After the meeting, James Ritchie in his book entitled 'To Canada with Emigrants' said that he was amazed to find: "a mental vigour and active memory rare in one so aged. She told me anecdotes of myself as a boy that I had quite forgotten, and retains in old age the enthusiasm for which she was remarkable when young." Susanna was 79 years old.

14th May 1883: Catharine plans to visit Susanna

Susanna was ill early in 1883 and Catharine went to visit her. The journey was too long to complete in a single day, and Catharine wrote to Ellen Dunlop on 14th May asking to be put up for the night en route. Catharine wrote: "Now my dear friend it is possible I may have to pass up to Toronto to see my poor sister Mrs Moodie, who has been very – very ill lately and is too weak to bear a journey to Lakefield for change of air, as she had purposed, and I have nearly made up my mind to go up to see her myself. We are all we two, of the old sisters in Canada. There are only four of all the old Stricklands left, two in England – Mrs Gwillym 85 – Jane Margaret 83 – myself 81 – and dear Mrs Moodie in her eightieth year – an aged sisterhood – who knows if indeed we may ever now meet on earth."

Catharine continued: "I am but a poor traveller at night so I think I will come down the day previous and go up by the early Toronto train so that I should not be bewildered by being at the station in a crowd at night. I am not going to make a long visit. I cannot afford any addition to my wardrobe which is not very grand for a city – but I only go to my sister's sick-room and not for going abroad to make visits among strangers. I know that you will take the old friend in for the night, and dear Charles will get the cab-man bespoke for taking me to the station in time to go by the morning train to Pt Hope to meet the Express – See what trouble I am always giving you dear friends." Catharine made the visit successfully and returned to Lakefield for the summer of 1883.

May 1883: Alice Fitzgibbon has returned to Canada

Alice Fitzgibbon had returned from England to Canada by the time Catharine wrote to Ellen Dunlop in May 1883. Alice then went to stay with her sister Geraldine Moodie and her family in Manitoba. There she became engaged and was married in the spring of 1884, when she became Alice Dunn.

16th November 1883: Catharine has found Susanna much changed

Catharine made a second trip to Toronto in 1883 to visit Susanna, and this time was able to complete the journey in a single day. In a letter to William Traill dated 16th November she told him: "You will be surprized to hear that I have been in Toronto – Indeed it was not for pleasure that I made the journey which I could ill afford but to see your poor aunt Moodie. I heard that she was in a very weak and failing condition both in mind and body – and so I made the effort as the Moodies had invited me for a few days visit – I was able to take the through line train from Lakefield to Toronto without changing cars – leaving Lakefield at half past two – I reached Toronto at 9.30 the same evening."

Catharine continued: "I found your dear Aunt up – but was very much shocked at the change in her. She looked aged and feeble and I found the fine intellect much weakened – more than I could have supposed – Only at times she would brighten up, and seem more like her old self, but it was like flashes of light on dull cloudy days.

"She seemed to improve much during my stay with her – which was only for ten days including the going and returning home. But she varies from day to day – Robt M said she was better for a few days after I left but fell back again – I think she feels the want of occupation as she reads little now, she neither sews nor knits and time hangs heavy on her – She can not paint nor write at all – Poor old dear it made me sad to see her thus."

There was a small bright side though. Catharine told Willliam: "One thing; she has plenty of money to obtain all that she requires – so Mr Vickers told me – but she fancies she is robbed of money, and clothes – This is a haunting idea and troubles her mind continually – and of course is vexatious to those about her."

While Catharine was away from Lakefield paying her second visit to Susanna, one of her Strickland nieces had unexpectedly become engaged to Philip Wigg, son-in-law to Robert Strickland and widower. Catharine told William: "I found all well on my return home – The first news of the day here current was that Fanny S, your cousin George's daughter a nice pretty clever girl, was engaged to her cousin Philip Wigg – and it was a great surprize to us all."

Catharine continued: "P and his lady love came down a week ago and all seemed merry as a marriage bell – The course of true love had run too smoothly to last and a few days ago we were told that the engagement was off. A great flare up – no one knows why. Fan is off to Toronto, Philip away, and the bubble has burst – and the affair is being discussed left and right, and no one tells the right story – We hear all, and say nothing."

Part 8: A late flowering

Catharine the celebrity; 'Studies of Plant Life in Canada' by Catharine Parr Traill; Susanna bows out; 'Life of Agnes Strickland' by Jane Margaret Strickland; Jane departs; Canadian descendents too numerous to mention; Sarah brings this Strickland family to an end in England

25th January 1884: Catharine begins to experience celebrity life in Ottawa

By the end of 1883, Catharine had almost finished work on her unpublished natural history material, and in January 1884 she went to Ottawa to stay with Agnes Fitzgibbon Chamberlin, so they could work together and get it ready for publication. Catharine made the journey from Lakefield in two stages, staying overnight in Peterborough with Ellen Dunlop and her husband Charles, and completing the journey on the second day.

On 25th January 1884, Catharine wrote to Ellen Dunlop to thank her, and described the second stage of her journey by train, which began with Charles Dunlop putting her on the train at Brockville. Catharine wrote: "The good Samaritan as I shall ever consider him took every care to place me in a comfortable car not too crowded and there I remained in my silence and solitude though not alone of course lonely" where she began to worry about the rest of her journey: "Well I gave up all thought of seeing the Col or Miss Fitzgibbon and just as I had resigned myself to my fate – At Connexion Station 30 miles from Ottawa – I heard a well known cheery voice say 'Oh Auntie I am so glad you are here.' It was dear kind Maimie FG – come down to meet me – and we had 'good times' – as the children say.

"All the weary feelings and anxious thoughts fled like melted snow away – and Maime was so quick and ready when we got to Ottawa among a street crowded with Cabs and men – she brought me bravely along – just knowing at once what to do and how to manage – though I should have been perfectly bewildered by the jostling crowd – of men and horses and boys pulling at one's sleeve – for Cab – Cab – Cab – but M- was an experienced traveller and we got on finely – but O it was cold! – and she wrapped me up covering me over head and all – till we reached the home and haven where I would be. A warm welcome and a warm fire side and a nice hot cup of tea and 'Richard was himself again' And very happy and I need not say most lovingly treated ever since by the good kind Col and my dear Agnes C and her two daughters and many friends."

Agnes Fitzgibbon Chamberlin, being the wife of a politician and businessman, knew many people in Ottawa, and Catharine's visit was an enjoyable adventure for her. Catharine told Ellen Dunlop: "On Monday Mrs C took me to call with her on Mrs Macpherson – and it was her day. I saw several strangers and had a kind greeting from the Genl – but they were all rather grand though very nice – Then we went to Professor Selwyns and I liked him and we got sociable at once."

Catharine was soon taken to sign the visitors' book at Rideau Hall, which had been the official residence in Ottawa of the Governor General of Canada since 1867. Catharine told Ellen: "Next day we had a charming drive to Rideau Hall to enter our names in the visitors book – We did not see anyone there – only wrote our names and retired – and Oh Ellen how I enjoyed the drive through the beautiful grounds and the dear snow laden evergreens of the woods – It was a treat and took me back to old times but the deep – deep snow! and the cold – last night was 26 below zero."

There had also been a small domestic adventure to report: "Yesterday we had a great scare with the chimney on fire and only three poor women to put it out – but as we are all bricks – We got safe out of that scrape – the roof so thick with snow there was no fear of that only within the house but it was overcome at last with vigorous water-works, a big syringe and hose – conquered the enemy – but drenched the poor firemen, or women, as well as the floors."

Catharine's life during this visit to Ottawa bore some resemblance to the life that Agnes had lived for many years in England. Catharine's purpose in Ottawa was to complete and promote her botanical and other natural history writings. In the process she had the opportunity to meet and discuss her work with experts. Among these was James Fletcher, the parliamentary sub-librarian who in 1886 would become the Central Agricultural Farm's first entomologist and botanist.

While in Ottawa, a letter from Sarah was forwarded to Catharine, and Catharine in reply gave Sarah news of her stay. On 29th January 1884, Catharine wrote: "My Dear beloved Thay, My Kate forwarded your most kind and welcome letter and the letter of credit which was indeed an unexpected gift to her and myself and I thank you my ever kind and generous sister for the money which will prove very useful at this time as I am as you will perceive at Ottawa with the dear niece Mrs Chamberlin and the good dear Colonel her husband."

Catharine was enthusiastic about her visit and told Sarah: "I am enjoying myself very much for all are so good and loving to the old auntie and I am paid more attention to here in Ottawa than I have ever been by the heads of the society being made much of for my literary talents which of course few care for at Lakefield." Her own interest in natural history in general, and botany in particular, was not shared by her friends in Lakefield, so when at home her conversations with friends and relations were on other matters. As she told Sarah: "there are always little matters to talk about beside Books – those that interest me most on Botany and flowers – and natural History have not much charm for any out of our own – but here I find many friends among the Professors and we get on charmingly."

Of the book which she was compiling, Catharine said: "I am encouraged by the Parliamentary Librarian Mr Fletcher and the head of the Geological Society Mr Macoun a great authority to try the publishing of my MS work on the 'Wild Flowers Ferns and Forest Trees of Canada' – which Mr Fletcher has most kindly revised and corrected for me – a great obligation – for his time is very precious."

Agnes Fitzgibbon Chamberlin was also working on the book as Catharine explained to Sarah: "Her designs and drawings are to illustrate the work. It is not to be like our former book but on a lesser scale as to size and we hope to make a popular volume that may go into the hands of a great many readers – Our former work was too costly – and the sale was limited to the few – But we must bring out the first edition by subscription to ensure ourselves from risk as I have no capital or money resources and Agnes could not venture to lose hers. Still my name is now well known, and my work valued far more than ever they were in former years when the people of Canada were in a different condition.

"Education has made vast strides since even our Flower Book appeared and the enlightened policy fostered by the English Governors have done much to raise a higher tone in the tastes and minds of the Canadians – There is not now the struggle for mere bread that there was – the cultivation of the mind is extending far and wide even to the remotest parts of the country you cannot think the progress that a few years have made among all ranks of the people."

29th January 1884: Plans are being made for Sarah's next Canadian visitor

About a year after Alice Fitzgibbon returned to Canada, plans were being put in place for Maime Fitzgibbon to take her place, and to pay a long visit to England. Catharine told Sarah in her letter dated 29th January 1884: "You will I am sure like your great niece Miss Fitzgibbon she is clever practical and very agreeable not pretty, but nice and ladylike and possesses much general knowledge and taste and the talent for writing which still belongs as a sort of heirloom to the Strickland race."

1st March 1884: Catharine attends a fete at Rideau Hall

When Catharine wrote to Ellen Dunlop on 2nd March 1884 she was still staying in Ottawa with the Chamberlin family. Agnes Fitzgibbon Chamberlin was negotiating with a possible publisher for their book and Catharine, who had been ill for a couple of weeks, was obliged to remain in Ottawa until everything had been agreed.

Catharine in telling Ellen about a fete she had attended at Rideau Hall wrote: "Now my dear Ellen I must tell you something about my yesterday's visit by card to the Governors Saturday night grand fete – Well it was indeed the grandest sight that I ever witnessed and I shall never forget the delight it gave me. The drive through the avenue among the snow laden trees was delightful the sky studded with stars and a splendid young moon just above the dark pine woods gave light enough to make every old leafless oak and silvery birch stand out from the darker evergreens in bold relief – The grounds about Rideau have the picturesque charm of hill and dale that are very charming to such as love natural scenery.

"As we drew nearer to the Hall I noticed a beautiful sight of a great vapoury cloud of smoke rising into the still air and spreading in fold after fold upwards, the lower part gilded till it appeared like a golden veil over the great solid banks of snow." At the next turn in the drive she saw "a glorious sight – Long lines of radiant light – reaching down from the summit of the great snow slide to its far off terminus among the trees in the valley – The light dazzled one – for the grand bon-fire in the centre of the grounds blazed up and made visible masses of people moving or in stationary groups watching the swift toboggans as they flashed past on their downward descent with a speed that almost took away my breath to see."

Catharine continued: "The Governor shook hands very cordially with me and thanked me for a note that I wrote a few days before – he had previously expressed his acceptance of the dedication of my book in handsome terms. The Marchioness was very friendly and kind, chatting as we stood side by side on the platform above the slide."

There was a log cottage in the grounds where they could warm themselves. Catharine told Ellen: "We went into the log cottage and got warmed by the stove but a log-fire would have been more in keeping with the cottage – which by the bye was handsomely panelled with varnished wood inside – it was not a real log cabin – for it was not rough and chinked and plastered as the log houses used to be. This would have been a palace for a settler in the old settlement days in the Back woods. We should have been thought too luxurious altogether and the house out of keeping with the rude furniture, diet and dress of that time."

Catharine found one draw back to the event though: "The only thing that I did not like was that when I was left in the tea-room everybody kept staring at me, and some edged nearly up to me, and I kept hearing – 'That's her – That's Mrs Traill' and so on, and short people stood on tiptoe, and others peered over shoulders and pushed those before them aside peering at poor me as if I had been the shew piece of the play. The poor old lioness squeezed herself into a corner (I believe some people expected her to roar or wag her tail) not being accustomed to being gazed at in that way – it was a little oppressive."

Catharine ended her letter on a reassuring note. She told her friend: "Now my dearest Ellen do not be afraid all the attention and flattery bestowed on me will turn my old head – it is pleasant from some, but seems almost too absurd from others – The only thing is – It is good for the book – as some will get copies out of curiosity now – Nor do I expect unadulterated praise – but some may like the pictures, and others the cover, and a few the letter press – and some will criticize – but that is the fate of those who 'Write a book'."

Catharine was able to leave Ottawa and return home soon after a deal had been agreed with a printer and publisher called Woodburn. Catharine noted in her diary: "Woodburn has offered to print and publish the work at his own risk. We of course are expected to get as much support from our friends and subscribers as we can to help the publication. Expences to be defrayed then half the profits are to be shared between Mrs C and myself but we are under no risk. This is the present proposal and we agree to his terms retaining the copyright of the MS – Mrs C of the drawings."

31st March 1884: Catharine is preparing to return to Lakefield

When Catharine wrote to her daughter Kate on 31st March 1884 about her homecoming, there was a good deal of down-to-earth economy in the letter. Catharine wrote: "we are to bring a sitting of fresh-laid eggs to get hatched on shares – as the breed is an extra good one, a cross between two good sorts" of chickens. Catharine had a contact who: "held out a hope that he would get a free ticket as far as Belleville – if not to Peterborough – so that you see dear I shall have some means in hand to pay for the wood and any necessary things. I have not bought anything for clothing since I got the silk dress altered and shoes; but cab, and car hire costs much in this place, the long walk into the city is more than I can manage."

Catharine had bought extra luggage to carry her belongings home. She told Kate: "I think I told you of the nice granite ware teapot which I got as a present and if I see fit I will bring a coffee pot to match it for you, and I got some good articles at the 5cts store that were very tempting – I could have got a nice tea tray – for only 25 cents but it would not have gone in the trunk and so I could not manage it – but it was a very great bargain."

Catharine told Kate that she was expecting to get some money from the printer before she returned home. She wrote: "I shall not you see come back quite empty handed so get anything you want that is needful – I would send money but I shall be home next week, and if you are in want ask dear kind Robt or Caroline and I will repay them at my return with thanks."

In the event, Catharine's journey was delayed a little longer than she had anticipated, because the thaw set in, rivers began running fast and high, and she had to wait until 9th April 1884 for the roads and bridges to be safely passable. When Catharine returned to Lakefield, her great-niece Maime Fitzgibbon accompanied her on the journey.

28th April 1884: Maime Fitzgibbon is nearly ready to go to England

In a letter to her son William dated 28th April 1884, Catharine gave him news of Maime Fitzgibbon. Catharine wrote that Maime: "was out in Manitoba three years ago and wrote a nice lively book while out there, is staying with us at this time and is going to England in June for a years visit to your Aunt Gwillym – she is very bright and clever and excellent company having the art of conforming to any situation rough or smooth – She says send my cousinly love to Willie and say, if I ever again go to the NW – I'll come and see him."

Catharine told William what Maime was doing: "At this minute she is busy with Katie mending broken china for I bought up a fine lot of brittle ware and when we came with pride of heart to set forth our china Lo not half a dozen whole articles remained to gladden the eyes of our mistress – It was an awful smash though packed by a first rate hand."

1884: Robert and Caroline Strickland move to England

Robert Strickland had retired early from direct involvement with the family businesses in Lakefield. He may have given financial support to Philip Wigg as his son-in-law, to help Philip establish himself in business, possibly the lumber business in Lakefield, and possibly buying up stock advantageously on an occasion when the Strickland family lumber business was in difficulty.

In 1884, Robert and Caroline Strickland began to consider England their permanent home, living in West Drayton, Middlesex near to their daughter Charlotte Taylor, whose husband was now the vicar of Harmondsworth, near Staines, Middlesex. To England with Robert and Caroline Strickland went their four-year old granddaughter, Agnes Wigg, daughter of Philip Wigg.

Philip Wigg's character and life were causing concern, and may have been part of the reason for Robert and Caroline removing to England and taking Agnes Wigg with them. However, the presence of a daughter in England with a growing family, Caroline's family roots in Southwold, and Robert's step-mother being in England and in poor health, might have been good enough reasons for them to move to England regardless of Philip Wigg.

1884: Sam's children in summary

Most of Sam's children remained in the Lakefield area. Robert Strickland seems to have passed responsibility for the family home, 'Homestead' on to his brother Roland before he moved to England. George and Roland appear to have been the two most successful in maintaining and developing the Strickland commercial interests, keeping the lumbering and milling operations going during economic downturns, presumably either recovering from, or avoiding bankruptcy in the past. Roland was prominent in local politics and is said to have been elected to the role of reeve of the village of Lakefield for at least five successive years in the early 1880s.

Sam's three married daughters (Maria Tully, Emma Barlee and Jane Blofield) all seem to have remained in or fairly near to Lakefield. Maria Tully died in 1884 leaving Kivas Tully a widower with three, or possibly two adult children.

Sam's son Walter, as already mentioned, became a surveyor, architect and engineer, earning his living away from the family businesses but geographically not distant. Henry Strickland lived in Ashburnham (Peterborough) where he had considerable success in real estate and other commercial activities as well as taking an active part in the town's social and athletic life.

Percy's business interests are less clear. At one point in the 1870s he is said to have been captain of a Strickland boat that plied the lakes north of Lakefield. He was a near neighbour of Catharine and this may have been why he was selected by Agnes to be a beneficiary under her Will. Francis Arthur Strickland is recorded on a published family tree as having died unmarried in 1858, aged 20, but the cause of his death is not mentioned.

The youngest of Sam's sons, Richard Gwillym Strickland, was in childhood a close friend of William Traill. For a time he was a farmer in Lakefield, but he moved to Grand Forks in the Dakota Territory where he bought land from Walter Traill, and he remained there with his family.

January 1885: Catharine's botanical work is published

Catharine and Agnes Fitzgibbon Chamberlin's book had the full title 'Studies of Plant Life in Canada; or, Gleanings from Forest, Lake and Plain' and began to appear in January 1885. It included twenty lithographic plates which made the production process slow, and it took several weeks for the first edition of 1,000 copies to be assembled and distributed.

Despite being 83 years old, Catharine decided to take 100 copies of the book instead of any cash payment, and she then sold her copies through her network of friends and relations. The task of selling and distributing these copies, and thereby obtaining some money for her work, kept Catharine and her friends busy for some time, and does not seem like the easiest or the most profitable course of action for her to have chosen.

Ellen Dunlop in Peterborough helped on several occasions and Catharine in a letter, thought to have been written in mid-January 1885, wrote: "I must thank you my dear Ellen for your assisting Kate in regard to the disposal of the books which indeed must have imposed trouble upon you and your good husband – more than ought to have been, could we have done otherwise in arranging this troublesome matter – and even now I must ask if you will further aid us by taking four of the books out or (ask my dear Mary – rather) to take two of the remaining number to send down to Birdie and Harriett at Montreal. One to be given to my grandson C Atwood and the other to Mr B Hutchinson, subscribers for the Book – And if you do not mind keeping the other two copies, one for Mr Wm Stewart, and the other for Miss Jackson whose address I do not know – I know my dear Ellen will not mind doing this for me."

Despite all her many relatives and friends in Canada, plus income from her newly published book, Catharine still wanted financial help from her sister Sarah, now aged 87. In a letter to her daughter Annie Atwood dated 14th February 1885, Catharine wrote: "Aunt G did not send as much as she used to and only a small sum to your sister this year – just £2 – so if it were not for the money coming in from the 'Plant Life' we should have been hard up to get along."

19th February 1885: Catharine is an acknowledged botanical writer

Reviews of Catharine's work 'Studies of Plant Life in Canada; or, Gleanings from Forest, Lake and Plain' published in Ottawa by AS Woodburn, confirmed her status as a botanical writer. The 'Week' is reported to have written on 19th February 1885, that although the book was: "immensely enhanced by the work of Mrs Chamberlin" Catharine had to be acknowledged as: "an authority upon the flora of this country." It praised her for her use of a "simplicity of style" that "insensibly charms the reader."

It is said that the reviewer of the 'Toronto Globe' on 7th February 1885 acknowledged that the book had successfully achieved its aim as outlined in the introduction, which was to be technical enough for use by students, but with sufficient literary charm to be enjoyed by those ignorant of botany. It added: "Mrs Traill by no means hopes without reason when she expresses a wish that her book may become in Canada what Gilbert White's 'History of Selborne' is to England, and she will find thousands of friends in Canada, who know her through pleasant hours spent with her former works."

The Rev Gilbert White had been born in 1720 in the vicarage at Selborne in Hampshire where his grand-father was the vicar. He loved his native village and kept detailed notes in his 'Garden Kalendar' and his 'Naturalist's Journal.' His book 'The Natural History of Selborne' was based on letters he exchanged with two distinguished naturalists – Thomas Pennant and Daines Barrington. In common with Catharine, the area he studied was geographically small, and his book and correspondence were written with great charm. It was published in 1788 and was, and remains very popular. According to an edition published in 1977, though perhaps a little difficult to believe: "it is reputedly the fourth most published book in the English language."

William Kirby, an admirer of Catharine's book wrote to express his pleasure at reading it, and suggested that she would be interested in some of the plants which had been protected by the wildness of the Niagara Falls. In replying to his letter, Catharine, in a letter dated 7th January 1886, showed the limits of her botanical studies. She wrote: "I confess that I have never seen the wonders of Niagara Falls. It is true that I have never been ten miles west of Toronto. It would be difficult to explain why, or why my floral gatherings and knowledge of the habitats of plants has been confined within limits so narrow – I have learned by life-long experience if I cannot overcome, to conform to adverse circumstances and draw from them all the good that can be obtained."

In speaking of this book in later years and of Catharine's studies in general, James Fletcher, when the Central Agricultural Farm's entomologist and botanist, is reported to have said to Catharine: "With regard to your disclaiming the title of botanist, all I can say is, I wish a fraction of one percent of the students of plants who call themselves botanists, could use their eyes half as well as you have done. I think indeed your work of describing all the wild plants in your book, so accurately that each one could have a name applied to it without doubt, is one of the greatest botanical triumphs which anyone could achieve, and one which I have frequently spoken of to illustrate the powers of observation."

2nd March 1885: Another of Agnes's namesakes dies young

Charlotte and John Taylor's eldest child, Agnes Ethel Strickland Taylor was another member of the extended Strickland family to die young. Aged only four, she died of meningitis on 2nd March 1885 at the vicarage in Harmondsworth, having been ill for a fortnight. Her father registered the death the following day.

8th April 1885: Susanna Moodie dies

By the end of 1884, Susanna was physically frail, her eyesight was weak and her mind had begun to wander. At this point, she was moved from Robert Moodie's home to the larger house of Katie Vickers, where there was room to accommodate a nurse to care for her.

Towards the end of March 1885, Catharine went to Toronto to visit Susanna. She found Susanna very well cared for, but very confused and no longer herself. In a letter to Ellen Dunlop dated 27th March 1885, Catharine wrote: "She looks a picture of neatness and is dressed so nicely with a lovely cap of mauve ribbons and warm delicate shawl and elegant lace collar and handsome dark dress and warm slippers. She looks a perfect picture as far as hands can make her – but she is much bent and requires support."

Catharine had to stop writing the letter at that point and finished it the following day. She explained: "My dear Ellen I have lost a mail and lost a day and now I find my letter will not reach you this week. The case is when I go into my sister's room I cannot leave her as she frets if I go away and when she comes in to me she keeps talking and rambles so that I lose all thought of any thing and every one else – What a strange change – what a wreck. Poor dear old sister – Well thank God she is unconscious of it herself. God be gracious and merciful to my dear sister. Her speech is very difficult to understand but her own hearing is good."

After staying for a week, Catharine returned to Lakefield, Susanna seeming much as she had been for some time. However, the tolling of a new church bell nearby on Easter Sunday, confused and upset Susanna, and set off a series of delusions. Her condition deteriorated and on Easter Monday she became unconscious. Katie Vickers sent a message to Catharine who returned just in time to sit at her sister's bedside for the last few hours of her life.

Susanna Moodie died on 8th April 1885 aged 82. Catharine in a letter to Annie Atwood told her: "The remains were taken to Belleville as she wished and her husband and two children will be buried in the new cemetery above the bay east of the city." The Moodie gravestone in Belleville cemetery is said to commemorate not only John and Susanna Moodie but also their two sons who died young – John Strickland Moodie (1838-1844) and George Arthur Moodie (1840).

By the time of her death, Susanna was recognised as one of the important figures in early Canadian literature, particularly because of her book 'Roughing It in the Bush'. John and Katie Vickers had ensured Susanna's material well-being after the death of John Moodie and, in spite of Susanna's insistence that she was extremely poor during her last years, she is said to have left in her Will, executed by John Vickers, an estate of $4,700

April 1885: Catharine fears for William's safety

While Catharine was in Toronto paying her last visit to Susanna, there was excitement and anxiety about another uprising by the Metis led my Louis Riel. Walter had moved away from the affected area several years before, but William Traill was still living and working there.

In her letter to Ellen Dunlop written from Toronto on 27th March 1885, Catharine said: "There is excitement in every house in the city. The volunteers are marched out today for Winnipeg – the report is that eight of the men who went against Riel and his rebels are killed and another fight imminent at Prince Albert on the Saskatchewan – but I think the rebels will be put down soon – Why did the Government let that Riel go loose to stir up mischief? – We shall hear more before night I think 250 volunteers left this day at noon from

Toronto but it will be a week before they reach the scene of action – I only hope Hargrave will not be moved to go out – or your boys." Catharine was referring here to her grand-son Hargrave (or Hargreave) Muchall, the son of her daughter Mary.

The Second Riel Uprising lasted for only three months and was unsuccessful, but it was several months before Catharine's mind was put at rest when a letter arrived from William telling her that he and his family were safe. In fact he had known nothing of the event until he read about it afterwards. A son of one of Catharine's friends was among the unlucky few to be killed in the fighting.

18th June 1885: Catharine passes family news on to William

In passing news on to William in a letter dated 18th June 1885, Catharine said: "From letters from Engd I find that your aunt Jane is in very poor health. She was dangerously ill all Winter – Your aunt Gwillym has gone down to Southwold to see her."

Catharine had recently received extra money from England, which made up for the small amount received at Christmas. Catharine told William: "You will be glad to hear that your good aunt Mrs Gwillym sent me yesterday a draft for £20 – which was most kind and helpful so you will know that I am in no need." This supplemented the $200 Catharine had made by selling the 100 copies of her book.

Catharine already had plans for some of the money, as she had told Annie a few months earlier. She had written: "I am going to get our kitchen boarded outside for the cold this year has been killing and though it will take a good bit of our book money it must be done – Your dear sister suffered greatly this winter from the cold when at work there and there has been a great consumption of the wood and a heavy wood outlay – for it is higher than it has ever been."

In her June 1885 letter to William, Catharine wrote: "I think your sister Kate wrote very lately she is not very strong but still not ill – Katie is at home now but will very likely leave us to go to Walkerton to stay with her aunt Sybella who wants her to take the place of governess to her children – We should miss the dear child very much. She is very good and nice and sensible and sweet and lady-like." Catharine's daughter Kate and grand-daughter Katie Traill were 53 and 18 years old respectively. These three females sharing the same Christian name were the only people who considered 'Westove' in Lakefield their permanent home.

22nd June 1885: Philip Wigg is in trouble

It may be that Philip Wigg was actually in prison when Robert and Caroline Strickland moved to England in 1884, taking Agnes Wigg with them. It is said that at some point he was in prison in Oswego NY awaiting trial for alleged business misdemeanours. The 'Daily Examiner' for 22nd June 1885 reported that Philip Wigg was being sued by a former partner in business, the Hon Mr Ross who had secured two judgements against Philip for amounts of $83,000 and $18,000.

On 22nd October 1885, Philip's estate 'Acle Hall' in Lakefield is said to have been listed for sale in the 'Peterborough Review'.

Winter 1885-1886: William visits Lakefield

William Traill made a long visit to Lakefield, starting late in 1885 and lasting until April 1886. After he returned to his own home, Catharine took a while to adjust, and in a tardy letter to Sarah dated 4th June 1886 she explained: "the presence and afterwards the separation from my beloved son engrossed my chief thoughts – I knew it was forever on this side the grave, that I should hear his voice and see his kind loving face – no wonder that my heart was sad at the thought that our parting was once for all in this world." William was 41 years old when he made the visit.

March 1886: The Atwoods move to Lakefield

In March 1886 Clinton and Annie Atwood let their farm and home on Rice Lake Plains, and moved to Lakefield. During the upheaval of moving, their children stayed with Catharine and Kate at 'Westove'.

William Traill was still in Lakefield when Annie and her husband arrived, and they arranged that one of William's children would move to the area to go to school. Catharine told Sarah: "William was so desirous that his second son – William – should have the benefit of an English education that he agreed to send him down to board with his Aunt Atwood and go to the school with his cousin Evan."

June 1886: William Traill's son arrives in Lakefield

By the time that Catharine wrote to Sarah in June 1886, William's son had arrived. Catharine said that William had put his son "under the care of a gentleman who brought him safe to Peterborough where his Uncle Clinton met him but Willie took a severe cold on the long long days and nights of travelling from Prince Albert to Winnipeg and on through Canada and has a very bad cough."

Catharine's home was said often to serve as a haven to many members of the family. Apparently, whenever her letters mentioned someone else's needs in time of ill-health, or other kinds of difficulty, they usually included the observation that such a person "will come to us." This is what happened when her grandson arrived after his long journey. Catharine told Sarah: "I am going to take him home to our house for change and to nurse him up a bit before he can begin his school studies."

June 1886: Agnes Fitzgibbon Chamberlin visits England

Susanna's daughter Agnes Fitzgibbon Chamberlin had one child by her second marriage, a daughter born in 1871 and named Agnes Gertrude Mary Chamberlin.

Maime Fitzgibbon had gone to England in June 1884, intending only to stay for a year but she was still there two years later. In June 1886 her mother, Agnes Fitzgibbon Chamberlin, went to visit her, taking her 15-year old daughter Agnes Chamberlin with her. Agnes Fitzgibbon Chamberlin's health had not been good and it was hoped that the sea voyage would strengthen her. She also hoped to progress the publishing in England of Catharine's latest Canadian book.

Catharine in her letter to Sarah dated 4th June 1886 wrote: "You will ere this reaches you have seen and welcomed the dear much loved niece Agnes Chamberlin and her pretty Agnes. I suppose while I am writing this letter to you, my dearest sister, Mrs Chamberlin is nearing England. I have felt very anxious about her health lately – and she was nervous too at the idea of the sea voyage and long journey, but I hope the former may have been restorative, and she will enjoy the rest and your society, and the reunion with her dear daughter. I shall often think of you and this my beloved niece, together, for you will be sure to love her and she you."

Catharine had been concerned about Jane's health and wrote: "I hope you found my dear sister Jane improved in health, when you were in Southwold – it is so long since I heard from her – or of her and she was not well when you last wrote." Jane was 86 years old and the biography that she was writing of Agnes, who had died twelve years earlier in 1874, was still unfinished.

In her letter to Sarah, Catharine gives information about their mother, the late Mrs Strickland by writing: "My dear Kate has been busy in her garden – planting out annuals while I am at work among the vegetable beds, as we greatly depend on them during the warm weather – neither she nor I ever care much for meat. We have planted a new bed of strawberries and I have trained and kept the raspberry plantation in good order beside sowing the peas, beans and all the root vegetables, so you see I am like the dear old Mother, a great gardener. My flowers are all perennials and wild flowers and ferns."

June 1886: Catharine's income diminishes

When Catharine sold the copyright left to her by Agnes, she had invested part of the money in order to have a regular source of income from the dividends, but her income from this source was in decline, as she explained to Sarah in June 1886. She wrote: "I had the disagreeable disappointment of finding that there was a deficiency in the half-yearly dividend when I got my check on the Ontario Bank, a reduction again in the interest of the investment of my dear Agnes's copy-right proceeds – and this is indeed my income – but for your most generous presents from time to time I know not how we could live – Thank God who has put it in your loving sisterly heart to aid me so faithfully – may he bless you dearest in all things for your goodness to me."

Catharine then explains where the money from the sale of her current book has gone. She said: "We had a busy Spring I had made arrangements to have the house painted and repaired, this I am glad to say has been done. I devoted the money that I got from my Book to that purpose and it was duly paid so that poor as I am I have gained a great increase in comfort and incurred no harrowing debt which is a satisfaction."

Summer 1886: Catharine's grandson William resembles Tom

Catharine told Sarah of her grandson's likeness to their brother. In June 1886 she wrote: "He is eleven years old, a very pretty likeness of our brother Tom at his age." She referred again to this likeness when she wrote to William a letter dated 30th August 1886, and also gave a hint of her earlier life. She wrote: "We think that your dear boy has grown taller since he came to Lakefield he has a pretty face and very bright expression and indeed seems to make a good impression on every one – to me he has a double charm he is so like my own dear brother Tom, just what your uncle Tom was as a boy of Willies age – he and I were dearly fond of one another all the days of our childhood and youth till his wife grew jealous of his love for me and parted us – so I love my dear young grandson for his dead uncle's sake and auld lang syne."

July 1886: Jane looks very poorly

Other members of the Strickland family were en route from Canada to England at the same time as Agnes Fitzgibbon Chamberlin. Catharine had told Sarah in June 1886: "Our nephew, George Strickland wife and daughter, are on their way to England and will pay their respects to you soon." George Strickland and his family stayed a few weeks in England and had returned to Canada by the time that Catharine wrote to William on 30th August 1886.

Jane continued to be in poor health as Catharine told William: "I am grieved to say that dear aunt Strickland continues very poorly. Your cousin George saw her and was shocked at her appearance she was so changed – The George Strickland party are home but I have not yet seen either of them." George Strickland was 53 years old and was the fourth of Sam's surviving sons.

Catharine told William at the end of her August 1886 letter: "Mrs Chamberlin had a poor state of health during the voyage and has never been well since. She did not make a long visit to her aunt G but went down to Southwold and when she wrote she was staying with her aunt Jane.

"I fancy your aunt G paid her board with aunt Jane but that is only conjecture – I do not think any business about my book had been effected – but Mrs C says she will try again before leaving Engd. She is ill and writes in low spirits and is to leave the old country in Sept. I dread the effects of the sea voyage for her – Her daughter Mary" (Maime) "is to remain to nurse her aunt Jane, and Aggie returns to Ottawa."

30th August 1886: Catharine still needs money from Sarah

As Catharine lived surrounded by family in Lakefield, and had numerous relatives in other parts of North America, it is puzzling that she should feel it necessary to make so clear to Sarah that she still needed money from her. Sarah may have had some feelings along the same lines, for she had been visited by several descendents of Sam and of Susanna who had the resources to cross the Atlantic and visit England for weeks if not months at a time.

On 30th August 1886 in her letter to William, Catharine wrote: "I have had no letter or donation from your aunt Gwillym this year – which has been a great disappointment, nor do I now expect any help from her unless at Christmas – it was the more needed this year for the Co have again reduced the dividend on the shares – However we will not despair. God in His goodness never forsakes us – never has done, and never will."

Later in her letter Catharine told William: "My sisters in England have been told that Walter is immensely rich! – and so that I can want for nothing – I believe it to be an immense mistake and very injurious both to my dear son, and me – I am sure Mrs Chamberlin would not do anything to prejudice my sisters, but these foolish people that talk about what they know nothing truly, do mischief without thought of the effect upon one by untrue reports from exaggerated sources."

Who the culprit in telling Sarah and Jane that Walter was rich is not stated, nor is it reported how Catharine got to hear about it. Walter had wide business interests and only his wife and two stepchildren to support, so supposing him to be rich, does not seem unreasonable. He did send money to Catharine, but there was also his sister Mary Muchall to be helped. Mary and her four children were struggling to support themselves, despite all being in very poor health, and their father Tom Muchall continued to have a problem with alcohol.

9th January 1887: Jane is better

Catharine received a letter from Jane at the beginning of 1887, as she told Sarah later the same month: "I got a very affectionate interesting letter from dear Jane about the time of my birthday" which was on 9th January "which I answered directly I was able to do so, but I have not been well. I was glad to learn that dear Jane was better."

24th January 1887: Sarah sends Catharine money again

Sarah's lack of donation to Catharine in 1886 seems to have been a one-off and on 24th January 1887 Catharine wrote to Sarah, a letter whose effusive thanks feel a little excessive unless the amount sent had been substantially more than usual. Catharine wrote: "Dearest Thay, My Kindest of Sisters, Your dear letter with its unexpected gift came by today's mail – How can I find words to thank you my dearly loved one for this additional proof of love that never wearies of doing me good."

Catharine said she had been beginning to wonder if some of her letters to England had gone astray: "I do not know if all my letters reached you. I wrote in the Spring, when I thought you were with dear sister Jane – again in June, or July and in October – and I was beginning at that time to feel anxious about not hearing from you for it was unusual."

They were both suffering from aches and pains, and Sarah seems to have had thoughts of going to Bath for treatment. Catharine wrote: "I read your precious letter not without tears – I hope and pray that these lines may find you in less suffering and if able to reach the hot baths you may find great relief from them and the use of the waters which have so often given ease to rheumatic pain."

Catharine here added a reminiscence from many years previously: "I remember many years ago it was in 1831 when I was in Bath with Mrs Leverton I used to see Mr Wilberforce drinking the water at the Pump." William Wilberforce had been a leader of the movement to abolish slavery. He died in 1833, aged 74 years. Catharine said of him: "He was attended by a nurse but so crippled – I used to watch the dear old man with great interest."

Of her own pains, Catharine told Sarah that she was: "still suffering from neuralgia which is obstinate; and very painful. Sometimes the pain flies to the shoulders and hands or to the hips and knees – but it is the head that is the great constant seat of pain."

7th March 1887: Jane's biography of Agnes is published

Jane's biography of Agnes was entitled 'Life of Agnes Strickland' and was published by William Blackwood and Sons, the publisher with whom Agnes had had a good working relationship. Advertisements began to appear at the end of February 1887 and continued to appear in a variety of papers during March. The launch date was Monday 7th March 1887 and the advertisements proclaimed: "This day published 'Life of Agnes Strickland' author of 'Lives of the Queens of England', 'Lives of the Queens of Scotland' etc by her sister Jane Margaret Strickland. With portrait engraved on steel. Post 8vo 12s 6d. William Blackwood & Sons Edinburgh and London."

The launch date may have been the earliest that could have been achieved given Jane's lengthy bout of ill-health. The presence of both Agnes Fitzgibbon Chamberlin and her daughter Maime Fitzgibbon in Southwold in 1886 may have speeded up the final stages of the work. However, an additional factor in the timing of the publication must surely have been the 300th anniversary on 8th February 1887 of the execution of Mary Queen of Scots.

The relevance of this event, and an understanding of the feelings about it, were summarised in a number of newspapers in Scotland. For example, the 'Aberdeen Evening Express' noted: "Now, as during her lifetime, Mary Stuart is still the personification of a creed and of a party, and consequently her actions are judged with all the partiality or all the animosity which religion and politics inspire. The controversy is the keener and the more stubborn that each party is able to find materials for the support of its own views in the records of the period."

Agnes, who made no secret of her partiality for Mary Queen of Scots, was mentioned in the article which continued: "On few questions in any history, or none of our own, is there such a bewildering array of conflicting witnesses ... They who, like Froude, would make Mary a monster of iniquity, 'a being earthly, sensual, and devilish beyond the proportion of nature', appeal to Buchanan and Knox as authorities for the view which they perhaps think it due to their religion to maintain. On the other hand, those who, going to the opposite extreme, like Miss Strickland, look upon her as an embodiment of purity and candour, have Lesley, and Blackmore, and Belleforest, and Brantome to bear out their opinion." This also explains the great care that Agnes took in marshalling her facts when writing this biography, which Agnes herself rated as her own most important work.

To launch the first biography of Agnes Strickland shortly after such an anniversary was good marketing on behalf of William Blackwood & Sons, boosting sales of past works as well as reviving interest in Agnes herself.

Jane's biography was widely and kindly reviewed. The reviews which the publishers selected and used in advertisements for the book are the following, and while being the most flattering, they do not (based on the newspapers currently available in the British Newspaper Archive) conceal any serious criticism:

"Penned by a sister's sympathetic hand, this record of one of the most gifted English women of the century is singularly well conceived and executed ... This bright, amusing volume is most agreeable reading – its pretty, prim, maidenly tone being wonderfully piquant ..." (Whitehall Review)

"The elegantly written memoir from the pen of her sister is somewhat tardy in appearance, but it has merit enough to reawake the past interest in its subject, and will be regarded by Agnes Strickland's admirers as a valuable record of her industrious life." (Scotsman)

"A charming tribute to the memory of the famous historian ... Miss Strickland has given us a really valuable book, and one which should rank in biography as high as her sister's does in history – higher praise we cannot give." (St Stephens Review)

While there was comment on the tardiness of the biography, this was slight, and no-one mentioned the obvious point – that Jane was far from young and had bad health, and that it was a substantial achievement for her to have written and published the biography at all. Jane had nearly reached her 87th birthday (which would fall on 18th April 1887) by the time her biography of Agnes reached the shops.

The review in 'St James's Gazette' read: "This is a sister's tribute to the memory of a deserving writer who helped to lighten the study of history to a generation which knew little of the popular treatment of great subjects.

"A happy uneventful life she seems to have led – not without honourable recognition of her labours from those whose praise was worth having ... It is touching to learn the reason why she refused a handsome offer to continue the 'Queens of England' into the Brunswick period. How describe the contest between Queen Caroline, the consort of George II, and her eldest son – the great-grandfather of her present Majesty – 'Without giving offence to whom they were loyally bound to revere and honour?' That was the question which Agnes and her sister and fellow worker, Elizabeth asked themselves, and answered with old-fashioned simplicity.

"The decision was the more honourable that money must have been a serious consideration to these ladies; on whom a pension of £100 a year from the Civil List was bestowed in 1870. Anything more frigid than the announcement of the grant, through Mr Gladstone's private secretary, can scarcely be imagined. But the pension was acceptable."

The review in 'John Bull' said: "Were more space at our command, it would be easy to dilate upon the fascinating individuality of Agnes Strickland who seems never, through her 78 years of unwedded life, to have made an enemy or lost a friend save through death. She is worthily depicted in these pages, written as they are by the sympathetic pen of her surviving sister, and largely consisting of the correspondence which Agnes conducted with indefatigable zeal and unvarying kindliness of heart.

"There are a few mistakes of diction ... and they will weigh as nothing in the scale with the careful memoirs of two sisters each of whom in her different way well deserves to be remembered for what they did in her generation."

Among the reviews of Jane's book was one written in Ulverston. Jane had recounted in her biography that Richard Gwillym and Sarah had met in Soulby's shop in Ulverston when Agnes was buying stationery in 1843. That event, and the subsequent engagement and marriage, had been included in Jane's book, and was proudly repeated on 17th March 1887 in Ulverston's local newspaper 'Soulby's Ulverston Advertiser and General Intelligencer'.

6th August 1887: Sarah joins in the social life near Tilford

Despite being 89 years old and a relatively recent arrival in Tilford, Sarah was among the many people who were listed as attending a garden party held by the Bishop of Winchester on 6th August 1887.

The local papers described the event: "Garden Party at Farnham Castle – Perhaps none of the preceding parties given annually by the Bishop of Winchester and Mrs Harold Browne at Farnham Castle passed off with more eclat than did the gathering in his Lordship's episcopal palace overlooking the ancient town of Farnham on Saturday. The sun shone forth ... the grounds, lovely at this season, were in many parts delightfully cool. The visitors began to arrive shortly after 4 o'clock and they were received on the edge of the lawn ... the party was large ... in the stone hall refreshments were provided ... Till 7 in the evening ... an enjoyable time was spent by all."

19th August 1887: Catharine goes foraging at Stoney Lake

When Catharine wrote to Ellen Dunlop a letter dated 19th August 1887, she showed herself still full of energy and enthusiasm for things botanical. She told Ellen she had just been: "for a long day to Stoney Lake on invitation from my good nephew George's kind wife. George paddled us up to Hurricane Point and landed us near a beautiful Cranberry Marsh a gem of a place and I got roots and grasses and mosses and all sorts of precious things – It took me all morning after we returned to plant and press and admire my treasures – I scrambled among the rocks with the aid of a stout stick and nearly wore out my new walking shoes – I got a new fern – a beauty and another that was so tall it came up to Kate's head and shoulders – and so stout was the root, that we could only manage to get two roots up to bring home – This is the 'Chain-fern' – This grand fern grew in such a wilderness that K was nearly lost in it – I did long for a free grant of a few acres of the rocky ground and that Marsh – The Cranberries did look so lovely."

1888 onwards: Catharine fills in some of the gaps in Jane's biography

Catharine had long believed that her generation of the Strickland family was exceptional and deserved to be remembered by their descendents, and possibly by the world at large. Sam had written a book about his early life in Canada, and Catharine had written some autobiographical essays about her early life in Canada. Susanna had written her famous book, 'Roughing It in the Bush', which purported to be auto-biographical, but contains an unknown and possibly large proportion of her own imaginings. Apart from these three works about the life of the three Stricklands who emigrated to Canada and their experiences with emigration, the only published book which might have told the family story was Jane's biography of Agnes.

Jane briefly recounted the lives of the young Agnes and Elizabeth but made no mention of the abilities of the rest of the family, and made scant mention of the family background and early life. Catharine felt this was inadequate and set out to remedy the situation by adding fresh works to the biographical and autobiographical pieces she had already written.

In a note of explanation written after she had become the only remaining member of her generation of the Strickland family, Catharine wrote: "I who have taken up my pen in old age to chronicle the events of my childhood and early youth am almost cheated into the belief that I see, and hear, and move among the dear companions of my childhood. And it is from memory painting of years gone by that I now enter upon my task knowing that nothing will be recorded in these pages that is untruthful or coloured from mere imagination.

"Much indeed will be omitted that involved other individuals not exactly connected and therefore out of the family record which is written for information of the descendents, some of whom can have no access to any knowledge of the early years of their English relatives but what can only be supplied by the surviving member of the family of which I remain the last. And as some of the names of the Strickland sisters have become matter of literary history, I wish that their memories should not cease, and so I write my chronicle."

She was determined to tell the truth and only the truth – but she omitted the determination also to tell the whole truth. Therefore, when it came to parts of the narrative which she deemed nobody's business, such as unhappy affairs of the heart, she restricted what she wrote. She hinted, slightly, that there was or were romantic hopes in Agnes's early life but made no further comment on such matters.

Catharine's memory in old age was extraordinarily good, and the verifiable facts in her accounts are correct. Unfortunately, like Jane, her recollections are incomplete. She described Elizabeth and Agnes specifically and threw some light on their father's character. She also covered the family life in general and gave some detail of the early life of Sam Strickland. However, she gave hardly any information about Mrs Strickland. She referred to Sarah without naming her, and both Jane and Tom are barely mentioned at all. Therefore, although Catharine contributed greatly to the information that remains about some of her family (and the early part of this book repeats much of her material) she left gaps which are regrettable.

1888: Jane has another book published

After the deaths of Agnes and Elizabeth, Jane owned the copyrights of their books relating the 'Lives of the Tudor Princesses' and 'Lives of the Stuart Princesses'. The last task that Jane completed in the world of literature was to edit and combine the Tudor and the Stuart princesses into one volume which was published in 1888 by George Bell and Sons. Although it was Jane who did the work of editing and combining her sisters' work, her own name was not mentioned in the published volume.

10th April 1888: Robert Strickland has family problems

In a letter to Katie Traill dated 10th April 1888, Catharine told some of the financial difficulties that the next generation was causing Sam's son Robert Strickland. Catharine wrote: "I have just been told that dear nephew Robt S arrived today – but I think it can hardly be true as he was advised not to return as there is some trouble caused by that selfish reckless son" (Arthur Strickland) "but I cannot tell what it is all about. Only I feel grieved for dear R and C – It is also reported that Philip has taken the child away and that if true will be a sore trial to Caroline but indeed dear Katie it is very hard to know what is true and what is false."

14th June 1888: Jane Strickland dies

Jane, despite her many years of ill health and to her own surprise, lived to pass her 88th birthday. She had suffered from bronchitis and asthma for many years but it was heart disease which caused her death. Jane survived for just over a year after the publication of her biography of Agnes Strickland, and died on 14th June 1888 at her home, 'Park Lane Cottage' in Southwold.

Maime Fitzgibbon was with Jane when she died, and registered the death four days later. She gave Jane's age correctly as 88 years and her occupation as authoress.

Notices of Jane's death appeared in the local papers, either as a simple note in the death column, or in a slightly more elaborate version which read: "Death of Miss Jane Strickland – Miss Jane Margaret Strickland died in Southwold on Thursday afternoon, 14th June 1888. The deceased was sister to the celebrated authoress, Agnes Strickland, to whom the world is indebted for 'The Lives of the Queens of England' and other works. The deceased assisted her sister in many of the works bearing her name." It may be this last sentence which led to some published statements that Jane was Agnes's anonymous co-author. This is not true. Jane was an author who had several books published under her own name, and she had an important subsidiary role in the later part of Agnes and Elizabeth's working lives, but she was never more than an editorial or secretarial assistant to them.

19th June 1888: Jane's funeral takes place

Jane's funeral was reported in the local paper. The report read: "Southwold – Funeral of Miss Jane Strickland. The funeral of the late Miss JM Strickland took place on Tuesday 19th June 1888 at noon. The coffin, of polished oak, with brass furniture, was conveyed in a hearse to the church, and carried from thence to the grave by bearers selected from the tradesmen and fishermen. The mourners were – Miss Fitzgibbon, Miss Coulsher, Mr Robert Strickland, Mr Charles Foster, Mr JE Grubbe (Mayor of Southwold), Mrs Ellis, Miss Simmons, Rev Grubbe and the servants. The service was performed by the Rev E Howlett. The arrangements were under the joint management of Messrs HJ Debner and Sons and Mr Thomas & Denny. The shops were closed during the ceremony."

Maime Fitzgibbon and Robert Strickland were the family mourners, while Sarah aged 90 was understandably absent. The presence of the Mayor, and the description of the bearers having been selected from local fishermen and tradesmen, both indicate that Jane had a degree of importance in Southwold. She was buried next to Agnes, and their graves are in St Edmund's Churchyard in Southwold, north east of the chancel.

22nd June 1888: Jane's obituary is very informative

An obituary notice appeared a week after Jane's funeral. It was very affectionate and gave many details about Jane's later life, and must have been written by some-one local to Southwold, but unfortunately the author was not named. The notice, which appeared on the 22nd June 1888 in 'The Daily Journal, and Suffolk, Norfolk, Essex and Cambridgeshire Advertiser' was inaccurate about Jane's birthplace, but as Jane was only eight years old when the family arrived at Reydon, the error is of little significance. The notice was headed: "The Late Jane Strickland (by a Special Correspondent)" and said: "Southwold has lately lost one of its most respected and beloved inhabitants, Miss Jane Margaret Strickland, sister of the historian of the 'Queens of England', herself a clever and varied writer.

"Miss Strickland, who was born at Reydon Hall, lived there and at Southwold nearly all her long life. She was very firm and true in her friendships, but did not care to make acquaintances among the many who came to Southwold and asked for an introduction. All who knew her felt it a great privilege and pleasure to see and chat with her, to hear her clever conversation, and to see her beautiful, animated face as she grew enthusiastic on any subject.

"Her knowledge and power of memory were extraordinary. I went to see her once after a tour in Italy, and was rather taken aback by finding that, though I had really studied the subject, I knew far less about it than she did, though she had never been out of England! The reason of this was that Miss Jane Strickland's great work was 'Rome, Regal and Republican', and for this she had thoroughly worked up the subject, and knew the buildings and streets of Rome as if she lived in that wonderful city. She also wrote a charming story of the Jewish captivity 'Adonijah', in which she showed accurate knowledge of the manners and customs and life in Rome in those days. She published other books, tales etc.

"Miss Jane Strickland never had the advantage of her elder sisters, Elizabeth and Agnes, in studying at the British Museum and in many valuable libraries in England, Scotland, France and Holland, but she had a marvellous memory, and could give chapter and verse for her historical statements, and the reasons why she preferred one history to another, though years had passed since she had seen the MSS upon which she relied.

"Miss Strickland always had weak health, but her industry was very great. She was an unusually rapid reader, but notwithstanding this she remembered what she read. Her last book was 'The Life of Agnes Strickland' published by Blackwood, which was favourably reviewed and has been read with great interest by many, as showing the life of one of the pioneers of literary women. Miss Strickland's last work was re-editing and amalgamating Agnes Strickland's 'Tudor and Stuart Princesses', which was published only a few weeks ago, and she was just wondering what her next work should be.

"Miss Strickland's tastes and powers were very varied. She was an exquisite worker, and even the day before her death was beginning a fresh piece of lace work, transferring and arranging the pattern. She had grown slightly deaf and was much troubled with bronchial asthma, but her blue eyes were bright and keen as ever, and her mind fresh and intelligent to the last. She was truly a good woman, and death, which she felt sure would come suddenly, had no terrors for her. It did come suddenly, and she passed away on June 14th without a struggle. She was laid to her rest on the 19th in Southwold Churchyard, by the side of her sister Agnes, followed by those who truly loved her, amid demonstrations of respect from the inhabitants of the place."

This moving, and only obituary written about Jane, contains more information about her, and implies a deeper level of affection for her, than has been found in any other document.

24th July 1888: Jane's Will is implemented plus a bit more

Jane's estate was valued at just under £2,000 net with no leaseholds. The two executors of her Will were her solicitor, Charles Foster (husband of her friend Mrs Foster) who lived in Thorpe near Norwich, together with Mary Agnes (Maime) Fitzgibbon who had been living with Jane at 'Park Lane Cottage'. The Will was written on 4th February 1887, and probate was granted on 24th July 1888, little over a month after Jane's funeral.

Jane left to Maime her: "freehold property in Southwold Suffolk consisting of a house called 'Park Lane Cottage' and gardens" and an adjoining cottage called 'West Cottage'. Jane also left to Maime:

"all manuscripts and copyrights upon which I have or may have any claim."

Jane had little in the way of money to bequeath but she left £400 to her niece in Lakefield, Jane Blomfield, a married daughter of Sam and her god-daughter as well as namesake. She left £300 each to her niece Kate Traill and to her nephew Henry Strickland. Henry was Sam's fifth child and third son. Why he was selected for a bequest is unexplained, as had been the bequest by Agnes to Percy Strickland. Percy had visited England but no mention has been found of Henry having done so. All Jane's furniture, plate, china, pictures and books were left to Maime. She left £10 to Emma Brown, her maid-servant or, as Jane would so charmingly have described Emma "her maiden."

Apart from paying expenses to her solicitor, Mr Foster, and other necessary matters, that was all that Jane's Will stated as bequests. Catharine was not mentioned. However when Catharine told William about Jane's death in a letter dated 4th August 1888, she wrote: "I had word of the death of your aunt Jane – she died very suddenly at last on the 14th of June." Without any further comment on Jane's demise, Catharine went straight on to tell William of the contents of the Will. She wrote: "in her will she left me £100 – your sister Kate £300 – Her Godaughter Jane Blomfield £400; and Henry Strickland £300 – this with something to an old Servt and her lawyer formed the money legacies, but there are personal bequests besides, but the date not being correct, these are thrown out by the executor as invalid – as next of kin your aunt G and I come in for a fifth each of the value and the remainder has to be divided among the nearest of the nephews and nieces – but that will hardly be worth the expences attached to correspondence and &c" The money to be divided between the next of kin would be any contents of Jane's bank account after funeral expenses had been paid, plus any shares etc which were the basis of her independent income, separate from the literary income which she had bequeathed to Maime.

Catharine continued: "To Mary Agnes Fitzgibbon the two houses and all they contain of plate china books MSS – and everything else is left so she will be well provided for. Aunt Gwillym gives her a hundred a year and other things suitable for her future maintenance – MFG- is also left executrix – I am very thankful for the money left to your sister as it and the hundred pounds to myself was unexpected as I looked for nothing from my sister Jane on our behalf." Catharine and Kate planned to use the money to buy additional land in Lakefield.

This is the same discrepancy between Catharine's narrative of Jane's Will as when she had told of Richard Gwillym's Will written in 1867. In neither of their Wills is there any mention of Catharine, but in both cases she thought she had been left a legacy. The implication is that Sarah gave £100 to Catharine when Jane died, as well as the unstated amount when Richard Gwillym died, on both occasions under the pretence of the money having been legacies.

4th August 1888: Philip Wigg is causing more trouble

Philip Wigg, Tom's grand-son and son of Adela Wigg, was continuing his troublesome life, and was being a heavy burden on Robert Strickland as a result. Robert's own son, Arthur had married and remained in Canada and, being a bit of a liability, necessitated Robert returning from England to Canada from time to time.

In her letter to William dated 4th August 1888, Catharine gave an account of the latest trouble Philip Wigg had caused: "Your cousin Robt S did not come out this year that wicked PW has nearly ruined his father-in-law and Arthur between them – so that R lost everything at the limits and was left in debt P refused to give up the books to his father-in-law – unless heavily bribed to do so – finally got the money under false pretences – went to England and blackmailed R & Caroline – got possession of little Agnes and refused to give her up unless money was given – got all his wife's jewels and then returned to Canada – not fulfilling his agreement he had got the money from Mrs R Strickland for. We heard that his health had again faltered and that he was in a Hospital again – but where, no one knows – A sad career is it not?"

Catharine was still busy writing and told William: "I have written much this Spring and Summer on a new work now very nearly finished – It is 'Notes for Young Naturalists' – I have also nearly completed the old family record and 'Seven Years of my life under the Pines' – This has been a large undertaking in the way of authorship at 86 years old – But I wished to leave something myself for my grandchildren as I have neither Gold – nor silver nor any personal property to leave besides what I told you my dear son I had left for the sisters – and that you know is very little – Now Kate will not be penniless – her aunt's legacy will be great boon to her."

28th October 1888: Money is being spent on 'Westove'

When writing to William Traill on 28th October 1888 Catharine mentioned his son William, who was still living in Lakefield. She reported that: "he grows a big lad now. He generally comes to see Grandmama on Saturdays or dines with us on Sundays."

Catharine had been away from 'Westove' for three weeks, staying with Ellen Dunlop in Peterborough, and she told William that when she returned: "I found that much had been done in my absence – the oak flooring laid and varnished in the dining and drawing-room and store room – A handsome arch to connect the hall and drawing room which gives the stove heat into the room – the upper hall and upper floor paper and painted and my room ditto – all this is done and looks well and will add to the comfort of the house not a little."

Catharine went on: "Now there is the outside work yet to do – the fencing of the new addition to the garden, and the veranda – and that will cost a good deal – but will add to the value of the property – We hope that by the New Year we may be able to pay all this outlay – as Miss F-Gibbon in her last letter said that she trusted the legacies would be paid in six months. Kate is bearing the chief part of the cost at her own charge as my means are not equal to the extra outlay."

In the same way that Agnes and Elizabeth had perpetually noted any historical information they came across, Catharine had a similar pattern of behaviour with regard to botany. As a footnote to her letter to William, Catharine added: "Thanks dear W for the seeds of the Prairie Anemone (A patens) it is also known as the Easter or Pasque flower and also for the little flower sent in your former letter. I have a book devoted to all the Rock Ferns and specimens you have sent me."

20th December 1888: Sarah provides a children's treat

Maime remained in England after Jane's death, sharing her life with Sarah. In 1888 Sarah gave a Christmas treat to the children of

Tilford, reminiscent of the treats given to the children of Ulverston by Richard and herself in years gone by. The local paper reported: "Tilford Children's Treat – On Thursday 20th December 1888, through the kindness of Mrs Gwillym, Abbot's Lodge Tilford, the children of the village were entertained in the schoolroom. After a capital tea the Rev WHF Edge (vicar) gave a magic lantern, which was highly interesting."

The report continued: "Oranges were distributed amongst the children, who were delighted with their treat, and gave cheers for their kind patroness. The ladies present were Mrs Gwillym, Miss Fitzgibbon, Miss Johnson, and Misses Julius." This seems to have been the first such treat that Sarah provided in Tilford.

4th June 1889: Sarah is being cared for

It seems that the properties in Southwold which Jane had left to Maime, were being used as a second home by Maime and Sarah, allowing them to spend time together there as well as in Surrey. When Catharine wrote to Sarah on 4th June 1889 in response to a letter just received, she wrote: "how glad I was to find you were enjoying your annual visit to Southwold. Do you take the warm sea water baths – I think you used to find them ease the rheumatic pains?"

Maime was now Sarah's companion, and Catharine wrote: "It is a great source of comfort and satisfaction to me that you have the dear good niece with you for we know her and I have always felt a great interest in her and know her value – and I trust she will never be tempted to leave you as long as you live. You could not have a more charming companion or one more trustworthy in every respect."

In addition in England, Robert Strickland was playing his part in ensuring that Sarah was looked after, lending practical help where needed. Catharine told Sarah: "I rejoice in dear Robert being so much appreciated for he is so truly worthy of your love for he is all love himself – God for ever bless him." As a postscript Catharine added: "I am so glad that dear Robert goes down to see you – and works in the garden for he has great skill – I think the orchard house must be very nice – I am glad Agnes FG is with you – she is indeed a treasure."

At the time Catharine wrote her letter, descendents of the Strickland family in England who could keep an eye on Sarah were few. The principal ones were Maime and Robert Strickland, although there may have been cousins and other relatives via Sarah's parents, plus great-nieces or nephews via Sam and Tom's descendents. Richard Gwillym's family was also there to make sure that Sarah was in good hands, both because of family affection, and also in their role as her heir with regard to Richard Gwillym's property.

By contrast, Catharine in Lakefield was surrounded by relatives, and had links with many more in other parts of Canada and the United States. In fact she had so many descendents, and there were so many relatives of herself, Sam and Susanna, that it was inconvenient to name them all. She ended her letter by writing: "I fear I have tired you my darling Thay with this long letter, and now I must say goodbye with much love from all my daughters, and the nephews and nieces who are many more in the second and third generation than I could name – they would take a long page or more – but all hold your name in love and respect. Thanks again for your sweet loving letter to your own faithfully attached and ever loving sister, Catharine Parr Traill."

June 1889: Catharine explains her finances to Sarah

In her letter to Sarah dated 4th June 1889, Catharine told what use had been made of the money that she and Kate had received as a result of Jane's death. She wrote: "I think my dear Kate was wise to buy the lot adjoining our premises – and she invested the residue at 6% – I also invested $400 – at the same rate – but I do not interfere with her money – she is so sensible. It is pleasant for her to feel her independence and indeed she is in all things now more capable of managing than I am myself and most unselfish she is and ever has been."

Some of the money had been used to improve 'Westove': "We enjoy the great comfort of the nice verandah which Kate put up that I might take the air outside under shelter and enjoy the garden and have a comfortable couch on it where I can be and read or work and rest when tired with working in the garden among the vegetables which I generally see to myself as the dear old mother used to do."

Catharine continued: "I am very like dear Mother in many of my ways and oh how like to her was my dear sister Moodie, when I bent over her coffin – I could have said – it is my dear mother so much did she resemble her, yet in life the likeness was not so striking."

Either Jane had more assets than expected or Sarah made an addition to Catharine's proper share, for Catharine told Sarah: "I was indeed surprized at the sum that was mentioned as an addition to the legacy left to me by dear Jane and deeply grateful I am to her memory and to Mr Foster and dear Agnes F for the admirable way everything has been managed by them."

Catharine and Kate had thought of buying another piece of land which would have linked the garden of 'Westove' to the river but had decided otherwise on the advice of "Walter" probably Walter Strickland, son of Sam. Catharine wrote: "he thinks it more advisable for me to put the proceeds of the Bill into the S(avings) Bank as the interest will raise the yearly income to about £40 of our currency that is with the yearly dividend from the Peterborough investment and the interest on the $400 – all together."

Catharine's investments had been through a worrying phase a few years earlier: "There was some trouble with the affairs of the Peterborough Real Estate Co – four or five years ago and they had to reduce the capital and also the interest – at one time we were afraid we should lose all – but I was advised to hold on – and so there is a reserve being made for the shareholders and by and bye we shall get back some of what was kept back but had it not been for your most kind and generous annual donation we must have been sorely pressed for even the necessities of life for you dear sister more than doubled the income and how can I be sufficiently thankful to you, and Kate no less so." At this time Catharine was 87 and Sarah was 91 years old.

13th September 1889: Catharine's finances are dealt a blow

Three months after telling Sarah that her investments had gone through a bad patch but things were now improving, it became apparent that Catharine's optimism had been misplaced. Catharine told the bad news to Robert and Caroline Strickland in a letter dated

13th September 1889 in which she wrote: "We hear that a further reduction is to be made to our scanty dividends or capital rather of the Peterborough real Estate – which seems to have very sandy foundations. I must go to Peterborough before the meeting on the 25th. I hope to see HS" (probably Henry Strickland) "– but he is always so busy – I can rarely get a sight of him to ask his advice and dear Mr Dunlop is so deaf – he does not hear me – Indeed, I too am getting very dull of hearing and my memory is failing fast – I must lay by my pen now dear friends for my hand is cramped – I will add a few lines before mailing this letter."

By the time Catharine continued her letter, worse news had arrived. She said: "I find by a statement received this day that affairs are not very promising for there will be no dividend this year on the shares which are now reduced again – It was indeed only $35 for the half year from Jan to June that we received, now nothing for Decr nor does it seem for another year. Therefore we must fall back upon the residue that I put into the S Bank for paying taxes, church rates, coals, food, clothing, medicines, and all the necessaries of life for a year to come."

Catharine was philosophic about her situation, trusting in God, as she always did, telling Robert and Caroline in her letter: "However, we have a resource that belongs to those who trust in God's care over them – and hitherto we have been preserved, fed, clothed and cared for, even when the way seemed narrowest and the clouds heaviest. It was His goodness that moved my dear sister Agnes to leave me the copyright share, which has up to the present date thus sustained us, aided by my beloved sister Sarah's generous yearly gifts – To her indeed I owe the comforts that we have enjoyed year after year – Now again I fall back upon my dear sister Jane's kind remembrance of us – so after all dear Friends – I need not fear for the future – I know that all necessary wants will be supplied." She also added: "let me Bless our gracious God for what he gives and for what in His Wisdom he with-holds. I know it is all right – so let it be."

Catharine gave Robert and Caroline an account of her daughter Kate and grand-daughter Katie. She wrote: "Katie has been away for three months and that has made some little difference in the business of the house. Kate has no time for correspondence when Katie is away – but we look for the dear girl this week or next – Her visit to Walkerton has been a sad one – the watching over a dear little baby cousin – till death took it to its home of joy and love above.

"I am very anxious at times about my dear Kate's health – the Doctor says the action of the heart is too weak, and advises care and rest and that is what she will not take. You know her habit of activity in the house and that her wish is to keep everything orderly, and to save me from the least fatigue. She sacrifices herself in every way – She has just gone out to read to Mrs Podger, who is declining daily and finds much comfort in my dear daughter's daily visits to her sick bed. Dear K hers is not a wasted life; unselfish, devoted, an example to those around."

Catharine's letter to Robert and Caroline responded to their family news and regretted the infrequency of letters exchanged: "We all were rejoiced to hear that dear Charlotte had been blessed in the gift of another darling babe I hope and trust that the dear little grand-daughter and mother are both well. We often long for news from you – It seems so rarely to come our way and I know the fault lies with ourselves I write so seldom and Kate has no time."

Of herself, Catharine wrote: "You know that I only leave the garden gate when any kind friend takes me up – as dear Mrs G Strickland does, from time to time to pass a pleasant day with her among her lovely flowers. I had been writing every day a little work which I hoped to get published – 'Notes for Young Naturalists' – but after the long Summer's labour it was not accepted, so I reconcile myself that it was not to be.

"My hearing is becoming so imperfect I fear to mistake or misstate what is patent to others – and forget so soon what passes. All the S families have been up to Stoney Lake hitherto – but a change has come from heat to cold and wind and rain will drive them back to their Lakefield homes."

Catharine was still exchanging letters with Sam's widow in England, Katharine Strickland, who was now very unwell. Catharine told Robert and Caroline: "I heard from dear Mrs Strickland last week. I fear each letter may be the last. I cannot bear to think of my youth and the cheerer of my age will be called to that mansion of bliss. Yet it may be that the summons will come first to myself."

23rd October 1889: Sarah supports local charities

Sarah continued to play a small part in Tilford society, and gave her support to a fund-raising event advertised in the local papers. The advertisement read: "Aldershot Institute. Grand Bazaar and Series of Entertainments in aid of the Funds and to pay off the Debt on the furniture, will be held in the Alexandra Hall (kindly lent for the occasion) on Wednesday and Thursday, October 23rd and 24th 1889 under the distinguished patronage of …" and then followed by a list of 24 people with Sarah in 7th position.

28th October 1889: Philip Wigg has visited Sarah

Philip Wigg had reappeared in England and was causing concern. In her letter to Robert and Caroline Strickland dated 13th September 1889 Catharine responded to some news they had sent her. She wrote, referring to little Agnes Wigg: "I felt very anxious when I heard that Agnes's father was at West Drayton. I hope that the beloved grand-child will not be taken away from its peaceful home with you. God forbid it."

Catharine made a similar comment when she wrote to Sarah a letter dated 28th October 1889 in which she wrote: "I was greatly surprised at P Wigg's audacity in paying you that visit. He is now again in Canada and at present in Toronto – As to that story of his marriage to a rich woman in Montreal. No-one believes one word of it – It is one of his canards to obtain credit – but no one puts any faith in him – It is sad to think of his wasted life with good talents and fine person and fair opportunities – but I do marvel at his intrusion at Abbots Lodge."

Unbeknownst to Catharine, Mrs George Strickland had written to Sarah in the belief that Catharine had lost everything with her investment in the Peterborough Land Co. She was worried that Sarah, believing Catharine to be in comfortable circumstances, might stop sending her money.

Catharine assured Sarah that she was not destitute, having reserve funds in the Savings Bank, but was grateful for the "enclosure, received that day." Sarah seems to have assured Catharine that she would care for Kate Traill's future. Catharine added: "I think my dear sister you have been a faithful steward of the riches entrusted to you."

23rd December 1889: Sarah gives another Christmas treat

Sarah again gave a Christmas treat for the children of Tilford in 1889. This was the second Christmas that Maime Fitzgibbon had been living with Sarah as well as the second year that Sarah had given a Christmas treat. It seems likely that Maime's presence was providing the extra energy that Sarah needed to carry out something which she may have wished to do in previous years, as a private memorial to Richard Gwillym. The event and the children for whom the treat was provided were too similar to past events held in Ulverston for the similarities to be coincidental.

The event was reported in the local paper as follows: "Tilford – Treat to Sunday and Day Schools – On Monday afternoon in Christmas week, 23rd December 1889, the children attending Tilford Sunday and Day Schools had an excellent tea provided for them at the schools, by the kindness of Mrs Gwillym, Abbot's Lodge.

"The vicar (the Rev WH Edge) amused the youngsters after tea by exhibiting some excellent dissolving views. The loud laughter and cheers of the children denoted how warmly they appreciated the kindness of Mrs Gwillym and the vicar. Mrs Gwillym and Miss Fitzgibbon were present during the afternoon. The latter assisted by the vicar, Miss Tilbury and Mr Smith (school master) attended to the wants of the little ones."

January 1890: Sarah lends items to an exhibition

The New Gallery at 121 Regent Street in London was opened in 1888 as an art gallery, and is now a listed building, headquarters formerly of Habitat followed by Burberry. In January 1890 a major exhibition of items associated with the Tudor period was opened, and continued until early March 1890.

The exhibition contained in the region of 2,000 items, filling the four rooms of the Gallery, and the balcony around the central hall. The catalogue of items on display was a hefty volume being over 300 pages long, with the index of those lending items covering 4 pages.

The list of those who lent items to the exhibition included people whose families had in the past made their collections available for Agnes to study, or who had helped her in other ways. They included the Duke of Devonshire, the Earl Spencer, Sir H Bedingfeld and Captain Cottrell Dormer. It was therefore fitting that the exhibition included three items which had belonged to Agnes and were now in Sarah's care.

Mrs Gwillym was listed as the lender and the items on loan were a portrait (8" by 6") of Queen Anne Boleyn which Agnes had bought, and which had been used as an illustration in the 'Lives of the Queens of England'. The other items were a portrait of Queen Jane Seymour (7" by 5 ½") and a bronze plaque portraying Edward VI.

28th March 1890: Katharine Strickland (nee Rackham) dies

In a letter to William dated 27th April 1890, Catharine told him of the death of Sam Strickland's widow. She wrote: "My most dear sister-in-law Mrs Strickland is no more. I know as yet little more than that your cousin Robt S was with her and her nephew Alfred Fowler – but her brother Mr Rackham and his wife came to the funeral."

Katharine Strickland had died on 28th March 1890 of heart disease and dropsy at the age of 84. She died in Aylsham in Norfolk.

Catharine told William: "I feel her loss deeply. No one here can be to me what she was in a spiritual sense – Sister and Friend most valued. She was four years younger than me – and one year less than my dear brother – she was 84 – I hear from England that your Aunt Mrs Gwillym is well and is now in her 93rd year – I in my 89th."

17th July 1890: Sarah Gwillym dies

Sarah may have been well in April 1890, but she died within four months of her sister-in-law. In a letter to William begun on 20th July 1890 Catharine told him: "I had a sad word by cable-gram telling me of the death of your Aunt my dear sister Mrs Gwillym which took place after much suffering on the morning of the 17th inst July.

"It was on the 13th that was the anniversary of her sister Agnes's death, whom she had survived 13 years. My sister Sarah was in her

93rd year – We had been parted for fifty-eight years – Yet I have felt her death deeply. We had been friends and companions sharing the same bed and chamber from our girlhood till I left home in 1832 – on the 20th of May never again to meet.

"For many days and nights my mind had been so impressed with the conviction that my darling sister was no more in life on earth I knew and felt that she was dead – for her spirit seemed to be with me as a surety – but though fore-shewn it came as a painful blow and for days I could not overcome my grief for her loss – I stand alone – the last and only one living of the sisters and brothers of my house – The golden chain is broken – One solitary link alone remaining."

By 1st August 1890 when Catharine continued her letter to William, she had received from Maime a letter with more news of Sarah's death. It was, Catharine told William: "a most interesting and sad account of my beloved sister's last days and hours. She seems to have had much suffering for a fortnight previous to her death but she knew that the change was drawing near for some time – she retained her consciousness and mental powers nearly to the last – she was not unprepared though she spoke little; but such indeed was her nature, and habit she was self-contained, and reticent on religious subjects or on any matter of serious importance at all times – I believe she was a Christian in faith and her works were done in proof of her belief. Greatly she will be missed by the poor – She had been very unselfish devoting a considerable part of her income to deeds of true charity – To myself she was a kind and helpful friend – And deeply do I regret her loss – I have had many deaths to mourn this present year. In the family three beloved dear ones. Your precious Aunt Strickland, your cousin George and now my dearest and last sister Sara."

24th July 1890: Sarah is remembered in Ulverston

Maime Fitzgibbon performed the same important and difficult duties for her great-aunt Sarah as she had done for her great-aunt Jane two years previously. She was with Sarah when she died, and four days later she registered the death. A short announcement of Sarah's death appeared in a number of papers, giving her age, where and when she died and describing her variously as the widow of Richard Gwillym, as the daughter of Thomas Strickland, and occasionally as the elder sister of Agnes Strickland. This last statement was wrong for Agnes had been older than Sarah by two years.

Both Sarah and Richard Gwillym were still remembered in Ulverston, and news of Sarah's demise soon reached the town. The local paper expanded a little on the bare facts of Sarah's life, the children's parties were fondly recalled, and the church recognised her role in the town by flying the flag at half-mast.

The local paper still bore the name of Mr Soulby, who had known Sarah and Richard over many years, and it carried a report of the event on Thursday 24th July 1890. 'Soulby's Ulverston Advertiser and General Intelligencer' said: "Death of Mrs Gwillym – Many old residents of Ulverston and district will learn with regret the death of Mrs Sarah Strickland Gwillym, widow of the Rev Canon Richard Gwillym, for 33 years vicar of St Mary's, Ulverston, who resided at Stockbridge House, and was chaplain to the earl of Harrowby.

"Mrs Gwillym, who died at Tilford, Surrey on July 17th, was in her 93rd year. She was a daughter of Mr Thomas Strickland of Reydon Hall, Suffolk, and elder sister of Agnes Strickland, author of 'The Lives of the Queens of England' &c. Her husband, the only son of Lieutenant Colonel Richard Gwillym of Bewsey Hall, Warrington and brother-in-law, of the late Mr Le Gendre Stailsie, of Huntroyde, died at Ulverston, in his 66th year, on November 29, 1867, and his remains are interred at St Mary's Churchyard. Mrs Gwillym has not been brought here for interment.

"On Sunday, the flag at the Parish Church floated at half-mast over the steeple, and at the evening service, Miss Benson played the 'Dead March in Saul'.

"On the occasion of the marriage of Canon and Mrs Gwillym, the carriage, at their home coming, was met at Oubas, the horses taken out, and they were dragged through the town to Stockbridge House. Mr and Mrs Gwillym had no children. Canon Gwillym was mainly instrumental in procuring the present peal of bells for St Mary's, for the restoration and rebuilding of St Mary's Church, for the erection of the Infants' School, and many other works of utility in the parish.

"We doubt not but that there are many living who still remember the delightful children's parties given by Mr and Mrs Gwillym at Stockbridge House. They were married in 1844."

Apart from this item, there were no obituaries to Sarah, and no report of her funeral has been found. She is buried in the churchyard of All Saint's Church in Tilford, in the plot next to the double grave of her brother and sister, Tom and Elizabeth Strickland.

Part 9: The sole survivor

Legacies and losses; Stoney Lake island homes; 'Pebbles and Pearls' by Catharine Parr Traill; "a wonderful old lady"; Catharine's end

6th August 1890: Sarah has left Catharine a legacy

Although Sarah's Will could not be implemented until the process of valuing her estate had taken place and had been agreed, Catharine was able to add a footnote when she finished her letter to William on 6th August 1890.

The footnote said: "Last night I got a letter from M FitzG – and to day possibly I may get more particulars – All she tells me is in a few words – that your aunt left me £500 – and your sister £1000 – that is a great gift – We know no more and you will be glad dearest Willie as it leaves no fear for any future needs not being supplied in my old age. Let us be very thankful; and bless the memory of the beloved sister who has thus cared for me and your good sister."

Despite the large sum of money that Sarah had left to Catharine and her daughter Kate, and the many boxes and gifts that had been sent from England to Canada over the years, Catharine still managed to feel discontented with the contents of Sarah's Will. In her letter to William Traill 20th August 1890 she wrote: "I felt sad that no token of personal love was left not even a book or any trifle of affection from sister to sister – It has pained me the fact that I only stood to her as a legatee like her nieces – neither more nor less!"

25th September 1890: Catharine greets the Governor General

Public acknowledgement of Catharine's achievements was shown by her being chosen to receive the Governor General and Lady Stanley when they visited Lakefield on Thursday 25th September 1890. The Peterborough newspaper 'Daily Evening Review' is said to have reported Lord Stanley's visit, as summarised below.

In his speech in reply to his welcome, Lord Stanley said "Great are the changes that have taken place since the old settlers first came here. It is a source of pride and satisfaction to be introduced to a lady who is known in England as well as here, and who herself is able to testify that in her lifetime these results have been achieved. When I speak of Mrs Traill you will understand that honor is due to such a name." After applause, Lord Stanley took Mrs Traill's arm and "gracefully" guided her "down to lunch."

Catharine described the same event when she wrote to William on 1st October 1890. She wrote: "The Govr Gen Lord Stanley paid a visit by invitation to Lindsay, to be present on some special occasion, and from Lindsay took steam boat – and came through the back Lakes I think to inspect the advantages of the navigation through to the Trent and Bay of Quinte so our little village had the honor of a visit of not quite 2 hours – and the good folks were left to their own resources for a suitable reception for many of the heads of the village were away – and there was really no Head to make suitable arrangements.

"Roland went up by steamer to meet the Governor. The village folk did wonders and got up Arches &c and made arrangements in the town Hall for an elegant evening tea, which twelve of our young ladies were to wait upon – and very pretty they all looked – But there was no lady to receive Lord Stanley – so it was laid upon me to do the honors and dear Mrs George S sent the carriage and the black ponies at 5 o'clock to take me to the hall.

"The upper room was very elegantly draped with flowers and wreaths – for receiving the party – I had a bad headache and felt unequal to the fatigue but when the kind Govr and his lady met me so cordially and frankly, all my little fear of failure ceased – You cannot think how truly kindly I was greeted, and I presented my copy of my Flower book to Lady Stanley who was apparently much pleased with this little mark of respect – I was surprized by the compt paid me by his Lordship and I fancy so too were some of the good people of Lakefield. Well – They went off by the night train amid huzzahs and a torchlight procession and God Save the Queen – by a Lindsay band – And having told you all this I will turn to other subjects."

Among the other subjects which Catharine mentioned to William were her finances and a literary commission she had received. On the financial front she seemed less enthusiastic about the benefit of Sarah's bequest to her. Catharine wrote: "We may not get the legacies for some months and then it may be some time before we get any interest from investments – so we have to manage the best we can – You see dear Will that I shall not have more than I have had (but Kate has her own to add and so we are not likely to be distressed in any way)."

Of the literary commission she wrote: "– but I am glad to do what I can to earn some little addition by writing – and I hope to get a few dollars from an engagement to write for a new magazine – 'The Young Canadian' – a monthly – The editor has applied for articles promising to pay for what I send – and has approved a small MS already. My subject is (Our) Indians, and I have plenty of matter to copy out from my old journals – and any little anecdote or information touching on the NW Indians would be very acceptable about the Crees or Blackfeet, or any of your new Indians in the country where you are now." William had been moved to increasingly distant postings with various promotions over the years. He was based at Fort St James at the south and eastern end of Stuart Lake in 1890 in what is now British Columbia.

1st October 1890: Maime's return to Canada may be imminent

After Sarah died, Maime Fitzgibbon returned to Canada, but exactly when she returned is not clear, possibly because she split her life between the two countries for a while. In a letter to William written on 1st and 3rd October 1890, Catharine brought him up to date on the whereabouts of the three Fitzgibbon sisters, thinking that Maime was to return to Canada in the near future.

Maime, the eldest of the sisters was 39 years old in 1890. Alice Dunn, aged 33, was a widow, and with two young children returned to Ontario and lived in Lakefield. Geraldine Moodie, aged 38, lived in Lakefield with her sister Alice in 1890 on a temporary basis before returning west to re-join her husband in Manitoba. There was also a brother, James Gerald Fitzgibbon, aged 37 in 1890, but his life did not become entangled with those of his English great-aunts in the same way as his sisters' lives had done.

Of Maime Fitzgibbon, Catharine in Lakefield wrote: "Maimie is coming to Ottawa probably this month. M will be here very likely as she wants to enter into some arrangements with me about MS and literary matters" but later in the same letter Catharine was less clear about Maime's location at that time. She wrote: "When Mary F Gibbon comes back to Canada she will most likely come to Lakefield and stay with us and if so I shall be busy writing as she wants us to bring out a volume together."

March 1891: Sarah's estate is valued

Administration of Sarah's Will was done jointly by Henry Feilden (or Fielden) Rawstone of 7 Suffolk Place, Pall Mall, Middlesex, gentleman, and Charles Foster of the City of Norwich, gentleman. The estate was valued at £15,782 10s 10d in March 1891. Henry Rawstone was a solicitor as well as nephew to Sarah's husband Richard, and Charles Foster was the solicitor who had already been an executor of Jane's Will. Sarah's last Will and Testament was written and signed on 31st October 1888, shortly after Jane's Will had come into effect.

Much of the source of Sarah's wealth was hers only during her lifetime and then passed to Richard Gwillym's heir, the Rev Robert Atherton Rawstone who, by the time Sarah wrote her last Will and Testament, had become Archdeacon of Blackburn.

Sarah left all her property in Tilford ('Abbot's Lodge' together with two cottages, 'South Bank Cottage' and 'Hill Side Cottage', in which her coachman and her gardener lived, and which had been left to her by Elizabeth) to her nephew Henry Rawstone, to whom she also left two houses in Rodney Street in Barrow-in-Furness (left to her by Agnes even though probably jointly owned by Elizabeth and Agnes) and any other unspecified property she may have owned.

Her money bequests were £500 to Catharine and £1,000 to Catharine's daughter, Kate Traill. During her period of widowhood, Sarah must have bought shares of her own with surplus income, as she had some shares which she was able to dispose of in her Will. She left all her Canadian shares to Robert Strickland, with no clue given as to the number of shares. Similarly she left to Richard Gwillym's godson, Richard Gwillym Strickland, £1,000 and all (but no number specified) her East India Railway shares.

Sarah left £500 each to Emma Barlee (widowed daughter of Sam), Jane Blomfield (daughter of Sam), to Agnes Fitzgibbon Chamberlin (daughter of Susanna) and to Robert Moodie (son of Susanna). To Robert Moodie she also left all her Dutch Rhonish Railway shares.

Some specific items of silverware Sarah left to Henry Rawstone and some she left to Agnes Mary Fitzgibbon (Maime) together with all the shares that she had the power to dispose of in the Liverpool London and Globe Insurance Company.

Sarah left £20 to each of Mary Ann Vickery and her sister Jessie Vickery, her coachman and her gardener. She left £10 to Letitia Douse (married sister of Mary Ann and Jessie Vickery) and £10 to her under-gardener. The Vickery family had been associated with Agnes, Eliza and finally Sarah for many years and had received a small legacy with the demise of each of them. In the case of Mary Ann Vickery, the legacies seem small given the length and nature of her working relationship between the families, particularly with Agnes. However, census data implies that the Strickland sisters provided for the long-term welfare of the Vickery family. In 1871, when Agnes was still alive and in good health, Mary Ann Vickery, aged 29, was the only person recorded as living in Park Lane Cottage, Southwold, and she was described as a general servant. In 1881, after Elizabeth had died, Jessie Vickery aged 39 was living in Eden Lodge on the Tilford Road, with her mother aged 71, and both had an annuity to provide them with an income. At this time, Mary Ann Vickery, aged 40, was living with Sarah at 'Abbot's Lodge' as her ladies maid. Ten years later, at the time of the 1891 census, and about nine months after Sarah's death, Mary Ann Vickery had joined her mother and sister living at Eden Lodge, and each of the three members of the family were able to describe themselves as 'now living on own means.'

Susanna's son Robert had died while Sarah was still alive. Sarah consequently wrote a codicil to her Will on 8th May 1889 leaving to Robert's widow Nellie, a lesser amount of £200 plus the railway shares intended for Robert. Sarah also added via this codicil, bequests of £100 each to her goddaughter Cecilia Frances (the eldest daughter of Henry Rawstone), to Miss Harriet Crompton of Cranleigh (probably a daughter of Richard's doctor and friend, Dr Crompton), to Robert Strickland's daughter Charlotte Taylor, and to Winifred Taylor (a daughter of Charlotte). There was no bequest to any descendent of Tom.

Sarah being the last member of her generation of Stricklands in England, she presumably had in her possession the personal effects, papers and memorabilia accumulated from Agnes, Elizabeth and Jane. There was no specific mention of these in Sarah's Will, apart from the catch-all of leaving all the residue and unspecified items to Henry Fielden Rawston, adding "the earnest request that he will assume the name of Gwillym as his surname after and in addition to the name of Rawstone and that he will also assume the arms and crest of the Gwillym family."

5th April 1891: Robert (and Walter) Strickland's families appear on the census

When the 1891 census was carried out on 5th/6th April there were still in England a few direct descendents of Thomas and Elizabeth (Homer) Strickland of Reydon Hall. In Middlesex were Robert and Caroline Strickland, both aged 60 and living in West Drayton in Middlesex with their 10 year old grand-daughter, Agnes Wigg. Despite the financial problems which Catharine had reported in her family letters, Robert was recorded as living on his own means. The family had two live-in servants – a 20 year old cook and a 17 year old housemaid. Their home was in a crescent between Station Road and Church Road, both of which still exist, as does their parish church of St Martin.

(In the 1901 census, the only change in Robert Strickland and his family's entry in the census, apart from adding 10 years to the ages of Robert, Caroline and Agnes Strickland Wigg, was that Robert no longer claimed to be living on his own means, instead he described his occupation as "Canadian Canoe importer.")

Robert and Caroline lived only a short distance from Harmondsworth where their daughter Charlotte and her husband, the Rev John Taylor lived with their five surviving children and four live-in servants – governess, cook, housemaid and nurse. The children were Winifred AS Taylor aged 9, John RS Taylor aged 7, Violet Grace S Taylor aged 5, Dorothy GS Taylor aged 1 and Harold MS Taylor aged 8 months. (The initial S seems to have denoted the name Strickland being regularly included, indeed, on the family tomb whose inscriptions can still be read in Harmondsworth churchyard, the name Strickland is given as part of the engraved surname. The tomb stands on the church side of the gate which links the garden of the vicarage to the grounds of the church and proclaims that a John Taylor was Lord of the Manor.)

Maime has not been found on the 1891 census. 'Park Lane Cottage' in Southwold was not itemised on the census, and if being used as a holiday home would have been unoccupied in April. 'Abbot's Lodge' in Tilford was being occupied by Sarah's former coachman and his family.

Walter Strickland was a 47 year old discount broker, living with his wife Emma, aged 39, in Walthamstow, Essex. They had four children, Agnes and Margaret Strickland aged 13 and 12 respectively, Walter aged 10 and Mary Diana aged 7. Walter therefore carried forward several family names starting with Agnes, the name of his famous aunt.

26th September 1891: Catharine enjoys a week at Stoney Lake

When Catharine wrote to William on 26th September 1891, the younger William Traill, Catharine's grand-son, had finished his education in Lakefield and had returned to his family.

Catharine wrote that on the 16th September 1891 she had received an unexpected visit from: "your cousin Mr Robt S-d. He was looking so well and bright and kind and loving we were glad to see him – His object was chiefly on his son Arthur's account and he left for Washington Territory where Arthur is, or was – desiring to get money to buy a farm or settle on a cattle ranch.

"Robt wisely delayed to send the money until he had seen the property. You know Arthur is not very reliable or prudent and though he has been out now for several years, he has sent no money for the support of his wife and five children – The poor wife has borne the loneliness and the care patiently hitherto in Lakefield, and her support has been from her own friends in Toronto, or from his parents. The look out for her future does not seem a promising one as far as we can judge from the past."

Of her own news, Catharine wrote: "Last week – our kind friend Mrs G Strickland invited your sister and me to spend a week at Fairy Lake Lodge – her pretty Stoney Lake summer house – and she sends the carriage for us so that we have no trouble or expense as we were conveyed to the wharf and went up in the Yacht.

"Young Clinton" (son of Annie and Clinton Atwood) "was disappointed of his longed for holiday as he was removed to Petrolia" in South West Ontario "as manager of the Branch Bank there; of course the position is an advance for him, but it was hard the removal just as he was ready to enjoy a fortnight with his family and take possession of his island and house up on the lake. It only requires the work of a good hand like Tim Sullivan for a couple of days to clear up the rubbish, and burn the brush heaps and level the rough places to make the island lovely. The views from it are beautiful – They are close to the Lillicraps, Mellors, Blomfields and Barlees, so I give the group the name of 'The Society Islands'.

"The pure bracing air of the lakes did me much good – I had been suffering from continual pain in my right knee and foot so that I could hardly move about for pain – but the change to the bright air did me the greatest good and I was able to get around with the aid of a stick even to get over the rocky ground – Now I feel the weakness again – in the limbs and the old cramps at night returning – There is a marked difference in the temperature directly we pass the locks. The less rapid water and lower level gave a soft warm drowsy air enervating and depressing, after the free bracing atmosphere of the larger, higher body of water and I felt the effect directly after our return to Lakefield."

23rd May 1892: Catharine's daughter Mary dies

Catharine's daughter Mary Muchall and her family had been living at 'The Rocks', the house which Catharine had bought for them in 1878 near her own home 'Westove' in Lakefield. In September 1891 Mary was showing signs of an illness which Catharine thought was malarial, and due to their basement having been flooded.

Mary died on 23rd May 1892. Her son Norman was in poor health and his condition deteriorated quickly after his mother's death. Within a year, he too was dead. Having tried to find work in Toronto and Montreal, he returned to Lakefield where, in poor health and with poor prospects, he committed suicide.

Before Norman's death, Catharine had a strange dream which she related to William Traill, in the letter which told of her grandson's death. She wrote: "I must here tell you of a strange dream which I had some months ago – I dreamed I found myself in a large empty building and in a spacious room the only objects were a Stretcher bed on which lay side by side wrapped in grave clothes my eldest sister E– and Agnes dead – my sister Jane came in with a vial in her hand which she said was left for me by E– who had discovered the secret of painless death to any one taking it – I took the vial in my hand preparing to take its contents – When these words were borne in unto me – as if by the Judge or an Angel 'God Did not call you Soul wherefore didst thou come?' And I wakened – The words seemed still to sound in my ears – 'Wherefore didst thou come' – and it has often occurred was it not a warning, to tell it to others – The sad words have indeed come back to me many times since – I named the dream many times but I do not know if my boy ever heard me."

After Mary died her three remaining children moved west in search of work. Her two daughters Caroline and Evelyne had poor health, and her son Hargrave did his best to support them. Mary's husband, Tom Muchall went to live at 'Westove' with Catharine and Kate, where he worked on the garden and did other small chores for them. His house, 'The Rocks' was rented out to provide him with a small income.

20th July 1892: Catharine has a fall

When she wrote to her grand-daughter Katie on 20th July 1892, Catharine and Kate Traill had just returned from another week's visit to Stoney Lake with Mrs George and Mary Strickland and others. While she was there, she had gone for a walk on her own and had a mishap. Catharine told Katie that she had: "got a pretty severe fall in the ravine – and I was all alone and had great difficulty in getting to the house. Fortunately there was hot water on the stove and I undressed myself and fomented the bruises and went to bed – Mary found me and got me some Pounds Extract and I got better before your Aunt and Mrs GS came in – but it was a great shake – and I felt very lame for many hours after.

"I could not venture out again and now I am all right and the aches and pains gone. It was a great mercy that no bone was broken for you know what a wild and rocky ground there is all about the ravine – overgrown with all manner of shrubs and wild flowers. It was trying to reach a plant among the rocks that caused the fall – I had been so cautious up to that time – and now I must be more on my guard and not indulge my love of scrambling over rocks after plants after this warning that I am too old for such gay frolics." Catharine was 90 years old.

In the same letter, Catharine showed that she was still quite spirited. She wrote: "Last week a party of surveyors came below the garden to prospect for a new line for the RR" (rail road) "I was in despair so I took my staff in my hand and went down to the water's edge and interviewed a stout middle aged Boss – in a grey hat and grey surtout.

"The man in grey seemed rather at first taken by surprize at the daring behaviour of the old lady – opposing so patriotic an attempt as carrying lines to interrupt my prospect which seemed of no earthly consequence in his eyes – I am afraid I remonstrated against the enormity of the proposed nuisance – He smiled and said my views were too limited he considered a line of such a RR was a prospect worth seeing – far beyond a parcel of trees or a sheet of water – no doubt he voted me an old bore, but 'Mrs Poyser had her say' – and I believe the said road is to go off at some other angle – at any rate we hope so – it would have been dreadful – the RR at our very door – I think we would have cleared out in disgust."

15th November 1892: Catharine tries to get her family memoirs published

Catharine had nearly completed her series of notes, essays, and memorials to her brothers and sisters. When they were finished, she wrote to a publisher named Messrs Scribner on 15th November 1892, in an attempt to get her recollections published. The firm must have been one that had not previously published Catharine's work, because she had to begin her letter by writing: "I will introduce myself to your notice as Mrs Catharine Parr Traill Authoress of 'The Back Woods of Canada' 'Canadian Crusoes' and many other works."

Catharine then put herself in the context of her family. She told Messrs Scribner: "I am the youngest but one of the Strickland sisters whose works are better known than my own by the American reader – Alas! – I am now the only survivor of these gifted sisters."

She told them: "I have by me a great deal of MS matter perfectly original never having been offered to any publishing House at home or in the US or in Canada never before published – which consists of a family record." Having outlined the various topics covered in the manuscripts, she assured them "it is no reprint and may be relied upon for perfect truthfulness – presenting pictures of old world life which will amuse if not astonish the reader."

Catharine acknowledged that further work would be needed. She wrote: "The hand of an expert would be needed to the better arrangement of the papers. Would Messrs Scribner feel tempted to read this MS – and enter into any correspondence with the Authoress? – Who is willing to accept any suggestion as to publication – only that she is not able to incur any risk herself."

In a postscript she added: "The memoir of Agnes Strickland having been already before the public the writing of the present MS only supplies the omissions and early portions of her life omitted by her biographer – but which will not be found uninteresting to the reader."

Catharine was unsuccessful in getting her work published. However, her manuscripts exist within the Canadian archives and have been used to a substantial extent in the early parts of this book, which cover family life in Bungay and at Reydon, as well as being used by Maime Fitzgibbon when she wrote a brief biography of her great-aunt in later years.

18th June 1893: Kate and Catharine become island owners

A year after his wife's death, Tom Muchall was still living at 'Westove'. When Catharine wrote to William on 18th June 1893, she said: "TM is still with us and likely to remain as far as I can see. He has worked hard to make my vegetable garden a success – and has put in crops in the home garden, a large piece of ground for him to cultivate for he is old and not very strong now." Tom had been twenty years older than Mary, and was in his 70s when Mary died.

Catharine with Kate enjoyed their visits to holiday homes on islands in Stoney Lake, where Catharine's health was better during the summer months than in Lakefield. Consequently Kate bought in the spring of 1893 the island 'Minnewawa', and that was where she and her mother spent part of their summer months in the following years.

Catharine told William: "I so seldom take pen in hand – now at ninety-two the brain gets duller. I have been wonderfully well this last Winter and Spring and Summer thus far – Yesterday I went up with K and Mrs Chamberlin and a pleasant party of relatives to see Kate's island. I did enjoy the wild scenery and the wild ferns and trees and flowers upon the island and the small house and its simple furnishings promise a delightful retreat – K rather expects to let it for some weeks during the hot season to secure interest on the outlay she made in purchasing the property.

"The island is about three acres in extent and there are some beautiful Oaks and pines growing upon it; how these fine trees escaped the greed of the lumberers I cannot tell – I was delighted with the luxuriance of the vegetation and the wild picturesque outline of the rocky mounts, and deep valleys. The little dwelling consists of a sitting room and two double-bunked bed-rooms; a small pantry and cupboard; shelves everywhere, and a cooking-house and stove."

The final, but perhaps the most important item of Catharine's letter to William, was to tell him that in addition to the island which Kate had bought, Catharine herself had been given an island of her own. She wrote: "My Dear Will, at last I may tell you that I am to be the dignified possessor of a few feet of Canadian freehold for the most liberal grant of Polly Cows Island has been granted to me as a reward for my literary services to the Domn of Canada." It is said that Catharine had wanted to own this particular island because it contained the grave of a young Indian girl, and she wanted to ensure the grave was left undisturbed.

Catharine continued: "I got a kind note from my friend Sandford Fleming – to whom I wrote asking him to put my petition for two small islands – near the Locks to be given to me – and he instantly went to the Head of Indian Affairs and obtained the promise of Polly Cows." Sandford Fleming was a Scottish-born Canadian railway engineer, and had been prominent among the young scientists and engineers who founded the Canadian Institute in Toronto in 1849. He retired from being Pacific engineer-in-chief in 1880 but continued to be a director of the Canadian Pacific Railway Company, as well as being a director of the Hudson's Bay Company. Following his retirement, Sandford Fleming worked hard for a number of public causes, although he never stood for public office. From 1880 until his death in 1915 he was chancellor of Queen's University in Kingston, Ontario.

Catharine in describing her island to William wrote: "It is a rock and not as much as half an acre in extent – The larger island is an Indian reserve but I can buy it for $25 – I think it mean if the price is not paid for it by the Ind Affairs manager but I had long set my heart on Polly Cow and now it is mine – The islands at the entrance of the Locks may in course of a few years become of more value. I will try to secure the bigger one by paying the tax upon it for next year. It is a lovely spot of trees and shrubs and founded upon a rock! We will make a call upon my island and take possession in the CP-T name." Catharine generally referred to herself, and always signed her name as Catharine Parr Traill. She summed up her feelings by saying to William: "You see dear I ought to be as happy as a Queen with my little kingdom to reign over."

Late September 1893: Catharine attends the local harvest festival

In a letter to William dated 6th October 1893 Catharine told how she was persuaded to go to a meeting in Lakefield. She wrote: "We had a great gathering last Thursday in the town hall and the

Lakefield English church. The harvest home was the occasion and everything was bright and beautiful. I was specially asked to attend and I did and was given a warm greeting by known and unknown friends – I was also at the Service in the evening but terribly tired and too deaf to hear a word but still it was good to be there and many were glad to see the old lady able to be seen among them again which has not happened now for several years."

6<u>th</u> October 1893: Catharine outlines her Will

Catharine took the opportunity when writing to William in October 1893, to outline to him the contents of her Will. She could do this because, she told him, she "had a quiet time for your sister K, the other K as they used to call Katie, and the little maid Minnie are all off today to Peterborough."

Catharine wrote: "I want to tell you that when in Peterboro – I left my deeds and my will such as it is with Mr J Burnham. In this when I am gone to my better home you will find that my sole means only amounted to four thousand dollars – all invested in small mortgages mostly int. 6 per cent – Of this I leave one thousand to your dear children or to you as their trustee. This with the deed of the little island in the Katchewanook Lake, and the big Bible, and two other books, is all I leave to you my ever dear son – The rest of the moneys are divided among the family. I had no power over the 'Westove' lot and house – it had been deeded to your sisters when I bought the little spot I have only a life interest you know."

Here Catharine was referring to the indenture, whereby Samuel Strickland, his son Robert and their wives, had given the property to Catharine's three daughters but "subject to the life estate therein of Catharine Parr Traill." This strategy ensured that the property could not be seized by any creditors of Thomas or Catharine.

Catharine continued: "It grieved me I had nothing to leave to your dear brother – not a single ornament for any of my dear grandchildren but none was left me by my sisters – The gold wedding ring is the only article of gold I own – that has never left my finger for sixty two years past."

The phrase 'but none was left me by my sisters' seems not only ungrateful but untrue. Agnes and Sarah had given Catharine a great deal over the years – money mainly from Sarah, boxes of clothing and material mainly from Agnes, and a first edition of each book she published from Agnes. These books alone, particularly if signed or kept with a signed letter from Agnes, would have provided numerous, worthwhile and valuable mementoes for Catharine to have passed on to other members of her family. In addition, Catharine had selected a gold cross from items of jewellery left by Agnes and sent to Canada, and both Agnes and Sarah had done their best to provide for Catharine in their Wills. When the contents of Reydon Hall were sold, Sarah said she would bid for items to be sent as keepsakes to Canada, but that everything was in such poor condition that she was puzzled as to what to select. In any case, it was surely Catharine's own responsibility, not her sisters, to ensure there were mementoes to pass on to her descendents, if that was what she wanted to do.

Kate also seemed to be spending for her mother's benefit, the money which her aunts had left to provide for her own future needs. Catharine told William that he would see: "how hard it was to make ends meet without the help that dear Kate has been obliged to give to keep ourselves free of debt – The money left to her you know she invested in building the house on the lot bought from Maury – the rent indeed has been expended by her in many things that came unexpectedly upon her, drains to the building – sheds – fences &c – Then she took upon her the needful repairs here, and adding a new woodshed, and kitchen and other things; painting &c to this house – I cannot tell you for I do not know what she did for the sick sister – Nor could these things be done without personal privation and taking from the capital which is not a large sum, as you know." This leaves the impression, possibly unjustly, that Catharine simply drifted through life in a financially thoughtless way, trusting on other people to come to her aid, which they always did.

6th December 1893: Catharine remembers Agnes and a poem

Catharine wrote to Katie Vickers on 6th December 1893, and in this letter quoted a poem that Agnes had written. Catharine wrote: "I often think of those sad lines written by your dear (to me ever dear) Aunt Agnes:

'O who would recall life's visions if they
Might recall with the roses the thorns of the day.
Or who for its brightest possessions now flown
The troubles and cares of the years they have known'."

Catharine continued: "I have not written those lines quite right but you will know her mind at the time she wrote, for she was then young and you know dear, youth has its heart sorrows, as well as those of riper years. Of all my dear sisters Agnes was to me the very dearest and best. She loved me dearly, and I almost idolized her."

The lines Catharine was recalling were from the poem 'The Close of the Year' which was included in 'Historic Scenes and Poetic Fancies' published in London by Henry Colburn in 1850, much of which had been previously published. The full poem has ten verses of four lines. The correct version of the lines that Catharine knew she had slightly mis-remembered, several decades after they had been written and published, is:

'Oh, who would retrace life's best journey, if they
Must recall with the roses the thorns of their way,
The pangs they have suffered, the cares they have known,
In the troubled review of the years that are flown?'

2nd May 1894: Catharine is still studying flowers and writing

In her letter written to William dated 2nd May 1894 Catharine explained that Kate had not written to William recently because of lack of time. Catharine wrote: "Her hands are always busy – for the old mother does nothing only just sewing and pottering in the garden drying her wild flowers writing scraps about them and doing little good to anyone."

30th September 1894: Susanna's daughters are looking after their mother's papers

In a letter dated 30th September 1894 in reply to a request for photographs of herself and her sisters, Catharine wrote: "I regret to say that I have no photo in hand of myself nor of my sisters, with the exception of those in the Queens of England of my sister Agnes. Of Agnes Strickland's letters I possess a few. I lost all her letters in the fire that left us homeless for a while and I could not part with the few letters I possess."

This may not have been entirely true, more a means of dealing with an unreasonable request, but Catharine showed that she was not the only family member treasuring the family memory when she continued: "Any information of the dear sister Mrs Moodie and the Sheriff can only be gained through her daughters, Mrs Vickers and Mrs Colonel Chamberlin. Mrs V is in possession of all her mother's papers &c – and she will not allow any one to interfere with them."

1889-1896: Strickland descendents cluster in Lakefield

Lakefield continued to be home to numerous descendents of Sam, Catharine, Susanna and Tom Strickland. As well as Catharine's family, Sam's descendents and the family of Tom's daughter Adela Wigg, some of Susanna's descendents also moved to Lakefield in the 1890s.

Susanna's widowed granddaughter, Alice Dunn having moved by 1889 to Lakefield with her two sons, Gwillym and Charlie Dunn, she remained there until the summer of 1896. She is said to have rented the house built by Kate Traill on the plot adjoining 'Westove'. Agnes Fitzgibbon Chamberlin sometimes came from Ottawa to visit her daughter, and by the spring of 1895 had a house near 'Westove'.

29th October 1894: Catharine's book 'Pearls and Pebbles' needs subscribers

After Sarah died, Maime Fitzgibbon returned to Canada and resumed her career as an author. In 1894 she had a book published in Toronto by the Methodist Book and Publishing House, which had recently begun publishing secular books under the guidance of William Briggs.

Catharine had long been at work on her manuscript which she called 'Notes for Young Naturalists' and by 1894 it was ready to be sent to a publisher. Maime encouraged Catharine to send her manuscript to William Briggs, and the work was developed into a book which had the title 'Pearls and Pebbles'.

The book began with a biographical sketch extending over 30 pages and written by Maime Fitzgibbon. Much of it covered the same ground as Catharine's own notes, but some additional and personal information came from Jenny, who had known Catharine in the 1830s and whose dying child Catharine had helped nurse. Jenny described Catharine when she arrived in Canada as: "sic a bonnie leddy, wi' her pink cheeks an' her blue e'en, an' she was sae lovin' and dear."

It was agreed that the book would be sold at a price of $1.00 and that Catharine would be paid the standard royalty of 10% of the published price. However, the deal was on the proviso that before publication, signatures would be obtained for at least 200 subscribed copies.

In a letter to Ellen Dunlop dated 29th October 1894, Catharine reported on the progress of her list of subscribers, which Ellen was helping to increase. Catharine wrote: "I knew that my kind friends in Peterborough would not fail but without your help I should never have asked anyone beyond yourself or dear Charles to subscribe for a copy. My kind Editor has a good list for the book, and Miss Fitzgibbon also, and Mrs Band sent me five names before I had named this book to her, that was very nice to begin with – And I know my Ottawa friend is at work – Mr Mills also from Guelph – I have names also from Toronto and hope in time to get the number required by Mr Briggs."

She continued: "Our kind parson brought one of the great church guns to call on me, Canon Logan, who asked me some questions – but did not ask me to put his name down. Mr Warren kindly did however – for 2 copies for himself."

March 1895: Catharine's book is a success

Catharine's book, whose full title was 'Pearls and Pebbles; or, Notes of an Old Naturalist, with Biographical Sketch' was published in December 1894 and was very successful. Over 750 copies had been sold by the end of March 1895 and a second edition was planned. It consisted mainly of short stories and anecdotes relating to the flora and fauna of Canada, interspersed with short pieces of poetry including one or two by Susanna and a full length poem mourning the death of a young child by Agnes.

It also contained a full length poem by Catharine in which she commemorates the graves of the early settlers who had to bury their dead near their own isolated homesteads, the graves being marked by some simple means such as: "a rough rail enclosure, a surface stone to mark where lay the sleeper, or a cross of wood, or a name rudely cut upon the living bark of some adjacent tree" but with the passage of time: "The lands have passed away from the families of the first breakers of the soil, and the peaceful dead are neglected in their lonely, unmarked resting-places, forgotten by man, but not uncared for by the Redeeming Love."

Catharine's poem of ten verses is entitled 'The Graves of the Emigrants' and compares the graveyards of England to the resting places of early emigrants. The first, fifth and last verses are as follows:

"They sleep not where their fathers sleep,
   In the village churchyard's bound;
They rest not 'neath the ivied wall
   That shades that holy ground;
...

Where, then, may rest those hardy sons
   Who left their native shore
To seek a home in distant lands
   Beyond the Atlantic's roar?
...

Where moss-grown stone or simple cross
   His silent record keeps,
There, deep within the forest shade,
   The lonely exile sleeps."

Maime Fitzgibbon sent two dozen copies of 'Pearls and Pebbles' to various people in London and Southwold. As a result, a London bookseller and publisher (Sampson Low, Marston and Company) is said to have requested 250 copies for sale in England.

Favourable reviews appeared in Canada, in England, and also in the United States, and some of the reviews were written by leading figures of their time. Principal George Grant of Queens' University is said to have written that he had read the works of Agnes Strickland and Mrs Moodie, but had been unaware that they had a sister "equal to themselves in literary power." He praised her ability to combine a "keen eye and trained powers of observation" with "fine poetic feeling and an intense appreciation of all that is beautiful and good."

Professor Goldwin Smith, an honorary professor at Cornell University and a former professor at Oxford University, had moved to Toronto in 1871 where he edited the 'Canadian Monthly'. He wrote a lengthy article, purportedly a review of 'Pearls and Pebbles' for the 'Illustrated London News' in late March 1895, but the article was also a general interest article about Canada, which he wove around his review.

In the part of the article most relevant to 'Pearls and Pebbles', Professor Godwin Smith wrote: "This book is a pleasant record of a very long life – passed in what the writer calls the backwoods of Canada. Backwoods they were when she came to them, but the peopled district of Ontario, with its smiling villages and homesteads, might now regard the name as an affront. Her delight has been the observation of nature, the fruits of which, gathered into this volume, form a sort of Canadian counterpart to White's 'Selborne'."

He continued: "Traill has seen changes. Looking to her diary of 1839, she finds notes of things that struck her in the first years of her sojourn in her forest home, but which now she seldom or never sees. Many of the plants and birds and wild creatures, once common, have disappeared before the march of civilisation. Her memory probably reaches back almost to the days when bears were seen in the neighbourhood of the populous and wealthy capital of Ontario, where you would now be as likely to see a mastodon. It certainly reaches back to the time when the air was annually darkened by migratory flocks of wild pigeons, which have now totally disappeared.

"In Ontario, where Mrs Traill writes, the year is made up of a hot and rather short summer, which ripens the paragons of apples; a beautiful autumn, with beautiful sunsets; a long and somewhat grim winter; and a spring which is not so much a season as a sudden break-up of winter. The district in which Mrs Traill lives around Lakefield has some pretty lake scenery. Still more has Muskoka, the summer resort of wealthy Torontians, who dot the shore and islands of its lake with cottages in which they enjoy a relief from business and civilisation.

"Mrs Traill expatiates with delight on the wild flowers. To the birds Mrs Traill has paid special attention. Besides her natural history and her pictures of scenery Mrs Traill has some interesting recollections of settler life. These reminiscences are growing scarce, and should be gathered before they fade."

December 1895: Catharine's 'Cot and Cradle Stories' is published

Following the success of 'Pearls and Pebbles', a fourth edition of 'Canadian Wild Flowers' by Agnes Fitzgibbon Chamberlin and Catharine Parr Traill was brought out by William Briggs in 1895. It was an edition limited to 500 copies of which 100 were numbered, dated and signed by Agnes Chamberlin, with the location Lakefield, Ontario also inscribed.

'Pearls and Pebbles' having been successful, the Methodist Book Publishing Company was willing to publish another book by Catharine, taking the whole risk on themselves and giving her 10% per copy of sales without having an initial list of subscribers. This next book, entitled 'Cot and Cradle Stories' again had Maime Fitzgibbon's involvement as editor, and was published at the end of 1895. It was not as popular as 'Pearls and Pebbles' possibly because 'Pearls and Pebbles', despite Catharine thinking of it as a book written to encourage in children a love of nature, was written in a style which was also suitable for adult reading whereas 'Cot and Cradle Stories' had the air of being a series of stories for parents to read to young children.

However, amongst the purely fictional tales about small animals in 'Cot and Cradle Stories', there are a couple of seemingly autobiographical stories. One of these described how five of the sisters asked their father to give them a piece of land to share and to cultivate outside the territory governed by the gardener. This he did, and Catharine described the gardens of the five sisters, who ranged from Agnes aged ten, down to Susanna aged three. Sam would have been too young to have had a garden and Tom would not have been born. There was no mention of twelve year old Elizabeth.

Following this story is an Editor's Note in which Maime Fitzgibbon paired the approach to gardening with the future lives of each of the sisters. Maime had from childhood known Catharine and Susanna, and she had lived with Jane and Sarah in their old age. The only one of the five sisters she had not known was Agnes. Robert Strickland was the only person who might have been in a better position to have commented on the sisters, but he may in conversations have helped Maime form her views. A shortened version of the Editor's Note is as follows.

Catharine described Agnes as laying out her garden in a methodical and intricate way which involved compasses and pieces of string to get circular beds and pathways. Maime wrote: "Agnes revealed her character in the methodical plan of her garden. Authoress of the Royal biographies, many poems, historical tales and several novels, she accomplished an enormous amount of work, writing her 'Lives of the Queens of Scotland' only a few chapters ahead of the printers, while at the same time fulfilling numerous social engagements, keeping up a large private correspondence, and accomplishing some of the finest and most laborious fancy work. Her systematic way of arranging her time enabled her to do much more and better work than she otherwise could have done."

Sarah had grown her plants in neat rows, and her plants were mainly aromatic herbs such as sage, lavender and lemon-thyme which the gardener praised and told her she would be a good housewife one day. Maime wrote: "The old gardener's prophecy ... was a true one ... She was the housekeeper of the family, and married the vicar of a large parish in the north of England, a rich man, who entertained a good deal – both his friends and the poor of his parish – and Sara was indeed 'a rare good housewife to a good husband'."

Catharine described Jane's garden as full of brightly coloured plants but with no pattern, mixing currant bushes with hollyhock with cowslips, adding more plants wherever there was room. Maime wrote: "Jane's garden, was also in a curious way an index of her life. She wrote many things on many subjects, her gamut ranging all the way from witty squibs to erudite histories and religious tracts. Her store of knowledge, apparently inexhaustible, was yet a kaleidoscopic collection of valuable material. Her love of colour was without artistic arrangement, but grand in its almost barbaric defiance of the rules of art."

Catharine, aged four, had tried to grow flowers by cutting daisy flowers and planting their stalks into the ground. When the daisies wilted and died she got disheartened and abandoned her effort. Jane teased her about it while Agnes and Sarah also laughed, but Agnes then consoled her young sister, tidied up the patch and helped her by planting fast-growing radishes and cress. Maime wrote: "In her choice of the buttercups and daisies ... she foreshadowed her love for the wild-flowers and ferns, and the valuable work she has done in bringing our Canadian flora to the knowledge of the world. All through life she has gathered gifts of her Heavenly Father ... and when the hot noonday sun of sorrow and sadness faded them, she has but turned again to the garden of her trust to replace them. She has owed much to the kindly help and sympathy of others, and has been ever as grateful as she was to Agnes when she sowed the useful mustard and cress in the garden under the wall."

Three year old Susanna dug a hole in her bit of garden, helped by Catharine. When asked why by their father, she said she was digging for gold and silver and other treasure, and kept on digging despite being told that she had mixed up the source of minerals with manufactured articles. Maime's comment about Susanna gives a different picture of her from that which seems to have emerged from this current work. Maime, writing about one of her own grandmothers, said: "Susie, who was possessed of the greatest of all gifts, the priceless gift of true genius, was ever questioning the reason of things, ever digging deep into the well of knowledge of life, ever seeking for the treasure of truth, and finding it in increasing beauty and wealth in the Book of Life. Generous, enthusiastic, a brilliant conversationalist, a true poet, and a graphic writer, Canadian literature owes much to her influence and her pen."

Elizabeth's absence from both the story and the assessment, seems a fitting reflection of her life.

5th January 1896: Catharine is interviewed

Book promotion brought about an interview with Faith Fenton, who visited Catharine early in 1896. Faith Fenton was a journalist and Canada's first female columnist, whose real name was Alice Freeman. Initially she had needed dual identity because journalism was thought a disreputable means for a woman to earn a living, and she was also a school-teacher, needing both jobs to maintain herself. In 1888 she had begun to write a women's column for 'The Toronto Empire' and as a result interviewed famous people, of whom Catharine was one. She had revealed her identity and become a full-time journalist in 1894.

Despite acknowledging a request from one of Catharine's grand-daughters that Catharine should not be described as "a wonderful old lady – Everyone does and we get so tired of it," Faith Fenton wrote "Yet there is no other phrase so true." Her article appeared in the 'Canadian Home Journal' in January 1896, and is said to have offered a warm and sentimental portrait, but also developed the theme that Catharine had to be regarded as a remarkable person for more than her longevity.

Catharine approved of the article, and in her letter to Ellen Dunlop dated 18th February 1896 wrote: "It was just a few days before my birthday that I had a nice visit from Faith Fenton and she sent me a copy of the Ladies Home Journal and the best memoir of my early life that has yet appeared."

20th September 1896: Catharine loses another grand-child

It was planned that on 21st September 1896, Catharine was to be taken to Peterborough to be introduced to Lady Marjorie Aberdeen, wife of the Governor-General of Canada from 1893 to 1898, who wanted permission to reprint some of Catharine's 'Cot and Cradle Stories' in a British publication for children called 'Wee Willie Winkie'.

The timing of the arranged meeting was unfortunate. Catharine's grand-daughter, Caroline Muchall was in very poor and declining health, and had been nursed and cared for at 'Westove' since early in 1896. The nursing and caring was shared between Kate and Katie Traill and by Evelyne Muchall, Caroline's sister. Despite their best efforts, Caroline Muchall died on 20th September 1896, the day before Catharine's intended meeting with Lady Marjorie Aberdeen which, of course, was cancelled.

When Catharine wrote to Ellen Dunlop on 23rd September 1896, she wrote sadly: "Now the last duty remains to lay her body to rest beside her dear Mother and brother. Mr Muchall arrived this morning by early train. I think Eva will go back to Coburg for a while with him – Dear Percy always comes to our aid in taking the funeral arrangements for us – It is so hard for women to attend and order these matters."

Of herself Catharine wrote: "I am good for nothing now in any way. My deafness tries me greatly – I seem to be shut out from knowing anything that is going on. Dear friends have been very sympathizing – especially dear Mrs Chamberlin – who is far from well herself."

30th October 1896: Catharine's writing is for the young

Throughout her life, much of Catharine's writing was aimed at children, and her later works were no exception. In a letter dated 30th October 1896, in reply to a complimentary letter from a stranger, Catharine wrote: "My last production is but a juvenile volume just one for 'Cot & Cradle'. It is simply a book of stories for the little ones – Some of the stories were written last summer while staying on a wild rocky island on Stony Lake – Of course it is but a simple book suited for simple folk – My role in writing has ever been for the young. I rarely aspire to any higher style." She hoped to inspire in children the love of nature which she herself felt.

Catharine had written a follow-up to her earlier work 'The Backwoods of Canada', which was in part a more thorough account of her emigration and in part a sequel. It was given the title 'Seven Years of My Life under the Pines' and there was talk of publishing it to follow on from 'Cot and Cradle Stories' but this did not happen and the book was not published.

December 1896: Catharine becomes an Honorary President

Catharine, in a letter to Annie Atwood dated 14th December 1896, described an honour paid to her in Peterborough. She wrote: "Last Monday Hampden Burnham came as a delegate from Col. Rogers and a committee of Gentn. to invite me to the Council Hall – and to accept my nomination as Honorary President of the Peterborough Historical Society, and so pressing was the demand for my presence, that though far from well I was induced to accompany Mrs Dunlop to the meeting.

"The President made a speech and said a great deal to my honour and glory with thanks for my presence at the meeting – Then I had in a few words to say 'Ta-Ta' and with Mrs D as vice- went home tired, feeling Grand – on the occasion, all the better pleased that I am not obliged to do or say or write anything – beyond my name in a big book.

"The same evening I was interviewed by a dear little school pupil who made a nice speech to me really beautifully worded to express his admiration of my writings and to give me a most judicious critique on my books 'Pearls & Pebbles' and 'Cot & Cradle' stories." Catharine added: "The child's approval was more to me than all the writers in the newspapers for it was genuine."

In 1896, as well as being made honorary president of the Peterborough Historical Society, Catharine is said to have been made an honorary member of the Canadian Women's Historical Society of Toronto.

20th February 1897: Catharine treasures two old pennies

Although she no longer had any relatives with literary experience in England, Catharine had in London a new helper and supporter. This was Emma Hubbard, a cousin of Clinton Atwood, who shared Catharine's love of nature. Emma Hubbard was an artist and wrote articles for the journal 'Nature'. Catharine had written a book entitled 'Sketchbook of a Young Naturalist' which had first been published in 1827. It was noticed that a London publisher used excerpts from it in a publication named the 'Sunday Magazine', and Emma worked on Catharine's behalf to get payment for use of the work.

In a letter to Emma Hubbard dated 20th February 1897, Catharine wrote: "I thank you gratefully dear Mrs Hubbard for your kind exertions. I am very glad of the cheque from young Mr Darton indeed Clinton got it cashed at the Montreal Bank in Peterborough.

"The difference in currency gave me $7.25cts beside two old English pennies which coins I had not seen for sixty years. The sight of the old coins so pleased me that I gave my dear Gson George Traill one, and treasured the other for a lucky penny, not to be idly spent – a relic for the love of the dear old country taking me back to the childish days when a penny was riches barley-sugar kisses, a luxury, and the pennies worth to be made a feast to share with Susie or the young brothers, all my juniors – In those days we earned our money by garden work – and the fruits of it I think were all the sweeter."

May 1897: Catharine donates her collection

Catharine is said to have attended the May 1897 meeting of the Peterborough Historical Society in order to present to the museum a collection of Indian relics that she had received over the years from her "Hiawatha friends", and a statement which she had written was read to the meeting.

Her statement showed that she had had friends among the people of Hiawatha for many years, and that she was interested in, and treasured the artefacts of their culture. Catharine is said to have written: "The flint weapons, spear-heads, arrows, bones and pottery, were a free gift to me from my esteemed friend Mrs M Jane Loucks, of Hiawatha, with the very interesting pamphlet (accompanying the collection) which was, with the relics, left to her by an aged native missionary from Minnesota, US ... My Indian friend told me that the aged man was in a very weak state, and died some time after he visited Hiawatha." Catharine signed the statement your "honorary president and friend – CP Traill."

May 1897: Catharine goes prospecting

Although Catharine had been concerned when there was the possibility of a railway line running in front of her home, she does not seem to have objected to the building work on the river which created a canal system and locks.

The noise disturbed her, but was born philosophically, and the work itself resulted in Catharine being able to hunt for specimens of geological interest on her own doorstep. In May 1897 in a letter to Ellen Dunlop, Catharine wrote: "opposite to my own garden the Canal men have laid stones till they have almost blocked up the carriage road. All the grass is covered with the broken rock – In fact we have a great rockwork – at our own door I go out and prospect for the Museum – staff in hand."

June 1897: Catharine applies to the Royal Literary Fund

Emma Hubbard was instrumental in obtaining money for Catharine from the Royal Literary Fund, the organisation which had sent £60 to Susanna in 1865. When Mrs Hubbard wrote to the Royal Literary Fund on 30th May 1897 she explained: "Joseph Darton had made extracts from his late serial 'Sunday' and sent me 30/-" (£1.50) "for Mrs Traill in acknowledgement of the passages he had selected. When Mrs Traill wrote to tell me this had reached her I was grieved to find how much was thought of even this small sum; and I have since felt very anxious that her income should in some way be supplemented."

She told the fund that Catharine was also a naturalist of note: "and one fern Aspidium Marginale has a 'var: Trailliae' named after her" and to strengthen her own credentials, Mrs Hubbard added: "For myself, although I am a stranger, yet probably ... the name of my brother Sir John Evans – President of the RS, is not unknown to you." Sir John Evans was President of a number of learned societies in the last quarter of the 19th century and was Treasurer of the Royal Society for twenty years. The letters RS presumably referred to the Royal Society.

In June 1897, Catharine wrote to the Secretary of the fund, wishing to make some points for him to pass on to the committee in addition to those that she had already made in answer to their questionnaire. Her main point was: "I state this fact, that though I am held in much esteem, for my literary work, I derive no income from any one of my publications in England, and in Canada only a small royalty on my last two books – Copies of which I send for the approval of your honorable and liberal society – and as vouchers for my character, and good faith, I have placed in the hands of my valued friend Mrs Hubbard – letters from persons of high standing and worth to whom I am personally known, and to whose testimony I can add many others if required to aid my cause." She added: "The aged authoress now fast advancing to her ninety sixth year claims to be the oldest English female writer now living and still writing."

Catharine's application was successful and she was given £150 in recognition of her need and her literary attainments. She sent a signed receipt to the Royal Literary Fund on the 17th June 1897 for £150, addressed from the home of Agnes Fitzgibbon Chamberlin at 'The Den', Lakefield, Ontario. When she wrote to Ellen Dunlop on the 12th August 1897 Catharine told Ellen: "I have laid it by as a fund that will be needed."

August 1897: Queen Victoria has read Catharine's letter

Other news in her letter to Ellen Dunlop showed that Catharine was still writing with style. She said: "Now within the last week I have had much pleasure through a letter from my valued friend Mr Edward Roper. After the great day of the Queen's Jubilee he sent me a very sweet photo likeness of her majesty – I received it just the time I was stepping into Sunbeam – very feeble and very lame – After we got settled at the island I wrote a long letter to Mr E Roper and gave him some account of the doings of the jubilee day and the doings at the dedication of the PHA" (Peterborough Historical Association) "which I knew would interest him – How the letter was written I cannot now say I forgot all about it but it had pleased him so much that he actually sent it to the dear Queen to read – And he says 'She did read it!' –

"and he received a reply of thanks and approval from the good Queen by the Secretary Sir Fleetwood Edwards expressing her thanks, and saying it was a wonderful letter from a person of ninety six years – She actually condescended to read this (as I fear very imperfect) letter herself. I had indeed wished to write to the good Queen myself but thought it would have been an act of presumption when millions were addressing her, my few words would never have met her eye or ear – So I did not. It was very good of Mr Roper to think of sending my letter to the dear Queen – and of her to notice it."

June 1898: Catharine loses her investments

Catharine's financial history contained a series of unlucky events, the last of which came in 1898 when her financial situation was again undermined, this time by the mismanagement of her investments, and those of others, by her agent in Peterborough, Mr John Burnham.

Catharine had invested $2,400, her inheritance from Sarah, with John Burnham in December 1890, hoping that it would yield her an annual return of $240. She had invested money with him before and by 1893, as she had told William, her total investment was $4,000 and all was with John Burnham. The only other money that Catharine possessed was the £150 which she had been given from the Royal Literary Fund the previous year which, fortunately, she had deposited in a local bank.

In a letter to Sir Sandford Fleming dated 2nd June 1898, John Lowe wrote that "nearly the whole Strickland family have also been stripped of their funds by trust in Mr Burnham, so they cannot personally do for Mrs Traill what they otherwise would have done." John Lowe was a brother-in-law of Agnes Fitzgibbon Chamberlin's husband, and the two men had once had a publishing business together.

Knowing of Catharine's need and being unable to help her directly, Mrs George Strickland and her daughter Mary also took action. They explained the situation to the former Governor General of Canada, Lord Lansdowne, whom they knew, and asked if Catharine might be put on the Civil List in recognition of her service to the Empire. Lord Lansdowne replied that a Civil List pension was not possible, but that he would arrange for a grant of £150 from the Royal Bounty Fund, on the condition that a fund for Mrs Traill "small or great" be subscribed to in the Dominion.

When Catharine wrote to Emma Hubbard a letter dated 28th June 1898, she knew that the request for a pension had been rejected, she wrote: "I think our dear Queen owes the old lady a pension – Well at ninety and seven – I merit her good will." On the other hand, Catharine wrote: "I cannot be too grateful for the gift of last year from the RL Association – but for that unlooked for timely aid – We should have felt the present loss in my yearly income severely – and that has been a great fund to rely on."

Catharine knew she would not receive a pension, but did not know of the possibility of a grant, conditional on a fund being raised by subscription, because George Strickland's daughter Mary and Agnes Fitzgibbon Chamberlin had set about organizing it without telling her. They produced a 'Confidential Circular' which consisted of a letter of tribute to Catharine, an outline of her financial difficulties, and an explanation of why a testimonial fund was needed.

June 1898: Catharine continues her botanical studies

Catharine in her letter to Emma Hubbard in June 1898 showed her continuing interest in, and knowledge of things botanical. She wrote: "I have just been in the wild garden and gleaned a few seeds which I send with this envelope thinking you might like to scatter them in your lovely garden or grove – They are among my favourite Canadian wild flowers though not the finest – The Red Columbine is an early flower, I am not sure the seedlings will give you any flowers until the second year's growth – The violets may – The yellow is Bryants flower.

"The Wild Ginger (asarabacca) is a curious plant – gives only one brown woolly bell flower – in May the root is aromatic. Our Fairy Fern Adiantum pedatum would live if I sent it in a tin case – only I fear to inflict postage on you – and am very stupid now at packing &c – My dear Grand-daughter – Katie Traill – is my great help in all little difficulties – she always seems to know the right thing to do."

Having dealt with botanical matters, Catharine alluded to the financial problems surrounding her, and the effect they were having on her. She told Emma: "I have lost much of my skill and knowledge – the late trouble pressed upon the aged head though it does not fret me – for I have lived through far greater trials than this – and strength was always given to me when it was needed – 'God is very

Good'." As far as the details of the financial crisis were concerned, Catharine wrote: "As yet I know very little how the business is to be settled not without much loss – that I know must be so I make myself contented to bear it."

Financial problems aside, Catharine was looking forward to visiting the family islands on Stoney Lake. She told Emma Hubbard: "We are soon thinking of spending a week or more at the island cottage – The fresh pure air and lake scenery always renovates me. The rocky island lies high up and I love the air of the pines." Catharine with Kate and Katie would be staying on Kate's island of Minnewawa, and there would be friends and family on nearby islands "– and" Catharine wrote "my Katie rows our skiff fearlessly – so that we never feel lonely. I fear I shall not be able to get along the rocks as well as I have done even with the aid of my good red cherry stick – I am more feeble than I was last year I must be less venturesome – and take the air lying on a couch on the veranda."

December 1898: Catharine receives her testimonial fund and grant

Through the efforts of Mary Strickland and Agnes Fitzgibbon Chamberlin, a testimonial fund of $1,000 was raised for Catharine. Lady Aberdeen led the list with a $50 contribution and the testimonial is said to contain the signatures of Canada's most influential men of science and literature, publishers and editors, friends, family and admirers. The fund was completed and the grant of £150 duly received from the Royal Bounty Fund by Christmas 1898. Catharine wrote a letter of thanks to Sir Sandford Fleming which was initialled as received in Ottawa on 28th December 1898.

Catharine wrote: "Your precious letter reached me last night by the kind hands of our pastor Mr Warren. You can hardly think how welcome it proved and surprize at the greatness of the donation was only equalled by the gratification of the manner and words that accompanied the Gift. How can I thank all the kindness of the generous givers of this large sum of money awarded to the aged Authoress – It does seem too great for such small service as has been given – Yet indeed, I feel happy in the assurance that in my small way I have served my beloved Sovereign's noble Dominion of Canada."

Catharine continued: "And in what words dearest Friend shall I thank you, and all my known and unknown friends in England and Ontario. I can only adopt the simple phrase used by the Indian women of the Hiawatha village – 'I bless you in my heart'."

Care had been taken to ensure that the money had been deposited somewhere which was both safe and accessible to Catharine. She told Sir Sandford Fleming: "It was so thoughtful to place the thousand dollars – at once to my credit in the P- Montreal Bank. I cannot add more at this time. Pray excuse the writing and all errors."

January 1899: Catharine is recuperating

Catharine had written her thanks to Sir Sandford Fleming even though she was ill in bed with a bad cough and cold. On 1st January 1899, just a few days before her 98th birthday, she wrote to Ellen Dunlop and told her: "When out of my bed my head has been so sadly confused that I could not think or plan anything. I hope that as the New Year has brought some improved state, I may enjoy some increase of strength of mind and body for a little while longer."

Catharine was still interested in local events but left Kate to pass on news of that kind. Catharine told Ellen: "The river is all frozen over – and the great Dredger is away – but we hear that the canal work is beginning next week close to the mill so we may look out for shocks soon – Kate will tell you when she is down all about the affair."

April 1899: Catharine has been ill again

Catharine had another bout of ill health before her next letter to Ellen Dunlop which was written on 24th April 1899: "I have been improving now for some days though still not able to walk alone – Still not suffering the severe pains in my feet, only the lameness & hot swelling. I believe it is gout. I put my clothes on about 12, and get drawn to the parlour, and again on the veranda to lie for some time on the couch in the air, and sun-bath – I can do nothing – but read and sew my patches – that is all!"

However, Catharine hoped to get to Stoney Lake in the summer. She told Ellen: "I hope I may get stronger before the time comes for the island and then I should enjoy the pure air of the lake – It has been a sad tax on my dear Kates – this long state of helplessness – but they do all for me that is possible and I have great cause for thankfulness to my merciful Father. The work on the canal gets daily now nearer – As yet I have borne the shocks very well but soon they will be closer as the diggers are at work on this side the red mill."

Catharine also gave family news "Mrs Douglas Moodie with her husband and two sons came last week and are to be installed at the Den, Mrs Chamberlin with them. We shall be glad for they are nice company for us all and pleasant neighbours."

June 1899: Catharine has another book ready for a publisher

On 1st June 1899 Catharine managed to write to Emma Hubbard after a couple of failed attempts in April and in May. Of her own health and life Catharine wrote: "I have been slowly recovering from a long state of bodily pain and still am but a poor cripple unable to walk alone even from room to room without the use of a stout staff – and the kind arm of my dear daughter or grand-daughter the last a ready help when free from school." Katie was a governess or teacher.

Catharine continued: "Yesterday Katie drew me into the village seated in state on a large wheeled chair the loan of one of my dear relatives – I had not been out of doors unless lying on a couch for four months with the exception of one aftn when Mrs Tate sent her light carriage for me to take a drive – but it proved too much for me then – It is gout – old English gout. Thanks be to the dear Lord, I am now only suffering with the swelling of the toes in a lesser degree.

"I am now able to dress myself and rise about 12 o'clock, and then seated on the rocking chair I am drawn into the sitting room or dining room or to rest on a couch on the veranda – twice I have walked with help some yards beyond on the grass in the grove where I can see the workers beyond on the canal – but I may not make too free of my returning health for I get a pull back and the heart gets troubled."

Catharine then mentioned a book which Emma Hubbard in England, and Catharine's grand-daughter Florence in Canada, were helping Catharine to produce, with Catharine herself planning to approach a potential publisher. Catharine wrote: "Florence thinks it might be best to send a few pages for your inspection and advice which will give you some idea of the nature of the little work – and I will write a letter myself to Mr Darton to introduce myself as the authoress of certain juvenile works written many years ago and published by the old firm of Darton & Harvey now seventy odd years ago – I will take the liberty of enclosing my letter under care to yourself."

Catharine continued: "I have not been able to write an introduction to this odd book so out of the usual line – only the novelty may prove attractive as in the present day what is out of the way and queer seems to be most valued – I was eighty years old before I wrote the first pages." The book was written for children on the subject of Canadian birds and the intended title was 'Mrs Margery Pie's History of the Birds of Canada'.

July 1899: Catharine visits Fairy Lake Island

Catharine managed to get to 'Fairy Lodge' and wrote to her grand-daughter Katie a letter which was begun on 10th July 1899. The journey to Fairy Lake Island had been difficult for her, and the weather had been chilly and windy for a couple of days with a thunder storm at night. Catharine had been ill for the first day or two of the visit but was beginning to recover. She told Katie: "I began to rally on Saturday a better night and yesterday aftn was fine and with the help of K-'s arm and the good stick I got a few yards up the slope and had a nice time with cushions on the rocks among the lovely grasses and shrubs beneath the pines. Lots of flowers and berries made me quite happy – A quiet time it was."

After visiting Fairy Lake Island, Catharine and Kate seem to have stayed briefly at another cottage on Stony Lake, before going to Kate's island of Minnewawa. There they finished their summer holiday before returning to 'Westove' and Lakefield.

August 1899: Catharine reaches the end

By August 1899 Catharine had learned that 'Mrs Margery Pie's History of the Birds of Canada' had not found a publisher, and

Emma Hubbard had returned the manuscript to her. Catharine was disappointed but not surprised.

In writing to Emma Hubbard on 27th August 1899, Catharine said: "My Dear valued Friend – Your kind letter came by our island post two days ago and yesterday brought back the MS parcel safely – What can I say in return to your loving service on my behalf – not the less precious though it failed – I was fully prepared for the result I know how cautious English publishers are in venturing upon any subject outside the beaten track – I thought the novelty of the idea might have been in its favor but was mistaken."

Catharine added: "I had many misgivings as to the merits of the composition &c – In fact I never see anything good in my writings till they are in print and even then I wonder how that event came to pass." She began a sentence: "When I meet with any commendable passage in my books I pause and question if I wrote it myself – or my editor – I had ..."

At that point Catharine said to Kate: "I am trying to write to dear Mrs Hubbard, but somehow I cannot get on with it." The letter was put away and was never finished, for Catharine died peacefully, aged 97, at 'Westove' two days later, on 29th August. She was buried in Lakefield Cemetery on 31st August 1899.

Part 10: Lasting fame?

Remembered in Canada

In Canada there is still a variety of evidence for the existence of Susanna Moodie, Catharine Parr Traill and Sam Strickland, greater evidence in fact than can be found in England of the family's existence or of Agnes's past fame.

Susanna's book 'Roughing It In the Bush' became a classic in Canadian literature, and both Susanna and Catharine's papers, with other items, have been stored in various Canadian archives.

A plaque in memory of Susanna Moodie was unveiled in Lakefield Memorial Park, Ontario, on 20th October 1966. There are said to be commemorative plaques marking the sites of Catharine's homes 'Wolf Tower' and 'Oaklands' on the Rice Lake Plains, with Catharine also named on a plaque in the Lakefield Memorial Park. Sam's 'Homestead' was said still to exist in 1999 and was then described as the most handsome mansion in Lakefield.

When Trent University in Peterborough Ontario opened in 1964, it named one of its three campuses Catharine Parr Traill College for women. The university opened with 100 students and by 2017 its annual enrolment had grown to almost 9,000 students. With this growth and the passage of time, the main campus names have changed, but Catharine is still commemorated in 'Traill College' which is described as the home base for the academic departments of English, Cultural Studies and Media Studies, together with the School for the Study of Canada. 'Traill College' is described as consisting primarily of a collection of old houses of architectural and historic significance, in a beautiful location near the centre of Peterborough.

The fact that 'Susanna Moodie, Letters of a Lifetime' (1985), and 'I Bless You in My Heart, Selected Correspondence of Catharine Parr Traill' (1996), were compiled by three Canadian academics,

Carl Ballstadt, Elizabeth Hopkins and Michael Peterman and printed by the University of Toronto Press, illustrates the place these two sisters have found in Canadian history. These books also ensure that a great deal of information about Susanna and Catharine remain in the public domain.

To mark the 50th anniversary of the National Library of Canada in 2003, a set of four commemorative stamps was issued, which consisted of two English-Canadian and two French-Canadian stamps. The National Archives of Canada selected Susanna Moodie and Catharine Parr Traill to appear together on one of the English-Canadian stamps, though unfortunately showing portraits of two Strickland sisters painted in England in the 1820s, and wrongly describing Sarah's portrait as a picture of Catharine Parr Traill.

Christ Church, the first small Anglican Church built in Lakefield using funds Sam raised in England in 1851/52, has long been superseded by a larger church on a different site. However, the original church still exists and houses a community museum, outside which is an information board with the heading 'Samuel Strickland 1804-1867'.

Forgotten in Britain

Descendents of the 19th century Suffolk branch of the Strickland family in England were very few, and in Canada were numerous. With the death of Sarah, the last in England of her generation, and the return of Maime Fitzgibbon to Canada, Strickland papers and memorabilia were mainly taken to Canada and became dispersed or destroyed.

However, the name Agnes Strickland was still very widely known in the first half of the 20th century, and in 1932 King George V was curious to see exactly what it was about 'Victoria from her Birth to her Bridal' that had so incensed his grandmother, Queen Victoria. Presumably unable to locate the copy in the Royal Library, he asked to borrow the copy that had been returned to Agnes, and which was at this time in Canada with descendents of the Strickland family. The books were lent to him and in due course were returned, wrapped in brown paper and posted from Windsor Castle.

In 2011 this copy of 'Victoria from her Birth to her Bridal' in two volumes, together with George Anson's letter requesting Agnes to collect the book and note the errors, and with the Windsor Castle wrapping paper used to return the copy to Canada after its loan to King George V in 1932, was sold as one Lot by auction at Sotheby's in London. It is recorded to have been sold for £11,250, ironically making Agnes's literary faux pas her most valuable work.

'Queen Victoria from her Birth to her Bridal' is almost the only one of the many books written by the Strickland family that cannot be obtained either in its original form (unless as an extremely rare copy) or as a new print-on-demand version (which tend to be missing any pictures or illustrations).

In 1940 was published the only biography of Agnes Strickland that has been written, apart from the one Jane wrote and published in 1887. It was written by Una Pope-Hennessy and, presumably being more easily available than Jane's in the days before print-on-demand, it became the source of information about Agnes. This is unfortunate as it is riddled with errors and inaccuracies which have now been repeated so often, particularly in Canada, that they have become wrongly accepted as fact.

Henry Birch, the vicar who married Catharine Parr Strickland to Thomas Traill in Reydon in 1832 was Una Pope-Hennessy's grandfather, and Una Pope-Hennessy (nee Birch) said that Agnes was her father's godmother and wrote: "The Strickland legend formed part of the back-cloth against which my childish years were set, with Agnes herself looming as a menacing, authoritative figure in the shadows. When in the nursery I gobbled up my mince and jibbed at eating my portion of sago-pudding, I used to be told it was a pity Miss Strickland was not in charge of me as she had a way of making children at her table eat their pudding first, whatever it was, and would then enquire sternly how much meat they needed."

So poor Agnes, who probably never had "any children at her table" was used by nursery maids or governesses to scare a very young Una Birch into good behaviour, and Una Birch later in life seems to have treated the nursery threats as founded on fact, and produced a biography accordingly.

Her biography was written very quickly. The closing lines of the book state that it was "Begun September 20th, 1938. Ended November 11th 1939." Britain declared itself at war with Nazi Germany on 3rd September 1939; and the biography was available for sale at a fund-raising event for the Red Cross which was held in Oxford Street London in the summer of 1940 with the title 'Agnes Strickland, Centenary of the Queens of England 1840-1940.'

Bearing in mind that Una Pope-Hennessy had been made a Dame for her work with the Red Cross during World War I, she may have been more concerned to finish her task in time to raise funds for a good cause, than with doing justice to someone who she gave the impression of disliking. Be that as it may, this fund-raising for a good cause is offered as an extenuating circumstance.

Una Pope-Hennessy's biography of Agnes was largely a re-hash of Jane Margaret Strickland's earlier book, but with added inaccuracies and with a change in tone from neutral to antagonistic. It was published and it was read, and her portrayal of Agnes has become accepted as truth which can be repeated, and poor Agnes's reputation has suffered as a result. On the positive side, Una Pope-Hennessy's biography of Agnes included a picture of the three portraits painted by Thomas Cheesman with the names Agnes, Susanna and Sarah associated with them.

In order to dispel suspicion that the only fault in Una Pope-Hennessy's biography is her description of Agnes, other examples of her handiwork illustrate that her errors were very wide-ranging. Una Pope-Hennessy wrote: "A good deal of the schooling imparted to the two elder girls by their father was passed on to the younger children by Eliza," which is correct, but Una Pope-Hennessy then goes on to write: "but some of it was not transmissible, and the capacity to write clearly and forcibly, though mastered by Eliza and Agnes under the tuition of Mr Strickland, was not developed in their younger sisters, who never progressed beyond rather feeble amateur accomplishment." Thus she dismissed the work of two celebrated pioneers of Canadian Literature, Susanna Moodie and Catharine Parr Traill.

The other member of the family who received substantial insult was Jane, who Mrs Pope-Hennessy described as: "a plainer, dumpier edition of Agnes whom she adored and whose willing slave and imitator she became." Jane did not look like Agnes and 'dumpier' means shorter and fatter. Jane had blue eyes, fair hair and was one of the tallest of the sisters while Agnes had black hair, and black or very dark eyes. As to being a "willing slave and imitator", Jane certainly helped with editing and letter-writing when Eliza and Agnes were under great pressure, and they paid her accordingly, but she did not imitate Agnes in dress, nor in opinions, nor in social activity.

Una Pope-Hennessy in her own biography of Agnes Strickland seems also to have made a good attempt to replace Jane's earlier biographical work. Mrs Pope-Hennessy wrote in her preamble: "Only one account of Agnes Strickland's career has ever been printed and that was tacked together by the worshipping sister, Jane Margaret, from material then neatly docketed, but now scattered or destroyed. In 'The Athenaeum' of the day (1887) it was condemned as the lifeless work of an unskilled biographer, but though open to the charges of inaccuracy, confusion and inadequacy I have found it a most useful sourcebook." Indeed she did, the two biographies follow almost the same path, the difference being mainly in tone, not in content.

Una Pope-Hennessy could have selected a quote from the many positive reviews of Jane's biography, some of which have already been quoted, but in addition there was a review in the 'London Daily News' which said: "... Miss (Jane) Strickland has fulfilled her pious task with loving care and discretion, and has given us a pleasing sketch of a life ... Like most lives of literary persons it is wanting in stirring incidents, but certainly not in interest ... The author's pages are perhaps none the worse reading for a little unconscious humour here and there." The fact that the only quote given by Mrs Pope-Hennessy is a negative one which has not been found in a search of the British Newspaper Archive, the archive which provided the many reviews herein quoted, and none of them negative, reflects rather badly on Mrs Pope-Hennessy. It does, however, help explain why her description of Agnes, and not Jane's, is the one which has taken hold in Canada.

In 2011 was published as part of the Continuum Histories, a work entitled 'Lives of the Queens of England.' An introductory page explained that the purpose of the series was "to attract a new generation of readers to some of the greatest narrative history ever written. Each volume includes a dramatic episode from a major work of history, prefaced with an introduction by a leading modern author." The book had an introduction written by Antonia Fraser who goes a little way at redressing the balance by describing 'Lives of the Queens of England' as opening "a whole new school of vivid utterly readable history" and saying that "Agnes Strickland, a hundred and seventy years ago, was a pioneer."

Buildings of relevance to the Strickland family still exist in England, albeit altered since the 19th century. Reydon Hall in Suffolk and Stockbridge House in Ulverston, have now both been given the protection of being listed buildings on account of their architecture. In the Orkneys, a building at 'Westove' which might have been part of Thomas Traill's family estate, has also achieved some recognition, but of a type in keeping with Thomas Traill's experience. It has been placed on Scotland's 'Buildings at Risk' register.

In 2016, Southwold's small local museum had no information to offer regarding Agnes Strickland. The only item they had about the Strickland family was a 20-page booklet entitled 'The Strickland Canadian Pioneers' which gave a brief history of Susanna and Catharine and which had originally been written in 2002. The cover carried the pictures of Susanna and Sarah painted by Thomas Cheesman, describing them as pictures of Susanna and Catharine.

Given the important financial part that Sarah played in Catharine's life, as well as the help Sarah gave to Jane and to Tom, to Geraldine and Maime Fitzgibbon, and to Catharine's daughter Kate, it somehow seems fitting that her face should be widely familiar, even if wrongly named. Sarah was described as the beauty of the family and the care with which her portrait was painted, and its repeated selection for reproduction when a picture of Catharine is required, indicates what a pleasing face she had.

The only other memory that has been found of Agnes in Suffolk was found in the village of Hoxne which remains very proud of its association with St Edmund, who was murdered in the vicinity of the village. In 2019 (and probably for some time before and continuing thereafter), the village church had a display of items associated with the history of St Edmund which included a copy of Agnes's booklet, written in 1870 and entitled 'The Royal Christian Martyr; St Edmund, the last King of East Anglia.'

On the wider national stage, Agnes Strickland was remembered by the staff of The National Portrait Gallery in London when they included her in an exhibition of eminent Victorians. This display was still in place when the National Portrait Gallery closed in March 2020, prior to a lengthy programmed closure.

Postscript

Following the original publication of this book in July 2020 under the longer title of 'The Strickland Family of Suffolk (1758 to 1899)', events have been held in Southwold, articles have been published in Suffolk and Ontario, and trans-Atlantic contacts have been made. Catch up with these and other developments by visiting www.thestricklandfamily.org

Acknowledgements

Books bought for this project, including most of the works of the Strickland family, were sourced either from independent bookshops and booksellers, or via abebooks.co.uk, which also made it possible for me to trace and purchase ephemera associated with members of the Strickland family.

This book has been published with the good offices of Becky Banning and others at Grosvenor House Publishing Ltd. It has been moved between my venerable desk top computer, and the electronic wizardry of the modern publishing world by means of the essential help of Peter at 'My PC Helper'.

My grateful thanks to all those involved in the above enterprises, named and unnamed, who have made it possible for me to allow members of the Strickland family to tell their own stories.

Thanks also to Tony Crabb for his great enthusiasm and encouragement, and to my son Oliver for his patient and careful reading of my book.

Of course, any errors or omissions, and any other such misdemeanours of which I may accidentally have been guilty, are my own responsibility.

CM Fisher
May 2022

Appendix 1: Family members and key dates

Thomas Strickland (c 1758 – May 1818)

Elizabeth Strickland (nee Homer) (1773 – September 1864)

Children of Thomas and Elizabeth Strickland:

  Elizabeth (Eliza) Strickland (December 1794 – April 1875)

  Agnes Strickland (August 1796 – July 1874)

  Sarah Strickland Strickland (Thay) (c 1798 – July 1890)
    m Robert Childs (1786 – December 1837)
    m Richard Gwillym (August 1802 – November 1867)

  Jane Margaret Strickland (April 1800 – June 1888)

  Catharine Parr Strickland (January 1802 – August 1899)
    m Thomas Traill (c 1793 – June 1859)

  Susanna Strickland (December 1803 – April 1885)
    m John Wedderburn Dundar Moodie (c 1797 – October 1869)

  Samuel Strickland (November 1805 – January 1867)
    m Emma Black (1805 – October 1826)
    m Mary Reid   (? – 1850)
    m Katharine Rackham (1806 – March 1890)

  Thomas (Tom) Strickland (c 1807 – September 1874)
    m Margaretta Adela Thompson (c 1812 – January 1863)

Appendix 2: Principal works of the Strickland family

Agnes Strickland	'Lives of the Queens of England' 'Life of Mary Queen of Scots'
Elizabeth Strickland	anonymous co-author of 'Lives of the Queens of England'
Susanna Moodie	'Roughing It in the Bush'
Catharine Parr Traill	'The Backwoods of Canada' 'Studies of Plant Life in Canada'
Jane Margaret Strickland	'Life of Agnes Strickland' 'Rome Regal and Republican'
Samuel Strickland	'Twenty Seven Years in Canada West'

Appendix 3: References

Main sources and references:

'Life of Agnes Strickland' by Jane Margaret Strickland, originally published in 1887 by William Blackwood and Sons, Edinburgh and London
Library and Archives Canada including 'Traill family collection'
'Twenty-Seven Years in Canada West VI, or The Experience of an Early Settler (1853)' (in 2 volumes) by Samuel Strickland, originally published in 1853 by Richard Bentley, London
'Susanna Moodie; Letters of a Lifetime' edited by Carl Ballstadt, Elizabeth Hopkins and Michael Peterman, published in 1985 by University of Toronto Press
'I Bless You in My Heart; selected correspondence of Catharine Parr Traill' edited by Carl Ballstaft, Elizabeth Hopkins and Michael A Peterman, published in 1996 by University of Toronto Press
British Newspaper Archive
Letters written to James Bird by members of the Strickland family, and other letters written by Agnes Strickland from 1827 to 1865, plus other miscellaneous items of relevance, held in the Suffolk County Archives
'The Backwoods of Canada' by Catharine Parr Traill, originally published in 1836 in the Library of Entertaining Knowledge series by Charles Knight, London
Wills and Probate Records 1858 to 1996 and General Register Office

Ancestry.co.uk
London Metropolitan Archives
National Portrait Gallery, London
'Lonely Planet Canada' published April 2017
NewspaperArchive.com
Oxford Dictionary of National Biography
'Suffolk, East, the buildings of England' and 'Suffolk, West, the buildings of England',
    Pevsner Architectural Guides 1974 edition (Surrey County Library)
'Half Fashion and Half Passion': The Life of Publisher Henry Colburn' by Veronica Melynk; A thesis submitted to The University of Birmingham for the degree of Degree of Philosophy
'A Charge Delivered to the Clergy of the Diocese of Chester' by John Bird Sumner in 1844

Other sources and references include:

'Pearls and Pebbles; or, Notes of an Old Naturalist' by Catharine Parr Traill with 'Biographical Sketch' by Mary Agnes Fitzgibbon, published in 1895 by William Briggs, Toronto
'Cat and Cradle Stories' by Catharine Parr Traill, edited by Mary Agnes Fitzgibbon, originally published in 1895 by William Briggs, Toronto
'Roughing It In the Bush' by Susanna Moodie, originally published in 1852 by Richard Bentley, London; 1986 edition with Introduction by Margaret Atwood, published by Virago
'Some Account of my Life and Writings: An Autobiography' by Sir Archibald Alison (1792 – 1867) (British Library)
'Wits and Beaux of Society 1860' by J & P Wharton (British Library)
'The Natural History of Selborne' by Gilbert White; 1977 edition with Introduction and Notes by Richard Mabey, published by Penguin Books
'Disraeli' by Robert Blake, published by Eyre & Spottiswoode, London in 1966
'The Compleat Angler' by Izaak Walton and Charles Cotton, Edited with Notes by John Buxton, Introduction by John Buchan; first published by Oxford University Press in 1935

'The Brontes' by Juliet Barker; edition published in 1995 by Phoenix, a division of Orion Books Ltd

'Agnes Strickland's Lives of the Queens of England, Introduced and Selected by Antonia Fraser'; published by the Continuum International Publishing Group in 2011

'Agnes Strickland, Biographer of the Queens of England 1796-1874' by Una Pope Hennessy, published in 1940 by Chatto & Windus, London

'Sisters in the Wilderness, The Lives of Susanna Moodie and Catharine Parr Traill' by Charlotte Gray, published in Canada by the Penguin Group in 1999

'The Story of Southwold' edited by M Janet Becker; published in 1948 by F Jenkins, Southwold

'East Anglia' by James Ewing Ritchie published in 1893 by Jarrold & Sons, London

'To Canada with Emigrants' by James Ewing Ritchie published in 1885 by T Fisher Unwin, London

'The Story of Tilford' published in 2000 by John E Franklin

'Letters of Love and Duty. The Correspondence of Susanna and John Moodie' by Ballstadt Hopkins and Peterman published in 1993

Archives at Barrow Library, Lancashire

The Morgan Library and Museum, New York

plus many miscellaneous websites dedicated to specific events, buildings or places, including:

St Mary's Church, Bungay, Suffolk

Wrentham Chapel, Suffolk

The History of Printing

The William Hone Bio Text correspondence with Robert Childs

historyofyork.org (fire in York Minster 1829)

ottawamatters (Ottawa Fire of 1870)

greatchicagofire.org (The Great Chicago Fire of 1871)

museumsontario.ca (Christ Church Community Museum, Lakefield, Ontario)

Trent University (Traill College)

Encyclopaedia of Canada

as well as the giants with their apparently endless supply of information available online.

Picture Credits

Reydon Hall, Suffolk artist and date unknown; credit Library and Archives Canada C-030779

Agnes, Susanna and Sarah Strickland by Thomas Cheesman; as used by Una Pope-Hennessy in 1940 courtesy of Mrs Moodie and Mrs Badgely; widely re-produced elsewhere

Agnes Strickland by John Hayes 1846
Agnes (or Eliza?) Strickland by Charles Gow 1844
Agnes Strickland by Wheeler & Day, Oxford circa 1865
All © National Portrait Gallery, London

Susanna Moodie circa 1850; photographed by G Stanton of Toronto; originally used by courtesy of Miss Kathleen McMurrich and re-produced elsewhere

Christ Church, Anglican Chapel, Lakefield, Ontario photographed in August 1925; credit CP Meredith/Library and Archives Canada/PA-026801

Richard Gwillym circa 1860; credit M Bowness, Ambleside/Library and Archives Canada/PA-201402

Catharine Parr Traill, Mrs Traill, February 1884; credit Topley Studio/Library and Archives Canada/PA-802715

'Westove', Lakefield, Ontario, Mrs Catharine Parr Traill's house 'Westove'; credit Meredith, Colborne Powell/Library and Archives Canada/PA-026903

www.ingramcontent.com/pod-product-compliance
Lightning Source LLC
Chambersburg PA
CBHW031225170426
43191CB00030B/69